San Diego Christian College
2100 Greenfield Drive
El Cajon, CA 92019

FINANCING SPORT
2nd Edition

FINANCING SPORT
2nd Edition

Dennis R. Howard, PhD
UNIVERSITY OF OREGON

John L. Crompton, PhD
TEXAS A&M UNIVERSITY

FITNESS INFORMATION TECHNOLOGY

A Division of the International Center
for Performance Excellence

West Virginia University
262 Coliseum, WVU-PE
P.O. Box 6116
Morgantown, WV 26506-6116

Titles in the Sport Management Library

Professor Packets now available at no charge for many of our bestselling textbooks. Visit www.fitinfotech.com for details.

Library of Congress Card Catalog Number: 2003108982

ISBN 13: 978-1-885693-38-9   ISBN: 1-885693-38-9

Copyeditor: Sandra Woods
Cover Design: Jamie Merlavage
Managing Editor: Geoff Fuller
Production Editor: Jamie Merlavage
Proofreaders: Jessica McDonald, Corey Madsen
Indexer: Jessica McDonald
Printed by Sheridan Books

10   9   8   7   6

Fitness Information Technology
A Division of the International Center for Performance Excellence
262 Coliseum, WVU-PE
P.O. Box 6116
Morgantown, WV 26506-6116 USA
800.477.4348 (toll free)
304.293.6888 (phone)
304.293.6658 (fax)
Email: icpe@mail.wvu.edu
Website: www.fitinfotech.com

Dedication

My heartfelt gratitude is extended to my wife and partner in all respects, Lin, who sacrificed much during the many years and long hours it took me to complete this project. Her keen editing skills are evident throughout the book. I also dedicate this book to my mother, Betty, and my two wonderful sons, Tim and Dan, for their continuous love and support.

Dennis Howard
Eugene, Oregon

To Liz, my friend, my rock, my foundation, my salvation, my all; and to Joanne and Christine, the joys of our lives.

John Crompton
College Station, Texas

Acknowledgments

A project of this magnitude cannot be completed without the support of many individuals. We would like to recognize the many professionals whose support, writing, advice, and commentary were invaluable to the preparation of this book.

Jeff Birren, Oakland Raiders
Lin Bone, University of Oregon
Rick Burton, National Basketball League, Australia
Richard Campbell, California State University, Bakersfield
Tim DeSchriver, University of Massachusetts
John Eichhorst, Howard, Rice Law Offices
Daniel Funk, University of Texas, Austin
Tom Hof, Ohio State University
Jeff James, Florida State University
Jim Kotchik, Portland Trailblazers
Katy Lenn, University of Oregon Library
Robert Madrigal, University of Oregon
Dan Mahony, University of Louisville
Duane McLean, Seattle Seahawks
Gregg Olson, Silicon Valley Sports & Entertainment
Janet Parks, Bowling Green State University
Jelinda Pepper, Texas A&M University
Andy Roundtree, Anaheim Sports
Trevor Slack, University of Alberta
Jeff Stinson, University of Oregon
Paul Swangard, University of Oregon
Marguerite Van Dyke, Texas A&M University

Contents

Detailed Contents

Preface

Over a decade ago we began work on this project. *Financing Sport* began with a phone call from Janet Parks, a professor of sport management at Bowling Green State University and Editor-in-Chief of the Sport Management Library Series, asking me to take on the task of writing the first comprehensive text on the topic of sport finance. Knowing I would need the best help available to achieve the promise of this book, I called on my good friend John Crompton. John and I had collaborated on a similar project earlier in our careers when we co-authored *Financing, Managing, and Marketing Park and Recreation Resources.* Our first book was in print for 20 years. John Crompton is the most prolific and influential writer in the parks, recreation, and tourism field, has done ground-breaking work in the area of public-private partnerships, and is a leading expert on a range of public finance topics. John's contributions to *Financing Sport* are immeasurable; in addition to assuming primary responsibility for many chapters, his fine mind and expert editing touch are evident throughout the book.

The reaction to our first edition of this book, published in 1995, was gratifying. The book has been adopted by many universities around the world and has been translated into Chinese and Japanese. We were also very pleased that one of our intended audiences, sport industry professionals, has used *Financing Sport* as a resource. We had hoped to complete a revised edition several years ago, but my move from Ohio State to the University of Oregon, as well as John's obligations to many other projects, left little time for the book through the late 1990s. However, we began a serious commitment to the second edition in the spring of 2000.

Although the organization and structure of this edition are fundamentally the same as the original, the content is almost completely revised. Rather than simply updating sections of various chapters—common to most new editions—we approached each chapter as though we were writing the book for the first time. The business of sport is fast paced and ever changing. We wanted the content to capture the many new and creative ideas managers in sport organizations have implemented in response to their dynamic work environment. The second edition maintains its original focus on conventional income sources available to sport organizations, including ticket sales, premium seating options, concessions, and the sale and execution of corporate sponsorships.

Three new chapters have been added. Chapter 1 sets the context for the book by describing the economic magnitude and factors influencing the growth of the sport industry. Chapter 7, Sports Enterprises' Sources of Revenues, focuses on three major innovations in venue development that have transformed the revenue-producing capability of sports teams: premium seating, the sale of naming rights, and the sale of personal seat licenses (PSLs). These new revenue sources grew into prominence after the publication of our first edition. The third new chapter, The Sale of Broadcast Rights (Chapter 10), was contributed by Mary

Hums, a professor in the sports administration program at the University of Louisville, and Tim Ashwell, who teaches communications at the University of New Hampshire. Given the growing importance of broadcast revenues to the operation of sports properties, we are grateful these authorities on sports media have provided such a thorough explanation of how broadcast rights are sold and marketed.

Equally gratifying was Chris Bigelow's willingness to update his chapter (Chapter 11) on the many critical issues managers face in developing and operating concession and souvenir sales. He is the president of the Bigelow Companies, and a leading food and beverage and merchandise consultant to stadiums, arenas, and sports teams in North America. From no other source will students and sport managers obtain such crucial "trade secrets" and insights into how to maximize the potential of concession sales for their organizations. Finally, we draw on Daniel Mahony's considerable background and experience in ticketing operations to help us with sections of Chapter 9 dealing with the organization and execution of ticket sales. Dan is currently serving as the Chair of Health, Physical Education and Sport at the University of Louisville.

The second edition maintains a strong practical orientation. Numerous vignettes or mini-cases drawn from actual practice are interspersed throughout the book. We believe students enjoy knowing how capital financing and revenue acquisition practices are actually being used by sport organizations, and include numerous real-world examples to illustrate many of the best practices employed by sport managers. It is our hope that this "nuts and bolts" treatment will allow readers to confidently transfer the methods to effective practice.

Dennis R. Howard
Professor of Sports Marketing
Charles H. Lundquist College of Business
University of Oregon
Eugene, Oregon

John L. Crompton
Distinguished Professor of Recreation, Park and Tourism Sciences
Texas A&M University
College Station, Texas

SECTION I:
THE FINANCIAL CHALLENGES FACING SPORT MANAGERS

Photo courtesy of University Oregon Athletic Department.

Chapter One

Sport in the New Millennium

There is no consensus on the economic magnitude of sport. Estimates vary widely. This is because *sport* is not recognized as an official industry in the Census Bureau's North American Industrial Classification System. This classification divides the economy into 20 sectors or major economic activities. Sport is not designated as one of these major economic activities and sport-related activities are scattered across 8 of the 20 sectors.[1] Each of these 8 sectors has multiple subsections into which economic activities are classified. Thus, there is no official "sports industry." Rather there are multiple industries that engage in activities that, to a greater or lesser extent, pertain to sport.

Adding or reconciling sales or financial data from each of these multiple, separate classifications is difficult because of the overlap from one category to the next. In some cases, simply adding numbers across categories may lead to double counting, whereas in others the true economic magnitude may be underrepresented. The lack of a single, official, aggregate figure provided by a government agency leaves a void that several analysts have sought to fill. Inevitably, they use different assumptions and, thus, produce very different estimates. At the end of the 1990s, estimates of total spending related to the production and consumption of sports goods and services ranged from $213 to $560 billion.[2]

The authors believe that the estimate provided by the *Sports Business Journal's* analysts at the beginning of the new century provides a solid starting point.[3] This estimate of the total economic activity related to the production and consumption of organized sport was $213 billion. Their analysis divided sports expenditures into the 15 discrete categories shown in Table 1-1.

Care was taken to conservatively prescribe each of the categories. For example, Spectator Sports was limited to on-site spectator expenditures (e.g., tickets, concessions) in contrast to most previous studies, which included vague estimates of money spent by radio listeners and television viewers. The analysts used actual hospital billing records in conjunction with appropriate insurance injury codes in determining the $4.1 billion Sports Medical Treatment category.

Table 1-1 Consumer Spending on Organized Sport $213 Billion a Year

Advertising $28.25 billion
- Network telecasts: $5.66 billion
- National cable: $1.39 billion
- Regional: $470 million
- Print: $1.8 billion
- Stadium/arena signs/billboards: $16.68 billion
- Radio $2.25 billion

Endorsements $730 million
- Endorsement value of top 80 athletes and coaches: $486 million
- SBJ and industry analysts project that this total represents two-thirds of all endorsements.

Equipment/Apparel/Footwear $24.94 billion
- Active sportswear used in competition: $8.73 billion
- Active athletic footwear used in competition: $6.93 billion
- Equipment used in competition: $9.28 billion

Facility Construction $2.49 billion
- Stadium/track construction: $1.7 billion
- Arena construction: $790 million

Internet $300 million
- Revenue from advertising: $295.5 million
- Revenue from access fees: $4.5 million

Licensed Goods $15.1 Billion
- Apparel/footwear: $8.8 billion
- Home (housewares, furniture, hardware, etc.) $990 million
- Media (electronics, software, videos, music, books, toys and games): $3.63 billion
- Misc.: $1.68 billion

Media Broadcast Rights $10.57 billion
- Big Four pro league telecast rights: $8.87 billion
- Collegiate telecasts: $987 million
- Other telecasts: $270 million
- Radio: $443 million

Professional Services $14.03 billion
- Agents: $220 million
- Marketing agencies: $2.37 billion
- Facility management and consultants: $5.74 billion
- Financial and insurance services: $5.7 billion

Spectator Sports $22.56 billion
- General admission gate receipts: $10.47 billion
- Premium seating: $3.25 billion
- On-site game-day concessions/merchandise/parking: $8.84 billion

Sponsorships $5.09 billion
- Events, teams, leagues, broadcasts: $5.09 billion

Medical Treatment $4.1 billion
- Baseball: $1.45 billion
- Football: $1.16 billion
- Basketball: $759 million
- Soccer: $314 million
- Softball: $150 million
- Other: $267 million

Travel $44.47 billion
- Expenditures for transportation, accommodations and meals for
- Spectators: $40.82 billion
- Colleges: $1.09 billion
- Big Four pro leagues: $295 million
- Other: $2.26 billion

Publications/Videos $2.12 billion
- Magazine circulation revenue: $922 million
- Videos/video games $752 million
- Books: $450 million

Gambling $18.55 billion
- Legal sports wagers: $2.3 billion
- Horses/greyhounds/jai alai: $15.33 billion
- U.S. Internet: $920 million

Team Operating Expenses $19.23 billion
- Big Four pro league player salaries: $5.24 billion
- Big Four operating expenses: $7.0 billion
- Colleges: $4.3 billion
- Others: $2.69 billion

The same kind of precision was used in estimating spending related to sport-related travel. Rather than using the traditional broad category label of Sports Tourism, analysts purposely chose the more restrictive label of Sports Travel. Previous studies commonly used straight-line estimates that assumed that sports accounted for 25% of all tourism expenditures. This unsubstantiated assumption has led to greatly exaggerated sport tourism figures. *The Sports Business Journal* researchers narrowed their consideration of travel to that done exclusively for the purposes of attending and competing in organized sporting events. In the case of major league sports, tourism visitors account for no more than 5% of attendance.[4] Travel expenditure estimates were based on data furnished by the Travel Industry Association, U.S. Travel Data Survey, and from league and team travel spending reports.

Although the definition of sports business used by the *Journal* was fairly inclusive, it did *not* include the fastest growing segment of the industry, *nonorganized recreational sports*. These more informal, participatory sports include a broad range of outdoor pursuits such as camping, hunting, fishing, and cycling, as well as a variety of popular fitness and exercise activities such as aerobic exercising and running and jogging. According to the National Sporting Goods Association,[5] in 2001, Americans spent almost $16 billion on equipment for just six activities. Bicycling led the way at $4.72 billion, followed in order by aerobic exercise ($3.84 billion), hunting ($2.20 billion), fishing ($2.07 billion), jogging and running shoes ($1.67 billion), and camping ($1.37 billion). By 2001, pleasure boating enthusiasts were spending $13.5 billion a year on acquiring and equipping new boats from skidoos to yachts. Table 1-2 shows considerable variation in expenditures across activities in the 5-year period between 1997 and 2001. Mainstream participation sports such as basketball (+61.3%), aerobic exercise (+29.4%), tennis (+16.3%), and soccer (+21.4%) registered impressive gains. Those activities trending downward included cross-country skiing (-53.6%), alpine or downhill skiing (-65.7%), and racquetball (-57%).

The Alternative Sports Boom

The fastest growing segment of sport spending at the beginning of the new millennium appears to be in the newly emergent "alternative," "extreme," or "lifestyle" sports, which are highly individualistic, free-spirited, adrenaline-rush activities. They include sports such as skateboarding, snowboarding, in-line skating, BMX biking, windsurfing, downhill mountain biking, whitewater kayaking, and the more extreme activities like bungee jumping, street luge, and sky surfing. Until the late 1990s, these activities existed on the fringe. For the most part, they were shunned by mainstream media, characterized as "pseudosports" or even denigrated as "parlor-room stunts" performed by antiestablishment teens.[6] By 2000, however, these so-called extreme sports had become mainstream. According to the National Sporting Goods Association,[5] over 80 million Americans, predominantly young males between 12 and 24 years of age, were spending billions of dollars annually on equipment and apparel to in-line skate ($251 million), snowboard ($235 million), and skateboard ($105 million). Even one of the most recent innovations in water sport, wakeboarding, which is water-skiing on what amounts to a snowboard, had sales close to $80 million.[6]

Table 1-2 Consumer Purchase of Mainline Recreational Sports Equipment

(In millions of dollars)	1997	1998	1999	2000	2001	1997 to 2001 % Change
Aerobic exercise	$2,968	3,233	3,396	3,609	3,841	+ 29.4
Archery	255	261	262	254	270	+ 5.8
Baseball/softball	304	304	329	319	316	+ 3.9
Basketball	186	298	293	291	300	+ 61.3
Bicycling	4,860	4,957	4,770	5,131	4,725	- 2.8
Bowling	156	156	160	162	169	+ 8.3
Camping	1,153	1,204	1,264	1,353	1,369	+ 18.7
Fishing tackle	1,891	1,903	1,916	2,030	2,070	+ 9.5
Football	80	80	84	86	89	+ 11.2
Golf	3,703	3,641	3,714	3,804	3,874	+ 4.6
Hockey & ice skates	168	169	140	138	142	- 8.4
Hunting & firearms	2,562	2,200	2,437	2,270	2,205	- 8.6
Jogging/running shoes	1,482	1,469	1,502	1,638	1,670	+ 12.7
Racquetball	49	49	44	36	28	- 5.7
Skin diving & scuba gear	332	345	362	355	348	+ 4.8
Skiing, alpine	723	718	648	495	475	- 65.7
Skiing, cross-country	69	66	40	34	37	- 53.6
Soccer balls	56	61	64	65	68	+ 21.4
Table tennis	36	35	41	41	41	+ 13.9
Tennis	319	313	338	382	371	+ 16.3
Volleyball & badminton	31	31	31	29	30	- 3.3
Water skis	56	56	51	60	59	+ 5.3
Athletic goods/ team sales	2,303	2,338	2,408	2,456	2,505	+ 8.8
Grand Total						$25,002

Source: National Sporting Goods Association (2002). *The Sporting Goods Market in 2002,* Mt. Prospect, IL: National Sporting Goods Association.

Alternative sports have had a particularly strong appeal to "Generation Y," 12- to 24-year-olds who increasingly have turned away from team "jock" sports to embrace the more free-spirited individualism of extreme sports. Many of these young participants appear to adopt a lifestyle that connects music and fashion to the alternative sports in which they engage.[6] Despite the hip, edgy, or antiestablishment image of these sports, corporations have been drawn to the increasing consumer strength of alternative sport participants. The annual spending power of 10- to 24-year-olds was estimated at $91.5 billion.[7] In addition, the spending potential of this youth market is expected to grow significantly over the next several decades. The 12-24 age cohort is currently growing at twice the rate of other age groups and is unlikely to level off until 2030.[6]

Figure 1-1
Growing Corporate
Investment in
Alternative Sports

Many companies see alternative sports as a conduit for reaching the hard-to-penetrate youth market. For example, Mountain Dew attributes its carefully cultivated "edgy brand image" as a sponsor of extreme sports as the primary reason for its being the fastest-growing soft drink in America in the early 2000s.

Perhaps the most prominent example of how mainstream extreme sports have become is the success of the annual Summer X Games. Originated by ESPN in 1996, the X Games are the premier event for alternative sports, the "Olympics of extreme sports." ESPN, in concert with ESPN2 and ABC, provides almost 20 hours of prime-time coverage, including competition in such activities as aggressive in-line skating, street luge racing, bicycle stunt riding, and sky surfing. Among youth aged 6-17, the X Games have become the second most appealing sporting event, exceeded only by the Summer Olympics.[8] In 2000, the event drew 270,000 spectators on site and over 5 million television viewers, including 37% of all male teenagers in the United States.[9] As might be expected, given the Games' popularity, corporations are investing substantially—an estimated $22 million in 2000—to align with the games as corporate sponsors. "Gold sponsors," such as Mountain Dew, Taco Bell, and Starburst Fruit Chews, have paid upwards of $2 million each to promote their association with the event to young consumers.

When consumer spending on mainstream and alternative participatory sports is added to the *Sports Business Journal's* $213 billion valuation of organized sport, the sum of annual expenditures exceeds $250 billion. At $250 billion, sport in its many manifestations, from organized to alternative, is a significant and growing segment of North America's economy.

The '90s Boom

The sports industry was a major beneficiary of the longest sustained period of growth in U.S. history—it provided the necessary condition for the impressive growth of many sports organizations. The most notable features of that decade included the following:

Sports Facility Construction Boom

Construction spending on new arenas and stadiums for major league professional sports teams was almost $16 billion in 2003 dollars during the 1995-2003 period. During the 1990s, over 160 new major and minor league ballparks, arenas, and racetracks were built in the United States and Canada (Howard, 1999).

Proliferation of Professional Sports Leagues and Teams

In the 1990s, almost 180 new professional sport teams came into existence, together with 13 new leagues (e.g., the XFL, National Rookie League, West Coast Hockey League). The total inventory of professional teams at all levels now exceeds 800. Unanticipated by analysts was the spectacular expansion of minor league hockey in the Sun Belt states and the emergence of women's sports leagues (i.e., Women's National Basketball Association, Women's United Soccer Association).

Increased Corporate Investment in Sport

Corporate investment in sport more than tripled from 1990 to $8 billion in 2000. The three most common ways in which companies align with sports properties are as follows:

Corporate sponsorships. Over 5,000 companies in the United States and Canada spent $5.92 billion sponsoring sporting events and teams in 2000, a jump of 14% from the preceding year.[11] The most common form of sponsorship occurs when a company pays a fee to have its company name or logo associated with a sports property, such as the PGA's *Buick* Open or *Gatorade's* sponsorship of the NFL's Punt, Pass & Kick program. Through sponsorships, companies attempt to capitalize on the appeal of the event to enhance the visibility and image of their brands or products.

Naming rights. One of the most prominent manifestations of corporate America's alignment with sport has been the number of naming-rights deals since the mid-1990s. In 1990, only a handful of professional teams played in corporately named venues. By 2001, 82 major league teams played in arenas or stadiums named for a company brand or product.[12] When the growing number of collegiate venues and minor league ballparks and arenas with corporate names is added to this list, the total exceeds 125. Early in 2001 the $300 million barrier was broken when Reliant Energy Company paid $300 million to name the home of the NFL's Houston Texans Reliant Stadium. In the 1980s, the biggest naming-rights deal was the $18.75 million entitlement of the Target Center in Minneapolis.

Premium seating. A few years ago, it was calculated that 114 teams in the four major leagues realized close to $1 billion from luxury suite revenues.[13] The great majority (over 75%) of these suite tenants are corporations with earnings that exceed $100 million annually. In addition, when the substantial number of season tickets purchased by companies for clients and employees is included—reputedly as high as 50 to 60% of the season tickets sold in NHL and NBA arenas—overall corporate investment in sport properties at all levels is substantial.

Annual Sporting Goods Sales Near $75 Billion

At the start of the new millennium, total expenditures for all sporting goods (footwear, apparel, equipment) and recreational transport (e.g., pleasure boats, bicycles, recreational vehicles, snowmobiles) approached $75 billion, an increase of almost 50% from the start of the previous decade.[5]

The Challenges Ahead

Ostensibly, the '90s boom suggested that substantial benefits are accruing to the owners and managers of sport organizations, as well to the fans and consumers of these establishments. As we enter the new decade, there are many more modern and sophisticated venues, much more sport products than ever before, and unprecedented levels of corporate support. However, at the same time, there are a number of serious challenges confronting managers. These include the increasingly competitive marketplace, emerging technology, and the need to do more with less.

Saturated Marketplace

Ironically, the prosperity that undergirded the unprecedented growth of the sports industry over the past decade has been the major contributor to one of the most serious challenges confronting sport managers: a *saturated marketplace.* Consumers now have more entertainment options available than ever before. Indeed, a respected national business publication proclaimed that the long-term robust economy that characterized the 1990s had stimulated the creation of so many new sport and entertainment alternatives that the United States now faced an "entertainment glut."[14]

Although new sports teams and properties (e.g., NASCAR, WWE, WNBA) expanded substantially, so did other entertainment options. Major entertainment and media companies like Disney, Time-Warner, and Viacom invested heavily in movie studios, broadcast and cable networks, online ventures, new record labels, and theme parks. It is projected that the total number of channels available to TV viewers will increase from about 75 in 2000 (mostly cable channels) to 1,000 by 2010, "when digital compression of TV signals makes room for hundreds of channels, and the linkage of TVs and computers becomes a reality."[14] At the same time, the exponential growth of websites is creating further choices for consumers. Some industry analysts are worried that there may already be too many choices, and consumers may be overwhelmed. As *Business Week* proclaimed, "It's a brutal battle, especially as audiences fragment amid the flurry of competing choices."[14]

As entertainment providers, sport managers are part of this highly competitive environment. Major investments made by entertainment conglomerates in the last decade are indicative of the positioning of sport as entertainment. For example, it was the entertainment value of the Atlanta Braves and Hawks on his television superstation that persuaded Ted Turner to acquire them, not his interest in baseball or hockey. Similarly, the Chicago Tribune Company purchased the Chicago Cubs to be the principal attraction of the Tribune's superstation.[15] A spokesperson for Comsat Enterprises, one of the largest cable suppliers in the United States stated, "We own the Nuggets because we're an entertainment company... We distribute entertainment. We package entertainment. We create entertainment."[15] Thus, when Comsat bought the Quebec Nordiques and moved the NHL franchise to Denver, and purchased a major interest in the Philadelphia Flyers and 76ers, the company had more entertainment to distribute, package, and create.[15]

Sport managers are competing for the scarce time and disposable dollars of the same consumers that all other entertainment companies are seeking to attract. The challenge of competing in such a cluttered marketplace is exacerbated because consumer spending on entertainment in the early 2000s slowed to around

6% annually.[14] This rate of entertainment spending was much smaller than the annual growth in investment in sport and entertainment properties. The problem is particularly acute in the spectator sports, a sector that is receiving a shrinking share of the amount of disposable income being spent on entertainment. During the 1990s, spending on spectator sports grew at a modest rate of around 2% per year, while personal investment in video, audio, and computer equipment increased at an annual rate of over 10%.[16]

It is evident that sport managers face more competition from both within and outside the sports industry than ever before. Finding ways to attract new, and retain existing, customers in an increasingly cluttered marketplace is a formidable challenge. Effective managers will take full advantage of technology to establish distinctive communication and service links with current and prospective customers by adopting a range of Internet initiatives likely to include electronic ticket sales and exchanges, chat rooms, and opportunities for fans to interact with players and coaches. They will implement powerful customer loyalty programs to reward and encourage repeat patronage and will demonstrate commitment to quality and customer service through the creation of satisfaction guarantee programs that eliminate a consumer's purchase risk.

Taking Advantage of Emerging Technology

The sports industry is only beginning to take advantage of the promise the Internet and other technology offers with respect to revenue generation and fan development. The early initiative by sports properties to adopt the technology was limited to getting online. Establishing an Internet presence usually involved creating a communication vehicle containing fan-friendly information (i.e., scores, player bios, schedules), "eye-popping graphics," and some interactivity.[17] It was not until the end of the 1990s that major sport entities began to develop coherent, long-term web strategies. Now almost all leagues and teams have established Internet marketing divisions, dedicated to capitalizing on the potential of the web to sell licensed merchandise, engender fan loyalty, increase ticket sales, and reach disaffected fans.

The President of AOL's Interactive Properties Group, who was also managing owner of the NHL's Washington Capitals, may provide the closest vision of how sports organizations will take full advantage of the Internet over the next decade. His team is using email (reputedly, he personally answered 10,000 email messages during his first year of ownership), AOL's Instant Messaging, Hotmail, live chats with players and coaches, chat rooms, and fan clubs in order to build a strong sense of community among fans. He expects the web to become a substantial revenue source. Even by the year 2000, the Internet had generated more income from ticket, merchandise, and sponsorship sales than the $8 million per year the club received from local television.[18]

Other sports organizations also are taking advantage of the Internet's ability to access their fans in a personalized manner. For example, the New York Yankees have induced more than 150,000 website visitors to register for their listserver. The San Francisco Giants established an innovative electronic ticket exchange program that is likely to become a model for other sports organizations.[19] Season ticket holders are able to use the Giants' website to sell tickets they cannot use at face value or higher. The exchange program is designed to reduce no-shows by at least

50% and to encourage high ticket-renewal rates by ensuring season ticket holders will not hold large numbers of unused tickets.

The key technological development of the near future is likely to be the convergence of Internet technology with television. Television and the Internet will converge into one delivery system in one of two contrasting ways: either as WebTV or webcasting. With WebTV (ABC dubs their version "Enhanced TV"), information accessed via the Internet is displayed on the television screen, whereas with webcasting (or netcasting), video imagery and audio are accessed directly from a personal computer. The first option brings the Internet to the television; the latter delivers live broadcasts, called streaming video or livecasting, directly to the PC user via the Internet. In either case, sport consumers will have the opportunity to instantly access game statistics (i.e., pitch count, third-down conversions), injury reports, and customized editorial comments while viewing digital-quality video.

The interactive aspect of the viewing experience eventually will allow a consumer to select a particular camera angle from which to view the action—for example, from the goalie's perspective. Quokka Sports provided early cutting-edge, "immersive" (user-active) live-event coverage on the Internet that allowed viewers to manipulate action sequences, such as America's Cup yacht races or to monitor Michael Johnson's biometrics during his Olympic sprint performances.[20] The integration of immersive coverage with the rapid growth of net-enabled cell phones (60 million people in the United States are likely to have access to Net livecasting by phone by 2003) is likely to transform the distribution and consumption of sport over the next decade.[20] Irrespective of the form of convergence or the extent to which it may occur, the integration of television and the computer will require managers to consider a range of critical issues, from how to both protect and enhance broadcast rights to how to fully leverage the considerable revenue opportunities related to virtual advertising, sponsorship, and merchandising.

It is conceivable that advances in technology will make paper tickets and ticket sellers all but disappear by the end of the decade, to be replaced by electronic tickets and electronic turnstiles. Fancard technology suggests that at some point fans will not have to bring money to the ballpark. The card-swipe technology will allow fans to purchase concessions and team merchandise while collecting points for prizes provided by the team. Fan cards allow teams to reward their most loyal fans while providing the organization with the ability to develop sophisticated databases on fan purchase behaviors (who buys what, how often, at what point in a game, etc.). Other exciting technological advancements that offer substantial potential for revenue growth include "smart" seats (small computer screens on individual seats that provide replays from different angles, game statistics, and the ability to place in-seat concession orders; Rofe, 1998), and virtual signage (computer imaging technology that allows television advertisers to superimpose messages on a playing field or in the stands that are seen only by television viewers[22]).

The revenue enhancement potential of the Internet for sports organizations is enormous. The New York Yankees became the "first pro sports team to turn cyberspace into a major seven-figure revenue source.[23] In a move similar to traditional broadcast deals, the Yankees sold their Internet rights to American City Studios (ACS), a website producer, for an estimated $3 million. ACS agreed to pay the entire rights fee in advance to produce and market the team's website. ACS, in return, kept 100% of the site-produced revenue from advertising, sponsorships, and subscriptions. Although it might be expected that one of America's most storied franchises could sell its Internet rights for a premium, the NFL, as a league entity, expects to raise the revenue bar much higher. The NFL Commissioner announced that he expected total league Internet revenues to hit $5 billion by 2004.[24]

Finally, from an international perspective, consider the revenue potential of the web for a renowned sports property like Manchester United, a perennial soccer powerhouse in the English Premier League. "Man U's" website attracts traffic from millions of avid soccer fans around the globe. As an illustration of its widespread support base, the team has 25,000 subscribers to its monthly fan magazine in Malaysia! Consider the financial windfall the club will realize when it is able to digitally stream live netcasts for its 60 games a year to all its supporters from Sheffield to Sydney. Even at a modest subscription fee of $10, the Internet telecast revenues will be gigantic.

Doing More With Less

Never before have sport managers faced as many complex challenges as those that confront them today. They face the daunting challenge of coping with declines in traditional revenue sources—tax support, media revenues, and in many cases, gate receipts—at the same time that costs are rapidly escalating. Maintaining programs even at current levels requires that sport managers learn to do more with less. At the beginning of the new millennium, only a handful of major league teams and only 48 of the 900-plus NCAA programs[25] operated without a deficit. As will be seen in the next chapter, a majority of both professional and amateur sports teams struggle to break even financially.

The fiscal challenge has caused managers to look beyond traditional financing concepts and strategies and to supplement them with new imaginative approaches. It is the basic theme of this text that managers of sport organizations are required to seek out scarce resources from a wide range of possible sources and to use their marketing and financing skills to ensure that the scarce resources acquired are allocated in such a way that they yield optimum social and economic benefits. These are exactly the requirements of an entrepreneur. Indeed, we view the contemporary sport manager as an entrepreneur. Increasingly, effectiveness in professional, collegiate, and other forms of amateur sport will be dependent upon managers' ability to aggressively seek out resources for their organizations. A major emphasis of this book is on providing readers with an in-depth understanding of the many traditional and innovative revenue acquisition methods available to sports organizations. It is the authors' belief that managers who are confident in their understanding of when and how to use a combination of these financing options will be in the best position to sustain and enhance the viability of their sports organizations.

The following quotation caught the authors' attention. It is extracted from a piece written in a national newspaper by a well-known commentator:[26]

Out of the clubs which form the League, it would probably be over the mark to say that one-sixth are beginning this season with a balance on the right side of their accounts. One result is that they are anxious to offer lower wages to their players. In spite of that some players are keeping up the prices happily.

My point is that football is being ruined by being a commercial speculation. Local team spirit is being shattered by the purchases of players from outside, and is being replaced by merely mercenary ambitions on the part of the players.

A large proportion of the clubs are so hard up that they can never hope to buy good enough players to rise to the top… We have developed, on the one hand, into a ring of financiers, who have captured sport for its value in the market, and, on the other hand, into a raucous, grasping multitude, who are good enough at pushing through the turnstiles, or bellowing at a player, or even battering a referee, but who have no notion of taking any decent exercise for themselves at any time.[26]

There are many in North America who would concur with the sentiments expressed by the writer and advocate that such flimsy foundations make the contraction of professional sports inevitable and perhaps desirable. However, the article appeared in *The Daily Telegraph,* an English national newspaper; its context was the English Premier League; and it was published in September 1900! The writer was bemoaning the transfer of a player from one club to another for $500 and a team spending $6,000 on a new ground. In 2002, an English Premier League player was transferred for a fee of over $50 million, and the new Wembley soccer stadium is projected to cost $1 billion. A large proportion of the clubs in 1900 were "so hard up that they could never hope to buy good enough players," but 90% of them are still in business 102 years later.[26] Clearly, sports managers have responded to the challenge to find new revenues in the past, and the authors are confident they will do so in the future.

Organization of the Book

The golden era of unparalleled growth and optimism that characterized the 1990s has given way to a future that is less certain. Successful managers will have to find ways to deal with greater competition in the marketplace than ever before, contentious player-management relations over distribution of revenues, and ticket prices that exceed the price-tolerance levels of many consumers. Helping managers to effectively cope with the reality of plateauing revenues and rising costs is the essential thrust of this book.

Although the focus of the book is on the two most visible segments of the sport industry, intercollegiate and professional sports, the methods and strategies of revenue acquisition discussed in its chapters can be adapted to a wide range of public and private sport organizations. Throughout the book, numerous references and examples are drawn from a variety of sport settings.

Sport organizations are likely to acquire financial resources from three generic sources, which are shown in Figure 1-2: the public sector, the private sector, and the sport enterprise.

Figure 1-2 Sources of Revenue for Sports Organizations

Private Sector Sources	Public Sources	Sports Enterprise Sources
• Investment capital	• "Hard" taxes	• Tickets, concessions
• Corporate sponsorships	• "Soft" taxes	• PSLs
• Donations	• Grants, subsidies	• Naming rights
	• Tax abatements	• Luxury seating
		• Licensed merchandise
		• Media fees

The public sector has traditionally assumed a significant role in the financing of sport organizations. Although government support may be axiomatic in the public recreation agency and collegiate contexts, some are surprised to find it is so pervasive in the professional sports arena. Consider the following:

> Modern professional sport in the United States exists as we know it as a result of the public policies of federal, state, and local governments. Without favorable tax treatment of the professional sports industry, antitrust exemptions for the NFL-AFL merger and Major League Baseball, and the broad antitrust exemption for the packaging of telecast and broadcast rights to league games, the economics and business operations of professional sports leagues would be dramatically different. Similarly, without the public financing of playing facilities, below-market rents for the facilities, tax exemptions, and other forms of subsidies provided by local and state governments, the economics and business operations of professional sports would be significantly different. This is just as true of those sports organizations and events that are not considered to be major league (i.e., the secondary sports market) as it is for the major league sports and premier sporting events.[27]

At the local government level, cities and counties have a long tradition of committing substantial tax monies in support of sport from youth programs to the construction and operation of stadiums and arenas for professional teams. However, in the past decade the sports landscape has been transformed by the commercial alignment of private companies with sports organizations in the form of event sponsorships (e. g., the Nokia Sugar Bowl) and stadium naming agreements (e. g., Reliant Stadium) that were valued at $8 billion per year by 2000. Finally, sports properties can generate substantial revenue directly from their own operations through the sale of admission tickets, concessions, licensed merchandise, and media rights. Since the mid-1990s, prices for attending sports events have risen at unprecedented rates. Ticket prices to major league sporting events doubled in the latter half of the 1990s. High-revenue-yielding premium seating options (club seats, luxury suites) displaced less expensive seating in all stadiums and arenas built in the 1990s. PSLs (permanent seat licenses), COIs (contractually obligated income streams), and a number of other revenue-enhancing innovations have become standard features throughout professional and collegiate sport in North America.

Before examining the major sources of revenue available to sport managers, chapter 2 provides a comprehensive overview of the two most visible segments of organized sport, professional sports and intercollegiate athletics. The intent of this introductory chapter is to furnish readers with insights into the many financial challenges and opportunities facing the thousands of sports leagues and teams operating in the United States and Canada at the major, minor, and collegiate levels. The economic status and prospects of professional and collegiate sports are analyzed, and recommendations for sustaining the financial viability of each sector are provided.

Section II of the book focuses on obtaining capital resources from the public sector and from investors. It describes the many public and private sources of capital for constructing and/or renovating sports venues. Chapter 3 examines trends in the cost and number of professional and collegiate facilities and discusses "who should pay" for the development of new sports facilities. Should sport facilities be financed primarily from public tax sources, or should teams and/or private owners pay their own way? The sources of momentum undergirding the large public investment in sport facilities are analyzed, and the contentious issues of opportunity costs and equity that invariably accompany public subsidy decisions are discussed. Invariably, economic impact analyses are undertaken to measure the magnitude of economic benefits purported to accrue from facilities, and these are central to debates on the public subsidy issue. For this reason, chapter 4 presents the principles of economic impact analysis and highlights the common errors that are made in applying this technique. The chapter provides a clear explanation of the steps involved in conducting legitimate economic analyses. Alternative justifications for public subsidy are explored in chapter 5, where it is suggested that the most powerful of these may be the "psychic income" residents receive from their association with a team or event.

When managers seek public sector funding, it is important that they have some understanding of the alternative options available for acquiring these tax dollars. Thus, chapter 6 provides an overview of the basic sources of taxation. Content includes a discussion of how various property and sales taxes are administered by governments and the manner in which they have been used to finance sport facility development. The chapter concludes with a review of the various kinds of tax-exempt and taxable bonds used to underwrite stadium and arena construction projects. Chapter 7 shifts the focus from public to private sources of capital development financing. The chapter identifies income generated by sport facilities from the sale of naming rights, luxury suites, and permanent seat licenses. Chapter 8 concludes the second section of the text by describing how government agencies and sports organizations can creatively combine public and private sources of capital to produce opportunities that neither could achieve alone. The chapter examines the principles that underlie funding partnerships between sports properties and public sector authorities. Numerous examples of successful joint venture arrangements are provided to illustrate how managers can leverage partnerships with other entities.

Section III of the book focuses on the financial resources that accrue directly from the operation of sport enterprises. Sports properties have historically relied on charged admissions, the sale of concessions, and the sale of radio and TV rights to finance their annual budget requirements. These traditional revenue sources are discussed in chapter 9 ("Revenues From Ticket Admissions"), chapter 10 ("Sale of Broadcast Rights") and chapter 11 ("Sale of Food Service and Souvenir Concessions").

Section IV is concerned with the solicitation of external resources. An increasingly prominent source of revenue for amateur and professional sports organizations is the sale of corporate sponsorships. Given the growing importance and sophistication of sponsorship sales and execution, four chapters are devoted to the topic. Chapter 12 provides an overview of the factors that have stimulated sponsorship growth and a detailed discussion of the benefits and risks associated with sponsorship agreements. The importance of matching the products and target markets of corporate sponsors, with those of the sports organization is the topic of chapter 13. The strategies and tactics involved in successfully soliciting sponsorships from corporations are covered in chapter 14. The sponsorship section concludes with a discussion in chapter 15 of the methods that corporations use to measure the impacts accruing from their sponsorship of sporting events.

For many youth-serving and collegiate sports organizations, fundraising constitutes an integral part of their annual operating budgets. Thus, the book concludes with a description of how sport managers can effectively organize and implement both annual donor and major gift programs from support groups. Forms of major giving, including endowments and trusts, are covered.

References

1. Li, M., Hofacre, S., & Mahony, D. (2001). *Economics of sport*. Morgantown, WV: Fitness Information Technology.
2. Broughton, B., Lee, J., & Netheny, R. (1999, December 20-26). The question: How big is the U.S. sports industry? *SportsBusiness Journal,* 23-29.
3. The making of the $213 billion sports business industry. (1999, December 20-26). *SportsBusiness Journal,* 24-25.
4. Noll, R., & Zimbalist, A. (1997). Sports, jobs, taxes: The real connection. In R. Noll & A. Zimbalist (Eds.), *Sports, jobs & taxes: The economic impact of sport teams and stadiums* (pp. 494-508). Washington, DC: The Brookings Institution.
5. National Sporting Goods Association. (2002). *The Sporting Goods Market in 2002*. Mt. Prospect, IL: Author.
6. Spanberg, E. (1998, November 9-15). Advertisers target teen trendsetters 1998. *SportsBusiness Journal,* 24.
7. Stouffer, J. (1998, November 9-15). X faithful may be young, but they're smart and savvy about their sports. *SportsBusiness Journal,* 29.
8. Ruibal, S. (2000, August 17). Trying to stay hip. *USA Today,* 3C.
9. Brown, P. (2000). This is extremely sporting. *New York Times,* Section 4, 2.
10. Howard, D. (1999). The changing fanscape for big-league sports: Implications for sport managers. *Journal of Sport Management, 13*(1), 78-91.
11. *IEG Sponsorship Report.* (2000, December 20). 1.
12. *Team Marketing Report.* (2000, May). 7-8.
13. Funk, D. (June, 1997). *Economics of professional sport franchises: The role of luxury suites and club seats in the construction of stadiums and arenas.* Paper presented at the 12th Annual North American Society for Sport Managers Conference, San Antonio, TX.
14. Stevens, E., & Grover, R. (1998, February 16). The entertainment glut. *Business Week,* 88-95.
15. Danielson, M.N. (1997). *Home team: Professional sports and the American metropolis.* Princeton, NJ: Princeton University Press.
16. Sports Business Research Network: (n.d.). Market research database. Retrieved September 30, 2001, from http://www.sbnet.com.
17. Duncan, M., & Campbell, R. (1999). Internet users: How to reach them and integrate the Internet into the marketing strategy of a sports business. *Sports Marketing Quarterly,* 8(2), 35-42.

18. Bernstein, A. (2000, May 1-6). Washington revolution: AOL honcho wants to fix a 'broken' industry. *SportsBusiness Journal,* 46.

19. Dickey, G. (2000, June 14). Giants' new ticket plan a winner [Electronic version]. *San Francisco Chronicle.*

20. Cummings, T. (2000, July 26). Major deals should improve ways to keep track of events. *San Francisco Chronicle,* E6.

21. Rofe, J. (1998, December 7-13). "Smart" seats nifty, but will fans byte? *SportsBusiness Journal,* 22.

22. Bernstein, A. (1998, June 22-28). High tech a (virtual) sign of the times. *SportsBusiness Journal,* 24, 36.

23. Bernstein, A. (1999, July 12-18). Yankees net lucrative web deal. *SportsBusiness Journal,* 1.

24. League notes. (1999, November 5). *Sports Business Daily* (14).

25. Lopiano, D. (2001, June 11-17). Division I cranks up the sports 'arms race.' *SportsBusiness Journal,* 33.

26. Boon, G., & James, D. (2002). *Annual review of football finance: Season 2000-2001.* London: Deloitte & Touche Sport.

27. Johnson, A. T. (1993). Rethinking the sport-city relationship: In search of partnership. *Journal of Sport Management,* 7, 61-70.

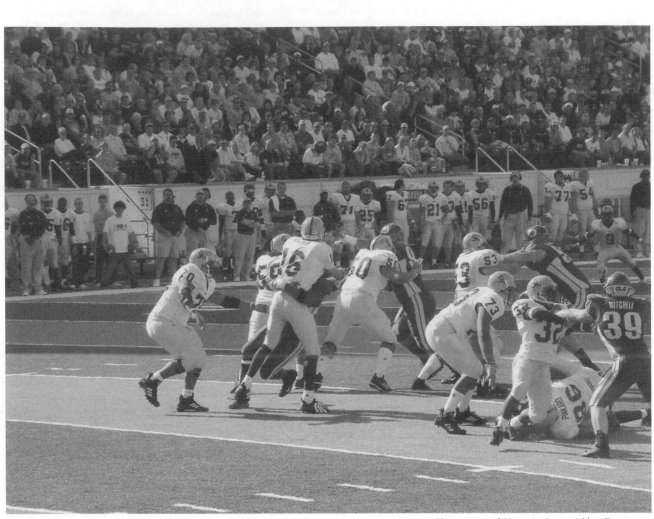

Photo courtesy of University Oregon Athletic Department.

Chapter Two

The Challenges Facing College and Professional Sports

This chapter focuses on the current state, and future prospects, of the two most visible sectors of sport, professional sport, and intercollegiate athletics. Together, these two segments include over 2,000 sports teams in the United States and Canada, attract over 200 million spectators annually, and spend $15 billion a year producing games and sporting events. Both sectors grew substantially during the 1990s. The number of professional sports teams at the minor and major league levels increased from 476 in 1990 to 813 by 2001.[1] By 2000, 1,256 colleges and universities sponsored either National Collegiate Athletic Association (NCAA) or National Association of Intercollegiate Athletics (NAIA) men's or women's sports programs, or both, in the United States, up from 1,183 in 1995. In Canada, the 49 universities affiliated with the Canadian Intercollegiate Athletic Union sponsor a range of men's and women's sport teams.

Although both professional and collegiate sports teams generally prospered during most of the 1990s, both sectors face difficult financial challenges in the years ahead. As discussed in chapter 1, competition among the expanded number of sports properties, as well as from the myriad entertainment entities outside of sport, has become more intense. This chapter examines the many challenges confronting managers of college athletic programs and professional sport franchises. The intent is to provide the reader with an understanding of the issues that affect each of these spheres so the financial tools described later in the text can be applied effectively.

The Financial Status of Intercollegiate Athletics

By 2000, college athletics was a $4.0 billion enterprise.[2] The average annual budget for athletic departments with major football and basketball programs was $20 million in 2000. The high degree of commercialization in collegiate sport is evident in the high salaries of coaches, the emphasis on television contracts, the prominence of corporate sponsorships, and the emergence of licensing agreements. For the modern sport manager, charged with maintaining the financial solvency of a college sport program, the adage "It's no longer a game, it's a business" is a prevailing theme. It has been noted that "the imperative to become more businesslike is a dominant characteristic of big-time college athletics."[3] Texas A&M is typical of major college athletic departments:

> Once upon a time, athletic departments did little more than pay salaries, operate facilities, schedule games, and count gate receipts, but those days are long gone. Aggie Inc. has 177 full-time employees and about 500 part-time student workers—not counting 500 or so student-athletes. It retires debt on bonds for stadium expansion. It has an entire division devoted to tutoring athletes and monitoring academic performance. As part of its never-ending search for more revenue, it licenses radio broadcast rights and hunts for businesses willing to sponsor special events, from the TU (Texas) football game ($100,000 to call it the AT&T Lone Star Showdown) to a spring softball tournament (forty plane tickets from Continental Airlines to help defray the travel expenses of nationally ranked teams).[4]

Although critics assail the intense commercial entertainment emphasis or corporatization of "College Sports, Inc.," the indisputable reality of modern collegiate sports is that its day-to-day governance is shaped largely by financial considerations of cost containment and income generation. More than three fourths of the largest collegiate athletic programs are losing money.[2] Smaller college programs at the Division III and NAIA levels are experiencing even greater financial pressure, with 75 to 90% reporting deficits. A former executive director of the NCAA commented, "You can probably count on your two hands the number of athletic departments that actually have a surplus annually."[5] This may be hyperbole, but an NCAA study of the financial condition of its member schools found that only 16% of the Division I and II athletic programs reported more revenue than expenses in 1999.[2]

As shown in Table 2-1, only the largest athletic programs are able to operate on a financially self-sufficient basis. Division IA schools, on average, generated $20 million in revenues from the operation of athletic programs largely from ticket sales, media contracts, and fundraising. At the same time, however, annual operating costs at the Division IA level averaged $20 million, indicating that collegiate athletics at the highest level is essentially a break-even proposition. Although a $20 million budget buys an average Division IA athletic program, if the goal is to be among the best 25 all-round athletic programs, the budget need rises to about $36 million.[6] Athletic programs at all other levels did not come close to generating revenues sufficient to cover the cost of operating their sports programs. Sports programs at the Division IAA and IAAA levels averaged annual operating deficits in excess of $2 million.

With costs exceeding revenues for all but a small number of programs, athletic departments have had to depend on substantial institutional support. In 1999, universities contributed $1.3 million on average to support their athletic programs. Institutional support comes in a variety of forms. A number of athletic programs in state-supported or public institutions like the universities of Minnesota and

Table 2-1 Mean Revenues and Expenditures of
NCAA's Division I and II Athletic Programs

Including School Support

Division	Total Revenues	Total Expenses	Net Profit/(Loss)
I-A	$25,100,000	$23,200,000	$ 1,900,000
I-AA	$ 5,600,000	$ 6,800,000	$ (1,200,000)
I-AAA	$ 5,100,000	$ 5,500,000	$ (400,000)
II (w/football)	$ 1,900,000	$ 2,300,000	$ (400,000)
II (no football)	$ 1,200,000	$ 1,600,000	$ (400,000)

Excluding School Support

Division	Total Revenues	Total Expenses	Net Profit/(Loss)
I-A	$22,600,000	$23,200,000	600,000
I-AA	$ 3,400,000	$ 6,800,000	($ 3,400,000)
I-AAA	$ 2,700,000	$ 5,500,000	($ 2,800,000)
II (w/football)	$ 1,000,000	$ 2,300,000	($ 1,300,000)
II (no football)	$ 500,000	$ 1,600,000	($ 1,100,000)

Profits and Losses by Sport

Division	Total Revenues	Total Expenses	Net Profit/(Loss)
I-A Football	$10,920,000	$ 6,170,000	$ 4,750,000
I-AA Football	$ 810,000	$ 1,310,000	($ 500,000)
I-Men's Basketball	$ 3,640,000	$ 1,970,000	$ 1,670,000
I-Women's Basketball	$ 360,000	$ 1,098,000	($ 738,000)
I-Men's programs	$15,800,000	$10,900,000	$ 4,900,000
I-Women's programs	$ 1,400,000	$ 4,600,000	($ 3,200,000)

Source: Fulks, Daniel. (2000). *Revenues and expenses of Divisions I and II intercollegiate Athletics programs: Financial trends and relationships—2001.* The National Collegiate Athletic Association.

Oregon receive direct subsidies from their respective state legislatures. A great many others receive mandatory (e.g., University of Illinois) or optional (e.g., University of Texas) student athletic fees annually. Indeed, a growing number of school athletic programs have been sustained only as a result of student fees. Students at the University of California at Davis approved a fee increase that kept as many as ten sports from being eliminated as varsity activities. The University's sports program faced a cut of at least $600,000, which would have forced the elimination of up to half of its 20 sports teams. An aggressive lobbying campaign by a booster group called Students Supporting Athletics was able to persuade nearly two thirds of the students to vote in support of paying $34 more each quarter to rescue the sports program, the Student Health Center, and other programs that faced cuts. The increase remained in effect for three years, after which students voted on continuing it.

As Table 2-1 indicates, subsidies provided from institutional sources allowed Division IA programs on average to report a "profit" of $1,900,000 and for schools in lower classifications to show smaller losses. The only true profit center for Division IA schools, however, is football. Over 70% of the Division IA schools responding to the NCAA survey reported their football program operated with a surplus. Indeed, the average profit margin reported by the nation's biggest football programs was an impressive $3.8 million. In many institutions, football must support the entire intercollegiate athletic program for both men and women. Thus, *Fortune* magazine referred to the University of Texas Longhorn football program as a "Grade A cash cow.[7]" The athletic department credits the team with generating 80% of the department's $45.3 million in overall revenues in 1999: "That's $36 million from tickets, individual donations, rights fees, sponsorships, hot dogs, beer and other sources.[7]" A hundred miles to the east, at Texas A&M University, the athletic director proclaimed, "Football pays for everything."[4] The revenue disparity between football and the rest of the school's sports programs is enormous. "Every other sport except men's basketball hemorrhaged red ink," with baseball losing $450,000, women's basketball losing $787,000, and softball losing $525,000.[4] Altogether, 17 sports at Texas A&M lost $6.2 million. Fortunately, football turned a $7 million surplus.

It is worth noting that the financial growth in intercollegiate athletics has been mirrored by a similar investment in intramural activities. During the 1990s, there was substantial investment in recreation centers constructed on campuses. In 2002, the National Intramural-Recreational Sports Association reported that its 725 member institutions had 1,546 recreation centers, almost half of which had been built since 1995, including 25% built since 2000. Although centers at larger schools can cost over $100 million, even small schools are being pressured by competitive forces to spend $20 million or more on combined intramural-intercollegiate centers. These investments reflect the rising expectations of college students about the amenities a college must have for it to be attractive to them. Schools have found that elaborate recreation centers with cybercafes as well as exercise equipment and playing courts for basketball and volleyball are important ways to attract and retain students.[8]

Cost Control Struggle

Total expenses for Division IA programs have almost tripled over the past 15 years, from $6.9 million in 1985 to $20 million in 1999.[2] Two factors that account for most of the increase are escalating tuition costs and gender equity. Tuition at the average public university rose 234% between 1980 and 1995.[9] This leads to a commensurate increase in costs to support scholarship athletes so that at the University of Alabama, for example, the costs increased from $3 million in 1988 to approximately $6 million annually in 2000. Federal (Title IX) and state legislation mandated gender equity in the provision of men's and women's intercollegiate sports. The NCAA responded by prescribing that investment in women's sports be equivalent to their proportion of representation in the student body. However, women's sports at most institutions currently contribute no more than 5% to 10% of the total revenues generated by average collegiate athletic programs.[2]

The response options of athletic departments to these pressures are either to create ways to add revenue or to cut costs. However, some are dubious that much, if any, progress will be made toward the second alternative. The athletic director at the University of Texas claimed, "It's clear that we're not going to be able to limit spending" for college athletics. Carrying the point further, he asserted, "There's a tendency in college athletics, like Congress, to spend if you have it."[10] And spend they have. According to figures released by the NCAA in 1999, from 1982 to 1999, athletic department expenses for almost all NCAA-affiliate athletic departments climbed over 300%.

It will be difficult to reduce the current level of costs given higher tuition costs and gender-equity compliance requirements. Other requirements constraining cost reduction options include the NCAA mandate that "even the smallest Division I schools" sponsor a minimum of 14 teams (7 men's and 7 women's) and spend a minimum of $500,000 on athletic scholarships in nonrevenue sports. The dilemma facing the average Division I institution is that nonrevenue men's and women's sports generate only 8% of an average athletic department's revenues, but account for 28% of its costs.

The situation confronting the University of Oregon Athletic Department is illustrative of the wide difference between revenue and nonrevenue sports. In 1998-99, football and men's basketball generated $16.8 million in gross revenues against $9.8 million in expenditures. The other 12 nonrevenue sports earned a total of $776,289, whereas their aggregate costs amounted to $5.3 million. The Athletic Director commented, "Football and basketball continue to carry them [non-revenue sports] at levels that are being mandated. If it weren't for institutional support [annual State of Oregon appropriations of $2 to $3 million] we'd have a tough time making it."[11]

The mounting insolvency of most college athletic departments has focused attention on the need to rein in escalating expenses. The NCAA established a special committee to identify ways in which athletic programs could realize cost savings.* One option given serious consideration was to replace the traditional practice of awarding athletic scholarships to cover the complete cost of tuition and room and board, with a substantially less costly aid package based on the financial capability of each athlete's family. Serious challenges face the radical shift from "full-ride" to "need-based" athletic scholarships. A former NCAA executive director expressed concern about the equity of a financial aid package based on need, commenting, "Some athletes would receive no aid. So then you get into a fairness question. Just because this individual's parents saved their money, it will cost them as opposed to somebody else that hasn't been so frugal."[12] In spite of this concern, it is likely that college presidents are likely to view this proposal as a viable approach to controlling the single greatest expense of college athletic programs.

In an effort to reduce growing deficits in their athletic programs, university presidents of the eight Big Sky Conference institutions imposed dramatic cost-containment requirements on their league's football programs. Faced with declining state funding and demands for gender equity, the presidents mandated a reduction of six football scholarships a year per school, beginning in 1994. By the start of the 1996-97 season, league schools were limited to 45 scholarships.

*Reducing the expense of Division IA football has been a focal point of NCAA cost-containment efforts. Since the early 1970s there has been a steady reduction in football scholarships from no cap in 1971 (most Big 12 schools had 130-150 scholarship players) to 92 in 1993 to 85 overall in 1995.

Given the limited potential for serious cost containment and the relentless demands for more revenue, it is not surprising to see emphasis placed on finding new income sources. As one critical observer of college athletics noted, it is becoming difficult to separate college athletic programs from professional sports: "Professional franchises showed the way to new revenues and now colleges are following."[13] Luxury suites, naming-rights deals, and corporate sponsorships have all become increasingly prominent aspects of the college sports landscape.

The current reality of college athletics is far from its popular perception as a "cash cow" for higher education. Spiraling costs, increased competition, and flat or declining revenues have all combined to place intercollegiate sports programs under severe financial pressure. A large majority are operating at a deficit. Grappling with budget issues—revenue generation and cost containment—will be key issues confronting collegiate sport managers for the foreseeable future.

The Impact of Title IX

In an environment of rising costs, athletic administrators now are also required to confront the enormous financial implications of finally complying with Title IX. A series of dramatic events in the early 1990s required colleges to make a serious commitment to addressing the gender equity issue. For almost two decades after the passage of Title IX of the Education Amendments Act in 1972, many college athletic programs paid only lip service to the notion of equal treatment of sexes. Then, beginning in 1991, in quick succession, three developments gave Title IX great momentum:

> A Supreme Court ruling in the Georgia case, *Franklin v. Gwinnett Public Schools,* for the first time permitted stiff monetary penalties for Title IX violations.

> The Office of Civil Rights identified "discrimination on the basis of sex in athletic programs" as a priority in its overall enforcement strategy.

> The Big Ten Council of Presidents adopted a resolution requiring conference schools to achieve a ratio of at least 40% female athletes to 60% male athletes by August, 1997.

The situation facing the Big Ten when it embarked on Title IX compliance illustrates the substantial financial challenges confronting schools working toward bringing about greater gender equality in college sports. An overall shift of 10% in gender representation was required to meet the conference's 40% minimum female participation goal. When the 40-60 proposal was adopted in 1992, 6,650 athletes represented conference schools in varsity competition. Approximately 2,000 (or 30%) were women. To attain the 40-60 ratio, three broad strategies were available:

1. If the number of male athletes was not to decrease from the existing total of 4,650, then 1,100 females would have to be added, which would increase the total to 7,750 athletes.

2. If no women were added, then there would have to be a reduction of 1,650 men, reducing the total number of athletes to 5,000, of whom 2,000 would be women.

3. If the overall number of athletes was to remain unchanged, then 660 men would have to be replaced with an equal number of women to attain the 60-40 ratio.

Given the severe financial constraints facing most institutions, the added strain of increasing the total number of athletes to 7,750 by adding 1,100 females seems an improbable scenario. The more feasible scenarios are options 2 and 3, which mean men's teams would have to be eliminated.

Although some schools and conferences had taken proactive actions on their own, real across-the-board progress in the 1990s emerged as a result of more rigorous enforcement of compliance standards by the U.S. Department of Education's Office of Civil Rights. The basic requirements set forth by the Office of Civil Rights require schools to meet one of three criteria, often referred to as the "three-part test":

1. The "substantial proportionality test" requires that women athletes receive participation opportunities and resources proportionate to the women in the student body at large. To be in full compliance with this test, a school must (a) offer varsity sport participation opportunities to women within an allowable difference of no more than 5% of the proportion of women in the general student population; and (b) allocate scholarship monies proportionate to the percentage of female student athletes in the athletic department.

   On a campus in which women represented 48% of the total undergraduate enrollment, to be in full compliance with both provisions of the proportionality test, no fewer than 47% of the athletes would be women, receiving no less than 47% of the athletic department's scholarship support.

2. The university demonstrates a consistent history of expanding and improving women's sports programs.

3. The university's athletic department is fully meeting the needs and abilities of its female student athletes.

In order to meet any one of these tests, athletic departments have responded in one or a combination of three ways: (a) by securing more money in order to add more women's sports; (b) by redistributing resources from men's to women's programs; and (c) by cutting existing men's sports. To date, roster capping and the elimination of men's programs have been the most common approaches used by departments to comply with Title IX.

During the 1990s, every men's nonrevenue sport, with the exception of golf, lacrosse, and track, lost teams or participants. Over 400 men's athletic teams have been abolished in order to meet Title IX. Between 1992 and 1997, 3.4 men's positions on college teams were cut for every woman's spot created.[14] Coaches from those men's sports that have been affected the most severely such as swimming, wrestling, and gymnastics have unsuccessfully lobbied Congress to eliminate the proportionality test. A spokesperson for the U.S. Track Coaches Association stated, "The intent of Title IX is not to have discrimination, and clearly there is."[15] However, the Executive Director of the Women's Sports Foundation argues that the coaches are attacking the wrong target: "The problem is financial-football and basketball expenses have gone up faster than revenues. Instead of forcing the big budgets to take a smaller piece of the pie, they cut minor men's sports and then blame Title IX."[15] She points out that substantial new revenue is being injected into athletic departments, but it "is being used to fuel the arms race being fought in college football and men's basketball. NCAA research shows that of every three new dollars going into college athletic programs over the last five years, two go to men's sports and only one to women's sports."[16] Her position is that schools should be required to retain all men's sports programs while they bring women's sports into compliance with Title IX.

Although football in particular is for many big schools the major source of revenue, it is also by a significant margin the most expensive sports program to operate, consuming on average almost $5.3 million annually or 24% of a Division IA athletic department's total budget. Some believe that substantial savings could be realized by cutting back the funds allocated to football. For example, as much as $500,000 in savings a year could result from cutting in half the number of grants-in-aid or scholarships awarded by Division IA football programs, but such proposals have been met with aggressive resistance from coaches and many senior athletic department officials who believe a significant reduction would seriously diminish the quality and, thereby, the marketability of collegiate football. As one senior NCAA official declared, "It [further cuts] would be akin to killing the Golden Goose." Although the impact of any reduction is unclear, it appears unlikely that cuts in the number of scholarships for football at the Division IA level will be made.

Although the courts have provided the legal authority for advancing the interests of women athletes, managers of college athletics have to assume moral responsibility for ensuring an equitable balance between men's and women's sports opportunities on college campuses. Finding new revenues and implementing cost-containment strategies to achieve the goal of gender equity are major fiscal challenges facing sport administrators. The courts have finally decreed that there will be no compromise on the issue of gender equity, so these are challenges that must be met aggressively.

The Financial Status of Professional Sports

Growth of Professional Sports

In chapter 1 it was noted that there has been substantial growth in professional sports at all levels over the past decade. The number of teams in the so-called Big 4 major leagues grew from 103 franchises in 1989 to 123 by 2001. During that time, the NHL added eight expansion teams, MLB added four, the NFL added three, and the NBA added five new teams. In addition, several new leagues were launched in the 1990s with aspirations of becoming prominent national properties, most notably Major League Soccer (MLS) and the Women's National Basketball Association (WNBA).

The most spectacular growth in professional team sports, however, occurred at the secondary level, where the so-called minor league teams, particularly in hockey and basketball, have expanded in numbers substantially (Table 2-2). By 2000, over 140 minor league hockey teams were playing in arenas throughout the United States

Table 2-2 Listing of the Minor Leagues in North America

Football
Arena Football League
Arena Football 2
Canadian Football League
Indoor Professional Football League

Baseball
Appalachian League
Atlantic League
Arizona Fall League
California League
Carolina League
Eastern League
Frontier League
Florida State League
International League
Midwest Baseball League
New York-Penn Baseball League
Northern Baseball League
Pacific Coast League
Pioneer Baseball League
South Atlantic Baseball League
Southern Baseball League
Texas Baseball League
Texas-Louisiana Baseball League
Western Baseball League

Basketball
ABA 2000
Collegiate Professional Basketball League
International Basketball League
National Basketball Development League
National Rookie League
United States Basketball League

Hockey
American Hockey League
Central Hockey League
East Coast Hockey League
Ontario Hockey League
Quebec Major Junior Hockey League
United Hockey League
United States Hockey League
West Coast Hockey League
Western Hockey League
Western Professional Hockey League

Soccer
National Professional Soccer League
World Indoor League

Roller Hockey
Roller Hockey International, Inc.

and Canada. Only baseball, with a total of 188 franchises, has more minor league teams. Four new basketball leagues were launched in 2000 alone, including the International Basketball League, the National Rookie League, the College Pro League, and the ABA 2000; and what is probably surprising even to ardent football fans, by 2001 over 60 professional football teams, *in addition* to the 32 NFL franchises, operated in cities throughout the United States and Canada.

The Arena Football League (AFL) may be the single most successful league property launched in the last 15 years. The AFL has expanded from 4 teams at its inception in 1987 to 16 teams in 2002. It has grown from one to two separate leagues with the creation of its own minor league, called AF2, in 2000. In 2002, there were 50 indoor football teams playing under the auspices of the Arena Football League.

Arena football is a hybrid version of the outdoor game with similar scoring, rules, and the basics of blocking and tackling. The major differences are that it is played indoors, on a surface half the size of a regulation football field, surrounded by padded dasherboards, similar to hockey. The result is a game called the "50-Yard

Indoor War" or the "Brawl Inside the Wall."[17] The league's tremendous success is predicated on providing a high-energy spectacle complete with laser shows and fireworks at family-affordable prices (the average ticket price in 2000 was $12). The Commissioner of the AFL observed, "The NFL is the Nieman-Marcus of pro sports. We just want to be the Wal-Mart."[17] The AFL's unique "Fans Bill of Rights" (Figure 2-1) is a public declaration of their fan-first orientation.

Professional sports, like other facets of the economy, are undergoing globalization. Among the major leagues, the NFL has led the way by sponsoring a European League and playing an early game each season in a part of the world where it is believed the NFL presence can be expanded—for example, Japan and Mexico.

The NBA employs a growing number of foreign players, and its games are shown on television in over 200 countries. The NBA's globalization efforts appear to be pursuing two tracks. First, the NBA announced an intention to expand into Europe with a target date of 2006. This may be done by (a) the NBA's adopting "alliances" with European clubs, many of which have already contacted them; (b) the NBA's taking over an existing league; (c) forming a new league comprising existing European teams, which would withdraw from their national competitions; or (d) awarding franchises to a number of European cities that would become members of the NBA.[18]

The second track to globalization for the NBA may lie in the exploitation of the home markets of its existing foreign players. The Houston Rockets drafted Yao Ming, a 7'5" center from China. Like Li Tie, whose situation is described in Figure 2-2, Yao is the most well-known athlete in his sport, and basketball vies with soccer as the most popular sport in China. With China's population of 1.3 billion, its economy growing at 7% per year, and a 98% awareness of the NBA among teenagers in the major Chinese cities, the NBA believes there is substantial potential and revenue from merchandise sales and television deals.[19]

Figure 2-1 Arena Football League Fan's Bill of Rights

- We believe that every fan is entitled to a wholesome environment for guests and family members, free of violence, profane gestures, and language or rude behavior that could in any way interfere with a first class entertainment experience.

- We believe that every fan demands that we maintain absolute respect for the game of Arena Football and maintain the integrity of the finest fair competition at all times.

- We believe that every fan is entitled to a total entertainment experience at an affordable cost for all members of the family from the time they arrive the arena to the time they depart.

- We believe that every fan is entitled to interact with and have access to players and coaches for autographs and conversations in recognition of their support at every game.

- We believe that fans expect us to honor our country and to be involved in our communities to make contributions for a better, safer, and more positive place to live.

- We believe that fans should know that we are committed to serve and not to be served, to give and just not to take, and to inspire and encourage people to higher levels of personal and professional achievement, growth, maturity, and respect for each other.

Baseball is now an Olympic sport with rapidly growing markets emerging in Southeast Asia, Latin America, and the Caribbean. Players from these regions regularly appear on MLB teams. As their numbers increase, it seems likely that MLB will follow the initiatives of the NFL and NBA. Who knows? In the not-too-distant future, the World Series may be a real world series with games between teams representing the best baseball nations in the world instead of a national championship for club teams in North America!

Soccer is one of the few aspects of globalization not dominated by the United States. Almost all the world's best players display their talents in one of the top four leagues: English Premier League, Italian Serie A, German Bundesliga 1, and Spanish Primaera Division. Hence, the international interest in the major clubs in these leagues is extraordinary as the vignette in Figure 2-2 illustrates.

Figure 2-2 A Globalization Vignette: 360 Million Watch a Routine Premier League Soccer Game

Everton Football Club is located in the city of Liverpool, and the soccer club has played in the English Premier League for 100 years, which is longer than any other team. In recent years it has tended to finish in the lower rather than the upper half of the 20 team league, but has avoided relegation (the bottom three teams each year are relegated from the Premier League to the Division I League, and replaced by the top three teams from the Division I League).

Despite the team's distinguished heritage and pedigree, the lack of recent success made obtaining shirt sponsorship challenging. Eventually they signed an agreement with Kejian, which is a Chinese mobile phone company. Soccer fever had taken hold in China after the national team qualified for the World Cup for the first time in 2002. The team lost all three games it played, but China's youth were taking up soccer faster than any other sport and enthusiasm was high. As a condition of their multi-million dollar annual fee, Kejian acquired not only the shirt sponsorship, but also required that Everton include two players from the Chinese national team as members of their playing squad! In addition to generating awareness in England of their company, Kejian also wanted to win the affection of the tens of millions of soccer fans in China for helping two of their players break into one of the world's major soccer leagues for the first time. Thus, Li Tie and Li Wei Fung arrived at Everton!

The Everton coach was skeptical and unhappy that his front office had foisted onto him two players whom he had never seen or heard about. However, Li Tie was the best and most well-known player in China, while Li Wei Fung was also a member of the national team. Li Tie's autobiography sold 100,000 copies in China within two weeks of its release and he enjoyed the "iconic status of a demigod." The Chinese sent media representatives to England to cover the players' progress. Li Tie turned out to be a fine player—good enough to play regularly on the Everton team.

Four months into the nine-month, 38-game season, Everton played Manchester City, another team positioned in the middle of the Premier League in what would normally be considered a routine game arousing little interest beyond the fans of these two clubs. However, after seeing Everton's success with Li Tie, Manchester City signed Sun Jihai who was the second most well-known player on the Chinese team. A host of Chinese journalists made the 6,000 mile trip for the game, and it was shown on CCTVS, the state-owned national sports channel. The game was watched by 360 million people!

Fortuitously, there was a large Chinese community in Liverpool. Liverpool is twinned with Shanghai while its Chinatown is the oldest in Europe, dating back to the late 19th century. Just as the shipping industry first induced Chinese sailors to settle around the city's busy docks, so soccer became the city's new Sino-British link. Tens of millions of Chinese became fans of Everton! Everton immediately became the biggest player in the rapidly emerging Chinese soccer market, which has potential for generating substantial sales from sales of replica uniforms and club paraphernalia.

For the Manchester City game, Kejian flew dozens of Chinese executives to the game where they enjoyed the hospitality of both the company and the club. The club has sold a dozen luxury suites to companies that do business in China. One of these companies' CEOs said, "One of the first things Chinese business people say to me when they come over is can I get them tickets to the Everton soccer game? My box is always full."

There were 191 million mobile phones in circulation in China, but most young people wanted Nokias, while Kejian was seen as a bit uncool. Li Tie and the association with top-flight soccer changed all that. Kejian now has the image of being cool and the phone to buy in China, and the company has gained valuable exposure to new markets in Europe.

Source: Adapted from Kay, O. (2002). All quiet on Western front for pioneer Li. *The Times*, August 24.

Emergence of Women's Professional Sports Leagues

Women's sports emerged as a component of the professional sports mosaic in North America over the last half of the 1990s. The talent pool produced by the achievements of Title IX, the resultant success of women's national teams on the world stage at the summer and winter Olympics, and the 1999 Women's Soccer World Cup provided impetus for the launch of several women's sports leagues. The seminal event in the history of women's sports in the United States was probably the national team's dramatic penalty-kick shootout victory over China in the Women's World Cup final in 1999. With an estimated 36.6 million U.S. viewers, this was the most watched soccer match in the history of U.S. network television, and the crowd of 90,185 at the Rose Bowl was the largest ever for a women's sporting event. By comparison, the combined viewership on ESPN and ABC of the live and taped telecasts of the U.S. men's soccer World Cup quarter-final game against Germany in 2002 was 6.8 million viewers, even though this was the best ever performance by a men's U.S. team in the World Cup.

In the late 1990s, new women's leagues were established in basketball (WNBA and the now-defunct American Basketball League), soccer (WUSA), and softball (WPSL); and plans for a professional hockey league in the United States and Canada are under consideration. A crucial factor in both the development and sustainability of these new properties has been corporate support. Women's sports properties accounted for $600 million of the $4.5 billion that corporations spent on sports in 1999.[20] Corporations began to realize that women's sports could provide a highly effective platform for reaching women, who make 80% of a household's purchase decisions in the United States. As the Executive Director of the Women's Sports Foundation asserted, women are now serious consumers of sport who are "no longer watching soap operas and talk shows from 10 a.m. to 2 p.m."[20] Indeed, in the United States more than half of women now engage in some form of regular exercise, and one third of all high school girls participate in one or more varsity sports.

One sports property that has flourished as a result of corporate America's growing interest in aligning with women's sports has been the Ladies' Professional Golf Association (LPGA). The women's golf tour experienced a remarkable increase in corporate support over the last decade, with sponsor-supported prize money more than doubling from $17.1 million in 1990 to $36.2 million for the 2000 season.[21] Although the LPGA continues to grow, the experience of the WNBA and the WPSL indicates that women's sports properties will continue to struggle to find a secure niche in a cluttered sports marketplace. After a successful debut season in 1997, the NBA-owned WNBA found it difficult to maintain its initial momentum. During the 2000 season, league-wide attendance slipped 11%, and the league reportedly continued to lose money.[22] On the plus side, however, television ratings, although modest, grew 5% during the league's fourth season, and the WNBA was able to add six new corporate sponsors. Since its inception, the league has steadily expanded from its original 8 teams to 16 teams in 2001.

Analysts are less sanguine about the WPSL's future. The league, launched in 1997 as Women's Pro Fastpitch, has struggled to find its niche in the competitive sports market. Instead of achieving its initial goal of expanding to at least 12 markets to establish a national presence, the WPSL declined from the six original teams to just four franchises by the end of its fourth season. Given its severely contracted state, the league faced major challenges in sustaining sufficient fan and corporate support to ensure its future.

Although women's sports properties offer exciting, more family-affordable entertainment options to consumers than do their more established male competition, their struggles are magnified because they are trying to establish a toehold in an already-crowded marketplace. Finding and connecting with those select individuals in any given market who are most appreciative of, and responsive to, women's sports will be crucial to establishing a sustainable market presence. Demonstrating that women's sports enable companies to meaningfully reach audiences different from those who watch traditional men's sports will be a key towards securing adequate corporate support. Finally, controlling costs in order to ensure the delivery of affordable and accessible entertainment will help to further differentiate women's sports from much of its more established male competition.

Other Successful Sports Properties

Growth over the past 10 to 15 years has not been confined only to team or league sports. Indeed, the fastest-growing sports property of the 1990s was NASCAR. Ticket sales for the stock car circuit in the 1990s increased by 91%, and television ratings increased over 40% from 1996 to 1999.[23] The latter achievement is most notable because this growth occurred during a period when overall TV viewing for other sports properties, even the NFL, declined. By 2000, NASCAR had supplanted the NHL as the fourth-largest major sport in terms of gross revenues, which were projected to exceed $3.4 billion by 2006.[23] In 2001, NASCAR began a 6-year, $2.4 billion TV rights deal with Fox and NBC. The agreement, which quadrupled NASCAR's previous television deal, pushed America's prime auto-racing circuit well past two of the big four sports properties. The NASCAR package was almost four times greater than the current NHL television deal and more than twice the value of MLB's contract.[24] The reason Fox and NBC were willing to pay a premium to air NASCAR events is that, by 1999, Winston Cup Races were drawing the second-highest ratings for televised sports, trailing only the NFL.

Another sports property that has become a big financial success in recent years is the U.S. Open Tennis Championships, arguably the single most profitable sporting event in North America. Total revenues grew to $135 million in 2000, with corporate sponsorship support almost doubling from $14 million in 1995 to $27 million by 2000. The United States Tennis Association reported an income of $90.29 million after expenses, so the net operating profit represented 69% of total revenues.[25] The profit margin is remarkable when compared to that of most major league teams, which claim to operate at a loss.

Finally, the late 1990s and early 2000s saw the growth of many new "niche" sports, like billiards, lacrosse, and pro rodeo. These sports attract a small but avid following, and their appeal is often confined to a particular region. Lacrosse, a game historically confined to the east coast and pockets of interest in the Midwest, has established two professional leagues, the indoor National Lacrosse League and the more recently established outdoor Major League Lacrosse (MLL). Again, as with any new sports venture, an essential ingredient for success is corporate sponsor support. With the niche sports, the ability of the property to tap the intensity of the sports fan base is the key to generating sponsor involvement. As one analyst suggests, "The intensity of the fan base is often far more important than its actual size."[26] MLL was able to leverage the league's natural appeal to lacrosse enthusiasts in signing its first three major sponsorship deals with Sports Helmets, Great Atlantic (a lacrosse catalog), and stick maker Warrior Lacrosse for more than a million dollars.[27]

Complementing the extensive involvement of corporations has been the evolution of cable television as the second key element in the growth of niche sports. Cable channels such as ESPN, ESPN2, and the 13 regional sports networks around the country are in constant need of new programming to fill their 24-hour schedules. For example, it was anticipation of the expansion of professional rodeo into network television that persuaded the owner of the MLB Texas Rangers and NHL Dallas Stars to buy the Mesquite rodeo in 1999. (Mesquite is a suburb of Dallas.) His instincts were verified in 2001 when the Professional Bull Riders World Challenge event graduated from ESPN2 to NBC in the fall of 2001.[28] The demand to fill cable programming has created attractive exposure opportunities for other niche sports like track and field, bowling, and bass fishing on a national level and for lacrosse and roller hockey on a local or regional level.

The long economic boom period of the 1990s and consumers' willingness to spend and watch sport in record levels, along with cable networks' almost insatiable appetite for sports programming, combined to foster an unprecedented environment for the growth of sports in the United States and Canada. At the start of the new millennium, over 800 professional sports teams were operating in North America, almost double the number in existence in 1990.

The Economic Reality of Professional Sports

In 2001, the estimated total market value of the 123 franchises across the four major leagues in the United States and Canada was approximately $30 billion,

Figure 2-3 Economic Value of the Major Leagues

Major League Baseball
Founded: National League in 1876. American League in 1901.
Teams: 30. *Commissioner:* Bud Selig. *Gross Revenues:* $2.79 billion.
Net Worth: $6.55 billion.

National Hockey League
Founded: 1917. *Teams:* 30. *Commissioner:* Gary Bettman.
Gross Revenues: $1.82 billion. *Net Worth:* $3.75 billion.

National Football League
Founded: 1920. *Teams:* 32. *Commissioner:* Paul Tagliabue.
Gross Revenues: $3.51 billion. *Net Worth:* $12.80 billion.

National Basketball Association
Founded: 1946. *Teams:* 30. *Commissioner:* David Stern.
Gross Revenues: $2.1 billion. *Net Worth:* $6.01 billion.

more than doubling their market value in 1990. The relative economic valuation of each league is shown in Figure 2-3. The cumulative revenues generated by teams in the big four leagues in 2001 edged over $10 billion.

Despite their value and the magnitude of their financial resources, a majority of teams *claim* they are *losing* money on an annual basis. Consider the following data:

> Since 1993, net income has steadily declined across all leagues except for the NFL; the average net earnings reported in 1999-2000 were just 4%.

> Seventy-five percent of the teams in the NHL and 70% of the teams in MLB reported finishing in the red in 1999-2000.

> Since 1994, MLB claims to have lost between $200 to $300 million each year. During the 2000 season, NHL teams reported their aggregate loss was $150 million.[29]

Although discussion in this chapter focuses on the U.S. major leagues, most of the issues discussed are generic among major professional sports leagues across cultures. For example, the 20-team English Premier Soccer League reported revenues of $2.4 billion in 2001 compared to revenues of $255 million in 1992. The leading U.S. sport economist observed, "The English Premier League is roughly comparable to MLB, the NBA, and probably behind only the NFL in profits per team and average franchise value, while its best teams are comparable to the best in any league, including the NFL."[30] Despite this apparent level of success and the extraordinary increases in revenues, only 12 of the 20 teams in the Premier League reported operating profits.[30]

Professional sport executives attribute the failure of franchises to make a profit to their inability to generate sufficient revenues to meet the acceleration in operating costs that has occurred in the past decade. However, there are considerable differences in estimates of the profitability of professional sports teams. For example, in 2001 the MLB commissioner announced that the combined operating *losses* of the 30 MLB teams were $232 million, but *Forbes* magazine reported the combined operating *profits* of the teams in that year were $75 million.[32] Many analysts have suggested that major league teams' purported losses are the result of creative accounting and are paper rather than real losses. All agree that whatever the operational financial status of the franchises, their owners enjoy substantial capital appreciation of their assets. These economic reality issues are reviewed in this section.

Revenues Not Keeping Pace With Expenses

The fundamental problem for many teams is that although revenues are rising, costs are increasing at a more accelerated rate. The profit and loss reports of professional sports at the individual team level suggest that a number of teams are facing financial problems. The Anaheim Angels reported more than $42 million in operating losses during the first three seasons of the Walt Disney Company's ownership of the MLB team.[33] Over the same timeframe, from 1997 through 1999, the NHL's Vancouver Canucks reported losses of C$91 million.[34] Surprisingly, many of the teams at the top of their respective leagues are reporting serious losses. One year after winning the NBA Championship, the San Antonio Spurs claimed that the team lost $6 to $7 million in 1999 and projected losses of $30 million by 2002. Even the venerable NFL team, the Green Bay Packers, reported an operating loss of nearly $500,000 in 2000. During the 2000 season, the Packers' expenses, primarily players' salaries, increased at a rate three times greater than team revenues. The Arizona Diamondbacks reported an operational loss of $15.8 million in 2000. In an effort to bring a winning ball club to Phoenix in only its second year of operation, the MLB expansion team doubled its payroll to $70 million in 1999. Despite the team's excellent performance on the field, attendance declined, as did revenues. As a result, the team had to make a cash call of $24 million to its owners/investors in order to meet the Diamondbacks' large payroll.[35]

The Cleveland Indians appear to offer an example of how challenging it is even for successful teams to make money in the current economic environment. After the opening of Jacobs Field in 1996, the Cleveland Indians were one of the most successful teams in all of professional sports. The team presold over 3 million tickets every year. Yet the franchise claimed, in a Securities Exchange Commission (SEC) filing, that only their successful appearance in postseason playoffs allowed them to turn a modest profit. Excerpts from a prospectus filed by the Cleveland Indians with the SEC to offer a $73.6 million public stock sale stated the following:

> Management believes that the Indians' local revenue potential has already been realized, and that future increases in net income are likely to be substantially less than in the past five years. Without the contribution of postseason playoff revenues, the team would not have produced a profit in 1997.

Creative Accounting

Although league officials and team owners consistently report that their franchises are losing lots of money, the actual extent and magnitude of these claims are difficult to substantiate. Very few professional sport teams are publicly held corporations. Ownership in most cases is mainly in the hands of private individuals, families, or closely held corporations, all of which are under no legal obligation to disclose detailed financial information about their team's operations. Financial experts and players' association representatives repeatedly have challenged the authenticity of the owners' claims of financial distress, claiming that "creative accounting" procedures used by the owners made the teams' financial positions look much worse than they really were.

Baseball teams have been described as "physical embodiments of tax accountants' minds."[36] There are four main legal accounting maneuvers used by team owners to make it appear they are losing money from their investment in the team rather than making money.[37] The result of these strategies is that owners increase their personal wealth from their investments, while submitting financial reports to the Internal Revenue Service showing their teams made losses.

First, owners and their dependents may receive salaries or fees from their teams. For example, in a court case it was revealed that the owner of the Philadelphia Eagles paid himself an annual salary of $7 million. Thus, the owner was making $7 million a year more on his investment than he appeared to be. The team may also purchase services from other companies controlled by an owner, for example, legal, public relations, or information technology services. To the extent that these services are either superfluous or charge more than market rate, the added costs to the franchise are merely revenues retained by the owner via another vehicle.[37]

An owner who controls the team, the stadium, and the team's broadcast and television outlets, or some combination of these, has multiple opportunities to create accounting losses by shifting revenues among the entities. They can be shifted at the owner's discretion to whichever entity best suits the purpose at hand. For example, in a carefully documented case, a former owner of the Florida Marlins claimed the team lost $30 million when winning the World Series in 1997. However, revenues from luxury suites, premium seats, naming rights, parking, signage, merchandising and concessions were all attributed to the stadium that he also owned, not to the team. The estimated revenues from these sources were $36 million. In addition, the value of the media outlet increased by $40 million in that year as a result of the team's success. Hence, the reality was that the team's activities resulted in a net gain to the owner of $46 million, rather than the $30 million loss he reported.[38]

The third accounting maneuver stems from the type of corporate structure used by the franchises. Many of them are "subchapter S" corporations.[37] These are limited to having no more than 75 shareholders, and these corporations do not directly pay income taxes. Rather, the income gains or losses and taxes are computed at the corporate level, but they are passed through to the shareholders and reported by the shareholders on their individual 1040 federal income tax forms according to their proportional share of the ownership. The advantages of this arrangement are illustrated in the following example:

A partnership of 10 owners contributed equally to the purchase of a professional franchise for $200 million. In a given year, the team reported an annual operating loss of $30 million. Owner A, who was a member of the partnership, had a taxable income of $2 million in that year. He filed a joint tax return with his spouse and so was required to pay $638,000 in federal income taxes on his earned income. However, he also received $3 million in losses as his one-tenth share of the subchapter S corporation's losses. When this is included in his tax return his $2 million taxable income falls to zero. Thus, he saves $638,000 that he would otherwise have had to pay to the federal government in income taxes. Further, he can carry forward the additional $1 million in losses to the following year and use it to offset his taxable income in that year.

A former president of the Toronto Blue Jays reputedly stated, "Under generally accepted accounting principles, I can turn a $4 million profit into a $2 million loss, and I can get every national accounting firm to agree with me."[38] This was a reference to the roster depreciation allowance provided to the owners of professional sports teams, which is the fourth legal accounting procedure used to support the façade that most professional sports teams lose money. Under a special provision, called the "Veeck Tax Shelter Convention," the IRS allows owners to claim half of what they paid to purchase a team as depreciation on player contracts. Bill Veeck was an imaginative, pioneering baseball team owner who convinced the IRS that the player roster is like a piece of machinery or building that wears out over time, so like these items, the roster should be depreciable over time.[37] Specifically, the owner can assign 50% of the franchise purchase price to player contracts. Then, for tax purposes the roster can be treated as a declining or "wasting" asset, depreciating the value of the contract over a 5-year period. The following illustration clarifies how an owner can take advantage of this tax sheltering provision:

> Suppose someone buys an NFL team for $200 million. The new owner assigns 50% of the purchase price to player contracts, (the maximum allowed under the law), that is, $100 million, and then depreciates the contracts over five years at $20 million per year. Suppose that revenue is $100 million per year, and that costs, exclusive of player contract depreciation, are $90 million. Then, for the first five years of operation of the team, the books of the team will look like this:

> Revenue . . . .$100 million
> Less Costs . . . . $ 90 million
> Less Depreciation . . . $ 20 million
> Pretax profits . . . . . - $10 million

The depreciation of $20 million is simply a bookkeeping entry with no actual cash expended to cover this expense, so a $10 million profit is transformed by legitimate accounting procedures to a $10 million pretax loss. However, the owner will have revenues of $10 million in his or her pocket. Some analysts believe that this tax-shelter enhances the after-tax return to an owner to such an extent that it increases the value of a team by as much as 40%.

Capital Appreciation

In addition to the special tax benefits they receive, owners of sports teams have been able to count on steep increases in the market value of their teams. Historical records of franchise sales indicate that team sales prices have increased at double-digit rates over the past 30 years. In 1920, George Halas paid $100 for the Chicago Bears. In a more contemporary context, in 1984 the owner of the Denver Broncos paid $70 million to purchase the team. A decade later, the Tampa Bay Buccaneers were sold for $197 million. By 2001, according to *Forbes* magazine, all three of these NFL franchises were estimated to be worth around $500 million.

As Table 2-3 indicates, huge capital gains are not confined to NFL teams. From 1995 to 2001, the average value of MLB teams *increased* by $179 million, at an annual rate of appreciation of around 19%. Both the NBA and NHL also demonstrated impressive double-digit gains. As one commentator noted,

> Team values have risen quite handsomely and this doesn't happen, typically, to assets that lose money over time. Just as typically, very wealthy people do not line up to gain access to an asset priced at hundreds of millions if they anticipate large losses.[37]

Although the cost of ownership continues to rise steeply, it appears that there are still more wealthy individuals interested in buying teams than there are available franchises. As long as demand exceeds supply, the value of professional sport franchises will continue to climb. Although so-called psychic income benefits (e.g., prestige, status, fame, fun) remain as compelling motives for team ownership, contemporary owners of professional sport franchises also recognize that well-managed sport properties afford them abundant tax-sheltering benefits and the prospect of an attractive return on investment over the long haul.

The Leagues' Declining Health

Three issues are indicative of the declining health of the major leagues: falling attendance, declining ratings, and an economic disconnect with their fan base. Each of these issues is discussed in this section.

Falling Attendance

Almost half of the teams in the four biggest leagues reported flat or declining attendance in 2001-2002. During the 2002 MLB campaign, almost 40% of the league's total seating inventory went unsold. Indeed, in 2002, 22 of the 30 MLB

Table 2-3 Average Value of League Teams From 1995–2002 (in millions)

League	1995	1996	1997	1998	1999	2000	2001-02	$ Diff	% Annual Increase
NFL	$160	$177	$202	$285	$380	$423	$531	+$371	20.1%
NBA	$113	$127	$150	$170	$183	$207	$223	+$110	12.0%
MLB	$107	$111	$115	$134	$194	$233	$295	+$188	18.6%
NHL	$ 71	$ 74	$ 90	$125	$135	$148	$157	+$ 86	15.1%

Sources: Information compiled from *Financial World, Forbes Magazine,* and *Sports Business Journal* articles published before February 2003.

clubs reported attendance declines, with 10 of those teams posting double-digit losses (ranging from -11.3% to -38.8%) when compared to the 2001 season.

In the 2001-2002 season, the NBA experienced its first increase in overall attendance since 1997-1998. Although league attendance was up a modest 1.2% in 2002, the increase reversed a 5-year trend in which the NBA's average attendance had fallen by about 2%. However, during the 2001-2002 season, 12 of the NBA's 29 teams showed declines.

The NHL also showed a modest resurgence in fan interest in 2001-2002, reporting a league-wide increase of 1.2% over the previous season. Although encouraging, this improvement still left the league short of attendance levels achieved in the mid-1990s. Attendance eroded steadily over the last 4 years of the 1990s, with the league-wide percentage of capacity figure falling from 93% in 1996-1997 to a low of 88.9% during 1999-2000. The positive step in 2002 (overall, the league sold 91.5% of its seating inventory) is particularly important for NHL teams because they are dependent on gate receipts for 60% of their total revenues. Twelve of 30 NHL teams reported attendance declines in 2001-2002.

Only the NFL has been able to sustain consistently high attendance levels through both the 1990s and 2000s. In most markets, NFL teams benefit from the basics of supply and demand. With a smaller inventory of games to sell (10 total, including 2 preseason and 8 regular-season home games), and a large and enthusiastic fan base in most markets, many NFL teams have been able to sell consistently over 95% of their available seating capacities. However, not every NFL team has been impervious to attendance problems. Over much of the 1990s and early 2000s, the Raiders both in Los Angeles and in their present location in Oakland (relocated to Oakland in 1995), as well as the Arizona Cardinals in Phoenix and the Seattle Seahawks have struggled to fill all the seats in their stadiums. What may be more troubling is the rising number of "no-shows" (no longer reported by the league) in many NFL stadiums. An example is the Carolina Panthers, who, in only their third year of operation, saw an average of more than 7,000 no-shows per game. That was a 317% increase in empty seats compared to their inaugural season.[37] No-shows are those fans who have purchased tickets but, for whatever reason, do not attend the game. Although the team does receive ticket revenue from the pre-purchased ticket sales, it does not benefit from the additional spending associated with game attendance from such sources as parking and concession sales. As will be discussed in later chapters, these ancillary sources of revenue can be considerable.

Declining Ratings

Most league executives, particularly in the NFL and NBA, profess relatively little concern about stagnant or sagging attendance, proclaiming that the typical fan is now a television fan. Certainly, more sports programming is available on free or cable television than ever before. With the emergence of regional sports networks to compete with ESPN's delivery of around-the-clock broadcasting, fans now have unprecedented opportunities to watch their favorite teams. Although the four major networks devote an increasing portion of their programming to sports—which in aggregate exceeds 2,000 hours each year—unfortunately, fewer viewers appear to be watching games involving teams from MLB, the NBA, NHL, or NFL. Ratings for all four leagues have been sinking for the past decade.[41] Between 1987 and 2000, ratings for MLB were down 30%; for the NBA, 14%; and for the NFL, 22%.

At least two plausible explanations have been offered for the ratings decline. Some, like the president of the NFL, believe the glut of entertainment options increasingly available to fans has diluted network numbers. There are more people watching sports on television, but they are watching it on a lot more channels. According to him, "The sports fan has so many choices now, but when you compare our ratings to the rest of network television, we are still delivering the numbers you can't find elsewhere."[41] Indeed, the NFL's approximate 25% household share (for regular-season games) is unmatched by any other sporting event with the exception of the Summer Olympic Games.

Economic Disconnect

A more ominous explanation for the league rating declines is that working-class and middle-class families, the traditional bedrock fans of professional sports, are gradually losing interest in watching major league games because they no longer can afford to attend them. There is ample evidence of a growing economic disconnect between professional sports and most Americans. Table 2-4 shows the steady and substantial increase in the cost of attending games across all four leagues. Using the Fan Cost Index (FCI) created by *Team Marketing Report,* which estimates the average cost for a hypothetical family of four to attend a professional team sports event, comparisons are provided for the major leagues over an 11-year period.

Table 2-4 The Rising Cost of Attending Major League Sports			
League	1990-91	'02–03	% Change
MLB	$ 77.41	$148.61	+ 92%
NBA	$138.82	$254.88	+ 84%
NFL	$152.55	$290.41	+ 90%
NHL	$132.62	$240.43	+ 81%

*Based on fan cost index (FCI) calculated by TMR to represent average cost for family of four attending a major league game. (2 adult and 2 child's tickets, 4 sodas, 4 hot dogs, 2 beers, 2 programs, 2 caps)

Sources: *Team Marketing Report* (through April 2003) and *USA Today,* January 22, 1998, p. 3C

The results show the price of attendance rising four to six times greater than the rate of inflation. The NBA and NHL lead the way, with more than 100% price increases over the decade. In 2002, at an average of $50.10, the cost of a ticket to attend an NBA game had eclipsed that of all of the other leagues, but the NFL and NHL were not too far behind, with ticket prices averaging $50.02 and $49.86 respectively. For a family of four to attend an NHL ($274.66) or NFL ($290.41) game during the 2002 season amounted to about 30% of an average household's weekly earnings. Even MLB, which takes pride in being pro sports' biggest bargain, raised its cost of attendance by 88%. It is clear that attending a live major-league sport event is now beyond the reach of most of the population. Indeed, 9 of 10 Americans say ticket prices are so high that it is difficult for them to attend a professional sporting event.[10]

Data confirm the increasingly narrow demographics of those attending big-league games. They indicate that middle-income and blue-collar fans have been replaced by more affluent spectators. A columnist proclaimed, "Going to ball games is becoming a perk of the new rich."[42] His proclamation is given credence by a report indicating that the average household income of Washington, D.C., area residents attending Baltimore Orioles games was $87,500,[43] Whereas the average household income of those residing in the Baltimore-D.C. area is around $53,000.

It was reported that although there was a 10.1% decrease between 1995 and 2001 in the number of spectators at MLB games whose household incomes ranged from $30,000 to $49,999, there was a 67.9% increase in the number whose household incomes ranged from $100,000 to $149,999.[32] Other compelling evidence indicating the gentrification of big-league baseball appeared in *American Demographics*.[44] Analysis found that adults with household incomes of $75,000 and above were 72% more likely to attend MLB games than were households with aggregate incomes of less than $35,000. When only such a narrow segment of the market (13.6% of households had incomes in excess of $75,000) can afford to attend professional sporting events on a regular basis, it is not surprising to find fan interest dissipating for both live and televised offerings of major league sports. It has been suggested that the greatest danger facing professional sports is fan apathy.[41] For example, a 1998 *Los Angeles Times* poll reported that almost two thirds of respondents did not consider an NFL team in the Los Angeles area to be of any importance to them.

With ticket prices displacing all but the most affluent consumers, teams—particularly in the NBA and NHL—have devoted an increasing proportion of their seating inventory to corporate ticket buyers. A survey conducted by the NBA's Minnesota Timberwolves found that 62% of season tickets sold in the lower bowl of their arena were owned by corporations.[40] Although teams may be able to sell an increasing share of their most expensive tickets to businesses, the trend leads to other problems. It has been pointed out that

> the corporate fan, who has replaced the core fan, is a fickle beast, choosy about which game he'll use his precious free time to attend. Mid-week against the Milwaukee Bucks, or the Nashville Predators? That's a pass. If the suit bothers to give the tickets away, he's likely to hand them over at the last minute to some secretary in Personnel, who might prefer to be home watching Regis make people sweat.[40]

It's no wonder, then, that no-shows are a growing concern to the major leagues. Some teams, like the NBA's Charlotte Hornets, were filling less than half the number of seats that were actually sold late in the 2002 season.* Sold but unfilled seats or unused tickets can have serious financial repercussion because "when no one is in that seat, not only do we lose the value of the ticket, we lose concession money, merchandise money, and program money."[40]

Although pricing is a serious issue facing the managers of professional sports teams, a poll commissioned by *Sports Illustrated* indicates there are a number of other serious issues that managers must address (Figure 2-4).

---

* At the end of the 2001-02 NBA season, the Hornets' franchise relocated to New Orleans.

Figure 2-4 Reasons Fans Stay Home

SI commissioned the Peter Harris Research Group to conduct a scientific national survey of sports fans on issues related to attendance at MLB, NBA, NFL, and NHL games. The 874 fans polled attended an average of 10.3 pro or college basketball or football games in the past year and 39.5 games in the past five years. The top 10 reasons, with percentages of fans citing them, that made respondents less likely to fill a seat at a sporting event are as follows:

Total cost to attend	57%
Comfort of watching games at home	41%
Players' behavior during games	41%
Traffic and parking	38%
Increase in sports on TV	35%
Lateness of games	26%
TV replay and analysis	22%
Unlikelihood of getting good seats	19%
Change in how local team is doing	14%
Change in family's interest in game	13%

Controlling Player Costs

The single greatest operational expense for major league teams is player costs. Player payroll costs represent about two-thirds of the total operational expenses incurred by teams.[45] Salary increases during the 1990s in every major sports league were extraordinary. As Table 2-5 illustrates, the NBA led the way. In 1991, the average NBA player was almost a millionaire. Ten years later, the average had more than trebled to $3.53 million. From 1990 through 2001, player salaries increased more than 2-1/2 times in all four major professional leagues.

The deputy commissioner of the NBA declared, "We have an economic system that we think is out of whack."[29] This declaration was not a revelation to those who owned or operated those franchises. The owners are ultimately responsible for paying the players' salaries, but the chairman of the Chicago White Sox and Bulls expressed frustration at the lack of constraint demonstrated by fellow owners by commenting, "In paying ballplayers, we are at the mercy of our *dumbest* competitor."[29]

Each of the four major leagues has attempted, with varying degrees of success, to bring spiraling salaries under some form of control. The varying systems, involving "hard" and "soft" salary caps, free agency constraints, and luxury taxes, have all been designed to act as a "drag" on the rapid inflation of player salaries. In every instance, however, owners' efforts to impose a constraint on roster costs have met with fierce resistance from the collective bargaining unit or players' association representing the interests of players in each of the leagues. Every league endured at least one labor conflict over the past decade. Major League Baseball has led the way with six lockouts or strikes since 1972. The following sections provide

Table 2-5 League Salary Increases From 1990-91 to 2002-03

Year	MLB	NFL	NBA	NHL
2002-03	$2,555,476	$1,316,000	$4,540,000	$1,640,000
1999-00	$1,938,849	$ 996,000	$3,170,000	$1,350,000
1997-98	$1,341,000	$751,000	$2,600,000	$1,200,000
1993-94	$1,012,424	$645,000	$1,350,000	$ 430,000
1990-91	$597,537	$351,800	$ 990,000	$ 320,000
Increase	328%	274%	360%	413%

Sources: National Football League Players Association, National Basketball Players Association, National Hockey Players Association, Associated Press.

an overview of the current state of each of the major leagues with respect to their ability to control or constrain player salaries.

National Football League

In 1993, the NFL owners signed a collective bargaining agreement (CBA) with the NFL Players Association ending a 5-year labor dispute. Under the agreement, for the first time, players whose contracts had expired were allowed the right as "free agents" to move to a team willing to make the best offer. In exchange for free agency, the players and owners agreed to a salary cap under which teams were restricted to spending not more than 64% of the league's "designated gross revenues" on player salaries. (In effect, this pool of money included the combined gate receipts of NFL teams and the monies from the league's national television contract.) The CBA also established a minimum, guaranteeing players no less than 58% of the designated revenues. The salary cap or payroll maximum in 1994 was $34.6 million. As league revenues have grown, so has the amount teams can pay their players. By the 2002 season, the salary cap had reached $71.1 million, up from $64.5 million in 2000.

Players, however, or more accurately the agents representing players in contract negotiations, were able to circumvent the imposed salary ceiling shortly after the CBA agreement went into effect. They negotiated a loophole, sometimes referred to as the "Sanders Provision" after Deion Sanders, the first player to secure the arrangement. It allows teams to pay players substantial up-front signing bonuses, but count only a small portion of the bonus payment toward their cap. Teams are allowed to prorate the amount of the bonus over the length of the player's contract. So hypothetically, let's say Deion Sanders signed a $50 million deal with the Washington Redskins for 5 years, including a $10 million signing bonus. For cap purposes, even though the Redskins could have paid Sanders as much as $18 million in Year One of the agreement—$10 million up-front bonus and $8 million in salary (assuming a salary payment schedule of $8 million per year for 5 years for a total of $40 million)—the team would only have to count $10 million against their cap ($8 million in first-year salary and $2 million as a pro rata share of the signing bonus). Although the team actually paid out $18 million, due to the signing bonus loophole, it had to charge only $10 million toward the team's salary cap. This is why the Washington Redskins' team payroll in 2000 was $88 million,

Table 2-6 A Comparison of the Annual Average NFL Caps and Team Salaries

Year	NFL Cap ($ millions)	Ave. Team Salary ($ millions)
1993		$39.3
1994	$34.6	37.0
1995	37.1	42.5
1996	40.7	45.7
1997	41.4	43.4
1998	52.4	61.4
1999	57.3	65.8
2000	62.2	

Source: *Sports Business Journal,* January 31, 2000, p. 30.

which was over $25 million above the NFL's cap. The team had a total base salary expenditure of $31 million and signing bonus payments of around $56 million.[46]

The data in Table 2-6 show that the average NFL payroll exceeds the cap every year. However, it should be noted that these are average data, and an examination of individual cases shows wide variation ranging from far below the cap to others far above it.[37]

What allows some teams the ability to maintain salary expenditures well above the cap is that some NFL owners have been able to generate significant additional income that does not have to be shared as part of league-wide revenues such as income from luxury suites, concessions, naming-rights deals, and in-stadium signage. So, for example, because the Redskins play in a stadium owned by the team that generates close to $100 million in annual revenues, most of which is exempt from the league's shared designated gross revenue system, the team is capable of paying the huge bonuses that do not count entirely against the cap.[46]

Although teams that play in lucrative stadiums have an economic advantage, the league's underlying economic structure has created substantial financial parity among NFL franchises. The NFL has the greatest amount of revenue-sharing among its owners, where as much as 77% of the total revenues generated by the league is shared among its 32 teams. Revenues from the NFL's national television broadcast contract alone provide each team with a substantial annual payout. Over the course of the 8-year television deal, each NFL team will receive an equal share, progressively growing to $85 million by the final year of the agreement in 2005.

In 2001, the NFL changed its gate revenue sharing plan. Previously, gate revenues from each game were shared equally between the home and visiting teams. The post-2001 arrangement required 40% of each game's gate revenues to go into a common pool from which each team in the league received an equal distribution, whereas the remaining 60% was shared equally by the home and visiting teams. The effect was to reduce both the contributions made to the collective welfare by the high-gate teams and the revenues received by the low-gate teams. This was done to increase the incentive of low-gate teams to improve their revenue performance.[37]

The result of the extensive revenue sharing in the NFL is that it is the healthiest of all the major sports leagues in North America. Because it has the greatest financial parity, the NFL also benefits from having the greatest competitive parity. During the 1999 season, 13 of the league's then-31 teams finished with records between 7 wins and 9 losses and 9 wins and 7 losses.[47] The NFL has the highest and most consistent team valuations, the strongest television ratings, and the most ardent fan following.

In the spring of 2001, the *Los Angeles Times* newspaper released confidential information about the financial performance of every NFL team from 1995 through 1999. Subsequently, the NFL data originally placed on the *Times* website was republished in full by *Sports Business Journal.*[48] The data, representing the actual audited financial statements of all 31 (at the time) NFL franchises, had been entered in evidence in a trial held in Los Angeles between the NFL and the Oakland Raiders in a dispute over whether the Raiders or the league held franchise rights to the Los Angeles market. The financial statements provided a detailed breakdown of each team's revenues, expenses, and net operating income over a 5-year period. While too voluminous to republish in this book, readers interested in gaining an in-depth understanding of the economics of the NFL are encouraged to carefully review the team performance data reproduced in the *Sports Business Journal.* To date, the NFL data provide the most complete and credible information on the financial performance of a professional sports league in North America.

National Basketball Association

After remarkable growth through most of the 1990s, the NBA luster faded somewhat in subsequent years. With the retirement of mega-star Michael Jordan and his magical championship run with the Chicago Bulls in 1998 and the labor dispute that led to the cancellation of 464 league games in 1999, league attendance steadily declined, TV ratings sank to the lowest in years, and merchandise sales plummeted.[49] According to some analysts, at least two thirds of the league's 63% slide in playoff television ratings through 2000 could be attributed to Jordan's retirement.[50]

After negotiations over a new collective bargaining agreement (CBA) collapsed in June 1998, NBA owners locked out the players for the third time since 1995. The struggle occurred over how much of the league's $2 billion in gross revenues would be shared with the players. The NBA claimed that the league operated at a deficit during the 1997-98 season for the first time in almost 20 years. League officials attributed the steady decline in the league's operating profits to rapidly escalating player salaries, which in 1997-98 amounted to 57.2% of the league's total revenues. Under the existing labor contract, the players' share was projected to reach 61% during the 1998-99 season. Negotiations stalemated when the owners wanted to impose a fixed limit on salaries at 48% of the total NBA revenues. The NBA Players Association held out for a 60% share.

After a 190-day lockout, resulting in an abbreviated 50-game season (regularly 82 games), the NBA and its players reached a settlement in January 1999. The new

6-year CBA ensured players would receive no less than 48% and no more than 55% of the league's pooled revenues, referred to as "Basketball Related Income." Most important to the owners, the new agreement afforded teams greater financial stability by setting caps for maximums on the salaries players could earn based on the number of years of service they had in the league. Under the new agreement, players with 0 to 5 years of NBA service were capped at $9 million per season; players with 6 to 9 years of league experience were capped at $11 million; and veterans with 10 or more years of service could earn a maximum of $14 million per season. The new CBA also built in some long-term cost control by setting a fixed or maximum limit on salary increases at 10%. In an effort to encourage roster stability, however, the agreement stipulated that a player re-signing with his existing team could receive a pay raise of 12.5% per year over the length of his contract. The new agreement, although costly, provided the NBA with a clear advantage over all the other leagues: the ability to control and anticipate its greatest expense, which is player salaries.

Major League Baseball

During the 2002 baseball season, players and owners narrowly averted what would have been baseball's ninth work stoppage in the last 30 years. With only hours to spare before a strike deadline, agreement on a new 4-year collective bargaining agreement was reached. The 2002 agreement represented the first time since 1970 that players and owners accepted a new labor agreement without a strike or lockout. In 1994, negotiations broke down between the owners and the powerful MLB Players Association, resulting in a 7-month strike that led to cancellation of the 1994 World Series and a shortened 1995 season. Heading into the 2002 season, many analysts believed that MLB still had not fully recovered from that damaging labor dispute.[51] In previous negotiations, players had successfully resisted the efforts of owners to impose any kind of serious constraint on salary growth. Unlike the NFL and NBA, MLB had no salary cap provision, and prior to the 2002 agreement MLB had no real mechanism in place to constrain salary inflation. Consequently, baseball payrolls grew at almost 300% in the 1990s (Table 2-5).

Nowhere is the gap between the "haves" and "have-nots" more evident than in baseball. Over the last decade, the revenue disparity between large-market and small-market teams has grown dramatically. In 2001, the New York Yankees generated over $242 million in gross revenues, compared to the Minnesota Twins' $56 million and Kansas City Royals' $63.7 million—disparities of $186 million and $178.3 million, respectively. For this reason, the Yankees were able to afford a payroll of around $135 million, whereas that of the Royals was $47 million. In all, five teams—Boston Red Sox, New York Mets, San Francisco Giants, Seattle Mariners, and New York Yankees—had revenues above $170 million in 2001. At the same time, five teams—Cincinnati Reds, Florida Marlins, Kansas City Royals, Minnesota Twins, and Montreal Expos—had revenues of less than $70 million. A primary cause of the disparities is local television and radio revenues. For example, the Yankees received about $56.7 million from these services in 2002, whereas the Expos accrued $536,000.[52]

A blue-ribbon panel commissioned by MLB to evaluate the economic conditions and prospects of the league reported that teams with the highest payrolls had won almost all of the postseason playoff series games since the settlement of the 1994 strike. The study found that no team that was not in the top tier or upper 25% of payroll spending won a single World Series game over the previous five seasons. Although, occasionally, relatively poorer teams have successful seasons, like the Oakland A's and Minnesota Twins in 2002, the preponderance of evidence supports a leading baseball analyst's contention that "the single biggest indicator of a team's opportunity for success from one year to the next is whether the team's payroll is among the top few teams in the league. Period."[53]

The competitive imbalance prevailing in MLB is the league's most pressing challenge. A leading sports publication declared that "as many as two-thirds of the teams in major league baseball have no chance of contending for the World Series—now, or anytime soon."[54] Attempts to address the serious disparity have not been successful. The owners' thwarted attempt to institute a salary cap precipitated the damaging players' strike that ended the 1994 season.

Although the 2002 agreement did not institute a salary cap, the new labor pact significantly altered the economic structure of MLB. The settlement substantially increased revenue sharing among teams and imposed a luxury tax on the payrolls of high-spending teams. Specifically the agreement that endures until December 2006 stipulated the following provisions:

Revenue sharing. The plan requires that each team contribute 34% of its local revenues (up from 20% in 2002) to a pool that is redistributed equally to all 30 MLB teams. It is estimated that the increased revenue-sharing provision will transfer $1.032 billion from richer to poorer teams over the 4-year term.[55] The Yankees contributed $50 million in the first year of the agreement, whereas low revenue teams like Oakland and Minnesota were significant beneficiaries, each receiving over $20 million in additional revenue from the redistribution plan.

Luxury tax. To place a drag on salaries by the richest teams, a tax was placed on those teams whose payrolls exceed set thresholds. At the start of the negotiations, owners proposed a 50% tax on payrolls above $98 million (including 40-man rosters and benefits). Although initially opposed to the luxury tax, players eventually agreed to a tax on payrolls at substantially higher threshold levels. In 2003, the tax was levied on that portion of a team's payroll that exceeded $117 million. This was raised to $120.5 million in 2004, $128 million in 2005, and $136 million in 2006. The tax rates imposed on teams exceeding the thresholds also varied by year and by the number of times a team violated the threshold, according to the following terms:

Luxury Tax Rates

Threshold Violations	'03	'04	'05	'06
First time over	17.5%	22.5%	22.5%	No Tax
Second time over	30.0%	30.0%	30.0%	30.0%
Third/Fourth time over	40.0%	40.0%	40.0%	40.0%

Under this arrangement, a team with a payroll of $165 million in 2003 would pay a luxury tax of $8.4 million. The team would pay 17.5% on every dollar it spent beyond the $117 million threshold, or $48 million (17.5% X $48 million = $8.4 million). The monies collected from the luxury tax were earmarked for player benefits and a fund dedicated to developing players in countries lacking organized baseball.

Minimum salary. The minimum salary for major league players was increased from $200,000 to $300,000. For players splitting time on minor league rosters, the minimum salary was $50,000.

Drug testing. All players were subjected to random drug tests for illegal steroids during the first year of the agreement. If 5% or more tested positive, mandatory random testing would take place over the next 2 years. If fewer than 2.5% tested positive in consecutive years, mandatory drug testing ended. The first time a player tested positive, he went into a treatment program. Repeat violations were subject to penalties ranging from a 30-day to a 2-year suspension.

The new collective bargaining agreement was reached just before this text went to press, so there was not sufficient time to assess the impact of the deal. Most early appraisals were cautiously optimistic about the extent to which the new contract would effectively address baseball's chronic competitive imbalance problem. "This agreement isn't perfect... but it takes real steps to help small-market teams compete with big-market teams"(p. 1D).[56] Another analyst concluded,

> The changes will not dramatically change the sport. But, the modification will nudge the game into a healthier place... The dream that all fans and franchises should carry into spring training, that their team has a fighting chance to win, is a little closer to reality. (p. C1)[57]

One key element to determining the degree to which the new contract will effect meaningful change is the extent to which owners of smaller revenue teams reinvest monies received from revenue sharing into increased payroll. The agreement does not require owners receiving redistributed revenues to spend the money on improving their player rosters.

National Hockey League

The National Hockey League is in the most precarious financial position of any of the major leagues. Like MLB, it has minimal revenue-sharing, but it has no mechanism in place to control salary growth. The league was locked into its collective bargaining agreement until 2004. The existing agreement established a cap only on rookie salaries, set at a maximum of $975,000 per season. The agreement provided few restrictions on free agency. The result was that player salaries grew at a much faster rate than team revenues.

The league's economic troubles have been exacerbated by several other problems.

With a relatively small national television contract (teams received $4.3 million per year at the end of the 1990s, compared to the NFL's $60-70 million), NHL teams depended on gate receipts on average for 60% of their overall revenues. This situation made it particularly difficult for the 14 or 15 teams that experienced attendance declines in recent years. With no provision for sharing gate revenues—home teams keep 100% of ticket sale income—the revenue imbalance has widened among NHL teams.

The financial stress has been particularly acute for the NHL's Canadian franchises. The six Canadian hockey teams have been burdened by a weak Canadian dollar and high Canadian taxes. The purchasing power of the Canadian dollar has slipped 30% in value compared to the U.S. dollar over the last decade. The declining value of Canadian currency has created an especially stressful milieu for Canadian teams. Although the franchises collect revenue in their native currency, to stay competitive with U.S.-based teams they have to pay salaries in U.S. dollars. In early 1999, the currency exchange difference on a $50 million payroll would have been about $20 million. The Montreal Canadiens pay property taxes on their arena of around $10 million per year, which is triple the combined taxes paid by all the U.S.-based NHL teams.[58] There appears to be no relief in sight for the Canadian franchises. In 2000, the Canadian Federal Government withdrew a tax credit plan that would have provided teams C$2 million a year, claiming there was no public support for the plan.

One bright note for the NHL is the television agreement the league signed with ABC/ESPN in 2000. The 5-year broadcast contract through the 2005-06 season pays the league $600 million, a significant increase over its previous contract with Fox, which paid the league $200 million. However, with no meaningful revenue-sharing proposal in sight and the likelihood of uncontrolled salary growth through at least 2004, the short-term financial prospects for many NHL teams look grim. In 1999, it was estimated that 20 of the NHL's then-28 teams were losing money.

It will be interesting to see whether the NHL commissioner's prescription for a "prosperous NHL future" will ever be realized. In his State of the NHL Address in 2000, the Commissioner offered the following plan:

> Continue to increase revenues by moving into even more new money-generating arenas and stimulating interest in hockey internationally.

> Slow skyrocketing salaries with judicious personnel decisions and, ultimately, through a new collective bargaining agreement.

> Promote, promote, promote to build a younger and broader fan base. [59]

Summary

Professional sports and intercollegiate athletics comprise over 2,000 sports teams in the United States and Canada, which attract over 200 million spectators annually. Both sectors prospered during the 1990s but face difficult financial challenges in the new millennium.

The governance of collegiate sports is shaped largely by financial considerations of cost containment and income generation. Costs exceed revenues for all but a small number of programs, so most athletic departments are reliant on substantial institutional support. The two factors that account for the escalating cost of athletic programs are increases in tuition costs and the mandate for gender equity. Increasing tuition costs means that athletic departments have to fund more money to pay for scholarships. The Federal Title IX legislation mandates that investment in women's sports be equivalent to their proportion of representation in the student body. However, women's sports at most institutions contribute only 5% - 10% of total revenues from collegiate athletic programs. To meet this mandate, colleges have resorted to cutting men's programs as well as adding women's programs because they lack the resources to meet the mandate solely by adding women's programs.

Professional sports enjoyed unprecedented prosperity in the 1980s and 1990s with expansion in the number of franchises in the four major league sports, expansion in all the minor leagues, and the creation of an array of new sports professional leagues. Part of future expansion is likely to take the form of increased globalization. Women's sports are rapidly emerging as a component of the professional sports mosaic in North America, and there has been growth in niche sports, which have a relatively small but avid following. This growth has been aided by the multitude of cable television channels that are in constant need of new programming to fill their 24-hour schedules.

The estimated aggregated value of franchises in the four major leagues in North America exceeds $30 billion, but a majority of teams claim they are losing money on an annual basis because revenues are not keeping pace with expenses. However, many analysts believe that these losses are the result of creative accounting and, in reality, that most of the franchises are profitable. The creative accounting may take four forms: (a) Owners and their dependents may receive substantial salaries or fees from their teams; (b) revenues may be shifted from the franchise to the stadium or media outlets that owners also often control; (c) franchise losses are used to shelter owners' other earned income so income taxes do not have to be paid on it; and (d) the roster depreciation allowance creates a substantial tax shelter. Although the return on investment based on annual operating income may not be obvious, the capital appreciation and profitability of franchises are apparent to all. The value of professional sports franchises has been appreciating at double-digit rates annually for the past 30 years.

Three issues are indicative of the declining health of the major leagues. First, attendances have plateaued or are in decline at many teams. Some of this problem is hidden by official attendance figures that include no-shows, and the number of no-shows is rising. Second, although the four major networks devote an increasing portion of their programming to sports, fewer viewers are watching. Ratings for all four major leagues have consistently declined over the past decade. A third indicator of declining health of the major leagues is the economic disconnect between the ability of the traditional bedrock fans to pay to watch their teams and the rapid rise in the cost of going to games. Attending a live major-league sport event is now beyond the reach of most of the population.

The single greatest operational expense for professional teams is player costs. Salary increases in the last decade have been extraordinary. Each of the four major leagues has attempted, with varying degrees of success, to bring spiraling salaries under some form of control. These efforts have been resisted by the players, and all of the leagues have endured at least one labor conflict in the past decade on this issue. It seems likely the leagues will continue to strive to control and constrain players' salaries.

1. *The Sport Summit Sports Business Directory.* (2001). Bethesda, MD: E.J. Krause and Associates.
2. Fulks, D. (2000). *Revenues and expenses of Divisions I and II intercollegiate athletic programs: Financing trends and relationships - 1999.* Indianapolis, IN: National Collegiate Athletic Association.
3. Hart-Nibbrig, N. , & Cottingham, C. (1986). *The political economy of college sports.* Lexington, MA: Lexington Books.
4. Burke, P. (1999, March). Inside Aggie Inc. *Texas Monthly,* 46-50.
5. Zimbalist, A. (1999). *Unpaid professionals: Commercialism and conflict in big-time college sports.* Princeton, NJ: Princeton University Press.
6. Pollard, J. (2001, November). Person to person. *Athletic Business,* 12.
7. Johnson, R. (1999, December 20). How one college program runs the business: Inside longhorn inc. *Fortune, 140*(12), 160-174.
8. Dreyfuss, I. (2002, August 4). Rec centers help colleges attract students. *The Eagle,* A3.
9. Sperber, M. (2000). *Beer and circus: How big-time college sports is crippling undergraduate education.* New York: Henry Holt and Company.
10. Krupa, G. , & K. Dunnavant. (1989). The struggle with the downside. *Sports Inc.* January 2, 33-38.
11. From lecture delivered by Bill Moos, Director of Intercollegiate Athletics, University of Oregon to students at the Charles H. Lundquist College of Business, University of Oregon, May 12, 2000.
12. Moran, M. (1992, June 6). Campus changes coming, like it or not. *New York Times,* B5.
13. Opdyke, J. (2000, August 23). An athletics arms race. *Wall Street Journal,* B1.
14. Will, G.D. (2002, May 27). A train wreck called Title IX. *Newsweek, 139,* 82.
15. Gardman, A. (2000, September 7). Coaches lobby for Title IX changes. *USA Today,* C4.
16. Lopiano, D. (2001, June 11-17). Division I cranks up a sports "arms race." *SportsBusiness Journal,* 33.
17. Fitzgerald, B. (2000, July 25). Arena football dreams bigger than the field [Electronic version]. *San Jose Mercury.*
18. Whittell, I. (2002a, March 12). NBA declares intention to expand into Europe. *The London Times,* 39.
19. Whittell, I. (2002b, June 12). Rockets poised to propel Yao into big league. *The Times,* 39.
20. Reynolds, M. (1999, June 23-29). Women's sports: A growth industry. *SportsBusiness Journal,* 5.
21. Williams, L. (2000, August 10). LPGA at 50: Progress but still not parity. *New York Times,* D4.
22. Mullen, L. (2001, May 14-20). WNBA nets pluses. *SportsBusiness Journal,* 18.
23. Poole, M. (2000, August 7-13). NASCAR faces questions, not crisis, as market determines future. *SportsBusiness Journal,* 13.
24. King, B. (1999, November 15-22). NASCAR goes prime time. *SportsBusiness Journal,* 1, 11.
25. Kaplan, D. (2000, August 28-September 3). Open is big financial success, too. *SportsBusiness Journal,* 25.
26. Cawley, R. (2000, July 10-16). Small sports fight for survival. *SportsBusiness Journal,* 25.
27. Bernstein, A. (1999, December 20-26). Lacrosse league will open with tour. *SportsBusiness Journal,* 11.
28. Shropshire, M. (2001). Follow the bouncing cowboy. *Sports Illustrated, 95*(13), 37.
29. Howard, D. (1999). The changing fanscape of big-league sports. *Journal of Sport Management, 13*(1), 78-91.
30. Boon, G. , & Jones, D. (2002). *Annual review of football finance: Season 2000-2001.* London: Deloitte & Touche Sport.
31. Noll, R. G. (2002). The economics of promotion and relegation in sports leagues: The case of English football. *Journal of Sports Economics, 3*(2), 169-203.
32. Who's counting? (2002, June). *Athletic Business,* 13.
33. Shaiken, B.(1999, August 12). Time to sell the Ducks? *Los Angeles Times,* C12.
34. Kerr, G. (2000, January 6). Emperor has no clothes. *Toronto Globe & Mail,* A12.
35. Gilbertson, D. (2000, August 15). Has Phoenix maxed out? *Arizona Republic,* C3.
36. Whitford, D. (1993). *Playing hardball: The high-stakes battle for baseball's new franchises.* New York: Doubleday.
37. Fort, R. D. (2002). *Sports economics.* Upper Saddle River, NJ: Prentice Hall.
38. Zimbalist, A. (1992). *Baseball and billions.* New York: Basic Books.
39. Quirk, J., & Fort, R (1999). *Hardball: The abuse of power in professional team sports.* Princeton, NJ: Princeton University Press.
40. Swift, E. M. (2000). Hey fans: Sit on it! *Sports Illustrated, 92*(20), 70-85.
41. McGraw, D. (1998). Big team troubles. *U.S. News & World Report, 125,* 40-46.

42. Angell, R. (1998, June 17). Comment: Rudy awakening. *The New Yorker,* 74. 8-9.

43. Fehr, S. (1997, October 31). Pricey new sports venues help make Washington no. 1 for high cost tickets. *Washington Post,* C1, C5.

44. Dortch, S.(1996). The future of baseball. *American Demographics, 18*(4), 22-28-57.

45. Hubbard, S. Moore, D. , & Fischler, S. (1994). Sports salaries: Rocketing out of control. *Inside Sports, 16*(4), 58-69.

46. Lombardo, J. (2000, September 4-10). Redskins $88 million tops opening day payrolls. *SportsBusiness Journal,* 1.

47. Phillips, J., & Much, P. (2000). Overview of sports franchise valuation. *Inside ownership of professional sports teams.* Chicago: Team Marketing Report.

48. King, B. (2001). Special Report. NFL team financial performances. *Sports Business Journal,* September 3-9, 38-43.

49. Tagliabue, J. (2000, March 4). Hoop dreams, fiscal realities of NBA [Electronic version]. *New York Times.*

50. King, B. , & Mullen, L. (2000, June 5-11). As critics multiply, Stern says fans still love this game. *SportBusiness Journal,* 54.

51. Hunt, A. (2002, August 22). Major league baseball: A case study in mismanagement. *Wall Street Journal,* A13.

52. King, B. (2002, December 10-16). House sees some ugly MLB numbers. *SportsBusiness Journal,* 44

53. Justice, R. (2002, August 12). Players may set strike date. *Houston Chronicle,* A8.

54. Costas, B.(2000) *Fair ball: A fan's case for baseball.* New York: Broadway Books.

55. Bodley, H., & Brady, E. (1999, April 1). Baseball's new caste system. *USA Today,* C10.

56. Bodley, H. (2002, September 3). Details of the deal that kept the game on. *USA Today,* September 3, 3C.

57. Rosenberg, M. (2002, August 31). Labor peace is victory for fan, game, sanity. *Detroit Free Press,* 1D.

58. Miklasz, B. (2002, August 31). While there was no winner, players and owners combined for dramatic save at the end. *St. Louis Post-Dispatch,* C1.

59. *Inside the ownership of professional sports teams—2000.* National Hockey League. Chicago, IL: Team Marketing Report.

60. Robinson, A. (2000, June 9). Bettman says NHL in state of transition [Electronic version]. *Los Angeles Times.*

SECTION II:
OBTAINING CAPITAL FINANCING FROM PUBLIC AND PRIVATE SECTORS

Chapter Three

Trends in Sport Facility Investment

The interwoven nature of public and private investment in facilities is only one of three facets that constitute the fiscal interrelationship of governments and sports teams. In addition to *subsidizing sport facility construction,* governments may also provide infrastructure subsidies and operating subsidies.[1] Thus, for example, if city A contributes a relatively small amount of funds to build a new facility compared to those supplied by city B, it does not necessarily mean that city A provides a lower subsidy to its franchise. The outcome may be the reverse of this if city B provides much higher infrastructure and operating expenses to its franchise than city A does.

Infrastructure subsidies reflect the amount that government entities fund for acquisition of the site and for such services as water, electricity and roads, police (both for security and for traffic management), fire safety, and ambulances. Government entities may pay all or part of these costs. *Operating subsidies* are defined in lease agreements between the government entities (e.g., cities, stadium authorities) that "own" the venues and the teams who play in them. Most teams pay no, or minimal, rent; receive some or all of concession, parking, and signage revenue; require government to maintain and renovate the venue; and pay no, or minimal, property taxes. All of these are sources of revenue foregone by government entities that they would normally be expected to receive. These foregone revenues constitute a substantial subsidy to the franchise.[1]

Investments in professional sports facilities have increased exponentially over the past decade, and their rate of growth is unprecedented. This chapter commences with an analysis of trends in the number and cost of new stadiums and arenas constructed for franchises in the four major leagues in North America and of the relative contributions to those projects made by the public sector and by the franchises. This is followed by a discussion of the factors that have contributed to the trend of increasing private sector investments in these facilities in recent decades. The primary sources of momentum undergirding the public sector investment in facilities for professional teams are reviewed. The chapter concludes by presenting a framework that explains the rationale for public subsidy.

**Trends in the Cost
and Number of Major
League Facilities**

Ascertaining the cost of constructing a major sports facility often is not a simple task, because in addition to the cost of the facility itself, there are likely to be other costs associated with its construction. These may include the cost, or the opportunity cost, of land; the cost of infrastructure such as enhanced roads, utilities, or parking; and the cost of relocating existing residents or businesses to other sites. Decisions have to be made as to which of these ancillary costs, and what proportion of them, should be included in the calculation of a facility's cost.

For example, the cost of Reliant Stadium, which was constructed to house the Houston Texans NFL expansion franchise, is listed by the team and other sources as $367 million. However, the stadium was built to replace the Astrodome, home of the Houston Oilers, the city's previous NFL franchise, and the MLB Houston Astros; and it was located on the same site adjacent to the old facility. Harris County, which owned the 350-acre site of prime Houston real estate on which these facilities were constructed, effectively donated it to the project, together with all the existing car-parking and infrastructure on the site. Texans officials estimate the value of these assets at approximately $325 million. Thus, when these assets are included, the "real" cost of Reliant Stadium is close to $750 million rather than the $367 million figure that is widely cited.

The challenge of ascertaining costs accurately is further illustrated by the baseball and football facilities constructed in Baltimore in the 1990s for the Orioles and Ravens. These are listed in Table 3-1 as costing $235 million and $223 million, respectively. One commentator[2] itemized the costs attributable to the two venues as follows:

Buying the land, relocating businesses, ...$ 100 million
and clearing the site

Relocating railroad tracks and rehabbing . . . .$ 18.6
station and the signature warehouse

Baltimore City contribution of some . . . .$ 48.2
of its federal highway funds to rebuild
a street and construct a new
highway access ramp

Construction of the baseball ballpark $106.5

Construction of the football stadium $190

Construction of a parking facility . . . .$ 10

                                        Total $473.3

This example illustrates three points. First, as the Reliant Stadium example suggested, the actual stadium cost may be less than 50% of the project cost. Thus, the Orioles' park was constructed for $106.5 million, but in Table 3-1 the total project cost of the ballpark is reported as being $235 million. Second, there is a discrepancy between the above itemization and the $458 total listed for the two facilities in Table 3-1, a discrepancy that suggests that some of the costs were not attributed to the facilities in the "official" statement of costs, given in the city's press releases. Third, the allocation of associated costs to a facility beyond its direct construction cost is likely to be somewhat arbitrary, because often it is unclear which improvements have been undertaken because they are essential to the project and which because they contribute to generally upgrading the locale.

These kinds of issues make it difficult to compare the cost of one facility with that of another, and they explain why statements in the popular press or professional literature specifying a facility's cost may differ. The most reputable source for this type of information is widely considered to be the Street and Smith *SportsBusiness Journal*.[3] Hence, this was used in the analysis presented here, with four amendments. The costs shown on the *SBJ* list were cross-checked with other sources. Because of the difficulty of allocating costs, discrepancies of less than 10% were ignored. However, as a result of this cross-check procedure, four of the *SBJ* costs were changed:

	SBJ Cost	*Amended Cost*
Fleet Center (Boston)	$275 million	$160 million
Key Arena (Seattle)	$119	$ 75
Corel Centre (Ottawa)	$274	$145
Molson Center (Montreal)	$315	$230

The reason for the overstatement of the Fleet Center and Key Arena costs is unknown. In the case of the Corel and Molson Centers, at least part of the overstatement may be attributable to a failure to convert the costs in Canadian dollars to U.S. dollars.

Description of the Trend Tables

Tables 3-1, 3-2, and 3-3 list the facilities in which professional franchises in all four major leagues played at the time this book was written. The facilities listed in Table 3-3 are separated from the others because they are "outliers." That is, they are much older, do not group into coherent cohorts, and are too few to be useful as reliable indicators of trends over that extended 1912-1958 period. Jacksonville's ALLTEL Stadium is omitted because its original construction cost was not available. In cases where teams were in transition—playing in one facility but shortly to move to another that was being constructed—both facilities are listed (examples include the Houston Rockets, Dallas Mavericks/Stars, San Antonio Spurs, Denver Broncos, and Pittsburgh Steelers). This means there is a small amount of double counting included in the grand totals at the end of the tables that aggregate the investment in all facilities.

Columns 3 and 4 of the tables show the date and historical cost of construction. These data omit any subsequent renovation cost associated with the facilities. Prominent examples of extensive renovation include $100 million invested in the 1966 Anaheim Angels field in 1998; $200 million at the 1966 Madison Square Garden in 1991; $100 million at the 1966 Network Associates Coliseum in 1996; $102 million in the 1966 Oakland Arena in 1997; $295 million expansion and modernization of the Green Bay Packers' venerable Lambeau Field; and $138 million at Jacksonville's ALLTEL Stadium in 1995. The exclusion of renovation costs that in total exceed $1 billion means that the aggregate totals at the end of the tables

Table 3-1 Historical and Inflation Adjusted Costs for Stadiums 1961-2003 (2003 Prices)

Facility	Tenant	Year Opened	Cost (Million $)	C.C. Index	C.C.I. Adjusted	Public Contribution	% Public	% Private
Dodger Stadium	Los Angeles Dodgers	1962	$27.7	15.1	$219.4	$4.7	17	83
Shea Stadium	New York Mets	1964	$24.0	16.2	$177.2	$24.0	100	0
Busch Stadium	St. Louis Cardinals	1966	$24.0	17.6	$163.1	$19.0	79	21
Network Associates Coliseum	Oakland Athletics/Raiders	1966	$25.0	17.6	$169.9	$25.0	100	0
Edison International Field	Anaheim Angels	1966	$25.0	17.6	$169.9	$24.0	96	4
Qualcomm Stadium	San Diego Padres/Chargers	1967	$27.0	18.6	$173.6	$27.0	100	0
Total 1961-1969			**$152.7**		**$1,073.1**	**$123.7**		
Average Facility Cost			**$25.5**		**$178.8**	**$20.6**	**82.0**	**18.0**
Cinergy Field	Cincinnati Reds/Bengals	1970	$55	23.9	$273	$55.0	100	0
Three Rivers Stadium	Pittsburgh Pirates/Steelers	1970	$35	23.9	$175	$35.0	100	0
Foxboro Stadium	New England Patriots	1971	$61	27.4	$267	$0.0	0	100
Texas Stadium	Dallas Cowboys	1971	$35	27.4	$153	$35.0	100	0
Veterans Stadium	Philadelphia Phillies/Eagles	1971	$50	27.4	$216	$50.0	100	0
Arrowhead Stadium	Kansas City Chiefs	1972	$53	31.2	$203	$53.0	100	0
Kauffman Stadium	Kansas City Royals	1973	$51	33.7	$179	$47.0	94	6
Ralph Wilson Stadium	Buffalo Bills	1973	$22	33.7	$78	$22.0	100	0
Superdome	New Orleans Saints	1975	$168	39.3	$511	$168.0	100	0
Giants Stadium	New York Giants	1976	$68	42.7	$190	$68.0	100	0
Olympic Stadium	Montreal Expos	1976	$231	42.7	$648	$231.2	100	0
Pontiac Silverdome	Detroit Lions	1976	$56	42.7	$157	$56.0	100	0
3COM Park	San Francisco 49ers	1980	$32	57.6	$66	$32.0	100	0
Metrodome	Minnesota Twins/Vikings	1982	$75	68.0	$132	$68.0	91	9
RCA Dome	Indianapolis Colts	1984	$78	73.7	$127	$48.0	62	38
Total 1970-1984			**$1,069**		**$3,375**	**$968**		
Average Facility Cost			**$71**		**$225**	**$65**	**89.0**	**11.0**
Pro Player Stadium	Florida Marlins/ Miami Dolphins	1987	$145	78.4	$221	$30.0	20	80
Sky Dome	Toronto Blue Jays	1989	$383	82.1	$558	$241.6	63	37
Tropicana Field	Tampa Bay Devil Rays	1990	$138	84.2	$196	$138.0	100	0
Comiskey Park	Chicago White Sox	1991	$150	86.0	$209	$150.0	100	0
Georgia Dome	Atlanta Falcons	1992	$210	88.7	$283	$210.0	100	0
Oriole Park at Camden Yards	Baltimore Orioles	1992	$235	88.7	$317	$220.0	94	6
Alamo Dome	San Antonio Spurs	1993	$195	92.7	$252	$195.0	100	0
Ballpark at Arlington	Texas Rangers	1994	$191	96.2	$237	$161.0	84	16
Jacobs Field	Cleveland Indians	1994	$175	96.2	$218	$175.0	100	0
Total 1985-1994			**$1,822**		**$2,490**	**$1,520.6**		
Average Facility Cost			**$202**		**$277**	**$169**	**84.6**	**15.4**

Table 3-1 (Continued)

Facility	Tenant	Year Opened	Cost (Million $)	C.C. Index	C.C.I. Adjusted	Public Contribution	% Public	% Private
Coors Field	Colorado Rockies	1995	$215	97.3	$264	$168.0	78	22
TransWorld Dome	St. Louis Rams	1996	$290	100.0	$347	$290.0	100	0
Ericsson Stadium	Carolina Panthers	1997	$248	103.6	$286	$50.0	20	80
FedEx Field	Washington Redskins	1997	$251	103.6	$289	$70.5	28	72
Turner Field	Atlanta Braves	1998	$235	105.3	$267	$0.0	0	100
PSINet Stadium	Baltimore Ravens	1998	$223	105.3	$264	$200.0	90	10
Bank One Ballpark	Arizona Diamondbacks	1998	$354	105.3	$402	$253.0	71	29
Raymond James Stadium	Tampa Bay Buccaneers	1998	$169	105.3	$191	$169.0	100	0
Adelphia Coliseum	Tennessee Titans	1999	$292	107.8	$324	$234.0	80	20
Cleveland Browns Stadium	Cleveland Browns	1999	$314	107.8	$348	$293.0	93	7
Safeco Field	Seattle Mariners	2000	$534	110.6	$577	$372.0	69	31
Comerica Park	Detroit Tigers	2000	$300	110.6	$324	$100.0	33	67
Enron Field	Houston Astros	2000	$248	110.6	$268	$169.0	68	32
Pacific Bell Park	San Francisco Giants	2000	$330	110.6	$357	$10.0	3	97
Paul Brown Stadium	Cincinnati Bengals	2001	$450	113.8	$473	$450.0	100	0
New Mile High Stadium	Denver Broncos	2001	$400	113.8	$420	$300.0	75	25
Miller Park	Milwaukee Brewers	2001	$394	113.8	$414	$304.0	77	23
PNC Park	Pittsburgh Pirates	2001	$262	113.8	$275	$222.0	83	17
Heinz Field	Pittsburgh Steelers	2002	$252	116.6	$258	$175.5	70	30
Ford Field	Detroit Lions	2002	$325	116.6	$333	$115.0	35	65
Reliant Stadium	Houston Texas	2002	$367	116.6	$376	$252.0	69	31
Seahawks Stadium	Seattle Seahawks	2003	$400	119.6	$400	$300.0	75	25
Great American Ballpark	Cincinnati Reds	2003	$334	119.6	$334	$300.0	90	10
Total 1995-2003			$7,186.0		$7,795.5	$4,527.0		
Average Facility Cost			$312.4		$338.9	$196.8	62.0	38.0
1962-2003 Total			$10,229.2		$14,734.1	$7,139.5		

*The C.C. Index for years 2002 and 2003 is projected.

underestimate the total real investment in sports facilities currently in use over this period. Allowances for depreciation have not been made in these calculations.

The historical costs in column 4 of Table 3-1 suggest the Olympic Stadium in Montreal, built in 1976 for $231 million, cost almost 50% less than the Detroit Lions' Ford Field constructed in 2002 for $325 million. However, such a conclusion would be flawed because it ignores the impact of inflation. Obviously, $100 in 1976 purchased substantially more materials and labor than did the same amount in 2002. To meaningfully interpret trends in costs, it is necessary to take inflation into account. Thus, the question to ask is, "If the Olympic Stadium had been constructed in 2002, would it have cost less than Ford Field, all else being equal?"

This question is answered in columns 5 and 6. The U.S. Bureau of Census identifies a number of organizations that track inflation in specific spheres of the economy and annually develop indexes that adjust for it. The most reputable

Table 3-2 Historical and Inflation Adjusted Costs for Arenas 1961-2003 (2003 Prices)

Facility	Tenant	Year Opened	Cost (Million $)	C.C. Index	C.C.I. Adjusted	Public Contribution	% Public	% Private
Mellon Arena	Pittsburgh Penguins	1961	$22.0	14.7	$179.4	$22.0	100	0
Oakland Arena	Golden State Warriors	1966	$25.5	17.6	$173.3	$25.5	100	0
Madison Square Garden	New York Rangers/Knicks	1968	$133.0	19.9	$799.3	$133.0	100	0
Total 1961-1969			$180.5		$1,152.0	$180.5		
Average Facility Cost			$60.2		$384.0	$60.2	100.0	0
Nassau Veterans	New York Islanders	1972	$28.0	31.2	$107.3	$28.0	100	0
Skyreach Center	Edmonton Oilers	1974	$11.9	35.9	$39.6	$11.9	100	0
Compaq Center	Houston Rockets	1975	$18.0	39.3	$54.8	$18.0	100	0
Joe Louis Arena	Detroit Red Wings	1979	$27.0	45.8	$70.5	$27.0	100	0
Reunion Arena	Dallas Mavericks/Stars	1980	$27.0	57.6	$56.1	$27.0	100	0
Continental Airlines	New Jersey Nets/Devils	1981	$85.0	62.9	$161.6	$85.0	100	0
Pengrowth Saddledome	Calgary Flames	1983	$73.0	72.4	$120.6	$73.0	100	0
1970-1984			$269.9		$610.5	$269.9		
Average Facility Cost			$38.6		$87.2	$38.6	100.0	0
Arco Arena	Sacramento Kings	1988	$40.0	80.4	$59.5	$0.0	0	100
Bradley Center	Milwaukee Bucks	1988	$90.0	80.4	$133.9	$0.0	0	100
Charlotte Coliseum	Charlotte Hornets	1988	$58.0	80.4	$86.3	$58.0	100	0
Palace of Auburn Hills	Detroit Pistons	1988	$70.0	80.4	$104.1	$0.0	0	100
TD Waterhouse Arena	Orlando Magic	1989	$110.0	82.1	$160.2	$110.0	100	0
Target Center	Minnesota Timberwolves	1990	$104.2	84.2	$148.0	$66.0	63	37
Delta Center	Utah Jazz	1991	$102.6	86.0	$142.7	$24.6	24	76
America West Arena	Pheonix Suns/Coyotes	1992	$95.0	88.7	$128.1	$45.0	47	53
Arrowhead Pond-Anaheim	Mighty Ducks	1993	$120.0	92.7	$154.8	$120.0	100	0
San Jose Arena	San Jose Sharks	1993	$168.0	92.7	$216.8	$136.0	81	19
Gund Arena	Cleveland Cavaliers	1994	$152.0	96.2	$189.0	$152.0	100	0
Kiel Center	St. Louis Blues	1994	$171.5	96.2	$213.2	$36.5	21	79
United Center	Chicago Bulls/Blackhawks	1994	$175.0	96.2	$217.6	$10.0	6	94
1985-1994			$1,456.3		$1,954.2	$758.1		
Average Facility Cost			$112.0		$150.3	$58.3	49.4	50.6
Fleet Center	Boston Celtics/Bruins	1995	$160.0	97.3	$196.7	$115.0	72	28
General Motors Place	Vancouver Grizzlies/Canucks	1995	$160.0	97.3	$196.7	$160.0	0	100
Key Arena	Seattle Super Sonics	1995	$74.0	97.3	$91.0	$74.5	63	37
Corel Centre	Ottawa Senators	1996	$145.0	100.0	$173.4	$0.0	0	100
First Union Center	Philadelphia 76ers/Flyers	1996	$217.5	100.0	$260.1	$32.0	15	85
Gaylord Entertainment Center	Nashville Predators	1996	$144.0	100.0	$172.2	$144.0	100	0
HSBC Arena	Buffalo Sabres	1996	$127.5	100.0	$152.5	$56.1	44	56
Ice Palace	Tampa Bay Lighting	1996	$161.8	100.0	$193.5	$102.0	63	37
Molson Center	Montreal Canadiens	1996	$230.0	100.0	$275.1	$0.0	0	100
Rose Garden	Portland Trail Blazers	1996	$262.0	100.0	$313.4	$35.0	13	87

Facility	Tenant	Year Opened	Cost (Million $)	C.C. Index	C.C.I. Adjusted	Public Contribution	% Public	% Private
MCI Center	Washington Wizards/Capitals	1997	$260.0	103.6	$300.2	$60.0	23	77
National Car Rental Center	Florida Panthers	1998	$212.0	105.3	$240.8	$184.7	87	13
Air Canada Centre	Toronto Raptors/Maple Leafs	1999	$178.3	107.8	$197.8	$0.0	0	100
American Airlines Arena	Miami Heat	1999	$213.0	107.8	$236.3	$39.1	18	82
Conseco Fieldhouse	Indiana Pacers	1999	$183.0	107.8	$203.0	$79.0	43	57
Pepsi Center	Denver Nuggets/Col. Avalanche	1999	$170.0	107.8	$188.6	$8.8	4	96
Philips Arena	Atlanta Hawks/Thrashers	1999	$213.0	107.8	$236.3	$62.5	29	71
Raleigh Ent. And Sports Arena	Carolina Hurricanes	1999	$158.0	107.8	$175.3	$92.0	58	42
Staples Center	Los Angeles Lakers/-Clippers/Kings	1999	$375.0	107.8	$416.0	$12.0	3	97
American Airlines Center	Dallas Mavericks/Stars	2000	$427.0	110.6	$461.7	$125.0	27	73
Nationwide Arena	Columbus Blue Jackets	2000	$150.0	110.6	$162.2	$0.0	0	100
Xcel Energy Center	Minnesota Wild	2000	$130.0	110.6	$140.6	$130.0	100	0
Houston Arena	Houston Rockets	2002	$175.0	116.6	$179.5	$175.0	100	0
SBC Center	San Antonio Spurs	2002	$175.0	116.6	$179.5	$147.0	84	16
1995-2003 Total			$4,701.1		$5,342.4	$1,833.7		
Average Facility Cost			$195.9		$222.6	$76.4	39.4	60.6
1961-2003 Total			$6,607.8		$9,059.1	$3,042.2		

* The C.C. Index for year 2002 is projected

Table 3-3 Historical and Inflation Adjusted Cost of Facilities Constructed Between 1912-1958 (2003 Prices)

Stadium	Tenant	Year Opened	Construction Cost Million $	C.C. Index 1913=100	C.C.I Adjusted Cost	Public Contribution	% Public	% Private
Fenway Park	Boston Red Sox	1912	$0.4	91	$29.6	0	0	100
Wrigley Field	Chicago Cubs	1914	$0.3	89	$22.7	0	0	100
Yankee Stadium	New York Yankees	1923	$3.1	214	$97.5	0	0	100
Soldier Field	Chicago Bears	1924	$7.9	215	$247.2	7.9	100	0
Mile High Stadium	Denver Broncos	1948	$0.3	461	$4.4	0	0	100
County Stadium	Milwaukee Brewers	1953	$5.0	600	$56.1	5	100	0
Lambeau Field	Green Bay Packers	1957	$1.0	724	$9.3	1	100	0
Sun Devil Stadium	Arizona Cardinals	1958	$1.0	759	$8.9	1	100	0
Total			$19.0		$475.5	$14.9		
Average Facility Cost			$2.4		$59.4	$1.9	50.0	50.0

construction cost index (CCI) is produced by *Engineering News Record*,[4] a trade magazine published by McGraw Hill. The CCI is a national average that is shown in column 5. The CCI was used to adjust all the historical costs in column 4 to 2003 dollars. Thus, in 2003 the numbers in columns 4 and 6 are identical, but the index is used to increase all the historical costs preceding 2003 to account for inflation. Olympic Stadium's $231 million cost in 1976 translates into $648 million in 2003 dollars when inflation is taken into account. Hence, instead of concluding that Olympic Stadium cost 50% *less* than Ford Field, the appropriate conclusion is that it cost almost 100% *more* than Ford Field.

Column 7 reports the dollar amount to which each facility was subsidized with public resources at the time it was built. Columns 8 and 9 show the proportion of each facility's cost that was contributed by the public and private sectors.

The Evolution of Facility Funding

The year cohorts in Tables 3-1 and 3-2 are 1961-1969, 1970-1984, 1985-1994, and 1995-2003. These were selected as comparison cohorts because it is believed they approximate demarcations of distinctive phases through which the financing of stadium and arena facilities to accommodate major league franchises has evolved.

In the earliest days of major league franchises, almost all teams fully financed their own facilities. Indeed, the only exceptions to the norm were the Los Angeles Coliseum (1923), Chicago's Soldier Field (1929), and Cleveland's Municipal Stadium (1931), which were all built with the intention of hosting the Olympic Games.[5] Tables 3-1 and 3-2 show that by the 1961-1969 decade, this situation had been reversed. One commentator suggested the following reasons for this reversal and the emergence of public subsidy:

> The Depression and World War II drained the resources of major league baseball, leaving no money to build new stadiums or refurbish aging ballparks. After World War II, private stadium development became more daunting, as urban land prices rose rapidly, large parcels became more difficult to assemble, and land requirements increased because of the need to provide parking.[6]

This decade may be termed the *Gestation Era*. It marks the beginning of a period in which the norm was for governments to finance and construct facilities for the franchises. After building the new stadiums and arenas, local governments became the landlords of the facilities in which professional sport franchises were primary tenants. The arrangement was established through a lease agreement in which the team as tenant and government entity as landlord negotiated the terms under which the team would use the venue. The lease specified the annual rent payment the team would pay and spelled out the extent to which the two parties would share specific venue revenues such as those derived from parking and concessions. Interest in professional sports in this era was confined primarily to the Northeast and upper Midwest, because that is where most of the franchises were located and there was little widespread television interest.

The trend of local governments' assuming primary fiscal and operational control of sport venues reached its zenith in the *Public Subsidy Era*. During this period, which stretched from 1970 to 1984, the popularity of professional sports grew substantially. Growth occurred in the number of franchises, in venue attendance, and in television viewing. The value of franchises increased exponentially. Funding expectations were set by the precedents of the Gestation Era, so funding was widely perceived to be the exclusive responsibility of public entities primarily using either general obligation bonds or revenue bonds redeemed by some form of sales tax. In Tables 3-1 and 3-2, 18 of the 22 facilities listed as being constructed in this period were 100% funded by governments, and two of the remaining four were over 90% subsidized.

The high level of subsidies that characterized the Public Subsidy Era coincided with the most active period of expansion and relocation of professional teams ever to occur in North America, which transformed major league sports teams from a regional phenomenon to a national phenomenon. Before this shift, enacted either through migration or expansion of sports teams to Sunbelt cities, major league sports teams were almost entirely confined to major cities in the Northeast and upper Midwest. The advent of jet travel and the emergent growth and prosperity of cities in the Sunbelt region made it profitable for the leagues to place teams in those enthusiastic and untapped markets.

Owners quickly realized that representatives in western and southern cities were willing to provide fully subsidized playing facilities as an inducement to relocate or expand. Precipitated by the move in the 1950s of the MLB Braves, Dodgers, and Giants from Boston and New York City to Milwaukee, Los Angeles, and San Francisco, respectively, there was an ongoing emergence of teams in southern and western cities. In almost every instance, local and state governments, eager to attract a team, provided generous venue arrangements to team owners. As shown in Table 3-4, government generosity resulted in public subsidies reaching an all-time high during this period. From 1970 through the mid-1980s, local and state governments contributed 93% of the development costs for major sport venues built in the United States and Canada.

Table 3-4 Proportion of Public and Private Sector Funding by Era

Era	Stadiums		Arenas		Totals	
	% Pub	% Priv	% Pub	% Priv	% Pub	% Priv
Gestation (1961-1969)	82%	18%	100%	0%	88%	12%
Public Subsidy (1970-1984)	89%	11%	100%	0%	93%	7%
Transitional Public-Private Partnership (1985-1994)	85%	15%	49%	51%	64%	36%
Fully-Loaded (Private-Public Partnership) (1995 – 2003)	62%	38%	39%	61%	51%	49%

During *The Transitional (Public-Private Partnership) Era,* from 1985 to 1994, governments assumed a progressively diminishing proportionate role in the financing of major new sport facilities. The transition from almost complete government responsibility to increased team financial participation was largely the result of four factors that are discussed more fully in the next section of this chapter. Prominent among them was the enactment of the Deficit Reduction Act of 1984, which prohibited the use of tax-exempt bonds to finance luxury boxes, and the Tax Reform

Act of 1986, which stated that tax-exempt bonds could not be used to finance sports facilities if more than 10% of a facility's revenues came from a single tenant such as a professional sports team. These two Acts are discussed in more detail in chapter 6.

It was the intent of these acts to discourage cities and states from issuing tax-exempt bonds, which had been the traditional source of capital financing for professional sports facilities. Tax-exempt interest rates are generally 2% *lower* than rates for taxable bonds. It was anticipated by the sponsors of these new laws that they would require governments to issue taxable bonds for these purposes and, thus, discourage public-sector financing of facilities for professional teams. An interest rate difference of 2% on $200 million in borrowed capital over 20 years could *add* $20 million to the overall project cost. It was thought that the increased cost of using these traditional financing methods would make it more difficult for government agencies, both fiscally and politically, to assume the entire cost of financing major sport venues. In some instances this anticipated outcome probably occurred, but in others the cities responded by offering more generous leases that required the franchises to pay less than 10% of a facility's debt charges, thus enabling tax-exempt bonds still to be issued. The rest of the funds needed to retire the debt were often redeemed from other revenue sources such as sales taxes, car-rental fees, and bed taxes. The result was more complex financing structures in which cities used these other revenue sources, but in which franchises' contributions often also were more substantial (Tables 3-1 and 3-2). The development of more luxurious, fully loaded venues in the early 1990s demonstrated to governments and their taxpaying electorates that new facilities, especially arenas, had the capability of generating revenues sufficient to pay a considerable share of the construction costs.

During this transitional period, the first public-private partnerships, or joint ventures, of government agencies and team owners emerged. These projects were characterized by teams' contributing a substantial, albeit minority, share of the venue's development costs. Notable public-private partnerships of this period were the America West Arena in Phoenix, Gund Arena and Jacobs Field in Cleveland, and the Target Center in Minneapolis. The shared-cost model became an acceptable development formula for both parties. Government officials who were anxious to find a solution for accommodating a franchise's demand for new facilities found public-private partnerships effective in ameliorating taxpayer resistance to expensive public subsidies. Teams, on the other hand, were willing to make a significant up-front contribution with the expectation that they would realize far greater financial returns from the incremental income produced by the new, fully loaded facility.

Typically, during this period, the public-private development agreements between teams and local government entities were accompanied by lease agreements that were generous to the franchises, guaranteeing them a majority, if not all, of the revenues from luxury suites, concessions, parking, and sponsor agreements. Although joint ventures became prevalent during the early 1990s, a number of major projects at that time, particularly stadiums, still were completely underwritten with public monies. Both St. Louis and Baltimore, for example, each anxious to lure NFL teams back to their cities, provided fully subsidized, state-of-the-art facilities to induce teams from Los Angeles and Cleveland, respectively, to relocate to their communities.

The remarkable growth in the popularity of professional sports during this era was accompanied by the desire of corporations to be associated with them. This was manifested in corporations' willingness to pay high prices for luxury boxes and associated amenities: "The corporate customer is relatively price-insensitive, but he demands his creature comforts."[7] In turn, corporate support provided impetus for the franchises to transition from basic multipurpose facilities into elaborate single-sport facilities. By the year 2000, 60% of season tickets in the NBA and the NFL were corporate purchases.

The "Fully Loaded" (Private-public) Era from 1995 to 2003 was an era of extraordinary proliferation in which 47 major new facilities were constructed. This represents approximately 45% of the total inventory of major league franchise facilities. In most cases, facilities from which teams moved were not physically obsolete; rather, they were commercially obsolete. The overwhelming characteristic of this era was the escalation in facility cost, which accompanied the owners' accelerated demands for excellent, deluxe, elaborate facilities, and the ability of these fully loaded arenas to generate substantial revenues. Most facilities are now financed through private-public partnerships. This description reorders the two sectors compared to the Transitional Era (i.e., private-public rather than public-private) to reflect the private-sector role moving towards being the primary source of funds. The increased contributions from the franchises reflect the growing unwillingness of taxpayers to wholly fund these projects with property taxes. This has resulted in financial structures being more creative, innovative, and intricate. The multiple parties involved and the complexity of the financing and partnership arrangements mean that the planning and construction period is often much longer than it was in previous eras.

How Much and Who Pays?

Tables 3-1 and 3-2 show that when expressed in 2003 dollars, the total investment in the stadiums and arenas being used by major league teams at that time was $23.8 billion—$14.74 billion for stadiums and $9.06 billion for arenas. Of this $23.8 billion, $13.14 billion (55%) was invested between 1995 and 2003. Governments' share of the $23.8 billion was approximately $15.2 billion (64%).

These calculations of total investment refer only to facilities then in use or shortly to be in use. In 2003, 56% of teams were playing in facilities constructed after the start of 1990. In most cases, teams playing in facilities constructed in the last decade abandoned a facility elsewhere, and many of those had been built since 1960. If the costs of those casualties of the upgrading process were included, then the total investment in major league sport facilities would be substantially higher. Similarly, the large investments in renovation and expansion of some facilities, illustrations of which were cited earlier in the chapter, are not included in these investment calculations.

Table 3-5 Comparison of Old and New Facility Costs for Selected Teams

TEAM	OLD FACILITY COST (2003 ADJUSTED $'S)	NEW FACILITY COST (2003 ADJUSTED $'S)
Houston Rockets	54.8	179.6
Dallas Mavericks/Stars	65.4	461.7
Milwaukee Brewers	53.4	414
Pittsburgh Steelers	175	265
Denver Broncos	4.2	420

The aggregate increase in investment is attributable both to an expansion of the professional leagues and the replacement of facilities for existing teams. The change in magnitude of costs when teams change facilities is vividly illustrated by comparing the "transitional" facilities included in Tables 3-1, 3-2, and 3-3; that is, those stadiums and arenas that were abandoned soon after the 2001 season as teams moved into new facilities. Teams that were in this category are listed in Table 3-5. The cost differences, even when expressed in inflation-adjusted terms, are dramatic and reflective of the high-quality standards that characterize the contemporary Fully Loaded Era of facility development.

The persistent and substantial downward trend in level of public subsidy is clearly evident in Table 3-4. Gradually, over the past 30 years there has been a dramatic shift toward franchise owners' assuming a greater share of development costs of the venues in which their teams play. This shift is most apparent in arena construction. Until 1984, local governments had assumed complete responsibility for financing arenas dating back to 1961, but beginning in the mid-1980s, governments assumed a significantly diminished role in arena financing. By 1995, primary responsibility for arena construction had reverted to franchise operators, with team owners supplying almost two thirds of the construction financing. Although not as dramatic, the trend toward greater owner financing is also evident with respect to recent stadium construction. Since 1995, owners have contributed 38% of the capital necessary to build new stadiums, a major increase over the 15% share they assumed through the mid-1980s.

The pivotal year in the shift in responsibility for arena financing was 1988. In that year, the Palace at Auburn Hills was built for the Detroit Pistons. It was a catalyst facility, because it was the first of the single-purpose, elaborate special-purpose arenas. In the same year, Arco Arena in Sacramento also opened. Both facilities were financed completely from private sources. In each instance, the owner-financed projects were capitalized on the basis of the arena's ability to generate income sufficient to pay for the cost of construction. The Bradley Center in Milwaukee, also built in 1988, was entirely underwritten by a $90 million gift to the State of Wisconsin from the Bradley family.

These privately developed venues, particularly the owner-financed projects, had a transformational effect on sport facility financing. The impact is clearly evident in

Table 3-4, where the swing toward more private investment in arenas in the Transitional and Fully Loaded Eras is obvious. In the most recent era, from 1995 to 2003, $4.70 billion was spent on building 24 new major arenas in the United States and Canada (Table 3-2). Of that amount, only 39% was contributed from public sources. In a little over a decade, arena financing moved from being almost exclusively publicly subsidized to being primarily financed by franchise owners. However, it is important to point out that in real dollar terms, the average cost of arenas in this most recent era was over $222 million (Table 3-2). Thus, 39% of the average cost is $86 million, which in real dollar terms exceeds the contribution government was making in the 1969-1984 era when it was paying 100% of the cost!

In the three eras up to 1994, government was almost the exclusive provider of funding for stadiums. The notable exception was Joe Robbie (subsequently renamed Pro Player) Stadium built in 1987, which was the first fully loaded stadium. The privately financed facility was funded primarily by the $90 million raised from its 183 luxury suites and 10,209 club seats.

The franchise owners' early responses to this stadium precedent were less enthusiastic than were the responses to the prototype new arenas. However, in the post-1994 era, there was a marked change, because among the 23 stadiums built in that period, government's contributions fell to 62% of the $7.14 billion invested. This proportion is still substantially higher than the subsidies provided to arenas over the same period, which is attributable to the greater difficulty of generating revenues in stadiums. Although the emergence of premium seating has resulted in substantial increases in stadium revenues, the limited versatility and supplementary use capability of football-only and baseball-only venues, and constraints imposed by the weather, make it difficult for such facilities to generate as much revenue as arenas do.

This is particularly true when the venue's primary, or anchor, tenant is an NFL football team. Most NFL franchises will play two preseason games and eight regular-season games in their home stadium. In a particularly successful season, a team may play one or two postseason playoff games at home. Thus, the best-case scenario is that an NFL team will occupy its home venue on 12 dates a year. This makes it challenging to produce substantial revenues, even if the football dates are supplemented with occasional concerts, and even in the largest stadiums. FedEx Field, home of the traditionally well-supported Washington Redskins, in a standard 10-game season can accommodate slightly over 800,000 spectators. The Staples Center, by comparison, from its three primary tenants alone (Lakers, Clippers, Kings) attracted over 2 million patrons in the 2000-2001 season. When 100 additional events occurring in the facility are taken into account, the Staples Center generates more than three times the number of tickets sold, hot dogs consumed, and cars parked when compared to the most populated NFL venue.

New facilities built in Denver and Houston exemplify the current status of who pays for football stadiums. Voters approved subsidies of approximately $300 million and $250 million in Denver and Houston, respectively, for the construction of new stadiums. The estimated cost of each venue was approximately $400 million. The owners of the Broncos and Texans were required to commit $100-$125 million of their own funds toward each project and to guarantee responsibility for any cost overruns. Thus, the relative contributions to the projects were 70-75% public and 25-30% private.

With 81 home games during the regular season, it is easier for MLB stadiums to produce a positive net operating income. Some teams, like the San Francisco Giants, achieve this by aggressively marketing their ballpark, Pacific Bell Park, as the site for a variety of events beyond baseball. In addition to concerts and other public events, it is rented to local corporations for company outings so employees and their families can have the experience of playing baseball at a major league park.

Even though owners now typically pay a greater proportion of stadium construction costs than they did in previous eras, most football and baseball franchises are more profitable as a result of playing in fully loaded venues and being supported by sponsorship, licensing, and media income streams. This trend of the franchises' paying a proportion of the costs has stabilized the magnitude of government subsidy for stadiums. The data in Table 3-1 show that in real dollar (2003) terms government subsidy of stadiums over the past three decades has been relatively stable. The average subsidy of a stadium in the four funding eras in real dollars (2003):

Gestation Era	1961 - 1969	$147 million
Public Subsidy Era	1970 - 1984	$200 million
Transitional Era	1985 - 1994	$234 million
Fully Loaded Era	1995 - 2003	$210 million

Conceptually, an argument has been made that the public subsidy of teams in larger cities should be smaller than that in less populated cities because the larger cities offer more earning potential for the franchises and the leagues. "They have the concentration of wealth that team owners and organizations seek to maximize their profits."[8] The authors making this assertion used the negotiations between the city of Houston and the Houston Rockets to illustrate their point, and the argument is developed in Figure 3-1. Unfortunately, the logic they developed appears to have been disregarded in the political calculus because it did not prevail. Table 3-2 shows that the Rockets' new $175 million facility was 100% subsidized by the city of Houston. Nevertheless, these data illustrate why smaller cities are likely to have the most difficulty attracting teams and retaining them and why teams in those cities are likely to be most strident in their demands for large subsidy from the public sector.

Trends in the Minor Leagues and Colleges

The trend for dramatic investment increases in facilities extends beyond the major league, to the minor leagues and collegiate facilities. The investment increases have been particularly pronounced in minor league baseball, where over 70 new stadiums were opened in the 1990s. Two stimuli have driven these increases. First, there has been a resurgence of interest in the minor leagues. In 2001, the aggregate attendance at minor league games exceeded 38.8 million, the highest attendance since 1949 and the second highest in the 100-year history of the minor leagues. In 1949, there were 448 teams in 59 leagues, whereas in 2001 there were

Figure 3-1 Why Larger Cities Should Pay Smaller Subsidies Than Smaller Cities

Larger markets result in more revenue opportunities for teams. Revenue from sources such as local broadcasts, merchandising, larger crowds, more alternate events in the arena, and sponsorship are likely to be more substantial in larger than in smaller markets. Since teams in the NBA retain all the income from these sources, the profitability of large market teams should be substantially higher, so they should require less public subsidy.

At the time the Houston Rockets were negotiating with the city of Houston for a new arena, the Houston market with 4.8 million residents was 50% bigger than St. Louis, which was the next largest market that did not have an NBA team. Characteristics of the other teamless markets available to the Rockets are listed below.

Market	Population	Regional purchasing income	Number of households with incomes above $150,000	Other pro teams
Houston	4,776,109	$88,900,192	58,637	2
St. Louis	2,866,973	$51,867,291	21,876	3
San Diego	2,854,630	$45,964,385	21,063	2
Norfolk	1,763,968	$24,277,660	6,629	0
New Orleans	1,732,671	$25,388,184	11,519	1
Louisville	1,510,942	$24,277,660	8,649	0
Las Vegas	1,321,834	$22,925,044	10,573	0

These data clearly indicate the superior earnings potential that Houston offers compared to the other options. A large public subsidy from one of the other teams may be appealing, but in the long term these data suggest no other market area is available that could generate as much income for the franchise as Houston.

Source: Rosentraub, M.S. (1997) *Major league losers: The real cost of sports and who's paying for it.* New York: Basic Books.

160 clubs participating in AAA, AA, and A leagues. These attendance increases have spawned an urge for bigger and better stadiums.

A second cause of major new investment was stimulated by Major League Baseball's incorporating Attachment 58 (A58) to the 1990 Professional Baseball Agreement. A58 specified minor league facility standards and compliance inspection procedures. It listed a comprehensive set of stadium specifications aimed at substantially raising the standards of these amenities, and minor league teams were required to comply with them. Existing stadiums were given until 1995 to meet these standards, which required most existing minor league stadiums to invest in substantial renovations or to rebuild. If teams failed to meet the new standards, then those franchises would lose their major league affiliation and their player development contracts, which are key to the financial success of minor league teams. Effectively, the teams would no longer be viable enterprises in these stadiums.

The A58 specifications had been carefully negotiated between MLB and the minor league franchise owners. The minor league owners accepted them with enthusiasm.[9] Approximately 95% of the 160 minor league teams play in publicly funded stadiums in the United States and Canada.[10] Thus, minor league owners saw this as an opportunity to pressure their host communities to invest in upgrading or replacing stadiums. If communities failed to do so, then the franchise would relocate elsewhere. Hence, most of the investment in minor league stadiums has been by local governments. The consensus among minor league officials is that A58 has, indeed, substantially improved the financial condition of many minor league teams.[9]

At the collegiate level, it is more difficult to find aggregate data on investments in stadiums and arenas. Obviously, college teams do not threaten to relocate to new sites, which means that a major stimulus for constructing new facilities is removed. Further, most college stadiums are likely to have been renovated and/or expanded rather than rebuilt. However, observation and anecdotal information suggest there has been a marked increase not only in the number of arenas built on college campuses, but also in their scale and the quality of amenities contained within them.

The best student athletes and the best coaches are attracted to institutions that have the best facilities. Because success is so strongly influenced by quality of facilities, as some colleges upgrade others are forced to match them or accept that they will attract only second-tier athletes and coaches. This process has sometimes been called "the 'arms race' of athletic facilities." The "arms race" has been fueled by the substantial increase in funds major colleges have received from football bowl payouts, football television fees, and the billion-dollar television fees for the NCAA Division I basketball tournament. It was further enhanced in the late 1990s by the extraordinary gains in the stock market, which led to an escalation in donations from supporters.

The institutions leading the way in facility, especially stadium, improvements at the beginning of the millennium were Ohio State, $350 million (of which $210 million was for the stadium renovation); California, $100 million; Penn State, $93.5 million; and Florida, $50 million.[11] Texas A&M spent $55 million on closing the north end of its football stadium, adding 10,000 seats and skyboxes, and making renovations to its softball, baseball, and track facilities. In all these cases, the objective was to increase the number of seats in the football stadium, especially luxury seats.

Like professional sports teams, a growing number of Division I-A schools are using the sale of premium seating as the basis for financing major facility improvements. Kansas State University provides an example of this growing trend. In 2000, the athletic department at Kansas State, in an effort to accommodate growing demand for its successful football program, spent $13.5 million on expanding its 31-year-old stadium. The "financial engine" for the expansion project was the construction of 2,000 additional club seats and 31 luxury suites. With club seats sold at $700 each for a 5-year commitment and suites leased for 5 years at $32,000 per season, the athletic department was able to comfortably meet the annual debt service of $1.6 million on the revenue bonds used to finance the project.[11]

In 2001, at least 43 of the 117 teams playing Division 1-A football were in the process of upgrading facilities. In the first 5 years after the formation of the Big 12 conference in 1996, the 12 member schools committed $700 million to upgrading facilities.[12] Thus, it seems the exponential investment in major and minor league professional facilities also is replicated to some extent in the collegiate context.

Factors Contributing to Enhanced Private Sector Investment in Major League Facilities

The primary trend identified in the first section was the shift towards franchise owners' paying a greater proportion of facility costs. The shift emerged in the Transitional Era (1985-1994), and it was further accentuated in the subsequent Fully Loaded (1995-2003) Era. In the discussion of these eras, two sources of impetus for the shift were suggested. First, the 1984 Deficit Reduction Act and 1996 Tax Reform Act were intended to stop favorable public financing mechanisms from being used to subsidize professional franchise facilities.

A second impetus was the enhanced revenue streams accruing to the franchises from generous lease agreements that gave them most or all of the revenues from luxury suites, personal seat licenses, concessions, parking, and sponsor agreements. In addition, over the past decade, franchises have received considerably increased annual revenues from broadcast rights, merchandising, licensing, and gate receipts. These exponentially increased revenue streams have resulted in a widespread perception that franchises should have the financial capacity to make substantial investments in the facilities they use.

A third contributing factor to enhanced private-sector investment in facilities is the generic trend over the past 25 years requiring the private sector to invest more in all public services and amenities from which they accrue benefits. During the 1975-76 financial year, the fraction of the gross national product accounted for by government spending fell for the first time in 50 years. This auspicious trend change marked the beginning of the tax revolt movement.[13] It spread widely and quickly across the United States, so by the end of the millennium, only six states were not constrained by some form of statutorily mandated tax limitation.[14] These statutory provisions were reinforced by the political actions of elected representatives who recognized that aspiration to, and survival in, office depended on their demonstrating frugality to the electorate.

In response to the revised political reality of having reduced tax funds available, governments have engaged in "load shedding," which is designed to shift costs that had previously been absorbed by the public sector over to the private sector. Hence, the shift shown in Table 3-4 of the private sector paying a higher proportion of the facility cost is consistent with the broad movement of government entities tending to adopt this *modus operandi* in all services with which they are involved.

Figure 3-2 The Growing Controversy Over Who Pays for New Sports Facilities

Source: Houston Chronicle, Thursday, August 31, 2000

A fourth factor that has contributed to the shift to more private investment is the increased public contentiousness of the merits associated with subsidizing major league facilities. The contentiousness invariably focuses on the issues of opportunity costs and equity. The cartoon in Figure 3-2 captures the atmosphere that prevailed in Houston when authorization was sought from taxpayers to subsidize a new arena. These issues are discussed in the following subsections.

Opportunity Costs

Opportunity costs are the benefits that would be forthcoming if the public resources committed to sports facilities were redirected to other public services. The issue was illustrated by a letter writer to the *Baltimore Sun* who had the following observations:

The city is full of ruined houses, the jails are overcrowded, the dome is falling off City Hall, there are potholes in the streets, crippled children can't get to school, taxes are up and services are going down—but we're going to have a sports complex.[15]

Similarly, an Illinois legislator during a debate on whether the state should subsidize a new stadium for the White Sox asked, "What in the name of heaven are we doing, when we can't take care of the children, we can't take care of the poor and we can't take care of the people who need our help?"[16] Given the immense fiscal crises confronting governments, especially in the major cities, and the numerous social and infrastructure needs requiring additional funds, it is incongruous and unconscionable to some that scarce public resources should be committed to such an apparently discretionary and relatively frivolous use.

Conceptually, for an investment of public money to be justified, it must meet the criterion of "highest and best use." That is, it should yield a return to residents that is at least equal to that which could be obtained from other ventures in which the government entity could invest. Opportunity cost is the value of the best alternative *not* taken when a decision to expend government money is made. Thus, "if an alternative generates $2 million of benefits net of subsidy, and a stadium generates $1.5 million net of subsidy, the stadium can be viewed as imposing a $0.5 million *loss* on taxpayers, not a $1.5 million benefit."[16]

It has been stated that "the issue of opportunity costs is the fundamental social issue associated with municipal investment in professional sports."[17] The key question is not whether an investment in sports is likely to be a profitable investment for the community. Rather, it is whether more benefits would be generated from any number of other opportunities such as investment in a local college, public schools, transportation infrastructure, health programs, or incentives to attract other kinds of businesses to locate in the community. The conundrum of priorities for the use of public tax dollars was highlighted in Cleveland. The day before the city council approved a large injection of public funds to build a new football stadium, the Cleveland public school system announced it would cut $52 million over 2 years, laying off 160 teachers and eliminating interscholastic athletics from a school system that its superintendent described as "in the worst financial shape of any school district in the country."[16]

Similarly, when the New York City council voted by 39 to 5 to spend $76 million to build a minor league ballpark in Staten Island for a Yankee farm team, a journalist pointed out that "the city will spend more money on this one palatial ballpark then has been spent for all public school sports for the last 10 years put together." He characterized it as "a $76 million summer jobs program for Hal Steinbrenner (son of George, owner of the Yankees) and 25 teenagers from Arizona and Florida."[18] Other illustrations of the type of issues raised by consideration of opportunity cost are given in Figure 3-3 and in the following example from Toronto:

Stadium projects can harm a city's already vulnerable capital spending program. At the same time Toronto debated whether to build a new domed stadium, which ended up costing close to $400 million, the city's budget for parks acquisition and maintenance was being squeezed. One city official estimated that the city needed 700 new acres of parkland to keep pace with demand, but the city had a budget of just $500,000 for parks acquisition. Other infrastructure needs that went begging included public transportation, housing rehabilitation, and expansion of the sewer system.[19]

Figure 3-3 The Opportunity Cost of a New Stadium for the Minnesota Twins

In the late 1990s, the Minnesota Twins repeatedly sought to persuade the Minnesota legislature to commit $300 million of public money to build them a new baseball park. They were unsuccessful. One of the reasons for the lack of public support was a highly visible campaign headed by a local minister who was outraged that public dollars would be used to fund a stadium for a billionaire owner and millionaire players, while "even a single child went to sleep hungry at night, even a single mother couldn't find adequate day care for her kids, or even a single teenager was adrift and unable to find job training" (p. 145). She pointed out that $300 million could pay for 840 teachers' salaries for ten years or 600 new police officers for ten years. She formed an organization called "Fund Kids First: When Kids Win, Minnesota Wins." Her passionate leadership and media visibility made her case convincing. She personified the notion of opportunity cost. She also offered a female perspective to the proposed project, pointing out that it was almost exclusively for the benefit of males:

> What strikes me about stadiums is that the entire community supports them through taxes and only men benefit. Men get to play in a ball park. They get to coach. Men mostly do the maintenance work. Men are mostly the vendors. I don't think it's a family game, the national pastime, or builds community. How can it? Women aren't allowed to play in it? (p. 250)

Emphasizing the opportunity cost of such a public financial commitment is a legitimate and important element in a funding debate. However, at the same time, another commentator offered the following perspective:

> Even a stadium subsidy of $350 million over a payout period of twenty years is a pittance compared to the state's total biennial budget of $22 billion. Take a $20 million annual tax bite to pay for a stadium, and it would amount to 0.1 percent of the state's two-year budget. Compare that to the $4 billion that public schools get, and this "priorities" argument seems flimsy. (p. 249)

Source: Adapted from Weiner, J. (1999). *Stadium games: fifty years of big league greed and bush league boondoggles.* Minneapolis: University of Minnesota Press.

Switching money from other activities (e.g., road building, public housing, or a business park) to a sports facility does not make the economy better off. The efforts of the mayor of San Jose to persuade the city's residents to approve a referendum allocating $265 million of public funds to a new stadium in which the Giants would play were strenuously opposed by the CEO of a prominent major high-tech company in the city. He objected to

> subsidizing a multimillionaire [the ball-club owner] with a quarter-billion dollar asset... This is a terrible investment when we're losing jobs and we

don't have enough teachers and police. [The owner's] no villain. He'd be a fool not to get the best deal he can. You look for suckers in these deals, which in today's world means government."[20]

There is an important caveat relating to the source of funds that needs to be inserted into this opportunity cost debate. It is that facility advocates seek funds for *capital* investments, whereas funding for such needs as hiring more teachers or police officers, or developing new health or welfare programs originates from cities' *operational* budgets. This means that choices between sports projects and social needs often are more rhetorical than real because capital and operating budgets are not directly substitutable. It is generally easier to persuade voters to commit tax funds for capital projects, especially if the source of funds is not property or sales taxes, than it is to persuade them (or their legislative representatives) to accept higher annual tax rates for operating budgets to attack social problems.

There are four main reasons that elected officials are much less willing to make substantial increases for services in operating budgets than they are to support major capital projects. First, capital projects have high visibility, and it is easy for elected officials to be associated with them. In contrast, there is not much high-visibility political kudos to be gained from hiring more teachers, welfare workers, or maintenance workers. Second, increases in operating budgets often are not endorsed by a referendum, so the resultant tax increases can be tied to those in office at election times and be a focus of criticism. Third, increases in operating budgets are effectively ongoing and forever, whereas capital investments are for a limited time period.

Finally, sport facility subsidies from capital budgets frequently are serviced by taxes imposed on noncity residents (these are discussed in chapter 6), whereas operational budgets derive primarily from a community's taxpayers. It may be argued that taxes derived from noncity residents used to finance sports facilities represent as much of an opportunity cost as those derived from property taxes. However, voters are less likely to perceive such taxes as having an opportunity cost because they are "special" taxes that residents are not required to pay. Because they are designated for a specific project and do not go into a city's general fund, these tax revenues are not subjected to the competition among different service priorities that characterizes the annual budget debate and highlights the opportunity cost issue.

The opportunity cost issue is especially galling among those residing in cities that authorized subsidies for facilities in the 1970s and 1980s and then watched as franchises departed after a relatively short period for better facilities elsewhere. Typically, the public subsidy was in the form of bonds repayable over a 20- or 30-year period. Thus, these communities continued to make annual multimillion-dollar debt payments on facilities that had become white elephants because they had no major league team. Meanwhile, there was no money available to rectify deteriorating schools, streets, and public services. This emphasizes that the risk on major sports facilities is carried exclusively by the public sector because it is the owner of a depreciating asset, which is another dimension of opportunity cost.

When public investment is committed to major sports facilities, it removes large amounts of land from the tax rolls. Especially in downtown areas, this land is likely to be high value; hence, the community's tax base is eroded. Borrowing for sports facilities also reduces the bonding capacity that a jurisdiction has available for other projects it may wish to undertake:

> Financing a new stadium in Jacksonville delayed a planned expansion of port facilities which, in the view of a critic on the city council, meant trading an investment in "10,000 very high-paying longshoreman-type jobs" for a sports project that would create "3,000 seasonal part-time, minimum-wage jobs."[6]

Much of the emotional rhetoric surrounding public investments in professional sports projects stems from the realization that the economic return from sports is slight; the benefits accrue disproportionately to wealthier segments of the community. For example, the Camden Yards complex in Baltimore ultimately results in an expenditure of $400 million from the Maryland State Treasury when interest charges on the debt are included in the cost.[16] The project was funded by revenue bonds supported by a specially created sports lottery. Hence, the bulk of the funds came from poor Baltimoreans who were the lottery's best customers. That $400 million could have been spent on the city's considerable needs for education or drug treatment from which the economically disadvantaged would have been most likely to benefit. A further irony of this situation is that a disproportionate number of those who paid for the ballpark—the buyers of Maryland lottery tickets who are relatively poor—are the least able to enjoy the events that occur in it, because ticket prices in the new stadium are so much higher than they were in the old stadium. Further, the City of Baltimore lost many of the 1,000 manufacturing jobs provided by the 26 companies that had existed on the Camden Yards site, as well as the property taxes that the food plants and other businesses on the site had generated.[15]

When employment measures of economic impact are announced, the implied intent often is to laud the new jobs that will accrue in the local economy. However, if the opportunity cost is considered, the number of new jobs created will inevitably be perceived as offering a relatively poor return on the public investment. In response to an advocacy group's study reporting that a new baseball stadium for the Minnesota Twins would cost the city $310 million and generate the equivalent of 168 full-time jobs, one economist remarked that if the money were "dropped out of a helicopter over the Twin Cities, you would probably create eight to ten times as many jobs."[16] The following comment refers to the state of Maryland's commitment of $200 million to attract the Baltimore Ravens NFL team:

> Without question, communities willing to put up $200 million to attract a new company can do better than a football team, which employs 71 workers and annually earns $80 million to $100 million. Compare: The state of Alabama pledged to Mercedes-Benz AG a package of tax cuts and incentives worth an estimated $300 million in order to land one of its factories. The plan is expected to employ 1,500 people directly and result in a spin-off of another 13,000 jobs. Using a pair of economic-impact studies, the Congressional Research Service estimated that each job created by the Ravens and their stadium will cost Maryland from $127,000 to $331,000. By contrast, the service said the state's "sunny day" fund, used to help attract and retain conventional businesses, creates jobs at an average cost of $6,250.[2]

The Equity Issue

Equity is concerned with fairness. In the context of allocating public resources, equity revolves around the question "Who gets what?" or, in normative terms, "Who ought to get what?" In the context of professional sports, two dimensions of equity emerge. The first dimension is relatively narrow and focused. It relates to who wins and who loses among the specific demographic groups located in the area where a major new facility is constructed. A city is not a unitary entity that is affected uniformly by a major public construction project. Such projects have a "tendency to displace groups of citizens located in the poorer sections of cities,"[21] either through mandatory relocation or more insidiously by substantial increases in housing and real estate values that may follow public improvements of the area. The people most affected by such displacement typically are those who are least able to organize and finance community resistance to such proposals. Although the context is a mega-event rather than a major sports facility, the findings reported in a study of the potential impacts of the Sydney Olympics on low-income housing illustrate this dimension of the equity issue:

> It concluded that previous mega-events often had a detrimental effect on low income people who are disadvantaged by a localized boom in rent and real estate prices, thereby creating dislocation in extreme cases. The same rise in prices is considered beneficial to home owners and developers. Past events have also shown that this has led to public and private lower-cost housing developments being pushed out of preferred areas as a result of increased land and construction costs. In the case of the Barcelona Games the market price of old and new housing rose between 1986 and 1992 by 240% and 287%, respectively. A further 59,000 residents left Barcelona to live elsewhere between the years of 1984 and 1992.

> In relation to Australia, past mega-events have led to

> - increased rental fees;

> - increased conversion of boarding houses to tourist accommodation;

> - accelerating gentrification of certain suburbs near where major events are held; and

> - a tendency for low income renters to be forced out of their homes.[22]

The second dimension of the equity issue is the financial nexus between who pays for and who benefits from major new facilities. Labor strife in professional sports has been characterized as a battle between "the haves and the have mores," but much of the dispute between the owners and players is over the allocation of "a revenue pool built by the tax dollars of citizens who can only dream of million-dollar salaries."[23]

In essence, the public subsidies transfer income from ordinary people to highly paid owners, executives, and players. It is this perversion of fairness, obvious inequity, and irrationality that is galling to many. The Mayor of Houston opposed providing a publicly provided stadium for the NFL Houston Oilers because he had "this terrific hard time with the idea that the average guys are called on to pay for this out of the taxes on their house, and then can't afford to buy a ticket."[6] Ironically, his successor supported a new stadium after the Oilers left the city, but he used soft rather than hard taxes to fund it.

The transferring of money from middle-class and blue-collar workers to an immensely profitable entertainment business offends the sensibilities. The essence of this inequity was captured in the headline of a *Newsweek* column discussing the move of Art Modell's NFL franchise from Cleveland to Baltimore that read "Modell Sacks Maryland: Average folks are building suites for rich fans so rich owners can pay rich players."[24] Another commentator suggested that there should be an adaptation of Winston Churchill's legendary remark after the air battle for Britain—"Never have so many owed so much to so few" to "Never have so few received so much from so many."[24]

To the ordinary taxpayer, public subsidy seems unnecessary. There is a disconnect between the everyday lives of taxpayers and the economics of professional sports. They are out of kilter. Players are paid too much. Owners' franchise values and profits are too high. Tickets are unaffordable. Forty-five individuals from the *Forbes* magazine list of the wealthiest 400 Americans (all with net assets exceeding $500 million) owned a direct interest in a team in one of the four major leagues at the end of the millennium.[5] Given these factors, the notion that public subsidy is needed seems ludicrous.

> On the subject of ticket prices one sports writer observed that [what] goes unsaid in the campaigns to get public money approved is the facilities are largely for *new* fans—wealthier individuals and corporations that can afford the seats in these often, ironically, smaller stadiums and arenas. Cheap seats remain at these facilities, but not that many and not as close to the action as they used to be. The net effect is long-time fans and middle-income families are increasingly driven from the games, replaced by corporations that can buy larger blocks of tickets and use them as tax writeoffs.[25]

The irritation of many taxpayers with public subsidy was epitomized by the acronym formulated by opponents to a new stadium for the NFL's Chicago Bears: STINCS (This Stadium Tax Is Nothing but Corporate Subsidy).[24] If public subsidy were not there, then the teams would have to compensate for its unavailability by using more of their revenues to repay the annual facility debt charges. This would leave less money available to remunerate players, owners, and executives whose salaries appear outrageously excessive to ordinary people. Without public subsidies, these individuals would still receive very large salaries, but the obviously inequitable transfer of resources from ordinary taxpayer to millionaire beneficiary would cease.

However, the principle of the inequity described here is not unique to professional sports; rather, it is generic across all types of businesses. In recent years, it has entered the lexicon as *corporate welfare,* which has been defined as

> any action by local, state or federal government that gives a corporation or an entire industry a benefit not offered to others. It can be an outright subsidy, a grant, real estate, a low-interest loan, or a government service. It

can also be a tax break—a credit, exemption, deferral or deduction, or a tax rate lower than the one others pay.[27]

All of the subsidy elements cited in this definition have been given to professional sports franchises, but they are only one of many beneficiaries. Corporate welfare has a long history in the United States—perhaps starting with the tax abatement Alexander Hamilton received from the state of New Jersey or the major land grants given by the federal government to the railroads.[23] However, public subsidies did not become widespread or egregious until the economic downturn of the late 1970s and 1980s, when government entities, desperate to counter unemployment, competed with ever-growing subsidies to persuade companies to remain or to relocate to their communities.[23] It is estimated that a corporate welfare bureaucracy of 11,000 organizations and agencies now exists with access to city halls, statehouses, the Capitol, and the White House.[28] Today, it is unlikely that any business in any community would locate there without receiving a package of subsidy elements from the community. Hence, the subsidy question confronting elected officials in the context of sport facilities is also asked of them by all other sections of the private economy. In the concluding comments of an unprecedented four-part series of articles on corporate welfare in which professional sports was never discussed, *Time* magazine asked

> What's a Mayor to Do? A major employer wants to expand or build anew. Rather than simply doing so, the corporation stirs up a bidding war to see which city and state will pony up the most cash, loans and tax breaks in the form of economic incentives. If you're the mayor and the facility means jobs and income for your town, do you play hardball and risk losing the plan and the jobs? Or do you give in and hand out tax money, only to face a never-ending string of similar demands from others? Right now it's not much of a debate: the mayors cave.[27]

It is ironic that at the same time federal and state legislatures and both political parties have engaged in prolonged debates about ways to reduce welfare payments for individuals, they have substantially increased their contributions to corporate welfare. People who seek public assistance are frequently disdained, but this assistance is lavished on the wealthy owners of professional sports teams. Welfare is perceived to be morally corroding when recipients forego employment for public assistance, but schizophrenically, this corruption is not perceived to extend to professional franchises.

Although it is pervasive in all sections of the private economy, proposals to subsidize sports facilities invariably arouse more passion than corporate welfare offered to other types of businesses. There are two main reasons for this. First, the scale of the largesse is likely to be greater. Instead of $10-20 million for a new manufacturing plant, Table 3-1 shows that the subsidy for a stadium is likely to be $200 million. Second, the newsworthiness of professional sports, the high visibility of the beneficiaries, and their extraordinary levels of remuneration all ensure that a subsidy proposal will receive extensive publicity.

Although the proportion of private sector investment in major league facilities has consistently increased, the data in Tables 3-1 and 3-2 show that the public sector's contributions remain substantial. Further, despite their reduced role in financing capital facilities, public subsidies to franchises often have increased as a result of the teams' receiving more generous leases. This section of the chapter explores the reasons for that support.

In the 1960s, 1970s, and 1980s, the momentum for investment in major league facilities emanated primarily from two sources. First, the unique cartel-like status of the professional leagues allowed them to collaborate to restrict the supply of teams. This enables franchise owners to threaten to relocate, which provides them with substantial leverage to obtain public investment either from a threatened government entity or from a receptive, new host jurisdiction. A second traditional source of momentum has been the community power structure in which those who control "the system" often have a vested interest in new facilities.

In the Transitional (1985-1994) and Fully Loaded (post-1994) Eras, two additional sources of momentum contributed much to the acceleration of investment in new facilities.[29] They may be termed the increasing-costs stimulus and the competitive-balance rationale. The role of each of these four sources of momentum is reviewed in the following subsections of the chapter.

Owner Leverage

The baseball, football, basketball, and hockey leagues within which franchises play are unique in that they are exempt from normal antitrust rules that prohibit barriers to competition. The Sherman Antitrust Act of 1890 prohibited restraint of trade and all attempts to monopolize any part of an industry. However, it has generally been judged not to apply to professional sports. Essentially, the courts have viewed leagues as single entities, like McDonald's, with multiple franchise outlets, and the owners have the right to locate their "outlets" (teams) and dictate their terms of trade as they wish. Opponents have failed to make the case that teams should be considered independent business entities and, as such, be required to desist from restraining trade through collaboration. In *North American Soccer League v. NFL,* Supreme Court Justice William Rehnquist observed

> The NFL owners are joint venturers who produce a product, professional football, which competes with other sports and other forms of entertainment in the entertainment marketplace. Although individual NFL teams compete on the playing field, they rarely compete in the marketplace... The league competes as a unit against other forms of entertainment.[31]

The leagues are effectively cartels. A cartel is a group of firms that organize together to control production, sales, and wages within an industry. In addition to controlling the number of franchises, the leagues effectively operate as cartels in three major ways:

1. They restrict interteam competition for players by controlling the rights of workers (players) through player drafts, contracts, and trades, thereby reducing competitive bidding among teams for player services.

2. They act in concert to admit or deny new teams, and they control the location and relocation of teams.

3. They control the rights to the national over-the-air broadcast of games and create rules that enable teams to exercise control over their over-the-air local broadcast territories (i.e., the sale of home games not included on the national broadcast package and the right to protect the local listener/viewer market from infringement by broadcasts from other teams in the league).

The leagues have used their cartel-like power to limit expansion. In effect, leagues are able to specify not only how many teams will exist, but also where they will play.[23] Historically, the number of cities seeking professional sports franchises has outnumbered the available supply of teams. Major league sports appear to be a culturally unique experience for an influential segment of the U.S. population, in that they cannot be replaced by other forms of entertainment. Further, the increased popularity of professional sports has exacerbated the situation because it means that the size of population that can support a team is shrinking. This is exemplified by the presence of major league franchises in relatively small cities such as Nashville, Jacksonville, Charlotte, and St. Petersburg. This popularity also means that larger metropolitan areas are able to support multiple franchises. The imbalance of supply and demand creates a competitive environment that leads cities to escalate their offers of public inducements as they attempt to outbid one another for franchises. It has been noted that "teams manipulate cities by selling them against each other in a scramble for the limited number of major league teams. While the cities fight each other, the teams sit back and wait for the best conditions and terms."[18] If Major League Baseball, for example, had 40 or 50 teams rather than 28, then much of the leverage used to garner public subsidies would be removed.

The leverage potential of owners was first demonstrated and exploited by the shocking decision to move the Dodgers from Brooklyn to Los Angeles that is described in Figure 3-4. Franchise owners in subsequent decades have consistently demonstrated their readiness to take advantage of this leverage potential. Since 1950, there have been 47 franchise relocations in the four major leagues: MLB, 11; NFL, 9; NBA, 18; and NHL, 9. The moves of the Raiders from Oakland to Los Angeles and the Colts from Baltimore to Indianapolis were illustrative of relocations that occurred despite long histories of sellouts and financial and playing success.[31]

This leverage trend accelerated to the point where in 1995 it was estimated that 49 of the 113 major league franchises were considering a move unless they obtained a new arena or stadium or a more favorable deal from the government entity that owned their building.[32] Clearly, this was a factor in explaining the extraordinary proliferation of new facilities that were built between 1995 and 2003. An owner's threat to relocate a franchise elsewhere may be reinforced by the league's threatening to veto any proposal to replace that team with a new franchise in the future in the host community, implying that failure to meet an owner's demands will lead to the permanent absence of a franchise in the community. In the last two decades, almost every major city in the United States and Canada has been involved in negotiations with major league owners seeking to exploit their position of leverage.

In the 1980s and early 1990s, the city of St. Petersburg, Florida, was a primary victim of this tactic. In 1988, the city invested $130 million of public monies to

Figure 3-4 The Dodgers Move From Brooklyn to Los Angeles

No professional sports franchise had been as closely identified with its host city as the Dodgers were with Brooklyn. The club was by a wide margin the most important institution in the borough and for all Americans it symbolized the character, culture, and ethnic diversity of Brooklyn, whose population was outnumbered by only four other cities.

In the early 1950s the Dodgers were the most profitable franchise in baseball, drawing huge crowds and enjoying the most lucrative media contracts in the sport. However, the team's owner was concerned about the future economic viability of the franchise. He wanted the city to help him replace the deteriorating 35,000-seat Ebbets Field, one of the smallest in the league, at a new site in a better neighborhood more accessible to subway lines and with better parking facilities. As more middle-class fans moved to the suburbs, the automobile was becoming the prime mode of transportation to ball games.

Negotiations with the city for a new and more accessible ballpark got nowhere, so the owner turned his attention to Los Angeles. By the fall of 1956 the mayor of Los Angeles was urging him to move to the coast and recommending Chavez Ravine, a large, nearly vacant area adjacent to the downtown and near three freeways, as a possible location. The Dodgers' owner saw Los Angeles as a huge unexploited territory ripe for developing, with millions of potential fans living within driving distance and even more possible customers for pay-television broadcasts.

In November 1957 the owner agreed to trade Wrigley Field, the playing field of the minor league L.A. Angels, to the city in return for a 300-acre site in Chavez Ravine and pledges by the city and county to spend up to $5 million for public improvements, including access roads to the freeways. There was a lot of public opposition to this sweetheart deal because the city land had an estimated commercial value of $18 million, was the only decent-sized vacant public lot near downtown, and was required by law to be used for a "public purpose," which in many people's minds was public housing. A referendum held to approve the contract got a lot of support from local boosters and the print media, and passed by 24,000 votes out of a record 667,000 ballots.

The owner had hoped that the city would further assist him by building a new ballpark, but it refused to, based on the community's traditional hostility to bond issues and the sharp divisions created by the trade of Chavez Ravine.

Source: Adapted from Reiss, S. A. (1989). *City games: The evolution of American urban society and the rise of sports.* Urbana, Illinois: University of Illinois Press, pp. 236-237.

---

build a domed stadium for the express purpose of attracting a Major League Baseball franchise. Instead of attracting a team, St. Petersburg was cynically used by other teams to leverage more public funds from their existing communities. St. Petersburg was involved in serious franchise negotiations on six occasions, when they failed to consummate an agreement with the 1984 Minnesota Twins, 1985 Oakland A's, 1988 Chicago White Sox, 1988 Texas Rangers, 1992 Seattle Mariners, or the 1992 San Francisco Giants.[33] The Chicago White Sox, for example, who played in the oldest stadium in baseball, successfully parlayed a threat to move to St. Petersburg into receiving a fully state-funded ($150 million) ballpark, the new Comiskey Park, from the Illinois State Legislature. This prompted a local official in St. Petersburg to comment, "We've been used as a nuclear threat to other communities to make them give their teams whatever they want."[34]

The ability to act as a cartel and limit supply gives the leagues extraordinary power with which to intimidate cities. An example of this occurred when the owners of the San Francisco Giants committed to selling the team to a group in St. Petersburg in 1992. The owners subsequently withdrew from this commitment, and the first reaction of St. Petersburg officials was to seek substantial damages through the courts for breach of contract. However, they did not follow through with a suit because they realized that such an action would likely have led to an informal blackballing of the city, which would have negated any chance of St. Petersburg's ever obtaining a franchise. By collective action, baseball owners would have been able to enforce this informal sanction against St. Petersburg, and they could afford to do it because of the great demand for teams from other cities. In the end, the city's perseverance was rewarded. In 1997, MLB owners awarded St. Petersburg one of two expansion franchises. The new team, the Tampa Bay Devil Rays, occupies the domed stadium, which was extensively upgraded to accommodate the new franchise and is now known as Tropicana Field.

Expansion of the number of teams in a major league is a careful balancing act. From the owner's perspective, more teams means more competition for star players, which leads to higher salaries; fewer big-draw games played between traditional rivals; a smaller proportion of television revenues; a decrease in the value of their franchise as more become available; and a diminution in the quality of play and, hence, in the entertainment value of the product.[35] Nevertheless, there has to be the promise of expansion in order to deter new leagues from forming. However, any expansion should be slow enough to ensure there are enough cities without a franchise available that owners' threats to relocate to one of them from their existing host community have to be taken seriously. Thus, one reason the leagues schedule exhibition games in nonfranchised cities is to encourage those communities to visualize themselves as future hosts of franchises. It has been suggested that "having two or four potential cities seems the right number in most leagues; for example, in the case of Major League Baseball the current potential cities would be Washington, D.C., Las Vegas, Sacramento, and Portland, Oregon."[5]

Multiple franchises in a city also offer leverage potential or improvement because whenever a public subsidy concession is made to one franchise, then inevitably it will become an expectation for the others. Thus, when Cleveland developed new facilities for its baseball and basketball franchises but failed to do this for football, the owner of the NFL franchise moved it to Baltimore, commenting, "I wanted and was promised equal treatment and it wasn't forthcoming."[6]

Owner leverage also extends to the movement of franchises in the minor leagues, where parent clubs are continually pressuring their minor league affiliates to relocate if another community will provide improved playing facilities, better player accommodations, or more fans in front of whom to play. It was noted earlier in the chapter that this leverage was accentuated in 1990 by Attachment 58.

The leverage exerted by franchises stems not only from the fiscal packages offered by other cities, but also from the sunk costs incurred by their current host cities. It has been noted that

> the fundamental fact of life concerning stadiums and arenas is that once they are built, they are fixed in place, while the teams that use them are potentially mobile. This puts an enormous bargaining advantage in the hands of teams playing in publicly owned stadiums. Teams can exploit

their threat of leaving a city to wring out of the manager of the stadium rental agreements that leave the city pretty much holding the bag.[36]

A possible corollary of this observation is that the larger the equity investment made by franchises in facilities, the less likely they are to relocate. Such facilities are likely to be difficult or impossible to sell, so relocation may mean teams would lose their equity investments in facilities. Hence, the increased share of franchise funds that is characteristic of recent facility construction (Table 3-4) may enhance franchise stability in the coming years.

The Community Power Structure

Franchises, and the construction of stadiums and arenas that accompany them, tend to be enthusiastically recruited by powerful vested interests in communities such as banks; real estate developers; elements of the tourism industry like restaurants and hotels; legal firms; insurance companies; construction firms; and potential suppliers of merchandise, equipment, and other services and materials. Consider, for example, the role of bond lawyers who are hired by a government entity as consultants to develop the legal documentation associated with issuing bonds. If a major bond issue of the magnitude required to fund a stadium or arena is approved, their fee is likely to approximate $1 million.[15]

Major league sports exemplify the classic interest-group dynamic whereby economic benefits are conferred on a numerically small set of actors, whereas the costs are widely distributed among the general public. Thus, team owners and other proponents are likely to have both the incentive and the resources to invest heavily in a pro-team publicity campaign soliciting public support for a proposed subsidy, whereas opponents are unlikely to have either the incentive or access to similar resources. Professional sports offer a classic illustration of the application of organized-interest perspective, which states that organized interests

> seek special benefits, subsidies, privileges, and protections from the government. The costs of these concentrated benefits are usually dispersed to all taxpayers, none of who individually bears enough added cost to merit spending time, energy, or money to organize a group to oppose the benefit. Thus the interest group system concentrates benefits to the few and disperses costs to the many. The system favors small, well-organized, homogeneous interests that seek the expansion of government activity at the expense of larger, but less well-organized citizen-taxpayers.[5]

The difference in incentive between supporters and opponents of new facilities is explained by the distribution of benefits and costs that accrue from a new facility. Substantial financial benefits accrue to team owners and a select number of others, motivating them to become politically active. In contrast, the cost to ordinary residents is likely to be $25-$50 each per year in additional taxes, which may be too small to motivate them to engage in active opposition.[16]

Similarly, the resources available to community elites and owners are likely to be substantial. The actions of the owner of the Seattle Seahawks are illustrative. The owner needed to expedite the placement of a football stadium referendum on the Washington state ballot before his option to buy the Seahawks expired. He offered the state $4.2 million to avoid the time-consuming signature-gathering phase that is usually required to authorize a proposal on the state ballot. The state legislature accepted and agreed to schedule the vote as a special referendum for which the owner agreed to meet the costs. A special election made it likely that although all those supporting the stadium would vote, those who were ambivalent would not bother voting. In a regular general election the advocates would probably have constituted a smaller proportion of the total electorate. The owner then spent a further $5 million in 6 weeks on a public relations campaign to persuade the public to vote positively, which they did.[16] The opposition spent only $160,000. These business interests are the major "movers and shakers" in their communities and are able to influence decision makers because they play a prominent role in political campaigns. Figure 3-5 describes how the community power structure in Hamilton County, Ohio, was able to move from having only 19% of voters support a tax increase to pay for new facilities for the Cincinnati Bengals (NFL) and Reds (MLB) to winning a referendum on the issue with 61% approval.

Elected leaders may be able to reciprocate the support they receive from the business elite and consolidate their own political position through the subtle patronage of key supporters that large-scale projects sometimes foster. This latter role was identified by a commentator in Detroit, who after ten years of watching the city's politicians maneuver to build a new baseball stadium concluded:

> The local politicians, particularly the mayor and the county executive, know that they get far more mileage out of having a big new project than out of a renovation. They have the ability to say who gets the contracts, whose land is used, which developers are employed, which bond attorneys do it—and all of these people are the people who contribute to their war chest. That's why expensive projects like new stadiums win out over small-scale ones. . . Not because they are intrinsically better for the city, or better for the team or anything. There is a political interest in doing it.[15]

Major projects such as shopping malls, business parks, airports, professional sports facilities, or whatever are favored by some elected officials because they believe the projects will be perceived as highly visible, tangible evidence confirming that a community is "moving forward." It is anticipated voters will view such projects as bold initiatives that are manifestations of elected officials' leadership ability. Some politicians, especially mayors and governors, have built careers around the development of major sports facilities. Politicians recognize the popularity of professional sports and, regardless of their personal views of the merits of a case, are likely to look for ways to facilitate an association with such projects to enhance their own popularity. Decisions relating to subsidies for sports franchises ultimately are invariably based on a political rather than economic benefit-cost calculus even though the latter may be the public overt manifestation of the issue.

It has been noted that "because lower price tags increase political acceptability, supporters often overestimate revenues and understate public financial obligations for arenas and stadiums."[6] This strategy of unreasonably optimistic projections helps minimize voter opposition to the projects when they are voted upon, but increases the public subsidy required in the future beyond that promised. For example, the Louisiana Superdome was sold to voters in 1966 as a $35 million project, but the ultimate cost was $163 million. Once such projects are approved

The residents of Hamilton County, Ohio, ratified a .5% sales tax increase which raised $540 million to build two new stadia in Cincinnati for use by the Bengals football and Reds baseball franchises. Before the referendum campaign launched by the supporters of this proposal, a telephone poll of 750 Cincinnati residents contacted by Louis Harris and Associates for the Cincinnati Enquirer found little support for public financing: Nearly 60% opposed the construction of a new stadium for the Reds and Bengals, with 17% favoring such a project; 17% supported the construction of two new stadia and just 19% supported a tax increase to pay for such projects. Despite this initial lack of support, the prostadia interests were able to launch a campaign which resulted in 61% supporting a tax increase to build two stadia.

The prostadia coalition commissioned an economic impact study that said the construction of two stadia would bring about a one-time economic benefit to the county of $1.13 billion; the annual economic impact of the Reds and Bengals operating in the new stadia would be $296 million; the new stadia would support 6,883 jobs; and about half of the sales tax increase would be paid by non-Hamilton County residents. Those opposing the stadium also released an economic impact study that challenged the validity of these findings.

The principal means by which those pro and con the issue communicated with the public was the media. The difference between the two campaigns' resources was enormous. The pro-tax group had the support of major corporations and businesses, while the anti-tax group had no large underwriter. One side raised small contributions by passing the hat, whereas the other side had the Cincinnati Business Committee assigning four- and five-figure contribution quotas to individual firms. The campaign managers of the prostadia campaign raised more than $1.1 million, whereas the opposition group spent less than $30,000. The pro-tax side received substantial contributions from the Bengals ($300,000), Cincinnati-headquartered Procter & Gamble ($77,000), the Northern Kentucky Chamber of Commerce ($35,000), the Cincinnati Area Board of Realtors ($30,000), and home-based companies Kroger ($23,000), Cincinnati Bell ($16,000), and Cincinnati Gas & Electric ($13,000), whose parent company recently purchased the naming rights (Cinergy Field) of the former Riverfront stadium. The following table gives a breakdown of the 42 major ($5,000 or more) contributors' economic interests. They account for 73% of the funds raised. An examination of contributions between $1,000 and $4,999 identifies another $90,000 from 45 additional contributors with similar interests.

by voters, they have a momentum that is unstoppable.[6] No city is going to allow a partially completed major facility to sit there as a highly visible derelict monument to its administrative incompetence. Thus, when cost overruns occur, the initial investment in the building ensures additional public funds will be forthcoming to complete it.

From a political perspective, whether a sports facility performs as projected in the pro forma financial statements often is not of central concern to officials. It is likely to be many years after the project was authorized before any negative financial outcomes emerge, by which time those who authorized it may no longer be in office. Further, if the financial targets are not met, the community may still have a professional franchise and facility of which it can be proud. In contrast, if public investment in a business park or a shopping mall fails, there are no redeeming community benefits.

Economic Interests of Major Contributors ($5,000 or more)

Category	n	Amount ($)
Sports franchise	1	300,000
Manufacturers	6	108,000
Wholesale and retail	4	73,500
Local economic development	3	70,000
Insurance	5	67,500
Services	6	58,000
Financial services and banking	6	53,000
Real estate	3	40,000
Trade associations	3	25,000
Hotel and restaurant	3	18,000
Miscellaneous business	2	15,000
Total		828,000

Those who stood to gain the most from public funding of the sports stadia were prominent in financially supporting the Issue 1 campaign. The Cincinnati Bengals made by far the largest single contribution. Real estate interests with a stake in the development of downtown and riverfront properties, financial institutions that stood to profit by the sale of bonds, and flagship corporations with an interest in protecting the overall business climate of the city as well as their roles as civic leaders were conspicuous in their generosity to the pro-tax campaign. Although the prostadia coalition had many smaller contributors, over 80% of its million dollar campaign was raised from fewer than 100 businesses. After the election, the owner of the Reds wrote a $41,000 check to retire the organization's campaign debt.

The prostadia organization also benefitted from its association with established local organized institutions such as the Cincinnati Business Community, the Greater Cincinnati Chamber of Commerce, the Northern Kentucky Chamber of Commerce, and the leading spokespersons for City Council and County Commission. With its abundant resources it was able to hire professional campaign management and consulting services. On the other hand, the opposing group was a much more heterogeneous collection of people who operated with the double disadvantage of volunteer leadership and woefully inadequate resources. Their spokesman explained that "without money we could not take advantage of the volunteers" available.

The pro-tax group had all the trappings of a modern campaign for major public office, and the anti-tax group almost none. They had a take-no-prisoners approach to the referendum. Its goal was to "set the terms of the debate, shut them down at every opportunity, marginalize the opposition" while maintaining "complete credibility at all times." The television and radio campaign was impressive in magnitude, as were the major efforts made in direct mail, telephone contact, and yard signs. The campaign benefitted from professional consulting, daily tracking phone polls, and a major "Voter ID/Get-Out-the-Vote" effort.

The telemarketing effort (i.e., voter identification) was one of the most impressive and effective aspects of the prostadia campaign. With a "scope that was unprecedented" for Ohio politics, paid staffers called hundreds of thousands of registered primary voters to determine their stance on Issue 1. "Pro" voters received an offer of a yard sign and a chance to volunteer. "Neutral" voters were probed as to what would move them. These undecided voters received follow-up informational mail and an extensive phone call by volunteers about their reservations in the closing weeks of the campaign.

The labor force to make the thousands of follow-up calls, to erect an estimated 10,000 yard signs, and to mount the election day push came from hundreds of young sports fans who were there from the beginning of the campaign. Many had been solicited from Bengals' season ticket holders and were regarded as the campaign's most important resource.

The pro campaign was also fueled by the cheerleading boosterism of the local media, including sports talk radio. The leading opposition spokesman complained that the media was not evenhanded, especially in the final weeks of the campaign. He called the one-sidedness of local radio superstation WLW ("The Big One" and "The Home of the Reds/Bengals") "shameless."

Despite heavy rain on election day, a record 49.5% of eligible voters participated in the election and the issue passed easily with 61% approval.

Source: Brown, C. & Paul, D. M. (1999). Local organized interests and the 1996 Cincinnati sports stadia tax referendum. *Journal of Sports and Social Issues, 23*(2), 218-237

In a referendum campaign, paid and free media access is the principal means by which those who are pro and con the issue communicate to the voters.[38] The local media are likely to be strongly supportive of public subsidy for major league facilities because of the added news and sports interest a franchise brings:

> Sports editors freely acknowledge the symbiosis that exists between the news media and pro sports. Newspapers create excitement among fans, who drive up ticket sales. And while pro teams themselves don't create a lot of advertising, a thriving franchise attracts readers to the paper who might not otherwise pick it up. In Seattle, press runs of newspapers the day after a game are increased by anywhere from 10 to 20 percent, depending on which team played and whether it won or lost.[16]

The impetus for media support may extend beyond this mutual symbiosis. In some cases, media owners may have a vested interest in government investment. An egregious example of this occurred in the 1970s when the publisher of the *Minneapolis Star Tribune* raised $10.5 million to help city officials buy land for the Metrodome and in exchange received the right to develop 200 acres of land surrounding the site. The staff of the *Star Tribune* paid for a full-page advertisement in the newspaper, disassociating themselves from the paper's Metrodome coverage.[16]

Potential for media conflicts of interest is enhanced as increasing numbers of media owners become owners of professional sports franchises. Three of the largest media corporations in the United States—Disney, News Corporation, and AOL Time-Warner—control the Los Angeles Dodgers, Atlanta Braves, Atlanta Hawks, Anaheim Angels, and the Mighty Ducks of Anaheim. *The Chicago Tribune* owns both the Cubs and their broadcast outlet, WGN. The *Arizona Republic* newspaper is a part-owner of the Arizona Diamondbacks, which places the paper in an interlocking relationship with the majority owner, who owns three of the four major league teams in Phoenix (Cagan & DeMause, 1998). Media owners invariably maintain that an impenetrable wall between reporters and management protects society against conflicts of interest. However, this is unlikely to be convincing to skeptical opponents when these media add their voice in support of public subsidizing of the owners' teams.

The central role of the media was explicitly recognized by the former Australian premier who was a key member of the group that organized Sydney's bid for the Olympic Games:

> Early in 1991, I invited senior media representatives to the premier's office, told them frankly that a bid could not succeed if the media played their normal "knocking role" and that I was not prepared to commit the taxpayers' money unless I had their support. Both News Ltd. and Fairfax subsequently went out of their way to ensure the bid received fair, perhaps even favourable, treatment. The electronic media also joined in the sense of community purpose.[22]

The elite business and political interests in a community that control much of its decision making have a number of incentives to work enthusiastically to invest public funds in a major league facility. This coalition controls "the system," that is, the financial, knowledge, information dissemination, and legal resources needed to bring a major project to fruition. Their control over political decisions enables them to dictate the timing of referendums, evaluate the vehicles that may be used to avoid referendums, the size of the jurisdiction that should fund it (city, region, state), the revision and resubmission of proposals that failed, the nature of the partnership, and a myriad of other details. Their ability to set and control the agenda provides elite interests with an overwhelming advantage.

The actions of the elite are legitimized by fans who want a sports franchise in their community and who are likely to be vociferous in their advocacy. The word "fan" is short for "fanatic," and such people are likely to be sufficiently myopic in their focus that they do not care if the project means that a majority of their fellow taxpayers who are not fans will have to pay for it also. The political and economic power of supporters and the difficulty of forming and sustaining organized opposition without resources make it challenging for those who oppose such projects to be heard. Further, although those supporting investment of public funds in a franchise base their arguments on *particular* benefits that they believe will emerge, those opposed are often able to base their case only on the less convincing grounds that *general* benefits will accrue to the city if these resources are allocated elsewhere. Thus, the opposition's case often lacks the focus and conviction that supporters are able to inject into the debate:

> Citizens can make the argument that sports and stadiums are poor development tools and that $200 million can be better spent on education, police, or housing programs; but such arguments often carry little weight, because the results of such spending are undramatic and recipients of the services are unorganized and sometimes even hostile. There is no guarantee that spending the money on education, for example, would markedly improve schools; the money, after all, would not transform the system but would go to the same bureaucracy and neighborhoods, without alleviating the problems of poverty and alienation they are experiencing. Why then, bother to shift the $200 million from the stadium project to the education system?[19]

It has been pointed out that those who select the sites for major sports facilities "are drawn to sites where local inhabitants, often poor or members of minority groups, lack political influence; and they seek to avoid areas where residents and businesses have the political wherewithal to protect their turf."[6] Thus, for example, the largely black South Armour Square neighborhood in Chicago failed in its intensive community effort to spare 500 households from being displaced by the construction of the new Comiskey Park. When opposition does emerge, it can frequently be undermined by offering benefits to appease opponents. Thus, the displaced residents of South Armour Square were compensated by $10 million. This was considerably more than was legally required but was paid to forestall a lawsuit that may have delayed or blocked construction on that site. Similarly, in Baltimore, the Waverly Improvement Association agreed to drop opposition to a new stadium, in return for increased funds for rehabilitation of their neighborhood and enforcement of housing codes to drive out slumlords.

The effectiveness of the community power structure is apparent in the results achieved. In the 1990s, 20 of the 24 bond referendums for major league sports facilities were passed (these are listed in chapter 6 in Table 6-2). The four that failed were eventually funded without a public vote, and their level of funding was substantially higher than the average of those approved by referendum. When not constrained by the need to win a majority in a public vote, it appears that the community power structure is able to commit larger amounts of public funds to the projects.[1]

There are two other facets of referendums worth noting. First, a team's goal is to extract from government the maximum amount a majority of voters will approve. Hence, if 65% of voters approve a referendum, then the franchise owners are likely to conclude that they requested too little. If they are successful in receiving the maximum amount of tax funding, then the approval vote should resemble 51% to 49%.

The second facet to note is the bias inherent in the process to ratchet up the quality of facility that is approved. Invariably, advocates specify a facility incorporating elements that make it superior to, and more expensive than, any similar amenity in the country. The only options in a referendum available to voters are approval or disapproval. There are likely to be many voters who would prefer to approve a fully loaded facility that was not the "biggest and best in the nation" and cost somewhat less. However, voters do not have that option. Hence, they reluctantly vote for the new "Taj Mahal" because to vote against it would risk losing the franchise.[1]

The Increasing Costs Stimulus

In the past decade, players' salaries and the cost of purchasing professional sport franchises have both escalated exponentially. This has made it more challenging for owners to receive satisfactory returns on their equity investment if they rely for most of their revenues only on gate receipts and television income. The solution to resolving this conundrum was to develop facilities that featured new revenue opportunities: luxury suites; club boxes; elaborate concessions; catering; parking; advertising; naming rights; theme activities; and even bars, restaurants, and apartments with a view of the field.[46] Figure 3-6 lists the elements that need to be included for a facility to be considered state-of-the-art.

Figure 3-6 Elements in a "State of the Art" Facility

(1) **Luxury Suites:** The more the merrier—with fifty to seventy-five being the absolute minimum. These suites should also annually generate at least $75,000 to $100,000.

(2) **Preferred or Club Seating:** At least 500 to 2,500 seats that have an additional fee associated with the purchase of these seats. These seats give the team more revenue and the patron additional benefits.

(3) **Stadium Arena Club or Restaurant:** This can offer benefits to either the preferred seat patrons or to the team's whole fan base. Ideally, such facilities should also be accessible on non-game days.

(4) **Novelty Shops:** The old days of mere concession stand selling small trinkets are passed. New facilities must have a number of small shops dedicated to a variety of specialized items. For example, Chicago's United Center has a store called "Fandemonium" that sells everything from T-shirts, to special Harley-Davidson motorcycles, to golf carts decorated in the colors of the Chicago Bulls and Blackhawks.

(5) **Hall of Fame:** While these shops do not directly generate revenue, they can make fans "wax nostalgic," which can encourage them to buy vintage caps, jerseys, etc.

(6) **Concession Stands:** The days of the typical cold hot dog and flat beer are also long gone. New facilities must offer a variety of dietary and beverage choices. Vegetarian and foreign cuisine are also requirements at any facility. Some facilities offer special "kids-only" stands that offer mini-servings and special kid items, such as peanut better and jelly sandwiches. Also, there need to be large numbers of points of sale with televisions at each stand so fans do not miss a single play.

(7) **Auxiliary Developments (Microbreweries, Hotels, Theaters, Etc.:** The hottest trend in sports facilities now is to incorporate other entertainment options designed to lure the fan to the sports complex, even on non-game days. For example, the Sandlot Brewery at Coors Field generates over 1,000 barrels of beer a year, while Toronto's Skydome lures numerous patrons to its hotel and Hard Rock Cafe.

(8) **Automated Teller Machines:** With such a variety of spending options, a state of the art facility will want to give its patrons a number of ways to access their money. It should also go without saying that all stands and stores will accept credit cards as well, and every major league sports facility has an ATM on site.

(9) **Wide Concourses for Signage:** Wide concourses allow for the inclusion of more revenue generators and allow fans to move about freely. Of course, they also allow for the inclusion of another popular revenue generator: signage.

(10) **Restrooms:** With all of these concession stands, there is a need for restrooms designed to aid in the fans' comfort. Again, the more the merrier, as fan comfort is a key concern. Baby changing tables in the womens' and men's bathrooms are also a plus. Of course, advertising can be installed here as well.

(11) **Other Signage:** The inclusion of advertising along the outfield walls and base lines is also a requirement. Of course, it should be done in a tasteful manner that does not detract from the game on the field.

(12) **Scoreboard with Replay Capability:** In this "instant replay" conscious world, a large scoreboard that can offer visual replays of highlights from the current game and other games from around the country is a necessity. Permanent scoreboard offering out-of-town scores is also a requirement.

(13) **A Large Number of Comfortable Seats:** Depending on the sport, a minimum number of easily accessible, comfortable seats need to be in the facility.

(14) **Adequate On-Site Parking:** Such parking should be safe and close to the facility if at all possible, thus allowing the team to control these revenues for itself.

(15) **Corporate Name:** All new facilities will have to have a corporate name, and account for such revenues through additional taxpayer dollars, in order to be considered state of the art.

(16) **Administrative Offices:** Finally, a facility should have sufficient office space to allow the team to conduct its day-to-day operations comfortably and economically (i.e., rent free).

Source: Greenberg, M.S., & Gray, J.T. (1996) *The Stadium Game*. Marquette University Law School: National Sports Law

It was noted earlier that the first of these elaborate, single-purpose, enhanced revenue-producing facilities was the Palace at Auburn Hills, constructed in 1988 for the NBA's Detroit Pistons. The arena was designed to hold 180 luxury suites and over 2,000 club seats, and the $12 million generated annually from these sources covered the arena's debt service. Both the number and quality of these premium seating options were unprecedented. In the late 1980s, most arenas had only a small inventory of suites. Indeed, two other major arenas built at the same time as the Palace, the Charlotte Coliseum and Miami Arena, contained only 12 and 16 luxury suites, respectively. The large inventory of suites and club seats was presold, generating $18 million in annual revenues. The $13 million derived from luxury-suite sales alone serviced the facility's annual construction debt payments. In contrast, the NBA Hornets, occupants of the newly constructed Charlotte Coliseum, in 1989 received just $989,000 in total revenues from the 12 suites available. As early as 1991, analysts declared the Charlotte Coliseum "economically obsolete."[46]

The success of the Detroit Pistons arena precipitated what might be called a "Palace Revolt." It was the first to demonstrate the income-generating capability of a fully loaded sports venue. Its success prompted owners across all leagues to push for their own sports "palaces" incorporating the latest technology (fiber optics), a wide array of revenue-generating amenities, and enhancement of more basic service elements, such as increased number and improved quality of restrooms. Thus, by the year 2000, the average NBA arena contained 82 suites and 2,152 club seats.[40]

Although the Palace showed the way, subsequent arenas have taken the return on investment capability of these facilities to an entirely different level. The substantial income-generating ability of a contemporary arena is exemplified by the Staples Center. Although the Palace at Auburn Hills generates gross revenues of $40 million per year, the $375 million Staples Center, which began operating one decade later, produced more than $120 million in venue-generated revenues during its first year of operation.[41] Home to four major league teams (NBA's Lakers and Clippers, NHL's Kings, and WNBA's Sparks) as well as an arena football league team, the venue is guaranteed at least 156 dates per year from the regular league games alone. Including playoff games and the numerous concert and cultural events the arena hosts annually, in 2001 the Staples Center booked 250 events.

Cleveland Browns Stadium, pictured under construction in Figure 3-7, is a good example of the income-generating capability of stadiums built in recent years. From premium seating alone (151 luxury suites and 8,600 club seats), the NFL Browns receive $27 million annually. When income received from the sale of in-stadium advertising (primarily scoreboard and concourse signage) and from concessions and parking is included, then stadium revenues increase to almost $50 million per year. In addition, the Browns realize approximately $35 million from the sale of regular season tickets. During their first season in the new stadium, the Cleveland Browns reported a $36 million net operating profit, which was the second-highest profit margin of any NFL franchise. It was exceeded only by the Washington Redskins, who play in a larger stadium with an even greater number of luxury suites (280) and club seats (15,044). In 1996, the Redskins ranked 17th in stadium-generated revenues ($24.6 million) among the then 31 NFL teams. In

Figure 3-7 Income Streams from a Fully-Loaded Facility

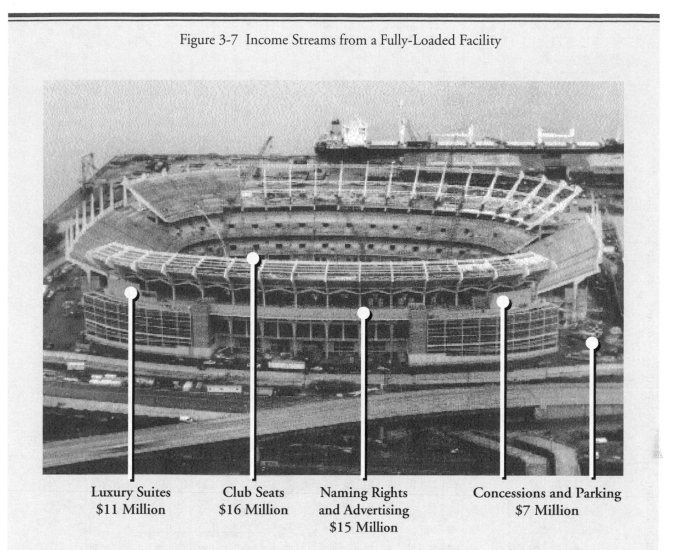

| Luxury Suites
$11 Million | Club Seats
$16 Million | Naming Rights
and Advertising
$15 Million | Concessions and Parking
$7 Million |

1997, the team moved to their new 80,000-seat stadium, FedEx Field, and quickly rose to the top of the league in venue-generated revenues. By 2000, the Washington Redskins' revenues from stadium operations exceeded $85 million.[42]

Transforming the bland, obsolete, multipurpose facilities of the 1970s and early 1980s into today's state-of-the art facilities by retrofitting them generally was found to be prohibitively expensive. In most cases, it was deemed more cost-efficient to build a new facility. In addition, the innovation, freshness, and excitement associated with a new facility were more likely than a renovation to arouse interest among the media and potential patrons. This excitement translates into an ability to raise ticket prices, which, on average, rose 35% when a team moved into a new facility.

The rapid shift in definition of what constitutes a high-quality facility rendered facilities obsolete quickly. For example, the Metrodome in Minneapolis was constructed in 1982, but 13 years later in 1995 the Minnesota Twins' president said that "[t]he fact is that the Metrodome no longer provides enough revenue to keep this team. This facility is non-competitive from a financial standpoint."[43] The Florida Panthers NHL team and the Miami Heat of the NBA shared Miami

Table 3-6   Analysis of Attendance Levels of Major League Teams Occupying New Venues Between 1995 and 1999

BASEBALL	1995	1996	1997	1998	1999	2000	2001	2002	Pre-Post	1st-2nd Yr % Diff	1st-3rd Yr % Diff	1st-5th Yr % Diff
Arizona Diamondbacks	-	-	-	3,602,856	3,019,654	2,942,251	2,735,821	NA	NA	-19.3%	-22.5%	-
Atlanta Braves	2,561,831	2,901,242	3,463,988	3,361,350	3,284,897	3,324,304	2,832,530	NA	19.4%	-3.0%	-5.5%	-22.7%
Colorado Rockies	3,390,037	3,891,014	3,888,453	3,789,347	3,481,065	3,293,354	3,168,579	NA	NA	14.8%	12.8%	2.7%
Tampa Bay Devil Rays	-	-	-	2,506,023	1,562,827	1,549,592	1,298,075	NA	NA	-60.3%	-61.7%	-
								AVG	19.4%	-17.0%	-19.2%	-10.0%

FOOTBALL	1995	1996	1997	1998	1999	2000	2001	2002	Pre-Post	1st-2nd Yr % Diff	1st-3rd Yr % Diff	1st-5th Yr % Diff
Baltimore Ravens	512,392	471,665	475,236	549,528	547,118	551,695	554,886	NA	15.6%	-0.4%	0.4%	-
Carolina Panthers	441,625	545,830	465,530	489,624	489,515	478,211	579,080	NA	23.6%	-17.2%	-11.5%	-14.1%
St Louis Rams	496,486	484,896	518,468	431,114	520,926	528,420	528,829	NA	NA	-2.3%	4.4%	4.9%
Tampa Bay Buccaneers	473,587	333,350	543,504	518,048	522,691	524,775	524,468	NA	63.1%	0.1%	1.2%	-
Tennessee Titans	-	-	224,221	299,552	528,891	547,532	550,393	NA	76.6%	4.9%	4.1%	-
Washington Redskins	413,150	427,740	602,592	542,096	619,749	647,424	624,374	NA	14.2%	-11.1%	2.8%	3.6%
								AVG	38.6%	-4.3%	0.0%	-1.9%

BASKETBALL	1994-95	1995-96	1996-97	1997-98	1998-99**	1999-00	2000-01	2001-02	Pre-Post	1st-2nd Yr % Diff	1st-3rd Yr % Diff	1st-5th Yr % Diff
Atlanta Hawks	504,807	496,669	585,793	715,452	331,831	601,138	560,330	506,110	NA	-7.3%	-18.8%	-
Boston Celtics	565,820	732,841	664,022	743,422	440,602	683,608	629,201	659,751	29.6%	-10.4%	1.4%	-7.2%
Denver Nuggets	704,011	675,717	461,406	483,791	296,965	637,698	619,300	633,846	NA	-2.9%	-0.6%	-
Indiana Pacers	655,028	673,967	636,735	645,302	404,536	752,145	733,444	686,537	NA	-2.5%	-9.6%	-
Los Angeles Clippers	438,254	414,560	400,637	408,693	256,568	559,714	601,587	740,185	NA	7.5%	32.2%	-
Los Angeles Lakers	591,125	649,634	697,159	691,994	430,007	771,420	776,336	778,877	NA	0.6%	0.9%	-
Philadelphia 76ers	507,809	489,327	626,478	655,417	436,444	756,929	805,692	842,976	28.0%	4.6%	-	28.6%
Portland Trailblazers	515,520	848,055	852,799	823,070	486,556	835,078	831,376	797,821	8.8%	0.6%	-3.0%	-1.6%
Washington Wizards	701,084	688,354	700,646	801,240	402,481	616,593	638,653	847,634	14.4%	-	-19.3%	5.8%
								AVG	20.2%	-1.2%	-2.1%	6.4%

HOCKEY	**	1995-96	1996-97	1997-98	1998-99	1999-00	2000-01	2001-02				
Boston Bruins	342,218	**716,434**	637,575	619,191	668,290	669,237	632,746	631,546	NA	-12.4%	-15.7%	-7.1%
Buffalo Sabres	361,537	563,012	**693,379**	641,034	737,275	736,174	731,438	705,828	NA	-8.2%	6.3%	5.5%
Colorado Avalanche	-	656,697	658,501	658,501	658,501	**738,395**	738,287	738,287	19.0%	0.0%	0.0%	-
Florida Panthers	340,619	544,439	602,823	602,244	**785,515**	655,260	601,857	659,440	25.9%	-19.9%	-26.0%	-
Los Angeles Kings	369,548	555,591	504,190	533,800	524,599	**677,264**	658,340	687,002	29.1%	-2.8%	1.4%	-
Montreal Canadiens	407,144	750,640	861,082	852,515	850,371	828,437	824,308	821,140	14.8%	-1.0%	-1.3%	-4.5%
Nashville Predators	-	-	-	-	**633,984**	680,582	635,374	606,347	NA	2.5%	-4.4%	-
Ottawa Senators	237,106	530,155	630,196	**684,126**	705,991	717,852	729,515	693,684	8.6%	3.2%	4.9%	1.4%
Philadelphia Flyers	411,848	711,391	**791,753**	800,285	804,105	804,169	802,805	802,337	11.2%	1.1%	1.6%	1.4%
Tampa Bay Lightning	478,419	**774,391**	713,891	568,539	471,948	557,618	611,173	644,610	-9.2%	-25.6%	-51.2%	-16.8%
Vancouver Canucks	334,379	**729,629**	710,136	684,748	647,913	600,319	697,717	726,226	NA	-2.6%	-6.6%	-21.5%
Washington Capitals	339,816	621,355	646,234	607,364	**708,351**	593,670	636,914	710,990	16.6%	-19.3%	-11.2%	-6.2%
AVG									14.5%	-7.6%	-8.5%	-6.2%

**Indicates shortened season due to labor stoppages in the NBA (1998-1999) and NHL (1994-1995)

Source: *Team Marketing Report*

Arena. In 1998 and 1999, both teams moved to new facilities, leaving the old arena without a major league tenant just ten years after it was built.

The New Facility Honeymoon Effect

The data in Table 3-6 report attendance figures from 1995 to 2001-2002 for the 31 major league teams that moved into new venues between 1995 and 1999. Attendance was provided through the 2001 season for NFL and MLB teams and through the complete 2001-2002 regular season for clubs in the NBA and NHL. Attendance in the year that the team moved into its new facility is highlighted in bold and underlined.[a]

Two questions were addressed by the data in Table 3-6. First, is there a prolonged attendance spike or honeymoon effect after a new venue is built? The data show that teams experienced a dramatic surge in attendance during the first year. Average attendance increased 22.2% during the initial year in which teams occupied new venues. However, the "after" occupancy comparisons provided in Table 3-6 show that 63% (19 of 30) of the teams experienced a decline in attendance between the first and second years of occupancy in a new facility. Three of four baseball teams reported declines after the first year, ranging from a modest dip in Atlanta (3.0%) to a free-fall plunge of 60% in Tampa Bay. NBA teams occupying new arenas reported the best record of the four major leagues with "only" half the teams reporting attendance losses after the first year and only one club suffering a double-digit decline in year 2 (Boston Celtics at 10.4%).

Although several teams showed improvement from years 2 and 3, in absolute terms, 16 of 30 (53%) franchises were drawing fewer fans in year 3 than in year 1. The attendance pattern improved slightly by year 5, with half (8 of 16) the teams reporting increases over first-year occupancy totals.

[a]Two anomalies should be noted. First, the Tampa Bay Buccaneers started playing in Raymond James Stadium in 1998. However, seating availability was tied to the purchase of season tickets in 1997 season, so the impact on attendance was felt in 1997. Second, several teams started playing in their new venues after the start of a season. For each of the following teams, the first full season in the new area was highlighted (Atlanta Hawks, Miami Heat, Montreal Canadiens, and Washington Capitals).

It appears that initial fan exuberance is confined largely to the first year of occupancy. The data suggest that in a majority of cases there is a decline in attendance after the excitement of the first year's transition. In some cases, this decline is substantial. However, the lower second-year attendances were likely to be sustained and did not substantially decay over the following 3 years.

This second question asked, "Are attendance levels higher in the new facility than they were in the old?" The "before and after" comparison provided in Table 3-6 indicates that with few exceptions, attendance improved dramatically as a result of moving to a new facility.

The positive impact of relocation was most evident in the first year of new occupancy. During their inaugural season in the new building, all 15 teams for which comparisons could be made reported average attendance gains of 24%. Most teams were able to sustain this relative advantage into the third and fifth years of occupancy. In the fifth year, 9 of 10 teams for which comparisons could be made showed appreciable gains in attendance over totals reported for the year preceding their moves to new facilities.

The increases for football and basketball franchises were substantially higher than those for baseball (but only one facility was available for comparison) and hockey. Although the expanded seating capacity of many of the new facilities can explain much of the attendance increase (e.g., the Portland Trailblazers' move to the new Rose Garden expanded the team's available seating inventory by more than 60%), a few franchises moved into facilities of equivalent or, in one or two cases, smaller size (e.g., Atlanta Braves).

Only four baseball franchises moved to new ballparks in this 1995-2001 period, and three were expansion franchises, so the only pre-post data available were for the Atlanta Braves, which experienced a 19.4% increase. Among NFL franchises, the substantial overall jump of 26.8% was largely a result of a significant attendance increase in Washington, DC, where the Redskins experienced a 40.9% improvement during their first year in their new stadium. All NBA teams moving to new arenas reported double-digit attendance gains, headed by the Portland Trailblazers' 64.5% improvement in their first year in the Rose Garden. Before-and-after data were available for seven NHL teams and showed that attendance totals were generally higher in the new facilities than levels achieved prior to the move.

Team performance may account for some variation in attendance. A dramatic example of this was the Philadelphia 76ers' performance in the 2000-2001 season, when they reached the NBA Finals and reported a 28.7% increase compared to their first season in the new venue. However, the relationship between winning and fan support is not consistent. Although some teams like the Colorado Rockies were able to sustain high attendance levels in the face of consistent subpar team performance (the team had a losing record in its first 4 years in Coors Field), a number of high-performing teams like the Atlanta Braves and Arizona Diamondbacks experienced consistent attendance erosion after the first year in their new ballparks. For example, the Diamondbacks' attendance dropped almost 20% the year after they advanced to the National League Championship Series. Thus, attendance declines cannot be attributed solely to poor performance.

These trend data indicate that the novelty effect associated with a team's move to a new facility declines substantially after the first year. However, for most teams, the declines are not accentuated after the second year. Despite the inability of new venues to sustain high levels of attendance, the data show that teams are invariably better off than they were in their old facilities. Attendance remained higher for 9 of 10 teams in their fifth year of occupancy than for the year preceding the relocation.

The Competitive Balance Rationale

The lack of competitive balance among teams is most pronounced in MLB and the NHL, which do not share revenues among the owners. Thus, those teams in smaller cities with lower gate attendances and smaller television markets have difficulty in competing with teams in larger cities. Without the revenue streams associated with new facilities, their noncompetitiveness seems inevitable. Even where there is revenue sharing of gate attendance (NBA) and television revenues (NFL and NBA), there is still disparity between those that have facilities with high revenue potential and those that do not.

Income derived from the lease of premium seating (luxury suites and club seats) is not part of the revenue-sharing arrangement of either league. Therefore, teams like the Dallas Cowboys (with 350 suites) and the Los Angeles Lakers (with 160 suites from $197,500 to $307,500 per season) are able to generate millions of dollars that are retained exclusively by their franchises. These teams have a substantial financial advantage over teams that are playing in facilities with limited premium-seating sales opportunities. In 2001, the Charlotte Hornets netted less than $1 million from the 12 suites (from $73,500 to $126,000 per season) available in the Charlotte Coliseum, placing them at a severe competitive disadvantage to the Lakers and many other teams in the NBA.

Teams with fewer resources to expend on players cannot remain competitive on the playing field. This is likely to create a spiral: Poor results lead to lower attendance and revenues, which lead to fewer resources to expend on players, which lead to poor results, etc. In these situations, teams are likely to argue convincingly that their only salvation is an injection of public funds to help them build a new stadium containing the desired revenue-enhancing amenities.

Meanwhile, because of the shortage of teams, owners are likely to use their leverage to encourage other cities to negotiate to host the franchise. This strategy was used effectively by the White Sox in their last 1980s effort to pressure Chicago for a better stadium, using the threat to move to St. Petersburg if such a facility was not forthcoming:

> The White Sox used their momentary poor standing to gain higher profits and a more favorable lease with the Chicago government, and, eventually, a new stadium. By stripping the team of top players, the owners in three years (1985-88) reduced its payroll from $9.1 to $5.8 million, barely half of the major league average of $11 million. With revenues of about $30 million annually, the team increased its short-term profits substantially. And, of course, the club's management used short-term failure not only to initiate cost-cutting measures but to press for a more lucrative

long-term relationship with the city. The White Sox were in good position to make demands on public authorities because of their lack of success on the playing field. The franchise could claim that it could not build a competitive team because an inadequate stadium and a burdensome lease restricted its resources. As is often the case in negotiations over sports facilities, nothing succeeded like failure.[19]

This argument that franchises performing poorly on the playing field need public subsidy for a fully loaded facility to enhance their revenues so they can better compete in meeting the salary demands of the best players has a long-term pernicious effect that has been portrayed in the following terms:

> This pattern suggests a kind of "Gresham's Law" ("bad money drives good money out of circulation") for stadiums, with publicly owned stadiums operating at a loss acting to drive privately owned stadiums out of business. The notion behind the Gresham's law for stadiums is this. Any team that owns its own stadium or that rents from another team has to compete in the market for players with all other teams in its sport, including those that play in publicly owned stadiums.
>
> Teams that play in publicly owned stadiums are subsidized. They are charged lower rental rates than are teams playing in privately owned facilities, because the rents charged by privately owned facilities have to cover the operating costs for these facilities, if they want to stay in business. This puts the teams playing in publicly owned stadiums at an economic advantage—their costs are lower. And this provides a powerful incentive for teams playing in privately owned stadiums to lobby for the construction of publicly owned facilities or to move to cities that provide such subsidized stadiums.[44]

The Rationale for Public Subsidy

The public's view on the appropriateness of public subsidy for sports facilities is divided. Between 1997 and 2001, almost 40% of the public referendum proposals to subsidize sports facilities were rejected. The converse of this is that over 60% were approved. These approvals suggest that a majority of residents in these communities perceived the benefits that accrue from sports facilities to be sufficient to outweigh the opportunity cost and equity issue that opponents raised.

Economists have developed a useful framework for examining the rationale for public subsidy. Too often, "the squeaky wheel gets the grease." That is, those who are most powerful, vociferous, and persistent win the case through emotional rhetoric, rather than on rational grounds. In an effort to counter this, the economists' framework conceptualizes a rational approach to the issue. It classifies all types of goods into one of three categories: private, merit, or public goods. The debate about whether or not there should be public subsidy and, if so, at what level, revolves around the classification of the good. The differences among the categories are summarized in Figure 3-8.

Figure 3-8 Differences Between Goods with Public, Merit, and Private Characteristics

Type of good continuum

PUBLIC GOOD	MERIT GOOD	PRIVATE GOOD
←		→

Who benefits?

All people	Franchise owners benefit most, but all members of the community benefit somewhat	Franchise owners

Who pays?

The community	Franchise owners pay partial costs	Franchise owners

If a project exhibits the characteristics of a *private* good, its benefits accrue exclusively to the franchise and spectators at the games. If there are no benefits or profits received by the general community, then it is reasonable to expect the franchise to pay all the costs, and there should be no public subsidy. At the other end of the continuum, a *public* good is perceived by a community as contributing health, knowledge, safety, or welfare benefits to all residents in the community. Because all residents benefit, it is equitable that they should all pay through the tax system, so public subsidy would be appropriate.

Many projects lie between the pole anchors of the public-private continuum. Such projects are called *merit* goods. These are private goods that have been endowed with the public interest, and this appears to represent how most communities currently conceptualize major league sports facilities. That is, part of their benefit is perceived to be received by the franchise owner and spectators at the game, but part also accrues to the public in general. In this case, it is not reasonable to expect franchise owners to pay all the costs because spillover benefits are received by the whole community. Thus, franchise owners should be subsidized to the extent that benefits to the whole community are perceived to occur.

An important point in understanding this public-merit-private classification is that the decisions as to where a sports facility project should be located along the continuum shown in Figure 3-8 are defined through political processes. Hence, this position may ebb and flow with changes in the values of a community, and it is likely that sports projects will be defined differently in different communities depending on a community's perceptions of the extent of spillover benefits. Franchises typically stress the spillover benefits that will accrue to the community in order to persuade elected officials and taxpayers that their facilities are public goods that should be at least partially paid for through tax revenues. In contrast, the efforts of subsidy opponents are directed to arguing that there are no general community benefits and to shifting perceptions of a project to the private end of the continuum so franchises will have to pay the full cost. The actual point on the continuum at which a particular project is located, and thus the magnitude of public subsidy, will depend on the persuasive power and political strength of the two sides.

The spillover effects that the proponents and opponents of sports facilities debate can be classified into five categories: (a) direct economic impact, (b) increased community visibility, (c) enhanced community image, (d) stimulation of other development, and (e) psychic income. Because these issues are central in determining the proportion of contributions to facility cost paid by government entities and franchise owners, they are addressed in detail in chapters 4 and 5.

The primary argument offered by proponents of subsidy invariably is that major sports facilities produce substantial economic benefits for the community. Hence, it is common practice for the supporters of new venues to procure the services of a nationally known consulting firm to demonstrate the substantial economic benefits that a new sports facility will provide for a community or region. The supporters are often an organized confederation of powerful vested interests (a community's powerful elite who were described earlier in the chapter) that commission the economic impact study either from their own resources or by applying pressure to elected officials to underwrite such a study. The standard operating procedure is for the consulting firm to produce an economic impact study that purports to scientifically document the economic contributions of the project. Typically, the results of their analysis are presented as objective evidence that the economic benefits (jobs, widespread income dissemination, tax revenues, etc.) produced by the new sports venue clearly outweigh the cost of public investment.

Despite a broad consensus that the benefits claimed by economic impact studies are frequently outrageously exaggerated, the vested interests that commissioned the study use the exaggerated figures to create a public impression that the new facility is a good community investment. They again draw on their considerable resources, both monetary and political, to ensure the study's findings receive widespread visibility in the local area. Because of the crucial role of economic impact studies in the public debate of who should pay, chapter 4 is devoted to an in-depth discussion of how these studies are conducted.

The other four categories of spillover benefits are the focus of the discussion in chapter 5. Although these are frequently less prominent in the political debate, there is a growing consensus among the cadre of academics who analyze, research, and write about the economics of major sports facilities that a stronger case in support of public subsidy often can be made based on the potential spillover benefits of one or more of these four categories than on economic impacts. It appears that a gradual shift is occurring in which proponents of sports facilities are placing less emphasis on their likely economic impact and more on the potential benefits emerging from increased community visibility, enhanced community image, stimulation of other development, and psychic income, benefits that are discussed in chapter 5.

Summary

Sports teams are relatively small business enterprises. The following observations provide perspective and context:

- Let us remember that Americans spend nearly three times as much money on flowers, seeds, and potted plants as they do on spectator sports.[45]

- A major university is not only larger than any sports team, but many exceed the size of an entire league.[39]

However, sports are a major element in Western cultures. Teams are cultural icons with which people in society identify, and in the United States this has resulted in taxpayers' being willing to pay substantial subsidies to these entities.

The recent rate of growth in professional sports facilities is unprecedented. Facility funding has passed through four eras. In the 1961-1969 Gestation Era, professional sports franchises were primarily confined to the Northeast and upper Midwest, and facilities were constructed for them by government entities. Government entities continued to be the almost exclusive provider of facilities in the Public Subsidy Era (1970-1984), when professional sports franchises expanded to reach a national rather than a regional audience. The Transitional (Pubic-Private Partnership) Era from 1985-1994 was characterized by more complex financing arrangements for facilities to which franchises now contributed and a transition from bland multipurpose facilities into elaborate, fully loaded, single-sport facilities. The Fully Loaded (Private-Public Partnership) Era (post 1995) was an era of extraordinarily proliferation of these facilities and marked escalation in their cost.

The total investment in the stadiums and arenas being used by major teams approaches $24 billion. In the recent Fully Loaded Era, only 39.4% of the $4.70 billion spent on arenas came from government, whereas before 1985, government had been the exclusive provider of funds. Among stadiums, governments contributed 62% of the $7.12 billion invested during the Fully Loaded Era. Although the proportion of cost contributed by public entities was lower, the dollar value remained essentially unchanged, reflecting the much higher cost of more recent facilities. In real dollar terms, the average cost of stadiums increased from $179 million in the Gestation Era (1961-69) to $340 million in the Fully Loaded Era (post 1994). The average costs for arenas ranged from $87.2 million in the 1970-84 era to over $222 million in the Fully-Loaded Era (post 1994). The escalating costs and improvements in quality that occurred in major league facilities were mirrored in minor league and collegiate facilities.

The focus of this chapter has been limited to explaining the changing relationship between the public and private sectors in financing major league facilities and the reasons that explain the dynamics of this relationship. It is recognized that this is only one dimension of the complex financial relationship between cities and major league franchises. Other dimensions include the extent of in-kind contributions for which cities may take responsibility (e.g., provision of land, roads, utilities) and the terms of leases that embrace a wide array of issues, including the distribution of revenue streams, maintenance and renovation of the facility, and scheduling of the facility for events unrelated to the team's franchise.

Data in the chapter show that the proportionate investment of public resources into facilities has declined, but the net annual public subsidy to the franchises often has increased. This is because although the facilities now generate more and higher revenue streams than those of earlier generations, the public sector entity often receives less income from these revenue streams than in earlier eras.

Using the data reported earlier in the chapter relating to the average cost of stadiums in real dollars in the four funding eras, the following scenario can be developed. A Public Sector Era (1970-1984) facility costing $200 million may have been 100% publicly funded, with the franchise paying a rental of $2 million per year. The average cost of a new version of the stadium built in the post-1994 Fully Loaded Era would be $339 million, of which the public sector would pay on average only 62%. However, the 62% translates to $210 million in real dollars, so the dollar contribution is higher; and if no rent or other revenue stream is paid to the city, then this represents an increase, not a decrease, in the net public subsidy.

Despite potential distortions to the financial relationship that these other dimensions provide, the issue of the extent of public subsidy and its relationship to private investment in major league facilities remains critical because the taxpayers frequently are required to vote on whether public resources should be invested in such projects. In contrast, many other dimensions of the financial relationship can be negotiated by small special-interest groups and supportive government officials without involving the broader public.

Four factors were identified as contributing to the shift towards franchise owners' paying a greater proportion of facility costs: first, the 1984 Deficit Reduction Act and 1986 Tax Reform Act; second, the enhanced revenue streams accruing to the franchises from generous lease agreements with public jurisdictions; third, the general trend over the past 25 years requiring the private sector in all segments of the economy to invest more in all public amenities and services from which they accrue benefits.

The fourth factor reflects the reality that when proposals emerge to commit public resources to constructing facilities for professional sports franchises, such proposals are invariably contentious. The commitment of private sector funds is likely to alleviate some of the contentiousness. The points of contention usually revolve around the issues of opportunity costs and equity. *Opportunity costs* refers to the benefits that would be forthcoming if the public resources committed to sports facilities were redirected to other public services. The equity issue is concerned with the fairness of transferring income from ordinary people to highly paid players, owners, and executives. Although this type of corporate welfare is pervasive across all sections of the private economy, it arouses especially high passions in this context because of the relatively high subsidies involved and the newsworthiness of professional sports.

Four primary sources of momentum undergirding investment in major league facilities have been identified. First, owners have leverage to persuade host communities to build new facilities, leverage that derives from the leagues' being exempt from normal antitrust rules that prohibit barriers to competition. This enables the leagues to ensure that demand always exceeds supply, which encourages cities to escalate their offers of public inducements as they attempt to outbid one another for franchises.

Second, the elite business and political interests in a community who control much of the decision making have a vested self-interest to enthusiastically support public subsidies of major league facilities. This coalition of business leaders, elected officials, and the media controls "the system"—that is, the financial, knowledge and legal resources needed to bring a major project to fruition.

Third, the escalating costs of players' salaries and the cost of purchasing a franchise provided a stimulus to develop fully loaded, elaborate, single-sport facilities containing an array of new and enhanced revenue opportunities. There is widespread belief that the level of excitement generated by a new facility translates into substantially higher attendances. This is generally true, but there is generally consistent attendance decay after the first year. A final source of momentum for facility development is the claim that small franchises are unable to compete on the playing field with those in large markets without public subsidy and fully loaded facilities, because smaller franchises have such small revenue streams. Less revenue translates into reduced ability to meet the salary demands of the best players.

Economists classify all types of goods into one of three categories: private, merit, and public goods. The debate about whether or not there should be public subsidy, and, if so, at what level, revolves around the classification of the good. This offers a useful framework for examining the rationale for public subsidy of a sports facility. To justify such subsidies, a project has to demonstrate there are benefits to the community as a whole, beyond those that accrue to the franchise owner and spectators at the games.

References

1. Fort, R. D. (2002). *Sports economics.* Upper Saddle River, NJ: Prentice Hall.
2. Morgan, J. (1997). *Glory for sale.* Baltimore: Bancroft Press.
3. Stadiums and arenas: Public-private breakdowns. (2000, July 17-23). *SportsBusiness Journal,* 34-35.
4. Engineering News Record. (2001). *ENR cost indexes.* On the ENR web site.
5. Siegfried, J., & Zimbalist, A. (2000). The economics of sports facilities and their communities. *Journal of Economic Perspectives, 14*(3), 95-114.
6. Danielson, M. N. (1997). *Home team: Professional sports and the American metropolis.* Princeton, NJ: Princeton University Press.
7. Swift, E. M. (2000, May 15). Hey fans: Sit on it! *Sports Illustrated,* 70-85.
8. Rosentraub, M. S., & Swindell, D. (2002). Negotiating games: Cities, sports, and the Winner's Curse. *Journal of Sport Management,* 16, 18-35.
9. Baade, R. A., & Sanderson, A. R. (1997). Minor league teams and communities. In R.G. Noll & A. Zimbalist (Eds.), *Sports, jobs, and taxes* (pp. 452-493). Washington, DC: Brookings Institution.
10. Johnson, A.T. (1993). *Minor league baseball and local economic development.* Urbana, IL: University of Illinois Press.
11. Menninger, B. (1999, May 3-9). Byproduct of success: Money. *SportsBusiness Journal,* 21, 30-31.
12. Campbell, B. (2001, August 8). Big money on campus. *The Bryan-College Station Eagle,* 1, 5.
13. Crompton, J. L. (1999). *Financing and acquiring park and recreation resources.* Champaign, IL: Human Kinetics.
14. O'Sullivan, A. (2001). Limits on property taxation: The United States "experience." In W.E. Oates (Ed.), *Property taxation and local government finance* (pp. 177-207). Cambridge, MA: Lincoln Institute of Land Policy.
15. Richmond, P. (1993). *Ballpark: Camden Yards and the building of an American dream.* New York: Simon and Schuster.
16. Cagan, J., & DeMause, N. (1998). *Field of schemes: How the great stadium swindle turns public money into private profit.* Monroe, ME: Common Courage Press.
17. Swindell, D., & Rosentraub, M. C. (1992). Hammers and their use: Some issues involved in the selection of appropriate tools for public policy analysis. *Economic Development Quarterly, 6*(1), 96-101.
18. Sullivan, N. J. (2001). *The diamond in the Bronx: Yankee stadium and the politics of New York.* New York: Oxford University Press.
19. Euchner, C. C. (1993). *Playing the field: Why sports teams move and cities fight to keep them.* Baltimore: The Johns Hopkins University Press.
20. Fimrite, R. (1992, June 1). Oh give me a home... *Sports Illustrated,* 76, 50-52.
21. Wilkinson, J. (1994). *The Olympic Games: Past history and present expectations.* Sydney: NSW

Parliamentary Library.

22. Hall, C. M. (2001). Imaging, tourism and sports event fever. In C. Gratton & I.F. Henry (Eds.), *Sport in the city* (pp. 166-184). New York: Routledge.

23. Rosentraub, M. S. (1997). *Major league losers: The real cost of sports and who's paying for it.* New York: Basic Books.

24. Will, G. F. (1996, January 22). Modell Sacks Maryland. *Newsweek,* 124, 70.

25. Farrey, T. (1998, September 16). New stadiums, new fans available: *ESPN.com.*

26. Baade, R. A., & Sanderson, A. R. (1997). Bearing down in Chicago: Location, location, location. In R.G. Noll & A. Zimbalist (Eds.), *Sports jobs and taxes* (pp. 324-354). Washington, DC: Brookings Institution.

27. Barlett, D. L., & Steele, J. B. (1998, November 9). Corporate welfare, *Time,* 151, 36-54.

28. Barlett, D. L., & Steele, J. B. (1998, November 30). Five ways out. *Time,* 151, 66-67.

29. Greenberg, M. J., & Gray, J. T. (1996). *The stadium game.* Marquette University Law School: National Sports Law Institute.

30. Keating, R. J. (1999, April 5). Sports pork: The costly relationship between major league sports and government. *Policy Analysis, #339.* Cato Institute.

31. Quirk, J., & Fort, R. D. (1999). *Hard ball: The abuse of power in pro sports teams.* Princeton, NJ: Princeton University Press.

32. The holdouts. (1995, July 23). *Dallas Morning News,* Section J, 1.

33. Shropshire, K. L. (1995). *The sports franchise game.* Philadelphia: University of Pennsylvania Press.

34. Corliss, R. (1992, August 24). Build it and they ~~will~~ might come. *Time,* 139, 50-52.

35. Whitford, D. (1993). *Playing hardball: The high-stakes battle for baseball's new franchises.* New York: Doubleday.

36. Quirk, J. P., & Fort, R. D. (1992). *Pay dirt: The business of professional team sports.* Princeton, NJ: Princeton University Press.

37. Dye, T. R. (1994). *Politics in America.* Englewood Cliffs, NJ: Prentice Hall.

38. Brown, C., & Paul, D. M. (1999). Local organized interests and the 1996 Cincinnati sports stadia tax referendum. *Journal of Sport and Social Issues, 23*(2), 218-237.

39. Noll, R. G., & Zimbalist, A. (1997). Build the stadium - create the jobs! In R. G. Noll & A. Zimbalist (Eds.), *Sports, jobs and taxes* (pp. 1-54). Washington, DC: The Brookings Institution.

40. Bucking the trend in Milwaukee. (2000, April 9). *Stadium Insider,* 5.

41. Simers, T. J., & Wharton, D. (1999, October 10). How the game was played. *The Los Angeles Times Magazine,* 28-30, 128.

42. Abrahamson, A., & Farmer, S. (2001, May 14). [Electronic version]. *San Jose Mercury News.*

43. Around the horn: Twins want out of obsolete Metrodome. (1995, September 12). *Minneapolis News Tribune,* 1.

44. Quirk, J. P. (1987, January 18). The Quirk study: A close look at the two proposals [special report]. *St. Louis Dispatch,* SR8.

45. Weiner, J. (1999). *Stadium games: Fifty years of big league greed and bush league boondoggles.* Minneapolis: University of Minnesota Press.

46. Noll, R. G., & Zimbalist, A. (1997). Sports, jobs, and taxes: The real connection. In Roger G. Noll & A. Zimbalist (Eds.), *Sports, jobs and taxes* (pp. 494-508). Washington, DC: The Brookings Institution.

Photos courtesy of Robin Ammon, Jr..

Chapter Four

The Principles of
Economic Impact Analysis

In 1776 economist Adam Smith recognized that a legitimate role of government is to provide

> those public institutions and those public works, which, though they may be in the highest degree advantageous to a great society, are, however, of such a nature, that the profit could never repay the expense to any individual or small number of individuals, and which it therefore cannot be expected that any individual or small number of individuals should erect or maintain.[1]

The primary argument for the substantial public subsidization that was identified in the previous chapter invariably focuses on the economic benefits that advocates propose will be generated by sports facilities, but that cannot be captured by the stadium's public-sector investor directly. Proponents claim that sports facilities built for professional or collegiate teams improve the local economy in four ways. When it is events rather their facilities that are the focus of debate, then attention tends to be concentrated on the third and fourth of these points:

> First, building the facility creates construction jobs. Second, people who attend games or work for the team generate new spending in the community, expanding local employment. Third, a team attracts tourists and companies to the host city, further increasing local spending and jobs. Finally, all this new spending has a "multiplier effect" as increased local income causes still more new spending and job creation. Advocates argue that new stadiums spur so much economic growth that they are self-financing: subsidies are offset by revenues from ticket taxes, sales taxes on concessions and other spending outside the stadium, and property tax increases arising from the stadium's economic impact.[2]

Belief in the preeminence of economic value percolates through to minor leagues. Thus, when city managers were asked to identify the benefits that their communities derived from minor league professional baseball, 85% cited economic impact whereas other benefits were much less frequently mentioned.[3]

There is always likely to be public debate about the merits of investing substantial public dollars into relatively discretionary projects such as major sports facilities, and invariable economic impacts will be a central element in the debate. Thus, after an initial explanation of the conceptual rationale for economic analysis, much of this chapter is devoted to explaining the principles upon which the legitimacy and validity of economic impact studies depend. Particular attention is given to addressing the theoretical underpinnings of multipliers and their strengths, weaknesses, and limitations, because a review by the authors of a large number of economic impact analyses of sports facilities and events indicated that the multiplier was widely misunderstood and misapplied.

The goal in this chapter is to describe why and how economic impact analyses commissioned by proponents of new sports facilities produce mischievous numbers that consistently exaggerate the real economic impact by a factor of 10 or 15 times. Indeed, our conclusion after reading numerous studies prepared by consultants for project advocates is that if the decimal point in their final number is moved one place to the left, then the resultant figure is likely to be a much more accurate estimate of economic impact than the number they promulgate! We demonstrate how this occurs by reviewing common mistakes and deliberate distortions that abuse the integrity of economic impact analyses. This review is followed by a description of the costs that often accompany the development of sports facilities and events but that, unfortunately, are usually omitted from analyses. The final section of the chapter discusses how to collect and analyze data for an economic impact analysis and reviews results from 20 studies undertaken by the authors.

The Rationale for Economic Impact Analysis

Sports teams and events are business investments both for the individual entrepreneur or athletic department that organizes and promotes them and for the communities that subsidize and host them. Civic leaders anticipate that sports events will attract visitors from outside their jurisdiction whose expenditures represent an infusion of new wealth into the community. City officials are eager to promote economic development as a means of generating local tax revenues and providing jobs, because these issues are of prime interest to their constituents. A sports stadium or franchise is a high-profile project that gives widespread visibility to their efforts, and they invariably commission a study to emphasize economic gains that can be tied to the project. Although entrepreneurs or athletic departments have a directly measurable bottom line that evaluates their fiscal performance, communities need to assess benefits in a broader context.

Figure 4-1 illustrates the conceptual reasoning for commissioning economic impact studies to supplement financial information. It shows that *residents* of a community "give" funds to their city council in the form of taxes. The city council uses a proportion of these funds to subsidize production of a sports event or development of a facility. The *facility or event* attracts nonresident *visitors* who *spend money* in the local community both inside and outside of the events and facilities that they visit. This new money from outside the community creates *income and*

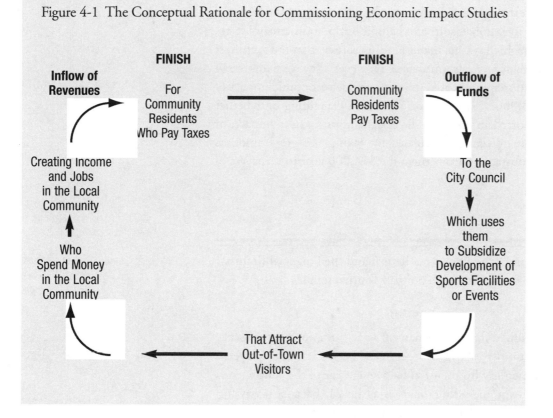

Figure 4-1 The Conceptual Rationale for Commissioning Economic Impact Studies

jobs in the community for *residents.* This completes the virtuous cycle of economic development. Community residents are responsible for providing the initial funds, and they receive a return on their investment in the form of new jobs and more household income.

In principle, the intent of the public agency is to provide seed money and/or in-kind resources to leverage substantial economic gains for the community. It is frequently argued that if public sector resources are not used to financially underwrite the cost of staging these sports events or facilities, then the consequent economic benefits to the local community will not accrue.

The purpose of economic impact analysis is to measure the broader economic benefits that accrue to a community. Sometimes the cycle shown in Figure 4-1 is perceived to start and end with the city council. This leads to a narrow definition of economic impact that includes only the taxes and revenues collected by local government from the event or facility. Such a narrow definition suggests the council should receive a satisfactory return on its investment from lease fees, admission revenues, increased sales tax revenues, or whatever. However, this approach is conceptually flawed because the money invested does not belong to the council; rather, it belongs to the city's residents. Economic impact is defined as the net economic change in the incomes of host residents that results from spending attributed to a sports event or facility. It is the return that *residents* receive that is important, rather than only that proportion of the total return that filters back to the council. Thus, in the context of this chapter, concern is with ascertaining how much residents receive in return for their investment.

The difference between a financial report and an economic impact report is illustrated in Table 4-1. When the sports federation in the city reported the financial consequences of hosting a national softball championship tournament, it reported to the city council, which was its major funding source, that the event lost $9,375. The council members were *not* impressed! However, they were impressed when the federation was subsequently able to report the net economic impact of the tournament was $273,000, $511,000, or $150,000, depending on whether economic impact was reported in terms of direct expenditures, sales impact, or impact on personal incomes (figures calculated by taking the gross amounts shown in Table 4-1 and subtracting from them the $14,000 cost to taxpayers of hosting the event).

Table 4-1 A Comparison of the Economic Return and the Financial Return to a City From Hosting a Softball Tournament

Context

All 37 teams that qualified for the tournament were from outside the local area. The average number of players per team was 15. Some players brought family and friends with them, so the average size of the contingent associated with each team, including the players, was 21. Because it was an elimination tournament, the length of time that the teams stayed in the community varied from two to six nights.

Economic Return

A survey of the players revealed the following:

Total expenditures in the local area
by players and their family and friends $287,000

An input-output model that calculated multipliers concludes the following:

Total economic impact on sales $525,000

Total economic impact on personal income $164,000

Financial Return

Income to the city parks and recreation
department from entry fees . . . .$ 4,625

Costs incurred by the department,
including manpower, to host the event . . . .$ 14,000

Net financial loss to the city . . . .$ 9,375

Pay-Back Period

The cost of constructing the softball complex was almost $2 million. Based on economic return to residents in terms of personal income, the capital cost of the complex would be repaid after 14 similar tournaments.

The capital cost of the softball complex that the city had constructed with tax funds was approximately $2 million, which means that, if the personal income measure of economic impact was used (the reasons for preferring this measure are discussed later in the chapter), the investment would pay for itself after 14 similar tournaments. How many other investments is a jurisdiction likely to have that pay for themselves in two years (assuming seven tournaments per year) and that continue to contribute $1 million to residents annually for the next 20 years? Sports agencies that present this kind of data in the form of an economic balance sheet to public entities demonstrating their contribution to economic development are likely to position themselves favorably in the minds of legislators and the general public.

The Mischievous Application of Economic Impact Analysis

"It's not what we *don't know* that hurts. It's what we *know* that just ain't true." Mark Twain's turn-of-the-century insight is remarkably appropriate today to an analysis of the techniques and tools employed by government officials in their policy-making roles. In this realm, the hurt can be measured in millions of tax dollars misspent on projects that in their planning stages appear beneficial. Much of the potential for real harm stems from what has become a common element in the evaluation of public works projects and economic development strategies: the Economic Impact Study.[4]

The political reality of economic impact analyses is that they are usually undertaken to justify a position that either a sports organization or community-elected officials have adopted or are proposing. Their point is not to find the truth, but rather to legitimize something the sponsoring group wants to "prove."

Community officials invariably commission economic impact analyses in response to increasing pressures holding them accountable for demonstrating the efficacy of tax-dollar allocations. They want to assure the public that government is making a "profit" in return for any subsidization it is giving to a private sports project and to convince taxpayers of the wisdom of the subsidy. Similarly, when such studies are commissioned by sport organizations, it is usually with the expectation that the results will reinforce the case for allocating public dollars to the project. In these circumstances there is a temptation to manipulate the procedures to strengthen the case.

Many of the consulting companies that are hired to do these studies possess respected national and international reputations for their work as accountants in auditing organizations' accounts. In that role, their integrity traditionally has been widely respected, although that reputation was tarnished by the accounting scandals in the early years of this decade. By hiring such consultants, advocates also are buying the aura of integrity and respect that accompanies the consultant's name. Sponsors rightly anticipate that the imprimatur of prestigious consultants will increase the credibility and public and political acceptance of the results and quell any questioning of the procedures used. However, in cover letters accompanying their reports, the consultants are careful to emphasize that the economic impact analysis is not analogous to an audit, that it is dependent on a host of assumptions given to them by the client, and that they extensively qualify their findings. Consider the following extracts from the cover letter accompanying a report from one of these national consulting agencies to their client:

> We have utilized sources that are deemed to be reliable but cannot guarantee their accuracy. [These sources are likely to include the advocacy group commissioning the study.] Moreover, estimates and analysis regarding the financial, economic and fiscal impacts associated with the stadium and team are based on trends and assumptions and, therefore, there will usually be differences between the projected results and actual results because events and circumstances frequently do not occur as expected and those differences may be material.

> The procedures we performed are limited in volume and extent and such procedures do not constitute an audit, examination, compilation or review in accordance with standards established by the American Institute of Certified Public Accountants and, therefore, we do not express an opinion or any other form of assurance on the information presented in this report.

Another consulting company with an international reputation that has completed many economic impact studies for sports facilities in its standard cover letter writes the following: "It should be noted that the analysis utilizes assumptions that were developed based on our market analysis, surveys with comparable arenas, hypothetical lease terms, and *conditions and assumptions provided by the City and developer*" (emphasis added). Thus the consultants offer no critique of the legitimacy of the assumptions given to them by the project's strongest advocates, but merely accept the assumptions as a given irrespective of how outrageous they may be.

These explicit and extensive qualifying statements invariably receive no visibility in the ensuing publicity announcing the report's results, as advocates tout only the outrageously high numbers that typically ensue. It is these qualifiers that provide the loophole that enables consultants to make unreasonable assumptions, engage in doubtful procedures, and announce mischievous results. It was not surprising, then, that one investigator who tried to gain access to a threshold number of these economic impact reports in order to evaluate their integrity reported that they were "cited time and again by the local media and the respective lobby groups keen to sway public opinion, and then they disappeared."[5]

Ostensibly, the people hired to conduct the studies appear to be both expert and neutral. However, "they are in truth the exact equivalent of an expert witness in a lawsuit who comes to testify in support of the side that is paying the expert's bill. An expert whose testimony harms his employer's case doesn't get much repeat business"[6]. The same commentator suggests, "The fees for the study are like a religious tithe paid to a priest to come bless some endeavor."[6]

This type of cynical comment about the integrity of economic studies is becoming increasingly pervasive. The cynicism is provoked by extravagant claims for the impact of visitor spending that many of these studies have made. The intent in this chapter is to arm sports managers with sufficient knowledge of basic principles so that they will be able to identify studies that are ethically challenged and distance themselves from them.

Because economic impact studies use complex procedures, produce quantifiable outcomes, and appear to be mathematically rigorous, often there is a presumption in the minds of bottom-line-oriented audiences who are unfamiliar with the technique that the analyses are "scientific," and hence, the outputs are objective and unequivocal. This impression of precision is seductive, but it is fallacious. These studies offer a misleading guise of statistical sophistication. Economic impact analysis is an inexact process, and output numbers should be regarded as a "best guess," rather than as being inviolably accurate. Indeed, if a study were undertaken by five different individuals, then it is probable that there would be five different results.

There are several points in an analysis where underlying assumptions can be made that will substantially affect the final result. Unfortunately, this means there is a temptation to adopt inappropriate procedures and assumptions in order to generate high economic-impact numbers that will position a project more favorably in the minds of the public. Sometimes such errors are the result of a genuine lack of understanding of economic impact analysis and the procedures used in it, but in other instances the errors are committed deliberately and mischievously to generate large numbers that support the advocates' position and mislead other stakeholders.

Consider the contrasting values placed on the San Francisco Giants when it seemed probable the franchise would leave Candlestick Park for a new stadium in San Jose. In San Francisco, which anticipated losing the franchise if voters in San Jose agreed to fund the stadium, the city's budget director reported she could document only a $3.1 million net gain to the city from the Giants. She placed this in the context of the city's gross economic product of $30 billion and pointed out this was 10,000 times as large, to emphasize how insignificant were the economic benefits of retaining the team. A professor of economics at nearby Stanford University was quoted as saying, "'Opening a branch of Macy's has a greater economic impact.'"[7] The low estimate reflected a belief that if the Giants did leave the city, much of the money that people spent at Candlestick Park would be deflected to other recreational activities in San Francisco. People would attend other events and engage in other activities in the city if they could not attend a Giants game, so there would be little net loss to the San Francisco economy. In contrast to the San Francisco officials, the Mayor of San Jose, who was trying to persuade the city's residents to approve a referendum allocating $265 million of public funds to a new stadium in which the Giants would play, announced results from a consultant's study showing that the same franchise would deliver to San Jose "'somewhere between $50 million and $150 million a year in economic benefits.'"[8]

In this section five principles whose inviolability is central to the integrity of economic impact analyses are reviewed: (a) exclusion of local residents, (b) exclusion of "time-switchers" and "casuals," (c) use of income rather than sales output measures of economic impact, (d) use of multiplier coefficients rather than multipliers, and (e) careful interpretation of employment measures. Mischievous manipulation of analyses invariably involves abusing one or more of these five principles.

Inviolable Principle #1: Exclusion of Local Residents

Economic impact attributable to a sports facility or event relates only to new money injected into an economy by visitors, media, vendors, sponsors, external government entities, or banks and investors from outside the community. Only those visitors who reside outside the jurisdiction and whose primary motivation for visiting is to attend the event, or who stay longer and spend more time there because of the event, should be included in an economic impact study.

Expenditures by those who reside in the community do not contribute to an event's economic impact because these expenditures represent a recycling of money that already existed there. There is no new economic growth, only a transfer of resources between sectors of the local economy. It is probable that if local residents had not spent their money at the sports event, then they would have disposed of it either now or later by purchasing other goods and services in the community. Twenty dollars spent by a local family at a sports event is likely to be twenty fewer dollars spent on movie tickets or other entertainment elsewhere in the community. Thus, expenditures associated with the event by local residents are likely merely to be switched spending, which offers no net economic stimulus to the community. Hence, it should not be included when estimating economic impact. Figure 4-2 elaborates on this issue.

Figure 4-2 Elaboration of the Concept of Substitute or Recycled Expenditures

How much more food do people eat because of the presence of a team? In other words, if a family eats dinner near the stadium or arena before a game, where did they not eat their dinner that night? If they would have eaten at a restaurant near their home, then the consumption of food as part of the sporting event is merely a transfer of expenditures from a restaurant near their home to one near the stadium or arena. This change of location for the expenditure certainly creates an impact in both areas—more spending near the facility and less in the neighborhood. But from the economy's perspective there is no growth or increase in spending levels, merely a transfer. Further, if the family would have eaten at home instead of at a restaurant, then the transfer of expenditures takes place between the supermarket and the restaurant, with consumption declining at the supermarket while restaurant sales increase. Again, there is economic impact in the sense that the restaurant may gain while the supermarket suffers, but the overall change in the community or city is not one of growth, but merely a transfer of activity from one vendor to another.

Source: Rosentraub, M. S. (1997). *Major league losers: The real cost of sports and who's paying for it.* New York: Basic Books.

This widespread admonition from economists to disregard locals' expenditures is frequently ignored, because when expenditures by local residents are omitted, the economic impact numbers become too small to be politically useful. For example, an internationally known consulting firm commissioned to undertake an analysis of economic benefits associated with the operations of the Green Bay Packers reported an annual impact of $144 million on Brown County. They blatantly and explicitly acknowledged breaking this fundamental principle by stating

> the spending and related benefits estimated in this report represent total annual spending and benefits occurring in Brown County as a result of the Green Bay Packers. It should be noted that no attempt has been made to estimate the portion of this spending and related benefits that is new to the area.

To accommodate the inappropriate decision to include local expenditures in an analysis, disconcerting new terms have emerged in consultants' reports. Some studies now report that an event or facility contributed $X million "to local economic activity." For example, the New York City Comptroller's office claimed that the Yankees, Mets, Rangers, Islanders, Devils, Knicks, Nets, Giants, and Jets accounted for $1.15 billion in "economic activity." Along with "economic activity" the synonymous terms *economic surge* or *gross economic impact* are now being used. For example, in a study for the Arizona Office of Sports Development, a nationally renowned firm of consultants stated, "A gross expenditures and economic multiplier approach was used in conducting this study, which is the most widely accepted approach in conducting these types of studies."[5] This statement is mischievous and disingenuous. It is the most widely *used* approach by consultants who are intent on producing a high economic impact number for their clients, but it is not "widely accepted" by anyone other than other consultants doing similar mischievous studies for similar client groups. Indeed, the authors are unaware of any reputable economist who has endorsed such a procedure. All of these terms have been concocted to describe all expenditures associated with an event or facility, irrespective of whether they derive from residents or from out-of-town visitors. This generates the high numbers that study sponsors invariably seek, but the economic surge, economic activity, or gross economic impact figures are meaningless. They are used by advocates to deliberately mislead other stakeholders for the purpose of boosting their advocacy position. Advocates are able to do this because most elected officials, media representatives, and residents mistakenly assume that economic activity, economic surge, and gross economic impact are legitimate measures of economic impact.

Studies of new sports-stadium impacts frequently include the economic impact accruing from construction. If the affected area of interest is the city and the facility is being constructed with city funds, then this investment is a substitute expenditure, not new money coming into the city. Either the money would have been spent by the city on another project, or it would not have been collected from taxpayers, who would then have spent it themselves—most probably somewhere within the city. Thus, city funds should be excluded from an economic impact analysis. However, if the money is coming from state or federal sources and would not have been granted to the city for other projects, then it can legitimately be considered as having an economic impact on the city.[9]

If federal or state funds were already designated to a city but were accelerated to facilitate building a new facility, then they should be excluded from consideration. For example,

> a previously approved Federal Transportation Administrative grant to improve the public transportation system in Atlanta was moved up six years due to the awarding of the Olympic Games to the city. This grant should therefore not be included as it would have taken place regardless of the Games.[10]

The author of a study measuring the economic impact of the Denver Broncos on the metropolitan Denver economy fully acknowledged that the inclusion of local resident expenditures was inappropriate:

> A limitation in most impact studies is in the implicit assumption that all first-round spending attributable to team or stadium activities is new spending for the local area—either export sales or import substitutions. Spending on sports may merely redistribute pre-existing local spending.[11]

Later in this Denver study the author notes

> The extent to which the money spent by local fans is "new money" and not simply a diversion of money destined for other local uses, is not known and cannot be determined. These local fan expenditures are an opportunity cost and an activity selected by the local population on which to spend a portion of their discretionary income.[11]

Despite recognition of the inappropriateness of this procedure, local residents' expenditures were included in the study anyway. Because 81% of Bronco spectators were revealed to be locals, presumably they accounted for a substantial portion of the reported $117 million economic impact. Elsewhere in the study, the author accurately states what he is really doing: "The study determined the amount of dollars that circulate in the Denver Metropolitan Area as a result of the Denver Broncos Football Club"[11] (p. 3). However, economic impact is not concerned with recirculation of existing dollars, only with the stimulus impact of new dollars. It is interesting to note that whereas this study of the Broncos identified an economic impact of $117 million, another study of the annual impact of a Major League Baseball team on Denver that respected the integrity of the inviolable principles projected $16.5 million—and the aggregate baseball attendance is many times larger and the season many times longer than those of football.

If there is evidence to suggest that a sports event keeps some residents at home who would otherwise leave the area for a trip, then these local expenditures could legitimately be considered as an economic impact because money has been retained in the host community that would otherwise have been spent outside it. It is usual to refer to this type of economic growth as *deflected* impact. It is deflected in the sense that instead of leaving town to watch a game, these individuals now spend their money on the local community. An attempt was made to measure this in a study assessing the feasibility of supporting an A-level minor league baseball team in Fort Wayne, Indiana.[12] Residents were surveyed, and almost 40% of households reported making a trip to another city to attend a sporting event, travel that represented a loss for Fort Wayne's economy. Almost 13% of this group who went to out-of-town games (representing 5% of the total sample) indicated they would cancel their trips if a team were located in Fort Wayne. It was calculated that they would contribute 12% of the total attendance at Fort Wayne games and their expenditures could legitimately be counted as new growth in the community's economy. Evidence of deflected impact is very difficult to collect and in most cases is likely to be tenuous, so the accepted convention by economists is to disregard all expenditures by local residents and to recognize that the resultant impact figure may be somewhat conservative.

Another issue related to the exclusion of any allowance for economic gain to the community accruing from local residents' expenditures was raised by the reviewer of a study of the economic impact of amateur sports on Indianapolis. He commented

> This study is a modest statement of the benefits, roughly analogous to viewing sports only from the view of producers and their employees—as net exporters. The trouble with that is that it ignores the utility to Indianapolis residents of the entertainment itself, as well as the services of restaurants and hotels and entertainment that would not otherwise exist.[13]

The point raises the following key questions: How many new and better restaurants, shops, and hotels do locals enjoy because the sports industry brings more visitors to town? How many of these entities might have gone out of business without the strategy?[13] The point is legitimate, but these very real opportunities that are created for Indianapolis residents are not readily measurable. Hence, they are typically excluded from economic impact analysis.

Inviolable Principle #2: Exclusion of "Time-Switchers" and "Casuals"

Expenditures from out-of-town visitors should be net of time-switchers and casuals. Some nonlocal spectators at an event may have been planning a visit to the community for some time, but changed the timing of their visit to coincide with the sports event. The spending in the community of these time-switchers cannot be attributed to the event because the spending would have occurred without the change, albeit at a different time of the year.

For major sports events, it is possible that prices in the community may be raised for their duration, so the expenditures of time-switcher visitors may be higher at that time than if they had visited at a different time of the year. However, most economists are likely to advocate that this increment be disregarded in the analysis, because of the difficulty of accurately assessing the magnitude of the increase across all sectors of the local economy. Rather, it should be recognized in the accompanying narrative as one factor contributing to the analyses measures' being conservative.

Casuals are visitors who were already in the community, attracted by other features, and who elected to go to the sports event instead of doing something else. For example, in a survey of the economic impact of the Chicago Cubs' spring training on Mesa, Arizona, many respondents reported they were out-of-state residents. However, the Mesa area is a prime location for "snowbirds." Large numbers of these retired people lock up their homes in the Midwest for the four or five coldest winter months and migrate south in trailer homes to spend the winter in the warmth of Arizona. When respondents were asked, "If the Chicago Cubs were to relocate to another state, would this affect your decision to visit Mesa, Arizona?" approximately half of the out-of-state respondents indicated it would have no effect. Thus, the expenditures of these casuals could not be attributed to spring training, because they were already in Mesa and it is likely they would have spent that money in the community on something else if there had been no spring training.

Expenditures by time-switchers and casuals would have occurred without the sports event, so income generated by their expenditures should not be attributed to it. However, if visitors who qualify as members of these two groups stay in the jurisdiction for more days than they would have done if the event had not been held, then their expenditures on those extra days should be included in the economic impact analysis.

Time-switchers and casuals can usually be disregarded when the event is a team sports tournament and its economic impact is almost all contributed by the participants and families or friends traveling with them. If a city hosts a softball tournament, for example, it is unlikely that any players on the teams that enter will be time-switchers or casuals. Their reason for visiting the community is likely to be exclusively associated with the team's tournament involvement. However, if much of an event's impact is generated by spectators rather than participants, or if it is the impact of a facility rather than an event that is being measured, then there may be substantial numbers of time-switchers and casuals.

Inviolable Principle #3:
Use of Income Rather Than Sales Output Measures

Economic impact can be expressed by a variety of different indicators, but almost all of them involve use of the multiplier concept. Hence, the notion of multipliers is explained before the discussion shifts to the relative merit of using income or sales measures of economic impact.

The Multiplier Concept

The multiplier concept recognizes that when visitors to a sports event spend money in a community, their initial direct expenditure stimulates economic activity and creates additional business turnover, personal income, employment, and government revenue in the host community. The concept is based on a recognition that the industries that constitute an economy are interdependent. That is, each business will purchase goods and services produced by other establishments within the local economy. Thus, expenditures by visitors from outside the local economy will affect not only the business at which the initial expenditure is made, but also the suppliers of that business, the suppliers' suppliers, and so on. However, some of the money spent by visitors leaks out of the city's economic system either to pay salaries or taxes to people or entities located outside the city or to buy goods and services from them. Only those dollars remaining within the host community after leakage has taken place constitute the net economic gain.

Frequently, studies apply a multiplier coefficient to direct spending estimates without explanation as to how it was derived or how appropriate it is to that particular community, so the naive stakeholder is left with the feeling that there is some magical process through which one dollar of spending eventually turns into two and perhaps even three. The great danger in the multiplier concept, and the way it is presented in research reports aimed at the policy maker, is that its basic concept and application are deceptively simple. However, the data and analyses needed to accurately measure a multiplier are complex, and the results require careful interpretation and explanation.

Multipliers are derived from input-output tables that disaggregate an economy into 528 industrial sectors and examine the flows of goods and services among them. In essence, an input-output model is an elaborate accounting system that keeps track of the transactions and flows of new money throughout an economy. The process allows a separate multiplier to be applied for each of the industrial sectors affected by the initial direct expenditure.

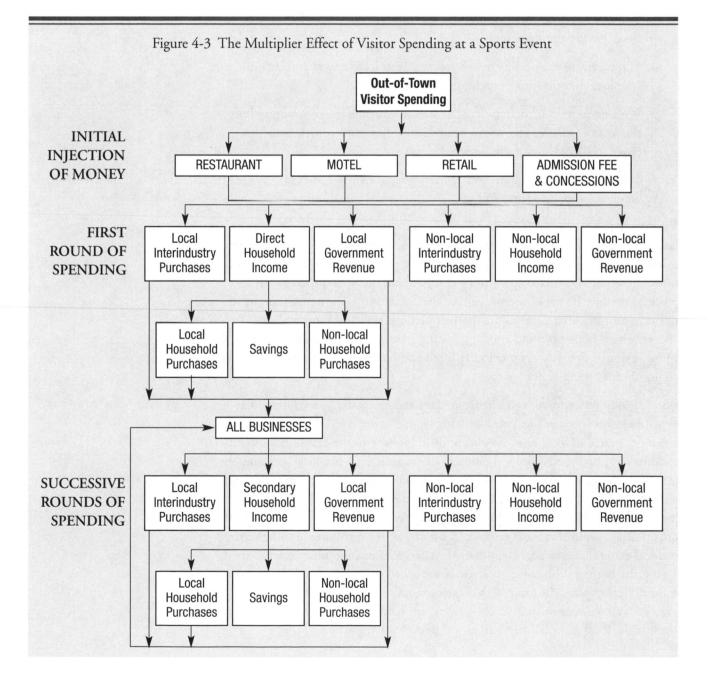

Figure 4-3 The Multiplier Effect of Visitor Spending at a Sports Event

The multiplier process is shown diagrammatically in Figure 4-3. To illustrate the process, the figure assumes that visitors spend their money at four different types of establishments in a community. Their initial injection of money constitutes the direct economic impact on the community. Figure 4-3 shows the six different ways in which each of the establishments receiving the initial funds could disburse the money it receives:

1. With other private sector businesses in the same jurisdiction (local interindustry purchases) to restock inventories to provide for future sales; to maintain buildings, fittings, and equipment; to pay insurance premiums; and for a myriad of other purposes.

2. With employees or shareholders who reside within the community in the form of salaries and wages or dividends that constitute personal income to them (direct household income).

3. With local governments as sales taxes, property taxes, and license fees (local government revenue).

4. With private sector businesses located outside the local jurisdiction (nonlocal interindustry purchases).

5. With employees or shareholders who reside outside the community in the form of salaries and wages or dividends that constitute personal income to them (nonlocal household income).

6. With nonlocal (e.g., state and federal) governments as sales taxes, income taxes, or taxes on profits.

The latter three categories of spending illustrate that the host city is part of a larger economy, and some money leaks out of the community's economic system to pay taxes to, or buy goods and services from, entities outside the community. Only those dollars remaining within the host community after leakage has taken place constitute the net economic gain to the community. The amount of the initial expenditures that remains in the jurisdiction from local interindustry purchases, direct household income, and local government revenue is subsequently spent in one of the six ways previously listed and thereby sets in motion a further chain of economic activity.

Because local government revenue from taxes and fees is likely to be immediately expended back into the local economy for services it provides, this money is considered a source of local economic stimulus. However, in the case of nonlocal interindustry purchases, nonlocal household income, and nonlocal government leakages (Figure 4-3), the direct revenue leaks out of the city and, thus, does not contribute any stimulus to the jurisdiction's economy. Also, some of the direct household income received by local residents may not be spent in the local economy. Rather, some of it may be saved, in which case it contributes nothing further to local economic stimulus (Figure 4-3). As far as the community is concerned, saving the household income received is similar to spending it outside the community. The effect is the same in that the economic stimulus potential is lost. Figure 4-3 also shows potential leakage from some household income being spent outside the local jurisdiction on nonlocal household purchases.

Some of the leakage shown in Figure 4-3 may not, in fact, be lost to the community. For example, it is possible that employees who reside outside the jurisdiction may spend some of their money within its boundaries, especially if the community is a major retail center for the area. This return of leaked funds is not shown in Figure 4-3 for two reasons. First, it is likely to be relatively small in many cases; second, it was concluded that including it in the figure would complicate rather than expedite understanding of the multiplier principle.

The visitors' initial expenditure is likely to go through numerous rounds as it seeps through the economy, with portions of it leaking out each round until it declines to a negligible amount. These subsequent rounds of economic activity reflecting spending by local interindustry purchases and local government revenues (Figure 4-3) are termed *indirect* impacts.

The proportion of household income that is spent locally on goods and services is termed an *induced* impact, which is defined as the increase in economic activity generated by local consumption due to increases in employee compensation, proprietary income, and other property income. The *indirect* and *induced* effects together are frequently called *secondary* impacts. In summary, there are three elements that contribute to the total impact of a given initial injection of expenditures from out-of-town visitors to a sports event.

Direct effects. These are the first-round effects of visitor spending; that is, how much the restaurateurs, hoteliers, and others who received the initial dollars spend on goods and services with other industries in the local economy and pay employees, self-employed individuals, and shareholders who live in the jurisdiction.

Indirect effects. These are the ripple effects of additional rounds of recirculating the initial visitors' dollars by local businesses and local government.

Induced effects. These are further ripple effects generated by the direct and indirect effects, caused by employees of affected businesses spending some of their salaries and wages in other businesses in the city.

These three different effects are illustrated in Table 4-2. In city A in Table 4-2, each dollar spent by visitors on food and beverages generated 24 cents in indirect sales and another 67 cents in induced sales. The induced effects stem from household spending of income earned from the direct and indirect effects. Similarly in city A, each dollar spent on food and beverages generated 31 cents in the local community in direct personal income, another 6 cents in indirect personal income, and 18 cents in induced income.

Defining Geographic Boundaries of an Affected Area

The distinction between who is a local resident and who is an out-of-town visitor is determined by where the boundaries are drawn defining the affected community. There is considerable flexibility and discretion in this decision. The geographic area of interest usually will be specified by those commissioning an economic analysis. *Local residents* could be defined as those living in a specific area within a city defined by zip codes or by city, county, state, or even national boundaries. If local residents were defined as living within national boundaries, then *out-of-town* visitors would be defined as foreigners visiting from other countries.

If more than one government entity—for example, city, county, and state—is involved in providing support resources, then it may be necessary to develop separate economic impact analyses consistent with the geographic boundaries of each entity. In this situation, visitors must be asked to recall or keep track of each of the places where they made their expenditures.

The size of the geographic area is likely to have a great influence on the size of the multiplier because the multiplier is substantially influenced by the structure of the host community. *Structure* refers to the degree to which businesses where visitors spend their money trade with other businesses within the affected area of interest, rather than with enterprises outside the defined geographical area. Thus, communities near major trade centers where the trade centers are located outside the local economy have smaller multipliers due to leakage than do similar communities that contain their own major trade centers.

The nexus to trade centers is a key element in assessing the likely economic consequences of sport franchises moving from downtown to suburban facilities. In such cases, much of the economic impact may remain in the downtown area where the business infrastructure is located. A referendum was held in Dallas on a financial package the city proposed to invest in a new arena for the city's NBA and NHL franchises subsequently called the American Airlines Center. If the referendum failed, then it was likely that the franchises would emulate the NFL Dallas Cowboys and move to the suburbs. Opponents to the public subsidy package argued that the city would lose little from the teams' move to the suburbs:

> Whether the arena is built in the city or the suburbs, it will have just about the same economic impact on Dallas and the metropolitan area. That's because most of the jobs generated by a new arena—from Dallas Mavericks T-shirt production to french-fry and hamburger bun distribution—will probably stay in the same place no matter where the stadium is, so long as it remains in the Metroplex. "What does Dallas care?" says one local economist. "Those hot dogs will get made at the same hot dog factory whether the teams play in Arlington or Dallas."[14]

As a general rule, a smaller community tends not to have the sectorial interdependencies within an economy that facilitates retention of monies spent during the first round of expenditures. Hence, much of the expenditure would be respent outside the local region, leading to a relatively low local economic multiplier. Conventional wisdom posits that the larger the defined area's economic base, the smaller the leakage that is likely to occur and the larger is likely to be the value added from the original expenditures. Thus, a multiplier coefficient for a small city is likely to be smaller than that for a multicounty area, which in turn will be smaller than the multiplier for a statewide economy. This principle is illustrated in Table 4-2, which reports multiplier coefficients from two of the communities in which the economic impact studies reported later in this chapter were undertaken. Note that the multiplier coefficients in city B, which has a population of 168,000, are substantially larger than those in city A, which has a population of 66,000.

Table 4-2 Multiplier Coefficients for Sales (Output) and Personal Income in Two Cities with Different Sized Populations

	SALES (OUTPUT) COEFFICIENTS						PERSONAL INCOME COEFFICIENTS					
	City A			City B			City A			City B		
	D	D+ID	D+ID +IDU	D	D+ID	D+ID +IDU	D	D+ID	D+ID +IDU	D	D+ID	D+ID +IDU
Food & Beverages	1	1.24	1.91	1	1.32	2.53	.31	.37	.55	.32	.39	.76
Retail Shopping	1	1.20	2.17	1	1.19	3.06	.32	.37	.64	.31	.36	.93
Lodging	1	1.33	1.87	1	1.36	2.44	.28	.36	.51	.32	.42	.75
Private Auto	1	1.22	1.56	1	1.25	1.89	.30	.35	.44	.32	.38	.58
Car Rental	1	1.32	1.65	1	1.34	2.12	.21	.29	.39	.18	.28	.52

D: Direct Effect **ID:** Indirect Effect **IDU:** Induced Effect

The trade-off in defining the geographic area within which economic impact is to be assessed has been articulated in the following terms:

> The smaller the area of focus the greater the number of those attending that would be classified as "visitors," that is, those attending from outside the region, and the greater would be the injection of new funds into the area's economy. Although the greater would be the leakage from any direct expenditures generated.[15]

Interpreting Alternative Measures of Economic Impact

Four different types of economic impact measures are commonly reported: (a) sales, (b) personal income, (c) value added, and (d) employment. Because the first three of these are all measured in dollars, they are often confused. A *sales* or *output* measure reports the direct, indirect, and induced effect of an extra unit of visitor spending on economic activity within a host community. It relates visitor expenditure to the increase in business turnover that it creates. Sales output is a rather esoteric measure with very limited practical value. It may be of some interest to economists interested in researching industry interdependencies, to business proprietors interested in sales impacts, or to officials in governmental entities who are interested in approximating sales revenues that may accrue from injections of funds into particular sectors, but it does not offer insights that are useful for guiding policy decisions of local elected officials.

The *personal income* measure of economic impact reports the direct, indirect, and induced effect of an extra unit of visitor spending on the changes that result in level of personal income in the host community. In contrast to the sales output indicator, the income measure has substantial practical implication for stakeholders because it enables them to relate the economic benefits received by residents to the tax resources that residents invested (Figure 4-1). The income coefficient reports the income per dollar of direct sales that accrues to residents, and it includes employee compensation and proprietor income. The *value added* measure is more expansive than the personal income indicator in that it includes other property income and indirect business taxes, in addition to employee compensation and proprietary income.

Table 4-2 reports the sales output and personal income indicators derived from two of the economic impact studies reported later in this chapter. The table illustrates two points that are crucial to properly interpreting and communicating economic impact measures. First, the coefficients are different for each category of expenditure that is listed. Thus, in city A, a $1 expenditure by visitors on gasoline (private auto) yielded substantially less personal income to residents than did a similar $1 expenditure on retail shopping (44 cents compared to 58 cents). However, it should not be assumed that the industry sectors with the highest multiplier coefficients contribute most to the local economy, because high volume of expenditures in a sector may compensate for a relatively low multiplier. Sectors with high multiplier values in which there are low levels of spending may not be as valuable as sectors with low multiplier values that have high levels of spending.

The second key point illustrated in Table 4-2 is that the values of sales indicators are substantially higher than those of *personal income* measures. For example, the table indicates that on average in city A, each $1 expenditure by visitors on accommodations will generate 51 cents in personal income for residents of the city, but business activity in the city is likely to rise by $1.87. If analysts do not clearly define which economic impact measure is being discussed, then there is a danger that inaccurate, exaggerated, spurious inferences will be drawn from the data as stakeholders are uninformed as to the differences between sales and personal income measures.

In an analysis of a sports event or facility, sales measures of economic impact are not of interest to local residents. The point of interest is the impact of visitors' expenditures on residents' personal incomes. Most government officials and taxpayers are likely to be interested only in knowing how much extra income residents will receive from the injection of funds from visitors. Their interest in value of sales *per se* is likely to be small because it does not directly impact residents' standard of living. Further, the use of sales indicators may give a false impression of the true impacts of visitor spending, because the highest effects on personal income are not necessarily generated from the highest increases in sales.

The conceptual model shown in Figure 4-1, which illustrates the rationale for economic impact studies, specifies that their purpose is to compare how much money residents invest in a sports event or facility with how much income they receive from it. The notion of sales transactions does not appear anywhere in the model, and from the perspective of residents and elected officials, it is irrelevant to the analysis. Nevertheless, because sales measures of economic impact are frequently three or more times larger than personal income indicators (Table 4-2), sponsors of economic impact studies invariably report economic impact in terms of sales outputs rather than personal income. The higher numbers appear to better justify the public investment that is being advocated, but they are meaningless for this purpose.

Inviolable Principle #4: Use of Multiplier Coefficients Rather Than Multipliers

The term *multiplier* is commonly applied to two different types of measures derived from the multiplier process, and this has created substantial confusion among practitioners, commentators, and researchers. Only one of these indices for which the term multiplier is used is of value to policy makers, and it is actually a *multiplier coefficient* rather than a multiplier. It has also been termed by different economists the "normal," "proportional," "true," or "unorthodox" multiplier. It is calculated by the following formula:

Direct + Indirect + Induced Effects

Injected Visitor Expenditures

Table 4-3A reports summary multiplier coefficients for the six sectors of the economy in which out-of-town visitors spent their money in the seven communities where the economic impact studies reported in the last section of this chapter were undertaken. Interpolating the numbers from city A in Table 4-3A to the formula indicates that the total personal income coefficient is .65:

$$.36 + .08 + .21 = .65$$

This personal income coefficient indicates that for every \$1 injected by visitors into the economy of city A, 65 cents of personal income accrues in the form of employee wages and salaries and proprietary income.

Table 4-3A Summary **Multiplier Coefficients** (normal multiplier) for the Six Industries on Which There Were Visitor Expenditures in the Seven Study Cities

City	Sales			Personal Income			Jobs		
	D	ID	IDU	D	ID	IDU	D	ID	IDU
A	1.00	1.26	1.88	.36	.44	.65	27.71	31.36	42.07
B	1.00	1.28	2.29	.42	.51	.90	28.87	32.57	48.46
C	1.00	1.26	1.78	.37	.46	.65	25.53	28.91	36.64
D	1.00	1.29	2.41	.39	.48	.89	26.78	30.94	49.38
E	1.00	1.22	1.83	.38	.45	.66	22.11	24.96	33.81
F	1.00	1.29	2.12	.38	.48	.80	24.39	28.18	40.68
G	1.00	1.22	2.15	.40	.47	.82	22.78	25.59	38.93

D: Direct Effect   **ID:** Indirect Effect   **IDU:** Induced Effect

Table 4-3B Summary Ratio (Incremental) **Multipliers** for the Six Industries
on Which There Were Visitor Expenditures in the Seven Study Cities

City	Sales			Personal Income			Jobs		
	D	$\dfrac{(D+ID)}{D}$	$\dfrac{(D+ID+IDU)}{D}$	D	$\dfrac{(D+ID)}{D}$	$\dfrac{(D+ID+IDU)}{D}$	D	$\dfrac{(D+ID)}{D}$	(D+ID+IDU)
A	1.00	1.26	1.88	.36	1.23	1.81	27.71	1.13	1.52
B	1.00	1.28	2.29	.42	1.22	2.17	28.87	1.13	1.68
C	1.00	1.26	1.78	.37	1.24	1.77	25.53	1.13	1.44
D	1.00	1.29	2.41	.39	1.24	2.32	26.78	1.16	1.84
E	1.00	1.22	1.83	.38	1.19	1.74	22.11	1.13	1.53
F	1.00	1.29	2.12	.38	1.27	2.10	24.39	1.16	1.67
G	1.00	1.22	2.15	.40	1.19	2.08	22.78	1.12	1.71

D: Direct Effect   **ID:** Indirect Effect   **IDU:** Induced Effect

In contrast, the formula for deriving a "ratio," "incremental," or "orthodox" multiplier has a different denominator, so it relates total income generated not to the initial change created by the injection of visitor expenditures, but to the direct income generated:

$$\frac{\textbf{Direct + Indirect + Induced Effects}}{\textbf{Direct Effects}}$$

Table 4-3B reports the summary ratio multipliers for the six industries in the seven study communities. Interpolating the numbers from city A in Table 4-3B to the formula indicates that the personal income multiplier is 1.81:

$$\frac{.36 + .08 + .21}{.36} = \frac{.65}{.36} = 1.81$$

This ratio multiplier indicates that for every $1 of personal income that accrues in the economy of city A, an additional 81 cents of indirect and induced income will be created. The size of the ratio multiplier is determined by the relative size of the direct effect.

A consensus has emerged in the economic impact literature that *the multiplier coefficient or normal multiplier should be used rather than the ratio multiplier* because the coefficient gives most guidance to policy makers. Despite this consensus, it is common practice for consultants reporting the economic impact of sports facilities to use the ratio multiplier measure because it generates larger numbers.

The ratio multiplier merely indicates that if $1 of direct income is created, a proportion of additional personal income will be created in other parts of the economy. It does not give a meaningful indication of the impact on personal income, because it does not include information on size of the initial leakage. Because the ratio multiplier is only a measure of internal linkage within an economy, to multiply it by visitor expenditures is meaningless. It is misleading, of no real value to policy makers, and should not be used.

In contrast, multiplying the personal income coefficients by visitor expenditures generates a very meaningful number for policy makers. Two decades ago, one of the pioneers of economic impact analysis in the tourism field advocated

> general abandonment of the multiplier approach and consequent removal of the confusion which it creates. It is difficult to envisage how or why such an inappropriate approach has gained such wide usage. Unlike the multiplier coefficient, it has no basis in economic theory and it provides misleading policy prescription.[16]

In the case of the sales measure of economic impact, the direct effect is synonymous with the initial visitor expenditure injected into the economy. This means that the denominator is the same in calculations both of the multiplier coefficient and the ratio multiplier. Hence, the sales output measure remains the same, irrespective of whichever approach is used.

Inviolable Principle #5: Careful Interpretation of Employment Measures

An *employment* multiplier coefficient measures the direct, indirect, and induced effect of an extra unit of visitor spending on employment in the host community. The employment multiplier reported in Table 4-3B shows that for every direct job visitor expenditures create in city A, an additional .52 jobs will be created elsewhere in the local economy. Again, the employment ratio multipliers in Table 4-3B offer no guidance to policy makers, whereas the multiplier coefficients in Table 4-3A, which purport to show how many jobs are created in the community as a result of the visitor expenditure, may be useful information.

Employment coefficients are expressed in terms of number of jobs per million dollars in direct sales. Table 4-3A shows the summary employment coefficients for the six industries in the seven study communities in which the economic impact studies reported later in this chapter were undertaken. The table indicates, for example, that in city A, for every $1 million in direct sales in these six industries by visitors from outside the area, 42 jobs would be created: approximately 27 direct jobs, 4 indirect jobs (31.36 - 27.71), and 11 induced jobs (42.07 - 31.36).

The state of Maryland committed $200 million for a stadium to attract the NFL Cleveland Browns to play in Baltimore and become the Baltimore Ravens. Findings from the economic impact study commissioned by the state were widely publicized in order to justify this investment of public funds. The study concluded that a Baltimore football team would bring the equivalent of 1,170 full-time jobs to the local economy, even though the team would have only 71 full-time employees, including the 50-man player roster.[17] Given that the team plays only 10 home games a year, the contention that it would beget 1,170 full-time equivalent jobs seems intuitively unreasonable. Part of this big number was attributable to the inclusion of locals, casuals, and time switchers in the calculation of monetary economic impact; but there are three other important caveats regarding estimates of employment that were ignored in the study and that should always be considered.

First, estimates include both full-time and part-time jobs and do not distinguish between them. The employment measure does not identify the number of hours worked in each job or the proportion of jobs that are full- and part-time. However, it seems reasonable to posit that local businesses are unlikely to hire additional full-time employees in response to additional demands created by a sports event because the extra business demand is likely to be sporadic and last for only a short time period. In these situations, the number of employees is not likely to increase. Rather, it is the number of hours that existing employees work that is likely to increase. Existing employees are likely to be requested to work overtime or to be released from other duties to accommodate this temporary peak demand. At best, only a few short-term additional employees may be hired. Hence, it is improbable that anything like 1,170 full-time jobs would be created by the Baltimore Ravens NFL team or that 42 jobs will be created in city A if an extra $1 million expenditure attributable to an event is forthcoming (Table 4-3A). The few jobs that do emerge will probably be short-term, part-time jobs. However, decision makers may easily be misled into assuming these are permanent full-time positions.

Second, the employment estimates assume that all existing employees are fully occupied, so an increase in external visitor spending will require an increase in level of employment within the jurisdiction. In the context of the front desk of a hotel, for example, the employment estimator assumes that the existing staff would be unable to handle additional guests checking in for overnight stays associated with a sports event. However, in many cases, they are sufficiently underemployed to do this, so additional staff would not be needed. The implication of employment multipliers is that without the injected expenditures, these jobs would not exist. In these situations, the employment coefficient is exaggerated.

A third potentially misleading corollary of employment estimates is that they imply all new jobs will be filled by residents from within the community. However, it is possible that some proportion of them will be filled by commuters from outside the community. In these cases, it is inappropriate to conclude that all the jobs benefit the community's residents.

The first and second caveats suggest that the employment multiplier coefficient is an inappropriate output measure for reporting the economic impact of short-term sports events. It becomes appropriate only when the focus in on sports facilities, such as golf courses, where the consistent flow of people to the enterprise suggests that jobs are likely to be full-time.

The Magnitude of Economic Impact From Professional Sports Franchises: Some Conclusions

Most professional sports franchises are located in major metropolitan areas. However, it is possible that a substantial part of the income received by a sports organization may be spent outside the local community for two reasons.[9] First, much of a team's business and practice operations may be conducted outside the city. Second, multipliers are based on the usual spending patterns of the proverbial "average person," and the athletes who receive more than half the money accruing to a franchise are not average people. They may reside for most of the year in a different community and spend most of their dollars there. One commentator observed

The biggest single expenditure of teams—player salaries—gets taken to the players' posh homes outside the local area. When I attend a game at Fenway Park, I am helping the economy of Boston less than that of Katy, Texas, where Red Sox pitcher Roger Clemens takes his $15 million salary. Even the skimpy wages of concessionaires and beer vendors tend to leave the city, according to reliable surveys.[9]

Given that their peak earnings time frame is relatively short, professional athletes may save more money than the average person does. Their wealth may result in the purchase of more luxury items that are not produced in the local economy. Their high incomes mean they pay a higher share of their income in income-related taxes that leak out of the local economy, and so they have proportionately less disposable income to spend locally. Most players and owners pay the top federal marginal tax rate of 39.1% and an additional 1.45% Medicare tax, so over 40% of their incomes leak directly to Washington, D.C. Outcomes such as these mean a large leakage occurs and the multiplier would be much smaller than the average multiplier used in software packages designed to calculate economic impact. If players do take money from the economy in these ways, then the spending on tickets that occurs by local people may result in a net loss to the economy, because if they had spent this money at small, locally owned businesses such as bowling centers or restaurants, more of it would have stayed in the local economy.

In contrast to this generalization, there is evidence that in some cases revenues that franchises receive from out-of-town visitors and other external sources such as television may tend to stay in the local area. For example, it was reported that 70% of expenditures by the Atlanta Falcons were made locally:

> 79 percent of the players and staff of the team live here all year; 39 of 58 players and 46 of 50 staff members live in Atlanta. Most field personnel are local residents, printing is local, the team uses Atlanta banks as well as an Atlanta based airline, and the team is locally owned.[18]

Thus, much of the visitors' revenues received by the Falcons was re-spent inside the local region, leading to a relatively high economic multiplier. Similarly, in the debate over financing a new arena in Dallas, advocates claimed

> It is important to realize that 75 percent of the $250 million in annual pro sports revenue comes into our community from companies outside the metroplex, the state of Texas, and even the U.S. in the form of licensing, sponsorships, media rights and advertising income. So what we really have are new national corporate dollars coming into the community, not recycled local dollars from local sports fans.[19]

The array of potential variables involved in determining the economic impact of sports teams means that there are likely to be wide variations. An estimate of the economic impact on household income of the NFL Texans on Houston is offered in Figure 4-4.

The findings of those who have independently evaluated the economic impact resulting from large public subsidies by local communities for sports team facilities, free from the pressures of a commissioning sponsor, are not encouraging. The findings from a series of such studies conducted in a variety of contexts by different

Figure 4-4 An Estimate of the NFL Texans' Economic Impact on Household Income in Houston

Impact of Television/Player Dollars	$ million	$ million
1. Team salaries from television money	75.00	
2. Income taxes	-25.00	
3. Income multiplier of 1.0 = Subtotal		50
Impact of Visiting Fan Dollars		
4. Ticket revenue from out-of-city visitors	6.3	
Concessions revenue from out-of-city visitors	1.6	
On-site revenue	7.9	
Off-site revenue	5.1	
Income multiplier of 1.0 = Subtotal		12
5. Total		62

Explanation of Data in the Table

1. The NFL television contract of $17.6 billion over 8 years means that the Texans receive about $75 million per year from the New York based league. That's new money, and it approximates the Texans' salary bill for players. Thus, the economic impact of the television money depends on how much of it the players spend in the Houston area. In turn, that is influenced on how many live in Houston during the off-season, buying homes and spending money there. Because of the mild winters and lack of a state income tax many of them do live in the area.

investigators in the past 15 years are that there is no statistical relationship between sports facility construction and economic development.[20, 21]

These findings have led respected authorities in this field to conclude

> The overwhelming consensus of opinion in these studies is that the local economic effect of a sports facility is between nonexistent and extremely modest. If stadiums do not contribute to any increase in local economic activity, they cannot cause a significant increase in revenues from local taxes.[24]

Another analyst concluded, "The statistical evidence indicates that professional sports as a golden goose ranks among the most enduring and greatest sports myths."[17] He went on to observe the following:

> The NFL seems an especially poor investment for a city. The teams play only eight regular season and two exhibition games at home each year. And the new stadiums are uniquely ill-suited for other purposes. Researchers at the University of California at Los Angeles even claimed, in a study released in 1997, that the sports industry had actually grown in

2. Players are likely to fall into the highest income tax bracket (39.1%) and federal taxes leak directly out of the community.

3. Houston is the fourth largest U.S. city and thus is likely to have a high income multiplier, so a multiplier of 1 has been assumed yielding a subtotal for the new television/player income of $50 million.

4. It has been assumed that 15% of fans are from out of town. The only data available are the 13,000 personal seat license accounts and 1,000 of these were from out of state. Average ticket price is about $60, and it has been assumed that an out-of-town party of four will spend $60 on concessions, and an additional $200 on food, gas, accommodation, and other items in the city outside the grounds, which yields on-site revenues of $7.9 million and off-site revenues of $5.2 million.

5. The total "best guess" economic impact estimate is approximately $62 million. The city of Houston invested $376 million in public funds (Table 3-1) in building Reliant Stadium. Thus, its annual return on investment is approximately 16%. However, without the television income the return would be close to 3%.

Two points should be especially noted:

a) The national television contracts of the other major leagues are much less remunerative, so in other sports substantially less new money comes to a community from this source.

b) The Texans were a new franchise, so it was legitimate to attribute all the new economic impact to the new stadium. In cases where an existing franchise is moving into a new ground in the same community, the only new spending is any increments which exceed spending in the previous facility. All the remaining economic impact is merely displaced from the original stadium.

Source: Adapted from Berger E. (2002). Houston hoping to mine NFL gold. *Houston Chronicle*, August 11, ps 1A, 14A.

L.A. after the Rams and Raiders bolted. Other sports, including a slew of minor league ones, flourished with the diminished competition.[17]

The average per-team gross revenues of major league teams in 2001 were

National Football League . . . . $116.2 M

Major League Baseball . . . . $94.6 M

National Basketball Association . . . . $79.9 M

National Hockey League . . . . $60.6 M

Teams typically employ 70-130 people in their front offices and hire approximately 1,000-1,500 part-timers for unskilled, low-wage day-of-game jobs. Firms with annual budgets of this magnitude are valued in the development of any region's economy, but these gross revenues are relatively small when viewed in the context of the overall economic activity in even the smaller major league cities.[9] Table 4-4 shows that in no county in the United States does the proportion of jobs classified by the U.S. Department of Commerce Standard Industrial Classification system as "Professional sports or managers" exceed four-tenths of 1% of all jobs in the county.[27] To provide a sense of perspective, consider that the impact on the local economy of sports in Dallas is about the same as the coin-operated laundry and interior-design businesses. Car-rental and leasing businesses, for example, in the city generate almost ten times as much in annual receipts.[40] In the broader context of spectators, consider that Americans spend nearly three times as much money on flowers, seeds, and potted plants as they do on all spectator sports! "Sports may attract a great deal of attention, but they are not an economic engine, they will not generate a lot of jobs and they will not revitalize a city's economy."[9]

It is large dollar numbers that resonate with the media and elected officials, whereas precise definitions of what those numbers mean, typically, are given only cursory attention. This has created a trend towards expanding definitions of both the activity and geographic area of interest. With this in mind, sports advocates in some communities have commissioned studies identifying the value of the "Gross Sport Product" (GSP) in a given area. Such studies tend to embrace some or all of the categories of expenditures shown in Table 1-2, and their purpose is to raise the profile of the economic role of sport in a community or region. The resulting study will show a GSP of $x billion, which is likely to be large enough to capture the attention of the media and elected officials. This may represent less than 1% of the community's overall sales product, but that fact is likely to be lost under the glamour of the $x billion figure. The authors see little point to such studies. There would be no real downside to them if they were done with integrity, but, alas, most of the time they are not.

The consensus of discouraging findings in the scientific literature regarding the economic impact of sports stadiums appears gradually to be diffusing to the popular media, which are increasingly urging reduction of public funding to support sports facilities despite the media's symbiotic relationship with sport. Typical is the editorial in the *Toronto Globe Mail* that concluded, "There is no sound argument for the construction of publicly funded sports stadiums. Period. End of story. You can look it up."[29] The evidence relating to the economic impact of sports venues has been summarized as follows:

1. Sports teams themselves are small to medium-sized firms. They are clearly vibrant, even vital components of any city's economy, but no more

Table 4-4 U.S. counties with the highest level of professional sports employment when expressed as a percentage of all jobs

County (State)	%
Summit (OH)	.35
Fulton (GA)	.32
Baltimore (MD)	.26
Oakland (MI)	.24
Bronx (NY)	.19
Erie (NY)	.19
Queens (NY)	.18
Cook (IL)	.16
Marion (IN)	.16
St. Louis (MO)	.16
Suffolk (MA)	.16
Philadelphia (PA)	.13
Salt Lake (UT)	.11
Hennepin (MN)	.10

Source: Nunn, S. & Rosentraub, M. S. (1997). Sports wars: Suburbs and center cities in a zero-sum game. *Journal of Sport & Social Issues, 21*(1), 65-82.

so in economic terms than many, many other firms. By themselves, sports teams are not economic engines; they have too few employees and involve too few direct dollars to be a driving force.

2. The professional sports sector, even in areas with multiple teams, is a very small portion of any region's economy. In no county do professional team sports account for as much as 1 percent of the county's payroll or private sector jobs.

3. A substantial portion of the spending that takes place at arenas and ball-parks, and at restaurants and retail outlets near or in these facilities, is merely a transfer of economic activity within the market area. Some studies have shown that as much as four-fifths of the spending would occur in the absence of the team.

4. The majority of revenue collected by the team is used to pay players. However, players tend to save more money than do other people, and they tend to spend money in their "home" communities. More than half the funds spent by fans being used to pay players will not be respent in the local economy.[9]

Justifying public subsidy of minor league teams on the basis of their economic impact is particularly tenuous, because their impact is likely to be analogous only to that of a small local business. For example, a minor league baseball team's gross operating budget, with few exceptions, ranges from approximately $250,000 to $2 million, depending on the level of the league in which the team plays. This compares to the $7 million in gross sales reported by the average grocery store, which also employs more people on a year-round basis.[3] The lack of economic impact is apparent from the following data, which were derived from an analysis of minor league baseball teams:

A team employs 5 to 20 individuals beyond its 21 to 26 players and coaches. Some of these employees, if not most, will be employed on a seasonal basis and paid on a commission basis. Players receive a minimum salary of $700 a month during the playing season only (April to August). Workers beyond the concession stands and vendors may be volunteers or work on a part-time basis. The profits of a team with no local owners likely will be invested elsewhere.

Visiting teams stay at a hotel in the community, thus increasing that establishment's revenue, but not necessarily increasing employment there. The low per diem given to players (from $5.50 to $14.00) makes it unlikely they have a major impact on the restaurant and bar business. There are two to three umpires per game, a small number of fans occasionally may follow the visiting team to town and stay one night (in many cases they can return home the same night) and scouts and personnel from the parent club visit the community on an irregular basis.[3]

Figure 4-5 Anatomy of a Mischievous Economic Impact Study

THE DEAL

On January 12, 1999, Governor John Rowland signed a bill authorizing $374 million in state spending for a new stadium for the New England Patriots. The development agreement obligated the State of Connecticut to pay for a riverfront stadium in downtown Hartford that would serve as the new home of the NFL Patriots. Robert Kraft, the owner of the New England team, had agreed to relocate his team from the Boston-area pending approval of the new stadium.

In addition to providing a new 68,000-seat stadium rent-free, the state promised to pay Kraft as much as $175 million in cash over the first 10 years if he failed to sell out the stadium's 125 luxury suites and 6000 club seats. The taxpayers of Connecticut would pay to build new highway ramps and thousands of parking places to accommodate stadium traffic. The agreement also promised that the state would pay as much as $200 million for improvements and renovations over the lease period.

A BREAK-EVEN PROJECT?

From the inception of the idea of bringing an NFL team to the capitol city, Governor Rowland was an enthusiastic supporter of the stadium project. Several months prior to signing the stadium bill the governor authorized the hiring of an internationally known consulting firm to determine the economic impacts that a proposed new stadium would have with the New England Patriots as the primary tenant. The firm had a long track record of completing fiscal and economic analyses for proposed professional sport franchises.

The final draft of the firm's economic impact analysis, issued in November 1998, concluded that the stadium would more than pay for itself in 30 years. In fact, the analysts predicted that the cumulative economic benefits from direct and indirect spending and increased tax revenues would produce a $3.2 million *profit* by the time the stadium bonds were paid off over 30 years. At a news conference to announce the study's findings, Governor Rowland pronounced that the stadium would "create jobs, act as a catalyst for more development, and pay for itself."

In reaching the conclusion that the proposed stadium would be economically viable, the consulting firm applied commonly accepted techniques for conducting economic impact analyses. However, careful evaluation of several assumptions underlying the analyse clearly demonstrate how mischievous economic data are generated. The following figures, drawn directly from the consulting firm's report, illustrate the extent to which the conclusions greatly exaggerate the economic benefits attributed to the $375 stadium project.

1. Assumptions Inflate Direct Spending Estimates

Direct spending in 2001, the first year in which the stadium was projected to open (and the base year for all subsequent calculations), including both gross revenue spending at the stadium ($100 million) and attendee spending outside of the stadium ($7 million), was projected at $107 million. This direct spending figure was based on the following assumptions:

Assumption #1: The Patriots would sell 95% of their regular ticket inventory at an escalating average price of $50 to $63 for the first five years.

Facts: Achieving that performance standard would exceed the sales record of every new NFL franchise established in the 1990s. The Carolina Panthers over the first four years sold 87.3% of their regular season ticket inventory. The St. Louis Rams sold less than 90% of their available inventory in years 2 and 3 in their new stadium. In the fifth year of operation, the play-off bound Jacksonville Jaguars sold 92% of their seating capacity. From 1996 through the 2000 season, an NFL team on average sold 92% of its ticket inventory.

Assumption #2: The Patriots would sell 100% of their 6,000 club seats at $4,250 each for the first five years.

Facts: During the 1998 season, the first year in their new stadium (what is now named FedEx Field), the historically popular Washington Redskins were unable to sell 8,000 club seats. According to the Association of Luxury Suite Directors (ALSD), in 1999 the NFL overall sold 92% of the league's available club seat inventory. The average club seat price used by the consulting firm was almost two thousand dollars *above* the league-wide average which the ALSD reported was $2,500. [As part of the agreement, the State agreed to make up the difference if the club seats failed to bring in $20 million annually!]

Assumption #3. The Patriots would generate a concession sales per capita of $18.50 to $20.52 over the first five years of playing in the stadium.

Facts: Concession revenues, the income generated from the sale of food service items and souvenirs, are commonly tabulated on the basis of per capita sales—the total amount of concessions sold divided by the number of patrons. The consulting firm projected that the average attendee to a Patriots game would spend around $20 per visit on hot dogs, beer, souvenir pennants, etc. According to the leading authority on concession spending at sports venues, the per cap projection used by the Hartford stadium consultants was 33% above the NFL average. The Bigelow Companies reported that the amount spent on concessions at NFL venues averaged around $15.00 during the 2000 season.

2. Failure to Exclude "Local" Resident Spending

Assumption #4: The consultant claimed that "90% of the total spending ($107 million in 2001) would be incremental." They assumed that $9 of every $10 spent on attending Patriots games, amounting to $97 million in 2001, would be "export" dollars or new money entering into the Connecticut economy.

Facts: In their market analysis, the consultants acknowledged that most of the attendees would come from the Greater Hartford area, and most of the rest from within the state of Connecticut. A more reasonable assumption would be that 20% of the fans attending Patriots games would be traveling from outside the state, resulting in an estimate that 20% of the direct spending would be new or incremental money.

3. Use of Inappropriate Multiplier

Assumption #5: To account for the "total output" of economic activity (direct, indirect, and induced) that would result from ongoing stadium operations, the consultants applied a sales or output multiplier of 1.75. This allowed the analysts to claim that the total economic impact of the new stadium would be $170.3 million in 2001, growing to $200.6 by 2005.

$$1.75 \text{ (sales multiplier) X } \$97,083,000 \text{ (direct "incremental spending")}$$

$$= \$170.3 \text{ million (total output)}$$

Facts: Inviolable principle #3 in this chapter emphasizes that sales measures are inappropriate and income multipliers should be used. Residents are only interested in how much extra income they will receive from the injection of visitors' funds. Sales *per se* do not impact residents' standard of living.

4. Distorted Employment Claims

Assumption #6: By 2005, stadium construction and spending prompted by the operation of the stadium would create 3,240 FTE (full-time equivalent) jobs in the state.

Facts: The projected number of jobs was derived from the fallacious direct expenditure and "non-locals" data identified above. The report also fails to acknowledge that virtually all of the jobs which would emanate from the stadium project are likely to be part-time or seasonal, not full-time, with pay at close to minimum wage levels.

IMPACT OF ALTERNATIVE ASSUMPTIONS

If more reasonable assumptions are substituted for those on which the consultants based their economic impact, the results are quantumly different. Consider the following:

1. Direct Spending:	Revised	Consultant
If 90% (not 95%) of regular tickets were sold	$43,715,367	$46,144,000
If 92% (not 100%) of club seats sold at $2500 (not $4250)	$13,800,000	$25,500,000
If concession per cap were $15.00 (not $18.50)	$11,670,000	$14,393,000
	$69,185,367	$86,037,000

Using these three sources of direct spending, the revised assumptions reduce the consultants' estimate by almost $17 million in just 2001! The consultants' other sources of direct spending in the stadium are parking, novelties, and advertising. If their assumptions in these three areas and the outside stadium estimates remain unchanged, the total direct spending falls to $88.6 million from $107 million.

2. Incremental Spending Impact

If out-of-state attendees are projected to be 20% of the total attendance (rather than 90%), then the estimate of new direct or "incremental" spending would be $17.7 million (.2 X $88.6 million).

Remember that the key to economic impact is the infusion of new dollars from outside the local economy. It is fair to assume that a great majority of direct spending would be from local Hartford-area residents who would most likely be substituting their spending at Patriots games for other entertainment options in the local community. In any event, their spending would not be adding new dollars to the state's economy. Thus, the true economic impact related to the new stadium would be far less than projected by the consultants.

3. Personal Income Multiplier

If an average personal income multiplier of .75 were used, rather than the 1.75 sales multiplier used by the consultants, the economic impact would be (.75 X $17.7 million):

$$\$13.3 \text{ million}$$

We believe this is likely to be a much more accurate estimate of the economic impact of the new stadium on the residents of Connecticut in 2001 than the consultants' estimate of $170.3 million!

The analysis reported in Figure 4-5 illustrates the impact of different assumptions. The consultants reported an economic impact of a new stadium for an NFL franchise at $170.3 million per year, but the authors' analysis of their report indicated widespread abuse of basic principles. When these were followed, the authors projected the economic impact to be $13.3 million.

One of the authors was invited by a large U.S. city to undertake a study that would assess the economic impact on the area of a 10-day sports festival that incorporated over 60 events. A multistage sampling procedure was used to collect data from over 2,600 festival participants. Data from that study are used here to illustrate the egregious errors that occur when the central inviolable principles of economic impact studies described earlier are abused.

Illustrations of the Implications of Abusing the Inviolable Principles

Because it was a large city with extensive suburbs, the defined area for which the economic impact study was undertaken was delineated to include both the county within which the city's boundaries were confined and two surrounding counties that embraced the city's suburbs. These three counties essentially represented the integrated local trading area. If the study had been limited to a single county, the economic interrelationships between city and suburbs would have been ignored and the results would have been less representative of economic impact on the area.

Table 4-5 Economic Activity in City X Created by the Expenditures of Residents and Non-Residents Who Attended Sports Events

Items	Total Sales	Personal Income	Number of Jobs Created
Food & Beverages	109,196,634	48,238,234	3,110
Admission Fees	38,691,412	14,200,095	1,095
Night Clubs, Lounges & Bars	20,163,133	10,987,611	402
Retail Shopping	66,934,134	28,159,102	1,805
Lodging Expenses	47,872,258	19,922,456	1,148
Private Auto Expense	14,727,339	5,123,586	259
Commercial Transportation	22,146,640	9,126,217	370
Other Expenses	1,874,950	1,076,825	69
TOTAL	321,606,500	136,834,125	8,258

The data reported in Table 4-4 abuse four of the inviolable principles. The table reports "economic activity," not economic impact, because it inappropriately includes local residents in the analysis; it prominently displays economic activity in terms of value of sales as well as in terms of personal income; it includes time-switchers and casuals; and it displays total jobs created, failing to note that they are a combination of part-time and full-time jobs and that they are unlikely to be durable. From these results, the uninformed policy maker, media representative, or taxpayer may reasonably (but mistakenly) conclude that the economic impact of the city's festival was over $321 million and that it generated 8,258 full-time jobs.

In Table 4-6, local residents' expenditures were removed from the analysis, so the table now reports economic impact and not economic activity. The aggregated impacts are substantially lower than those shown in Table 4-5, but they are still exaggerated because they include time-switchers and casuals. A footnote introduces appropriate caveats regarding the number of jobs created.

Table 4-6 Economic Activity in City X of Expenditures by Non-Residents
Who Attended Sports Events

Items	Total Sales	Personal Income	Number of Jobs Created*
Food & Beverage	37,859,887	16,737,554	1,078
Admission Fees	7,837,688	2,875,055	222
Night Clubs, Lounges & Bars	4,555,057	2,478,865	91
Retail Shopping	23,545,491	9,909,880	635
Lodging Expenses	35,124,109	14,637,961	843
Private Auto Expenses	4,744,930	1,653,118	84
Commercial Transportation	10,710,664	4,340,311	179
Other Expenses	1,088,768	458,243	29
TOTAL	125,466,594	53,090,987	3,161

*This figure refers to both full-time and part-time jobs. It assumes the local economy is operating at full capacity and that there is no slack to absorb additional demand created by these events.

Respondents were asked questions that showed that 27% of nonlocal participants were time-switchers who would have visited the city if the festival had not been held, but the festival influenced their decision to come at that time. Another 43% of nonlocals were casuals who would have come to the city at that time, irrespective of the event. They went to the festival because it was an attractive entertainment option while they were in the community. Table 4-7 shows the impact on the city when these two groups were discarded from the analyses, because their expenditures would have entered the city's economy even if the event had not been held. In this survey, time-switchers and casuals were not asked if their stay had been extended because of the festival. If there were extensions, then that increment of their expenditures should have been added to the total. To that extent, the economic impacts shown in Table 4-7 are underestimates.

The data shown in Table 4-7, excluding the sales column, were used in the presentation of the study's findings to the sports festival's board. The results were scheduled to be presented to the city council the following week. At the conclusion of the presentation, some board members quickly challenged the results, arguing that they were much too low. They observed that 2 weeks previously, the city council had heard a similar presentation from the convention and visitors bureau relating to a professional rodeo event that the city hosted annually. The council had been informed that the economic impact of the 3-day professional rodeo event was almost $30 million. The conundrum confronting the sports festival board was posed in the following terms:

How can we possibly accept that this festival lasting for 10 days and embracing over 60 events had a smaller economic impact than a single 3-day rodeo event? The city council provides a substantially larger budget to the sports festival board to stage the festival than they allocate to the convention

Table 4-7 Economic Activity in City X of Expenditures by Non-Residents
(Excluding Casuals and Time Switchers) Who Attended Sports Events

Items	Total Sales	Personal Income	Number of Jobs Created*
Food & Beverage	7,371,629	5,088,151	328
Admission Fees	1,550,953	874,005	67
Night Clubs, Lounges & Bars	1,384,713	753,562	28
Retail Shopping	4,943,987	3,012,571	193
Lodging Expenses	6,655,528	4,449,879	256
Private Auto Expenses	824,220	502,541	25
Commercial Transportation	1,897,734	1,319,433	54
Other Expenses	213,126	139,305	9
TOTAL	24,841,890	16,139,447	960

*This figure refers to both full-time and part-time jobs. It assumes the local economy is operating at full capacity and that there is no slack to absorb additional demand created by these events.

and visitors bureau to host the professional rodeo event. When they compare the sports festival data that has been presented to us with those from the rodeo, there is a real possibility that the festival budget will be cut, because the festival costs much more to stage and its economic impact on the city appears to be barely half that of the rodeo.

When a copy of the rodeo economic impact study was reviewed, it was found that it abused four of the inviolable principles: It included local residents, time-switchers, and casuals, used sales output as the measure of economic impact, and implied full-time jobs resulted from the visitors' expenditures. The author's response in his subsequent presentation to the city council was to replicate the presentation made to the sport festival board, but then to extend it by referring to the rodeo study and showing that if those erroneous assumptions were applied to the festival, the comparative number to the rodeo's almost $30 million was over $321 million (Table 4-5).

This illustration demonstrates the wide range of numbers that purport to measure economic impact that may be presented to stakeholders from the same set of primary data. If a press conference was held in city X to report the festival's economic impact, the organizers could at one extreme announce that the *sales output* from *economic activity* associated with the festival was over $321 million (Table 4-5). At the other extreme, they could announce that the *economic impact* of the festival on *personal income* was approximately $16 million (Table 4-7).

The media, general public, city council, and other relevant publics are unlikely to be aware of the underlying assumptions, subtleties, and potential error sources associated with economic impact studies. This lack of sophistication and the apparent objectivity conveyed by the numbers make it tempting for advocates to act unethically.

Clearly, there is a dilemma. If the correct $16 million figure for city X is presented, the economic contribution of the sports festival is likely to appear relatively insignificant compared to that of other events that misleadingly announce the equivalent of the $321 million figure as their estimated economic impact. The relatively small impact of the festival is likely to translate into commensurately less political and resource support for it from decision makers and, perhaps ultimately, even withdrawal of appropriations for it. Acting ethically when others do not could critically damage the festival's standing.

Alternatively, some may rationalize that it is equitable to use the same set of measures to compare the economic contributions of sports events, even though the results of all of them are grossly misleading. If such a position is accepted, then abuses incorporated into one economic impact analysis become contagious, because when precedent has been established in one study, others are likely to feel compelled to knowingly perpetuate the abuse by incorporating the misleading procedures into their own analyses. If they fail to do so, then the economic impact attributed to their event or facility is perceived to be lower than that reported by others and thus less worthy of public investment.

Continued abuse of economic impact principles by advocates inevitably will lead to the technique's being discounted by decision makers. The author adhered to the inviolable principles in his presentation to the council, but at the same time, it was necessary to recognize the political reality of being compared to others who had reported misleading economic impacts to the city council. The conundrum was resolved during the presentation by identifying the erroneous assumptions that the rodeo event incorporated and demonstrating how the results of the sports festival study would be inflated if the same erroneous assumptions were incorporated into it.

Despite growing skepticism of the mischievous results emanating from advocacy studies, they are likely to continue to be commissioned as long as they contribute to two ends. The first one is to provide political cover for elected officials supporting the public subsidies. At the end of chapter 5 it is suggested that there is a better option for this purpose. The second end is to persuade at least a small number of people to vote in favor of a subsidy in a referendum. For example, in a community where 54% of voters are either undecided about the issue or opposed to a subsidy and 46% are in favor, a mischievous economic impact study that misleads only 5% of the voters can change the outcome. It has been pointed out that "if bogus studies can sway only a relatively few people, the interests that benefit from facility construction (the sports team, local contractors, construction unions, real estate operators, bankers) are motivated to produce them."[31] It was noted in chapter 3 that these powerful interests are able to raise substantial funds to promulgate the mischievous numbers in promotional campaigns so they become firmly entrenched without substantial challenge from opponents who lack those resources. For example,

> In June 1997 San Francisco and the state of Washington held referenda on whether to subsidize a new NFL football stadium. Both referenda won by tiny margins. In San Francisco, proponents outspent opponents by 25 to 1, while in Washington the spending ratio was an amazing 80 to 1! If as few as 2 percent of voters were misled by the incorrect claims about the

economic effects of the stadium proposals in these campaigns, the bogus studies determined the outcome in these elections. With the campaign spending so unequal, such an outcome surely is not implausible.[31]

Consideration of Costs

Unfortunately, sports events can generate substantial economic costs that often are forgotten in the euphoria surrounding development of a facility or an event. The numbers emerging from an economic impact study represent only the gross economic benefits associated with a project. Too often, only positive economic benefits are reported, whereas monetary costs and nonmonetary negative impacts inflicted on a community are not considered. Community stakeholders are likely to be more concerned with net, rather than gross, economic benefits. This involves identifying the costs associated with a facility or event and deducting their economic value from the positive economic impacts shown by an analysis. Clearly, if costs exceed the benefits then, even if there is a relatively high gross economic impact, the sports event or facility may not be a good investment for the community.

Incorporating costs into a study changes it from an economic impact analysis to a benefit-cost analysis. An economic impact analysis is designed to study the economic effect of additional spending attributable to a sports facility or event. It can usefully be compared with equivalent investments designed to create economic stimulus in other sectors of the economy to give decision makers guidance on prioritizing their investments. In contrast, benefit-cost analysis is designed to identify the return on investments made in sports events or facilities. A good example of a benefit-cost analysis was commissioned by the City of Indianapolis and is summarized in Figure 4-6.

The calculation of a rate of return based on a comparison of costs and benefits enables a city to assess the merit of its investment in sports vis-à-vis the likely return from investment of similar public resources in other sectors of its economy. In the authors' view, decision makers should be using benefit-cost analysis when evaluating alternative investments, despite the difficulties associated with deriving accurate costs. In addition to the monetary costs described in Figure 4-6, consideration should be given to three other types of costs: (a) impact costs, (b) displacements costs, and (c) opportunity costs.

Impact Costs

Impact costs may be both on-site and off-site. On-site costs include the costs of additional equipment or supplies, the cost of additional labor contracted by an agency to assist with an event, and the cost of the time invested in a project by the agency's existing employees. In Table 4-1, for example, the labor and equipment costs incurred by the city agency in hosting a softball tournament were tracked, recorded, and included in the analysis, so the economic impact net of on-site impact costs could be presented.

Figure 4-6 Compiling a Benefit-Cost Analysis

In the mid-1970s, leaders in Indianapolis searched for new ways to bring vitality to the city. One key strategy that emerged was to make Indianapolis a national center for amateur sports. In 1992 a benefit-cost analysis was commissioned to evaluate the effectiveness of this strategy between 1977 and 1991. The analysis excluded non-monetary costs and the opportunity costs of using sites for sports facilities, but it offers a reasonably good model of how to use benefit-cost analysis to identify return on monetary investments in sport.

The monetary "social costs" of creating the amateur sports industry were estimated at $124 million at the time they occurred. Most of this cost ($112 million) consisted of investments in sports facilities. Also

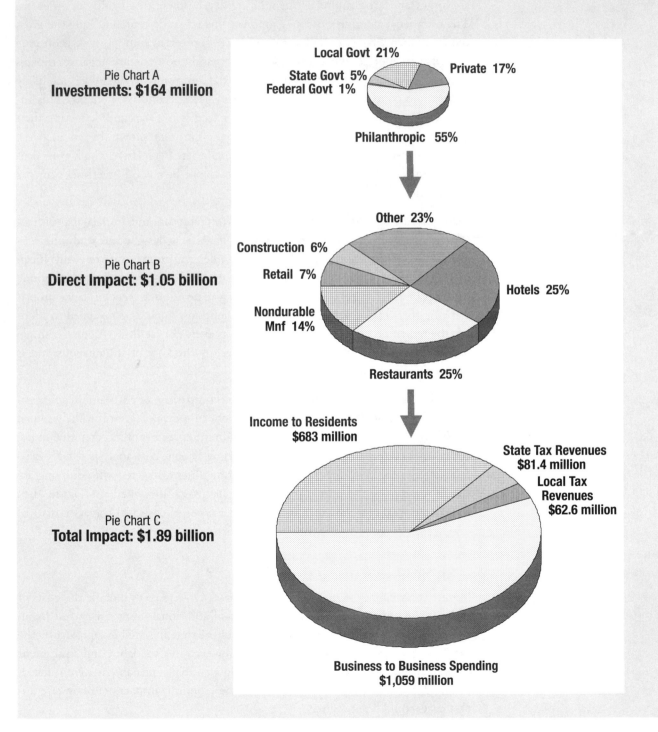

Pie Chart A
Investments: $164 million

Local Govt 21%
State Govt 5%
Federal Govt 1%
Private 17%
Philanthropic 55%

Pie Chart B
Direct Impact: $1.05 billion

Other 23%
Construction 6%
Retail 7%
Nondurable Mnf 14%
Hotels 25%
Restaurants 25%

Pie Chart C
Total Impact: $1.89 billion

Income to Residents $683 million
State Tax Revenues $81.4 million
Local Tax Revenues $62.6 million
Business to Business Spending $1,059 million

included were tax abatements, public safety services, and subsidies to organizations and facilities for operations. In 1991 dollars, the total investment amounted to $164 million. Pie chart A in figure A shows that over half of the investment came from philanthropic sources. These costs represent the amount of funds that would not have been invested in the local economy but for the amateur sports strategy.

Pie chart B shows the sectors of the Indianapolis economy that benefitted from the $1.05 billion attracted to the city by the amateur sports movement. This represents the aggregate spending by out-of-town visitors ($787 million) and expenditures by sports organizations and facilities from external sources ($213 million and $51 million, respectively). Since most of this money was in the form of visitor spending, it was not surprising that half of it went to hotels and restaurants.

Applying multipliers to the $1.05 billion direct economic impact yielded a total sales output impact of $1.89 billion. Pie chart C shows where these gross sales revenues eventually ended up. Over a third ($683 million) went as income to Indianapolis residents in the form of salaries and wages. A further breakdown of this $683 million revealed that while hotels and restaurants were the biggest winners in terms of direct economic impact, workers in other services industries actually ended up benefitting more (in total dollars) than those in the lodging or food services industries.

Table A summarizes the annual and total income and cost of investment flows. These investment and return figures can be converted into a rate of return once adjustments are made for the delays between the years in which the investment took place and the returns achieved. When adjustments for the timing are made, the rate of return on the investment is equivalent to an annual average rate of 64.1%, a figure that is substantially higher than that achieved in most business investments. In addition, this figure may be viewed as somewhat conservative because the amateur sports development strategy did not end in 1991. Returns from the investment will continue into the future.

Table A Annual Income on Investment Costs in Indianapolis
Generated by the Amateur Sports Strategy 1977-91 ($1991)

Year	Net Income	Investment
1977	960,000	1,000
1978	1,440,000	7,800,000
1979	3,770,000	2,088,000
1980	4,260,000	6,035,000
1981	3,380,000	14,793,000
1982	47,150,000	26,079,000
1983	46,050,000	25,131,000
1984	38,700,000	1,445,000
1985	34,410,000	3,119,000
1986	49,860,000	12,411,000
1987	147,340,000	42,966,000
1988	70,070,000	15,101,000
1989	75,600,000	2,806,000
1990	75,740,000	2,188,000
1991	85,180,000	2,052,000
Total	$683,910,000	$164,015,000

In addition to showing the return to residents, Figure B shows returns to the city and the state. The researchers found that the city's $35.1 million investment (in $ 1991) was more than recovered with a return of $62.6 million over the 15 years in the form of property and sales taxes. When cash flowed, these investments and returns represented a 23% average annual rate of return.

The state of Indiana fared even better, having collected $81.4 million in sales and income taxes attributable to the amateur sports industry between 1977 and 1991. The state's return on its $8.1 million investment averaged 65% per year.

Source: Schaffer, A., Jaffee, B.L., & Davidson (1993). *Beyond the games. The economic impact of amateur sports in Indianapolis, 1977-91.* Indianapolis, Chamber of Commerce.

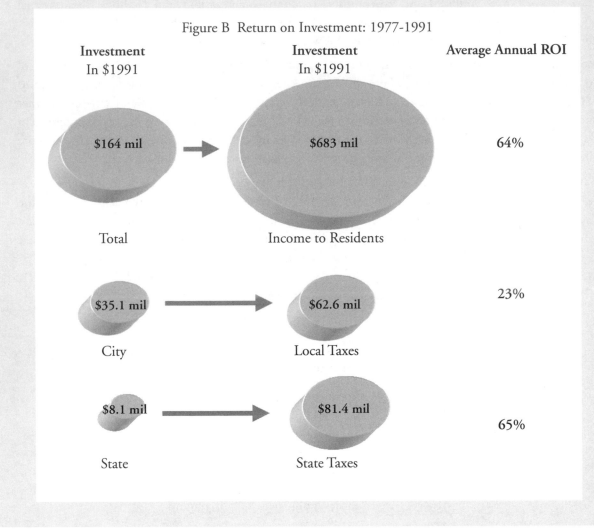

Figure B Return on Investment: 1977-1991

When large numbers of visitors are attracted to a sports event, they are likely to create extra demands on a community's services and inflict social costs on local residents. Off-site impact costs borne by the community as a result of an event may include such elements as traffic congestion, road accidents, vandalism, police and fire protection, environmental degradation, garbage collection, increased prices to local residents in retail and restaurant establishments, increased costs to other businesses seeking these new workers if there is a shortage of labor supply, loss of access, and disruption of resident's lifestyles. Translating some of these impacts into economic value is relatively easy (for example, costs of extra police or fire protection and off-site clean-up costs), but in other cases it is difficult, which is one reason why these costs are usually ignored. If some of these costs cannot be translated into economic values, they should at least be described, qualitatively assessed, and included in a presentation to a legislative body, so they are considered in an evaluation of an event's net benefits. An alternative approach is to monitor the level of residents' tolerance to these off-site costs during the event, and questionnaire instruments for this purpose have been developed.[32]

Displacement Costs

There is some likelihood that visitors from outside a community who are attracted by a major sports event may displace other visitors who otherwise would have come to the community but do not, either because they cannot obtain accommodations or because they are not prepared to mingle with crowds attracted by the event.

Data for economic impact studies are collected by surveying visitors who are in the area for the event. Thus, each of them is regarded as a source of new economic impact. However, if each of these visitors merely replaces another potential visitor who stayed away from the community because of the congestion associated with the sports event, then there is no new economic impact:

> What the survey technique cannot identify and sample are those not in the area that, but for the event, would have been. If the foxes held their convention in the hen house, this survey technique would attribute positive impacts to the foxes and never notice that all the hens were gone.[33]

NFL-sponsored studies of the economic impact of the Super Bowl on host communities typically generate large numbers. For example, the impact on Miami of the 1999 Super Bowl was reported to be $396 million, whereas in 2000 at Atlanta, the official number was a $292 million impact on the state of Georgia.[34] However, a study that compared January spending in six Super Bowl host cities to spending in that month in those cities during a series of non-Super Bowl years before and after the event found no increase. The study's author concluded, "The net economic impact of a Super Bowl is virtually zero."[34]

Multiple reasons were suggested to explain these results, most of which have been discussed previously in this chapter. However, a primary reason was the displacement effect. The six Super Bowls that were studied were held in the cities of Tampa, Miami, and Phoenix. Hotel rooms in January in these three Sun Belt cities are close to being fully booked.[33] Although the room is paid for, when the guest leaves early, it is empty. Consequently, there is no ancillary spending impact on restaurants, shopping, etc. In contrast, if the Super Bowl were not there, then the room would be filled with a guest spending at these other entities.

The displacement-cost principle was illustrated by events at the Atlanta Olympic Games:

> To the surprise of all, the masses never came. Further, those that came did not spend the money expected of them. The tour buses sat empty and the area's attractions remained relatively unseen. The Olympic consumer proved a very different marketing customer from the ordinary tourist or business traveler: an unpredictable hybrid—sports-mad, tight-fisted and uninterested in traditional tourist attractions. It has been estimated that on average, spectators at the Atlanta Games spent just $US15 a day after

accommodation and transport. Normal business travelers, by comparison, would spend $US350 a day and ordinary tourists about $US100 a day on a similar basis.[35]

Olympic guests had no interest in eating out, visiting attractions, or retail shopping because they spent so much time getting to venues and sitting through events that by the end of the day they wanted to relax in front of the television. Consequently, they spent much less than the regular visitor to Atlanta whom they displaced.

Another form of displacement should be mentioned. This occurs when an old facility is replaced by a new facility. In the Fully Loaded Era of the past decade, economic impact studies undertaken on the new facilities typically attributed all economic gains to the new facility. However, most of these were already accruing to the community from the old facility. Only the *incremental gains* uniquely attributable to the new facility constitute new economic income to the community. The other element of economic gains is merely displaced impact from the original facility.

Opportunity Costs

The general concept of opportunity costs was discussed in chapter 3. In the context of economic impact studies, it needs to be emphasized that a positive net economic impact does not mean that a sports event or facility necessarily should be supported, because the opportunity cost associated with this investment may be unacceptably high. Consider the following situation:

> Politicians in Denver did not exactly drop their jaws in shock when a Brown, Bortz and Coddington study projected a $16.5 million annual impact were the city to get a Major League Baseball team. It was more like a yawn. "It's nice, but I can't say we were all that impressed," said a mayoral assistant. "We just finished approving a convention center that's going to generate $200 million."[35]

The difference in economic impacts of these two types of facilities is attributable to who uses them. Sports teams primarily entertain local residents, whereas convention centers attract nonresidents to the community. Ironically, it is the sports team that is likely to be more popular politically because its contribution to the host community's quality of life is likely to be more obvious to most residents. In the above example, the city was able to invest in both enterprises. If resources had been available for only one of them and community politicians had selected the baseball option, the economic impact analysis would have been positive so the city would probably have supported the baseball opportunity. From an economic perspective, however, this would have been an unwise investment of public dollars that would have occurred only because the opportunity cost of not being able to invest in the convention center was not considered.

It is unfortunate that invariably it is only total economic benefits and costs that are measured, and their distribution is not considered. It was noted in chapter 3 that the economic rewards of sports projects tend to accrue to a small group of wealthy individuals. If these public funds were invested in health, education, or productive industry, it is likely that the result would be a wider distribution of benefits. One critic observes

> Most sports revenue goes to a relatively few players, managers, coaches, and executives who earn extremely high salaries—all well above the earnings of people who work in the industries that are substitutes for sports. Most stadium employees work part-time at very low wages and earn a small fraction of team revenues. Thus, substituting spending on sports for other recreational spending concentrates income, reduces the total number of jobs, and replaces full-time jobs with low-wage, part-time jobs.[2]

Thus, for example, if a baseball player's salary of $6 million were spread among 200 people earning $30,000, local dry cleaners, restaurants, and other businesses would do better and hire more workers.

Figure 4-1 showed that money used to create sports facilities and events has been contributed by community residents in the form of taxes. This represents an opportunity cost because residents are likely to have spent those funds in the community if the government had not taken them. In essence, the government may be perceived as spending it for them, so the net gain to the community is zero. Indeed, it may be argued that when residents are taxed to build a new facility, the negative multiplier effect of taxing residents is likely to offset any positive multiplier:

> Everybody who pays a dollar in taxes to support the facility must reduce his or her spending. The diminished spending goes round and round, just like the positive multiplier effect. The studies supporting stadium plans never mention that counter effect assuming that the cost of capital is free.[36]

The taxing process merely substitutes public expenditures for private expenditures, and the resources allocated to a sports event are denied to other sectors of the economy. This point has been articulated in the following terms:

> While governments may like to believe that their contributions are "productive," unless total receipts from outside the region are increased by the government financing contribution, all that is happening is that public funding is being substituted for private funding and there is no net economic benefit to the State—just a public cost.[4]

Expenditures by local governments are costs because they are financed by residents within the host community who therefore have to forego something else, and there is no extra generation of income. Thus, an expenditure on a sports facility by a local government cannot be considered an injection of new funds. If resources are injected into an economy from nonlocal governments, they can be considered as new money only if they would not have come to the community without the project. Thus, federal funds such as Community Development Block Grants, which are awarded to communities on a formula basis and have been used in some communities to partially fund sports stadiums, should not be included in economic impact analyses because they could legitimately have been allocated to a variety of alternative community projects.

Because stadiums are often constructed on valuable urban land, the opportunity cost of that land is sometimes substantial:

> The downtown stadium will use land that would be owned by the city and that has potentially valuable alternative uses. The true economic cost of the stadium should include foregone property taxes that would have been paid if the land had been sold or leased for private development, and it also should include foregone rents that could be earned from such alternative uses.[37]

Thus, in the context of constructing arenas or stadiums, the opportunity cost of donating public land or leasing it at a nominal rate for a project should be included in an analysis, but invariably this is not considered. If public land is given away in this manner, then the opportunity cost includes both the capital value of the land that the city forgoes *and* the economic benefits that would accrue if other types of economic activities were conducted on that site.

The emphasis placed on multipliers in economic impact analyses dealing with sports events or facilities may lead the unwary to suppose that there was some unique property conferred on income and employment generation resulting from such events or facilities that was not shared by other sectors of the economy. The inclusion of opportunity cost in an analysis recognizes that this is not the case: "It is the *comparative* size of the multiplier that is important, not simply the fact that a multiplier exists."[38] This commentator goes on to note that the empirical literature indicates visitor expenditure multipliers "at best probably reflect an average value added compared with other sectors. References to the multiplier as a significant advantage need to be seen in this context."[38]

Doing Economic Impact Analyses

This final section of the chapter describes the content of a questionnaire that the authors have used on numerous occasions to collect visitor expenditures, the basic data needed to undertake economic impact analyses. This is followed by a brief overview of IMPLAN (Impact Analysis for PLANning), which is the software package most commonly used in economic impact analyses. Finally, results from 20 analyses undertaken in a recent 12-month period by one of the authors are reviewed.

Collecting Expenditure Data

A prerequisite for accurate economic impact results is that the visitor expenditure data to which multipliers are applied is accurate. These expenditure data can be collected either by directly surveying visitors to the sports event who come from outside the community or by surveying the hoteliers, restaurateurs, retailers, etc., who receive the expenditures. The latter approach is least preferred because the data are likely to be less reliable. Businesses will experience difficulty in assessing what proportions of their customers' expenditures were from visitors and from locals and whether the sports event influenced visitors' decisions to come to the community.

The preferred approach is to survey visitors at the sports event. *Visitors* refers not only to spectators but also to participants, officials, media, sponsors, and vendors who come from outside the community. It is beyond the scope of this chapter to discuss sampling methods and the relative merits of alternative data-gathering procedures. Rather, discussion focuses on appropriate questions and question formats for collecting data.

A suggested questionnaire for collecting the information needed to calculate economic impact is shown in Figure 4-7. A major goal was that the questionnaire should be short. The shorter it is, the less time it takes respondents to complete, and the more likely it is that they will cooperate in the study. To achieve this goal, it was imperative that the questionnaire should contain only essential questions. The criterion used in developing it was "What will be done with the information from this question?" Questions that may have produced "interesting information" were not included unless that information was essential for calculating economic impact.

Question 1 was designed to differentiate between local and nonlocal respondents. Zip codes enable "the local area" to be configured in any way the study sponsor desires. Thus, *local catchment area* may be defined as selected areas of a city, by a city's boundaries, by a city and its suburbs, by a county, or whatever. Indeed, zip codes enable the economic impact of a sports event or facility on each of these different catchment areas to be calculated if the study's sponsors wish to do this, because it is easy for the computer to aggregate zip codes into any desired configurations.

Obviously, if the sports event of interest was scheduled for only one day, then Question 2 would be omitted. Responses to this question enable both per day-per person and per day-per visitor group economic impact data to be calculated. This permits communities to compare the economic impacts of events that have different time frames to ascertain which types of events offer best return to a community for the resources it invests. The per-day data also enable the results from events that are surveyed to be extrapolated easily to other similar events that may be of different duration and at which no surveying is undertaken.

Question 3 is designed to direct respondents' thinking towards the immediate group that is the unit of analysis used in the next question, which collects the financial information. The question also permits per-person and per-visitor group expenditures to be calculated that facilitate comparisons across an agency's events and extrapolation to nonsurveyed events.

Knowledge of the group size is essential in studies where the focus is on the economic impact generated by spectators, because in these cases total expenditures are calculated by multiplying the sample responses up to the total attendance. This is illustrated in the following calculation:

Total number of sports event visitors
from out-of-town 15,000

Average expenditure per respondent's
immediate group $30

Average size of immediate group 3

Total expenditures by out-of-town . . . . $\frac{15,000}{3}$ = $500 x $30 = $150,000
visitors to the event are

This calculation could not be made without knowing the group size. Group size is not needed in studies involving team sports because the team rather than the individual is the unit of analysis.

Figure 4-7 shows alternatives to questions 1, 2, and 3 described above, if the focus of the study is on the economic impact of a local sports tournament where the only spectators are likely to be friends and relatives of the participants. In the case of local sports tournaments, data are collected by randomly selecting a limited

---

Figure 4-7 Economic Impact Questionnaire

1.　　What is the zip code at your home address? _____

2.　　Which of the following days will you be attending this sports event? (Please circle all that apply)
　　　Friday　　　Saturday　　　Sunday

3.　　How many people **(including yourself)** are in your immediate group? (This is the number of people for whom you typically pay the bills—e.g., your family or close friends.) _____ people

Alternative questions 1 and 2 to be used (question 3 is omitted) in the context of a sports tournament
1.　　What is the name of your team? _____
2.　　How many players are there on your team at this tournament? _____

3.　　To better understand the economic impact of the (Name of Sports Event), we are interested in finding out the approximate amount of money you and other visitors in your immediate group will spend, including travel to and from your home. We understand that this is a difficult question, but please do your best because your responses are very important to our efforts. **DURING THE COURSE OF YOUR VISIT, WHAT IS THE APPROXIMATE AMOUNT YOUR IMMEDIATE GROUP WILL SPEND IN EACH OF THE FOLLOWING CATEGORIES:**

	TYPE OF EXPENDITURE	Amount spent in the (name of city) area	Amount spent outside the (name of city) area
A.	Admission / Entry Fees	_____	_____
B.	Food & Beverages (restaurants, concessions, etc.)	_____	_____
C.	Night Clubs, Lounges & Bars (cover charges, drinks, etc.)	_____	_____
D.	Retail Shopping (clothing, souvenirs, gifts, etc.)	_____	_____
E.	Lodging Expenses (hotel, motel, etc.)	_____	_____
F.	Private Auto Expenses (gas, oil, repairs, parking fees, etc.)	_____	_____
G	Rental Car Expenses	_____	_____
H.	Any Other Expenses Please identify: _____	_____	_____

Questions 5 and 6 are not required for sports tournaments.

5.　　Would you have come to the (Name of City) area at this time even if this sports event had not been held?

　　　Yes_____　　　No_____

5a.　If "Yes," did you stay longer in the (Name of City) area than you would have done if this event had not been held?

　　　Yes_____　　　No_____

5b.　If "Yes" (in 5a), how much longer? _____Days

6.　　Would you have come to (Name of City) in the next three months if you had not come at this time for this event?

　　　Yes_____　　　No_____

number of teams in the tournament and then surveying all (or as many as possible) of the players on the selected teams' squads. This procedure requires that both a participant's team name and the number of players on that team's squad be requested on the questionnaire. At the same time, players' or teams' zip codes are not required, because tournament organizers can provide information on which teams are local and which are from out of town. The days of a sports tournament are fixed, so question 2 is redundant. Similarly, because total participation is measured by teams and not individuals and the aggregate number of teams in a tournament is known by the organizers, question 3 is not needed. However, if question 3 is omitted, then the definition of immediate group, which is shown in parentheses in question 3, will need to be included in question 4. Thus, in the context of a sports tournament, questions 1, 2, and 3 described in previous paragraphs are replaced by the two alternative questions.

It would be inaccurate to capture only the expenditures of individual respondents because they may be paying for other people or, alternatively, others may be paying for them. The only way to avoid these error sources is to capture the expenditures of all members of the immediate group. Thus, the immediate group is emphasized in question 4.

It was noted earlier in the chapter that each category of expenditure has a different multiplier coefficient, so expenditures have to be identified by category. Experience has shown that nearly all out-of-town visitor expenditures associated with sports events fall into the first seven categories shown in question 4. If there is no admission charge or entry fee, then category A should be omitted. If expenditures are assigned to category H, it is important to specify what they were for, so they are assigned to the correct industrial sector in the multiplier model.

Question 4 requires respondents to give their expenditures both within the area of interest and outside that area. Economic impact studies are concerned only with the amount of money spent in the area of interest, so the information reported in the second column pertaining to expenditures outside the area is discarded. Even though it is not used, this information is requested because it causes respondents to think carefully about where they spent their money. If it were omitted, there would be a greater probability of respondents not reading the question carefully and incorrectly attributing all their trip expenditures to the host area.

Ideally, the headings on column one in question 4 would be defined by zip code (viz., "Amount spent in the following zip codes:_____"). This would ensure that the reported expenditures coincided with the selected configuration of the affected area, which is defined by zip codes. Unfortunately, most people, residents as well as visitors, are unlikely to know the boundaries of zip code areas, so a surrogate descriptor that respondents will recognize (usually the city or neighborhood name) has to be selected.

The expenditures reported in question 4 can only be approximations because (a) if respondents complete the questionnaire before they leave the event and the affected area, they have to estimate the additional expenditures they are likely to incur and (b) if they complete the questionnaire after the event and mail it back, then their recall memory may be faulty. This reinforces the realization that economic impact studies can only be "guesstimates."

Questions 5 and 6 are designed to identify time-switchers and casuals. These questions are not likely to be relevant in the context of sports tournaments because spontaneous, casual participation in such events is not possible, and experience has shown that the proportion of players who planned to come to the community at another time is negligible. Thus, the questionnaire used in the economic impact studies of sports tournaments consists only of three questions (alternate questions 1 and 2 and question 4), and the latter two are omitted (Figure 4-6).

Those who answer "yes" to question 5 are classified as casuals and are omitted from the study, unless they also answer "yes" to question 5a. These individuals were already in the community, but were attracted there by other factors. Their economic impact cannot be attributed to the event because it was not responsible for bringing them to the community, and if they had not elected to attend, then it is likely they would have spent their money somewhere else in the community. However, if the event causes them to stay in the jurisdiction for more days than they would have done if the event had not been held, then their incremental expenditures on those extra days should be included in the economic impact analysis. This information is captured in questions 5a and 5b.

Question 6 is designed to identify time-switchers. Those who respond "yes" changed the timing of an intended visit to the community to coincide with the event. They will be omitted from the analysis because their spending in the community cannot be attributed to the event because it would have occurred without the event, albeit at a different time of year.

The discussion in this section has referred only to the economic impact of participants or visitors of sports events. However, additional economic impact may be forthcoming from other groups such as professional athletes, vendors, media personnel, and coaches. If these groups are involved and their economic contributions are to be estimated, then each of them needs to be sampled because it is likely that different groups will report different expenditure amounts and patterns. This would require an additional item that would appear at the beginning of the questionnaire:

Which of the following are you?

**Spectator   Coach   Athlete   Media person   Sponsor   Vendor
Other_____**

Analyzing the Data

A decade ago, it was not feasible for sports managers to calculate with reasonable accuracy the multiplier effect of visitor expenditures in a community. To do this, trained economists had to be hired to construct an input-output model that could examine relationships within the local economy both between businesses and between businesses and final consumers. This required the collection of large amounts of data from local industries and was a complex, laborious, and expensive process. Thus, the only recourse to organizations wanting to incorporate an indicator of the multiplier effect was to use an arbitrary coefficient that purported to be "conventional wisdom." Such "guesstimates" had no empirical basis and often were unreasonably high because they were promulgated by advocates of the facility or event.

In recent years, this situation has changed with the widespread availability of IM-PLAN, which was developed as a cost-effective means of producing local input-output models.[39] Instead of building input-output models with primary data collected directly from local industries, IMPLAN is an input-output modeling system that builds its accounts with secondary data collected from a multitude of federal government agencies that were originally collected for other purposes.

There are two components to the IMPLAN system, the software and the databases. The software performs the calculations and is available for personal computers using a Windows format. The databases are updated annually and provide all the information needed to create the IMPLAN input-output models. They provide information from 528 different industrial sectors, closely following the accounting conventions used by the U.S. Bureau of Economic Analysis. The databases incorporate comprehensive data for the entire United States. They are available in standard form at the county, state, or U.S. level and can also be customized and made available at the zipcode level. Thus, an input-output model can be defined for a section of a city, a single city, a single county, several counties, a state, a group of states, or the entire United States.

Results of 20 Economic Impact Studies

Tables 4-8 and 4-9 summarize the results of 20 economic impact studies of sports tournaments and events that were undertaken by one of the authors in a 12-month period in seven U.S. communities: Boise, Idaho; College Station, Texas; Des Moines, Iowa; Everett, Washington; Grand Rapids, Michigan; Lansing, Michigan; and Scottsdale, Arizona. These communities were reasonably diverse in size and geographical location.

To avoid the possibility of embarrassment to any of the cooperating cities, their identities have been protected and have been replaced by letter symbols that are shown in the left-hand column. Columns 2 and 3 list the names of the events and their duration in days, respectively.

Sampling participants in team sports can be done by surveying either every nth team or every nth individual. In most cases, it is more convenient to sample teams because team members are often grouped together while waiting to play, practicing, or appearing at social gatherings. Column 4 in Table 4-7 shows that this was done in 11 of the 14 studies. In the remaining 3 studies, individuals were interviewed without reference to the teams they represented.

Column 5 reports the average size of the team squads. This information was obtained either from the questionnaire or from event organizers in those cases where teams were required to provide them with tournament rosters. Column 6 was derived by multiplying the data in columns 4 and 5.

Economic impact refers only to the expenditures of visitors who resided outside the community. Columns 7 and 8 list the number and percentage of teams from within the city (or individuals in the three cases where teams were not surveyed). They were excluded from the analysis. The number and percentage of teams or individuals from outside the city are reported in columns 9 and 10.

The total expenditure shown in column 11 is derived by extrapolating the expen-

Table 4-8 The Economic Impact of 14 Sports Tournaments

City	Event Name	Duration (# of Days)	# of Teams (# of Participants)	Average Size of Team Squad	# of Individual Participants	Teams from inside the city #	%	Teams from outside the city #	%	Total Expenditure	Per Team	Per Team Per Day	Per Team Member Group	Per Team Member Group Per Day	Sales	Personal Income	Jobs[a]
A	ASA Men's 40-Over Fastpitch National Championship	5	37	14	518	0	0.0	37	100.0	287,425	7,768	1,554	555	111	524,645	164,352	12.8
A	USS Swim Meet	3	24	45	1,079	2	8.3	22	91.7	124,999	5,682	1,894	126	42	236,852	64,201	5.3
A	Boys Soccer Tournament	3	68	15	1,020	5	7.4	63	92.6	128,519	2,040	680	136	45	247,085	69,493	5.7
A	Girls Soccer Tournament	3	70	15	1,050	0	0.0	70	100.0	160,956	2,299	766	153	51	305,070	85,889	6.8
A	Girls Fastpitch Invitational Tournament	3	69	12	828	15	21.7	54	78.3	184,517	3,417	1,139	285	95	351,588	99,811	8.0
B	Hoopin' Downtown Basketball Tournament	1	(584)	N/A	584	N/A	77.8	N/A	22.2	9,589	N/A	N/A	16	16	21,238	7,111	0.4
B	Great Plains Soccer Shoot Out Tournament	2	(1,800)	N/A	1,800	N/A	21.0	N/A	79.0	211,502	N/A	N/A	117	59	483,607	161,692	10.1
C	Magic Classic Softball Tournament	1	(900)	N/A	900	N/A	17.6	N/A	82.4	49,046	N/A	N/A	54	54	92,740	30,254	2.1
A	Whataburger Basketball Shoot Out	4	104	11	1,144	2	1.9	102	98.1	608,458	5,965	1,491	542	136	1,157,000	349,710	26.9
D	Girls U-14 Regional Softball Tournament	3	16	13	208	0	0.0	16	100.0	118,636	7,414	2,472	570	190	290,060	85,955	6.1
E	Invitational Youth Soccer Tournament	4	146	15	2,190	20	13.7	126	86.3	441,424	3,503	876	234	58	825,534	287,878	16.7
A	ASA Men's Fastpitch Softball Championship	3	28	14	392	1	3.6	27	96.4	93,219	3,453	1,151	247	82	176,903	50,904	4.0
A	ASA Men's B Fastpitch National Championship	5	60	14	840	2	3.3	58	96.7	386,999	6,672	1,334	477	95	730,973	211,870	16.7
E	Softball Tournaments	3 / 2 / 3	70 / 55 / 24	12	1,788	4 / 5 / 6	5.7 / 9.1 / 25.0	66 / 50 / 18	94.3 / 90.9 / 75.0	406,390	3,033	1,153	253	96	579,053	209,751	12.3

a. This figure refers to both full-time and part-time jobs. It assumes the local economy is operating at full capacity and that there is no slack to absorb additional demand created by these events.

ditures reported by the sample of external visitors to the total number of external visitors to the tournament. One of the dangers inherent in this procedure, especially if the sample is relatively small, is that a few extraordinary "outlier" responses in the sample can result in a large magnitude of error in the extrapolated results. Outliers are the very small number of respondents who report extraordinarily high (or low) expenditures, which would skew the study results because they are atypical. To rectify this potential error source, the data collected from the 5% of respondents reporting the highest expenditures and the 5% reporting the lowest expenditures were routinely discarded.

Columns 12 through 15 break down the total expenditure to a per-team average (divide column 11 by column 9), per team per day (divide column 12 by column 3), per team member (divide column 11 by column 6), and per team member per day (divide column 14 by column 3). The purpose of these breakdowns is to establish common denominators across tournaments of different duration, with different numbers of teams and different size squads. Standardizing the data in these ways facilitates the search for patterns and parameters in the data.

It was noted earlier in the chapter that there are multiple measures of economic impact. The three most commonly cited are reported in columns 16 through 18. The measures were derived by entering the total expenditure data reported in column 11 into the IMPLAN model by the seven categories shown on the questionnaire in Figure 4-6.

The data in Table 4-8 suggest the following:

1. The obvious and expected relationship that the larger the number of participants from *outside the community*, the greater the economic impact is likely to be.

2. If an overnight stay is not required, then the economic impact on the community is likely to be small. This exemplifies the retailing principle that the longer people remain in an area, the more they are likely to spend. Increasing visitors' average length of stay is the most efficient way to increase the economic impact of an event on the community. The highest total expenditures in column 11 correlate strongly with longer tournaments, which presumably required more overnight stays in the community. The two tournaments with the smallest economic impact were both one-day events. Such sports events appear unlikely to be sufficiently extensive or prestigious to attract visitors from far away and, hence, rely primarily on a relatively local clientele. For example, two thirds of city B's Hoopin' Downtown Basketball Tournament participants resided within the city, so the event's economic impact was minimal.

3. Per team member group-per day expenditures across the four boys' and girls' soccer tournaments were relatively consistent at $45, $51, $58, and $59, suggesting that an expectation of approximately $55 per day is likely to be a reasonable basis for estimating expenditures at youth soccer tournaments.

4. Per team member group-per day expenditures at the seven softball tournaments were $54, $82, $95, $95, $96, $111, and $190. The first and last

numbers were extraordinary and unlikely to be typical. The first number related to a tournament that lasted for only one day, so many participants were not required to stay overnight. The last number was caused by some of the teams traveling over 1,000 miles, and although the tournament was the trip's main purpose, the city's appealing location caused many to view the trip as a family vacation embracing other attractions in the area. This was reflected in the expenditures. The evidence of the other five studies suggests that an expenditure of approximately $100 per day is likely to be a reasonable basis for estimating expenditures at softball tournaments.

The format of the analysis shown in Table 4-9 is similar to that described in Table 4-8 with two exceptions. First, the columns relating to teams in Table 4-8 are not relevant to the analyses in Table 4-9 where the unit of analysis is individuals. Second, columns 8 and 9 relating to time-switchers and casuals did not appear in Table 4-8 because they were likely to be irrelevant in the context of sports tournaments.

The total expenditures shown in column 12 are derived from two sources: first, visitors who were attracted to the community by the event; second, the incremental amount spent by casuals and time-switchers, which could be attributed to an extension of their stay in the community because of the event.

The data in Table 4-9 suggest the following:

1. Large numbers of participants and spectators do not necessarily equate to a large economic impact. For example, the minor league baseball games in city C and the golf tournament in city D attracted 16,895 and 1,259 visitors, respectively. However, the economic impact of the golf tournament was substantially greater than that accruing from the baseball games (columns 12 and 15). This is explained by the baseball games' lasting only 1 day and only 28% of the spectators who visited city C coming for the specific purpose of watching the games. Further, it seems likely that many out-of-town visitors commuted to these games from proximate communities, so their spending on accommodations and food in the host community was likely to be small.

2. The importance of ascertaining the proportion of visitors who are time-switchers and casuals is demonstrated by the baseball games and the open golf tournament where time-switchers and casuals accounted for 32% and 16% of all visitors, respectively. If the questionnaire had asked only for their home address or zip code and, therefore, failed to differentiate them from out-of-town visitors who were attracted specifically by the event, then there would have been a substantial overestimation of the economic impact attributed to these events.

3. The extraordinary economic impact generated by a sporting mega-event is demonstrated by the first event listed in Table 4-9. This golf tournament was a stop on the men's professional tour. The very high total expenditure (column 12) not only reflects people staying multiple nights in the community and a large proportion of visitors from out-of-town, but also the relative affluence of the visitors. The almost $30 million estimate in Table 4-9 is limited to the expenditures of spectators and does not

Table 4-9 The Economic Impact of 6 Sports Events

City	Event Name	Duration (# of Days)	Mean Length of Stay of Out-of-town Visitors	# of Visitor Days	Participants/ Spectators from inside the city #	%	Casuals/Time Switchers #	%	Participants/[b] Spectators from outside the city #	%	Total[c] Expenditure	Average per Visitor per Day Expenditure	Economic Impact Sales	Personal Income	Jobs[d]
G	Open Golf Tournament	3	2.4	464,000	140,167	30.2	72,500	15.6	251,333	54.2	29,523,070	117	65,856,795	22,389,187	1,232.0
C	Two Minor League Baseball Games	1 day each	1.0	16,895	6,735	39.9	5,438	32.2	4,722	27.9	25,225	5	54,184	17,818	1.3
E	Triathlon Dash	1	1.1	482[a]	94	19.5	38	7.9	350	72.6	14,841	42	25,693	11,416	0.5
F	Motor Race	3	1.6	85,000	72,425	85.2	4,899	5.8	7,676	9.0	172,764	23	382,446	129,902	7.8
D	Women's Fitness Challenge	1	1.3	105,415[a]	83,795	79.5	0	0.0	21,620	20.5	559,246	26	892,808	429,238	23.9
D	American Junior Golf Association Tournament	4	5.4	1,259[a]	0	0.0	0	0.0	1,259	100.0	74,868	59	188,414	56,690	4.0

a. The attendance data provided by the agencies for these events were in number of participants, and for purposes of consistency these were transformed in this table to number of visitor days, which includes members of participants' immediate groups.

b. This figure consists of the number of out-of-town visitors whose primary purpose of visit was to attend the event (Out-of-Towners), and the number of out-of-town visitors whose primary reason for their visit was not to attend the event but extended their stay because of it (Extended Stayers).

c. This figure consists of the expenditures by out-of-town visitors and extended stayers.

d. This figure refers to both full-time and part-time jobs. It assumes the local economy is operating at full capacity and that there is no slack to absorb additional demand created by these events.

include those by the players, officials, and their entourages; the extensive number of media representatives; the hospitality expenditures of major companies; or sponsorships. Nevertheless, the $30 million expenditure dwarfs the aggregated economic impact generated by the other 19 sports tournaments and events shown in Tables 4-8 and 4-9.

4. Economic impact will be increased if visitors are encouraged and given good reasons by host communities to stay longer beyond the time frame of the event. For example, the 1997 Super Bowl host committee in Phoenix planned 106 events surrounding the actual game. Suggestions for extending a visitor's stay in the Super Bowl community include the following:[10]

> Schedule a significant attraction for the Monday or Tuesday following the Super Bowl (e.g., a headline name could perform in the host city the week following the game or another major sport match-up could be promoted).

> Encourage hotels and airlines to promote and offer 5- and 6-day extended packages.

> Schedule a parade for the winning team in the host city on the Monday after the game.

> Encourage the NFL to keep the NFL Experience open through Monday.

> Encourage corporate sponsors and other entities to schedule conventions or sales meetings in the host city after the Super Bowl.

> Attempt to persuade the NFL to schedule the game on the Sunday before the Martin Luther King Holiday (2 weeks earlier). If this could be accomplished, visitors would not be in such a hurry to leave the city as most would have the next day off.

Summary

The primary argument for the substantial public subsidies that are invested in many sports facilities and events invariably focuses on the economic benefits that are purported to emanate from them. Economic impact studies provide a broad framework that enables an estimate to be made of the amount of income that a community's residents receive as a result of the investment of those residents' tax dollars in sports facilities or events.

Economic impact is defined as the net economic change in a host community that results from spending attributed to a sports event or facility. It has been suggested that, "The key stage in public campaigns of stadiums is the release of official studies that estimate how many millions of dollars a sports team 'contributes' to the city's economy."[40] Economic impact studies are not value-free tools, because their results are dependent upon the assumptions that guide the analysis, assumptions that invariably agree with those of the study sponsor. Most economic impact studies are commissioned by sponsors who seek numbers that will support their advocacy position. Unfortunately, this often leads those undertaking the studies to adopt procedures and underlying assumptions that substantially bias the results in a direction desired by the sponsors. Indeed, most of these reports should be viewed as political documents designed to support an advocacy position rather than as legitimate studies of economic impact.

There are five principles whose inviolability is central to the integrity of economic impact analysis. First, expenditures related to a sports event by those residing within the defined impact area should not be included in the analysis because such expenditures represent only a recycling of money that already existed there.

Second, expenditures by time-switchers who were planning to visit the community for other reasons but schedule their visit to coincide with the event and casuals who attended the sports event but were in the community for other purposes and whose visit was not influenced by the event should be excluded from an economic impact analysis. Only the net increment of those expenditures attributable to increased length of stay because of the sports event should be included.

Three elements contribute to the total economic impact of out-of-town visitors. Direct impact is the first-round effect of visitor spending. Indirect impact is the ripple effect of additional rounds of recirculating the initial expenditures. Induced impact is the further ripple effect caused by employees of affected businesses spending some of their salaries and wages in other businesses in the city.

The three most commonly used multiplier coefficients are those for sales, income, and employment. Sales multipliers are not useful for assessing economic impact. The third inviolable principle is that household-income multipliers should be used for this purpose because the point of interest is the impact of the sales on household income and employment. Nevertheless, sales outputs tend to be used as *the* multiplier in economic analyses of sports events because they are substantially higher than income multipliers.

The geographic area within which economic impact is to be assessed will be specified by those commissioning the study. The larger the area's economic base, the smaller the leakage that is likely to occur and the larger the multiplier is likely to be. Only expenditures made by visitors within the boundaries of the defined area should be included in an analysis, not total spending because some of this is likely to have been expended in travel to or from the defined impact area.

The fourth inviolable principle is that multiplier coefficients ("normal," "unorthodox," or "true" multipliers) rather than "ratio" or "orthodox" multipliers should be used because the former give more useful guidance to policy makers. Despite there being a consensus on this issue among economists, ratio or orthodox multipliers are still frequently used to calculate the income that is returned to residents in sports events economic impact analysis because such multipliers generate much larger numbers.

The fifth principle requires that measures of employment output be carefully interpreted. These measures typically do not differentiate between full-time and part-time jobs, and in the context of sports events more are likely to be short-term, part-time positions. Further, these measures assume that all existing employees are fully occupied, so there is no spare capacity in the system and that all new jobs emerging will be filled by residents from within the community. Both of these assumptions are often challengeable.

The general consensus of impartial empirical studies is that professional franchises and the development of major sports facilities for them have no discernible positive impact on a city's economy. Indeed, there is evidence that in some cases they have a negative impact because of the opportunity costs incurred and the greater leakage out of the community frequently associated with professional sports franchises compared to other types of businesses. Reports commissioned by advocates indicating large positive economic impacts invariably arrive at their conclusions by breaking one or more of the five inviolable principles. Despite a growing awareness that the results from these reports are frequently bogus, they are likely to continue to be commissioned because they provide mischievous numbers for advocates to promulgate in promotion campaigns designed to convince residents to be supportive in referendums.

The numbers emerging from an economic impact study measure only gross economic benefits, and the costs and negative impacts on a community associated with a sports event are invariably not considered. Voters and decision makers need information on both sides of the equation to make informed decisions. In addition to the monetary costs incurred, considerations should be given to impact costs, displacements costs, and opportunity costs.

Impact costs may be on-site and off-site. On-site relates to the equipment, supplies, and labor costs incurred by the community at the event site. Off-site costs borne by a community may include traffic congestion, road accidents, vandalism, police and fire protection, environmental degradation, and so on.

Displacement costs occur when visitors to a sports event displace the revenues that would have accrued from other visitors who did not come to the community because of congestion and price increases created by the sports event. An alternative form of displacement is the replacement of an existing facility with a new amenity in the same community.

If a community subsidizes a sports event, facility, or franchise, then it cannot invest that money in another project. The return it could have received from the best alternative investment of the money is known as the opportunity cost. This should be incorporated in an economic analysis. The quality-of-life outcomes and the multiplier coefficient of these alternative investments may be as high or higher than that associated with the sports investment.

Data for calculating direct spending are generally collected by surveying visitors to the sports event who come from outside the community, including spectators, participants, officials, media, sponsors, and vendors. A short set of between three and six questions is sufficient to collect the needed information. The IMPLAN software is widely used for developing output measures of economic impact from the direct expenditures collected in the survey.

References

1. Smith, A. (1976). *An inquiry into the nature and cause of the wealth of nations* (Vol. 2, E. Cannan, Ed.). Chicago: University of Chicago Press. (Original published 1776)
2. Noll, R. G. (1997). Bread not circuses: Are new stadiums worth the cost. *The Brookings Review, 15*(3), 35-39.
3. Johnson, A. T. (1991). Local government, minor league baseball, and economic development strategies. *Economic Development Quarterly, 5*(4), 313-324.
4. Hunter, W. J. (1988). *Economic impact studies: Inaccurate, misleading, and unnecessary.* [Heartland Institute Policy Study #21]. Chicago: The Heartland Institute.
5. Hudson, I. (2001). The use and misuse of economic impact analysis. *Journal of Sport and Social Issues, 25*(1), 20-39.
6. Curtis, G. (1993, September) Waterlogged, *Texas Monthly,* 7.
7. Corliss, R. (1992, August 24). Build it and they ~~will~~ might come. *Time,* 139, 50-52.
8. Fimrite, R. (1992, June 1). Oh give me a home... *Sports Illustrated,* 76, 50-52.
9. Rosentraub, M. S. (1997). *Major league losers: The real cost of sports and who's paying for it.* New York: Basic Books.
10. Delpy, L., & Li, M. (1998). The art and science of conducting economic impact studies. *Journal of Vacation Marketing, 4*(3), 230-254.
11. Regan, T. H. (1991). *A study of the economic impact of the Denver Broncos football club on the Denver Colorado metropolitan economy.* Unpublished doctoral dissertation, University of Northern Colorado, Greeley, CO.
12. Rosentraub, M. S., & Swindell, D. (1991). "Just say no?" The economic and political realities of a small city's investment in minor league baseball. *Economic Development Quarterly, 5*(2), 152-167.
13. Schaffer, A. Jaffee, B. L., & Davidson, L. (1993). *Beyond the games: The economic impact of amateur sports in Indianapolis, 1977-91.* Indianapolis: Chamber of Commerce.
14. Barta, P. (1998, January 14). As arena vote nears, economists say much of the debate is irrelevant. *Wall Street Journal,* Section T, 4.
15. Burns, J. P. A., & Mules, T. J. (1989). An economic evaluation of the Adelaide Grand Prix. In G. J. Syme, B. J. Shaw, P. M. Fenton, & W. S. Mueller (Eds.), *The planning and evaluation of hallmark events* (pp. 172-185). Aldershot, England: Avebury.
16. Archer, B. H. (1984). Economic impact: Misleading multiplier. *Annals of Tourism Research, 11*(3), 517-518.
17. Morgan, J. (1997). *Glory for sale,* Baltimore: Bancroft Press.
18. Schaffer, W. A., & Davidson, L. S. (1984). *Economic impact of the Falcons on Atlanta.* Atlanta: Georgia Institute of Technology.
19. Lavelle, N. (1995, July 23) A new arena: Fair play? Go for the win. *Dallas Morning News,* J1, J10.
20. Lipsitz, G. (1984). Sports stadia and urban development: A tale of three cities. *Journal of Sport and Social Issues, 8*(2), 1-18.
21. Baade, R. A., & Dye, R. F. (1990, Spring). The impact of stadiums and professional sports on metropolitan area development. *Growth and Change,* 1-14.
22. Rosentraub, M. (1994). Sport and downtown development strategy. *Journal of Urban Affairs, 16*(3), 228-39.
23. Baade, R. (1996). Professional sports as catalysts for metropolitan economic development. *Journal of Urban Affairs, 18*(1), 1-17.
24. Noll, R. G., & Zimbalist, A. (1997). Build the stadium—create the jobs. In R. G. Noll & A. Zimbalist (Eds.), *Sports, jobs & taxes. The economic impact of sports teams and stadiums* (pp. 1-54). Washington DC: The Brookings Institute.
25. Walden, M. (1997, October/November). Don't play ball. *Carolina Journal,* 23.
26. Coates, D., & Humphreys, B. B. (1999). The growth effects of sport franchises, stadia and arenas. *Journal of Policy Analysis and Management, 18*(4), 601-624.
27. Nunn, S., & Rosentraub, M. S. (1997). Sports wars: Suburbs and outer cities in a zero-sum game. *Journal of Sport & Social Issues, 21*(1), 65-82.
28. Euchner, C. C. (1995, July 23) A new arena: Fair play? Take a walk. *Dallas Morning News,* J1, J10.
29. Emperor has no clothes. (1997, June 16). *Toronto Globe & Mail.*
30. Johnson, A. T. (1989). *Local government and minor league baseball: Survey of issues and trends* [Sports Consortium Special Report #1]. Washington, DC: International City Management Association.
31. Noll, R. G., & Zimbalist, A. (1997). The economic impact of sports teams and facilities. In R. G. Noll & A. Zimbalist (Eds.), *Sports, Jobs & Taxes: The economic impact of sports teams and stadiums* (pp. 55-91). Washington, DC: The Brookings Institution.

32. Ap, J., & Crompton, J. L. (1998). Development and testing of a tourism impact scale. *Journal of Travel Research, 37*(2), 120-130.

33. Porter, P. K. (1999). Mega-sports events as municipal investments: A critique of impact analysis. In J. Fizel, E. Gustafson, & L. Hadley (Eds.), *Sports economics: Current research* (pp. 61-73). Westport, CT: Prager.

34. Williams, P. (2001, January 15-21). Economic impact of Super Bowls tough, if not impossible, to gauge. *SportsBusiness Journal,* 21-22.

35. Ratnatunga, J., & Muthaly, S. K. (2000, September/October). Lessons from the Atlanta Olympics: Marketing and organizational considerations for Sydney 2000. *Sports Marketing & Sponsorship, 2*(3) 239-257.

36. Keating, R. J. (1999, April 5). Sports pork: The costly relationship between major league sports and government. *Policy Analysis #339.* Cato Institute.

37. Quirk, J. P. (1987, January 18). The Quirk study: A close look at the two proposals. *St. Louis Post-Dispatch,* Special Report 8.

38. Hughes, C. G. (1982, September). The employment and economic effects of tourism reappraised. *Tourism Management,* 2, 167-176.

39. Minnesota IMPLAN Group. (1997). *IMPLAN professional: Social accounting & impact analysis software.* Stillwater, MN: MIG inc.

40. Euchner, C. C. (1993). *Playing the field: Why sports teams move and cities fight to keep them.* Baltimore: The Johns Hopkins University Press.

Photo courtesy of University Oregon Athletic Department.

Chapter Five

Alternate Justifications for Public Subsidy

The discussion in chapter 4 suggested it is unlikely that the monetary returns from a major league sports facility will be adequate for taxpayers to recoup their investment in subsidizing it. However, increased public skepticism with the contention that substantial economic returns accrue from such investments does not necessarily mean subsidies should not be forthcoming. Rather, it means that proponents of public subsidies are required to demonstrate that there are alternate sources of spillover benefits that justify them. The question proponents have to answer is, "Can an annual subsidy of (say) $10 million for a facility be justified on grounds other than direct economic impact?" Four alternate sources of spillover benefits are most frequently proposed: increased community visibility, enhanced community image, stimulation of other development, and psychic income. Each of these alternate justifications is discussed in this chapter. The first three of these spillover benefits are perceived by proponents to be precursors to enhancing a community's tax base by attracting new businesses to the area, whereas psychic income recognizes that sports teams and events often engender community pride that is an element in a community's quality of life.

To simplify the exposition, the discussion focuses primarily on major league franchises. However, many of the principles apply to sports teams in other contexts. For example, many colleges benefit from the visibility, image enhancement, and psychic income that they derive from their athletic teams.

The focus on economic impact of facilities and events in chapter 4 offered a micro perspective of possible spillover benefits, but it ignored the macro perspective concerned with the broader impacts on urban development and community pride. It provided a text that lacked a context.[1] The shift in emphasis to these alternate justifications provides more context. Confining the discussion only to the direct economic issues is too narrow. There are likely to be many other investments a community could make that probably would bring a better economic return, but none would be likely to bring the publicity and community pride associated with sports.

However, after taxpayers and elected officials have considered these alternate justifications, there is still a cost-benefit calculus involved, because they still have to decide whether these benefits represent a satisfactory return on the public investment. Consider the case of Cleveland described in Figure 5-1.[2] Did Cleveland receive a satisfactory return on investment?

The question asked in Figure 5-1 also could be framed in a wider context and rephrased to ask, "Could all these benefits accrue without public subsidy?" If the protected cartel status of the major leagues was removed and an open market permitted, the response might well be affirmative. For example, the benefits of

---

Figure 5-1 Did Cleveland Receive an Adequate Return for Its Investment?

The public investment in Cleveland's downtown renovation included $218 million, $152 million, and $293 million to provide facilities for the MLB Indians, NBA Cavaliers, and NFL Browns, respectively. There was substantial additional public investment into Playhouse Square, the Great Lakes Science Museum ($55 million), and the Rock and Roll Hall of Fame and Museum ($92 million). Thus, total public investment exceeded $800 million. This investment stimulated private investment in 20 or so restaurants, several office buildings (including the $400 million Key Corp Tower Center and $95 million Bank One Center), four or five hotels, and a number of art galleries and small speciality shops.

The nexus between the sports facilities and subsequent private development appears to be tenuous. However, the facilities represented a clear commitment to the revitalization of downtown Cleveland, and this was a critical factor in the decision of major office and hotel developers to locate there. Within the city of Cleveland there has been debate as to whether the taxpayers received a good economic return on this very large public investment of funds. However, the debate has to be framed in a broader context than only economic returns. Cleveland is no longer known as "The Mistake by the Lake." It is no longer perceived as the city with a burning river, racial riots, a depressed and decaying downtown, and conflict between its political and economic leadership. Cleveland is seen as a "winner" with a downtown area that attracts residents, people from across the region, and tourists. Cleveland is now attracting more than five million people to its downtown areas for baseball, basketball, and football games, and other forms of entertainment. These five million people who attend events are coming to a downtown that just one decade ago was avoided.

What is the value of these improvements in image, in terms of community pride to Clevelanders and in attracting businesses to relocate? What is the value of creating vibrancy and excitement in the downtown area? What is the value of creating an atmosphere in which there is some degree of fraternization between racial groups, given the racial polarization that exists in Cleveland, as in many other cities? The image of a successful city creating an impression or an illusion of economic success and vitality certainly has value. Further there is a community-building benefit from sports stemming from a shared pride in the teams' performances. Are these benefits worth the $80 million annual public investment that is required to pay the debt charges on these amenities?

Source: Adapted from Rosentraub[2]

---

awareness, image, stimulation of other development, and psychic income discussed in this chapter can all be found at the soccer facilities of teams in the major European leagues in England, Italy, Germany, and Spain, and there is no government subsidy of those facilities.

Increased Community Visibility

A professional sports franchise guarantees a significant amount of media coverage for the city in which it is located. It keeps the community's name in front of a national audience. The importance of this exposure was recognized by an official in Washington, D.C., when the Redskins were considering a move from that city to Arlington, Virginia:

> Officials in Washington could only fear that getting Skinned meant the town would be rubbed off the map. "Brooklyn has never been the same since the Dodgers left," said the D. C. council chairman, whose own city lost two baseball clubs in the 1950s. "You don't even think about Brooklyn."[3]

If a city has a major league franchise, then each day across the nation when fans read their sports pages, that city's name will be there. A baseball owner noted to a reporter, "Tonight, on every single television and radio station in the USA, Seattle will be mentioned because of the Mariners' game, and tomorrow night and the next night and on and on. You'd pay millions in public-relations fees for that"[4] Further, sports teams usually generate favorable publicity, plugging troubled cities into "the good news network. . . 'We're OK,' say the sports pages."[4] The city will likely hold an all-star game once every 20 years or so and enjoy all of the national attention associated with it. Exposure will be further enhanced when the team makes the playoffs and especially when it appears in a championship final. In the case of these latter events, the exposure is accompanied by the luster of success.[2]

The desire to generate awareness for the community sometimes creates friction between public entities. Most commonly, cities may resent losing the awareness identity of "their" team to a regional or state entity. Thus, for example, after Denver invested substantial effort to acquire a MLB franchise, the team was named the Colorado Rockies instead of the Denver whatevers.[4] The loss of city identity to state or regional names has occurred in the case of approximately 20 major league teams.

On the other hand, there are cities that receive visibility from teams that play elsewhere and are subsidized by other communities. For example, the New York Giants and Jets play in East Rutherford, New Jersey, whereas Detroit benefits from being identified with the Pistons and Lions even though the teams play in Auburn Hills and Pontiac.[4]

The linkage between community exposure and team visibility is widely recognized. Proponents of public subsidies for sports facilities imply in their articulation of the relationship that it will aid recruitment of relocating businesses and, thus, lead to enhancement of a city's economic base. Thus, when Jacksonville was awarded an NFL franchise, a city leader commented, "T.V. sets in division rivals Cleveland, Pittsburgh, and Cincinnati will be showing Jacksonville's sunshine in the dead of winter, luring future tourists."[5] However, there is no empirical evidence that media visibility *per se* results in this desired sequence of events. Opponents would argue that such arguments are false premises. Nevertheless, they would probably have to accept that the media visibility has some value. Consider the following case:

> In the early spring of 1995, Michael Jordan "unretired" from professional basketball. The first game he appeared in after his "I'm Back" announcement was against the Indiana Pacers in Indianapolis. NBC seized the game for its Game of the Week and broadcast the return of his "Airness" to numerous countries. During various breaks in the action NBC displayed aerial and ground-level shots of Indianapolis's skyline, civic fountains and monuments, and downtown parks. On a glorious spring afternoon, Indianapolis received worldwide attention and publicity. That night each of the network news programs highlighted Michael Jordan's return, as did the following morning's breakfast news shows. In each of these newscasts Indianapolis was mentioned and was sometimes even highlighted. Did anyone move to Indianapolis because of that coverage? No, but what would Indianapolis have had to pay to get that kind of attention to help identify and market itself? Indianapolis received that attention because it is part of the cultural icon known as sports as a result of the presence of the Indiana Pacers basketball team.[2]

Some indication of the magnitude of exposure that occurs is given by the statistics cited in Figure 5-2 relating to media coverage of the Atlantic Falcons.[6] Efforts are sometimes made to attribute an economic value to this exposure. For example, a study undertaken by Chicago's Department of Economic Development reported that advertising executives claimed when the Chicago Bears football team won a Super Bowl, it produced publicity for Chicago equivalent to a $30- to $40- million promotion campaign.[7] The study does not describe the procedures used to derive this value, but a widely used method of obtaining a crude dollar-value measure of media exposure is to use prevailing advertising rates in the media in which it appears. Companies frequently use this approach to measure economic value of their sponsorship. The procedures involved and the merits and limitations of this approach are discussed later in this book in chapter 15 in the context of sponsorship.

The effectiveness of a sports event in raising awareness of a city was measured when the Winter Olympics were held in Calgary.[8] Samples were taken from a number of locations in both Europe and the United States, and changes were traced in respondents' awareness of Calgary during a 3-year period. The changes were dramatic. The nearby city of Edmonton served as a control place against which the magnitude of changes in Calgary's level of awareness was measured. Among the European sample in the 2 years preceding the Games, Calgary obtained unaided recall percentages of 10.1 and 12.0%, respectively, whereas comparable figures for Edmonton were 5.3% and 5.0%. The main impact of the Games was shown in the figures for the year in which the Games were held when Calgary's unaided recognition level jumped to 40.0%, whereas Edmonton's remained at just over 6%. Similar impacts were observed among the United States' samples, although the growth in awareness of approximately 23 points was not quite so dramatic as the 28-point gain recorded by the European samples.

Figure 5-2 Media Exposure Accruing to the City of Atlanta from the Falcons Football Team

On any given weekend last fall, the five major Atlanta-area newspapers devoted more than 1,000 column-inches to the Falcons and their opponents. The visiting team was mentioned prominently in each story.

When the Falcons travel, their coverage is at least as great, and probably larger, because they play in larger cities that are the homes of more publications than is Atlanta. Over the regular season, major stories featuring the Atlanta Falcons appear at least twice in the other three Western Division cities. These stories are circulated in the major metropolitan areas of the nation. And it is certain that the nation's 1,790 daily newspapers all carry at least the scores of professional football games, bringing the Falcons' name before countless readers and building Atlanta's image as a major-league city. With a 20-game schedule, 35,000 mentions of Atlanta are a certainty.

More than 130 radio stations in the Southeast carried the play-by-play action of all Falcons games, preseason and regular-season on the Mutual Broadcasting System. And a majority of the 7,000 radio stations across the nation broadcast daily sports reports with frequent mentions of the Falcons.

Nationwide television networks took the Falcons live into virtually every community in the United States, including the states of Alaska and Hawaii. Over 620 network affiliates (CBS, NBC, ABC) carry game reports including Atlanta scores. In the regular-season games which were carried by either CBS or NBC on regional telecast, the Falcons appeared on 364 television stations, and the ABC-TV Monday-Night Games of October 22 and November 5 appeared on 211 more stations. In addition, the four preseason games were televised to the Atlanta-area audience.

Four primary cable networks report sports extensively and frequently mention the Falcons during the season: Entertainment and Sports Programming Network (ESPN), in 37.5 million homes from the United Kingdom to Japan and Canada through Central America; Cable News Network (CNN), in 31.4 million homes in all 50 states and 28 other countries; USA Network in 29 million homes in all 50 states; and Home Box Office (HBO) in 14.5 million homes in the 50 states and Puerto Rico.

These few observations make it quite clear that Atlanta benefits from her professional football team, providing continued advertising and exposure to the rest of the world for the "next great...city." How much is this continued exposure worth? It is hard to say. So many factors are at work in determining a city's future that it is difficult to attribute success in growth to any one particular factor. However, every little bit helps, and few activities can yield the exposure produced by modern professional sports.

Source: Schaffer and Davidson[6]

The instrumental purpose and value of high exposure were articulated in the following terms in relation to the city of Adelaide's investment in its Grand Prix event:

> This is the first step in marketing Adelaide to international markets. Any promotion to create market knowledge of what Adelaide has to offer as an international visitor destination can only be effective after potential visitors know it exists and where it is. Achieving this prerequisite awareness is a considerable hurdle to be overcome. The cost and effort in doing so for a new long haul destination is quite high. Therefore the Grand Prix influence (of which the first year is only part of a cumulative process) is quite valuable in that it would be difficult to achieve by alternative means.[9]

In the case of mega sports events such as the Olympic Games or the Soccer World Cup, it seems possible that visibility may translate into economic impact through increases in tourism that extend beyond the period of the event. For example, Albertville, France, and Lillehammer, Sweden, both received long-term benefits from holding the Winter Olympic Games. The Games better positioned them to compete with the more well-known ski resorts in the Austrian and Swiss Alps. Similarly, the Olympics announced Barcelona to the world. The Director of the Catalan Tourist Board said, "After the Olympics, the city was put on the map. From that moment we have been a successful tourist city" (p. 14).[10] This statement was made seven years after the Games, so the benefit was not merely a short-term phenomenon. After the America's Cup races were held in Freemantle, Western Australia, the following was observed: "Based on the crowds which continue to come to Freemantle day and night, the town has become a major destination for tourists and local visitors in the year since it was 'discovered' by the Cup."[11]

It is conventional to refer to image as consisting of a mental reconstruction of a place in a person's mind. However, this traditional use of the term has been expanded to embrace a conceptualization of image as perceived reputation or character.[12]

Enhanced Community Image

Many cities consciously engage in what has become known as *place marketing*, which involves striving to sell the image of a place so as to make it more attractive to businesses, tourists, and inhabitants.[13] The pervasive popularity of sport in the media has persuaded many cities that sport may be a useful vehicle through which to enhance their image. Thus, some believe that major sports events and teams are the new "image builders" for communities.[14] In the construction years after World War II, this role was performed by tall building-tower skylines, large-span bridges, or manufacturing industries (for example, Motor City or Steel City). Today, as the economy has switched to a service orientation, major sports events and teams capture the imagination and help establish a city's image in people's minds. When the Houston Astrodome was built, it was the self-proclaimed "Eighth Wonder of the World" and was an important element in the city's effort to recast its image from "sleepy bayou town to space-age Sunbelt dynamo" (p. 104).[4] The most frequently cited example in the United States of using sports to enhance a city's image is Indianapolis, and its renaissance is briefly summarized in Figure 5-3.

In chapter 3, it was noted that major sports projects sometimes result in the displacement of poorer people living in the cities. There is a Machiavellian rationale related to image enhancement that supports these kinds of actions. Sport in cities traditionally has been associated with the urban working classes. It has been suggested this is "hardly the image that would be deemed to attract the 'right sort of people' to cities which already possess enduringly strong working-class reputations" (p. 131).[12] The increasing gentrification of sport effectively removes the working classes from the scene, replacing them with a more affluent clientele. It is believed this is likely to attract more affluent entities from the business and tourism sectors that, in the eyes of some, all contribute to upgrading and enhancing a city's image.

Figure 5-3 The Renaissance of Indianapolis

Indianapolis is most often cited as the city that most effectively used sports to change its image. It was a model that officials in many other cities sought to emulate, including Cleveland, Baltimore, Jacksonville, Memphis, and Charlotte. Before 1980, the only thing people thought of when Indianapolis was mentioned was its annual 500-mile auto race. The novelist Kurt Vonnegut. who was a native son, famously commented that the city was a cemetery that woke up for one day and then fell back comatose for the other 364! The city was derisively nicknamed "India-no-place" or "Naptown." Indeed, a consulting firm hired to suggest how the city may resurrect its downtown area commenced its presentation to political leaders by saying, "Gentlemen, the good news is your city does not have a bad image. The bad news is it doesn't have a good image. In fact, to many people in the county, Indianapolis has no image at all."

The downtown core of the city was dirty and filled with vacant, dilapidated buildings. Like many other old industrial cities, Indianapolis' businesses and residents had moved away from the central business district. The Director of the Indianapolis Department of Metropolitan Development recalled that in the late 1970s, the emptiness of the city led to some interesting Sunday afternoon excursions for local Jaycees (escorted by police):

> They were downtown with shotguns and bags, shooting pigeons.
> If you can image a downtown so desolate, there were roving guys
> with shotguns. We had nothing downtown. If our goal was to
> create a city nobody wanted to live in, we'd done it.

To address this problem, a plan was developed by elected officials, business leaders, and the major philanthropic institution in the city to collaborate and use sport as a foundation upon which to build an amenity infrastructure for the downtown area. The city's central geographic location, both within the state of Indiana and in the United States, was perceived to be an asset. The goal was to turn Indianapolis into the "Sports Capital of the U.S." It was anticipated that this would provide a positive image and national identity for the city, and would encourage other types of capital investment.

It was a comprehensive strategy which involved much more than two professional teams (Pacers and Colts), but extended to amateur sports and attracting a continuous flow of major sporting events. The vision was to create a vibrant downtown area through sports which would encourage other companies and residents to move there. There were existing institutions to build around: Indiana University Medical Center; the 27,000 enrollment Indiana-Purdue University campus; a large private-sector employer (Lilly); and government facilities employing thousands in state and local government.

Between 1974 and 1984, $1.7 billion in public, private, and philanthropic funds were invested in the construction of projects that were located in the downtown area. These included an impressive array of state-of-the-art sports facilities that continued to be constructed after the initial boom period throughout the 1980s. The facilities and their cost are listed in the following table: they account for approximately 10% of the total investment.

Facility	Year of completion	Cost in millions
Market Square Arena	1974	$23.5
Tennis Complex	1979	$7.0
Natatorium	1982	$21.5
Track & Field Stadium	1982	$5.9
Velodrome	1982	$2.5
BMX Track	1985	$0.05
Hoosier Dome	1984	$77.5
National Institute for Fitness and Sport	1988	$12.0
Soccer Complex	1987	$1.3
Regatta Course at Eagle Creek	1987	$0.07
Archery Range at Eagle Creek	1987	$0.05
Renovation of Golf Courses at Eagle Creek	1988	$2.6
World Skating Academy	1987	$7.0
Renovation of Sports Centre	1988	$1.0
	1990	$2.0
Little League Regional Headquarters	1990-91	$3.0
Total		$168.5

Although the public investment was substantial, 56% of total investment in the downtown area was from private sources and 8% from non-profit organizations (primarily the Lilly Foundation). Further, the state of Indiana and Indiana University were also major contributors, so the city's proportion of the total investment was only 16%.

The anchors to the sports strategy were the 60,300-seat Hoosier Dome, which cost $78 million in 1984, and the city's success in persuading the Baltimore Colts franchise to relocate there. When that move was confirmed, the Mayor of Indianapolis commented, "I was saying for eight years we were in the process of becoming major league; now we can say, I think without grandiose pomposity, that we are a major league city."

On another occasion the Mayor reiterated this theme:

> Yes sir, we're going all the way now. It's a wonderful thing for our community. It's a boost to the city's image nationally and to local morale as a symbol of major league status...We want people to sit up and say, "By gosh, that city has a lot going for it."

Successfully luring the Colts was a key to the success of Indianapolis' sports strategy. In the following decade, two dozen sports connected organizations, including one international and seven national sports governing bodies, established headquarters in Indianapolis: The Indianapolis sports movement captured widespread attention. The national and some international media carried a plethora of glowing reports about the city's transformation from "India-no-place" to "the star of the snowbelt," which was the title bestowed on it by an article in the *Wall Street Journal*.

Sources: Schimmel[1], Shropshire[15], Rosentraub[2], and Schimmel[16]

The potential of sports events in shifting a city's image was documented in the longitudinal study of the Winter Olympic Games on Calgary described earlier. In the year preceding the Games, the dominant element in the city's image was the annual Calgary Stampede, which was mentioned by 26% of respondents, whereas the Olympics received mention from 17%. In the year of the Olympics, the Games were referenced by 77% of respondents, whereas the Stampede was mentioned by only 11%. In that short period, Calgary had established itself as an Olympic city and benefited from the cachet that accompanies that title; it was no longer "the cowtown which holds the Stampede."[8] Another example of using a sports event to change a city's image is given in Figure 5-4, which describes how the Grand Prix motor race was used to spearhead the "Adelaide Alive" image that was intended to replace the Australian city's traditional, rather unexciting image.[9]

It seems likely that image enhancements based on a sporting event will decay over time. If the catalyst for change impetus initiated by an event is to be fully capitalized upon, there needs to be a coherent plan in place to sustain the initial momentum. The city of Manchester in the north of England is an old industrial city that has used sport as an initial catalyst and has carefully planned a strategy to nurture and sustain it:

> Manchester made two unsuccessful bids for the Olympics (for the 1996 and 2000 Games), but despite this apparent failure, successfully used the bids as a focal point for the reorientation of the city's image. Although the mega-event never took place in the city and the majority of the proposed sport facilities were not built, it is generally regarded that the city's holistic image was improved greatly as a result. In effect, the mere association with sport in general, and more specifically the Olympic Games themselves, replaced vague or negative perceptions of the city with more positive perceptions. Manchester has used the legacy of the bid in the form of, for example, images of sports facilities in promotional literature, in an attempt to connote a new era for the city, illustrating the symbolic and abstract purpose of much sport reimaging. The image enhancement in this instance does not utilise the functional value of the bid in providing an improved sport tourism product, but occurs on a more abstract, symbolic level which has enabled the holistic image of the city to receive a much needed boost.[12] (p. 141)

Figure 5-4 The Role of the Grand Prix in Changing the Image of Adelaide

Promotion of the Grand Prix by both the organizers and the sponsors focuses on the action and the glamour aspects which dominate the image of the event. The event becomes recognized as part of the Adelaide tourism product and hence strongly associated with the City's image. The Grand Prix has made an immediate impact on the State's tourism image. People now associate the Grand Prix with South Australia, and South Australia with the Grand Prix. Recent market research conducted in Melbourne supports this. Among Melbourne residents who said it was either extremely or highly likely that they would visit Adelaide during the next twelve months, 22% said the Grand Prix was a very important factor in their decision to visit South Australia. The perceived excitement and action of the Grand Prix, aptly captured in the Grand Prix marketing slogan 'Adelaide Alive', contrasts markedly with Adelaide's long-standing image in interstate markets as being 'quiet', 'boring', 'City of Churches', etc. The existing image has acted to inhibit consideration of Adelaide as a travel destination for many would be visitors. The Grand Prix influence in changing that image thus creates a greater market receptiveness to promotion of Adelaide as a travel destination.

The resources required to achieve such an impact on Adelaide's image by alternative means would be substantial, and hence the value of this tourism benefit is considerable. However, this is only a potential tourism benefit, since if the opportunity thus created is not effectively exploited then no tourism benefit is gained.

Source: Van der Lee and Williams[9]

There is much public sympathy for the adage that no place really can be considered a "major league city" or "first-tier city" if it does not have a major league sports team. The team is positioned as being symptomatic of a city's character and as defining external perceptions of the city. Proponents of public subsidy for facilities frequently frame the issue in these terms. Consider the following comments made by an advocate imploring voters to support a referendum requesting $125 million for a new arena in Dallas:

Do we want our community to be considered Major League or Minor League? Do we want to be a community of vision or a community that lacks vision?

A great step toward becoming a visionary community would be the construction of a state-of-the-art arena and focusing on maintaining and enhancing our existing sports and entertainment infrastructure. . . Our greatest obstacle is our reputation as a "Can't Do Community" rather than a "Can Do Community". . . In the past few years we have lost the World Special Olympic Games to Connecticut; major status and prestige for the

Cotton Bowl; and bids for the Goodwill Games, U.S. Soccer Federation and Womens Sports Foundation headquarters. Our lack of vision and leadership have become the brunt of jokes and ridicule among many prominent sports leaders and organizations throughout the world.[17]

Proponents of the new sports stadiums in Cincinnati developed similar arguments: "There is a whole bunch of . . . second-tier cities creeping up on our heels. Unless we continue to provide a viable exciting community, we're going to wake up and wonder how Nashville, Charlotte, even Albuquerque outran us. Cleveland's already done it."[18] The Cincinnati Chamber of Commerce warned the city's residents that it was on the verge "of becoming another Memphis" (p. 229).[18]

Despite these claims, the legitimacy of the premise that major league team equates to a major-league city is challengeable. "Do people view Charlotte, Jacksonville, and Nashville to be big-time locations and Los Angeles an also-ran place because the former have NFL teams, while the latter does not" (p. 103).[19] Large cities receive constant media attention. Their size ensures that a disproportionate number of newsworthy events occur there, both positive and negative. Hence, their image is molded by a host of symbols, events, people, and behaviors, so the incremental contribution of a sports event, facility, or team to the image of those cities is likely to be relatively small. Their contribution to the image of smaller cities is likely to be proportionately more substantial:

> While the largest cities viewed sports teams as an important piece of their overall cultural package, in many less populous cities the teams have become inextricably linked with the city's image. Cities such as Oakland, St. Louis, Kansas City, and Cincinnati—none of them among the top 25 cities in population—all have proved to be great sports towns; in many cases, their sports franchises constitute validation that these cities were in the "big leagues."

"Sports means more to Oakland," says the former city manager. "It makes less of a difference to New York, San Francisco, or Chicago" (p. 36).[20]

People frequently make judgments about the competence of a city's administration and its quality of life by extrapolating from snippets of information or from symbols. A sports team is a highly visible symbol. Thus, another dimension of the image issue relates to perceptions of the level of competency of a community's governance. A sports franchise may be considered by some as a symbolic embodiment of the city as a whole.[21] An analogous situation may also exist with major university sports today. Thus, a successful franchise, or the acquisition of a new franchise after competition with other communities, may be portrayed as being symptomatic of a community's economic and social health. For example, a leader in the campaign to attract the NFL Colts to Indianapolis from Baltimore stated, "If Indianapolis lands the Colts or any NFL team, it's going to do some amazing things for the city in terms of prestige, economic development, and in terms of enticing companies to locate to Indianapolis" (p. 144).[1] If a city successfully negotiates and implements a major sports event or franchise agreement, then the inherent complexity of the task and the extensive publicity these actions generate are likely to convey an aura of high competency upon the city's leadership.

Conversely, if a city loses a sports franchise, it may create the impression that local businessmen and politicians are incompetent, that the community is declining or a "loser," and that its residents lack civic pride. Indeed, it may be worse for a city's image to lose a major event or major league team than never to have had one at all. When the Colts left Baltimore, city officials stated it "inflicted a painful blow to the city's renaissance image that would slow economic development" (p. 144).[1] A case could be made that Indianapolis absconded with Baltimore's "major league city" status along with its football team. There was concern at the time that the city would also lose the Orioles, who played in the same old stadium that was a main stimulus for the Colts' leaving. If this occurred, many suggested that Baltimore "was rapidly moving back to being recognized only as the toilet stop on the drive between Washington, D.C. and Philadelphia" (p. 50).[15] This concern provided the urgent impetus to build two new stadiums, one for the Orioles and another to entice the new NFL Baltimore Ravens franchise to the city.

Those in leadership positions in cities where franchises leave–for example, the Raiders, Colts, and Cardinals—may forever be stigmatized in the eyes of many, irrespective of the intrinsic merits of their decisions. This may account for the reaction of the Illinois Governor who said "I'll bleed and die before I let the Sox leave Chicago"(p. 11) when the White Sox threatened to leave Chicago for St. Petersburg.[15]

Although association with sports teams generally is perceived to enhance a city's image, there is some risk that if a team is poor then it could create, or at least reinforce, a negative image:

> Cleveland's image as a failed city was reinforced by a long string of losing seasons by the Indians, who played in a dingy stadium tabbed the "mistake by the lake." Even the local media took to calling Atlanta "Loserville, U.S.A." during the years when the Braves, Falcons, and Hawks were going nowhere. Television also is a mixed blessing, despite efforts of local boosters to accentuate the positive for national audiences. No amount of public relations blather can disguise the fact that the weather in Buffalo is far from balmy during the football season, as viewers across the land watch games played in blizzards and Arctic cold. Television can project images of urban disorder as well as economic vitality, as did the 1989 Super Bowl in riot-torn Miami, reinforcing the city's reputation as a violent and dangerous place rather than reflecting, as the mayor and other leaders had hoped, "the changed reality and the changed image of Miami."[4] (p. 104)

The powerful impact of franchise movements on image in some communities was described by an urban economist reporting on his experience at a radio call-in talk show. The caller wanted him to discuss the decline of St. Louis that took place after the Cardinals left for Arizona. The economist had analyzed the St. Louis economy and found it had not suffered, indeed it had improved, after the Cardinals left; but the caller had the distinct impression that the city was in decline. The economist went on to report:

> It was not only the caller who believed St. Louis's image had declined. When we interviewed civic officials in St. Louis regarding the investments they made to attract the Rams from Los Angeles to the new domed stadium,

each told us they supported the concept because most people in America believed that "St. Louis's best days were behind her." So, image matters to people even if those of us who study the economic effects of stadia and teams conclude there is no real benefit from the presence of a team.[2] (p. 205)

Given the potential positive impact of a franchise on a city's image, those cities with most to gain from it are probably those that are in decline. They are most desperate to communicate signs of economic and social rejuvenation, and as the Indianapolis case shows, obtaining a major league franchise can be a successful strategy. Unfortunately, these struggling cities also are likely to be least able to make the major investments necessary for this strategy to succeed.

The discussions of awareness and image enhancement have focused on professional sports franchises, but most of the suggested outcomes apply also to the college context. Many colleges view their high-profile sports teams as promotional vehicles for the school and as a focal point with which students and alumni can identify. Sports teams are commonalities that cross disciplines and represent the school as a whole. All alumni cannot get excited about the excellence of the English or chemistry departments, because most of them have no relationship with those entities. However, all can unite and bond in support of "the team" because it is a common element—a beacon to rally around. The team characteristics of spirit, success, and camaraderie are metaphors and exemplars with which alumni and students identify. Sports teams also constitute the impression of the college held by most of the population who know nothing else about the school.

| **Stimulation of Other Development** | The contention that a sports event or facility will stimulate additional development and thus contribute to expansion of a city's tax base is at least in part a consequence of the increased visibility and enhanced image that cities believe will accrue from their investment. There are two principles that appear crucial to the ability of major sports facilities to serve as the "glue" for anchoring a downtown economic redevelopment project and attracting additional development to it. |

The first is the principle of having a threshold level of cumulative attraction. This builds on the notion that a given number of entertainment attractions will do more business if they are located adjacent or in proximity to each other, than if they are widely dispersed. This principle states that in order to persuade people to go downtown there has to be a threshold number or critical mass of complementary attractions, such as hotels, restaurants, specialty retailers, theaters, and other entertainment offerings. This was an explicit reason for selecting the Camden Yards site for the Orioles' new baseball park: "The basic rationale for selecting the site was that the presence of multiple attractions would induce more attendance both at Orioles games and other downtown attractions than either could generate in the absence of the other" (p. 255).[22] It is untenable to believe that a facility such as an MLB ballpark could induce substantial associated economic development given that it operates only for three hours a day, a few days a week, between May and September. There must be other reasons to visit the area when games are not being played. Indeed, in some contexts, a major sports facility may deter downtown development, because some potential relocators may see periodically full parking lots and street congestion as impediments to their business.[7]

The second, and related, principle to stimulating other development is to ensure the facility is part of an integrated, coherent, master plan for downtown redevelopment, rather than an ad hoc initiative that it is vaguely hoped may stimulate others to locate nearby:

> It matters if the city has developed a plan for integrating the stadium in its overall strategy for the downtown area or for the region. Too often there is virtually no planning but a good deal of hoping that the stadium or arena will "jump-start" the economy or region. By itself, a stadium or arena cannot jump-start even the small economy of a part of downtown. But as part of an overall plan or strategy, a stadium could be helpful and useful. Does such a plan exist, and what is expected or anticipated from the development of the stadium or arena?[22] (p. 205)

In the past, focus was on building a sports facility. Now, the vision typically is broader, and the broader vision is likely to provide more justification for public subsidy if it can successfully facilitate additional urban redevelopment. This broader vision has design implications. A facility cannot be a catalyst for development if it is an island built in the middle of a sea of surrounding concrete car park.[7] This isolates fans from other development, rather than integrates them. If the stadium is intended to stimulate other development, then fans should be channeled to it through carefully planned corridors to maximize secondary economic activity.[6] Further, the design should build upon and assimilate the character of surrounding structures (e.g., Camden Yards in Baltimore); otherwise, the facility becomes an ugly intrusion on the urban fabric instead of an indigenous component of it. Many new stadiums do not foster surrounding development because they are not physically interwoven with other components of the urban fabric. Rather, these stadiums are designed for quick entry and exit of suburban fans with automobiles. Even though they are technically inner-city parks, often their urban integration is limited to supplying parking facilities close to the downtown business district. In the Bronx, where community improvement was the primary justification for refurbishing Yankee Stadium, a local storekeeper observed, "That's an isolated place over there, people just drive in and out" (p. 294).[23] The project was widely acknowledged to have failed in its goal to be the major catalyst for the borough's rehabilitation. Similarly, a commentator on the news station discussing a proposed new stadium in Chicago observed, "Never have city and stadium been so detached from each other: The garages will attach to the park by elevated walkways, and thus fans who arrive by car will have the privilege of never actually setting foot on the South Side of Chicago."[21]

The antithetical goals of team owners and public officials who are seeking to use a new stadium to stimulate redevelopment of downtown areas were noted in the following observation:

> From the team's perspective the ideal location will be a site that is easily accessible, has visibility from major highways, and is compatible with the direction of existing and future population growth. It should not be surprising that the community goals of local officials often do not match the location criteria and business interests of team owners. As one interviewer commented, team owners are not in the urban redevelopment business.[24] (p. 319)

When Pittsburgh replaced Three Rivers Stadium with two new specialist stadiums, one for baseball and one for football, the city's goal was to use them to revive its inner core. They were part of a comprehensive plan that included making the proximate newer area attractive, creating easier access to it, removing clutter and dilapidated buildings, and improving infrastructure. One of its strategies to stimulate development was to cap game-day parking rates at its downtown garages at $3 to encourage fans to park downtown and walk across the river to watch the game. The hope was that this would help boost foot-traffic to restaurants, shops, and attractions in the renovated area.[25]

There is some evidence that economic development can be stimulated by hosting mega sports events. Indeed, some would argue that the cost of staging megaevents (both the monetary costs and the cost of adverse congestion impacts the host population) is so high that host cities can justify them only if they result in economic rejuvenation or a windfall of new sports facilities that the community does not have to pay for. The most prominent example is the Olympic Games. Since the Rome Olympics of 1960, using the Games to trigger large-scale urban redevelopment has been a primary justification used by host cities for becoming involved.[26] Even unsuccessful bids can result in urban renewal, as the regeneration may be seen as a prerequisite for a bid to be viewed as viable. In many cases, a bid for the Games provides the justification to "fast track" improvements that have long been talked about but not enacted. The hosting of a prestigious, highly visible event focuses the attention of elected officials and creates a sense of urgency and priority, so things get done that would otherwise not yet be done or be delayed.

This catalyst role was particularly prominent at the Summer Olympic Games in Barcelona. The Games produced major changes in urban infrastructure that transformed the city of Barcelona.[27] The city was opened to the sea, and a run-down coastal area was rejuvenated to include a new marina, leisure facilities, and attractive sandy beaches. There was major investment in new transportation systems including construction of a coastal ring road, modernization of the port and airport, and restructuring of the city's rail network. Other major improvements included renovating the sewer system, building residential facilities that served as the Olympic Village, and upgrading the urban technology and communications systems that were necessary to accommodate the world's media. Officials in Barcelona estimated that hosting the Games resulted in 25 years of development being collapsed into a 6-year period.

The types of development that proponents envisage may be stimulated by large-scale sports facilities can be classified under three headings: proximate development, complementary development, and general development.

Proximate Development

It was noted earlier that sports facilities are increasingly conceptualized as being part of an integrated redevelopment package that includes substantial proximate development. These facilities do afford urban planners the opportunity to steer their development to a desired location and to try and use them to jump-start economic development there. The use of a facility as a catalyst for attracting other development was the thinking underlying development of the $250 million MCI

Center in Washington, DC, which opened in 1992. It hosts the NBA Wizards; the NHL Capitals; the Hoyas, Georgetown University's basketball team; the WNBA Mystics; and a myriad of concerts and special events on nights with no games. In addition, it houses a sports museum with interactive exhibits, two restaurants, and a sporting goods store.

Prior to the opening of the MCI Center, the area in which it was located was a rundown, forgotten part of the city. Littered with vacant lots and buildings, it was a place where drug traders plied their trade and few outsiders ventured after dark. Today, the whole area has been transformed with new office buildings, hotels, restaurants, apartments, entertainment venues, and stores. The MCI Center has been the major catalyst for this development.[28]

The Center is serviced by all the area's Metrorail transit lines and is close to the corporations who pay for the luxury suites, club seats, and other corporate services. An estimated 50 to 60% of audiences at large MCI Center events uses public transportation. Games are scheduled for 7 p.m., which encourages downtown employees to head directly to the games after work and to use the restaurants and stores in the area as part of their visit.[28]

Sometimes a lapse in time between construction of a sports facility and emergence of associated proximate development is common. For example, many thought the opening of Atlanta's Turner Field might create a retail boom in the economically depressed neighborhoods around the ballpark, but retailers were slow to come to the area despite new housing and new residents. Vacant lots were cleared of debris and weeds, and new homes were built, but the number of residents and visitors to the area took a while to reach the threshold needed to attract retail investment. An official noted, "Five years ago that area was crack city. It's coming back, but it takes time. It needs more residential before retailers will come in" (p. 22).[29]

The renaissance of downtown Indianapolis described in Figure 5-3 was stimulated by sports projects, and they do appear to have been a successful catalyst for subsequent development. From 1980 to 1984, the years when the initial major investment in sports facilities was committed, 16 new restaurants were added to the downtown, and in those years the city had the fastest population growth of any of the 10 largest Midwest cities. The old deserted buildings were converted into condominiums and luxury apartments, and the upper-middle class residents who moved into them provided support for retail and services businesses that emerged.[1]

Figure 5-5 offers an example from the minor leagues where the city of Harrisburg, Pennsylvania, constructed a baseball stadium and purchased a franchise to anchor redevelopment of a rundown part of the city.[30]

Complementary Development

Complementary development may take two forms. First, it refers to new facilities constructed as part of a jurisdiction's commitment to hosting a megaevent. Frequently, many facilities already exist, but others also have to be developed to complement the existing inventory. Often these are paid for by entities other than the

Figure 5-5 The Harrisburg Senators: Catalyst for Urban Renewal

The Harrisburg Senators is a AA minor league franchise that plays in a ballpark on City Island in Harrisburg, the capital of Pennsylvania. City Island is located in the Susquehanna River and is the city's eastern border. Before the ballpark was built, and a franchise purchased to play in it, the island was popularly perceived to be dangerous and crime infested.

The stadium was planned to be the catalyst for the redevelopment of the island and as the island's central attraction. To consolidate its commitment to this goal, the city of Harrisburg purchased the franchise, so it is one of the few American professional sports franchises owned by a local government. In each of the following four seasons, the Senators won the class AA Eastern League's championship. Each year, the city has reported an operating profit on the team, and the capital value of the franchise has also substantially increased.

City Island now supports a recreational complex with playing fields, miniature golf, parks, horse-drawn carriages, and a variety of concessions. A state sports museum also has committed to the site. The team averages 4,000 fans per game and their presence, the success of the team, and the physical attractiveness of the stadium, have been the catalyst for the island's revitalization. The team has attracted suburbanites back into Harrisburg on summer evenings.

Source: Schoenfeld[30]

host community. The facilities legacy from the Atlanta Olympic Games listed in Table 5-1 illustrates this type of complementary development.[31]

A much more common form of complementary development refers to the upgrading or initiation of businesses as a result of the demand for their services that is directly created by a sport facility or event. In the case of most sports facilities, complementary development is likely to take the form of restaurants, bars, and souvenir stores. Coors Field, the home of the Colorado Rockies, is an example of this type of catalyst role.[32] It is credited with helping the revitalization of Denver's Lower Downtown or "LoDo" district. Restaurants, sports bars, and sports memorabilia stores opened with Coors Field to serve the over three million fans who attend Rockies games.

The potential in both number and range of ancillary businesses that can flourish in a parasitic relationship with facilities hosting major league sports franchises is relatively small and is decreasing. The new generation of fully loaded facilities is likely to capture much of the spending that used to occur in nearby restaurants, bars, and sports merchandise stores. It has been suggested that these new facilities are analogous to European walled cities, seeking to enclose all commercial activity and revenue flows within their confines.[19]

Other sports offer much more scope for complementary development. For example, when the America's Cup Challenge was held in Freemantle, Western Australia, it had the effect on the city of boosting development of both new marine-related industries and non-marine-related high technology businesses such as computer systems, advanced metals technology, and synthetic fibers. These products were prominently publicized in the Australian media during the

Table 5-1 Legacy of Olympic Venues (amounts in million dollars)

Facility	Total Investment	ACOG Share
Olympic Stadium	189	189
Georgia International Horse Park	90	28
Wolf Creek Shooting Complex	17	17
Stone Mountain Tennis Center	18	18
Lake Lanier Rowing Center	10	10
Georgia Institute of Technology Dormitories	194	47
Natatorium	24	21
Alexander Memorial Coliseum	1.5	1.5
Atlanta University Center	51	51
Stadiums – Morris Brown College/- Clarke Atlantic Univ	37	37
Basketball Arena – Morehouse College	11	11
Tennis Facility – Spelman College	1	1
Drug Testing Center – Morehouse School of Medicine	1	1
Interdenominational Theological Center	0.8	0.8
Georgia State University Gymnasium Renovation	2	2
Clayton County International Park	3	0
TOTAL	599.3	384.3

Note: Values shown only include portion of project budget dedicated to construction/renovation of permanent facilities.

Source: Atlanta Committee for the Olympic Games, HE Advisors and The Selig Center for Economic Growth, Terry College of Business, The University of Georgia (June, 1995). Referenced in Li et al.[31]

prolonged period of years during which the media were preoccupied with the America's Cup. The frequent references to high technology products and Freemantle created a nexus in many people's minds and stimulated such development in the area.[11]

Perhaps the most successful examples of using sport to generate complementary development are motor sports. Figure 5-6 describes some of the ancillary businesses that have been spawned by the presence of NASCAR headquarters and teams in the Charlotte area of North Carolina.[33] Similar ancillary development emerged in Indianapolis to support the multiple CART, Indy Racing League, and National Hot Rod Association teams that are based in the city:

- In 1992, there were approximately 200 motor sport related businesses in Indianapolis, but by 2001 it was estimated that this number had tripled and that 10,000 people worked in these businesses. In 1994, Indi-

Figure 5-6 NASCAR: Nurturer of Complementary Development

Charlotte is the defacto headquarters of NASCAR and numerous NASCAR related businesses are located in the area. At least 50 teams have it as their home base. Taking a cue from Hollywood, Mooresville, which is a small city on the edge of Charlotte, created its version of star maps, leading fans to race shops for tours and souvenir shopping. Essentially, motor sports has replaced the textile industry, which was declining in the area, as the key economic engine. An official observed:

> If you need it for racing, somebody makes it somewhere in town. The infrastructure is here to support racing. Parts suppliers, machine shops, coating companies. If you go any place else in the country and try to do this, you're going to be FedExing stuff back and forth every day. (p. 25)

NASCAR and the nearby Lowes Motor Speedway are primarily responsible for development of Concord Regional Airport, since 40 planes belonging to race teams are based at the airport. Those planes purchase $4.5 million worth of airplane fuel a year at Concord airport. When the Speedway hosts its three annual Winston Cup events, the airport traffic grows much heavier with sponsors and fans bringing in their planes. The NASCAR connection has created a community asset, because without it the airport would not be a viable enterprise.

Source: Spanberg[33, 34]

anapolis passed a sales-and-use tax exemption that became the cornerstone for promoting a motorsports boom in the city. A major hub of these ancillary businesses is a four block area south of the Indianapolis Speedway known as "Gasoline Alley," where an impressive array of suppliers, fabricators, chassis builders, and engine builders are located.[35]

General Development

It is sometimes suggested that views of a city and its skyline that appear on television as part of a sports program or the presence of a major league franchise *per se* aid in economic development. Thus, advocates for public subsidy of facilities are likely to state, "The team's presence on national television is the best advertising the city has. You never know who is watching an NFL game. Viewers may include convention planners, business CEOs, and relocation consultants, so the team's presence is a real benefit for the city." This type of optimistic statement exemplifies the belief that the big-league image will serve as a magnet and attract general development to the city that is neither complementary nor proximate. Such a positive outcome seems improbable because the publicity or the "winning image" of a team does not change any of the cost and market factors that influence business relocation decisions and economic development and growth.[2]

Some communities now have moved beyond this type of vague wishful thinking. They have sought to promote general development by harnessing the celebrity status of major events, teams, and players to open doors and gain access to key figures in business relocation decisions:

- Newcastle United is a soccer team in the English Premier Division. Located in the Northeast of England, the town of Newcastle had a long-standing image of poverty, crime, and unemployment that were a legacy of the demise of the shipbuilding and coal industries that had been its traditional economic base. In the 1990s, Newcastle United emerged as a top-class soccer team after many decades of mediocrity. As a result, they qualified to play in the prestigious European international competitions. The town's economic redevelopment officials saw an opportunity to leverage the team's participation in these competitions. When the team played in foreign cities or hosted foreign teams, key business leaders from those cities were identified. They were invited to the games as the town's guests; afforded opportunities to mingle with the Newcastle players; and offered tours of the city.[36]

After Jacksonville was awarded the 30th NFL team franchise, the city dubbed itself The Expansion City. It launched a campaign featuring a Jaguars helmet and the slogan "Get inside the NFL's head," which resulted in more than 150 inquiries from companies asking about relocation possibilities.[5]

Megaevents may offer similar leverage to engage and enlighten business leaders on the potential merits of expanding or relocating to the host area. Thus, soon after Atlanta was awarded the Olympic Games, officials in Georgia established Operation Legacy,[37] which is described in Figure 5-7.

Figure 5-7 Attracting Development: Atlanta's Operation Legacy

The goal of operation legacy was to use the Olympics to recruit 20 major companies or facilities to Atlanta and Georgia, which would create 6,000 jobs. Once every few months, about 40 top executives from a single industry—auto parts, communications, and agribusiness were some of the targets—were invited, with their spouses, to spend several days in the city and state. There was the usual wining and dining, including an evening at the governor's mansion, and panel discussions about economic developments, but the centerpiece was the Olympics.

The visitors could try their hand at trap and skeet shooting at the Olympic shooting range or do some white-water rafting on the new Olympic canoe and kayak course. The head of the Atlanta Olympic Committee spoke about the spirit and progress of the Games. The program then offered hospitality during the Games themselves to 200 executives and their spouses who looked to be the best prospects. An official stated, "We knew if we sent invitations talking about the Olympics, we could get their attention."

Source: Adapted from Ruffenach[37]

Psychic Income

In each of the previous four external benefits that have been discussed—economic impact (chapter 4), community visibility, community image, and stimulation of other development—the focus has been on using sports to reach *external* audiences, with the intent of encouraging their investment of resources in the community. In contrast, psychic income focuses *internally* on a community's existing residents. *Psychic income* is the emotional and psychological benefit residents perceive they receive, even though they do not physically attend sports events and are not involved in organizing them.

People may avidly follow "their" team through the media and engage in animated conversations with others about the team, but never attend a game. A commentary on the Baltimore Orioles observed

> The identification of a sports team like the Orioles with a city surely generates some pleasure for its citizens beyond that reflected in ticket sales. In this respect the economics of sports is much different from the economics of, say, apples. A fan can derive substantial pleasure from the Orioles and identify with them as "his" team without ever attending a game, but he gets no such pleasure from knowing that somebody is eating apples in Baltimore.[22] (p. 269)

If a new IBM plant opens in a city, elected officials and business leaders may get excited, but ordinary residents do not because the economic benefits appear intangible and impersonal to them. When a sports team comes to a city, a much broader segment of the population becomes excited and identifies with it. A sports team is an investment in the emotional infrastructure of a community. Sport has been eloquently described as "the 'magic elixir' that feeds personal identity while it nourishes the bonds of communal solidarity" (p. 5).[38]

Sports are not like other businesses. They are about "triumphs of the human spirit, community bonding, and family memories. They're about taking a break from the pettiness that divides us. They're about celebrating some of the things that make society whole: competition, victory, redemption" (p. 309).[39] Society has an emotional attachment to sports and receives a psychic income from them. The emotional involvement transposes some people from the dreary routines of their lives to a mode of escapism that enables them to identify with a team, personalize its success, and feel better about themselves. Life is about experiences, and sports teams help create them—albeit vicariously in most cases. When Tottenham Hotspur, a prominent English Premier League soccer team from London, went essentially bankrupt a few years ago, their bank did not foreclose on the unpayable loan by closing the ground and selling it and the other team assets as they would have done with any other business. The bank realized if they took this action, they would alienate a large proportion of the London population, lose tens of thousands of accounts in London, and be stigmatized forever. The bank absorbed the team's losses and the team continued to operate.[40]

Sports teams are a medium through which cities and their residents express their personality, enhance their status, and promote their quality of life to a national audience. Major league sports teams are much more than enterprises with economic benefits and costs:

They are first and foremost cultural assets, like art museums and symphony orchestras. Baltimore is a better place to live because of the Orioles and Ravens. Cleveland is a better place to live because of the Browns, Indians, and Cavaliers. Hosting a World Series is no substitute for operating a successful school system or fielding an effective police force, but it shouldn't have to be. A major league sports team, even a losing one, can be a wonderful community enhancement, like a bustling waterfront or a historic site.[39] (p. 315)

In some ways, sports teams may be perceived as being analogous to the arts. Most performing arts, museums, and visual arts organizations receive public subsidy. If they were removed from a community's social fabric, there would be a void. Indeed, the team's role as a central part of a community's social fabric was prominent in a court's decision to approve an injunction preventing the dissolution of the Minnesota Twins (Figure 5-8).

The relationship between sports teams and their fans is often referred to as "a love affair."[16] When a team leaves a community, it is the end of a "marriage." These are nuptial-like analogies. The pervasive influence of sports is exemplified by the extensive use of sports metaphors in everyday life. Knowing how to keep a straight bat, respond to a googly, bat on a sticky wicket, keep your end up, avoid being stumped, or duck a bouncer—these are cricketing phrases that are endemic in the English language of many civilized countries. Indeed, it has been suggested that "the language of sports is the symbolic glue that holds the entire social life world."[41] This might be hyperbole, but sport is a central topic of conversation in many social contexts. Another commentator noted,

> Holiday celebrations include sporting events; political statements are made through sporting events; even dating is tied to the high school sports scene. Fathers and their children develop relationships through sports, and increasingly women are also involved in team sports, building for them a cherished set of memories.[2] (p. 449)

Sports teams or events provide a tangible focus for building community consciousness and social bonding. They are an important part of the collective experience of urban dwellers because they tie residents together regardless of race, gender, or economic standing. They are one of the few vehicles available for developing a sense of community. "Fans who chant 'we're number one' are trumpeting the superiority of both their team and their town. In rallying around the home team, people identify more closely with a broader civic framework in the spatially, socially, and politically fragmented metropolis" (p. 9).[4] They generate civic energy. The strength of civic pride was illustrated in the brouhaha over the naming rights of the new stadium built for the NFL's Denver Broncos that is described in Figure 5-9.[42]

The use of facilities to create civic pride may be particularly important in communities where there has been a long period of decline that has demoralized residents. The Cleveland and Indianapolis cases in Figures 5-1 and 5-3, respectively, were illustrations of this. It was suggested in the mid-1990s that the success of the Dallas Cowboys at that time was instrumental in redeeming the collective self-esteem of the residents of Dallas:

Figure 5-8 The Minnesota Twins as Part of the Community Fabric

In 2001 MLB sought to reduce the number of teams by two and selected the Montreal Expos and Minnesota Twins for dissolution. A prime reason for their selection was the refusal of their cities to provide these franchises with new, "fully-loaded" stadiums. There was a public outrage over this decision in Minnesota. A financial analysis by the city showed that in the period since the Metrodome opened in 1982, the team received $216 million in public aid, while the owner originally paid $34 million and subsequently invested a further $130 million during this period. Hence, the public had a larger financial stake in the team than the franchise. Further, their lease required the Twins to play the 2002 season at the Metrodome.

When the city's agency, The Metropolitan Sports Facilities Commission, applied to the courts for an injunction prohibiting the proposed dissolution, it was granted. The judge in his ruling placed great emphasis on the team's contribution to the community fabric, stating, "The relationship between the Twins and the Commission is not a typical landlord tenant relationship. The relationship provides the State's citizenry and fans with substantial non-monetary benefits…"

Baseball is as American as turkey and apple pie. Baseball is a tradition that passes from generation to generation. Baseball crosses social barriers, creates community spirit, and is much more than a private enterprise. Baseball is a national pastime. Locally, the Twins have been part of Minnesota history and tradition for forty years. The Twins have given Minnesota two World Series Championships, one in 1987, and one in 1991. The Twins have also given Minnesota legends such as Rod Carew, Tony Oliva, Harmon Killebrew, Kent Hrbek, and Kirby Puckett; some of which streets are named after. These legends have bettered the community. Most memorably, these legends volunteered their time to encourage and motivate children to succeed in all challenges of life. Clearly, more than money is at stake. The welfare, recreation, prestige, prosperity, trade, and commerce of the people of the community are at stake. The Twins brought the community together with Homer Hankies and bobblehead dolls. The Twins are one of the few professional sports teams in town where a family can afford to take their children to enjoy a hot dog and peanuts at a stadium. The vital public interest, or trust, of the Twins substantially outweighs any private interest. Private businesses were condemned to build the Metrodome. In condemnation proceedings, the building of the Metrodome was deemed to be in the interest of the public. The Commission, the State, citizenry, and fans will suffer irreparable harm if the Twins do not play the 2002 baseball games at the Metrodome.

It is widely believed that the city's redemption from its darkest day – Nov. 22, 1963 – came with the rise of the Cowboys, their glamour and their glory sprinkling stardust upon the discredited city. Once it was blithely assumed that Dallas had somehow killed President Kennedy. Now, no matter who else may be accused of that crime – the CIA, the Mafia, Cuba, aliens – Dallas is no longer impeached. And J.R. is gone, too. Dallas is just the home of the Cowboys, the NFL champions, a franchise that has never seen its equal. *You know who I am.* I am Dallas; I am the Cowboys.[43] (p. 62)

Sports is a theater where Kipling's twin imposters of triumph and disaster run side-by-side and affect large numbers of people. It provides a theater of emotions to fantasize about and to casually share.[44] When a team or event is successful, benefits often accrue to the collective morale of all residents. A substantial proportion of a community emotionally identifies with "their" team or event and feels elation, anxiety, despondency, optimism, and an array of other emotions according to how the team performs. Some of these people may not understand the nature of the event or how the activity is performed. Nevertheless, the team constitutes "a common identification symbol, something that brings the citizens of the city together, especially during those exhilarating times when the city has a World Series champion, or a Super Bowl winner" (p. 176).[45] The emotional response of Atlanta residents, reported in Figure 5-10, to the news that the Olympic Games would be coming to their city illustrates the phenomenon of psychic income derived from collective community pride.[46]

Professional teams contribute to building a community's "sense of place."[44] In the context of Minneapolis, one commentator believed

> the Twins or Vikings or North Stars or Timberwolves have provided each of us and all of us with exquisite memories that attach us to our grandparents,

---

Figure 5-9 The Renaming of Mile High Stadium

The Metropolitan Football Stadium District is comprised of representatives from six counties in the Denver area who were responsible for the public funds used to subsidize construction of the new stadium for the NFL's Denver Broncos. The District interpreted its primary responsibility to minimize the tax obligation of residents in these counties. Accordingly it sold the naming rights to the new facility to the Invesco Funds Group, a subsidiary of a British corporation. Most of the money from the sale went to the team, but the District's share amounted to approximately $6 per resident in the District.

The name was augmented so the facility was officially titled Invesco Field at Mile High Stadium. Segments of the Denver public were outraged at the prospect of their beloved Mile High Stadium metamorphosing into Invesco Field. They said to the Stadium District, in essence, "We excuse you from responsibility to reduce public debt. We voted to spend our money for the stadium, and we'll pay for it without that kind of help. Keep Mile High."

The city's major newspaper announced that it would refer to the new facility as Mile High Stadium, rather than Invesco Field at Mile High Stadium. The newspaper's editor said this decision was the result of "listening, learning, understanding. And of giving the public its voice."

He argued that Mile High Stadium was "in the public minds, hearts, and on the public's tongue."

Mile High was an integral part of the heritage and legacy of the Broncos. The public perceived that they owned it and it was part of their identification with the team. Its widespread national recognition and reputation was a source of pride to many residents. The brouhaha showed that for many residents the psychic income they received from the name, and the imagery and associations that went with it, was worth much more than a tax saving of $6 each.

Source: Guzzo[42]

our parents, our neighbors, our siblings, our children . . . . Pro sports in a metropolitan area the size of the Twin Cities can especially become the collective memory of a diverse citizenry constantly seeking common ground.[44] (pp. 451-452)

The warmth derived from these kinds of connections is difficult to quantify in dollars; it sounds hokey and gets lost in the endless cynical wranglings between millionaire players and billionaire owners, between billionaire owners and public bodies. Nevertheless, this psychic income may be the strongest justification for investing public money into professional sports.

When Jacksonville was awarded a franchise to become the NFL's 30th team, it became a catalyst for unifying diverse groups in the city: "Linked by a mighty passion for football, the citizenry overcame the town's diverse history and pulled together—white bankers and black preachers on the same team—to sell out the 73,000 seat stadium in record time and grab the NFL's admiration" (p. B8).[5] However, the momentum created by this catalytic event needed to be sustained if Jacksonville was to shed its remnants of the Old South.

It has long been recognized that the emotional identification with sports teams has an extraordinary impact on the morale of many people. In recent years, a biological explanation for this has emerged.[47] Winning and losing have a direct effect on the chemical composition of our brains, particularly on levels of a neurotransmitter called serotonin. The social environment, not heredity, has been shown to be the critical determinant in serotonin levels. Winning raises these levels and losing lowers them. This at least partially explains the observation, "Every time we win, we're like a different country. Everybody's happy. Football (soccer) can bring peace" (p. 56).[45] People with low levels of serotonin are more depressed and aggressive than people with high levels. When individuals identify with the fortunes of their team and it loses an important game, unconsciously, they lose. They are more likely to feel depressed or become violent afterwards because their serotonin levels dropped. Antidepressant drugs such as Prozac work by raising serotonin levels.

The psychic income that people experience often is used by elected officials who seek to exploit the popularity of sport by linking with it. For example, they invariably seek association with victorious teams by organizing parades and ceremonies for teams in which they feature prominently, hoping the "feel-good" factor will spill over to aid their popularity as elected officials. As the vignette in Figure 5-11 suggests, politicians can probably aid their reelection chances if they can arrange for the election to coincide with an important sporting success with which their constituents identify, because the raised serotonin levels of constituents are likely to create a feel-good factor.

The vignettes in Figures 5-11, 5-12, and 5-13 are illustrative testimonials of the extraordinary amount of psychic income that can collectively accrue to those who identify with sports teams. There are clear similarities between this situation and those that exist in many professional and collegiate teams and their host communities in the United States. In Europe, the integration of nations into the European Union was eroding national boundaries, but sport remains a central pillar around which national psyches are constructed. Figure 5-11 describes the reaction

Figure 5-10 World Recognition Gives Atlantans a New Sense of Pride in Their City

Karen Twait was weaving her way to work through heavy eastbound traffic on Interstate 20 when the announcement came over the radio. "Suddenly horns started honking, and fists came out of car windows. Everywhere I looked people were screaming. It was incredible," said the 24-year old financial analyst who moved here from Tampa three months ago. "I started screaming too. And tears just started streaming down my face. It was so dramatic. I never expected so much emotion to come over me."

On the other side of the city, Robert Clark, 52, an Atlanta native and downtown businessman, was watching TV, getting ready for work. "I was startled," Mr. Clark said. ""I just broke down and cried when the guy said, 'Atlanta.' I don't know why. It's been more than 30 years since I cried. But I know I'll remember that day for a long, long time."

The instant the Olympic announcement was made Tuesday morning, a change swept through the city. The town rose up, rearranging a collective psyche that some say has long been subject to a Southern inferiority complex. Winning the Games seems to have finally ripened a town that's forever been on the edge of maturity.

Scores of people say they feel decidedly different now. They feel better about Atlanta, better about living here. Many people say they will never forget where they were and what they were doing when they heard the news, and they will long remember how they were moved. Anyone who has lived in a city that won the World Series or a Super Bowl will understand something of the feeling that swept through the city Tuesday. But Atlanta savored far more than a one-day seasonal victory.

Atlanta has long had an image problem. The town called Terminus that began as a transportation crossroads grew up as a drummers' town and remains one. It has always been a city where myth outstripped reality. Tourists will ask in vain to see vestiges of Scarlett's and Rhett's antebellum South, and must eventually confront the question: "What is there to actually see here?" In so many ways, Atlanta has been seen as Loserville, and not just in terms of sports.

"Atlanta has never become the city it wanted to be. Its history has been one of thinking it might have finally arrived, then finding that it hasn't," said Albert Scardino, whose editorial writing won a Pulitzer Prize at *The Georgia Gazette* in Savannah.

Atlanta has often been portrayed as being interested in little more than rampant development exceeded only be excessive boosterism, a sweltering clime, and a transplanted and transient population.

"Atlanta itself has no real identity," Mr. Robinson said. "You never have to ask what makes New York a great city, or Boston, or L.A., or San Francisco. You know why they're great. But Atlanta? The city has no real indigenous culture of its own. It's a city that has long been groping for its identity."

In the height of its most recent hoped-for glory, during the Democratic National Convention, the city was ripped again—called "The Big Hustle," a city built on lies, in *The Wall Street Journal.*

That changed Tuesday. With the Olympic Games, Loserville became Lusterville. "Winning the Olympics says Atlanta is a real city," Mr. Robinson said. "It says to the people who live there, 'Finally, we're a place. We have an identity.' For a lot of people, this legitimizes the identity of their city."

Walking the streets in the days since the announcement, it is not hard to find people who say their image of the city has changed overnight. "The problem we've had is that we've always claimed to be an international city. But let's face it, we have not been one," said Tony Bulthuis, 45, accounts director at Comfort Inns, who moved here from Amsterdam 22 years ago. "Now we don't have to make excuses for ourselves any longer."

When Ann Crawford, 32, moved here from New York four years ago, she thought it a sleepy town. "I had a sense of, 'Oh, my God, what have I done.' It was a big step for me, and it felt like a step backward."

"But today there is a real and new sense of pride," said Ms. Crawford, who works for the international exchange program American Field Service. "There's a sense that this is where it's happening. Everyone in the U.S. is envious of Atlanta today.""

Debbie Lee, 25, a traveling businesswoman who has been in Atlanta eight years, put it this way: "I have a lot of friends that wouldn't visit me in Atlanta, friends from Florida, New York, California. But now they'll all want to come."

The new-found optimism has spilled over to the city's most debated problems. "I'm hoping this will mean we'll finally do something about the homeless and needy," said Adrian Chester, 27, an Atlanta native who is a disc jockey at Dominique's nightclub. "Getting the Olympics is sort of like everyone's lottery ticket. It allows everyone to dream. And hopefully everyone will benefit."

Source: Bronstein[46]

of the French when their team won the soccer World Cup. In recent years, racial conflict in France has been more prominent than probably in any other European country, as relatively large numbers of immigrants from the former French colonies of Algeria, Morocco, and elsewhere entered the country. The stars of the French team were their darkest skinned players, but in the euphoria of victory these prejudices were cast aside as all France erupted with joy.

The French success in 1998 was followed by abject failure in the next World Cup in 2002 where the team was again favored to win, but became the first reigning champions to be eliminated in the first round since 1966. Their performance was described by a respected commentator as "the most pathetic defence of the crown in World Cup history" (p. 4).[56] Because France had embraced its 1998 win as the source of a national renaissance, it was inevitable that the team's ignominy would be viewed in a much broader context than a sporting event. There was a pervasive sense of humiliation proportionate to the high hopes that had preceded it. The presenter for France Instate television said, "This is an historic debacle, a massive catastrophe, a Waterloo,"[52] whereas another commentator reported that

> France choked with disbelief and anger over its premature ejection from the World Cup, a disaster that ended four years of football supremacy and fuelled a general malaise that has gripped the country since spring".[57] (p. 14)

The leader of the far-right political party took the opportunity to mock the defeat of the "rainbow" team that had been cast as the quintessence of the new integrated *noir-blanc-beur* [black - white - Arab] France, and a party spokesman said the defeat "sounded the death knell of pro-immigration propaganda"[57] (p. 14).

Measuring Psychic Income

When the New York Yankees floated the idea of the city's playing a major role in constructing a new $1 billion stadium for them, one respected commentator suggested that instead of subsidizing a new stadium, the city could just hand the Yan-

Figure 5-11 Viva Les Bleus

The World's biggest event is the Soccer World Cup. Like the Olympics, it is held every four years. In 1998, the host country was France, which in the preceding decade—and perhaps for longer—had been undergoing a crisis of identity. There were rifts in French society primarily caused by: (1) the growing globalization of the economy (for which, in France, read Americanization) and the associated usurpation or bastardization of the French language by English; (2) the inability to come to terms in the collective memory with Vichy and France's role in the Holocaust, or with resentments left over from the Algerian War; and (3) the growing complexity of the nation's racial profile.

The issue of racial conflict was particularly prominent as new immigrants from Algeria, Morocco, and elsewhere settled in the major cities where whole areas evolved into ghettos. Their situation was exacerbated by a poor economy with unemployment levels that were the highest for 50 years. Resentment towards the new immigrants was exemplified by the successes in elections of an extreme right wing political party that advocated bans on immigration and a resettlement program.

Whereas in England, Italy, Argentina, or Brazil there is an excess of passion for soccer, in France there is a lack of it. For this reason, most of the top-class French players play for clubs in other countries. It was in this relatively uninspiring context that the 32 national teams that had qualified for the 1998 World Cup finals arrived in France in 1998.

The French squad was the most ethnically diverse of the 32 teams. France emerged victorious from several early close games, and during the month of the World Cup tournament the interest of the French people grew with the success of the team. The stars of the team were the darker skinned players, but suddenly race did not seem to matter. In the space of a few weeks, under the influence of the victories, the 1998 World Cup was transformed from an international sporting event of the first order into a new social phenomenon, as the lives of French people, men and women alike (women having suddenly taken a passionate interest in the sport), were put on hold for a whole month in the summer. In helping reveal a lost or at the least half-hidden national identity, football generated an unbelievable feeling of identification with France's Blue-White-and-Red national flag.

In the semifinal game played in Paris, France defeated Croatia and there was a national outpouring of passion and nationalistic fervor. The Champs-Elysees was packed with 350,000 people exhibiting the most extravagant display of national rejoicing in living memory. The crowds were cheering, dancing, sounding horns and letting off fireworks.

Youths, many with their faces painted red, white, and blue, danced on bus shelters in the Champs-Elysees, and police, who would normally have arrested them on the spot, used traffic cones as megaphones to lead the cheers for the national team. The same scenes were repeated in cities throughout France, with the crowds chanting "Allez les Bleus!"

After the French defeated Brazil in the final in Paris four days later, the Champs-Elysees crowd was one million jamming the two mile long road and each of the 12 avenues surrounding the Arc de Triomphe. The crowds were an "ethnic rainbow" like the French team: whites, Arabs, blacks, Asians dancing arm in arm, their faces painted red, white, and blue. One member of the crowd said, "We are not just celebrating football. We are celebrating being French. Every country needs that. Better it should be after a football match, than after a war."

This was a phenomenal outpouring of joy from Parisians known for their cynicism. Everyone was kissing—everybody, blacks and whites, pensioners and small children. Never since the Liberation of Paris from German occupation in 1944 had the French people come together in such great numbers. Through the actions of 22 men kicking a piece of leather across an acre or two of grass, millions upon millions of people drew their sense of identity, their sense of pride, and their sense of themselves. This "feel good" factor was reflected in the political opinion polls where the President of France recorded his highest ever approval ratings the week after France won the World Cup.

The mood on the Champs Elysees bordered on hysteria, but it was joyous, human, witty, and warm. French people of all races exulted in their Frenchness. Most of the crowd had probably never been to a football match, but they derived substantial satisfaction from the team's achievements and identified with them as Frenchmen. The French team's soccer coach was credited as "succeeding where the politicians failed by giving back the country its self-esteem" (p. 24).[46]

For the Arab and black populations of France, it was an occasion when they could feel they belonged: when people of their own race were being feted by French people of all kinds. The multi-ethnic composition of the French national team temporarily united a nation that was habitually fragmented by race and class. One commentator noted, "The biggest losers of this World Cup were the National French. How can the leader of that party peddle his racism when France's victory has been brought about by blacks and North African players" (p. 24)?[46]

Thus, in the summer in 1998, France acquired self-confidence, won admiration for its modernity, found a new racial harmony, and discovered new role models—all through a sports team. However, the permanence of these changes was unknown. How permanent is the power of a game to transform identity, image, and national self-confidence? Did the victory crystallize a feeling that France was undeniably in the "big league" of nations and accepted as such by the rest of the world? Did the World Cup lift a long depression and show the way forward in terms of national identity? Was it a pivotal catalytic moment in the history of French society, or was it an ephemeral blip on the trend line which quickly returned to the status quo? Were political initiatives forthcoming to build upon and solidify the catalyst opportunity provided by reaction to the World Cup victory?

Sources: Dauncey & Hare,[45] Lang,[46] White,[47] MacIntyre,[48] and Lichfield[49].

kees $10 million each year. Even better, the city could pay a fixed incentive sum for each game won, with a million-dollar bonus for winning the pennant.[58] The latter proposal would tie the subsidy directly to winning, which is an important dimension of psychic income.

A similar level of subsidy, without the incentive, was initially rejected by the president of the Cuyahoga County commissioners when they were first approached to support a $130 million bond issue for the Cleveland Browns. Noting that this would cost $10 million a year for 30 years, he said, "That's a $1 million subsidy per game. I don't think the taxpayers in Cleveland want to subsidize the Browns like that" (p. 229).[39]

These sorts of ramifications emphasize the arbitrariness of the extent of subsidies negotiated by cities. Elected officials recognize the legitimacy and potential importance of psychic income, but have no scientific basis or framework to use to determine a subsidy's appropriate magnitude. The question to be assessed is, "How much should teams and/or facilities be subsidized by public funds to compensate them for the positive experiences they offer to residents in a host community who otherwise pay nothing for that experience?"

Economists have a technical term for psychic income—they call it *consumer surplus*. Consumer surplus is the surplus benefit that accrues to individuals that is not captured in ticket revenues by the team. Economists recognize that sports

Figure 5-12 Psychic Income from Cricket on the Sub-Continent

In June 1999, India played Pakistan in a one-day World Cup Cricket match played in Manchester, England. Everyday life on the sub-continent came to a halt. Tens of millions of workers stayed home. The roads were empty. Every television set, from the huge screens set up especially for the World Cup in every five-star hotel to the battered black and white set flickering at the back of the tea shop, drew its crowd like bees round a hive. A management consultant in Bombay calculated that India was over $6 billion the poorer due to World Cup cricket-inspired absenteeism.

The qualities of cricket that make it riveting to the sub-continent are its valor, elegance, charisma, defiance, team spirit, and the tantalizing flukes and freaks of fortune. For India and Pakistan, cricket is vicarious warfare: "IT'S WAR NOW" screamed the headline in Bombay's weekly *Blitz*. In a game between the two countries played in Calcutta earlier in the year, India's star batsman was hurt by a Pakistani bowler. The crowd rioted, the stadium had to be emptied, and the match was finished in front of empty stands. The association of cricketing fortunes with national fortunes is logically absurd, especially given the fluky nature of the abbreviated one-day game (normal international cricket games are five days long). But in a part of the world where national passions burn like cordite, it is unavoidable.

When Bangladesh went home early after having been knocked out of the World Cup, they still received a rapturous welcome because they did defeat Pakistan, their historical enemies, in an early game. The government declared a national holiday and Dhaka, the capitol, a city not known for its joyfulness, came alive with thousands of revelers dancing and singing. "The jubilation today," said the Prime Minister, at the grand civic reception, "reminds me of 16 December 1971 when men, women, and children came out of their homes to celebrate the victory of our independence war. Again, the whole nation has awakened for another victory."

Bangladesh did achieve a victory against Pakistan, but overall their team did poorly! The incredible reaction illustrates how poor and demoralized nations can derive remarkable psychic income and good feelings from sporting victories.

Source: Adapted from Popham[54]

teams produce a service for which some beneficiaries pay nothing, and they seek to identify what they would be willing to pay for it.

For many decades, a number of techniques have been proposed for measuring consumer surplus. This work has been spearheaded by resource economists who seek to establish an economic value for natural amenities such as parks, open space, wetlands, wildlife preserves, wilderness areas, and coastal habitats. Many taxpayers may never visit such resources but, nevertheless, derive satisfaction from knowing they exist and, thus, are supportive of expending tax dollars on them.

The preferred approach for measuring consumer surplus is the *contingent valuation method* (CVM). CVM places dollar values on goods and services not exchanged in the marketplace.[59] There is an emerging awareness that CVM is potentially a useful tool for measuring consumer surplus associated with sports teams and events. It is a survey-based approach to eliciting the level of subsidy that individuals would be prepared to pay to support a new facility for a sports team.

Another illustration of the prominent role of sport in the national psyche was "The Keane Saga," revolving around the participation of Roy Keane in the World Cup Soccer tournament held in Japan and Korea. Keane was the captain of both Ireland and the world's leading soccer club, Manchester United. He was widely recognized as one of the best half dozen players in the world. He was not only Ireland's outstanding player but also their inspirational leader.

Keane traveled with the Irish Team to Japan, but in their pre-tournament practices he forcefully and publicly criticized the team's coaches as being incompetent. They responded by banishing Keane from the team and he returned to Ireland. There was a huge outcry from the Irish public who believed their team would perform poorly without Keane. For a whole week, the major front page news headlines of both the Irish and UK national media were preempted by the Keane controversy. It dominated the nation's everyday life as "mass hysteria swept Ireland." Back in Japan, the issue divided the team.

The Irish Taoiseach (Prime Minister) intervened as an arbitrator, appealing to both sides for a reconciliation for the good of the country. A number of people, including the Taoiseach, offered to make a private plane available for the 14 hour flight back to Japan. Keane appeared on Irish television saying he wanted to play for his country. Half-a-world away the coaches threatened resignation if he was reinstated. The saga dragged on for a week "with the country holding its breath" that arbitrators would succeed in negotiating Keane back on to the team. They failed. Keane stayed home.

Source: Adapted from Caulkin & Lister[55]

To obtain valid and reliable results, the implementation of CVM requires technical expertise. However, the basic question posed to a representative sample of residents is straightforward. For example, "What is the largest sum of money you would be prepared to pay in taxes each year, rather than have the Kamikaze Klutz MLB team leave town?" The total consumer surplus (psychic income) is obtained by multiplying the consumer surplus of the average individual in a sample by the total number of taxpayers in the city. The following case illustrates this approach. A more detailed illustration is given in Figure 5-14.[60]

- CVM was used to identify the level of subsidy that would be acceptable to residents of Lexington, Kentucky, to support a new $100 million basketball arena for the University of Kentucky team, and a $10-$12 million baseball stadium which was intended to attract a minor league team to the community. A survey was mailed to a random sample of households in Lexington. It showed respondents had a relatively high level of enthusiasm for the basketball team, but that this did not translate into support for a large subsidy. The data suggested Lexington residents would support a subsidy of between $311,000 and $610,000 a year, which would service a capital cost of between $3.71 million and $7.28 million—far below the envisaged $100 million cost. The community's subsidy tolerance for the stadium was between $302,000 and $592,000, which would service a capital cost between $3.6 million and $7.06 million. Again, this was much lower than the $10-$12 million projected cost of the stadium.[61]

The CVM approach is equally applicable to a collegiate context. There is an on-going debate as to whether college athletic programs should be self-sufficient, operating independently of the university's operating budget, or whether they should be subsidized by student fees. Many students do receive psychic income from the successes of an athletic program, even if they do not attend the games. This suggests they may be prepared to subsidize those programs. The CVM approach could identify how much per student they would be prepared to pay, and this would give an indication of the level of subsidy that was appropriate.

When the appropriate amount of public subsidy has been ascertained, an alternative to subsidizing a facility would be to subsidize a franchise. This parallels the collegiate situation in that in those instances where general student fee support is forthcoming, the funds usually go to athletic programs rather than facilities. There are examples of this in professional sports, but they are not common. For example, the State of Louisiana agreed to pay the New Orleans Saints $12.5 million a year, which escalated annually in operating cash, to ensure the team's financial stability.[62] However, the preferred alternative in professional sports is to subsidize construction of a facility. There are at least five reasons for this:[19]

1. Constructing a facility may help to secure political support from labor unions, contractors, property owners, and other members of the community elite who will benefit from developing a facility.

2. Facility leases are for 20 to 30 years, so facilities are likely to be more successful than a direct subsidy in tying a team to the city.

3. A facility provides a team with potential rather than realized revenue, creating an ongoing incentive for the team to perform well and keep attendance high. Cash transfers from the city to the team would provide no incentive for team improvement.

4. If subsidies come only in the form of facilities, then they do not establish precedents for other potential subsidy recipients who do not need a facility for their activity.

5. As was noted in chapter 3, direct cash subsidies to wealthy team owners are more likely to fuel resentment from voters against politicians.

Some Conclusions

The prevailing contemporary financing model of facilities for professional sports teams is that their construction should be a private-public partnership. Discussion of the public-merit-private goods continuum at the end of chapter 3 indicates this is consistent with the definition of merit goods. This suggests that such facilities should be subsidized to the extent that benefits to the whole community are perceived to accrue. In chapters 4 and 5, these spillover benefits have been classified and discussed in five categories: (a) direct economic impact, (b) increased community visibility, (c) enhanced community image, (d) stimulation of other development, and (e) psychic income.

To this point, justifications for public subsidy have been almost exclusively externally overrated. That is, they have focused on the direct and indirect influence of facilities on encouraging individuals or entities from outside a community to in-

Figure 5-14 Psychic Income Value of the Pittsburgh Penguins

In October 1998, the Pittsburgh Penguins of the National Hockey League (NHL) declared Chapter 11 bankruptcy and were at risk of moving to another city or being disbanded by the NHL. The Bankruptcy Judge issued a permanent injunction against moving the Penguins to another city, since they "are woven into the fabric of the city and county and surrounding counties."

This situation provided a good context in which to undertake a CVM analysis of the value of the team to the community. There was no suggestion that a new arena be built for the Penguins, so the study focused exclusively on what the Penguins were worth to Pittsburgh. If new owners could not be found who would agree to keep the team in Pittsburgh, then an alternate scenario was that the Penguins could become publicly owned by the taxpayers. It was this scenario which was presented to a random sample of households in Pittsburgh. The mail survey posed the following questions:

> If the city of Pittsburgh were to buy the team, it would never leave Pittsburgh. But in order for the city to buy the team, pay off its debts, and challenge for the Stanley Cup, taxpayer money will be needed. One estimate is that each Pittsburgh household would have to pay $TAX each year in higher city taxes.

Four $TAX amounts ($1, $5, $10, and $25) were randomly assigned.

Then respondents were asked the discrete-choice willingness-to-pay question— "Would you be willing to pay $TAX each year out of your own household budget in higher city taxes to help keep the Penguins in Pittsburgh?"—and were given three response categories: "Yes," "No," and "I don't know." All respondents were then asked the open-ended willingness-to-pay question, "What is the most you would be willing to pay out of your own household budget each year in higher city taxes to keep the Penguins in Pittsburgh?" They were presented with the following "payment card" categories to choose in response to the question: "Zero," "Between $0.01 and $4.99," "Between $5 and $14.99," "Between $15 and $29.99," "Between $30 and $49.99," "Between $50 and $75," and "More than $75."

The data suggested that Pittsburgh residents were prepared to pay between $1.9 and $5.3 million per year to subsidize purchase of the team. When this was capitalized by using present discounted values, Pittsburgh residents valued the team at between $17.2 and $48.3 million. These amounts represent the lower and upper boundaries of the psychic income value of the team to Pittsburgh residents.

A consortium of local investors ultimately bought the team for $85 million, so the CVM values represented between 20% and 57% of the team's market value. The cost of building a new arena averages $223 million (Table 3-2). If these psychic income values are transposed to that context, then it suggests Pittsburgh residents would be prepared to subsidize between 8% and 22% of a new arena's cost in return for the psychic income benefits they receive. Although this is lower than the 39% average public subsidy of recent new arenas, there are a number of new arenas where the public subsidy does fall within this range (Table 3-2).

Source: Adapted from Johnson, Groothuis & Whitehead [60]

vest in them. The emphasis has been on their contribution to economic development. The first four of these five categories encapsulated this thrust. The prevailing paradigm is illustrated in Figure 5-15.

Figure 5-15 indicates that economic development may be fostered by the spending of visitors to a community whose reason for being there is directly related to the games played in the facility. Chapter 4 described the conditions under which this legitimately occurs and presented examples. It was concluded that economic impacts associated with major league teams are likely to be small, but in some other contexts (e.g., megaevents) they could be substantial.

The notion that economic development will result from increased community visibility and enhanced community image may be intuitively appealing, but it is a superficial nexus with scant empirical evidence to support it. Visibility that increases external awareness and positive image are both necessary preliminary stages of a purchase or location decision, but there are a profusion of other factors that enter into it. Neither of these attributes changes the underlying cost, labor, transportation, incentive, quality-of-life, and market factors that influence business location decisions. Any relationship between visibility and image and economic development appears to be tenuous at best.

The discussion earlier in this chapter suggests the argument that major facilities stimulate other development is convincing in only a very few cases (e.g., downtown redevelopment in Indianapolis and Cleveland). In these rare instances of perceived success, the sports facilities have been only one part of a comprehensive plan. The sports facilities themselves were not sufficient to stimulate a level of proximate, complementary, or general development that justified the magnitude of public subsidy invested in them.

Many studies have been reported that empirically explored the relationship between sports facility construction and economic development.[63, 64, 65, 66, 67, 68] Their findings are remarkably consistent. None have found any statistically positive correlation between new sports venue construction and measures of economic impact.[19] Indeed, the most recent of these studies reported that new stadiums and sports teams actually reduced per capita income in the host communities.[68] The explanation for this was discussed in chapter 4. The leisure expenditures captured by the stadium/team were not new, they merely displaced previous leisure expenditures those individuals made in the community.[19] Because many team players and owners do not live in the community, there is substantial leakage, whereas the earlier leisure expenditures were at businesses where the leakage was much smaller. In general, sports are too small a component of any economy to lead economic changes or to propel large-scale redevelopment efforts.[2]

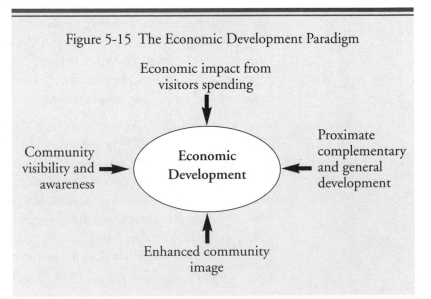

Figure 5-15 The Economic Development Paradigm

Economic impact from visitors spending

Community visibility and awareness

Economic Development

Proximate complementary and general development

Enhanced community image

Hence, the discussion in chapters 4 and 5 suggests that justification for public subsidy that relies on the emergence of economic development as the source of reasonable return for the public investment usually is flawed and unconvincing. In the context of facilities for professional sports facilities, the paradigm illustrated in Figure 5-15 generally has been found to be vacuous.

This has caused focus of the argument for public subsidy to be redefined away from economic impacts and economic development towards psychic income benefits. This is the new frontier. This redefinition enables decision makers to retain their integrity while supporting public subsidy of a facility. It is an alternative to the contorted and embarrassing shenanigans to which many of them have resorted to on this point. Instead of relying on the wistful "spin" that external sources will invest in the community as a justification for public subsidy of facilities, emphasis is shifting to measuring the benefits that accrue to existing residents living within the community. By shamelessly using flawed economic rationales to justify subsidies of major facilities, elected officials and other community elites are characterized as untrustworthy, manipulative charlatans with an agenda to sell. If a new psychic income paradigm is used for justification and scientific measurement is used to appraise the value of the psychic income and, hence, the subsidy invested, then these proponents could reposition themselves as responsible keepers of the public trust.[22]

The new psychic income paradigm is shown in Figure 5-16. Instead of focusing on visitors' economic impacts, this suggests that their important contribution is an increase in the "excitement quotient" in a host community (or area of it) that occurs when a large influx of visitors comes to it. Sometimes an ambiance of vibrance and vitality is created by a temporary influx of sports fans excitedly anticipating a game. This may be contagious and temporarily transferred to locals.

Increased community visibility may be a source of pride to residents who derive satisfaction from their community's name being widely disseminated across the nation. It reinforces their belief, and the belief of others, that they live in a community of stature. Similar emotions may be forthcoming from residents' perceptions of enhanced image stemming from being a major league or first-tier city and from living in a city that demonstrates to the rest of the world a positive "can-do attitude" towards major projects. Psychic income also may be derived from a community's effort to resuscitate a deteriorating area. The notion that "something is being done" may alleviate the collective community conscience, irrespective of the degree to which the outcome is successful.

Finally, there are the more obvious intrinsic dimensions of psychic income discussed in the previous section of this chapter. Sports franchises offer a forum for community excitement that expands to a sort of mass community ecstasy when they are successful. Emotional excitement stems from "the love affair" with the team, the tangible focus it offers for social bonding, and the enhanced collective self-esteem that emanates from a winning or widely respected team.

This shift in paradigms leads to the conclusion that instead of investing funds in commissioning flawed economic impact studies, proponents of public subsidies would be better advised to commission studies that measure the psychic income that residents ascribe to a sports team or event. This is likely to be substantial and to provide a more legitimate underpinning for subsidy of a sports facility. Consider the following example:

• For a stadium that receives a subsidy of $250 million in a metropolitan area with a population of five million, per capita costs are $50, and the per capita annualized cost of servicing the debt (interest, plus principal) to finance the stadium is $5. It does not vastly stretch credibility to argue that more than 50% of residents perceive they receive $5 worth of psychic income from the presence of a team. In such a scenario, it seems likely that a majority of citizens would vote in support of this subsidy in a referendum.[66]

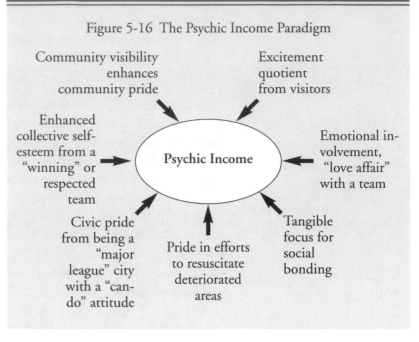

Figure 5-16 The Psychic Income Paradigm

Summary

The tendency to seek to justify investments in sports facilities on the basis of their economic impacts of visitation to them is myopic because there are other potential sources of spillover benefits. They are discussed under four major headings: increased community visibility, enhanced community image, stimulation of other development, and psychic income.

Major sports teams guarantee a significant amount of media coverage, providing considerable visibility for the communities in which they are located. There is an implication that this will aid recruitment of relocating businesses and, thus, lead to enhancement of a city's tax base. However, there is no empirical evidence that media visibility *per se* results in this desired sequence of events. In the case of megaevents, it does seem possible that visibility may translate into economic increases in tourism that extend beyond the period of the event.

Image traditionally referred to a mental reconstruction of a place, but this has now been expanded to embrace the perceived reputation or character of a place. Even though the premise has obvious flaws, there is much public sympathy for the adage that a place cannot be a major league city if it does not have a major league franchise. The team is positioned as being symptomatic of a city's character and as defining external perceptions of the city. Some may consider a sports team as a symbolic embodiment of the city as a whole. Thus, if a city successfully negotiates and implements a major sports event or franchise agreement, it may convey an aura of competence upon the city's leadership. Conversely, if a city loses a franchise, the loss may create the impression that the city's business and political leadership is incompetent.

Two major principles are crucial to the ability of major sports facilities to effectively anchor a downtown redevelopment project and attract additional development to it. First is the principle of a threshold level of cumulative attraction. This states that to persuade people to go downtown, there has to be a critical mass of complementary attractions. A sports facility alone will be inadequate. Second is the related principle that the sports facility be part of an integrated, coherent, master plan for downtown redevelopment, rather than an ad hoc initiative that it is vaguely hoped may stimulate others to locate nearby.

The types of development that proponents envisage may be stimulated by large-scale sports facilities can be classified under three headings: proximate development, complementary development, and general development. Proximate development is promoted when sports facilities are conceptualized as being one part of an integrated development package for an area. Complementary development refers either to the construction of additional facilities as part of the responsibility for hosting a megaevent or to the upgrading or installation of businesses as a result of the demand for their services that is directly created by a sports facility or event. General development is associated with the belief that the media visibility, big-league status, and image derived from a sports team will attract development that is not necessarily either proximate or complementary.

Psychic income is the emotional and psychological benefit residents perceive they receive, even though they do not physically attend sports events. Such people may follow their team through the media and take pride in it. In this sense, a sports team is an investment in the emotional infrastructure of a community. Sports teams and events provide a tangible focus for building community consciousness and social bonding. When a team is successful, benefits often accrue to the collective morale of all residents, and the collective self-esteem is enhanced.

Economists have developed measurement techniques that can be used to place a dollar value on psychic income. This value can be used to guide decision makers on the magnitude of public subsidy that would be appropriate for a facility. The empirical evidence generally does not support the prevailing belief that investments and expenditures made by businesses and individuals from outside a community as a consequence of a sports team or event are sufficient to justify the level of subsidy being made by communities. This economic paradigm has generally been found to be vacuous. The new psychic income paradigm appears likely to provide a more legitimate underpinning for these subsidies.

References

1. Schimmel, K. S. (1995). Growth politics, urban development, and sports stadium construction in the United States: A case study. In J. Bale & O. Moen (Eds.), *The stadium and the city* (pp. 111-155). Keele, Staffordshire, England: Keele University Press.
2. Rosentraub, M. S. (1997). *Major league losers: The real cost of sports and who's paying for it.* New York: Basic Books.
3. Corliss, R. (1992, August 24). Build it and they ~~will~~ might come. *Time, 139,* 50-52.
4. Danielson, M. N. (1997). *Home team: Professional sports and the American metropolis.* Princeton, NJ: Princeton University Press.
5. Thurow, R. (1995, August 18). NFL's arrival stirs Jacksonville's conscience. *The Wall Street Journal,* p. B8.
6. Schaffer, W. A., & Davidson, L. S. (1984). *Economic impact of the Falcons on Atlanta: 1984.* Georgia Institute of Technology.
7. Baade, R. A., & Dye, R. F. (1988, July). An analysis of the economic rationale for public subsidization of sports stadiums. *The Annals of Regional Science, 22*(2), 37-47.

8. Richie, B. J. R. (1989, June 3). *Mega sporting events and their role in the development and promotion of international tourism destinations.* Keynote address to the 4th annual conference of the North American Society of Sports Management.

9   Van der Lee, P., & Williams, J. (1986). The Grand Prix and tourism. In J. P. A. Burns, J. H. Hatch, & T. J. Mules, (Eds.), *The Adelaide Grand Prix.* Adelaide: The Centre for South Australian Economic Studies.

10. Steiner, S. (1999, March 18). Olympic leap into the hearts of tourists. *The Times,* 14.

11. Newman, P. W. G. (1989). The impact of the America's Cup on Freemantle-an insider's view. In G. S. Syme, B. J. Shaw, D. M. Fenton, & W. S. Mueller (Eds.), *The planning and evaluation of hallmark events* (pp. 46-58). Aldershot, England: Avebury.

12. White, A. (2001). Sporting a new image? Sport-based regeneration strategies as a means of enhancing the image of the city tourist destination. In C. Gratton & I. P. Henry (Eds.), *Sport in the city* (pp. 127-148). New York: Routledge.

13. Kotler, P., Haidler, D. H., & Rein, I. (1993). *Marketing places: Attracting investment, industry and tourism to cities, states and nations.* New York: Free Press.

14. Burns, J. P. A., & Mules, T. J. (1986). A framework for the analysis of major special events. In J. P. A. Burns, J. H. Hatch, & T. J. Mules (Eds.), *The Adelaide Grand Prix.* Adelaide: The Centre for South Australian Economic Studies.

15. Shropshire, K. L. (1995). *The sports franchise game.* Philadelphia: University of Pennsylvania Press.

16. Schimmel, K. S. (2001). Sport matters: urban regime theory and urban regeneration in the late-capitalist era. In C. Gratton & I. P. Henry (Eds.), *Sport in the city* (pp. 259-277). New York: Routledge.

17. Lavalle, N. (1995, July 23). Go for the win. *The Dallas Morning News,* 1J, 10J.

18. Brown, C., & Paul, D. M. (1999). Local organized interests and the 1996 Cincinnati sports stadia tax referendum. *Journal of Sport and Social Issues, 23*(2), 218-237.

19. Siegfried, J., & Zimbalist, A. (2000). The economics of sports facilities and their communities. *Journal of Economic Perspectives, 14*(3), 95-114.

20. Fulton, W. (1988, March). Politicians who chase after sports franchises may get less than they pay for. *Governing,* 2, 34-40.

21. Euchner, C. C. (1993). *Playing the field: Why sports teams move and cities fight to keep them.* Baltimore: The Johns Hopkins University Press.

22. Hamilton, B. W., & Kahn, P. (1997). Baltimore's Camden Yards ballparks. In R. G. Noll & A. Zimbalist (Eds.), *Sports, jobs and taxes* (pp. 245-281). Washington, DC: Brookings Institution.

23. Riess, S. A. (1989). *City games: The evolution of American urban society and the use of sports.* Urbana, IL: University of Illinois Press.

24. Johnson, A. T. (1991, November). Local government, minor league baseball, and economic development strategies. *Economic Development Quarterly, 5*(4), 313-324.

25. Jacobson, L. (2002, May 11). Three Rivers is down, Pittsburgh looks up. *National Journal.*

26. Essex, S., & Chalkeley, B. (1998). Olympic Games: Catalyst of urban change. *Leisure Studies,* 17, 187-206.

27. Tookey, K., & Veal, A. J. (2000). *The Olympic Games: A social science perspective.* New York: CABI Publishing.

28. Benfield, F. K. Ferris, J., & Vorzanger, N. (2001). *Solving sprawl: Models of smart growth in communities across America.* Washington, DC: National Resources Defense Council.

29. Glier, R. (2001, May 14-20). Turner Field yet to spark retail boom. *SportsBusiness Journal,* 22.

30. Schoenfeld, B. (2000, September 4-10). City runs first-rate ballgame. *SportsBusiness Journal,* 1, 57.

31. Li, M., Hofacre, S., & Mahony, D. (2001). *Economics of sport.* Morgantown, WV: Fitness Information Technology.

32. Greenberg, M. J., & Gray, J. T. (1996). *The stadium game.* Marquette University Law School: National Sports Law Institute.

33. Spanberg, E. (2001a, May 21-27). Airport took off when stock cars did. *SportsBusiness Journal,* 26.

34. Spanberg, E. (2001b, May 21-27). Entire region hears NASCAR's roar. *SportsBusiness Journal,* 25, 30.

35. Cavin, C. (2001, May 21-27). Big-leaguers to midgets, motorsports running flat out in Indy. *SportsBusiness Journal,* 26.

36. Hinde, S. (1994, October 30). City of gloom flourishes in northern boom. *The Sunday Times,* 12.

37. Rufflenach, G. (1995, October 30). The outlook: Atlanta hopes Games yield lasting benefits. *Wall Street Journal*, A1.

38. Lipsky, R. (1981). *How we play the game: Why sports dominate American life.* Boston: Beacon.

39. Morgan, J. (1997). *Glory for sale.* Baltimore: Bancroft Press.

40. Samuel, M. (2002, May 1). Why television must beware of making a monkey of fans. *The Times,* 33.

41. Lipsky, R. (1979). Political implications of sports team symbolism. *Politics Soc.,* 9, 61-88.

42. Guzzo, G. (2001, August 12). A triumph of public opinion. *The Denver Post,* 22.

43. Deford, F. (1996, September 9). Why cowboys became kings. *Newsweek,* 12, 62.

44. Weiner, J. (1999). *Stadium games: Fifty years of big league greed and bush league boondoggles.* Minneapolis, MN: University of Minnesota Press.

45. Quirk, J. P. & Fort, R. D. (1992). *Pay dirt: The business of professional team sports.* Princeton, NJ: Princeton University Press.

46. Bronstein, S. (1990, September 23). World recognition gives Atlantans a new sense of pride in their city. *The Atlanta Journal and Constitution,* R12.

47. James, O. (1997, June 8). The serotonin society. *The Observer,* 18.

48. Price, S. L. (2001, April 16). A good man in Africa. *Sports Illustrated,* 94, 56-59.

49. Dauncey, H., & Hare, G. (1999). *France and the 1998 World Cup.* Portland, OR: Frank Cass.

50. Lang, K. (1998, July 13). Soccer-mad France relives its crazy Liberation days. *The Sunday Times,* 24.

51 White, J. (1998, June). Why the World Cup matters. *Air Canada En Route,* 42-57.

52. MacIntyre, B. (1998, July 10). Paris parties as Croat supermen falter. *The Times,* 7.

53. Lichfield, J. (1998, July 12). For once united. *Independent on Sunday,* 19.

54. Popham, P. (1999, June 7). Bats replace guns in war for heart of Asian sub-continent. *The Independent,* 6.

55. Caulkin, G., & Lister, D. (2002, May 30). The Keane saga. *The Times,* 21.

56. Samuel, M. (2002b, June 12). France pays the price for lack of passion. *The Times,* 4.

57. Bremner, C. (2002, June 12). France mourns early exit of champions. *The Times,* 14.

58. Noll, R.G. (1996, April 11). Wild pitch. *The New York Times,* A25.

59. Loomis, J. B., & Walsh, R. G. (1997). *Recreation economic decisions: Comparing benefits and costs* (2nd ed.). State College, PA: Venture Publishing.

60. Johnson, B. K., Groothus, P. A., & Whitehead, J. C. (2001). The value of public goods generated by a Major League sports team. *Journal of Sports Economics, 2*(1), 6-21.

61. Johnson, B. K., & Whitehead, J. C. (2000). Value of public goods from sports stadiums: The CVM approach. *Contemporary Economics Policy, 18*(1), 48-58.

62. Foster, M. (2001, July 10). New Orleans paying Saints $12.5 million to stay. *USA Today,* B1.

63. Baade, R., & Dye, R. (1990). The impact of stadiums and professional sports on metropolitan area development. *Growth and Change, 21*(2), 1-14.

64. Rosentraub, M. (1994). Sport and downtown development strategy. *Journal of Urban Affairs, 16*(3), 228-239.

65. Baade, R. (1996). Professional sports as catalysts for metropolitan economic development. *Journal of Urban Affairs, 18*(1), 1-17.

66. Noll, R., & Zimbalist, A. (1997). The economic impact of sports teams and facilities. In R. G. Noll & A. Zimbalist (Eds.), *Sports, jobs and taxes* (pp. 55-91). Washington, DC: The Brookings Institution.

67. Walden, M. (1997, October/November). Don't play ball. *Carolina Journal,* 23.

68. Coates, D., & Humphreys, B. (1999). The growth effects of sport franchises, stadia and arenas. *Journal of Policy Analysis and Management, 14*(4), 601-624.

Photo courtesy University of Oregon Athletic Department

Chapter Six

Sources of Public Sector Funding

Over the last half-century, local governments have played a major role in building and operating sports facilities. Cities and counties often take the lead and, in many cases, exclusive responsibility for financing the development of sports facilities from big-league ballparks to community golf courses. The financing may be used to subsidize some combination of facility construction, infrastructure development, and operations.

As shown in chapter 3, the trend for local governments to assume primary fiscal and operating responsibility for major league facilities reached its peak during the 1970s and 1980s, a period in which many cities financed all or most of the cost of new stadiums and arenas. In recent years, teams and owners have paid a progressively larger share of the construction costs, but local government contributions still involve a considerable commitment of public tax resources, often over $200 million for new stadiums and arenas. In addition, there has been a tendency for government entities to offer franchises generous lease arrangements that also constitute a substantial subsidy to a franchise's operations.

The money used by government jurisdictions for these subsidies comes from a variety of different taxes. The chapter begins with a discussion of the property tax and the sales tax, because these are the traditional sources of revenue used by local and state governments to fund sporting amenities. These two forms of taxation are sometimes called "hard" taxes because (a) the burden of payment falls on all or a significant proportion of taxpayers in a jurisdiction; and (b) these taxes are *harder* to implement because they commonly require voter approval. The more general the tax proposed for a sports project, the broader the potential opposition is likely to be. The second section of the chapter discusses an array of "soft" taxes. These include the hotel-motel, or "bed" tax; taxes on rental cars; cigarette and liquor, or "sin" taxes; and the use of a tax on players' incomes. These are called soft taxes because they are borne by a select and relatively small proportion of taxpayers and are, therefore, politically easier to levy. These soft taxes are growing in importance in response to increased voter resistance to approving broad-based taxes for sports facilities.

Although hard and soft taxes provide the revenues necessary to pay the public's share of the construction costs, the financial instruments commonly used by cities and counties to actually finance new sport facilities are called *bonds*. The final section of the chapter provides an in-depth discussion of the various types of bonds available for sport facility construction. Bonds are long-term debt instruments that allow local governments to borrow *in advance* (typically from a bank) the money needed to underwrite construction costs. The revenues subsequently collected from the imposition of various taxes are pledged to repay the bonds over an extended period of time, typically from 15 to 30 years. The long-term repayment arrangement allows local governments issuing the bonds to pay off the construction debt in annual installments, thereby avoiding the need for large tax increases.

General Property Tax   **Hard Taxes**

For generations, the general property tax has been the backbone of local government finance. More than 96% of property tax revenues go to local governments (e.g., cities, counties, school districts). The property tax is to local government what personal and corporate income taxes are to the federal government. There has been some decline in its dominance, but it remains the preeminent source of revenue at the local level. In 1932, property taxes provided local governments with 97% of their total revenues.[1] Today, the aggregate figure has declined, but it still remains at approximately 70%, with the specific percentage varying quite substantially across jurisdictions.[2]

The dependence of local governments on the property tax stems from a lack of alternative revenue-generating options for most cities and counties. The potential of other taxes is limited. Local taxation of income, sales, or business could deter new business expansion and ultimately bring about shrinkage of the tax base. However, real property is immobile. Only a very substantial tax on land and buildings would induce people to move from their homes and places of work. Retail businesses must locate close to customers, and once committed, manufacturing establishments tend to stay because even severe property taxes represent only a small part of their overall operating costs. In short, real property offers a dependable base upon which local governments can safely levy taxes.

Theoretically, the property tax is consistent with both the ability-to-pay and the benefit principles of taxation.[3] To the extent that the value of property owned increases with income, those with greater ability to pay will pay higher taxes. Property tax serves as a benefit tax because its revenues are used to finance local government expenditures on services that benefit property owners and increase the value of their properties.

All property owners are required to pay the property tax; but churches, charitable organizations, educational institutions, and other governmental entities such as state and federal institutions are excluded from paying the tax in almost every state. Classes of exempt property also may include cemeteries (42 states), hospitals (40 states), and historic properties (13 states).[3] These exemptions can inflict

Figure 6-1 Types of property that may be subjected to taxation

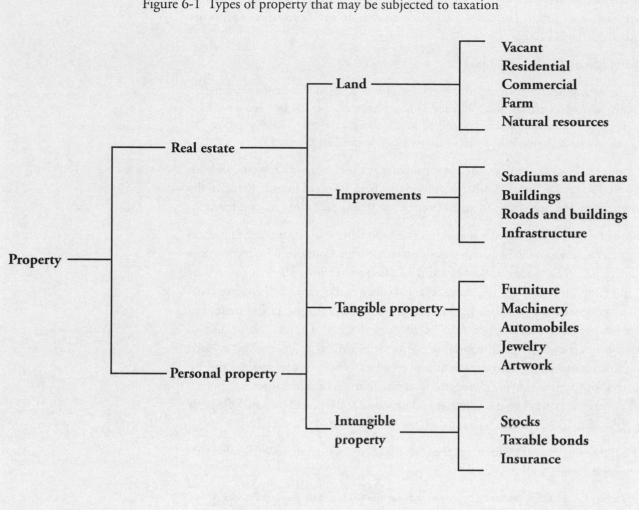

substantial financial problems on some jurisdictions. For example, a major state university located in a small city requires extensive support services from the city but provides no taxes to pay for those services.

Figure 6-1 shows a taxonomy of the types of property that may be subjected to taxation. The fundamental distinction is the difference between real property and personal property. Most variation across jurisdictions as to which of the property elements shown in Figure 6-1 are taxed occurs in the personal property category, which includes everything that can be owned but that is not real property. It is difficult for appraisers to locate, inventory, validate, and value both tangible and intangible personal property. Because of these difficulties, it has been noted that personal property frequently "is exempt by law; sometimes, by local practice. Seldom is taxation complete" (p. 292).[4]

Estimates of the value of real property are called *assessments*. The task of determining values of properties is assigned to an assessor, who is either appointed or elected. In most states, responsibility for assessing and collecting local property taxes falls to the county tax assessor. It is the assessor's responsibility to list on the tax rolls each parcel of taxable property within the jurisdiction and, on a specified date each year (often January 1), to place a value on each parcel in conformity with assessment rules.

Current market value is defined as

> the most probable price at which the property would be transferred in a competitive and open market under all conditions requisite to a fair sale between a willing buyer and a willing seller, neither of whom is under any compulsion to buy or sell and both having knowledge of relevant facts at the time of sale.[5] (p. 16)

A state's tax law may or may not assess property at the current market rate. Indeed, in only 19 states is assessed value supposed to reflect 100% of market value. In the other states, the practice is to assess property at below prevailing market levels.

Some of the states define assessed value as a fixed percentage of market value. Examples range from 70% in Connecticut to 10% in Louisiana. In some states (New York, New Jersey, Delaware, and Maine), the ratio is allowed to vary by local taxing unit. In 14 other states, the assessment ratio varies by property class. Such tax systems are usually referred to as *classified*. For example, in Colorado, residential properties are supposed to be assessed at 15% of market value and all other properties at 29%. Similarly, in Arizona, residential properties are assessed at a lower rate (10%) than is agricultural property (16%) or commercial and industrial properties (25%). Tennessee assesses commercial and industrial properties at 40% of market value, all other real property at 25%, and personal property at 30% of market value.[19]

The following example illustrates the consequence of using an assessed value that is different from market value:

> In Kay County, Oklahoma, the assessment ratio is 0.11. Thus, if a home is valued at $80,000, its assessed value for tax purposes in that county is $8,800. A tax rate of $5 per $100 assessed value would mean the homeowner would pay annual taxes of $440 to the county.

The intent of this practice is to create an illusion. Because the assessed value of the property is below market value, property owners may believe that they are getting a concession and, therefore, be less inclined to challenge the assessor's judgment. In fact, the actual tax payment made by the homeowner is likely to be the same irrespective of whether all properties in a jurisdiction are assessed at 100% or some lesser percentage of their market value.

Under normal circumstances, the overall assessment ratio has little impact on absolute property-tax burdens because assessment levels can be counteracted by differences in the statutory tax rate. For instance, suppose a municipality seeks $5 million from its property tax and the market value of taxable property is $80 million. If the assessment ratio is 100%, a property tax rate of $6.25 per $100 assessed value will yield the desired money. If the assessment ratio is 50%, a property tax rate of $12.50 per $100 assessed value will produce the desired revenue. Low assessment ratios will produce compensating statutory rate adjustments.[4]

The aggregate value of all the assessed property within a particular jurisdiction is referred to as the *tax base*. Once the tax base has been determined by assessment, the local government sets a *tax rate* to meet its revenue needs. Tax rates are usually expressed in terms of dollars and cents per $100 assessed value. The function of the property tax is to fill in the gap between the revenues that an agency's budget requires and the amount that the agency expects to derive from other local, state, and federal sources. Thus, tax rates are established by dividing the local government's budget (projected expenditures for one year) less anticipated income from nonproperty sources (e.g., sales taxes, fees, fines, federal and state funds) by the total assessed value of property. For example, assume that the total assessed value of property in a community is $400,000,000 and the tax revenue needed by a government unit amounts to $5,000,000:

(a) tax rate = $5,000,000/ $400,000,000 = 0.0125

This may be expressed as a tax rate of $1.25 per $100 assessed value. The relationship between the budget and total assessed value always determines the tax rate. For example, if a city increases its budget expenditures and the assessed value total remains stable, the tax rate goes up:

(b) tax rate = $6,000,000 / $400,000,000 = 0.0150

Conversely, if the assessed value or tax base goes up and the city budget remains the same, the tax rate will go down:

(c) tax rate = $5,000,000 / $500,000,000 = 0.0100

When the tax rate has been established, it is a simple matter to determine the amount of taxes that will be collected from individual homeowners. The calculation involves multiplying the approved tax rate by the assessed value of taxable property:

Tax Rate X Assessed Value = Tax Revenue due from property

Thus, if a property has an assessed value of $100,000 and a tax rate of $1.25 per $100 of assessed value, then the annual tax to be paid by the property owner would be $1,250. Although the tax rate most frequently is expressed in terms of dollars and cents per $100 assessed value, it is expressed in some states as a millage rate in terms of mills per dollar of assessed value. A *mill* is $0.001. Thus, a millage tax of 1 mill per $1 assessed value is equivalent to a tax of 10¢ per $100 assessed value or $1 per $1,000 assessed value. Tax calculations using both of these approaches are shown in Figure 6-2.

Property owners are obligated to pay their annual tax bill. If they fail to do so, then a tax lien can be attached to the property. This gives a jurisdiction the power to have the property sold and the proceeds from the sale applied to delinquent taxes, penalties, and accrued interest. However, if they believe the tax is too high, property owners have the right to protest and appeal the value at which their property is appraised for tax purposes. Each state establishes appeal procedures that jurisdictions must follow, and these are publicly announced. The procedures that property owners in Brazos County, Texas, must follow, for example, are specified in the announcement reproduced in Figure 6-3, which appeared in the local newspaper.

The newspaper headline in Figure 6-4 announces that the city council of College Station, Texas, decided not to raise the property tax in the coming year. Most residents in the community are likely to interpret this as meaning that the council is exercising tight cost controls and that residents' annual property tax payments will be the same next year as they were for this year. Claims of this nature are made frequently or implied by local elected officials and supportive media. However, such claims are likely to be grossly misleading because they ignore increases in the tax base. Later, in the body of the text in Figure 6-4, the reporter notes that the city budget is actually $5.2 million higher (9.6%) for the next year. Further, a city official acknowledges that if the unchanged proposed tax rate is approved, it would mean higher property taxes for residents whose homes have increased in value.

Figure 6-4 and the tax rate example (c) on the previous page illustrate how it is possible in communities where land values are escalating for a government body to announce, rather magnanimously, to taxpayers its plan to reduce the tax rate. Actually, its claim often is based on the assessed value of property having grown so much that the council can afford to reduce the tax rate substantially without losing any property tax revenue. Hence, even when reductions in the tax rate are announced, it is probable that the actual tax that the property owner is required to pay will increase.

To counter the possibility that taxpayers may be misled in this way, some states require all taxing jurisdictions to announce publicly their proposed *effective* tax for the coming year and to hold public hearings to discuss it before approving it. The effective tax involves reporting the total tax change that will take place. A typical announcement is shown in Table 6-1. It reports to taxpayers that, although the tax rate in the coming year remains the same, the taxes on an average home will increase by 10.56% compared with the taxes of the previous year because of the increases in the appraised value of homes.

Revenues collected from the taxes that cities and counties levy usually are placed into the general fund of the respective government units. The general fund consists of revenue from multiple sources including property tax, sales tax, user fees, fines, and intergovernmental transfers. The general fund finances almost all government services including sports facilities and programs.

Figure 6-3 Property tax protest and appeals procedures

Property Tax Protest and Appeals Procedures

The law gives property owners the right to protest actions concerning their property tax appraisals. You may follow these appeal procedures if you have a concern about:
· the value placed on your property
· any exemptions that may apply to you
· the cancellation of an agricultural appraisal
· the taxable status of your property
· the local governments which should he taxing your property
· any action taken by the appraisal district that adversely affected you.

Informal Review

Call or meet with staff appraisers at 1421 Waterfield #A101 (409-555-8731) Monday-Friday 8:00 am~5 pm. Appraisal Review Board policy requires that you meet with a staff appraiscr before the date of your hearing.

Review by the Appraisal Review Board

If you can't resolve your problem informally with the appraisal district staff; you may have your case heard by the appraisal review board (ARB). You must file a timely Notice of Protest by June 12. The ARB is an independent board of citizens that reviews problems with appraisal or other concerns listed above. It has the power to order the appraisal district to make the necessary changes to solve problems. If you file a written request for an ARB hearing (called a Notice of Protest) before the deadline, the ARB will set your case for a hearing. You'll receive written notice of the time, date, and place of the hearing. The hearing will be informal. You and the appraisal district representative will be asked to present evidencc about your case. The ARB will make its decision based on the evidence presented. You can get a copy of a protect form from the appraisal district office at 1421 Waterfield #Al01, Bryan, TX, or call 409-555-8731.

Note: You shouldn't try to contact ARB members outside of the hearing. The law requires ARB members to sign an affidavit saying that they haven't talked about your case before the ARB hears it.

Review by the District Court

After it decides your case, the ARB must send you a copy of its order by certified mail. If you're not satisfied with the decision, you have the right to appeal to district court. If you choose to go to court, you must start the process by filing a petition within 45 days of the date you receive the ARB's order. If the appraisal district has appraised your property at $1,000,000 or more, you must file a notice of appear with the chief appraiser within 15 days of the date you receive the ARB's order.

More Information

You can get more information by contacting your appraisal district at 1421 Waterfield #Al01, Bryan, TX (409-555-8731). You can also get a pamphlet describing how to prepare a protest from the appraisal district or from the State Comptroller's Property Tax Division at P.O. Box 13528, Austin, TX 78711-3528.

Deadline for Filing Protests with the ADD

Usual Deadline

On or before May 31 (or 30 days after a notice of appraised value was mailed to you, whichever is later). THE DEADLINE FOR FILING A PROTEST IS JUNE 12 FOR BRAZOS COUNTY APPRAISAL DISTRICT. Late protests are allowed if you miss the usual deadline for good cause. Good cause is some reason beyond your control, like a medical emergency. The ARB decides whether you have good cause.

Late protests are duc the day before the appraisal review board approves records for the year. Contact your appraisal district for more information. THE BRAZOS COUNTY APPRAISAL REVIEW BOARD EXPECTS TO APPROVE THE RECORDS BY JULY 18.

Special Deadlines

For change of use (the appraisal district informed you that you are losing agricultural appraisal because you changed the use of your land), the deadline is before the 30th day after the notice of the determination was mailed to you.

For ARB changes (the ARB has informed you of a change that increases your tax liability and the change didn't result from a protest you filed), the deadline is before the 30th day after notice of the determination was mailed to you.

If you believe the appraisal district or ARB should have sent you a notice and did not, you may file a protest until the day before taxes become delinquent (usually February 1). The ARB decides whether it will hear your case based on evidence about whether a required notice was mailed to you.

Figure 6-4 Property taxes may increase without raising the tax rate

Budget leaves property tax alone

By YVONNE SALCE Eagle staff writer

CS plan won't raise property tax rate

College Station residents won't see a property tax increase in the proposed budget thanks to the enormous amount of growth in the city, said the assistant finance director.

The College Station City Council received the city's proposed budget at Wednesday's workshop meeting. The $60.5 million proposal, which includes a number of additional staff members, is about $5.2 million more than the city budgeted last year. Charles Cryan, assistant city finance director, said the property tax rate of 44.50 cents per $100 property value will probably remain the same.

But because that rate is 5 percent above the effective tax rate of 42.38 cents per $100 property value, a public hearing must be called, he said.

If the proposed tax rate of 44.50 cents is approved, Cryan said, it would mean higher property taxes for residents whose homes have increased in value.

The effective tax rate is the rate that, using current property values, will generate the same amount of tax revenues as last year's tax rate.

Under Texas law, any increase of 3 percent or more above the effective tax rate requires a public hearing. The council voted to hold a public hearing Aug. 25 on the proposed budget. At that time, the council is expected to schedule a public hearing for the proposed tax rate, also call the ad valorem tax rate.

"There's no ad valorem tax increase because other revenue streams are growing fast enough," Cryan said, listing sales taxes as the big revenue maker. He said sales tax revenues are up $150,000 more than expected. For the coming year, Cryan estimates $9 million will be made from sales tax.

Table 6-1 Announcement of an "Effective" Tax Rate

	Last year	This year
Average taxable home value	$72,265	$79,893
Tax rate	$1.61/$100	$1.61/$100
Tax	$1,163.47	$1,286.28

Note: The above table compares taxes on an average home in this taxing jurisdiction last year to taxes proposed on the average home this year. Your individual taxes may be higher or lower, depending on the taxable value of your property. Under this year's proposal, taxes on the average home would increase by $122.81 or 10.56% compared with last year's taxes.

Property taxes are considered hard taxes because the burden of payment falls on all of the property owners of the jurisdiction. These taxes are also harder to impose because when they are used to finance capital projects, a public referendum granting approval is an almost universal prerequisite. Voters are given the opportunity to determine whether they want to pay additional property taxes in support of capital projects from schools to fire protection to building new stadiums.

The potential for using property taxes for sport projects has been made more challenging by laws enacted in 44 states that specify limits on revenues from property taxes. These limits take the form of (a) limits on tax rate for overall local spending, (b) limits on property tax revenue growth, or (c) limits on the growth in property assessment values.[6] These limits restrict the amount of property taxes that are available to meet cities' operating costs as well as their capital investments. However, many states do have an override option in their legislation that authorizes the limits to be discarded if voters approve increases beyond those limits in a referendum. In most states, an override requires a simple majority of the votes cast, but in a few instances, more onerous criteria have to be met. In the state of Oregon, for example, a "double majority" is necessary. Not only must 50.1% of the voters approve a property tax increase, but a majority of those eligible to vote must cast ballots. Because a 30% turnout for local elections is considered to be good, passing a property tax measure in such states can be highly problematic. In the state of Washington, a "super majority," or 60%, is necessary to pass a property tax measure. Given these conditions, it is not surprising to find that in the last 10 to 15 years, property-tax-financed major league sports facilities have been rare.

General Sales Tax

Sales taxes are the largest single source of state tax revenues and the second largest source of tax revenues for municipalities after the property tax. However, in some cities with large retail centers, sales tax receipts exceed those receipts received from the property tax. Local sales taxes tend to ride piggyback on taxes that the states levy, but the local rates are generally much lower than the state sales tax rates. The combined local-state general sales tax rates generally range from 3% to 10%, but the portion most commonly collected by cities and/or counties ranges from 1% to 2%.

Most sales taxes are imposed on nearly all transactions involving tangible products at the retail level but are not applied to the sale of services. Typically, food for at-home consumption and prescription drugs are exempted to reduce the regressive nature of the sales tax. (A regressive tax is one that bears more heavily on lower income groups than on higher income groups.) In some states, this exemption has been expanded to include clothing. Purchase of these essential items constitutes a higher percentage of the income of low-income families than of high-income families. Thus, if these items remained in the tax base, the sales tax would be regressive. In some situations, sales taxes have particular appeal to local residents because a large proportion of such taxes may be paid by visitors from outside the jurisdiction who, thus, effectively subsidize the sports amenities designed mainly for residents' use.

The general sales tax has been used to finance a number of major sports facilities over the past decade. As shown in Table 6-2, most sales taxes have been adopted over a regional or county-wide area. In metropolitan areas where the economic and image benefits associated with a professional franchise spill over into a number of municipalities, imposing the tax over multiple jurisdictions is a logical approach to financing a stadium or arena. When a general sales tax is imposed over a broader area, the magnitude of the tax needed to produce necessary revenues will be substantially smaller than a tax applied in a single municipality. County-wide sales taxes dedicated to funding new sports venues are relatively modest, rarely exceeding 0.5% (half a cent) on every dollar. As with the property tax, voter approval is generally necessary for a jurisdiction to levy a general sales tax because the burden of a general sales tax is borne by all residents.

Soft Taxes

Soft taxes are borne by a relatively small proportion of residents. Some of these taxes are targeted primarily at nonresidents. Thus, the Governor of Illinois speaking of the hotel-motel tax that underwrote a new ballpark in Chicago stated, "It's financed largely by out-of-towners. You can't get a better deal than that" (p. 277).[7] Other soft taxes are targeted at products that are perceived to have an adverse effect on society. The range of soft taxes is wide:

> Taxes on hotels, restaurants, and bars have been most popular because purveyors of lodging, food, and drink presumably are prime beneficiaries of professional sports; and these taxes have the added political benefit of being borne in part by visitors, rather than local taxpayers. The Louisiana Superdome was partially financed by a 4 percent hotel-motel tax; borrowing for the Metrodome in Minneapolis was backed by taxes on lodgings and liquor by the drink; a 1 percent tax on restaurant and bar bills provided funding for the Hoosier Dome in Indianapolis; half the cost of the Orlando Arena came from a resort tax; and Phoenix increased its hotel levy and added a tax on rental cars to finance the city's share of the American West Arena. Hotel guests and restaurant patrons throughout Illinois were taxed to underwrite state bonds for the White Sox's new park. In Cleveland, special taxes on cigarettes and alcohol were dedicated to financing Jacobs Field and Gund Arena.[7] (p. 276)

Table 6-2 Sports Facilities Financed by General Sales Tax

Jusrisdiction	Tax Increase %	Venue
Brown County, WI	0.5% increase	Renovated Lambeau Field
Hamilton County, OH	0.5% increase	Great America Ballpark
King County, WA	0.5% increase	Seattle Seahawks Stadium
Metropolitan Football Dist.	0.1% increase	Invesco Field at Mile High
SE Wisconsin Baseball Dist.	0.1% increase	Miller Park
Hamilton County	0.5% increase	Paul Brown Stadium
King County	0.5% increase	Safeco Field
Hillsborough County, FL	0.5% increase	Raymond James Stadium
Maricopa County, AZ	0.25% increase	Bank One Ballpark
Denver Metro Baseball Dist.	0.1% increase	Coors Field

In this section, we briefly describe the most common of these soft taxes used to fund sports venues: hotel-motel tax, car rental tax, alcohol and cigarette taxes, and player taxes.

Tourist Development Taxes

Since the mid-1990s, two types of selected excise or sales taxes have become the most popular approach to securing public tax support for the construction/renovation of major league sports facilities. Unlike the general sales tax, which is levied on a broad spectrum of sales transactions, tourist development taxes are imposed primarily on two expenditure categories: (a) the cost of occupying a hotel or motel room and (b) the cost of renting a car. In these cases, the burden of paying these taxes falls only on those using these services. The justification for levying these taxes is that tourist visitors will be the likely beneficiaries of new stadiums and arenas. This assumes that new sports facilities serve as attractions that lead to out-of-town visitors' occupying hotel rooms and renting automobiles as a part of their desire to experience a major league sporting event. However, it was noted in chapter 4 that spectators at most major league events are locals, so the rationale linking the use of primary tourist services to sport facility attendance is under increasing attack by the tourist industry. A Tourist Industry Association spokesman said, "It is really becoming ridiculous any way you look at it. It's nothing short of political cowardice. Cities are ready to tax people who won't be there to utilize it" (p.1).[8]

The potential downside of relying on tourism development taxes was evident after the September 11 terrorist attacks in 2001. The subsequent decline in travel and tourism meant that in some communities such as Chicago, the city had to consider increasing other taxes to make up the shortfall. Because tourism is subject to boom-and-bust cycles, contingency plans for rapid declines should be in place.

Hotel-Motel Tax

The most commonly applied tourist development tax to finance major league venue projects has been the hotel-motel tax, often referred to as the bed tax. According to the Travel Industry Association of America, approximately 20 cities in the United States currently use the lodging tax to support the development of sports facilities, whereas another 15 to 20 are seriously considering using the same tax to back tax-free bonds to finance stadium and arena construction.[9] The tax rate dedicated to a sports facility typically ranges from 2% to 5% of the price paid for a hotel or motel room in the jurisdiction where the tax is levied. However, the local bed tax is often combined with other service taxes imposed by the state and other local governments. In San Antonio, for example, a guest staying at a hotel pays a 2% charge for the purpose of financing the NBA Spurs' new downtown arena (SBC Arena) and an additional 6% Texas state tax and 9% city occupancy tax, for total checkout tax of 17% on top of the room charge. During San Antonio's biggest tourist month, April, the city typically collects almost $1 million from the portion of the bed tax dedicated to financing the new arena.[10]

The $200 million Georgia Dome in Atlanta was financed almost entirely from a hotel occupancy tax. The Dome's construction debt is covered primarily by money generated from half of a 7-cent hotel-motel tax collected in Fulton

County. In its first year, the bed tax raised nearly $11 million.[11] An additional 2% tax is levied on Chicago hotels to help pay for Comiskey Park, the home of the White Sox; a 4% lodging tax is imposed in two Louisiana parishes to help pay for the Superdome; a county-wide bed tax funds a major share of the debt for the domed stadium in downtown St. Louis; and the public tax contribution for the ballpark (Comerica) and football stadium (Ford Field) recently built in Detroit is derived in large part from a 2% county-wide hotel-motel tax.[12]

Car Rental Tax

The other tourism development tax that has been used frequently to finance sports facilities is a fee charged for car rentals. Over the last decade, taxes on automobile rentals have grown substantially, so they now average above 8% nationally.[13] In addition, local jurisdictions often add designed extra taxes to the base rate. In some communities, a designated extra charge has been imposed to finance new sport venues. For example, in Dallas, Tampa, and San Antonio, a 5% tax is added on to every car rental charge, and the funds are used to retire bonds issued to finance new arenas and stadiums in those communities. Thus, an individual paying a weekly car rental rate of $350 in Dallas would be charged an additional $17.50 tax, all of which goes toward retiring the debt of the American Airlines Center.

In Atlanta, having already committed half of the county's 7% hotel tax to build the Georgia Dome, the city decided to impose a 3% car rental surcharge to finance the $214-million Philips Arena, which provided a new home for the NBA Hawks and the NHL Thrashers. In the following section of this chapter, the 11 major facilities built since 1996 that have used car rental taxes to underwrite a major share of the construction costs are identified (see Table 6-4).

Although advocates argue that this tax is paid primarily by out-of-town visitors, the car rental industry in San Antonio stated that approximately half of all car rentals were booked by local residents.[14] Because half of the $120 million gross revenue in San Antonio is paid by locals, residents paid $3 million a year in new taxes to fund the NBA Spurs' new arena.

Sin Taxes

The so-called sin taxes are taxes imposed on the sale of alcohol and cigarettes. These taxes have been used occasionally to help finance the development of sports facilities. In Cleveland, for example, a variety of sin taxes were used to publicly finance three of the city's major sports venues: Jacobs Field (MLB Indians), Gund Arena (NBA Cavaliers and WNBA Rockers), and Browns Stadium (NFL Browns). The total public investment in these facilities is estimated at $620 million. The voters of Cuyahoga County approved the sin tax in a county-wide referendum in 1990 by a slim 52% majority. The original proposal called for the construction of two side-by-side, state-of-the-art facilities in downtown Cleveland: a ballpark to keep the Indians, who were threatening to relocate, and an arena to lure the Cavaliers from the suburbs back to the city center.

The construction costs for these new facilities were to be paid from the imposition of selected taxes on alcoholic beverages and cigarettes for 15 years. Specifically, the sin taxes included a $3 tax on every gallon of "spirituous liquor" sold in the county, 16 cents per gallon on the sale of beer, 32 cents per gallon on the sale of wine, and 4.5 cents on every pack of cigarettes sold in Cuyahoga County. In 1996, the voters approved by an overwhelming majority (72%) that these sin taxes be extended for an additional 10 years to finance the construction of a new $350 million stadium for the NFL Browns.

Although no other jurisdiction has used sin taxes at the level of magnitude adopted by Cuyahoga County, a few other cities have imposed taxes on liquor or cigarettes, or both, to help finance sport facilities. Thus, a portion of the revenue used to secure the $47 million bond that financed the RCA Dome in Indianapolis came from a cigarette tax. Similarly, the Seattle Mariners' ballpark is financed in part from a 0.5% tax levied on restaurant and bar expenditures in King County.

Player Tax

Over the past decade, a growing number of states and local governments in the United States and Canada have imposed a tax on income earned by visiting players. In many cases, this has been extended to those professional athletes playing on the home team whose year-round residences are in other states. Currently, all but seven states (Alaska, Florida, Nevada, South Dakota, Texas, Washington, and Wyoming) have laws that allow them to collect taxes on visiting players' salaries. In addition, 12 major league cities in the United States impose a city nonresident tax on professional athletes who perform in their municipalities (see Table 6-3).

The player income tax, sometimes referred to as the "jock tax," is based on a well-established legal concept that states may tax nonresidents on income received for services performed within their boundaries.[15] Generally, the player tax is based on the number of "duty days" a professional athlete spends working in a state or municipality. For example, in the State of Maryland duty days are defined explicitly as "game days, practice days, days spent in team meetings, promotional caravans, and preseason training camps."[16] The total number of duty days is used to calculate that portion of a player's overall salary that was earned in a particular state or locale. The tax is then assessed on that portion of total salary earned in that taxing jurisdiction. As indicated in Table 6-3, player tax rates range from less than 1% to almost 4%. Given the soaring salaries of professional athletes, player income taxes can result in a substantial revenue windfall for state and local governments. Some states are receiving $10 million annually from visiting athletes:[17]

Table 6-3 Player Income Tax Programs in U.S. Cities

City	Non-resident local tax	Non-resident state tax
Philadelphia	3.97%	2.80%
New York	3.02-3.80%	4.00-6.85%
Cincinnati	2.10%	0.691-6.98%
Columbus	2.00%	0.691-6.98%
Detroit	1.38%	4.20%
Kansas City	1.00%	1.50-6.00%
Pittsburgh	1.00%	2.80%
St. Louis	1.00%	1.50-6.00%
Pontiac, MI	0.50%	4.20%
Baltimore	0.25%	2.00-4.80%
Indianapolis	0.18%	3.40%

Source: Federation of Tax Administrators; county, city, and state governments

Consider Texas Ranger star Alex Rodriquez, who this year will make $22 million, or $135,802 in each of the 162 games on the major league schedule. When Rodriquez and the Rangers play a three-game series against the Anaheim Angels, the star shortstop earns $407,000 in salary. Complying with California's state tax, which tops out at 9.3%, means that A-Rod's total tax bill for his weekend in Anaheim is $37,851.[18] (p. 56)

The Province of Alberta has proposed a law that would assess a tax on visiting NHL players, on the basis of the number of games they play in Edmonton or Calgary, as well as on the base salary of home-team players in both cities. The 3.06% player tax is expected to net $6 million annually.[19] What makes the Alberta law unique is that the revenues generated from the tax would go directly to the two NHL teams in the province, the Oilers and Flames. In the United States, almost every individual state and local jurisdiction administering a player tax keeps all of the revenues. In most instances, these tax revenues are placed in the jurisdiction's general fund and not redistributed to local teams or used to subsidize the venues in which they perform. However, it is important to recognize that municipal expenses associated with staging games—traffic management, security, waste management, etc.—can be very substantial, and these are paid out of the general fund.

One exception to that pattern is the tax imposed on professional athletes by the City of Pittsburgh. The city levies a 1% tax on that portion of players' wages related to their play in Pittsburgh. All revenues collected from the tax, estimated at approximately $800,000 a year, are dedicated to helping the City retire its debt obligations on two new stadiums, PNC Park (Pirates) and Heinz Stadium (Steelers).

Although many state and local governments have been administering player income taxes for years, the nonresident tax is being challenged in several U.S. jurisdictions and in Alberta, Canada. In Pittsburgh, for example, concerns have been raised about the uniformity of the law that taxes a selected group of athletes (those playing major league baseball, football, and hockey) and not all entertainers such as musicians, comedians, and dancers.[20] The issue about the fair application of the tax also has been raised in Columbus, Ohio, where a 2% city tax is levied on players of visiting NHL teams such as the Detroit Red Wings and Pittsburgh Penguins, but not applied to players on the roster of the Toledo Mud Hens or other minor league baseball (AAA) teams playing in Columbus. In 2002, the National Hockey League Players Association filed a grievance against the NHL and the Alberta provincial government in anticipation of the province's implementing a tax on players for the number of games they played at Edmonton's Skyreach Center and Calgary's Saddledome.[19] The NHL Players Association viewed the tax as essentially a payroll tax because all of the revenue derived from the tax would flow directly to the teams. In effect, player salaries would be used to finance team operations, a use that the NHL Players Association claims contravenes the existing collective bargaining agreement between the league and its players.

Despite various legal challenges, player income taxes have become an established source of revenue in most states. To date, few of the taxes are administered in direct support of team operations (except for Alberta's proposal) or venue financing (except in Pittsburgh). However, there would appear to be considerable potential for the player tax to be used more widely towards these ends. The rationale for its greater application would be based on the benefit principle of taxation, which states that taxes are justified to the extent to which those paying the tax receive direct benefit.

With respect to player taxes, a strong case could be made that players would be significant beneficiaries of an improved venue. The rationale is strengthened in the case of those players in leagues with strong revenue-sharing agreements such as the NFL and NBA. Players in both of these leagues, by virtue of their collective bargaining agreements, are entitled to receive a majority of the gross revenues produced by each league, 63% in the NFL and 56% in the NBA. Gate receipts constitute a significant portion of the designated gross revenues shared with players. In chapter 3, it was noted that the new generation of sport facilities produces abundantly greater revenues than the stadiums or arenas they replaced. The Los Angeles Lakers, for example, more than doubled their annual income when they moved from their old arena, the Forum, into their new, state-of-the-art entertainment complex, the Staples Center. Hence, an argument can be made that players, particularly those in the NFL and NBA, are major beneficiaries of new facility development. More facility revenues ultimately translate into higher salaries. Thus, it would seem that proponents of new sports facilities could make a compelling case, based on the benefit principle, that a player income tax is a fair and appropriate source of development capital. One issue that must be taken into account, however, is whether athletes should be taxed differently from members of a community's orchestra, ballet, or opera. Any consideration of a players' tax should address the "fairness" issue.

Trends in the Use of Public Sector Taxes

Table 6-4 provides a summary of the types of taxes used by government agencies to finance construction of major new sporting facilities since 1990. It is evident from the table there is a trend toward the widespread adoption of tourist services taxes. Of the 24 major venues built largely through tax support between 1997 and 2001, 15 used either a car rental or hotel tax, or a combination of both, as the primary source of public financing. General sales taxes, albeit a far distant second, were the next most common source of public agency funding. Of the seven new facilities financed from the collection of regional or county-wide sales taxes, the only one approved by voters was the $160 million for the renovation of the Green Bay Packers' venerable Lambeau Field. The Packers spent $858,000 on the referendum lobbying Brown County voters to support a 0.5% increase in the general sales tax. Opponents of the referendum spent approximately $35,000.[21] Despite outspending the opposition 25 to 1 and the team's revered status in Green Bay, the referendum passed by only 53% to 47%.

Growing public resistance to stadium projects where local taxpayers bear a heavy burden is evident. Of the 10 public referendum proposals to subsidize sports facilities from 1997 to 2001, 4 were rejected by voters. Almost all of the measures that were defeated relied heavily on hard tax alternatives, most commonly a general sales tax. In vivid contrast, 5 of the 10 that passed during the same period were based on an increase in tourist development taxes. The Travel Industry As-

Table 6-4 Major League Stadiums and Arenas Summary of Referendums Related to Publicly-Financed Venues

Major League Baseball

Market	Facility (Team)	Referendum Year	Result	Taxpayer Support	Total Cost	Public Sources of Facility Financing	Open
Cleveland	Jacobs Field (Indians)	1990	Passed (52%)	$175M Passed (52%)	$175M	*Sin Taxes* - $3 on each gallon of liquor, 16 cents on each gallon of beer and 32 cents per gallon of wine sold in Cuyahoga County. Plus, 4.5 cents per pack of cigarettes sold in County.	1994
Dallas	Ballpark at Arlington (Rangers)	1991	Passed (65%)	$161M	$191M	*General Sales Tax* – 0.5% (one half cents) on goods sold in the City of Arlington.	1994
Milwaukee	Miller Park (Brewers)	1995	Defeated (36%)	$304M	$394M	Voters rejected state's request to use lottery monies to fund ballpark. Subsequently, legislature created 5-county stadium district with authority to impose 0.1% general sales tax in district. Team contributed approximately $90 million.	2002
Detroit	Comerica (Tigers)	1996	Passed (66%)	$100M	$300M	*Tourist Development Taxes* – 2% car rental tax and 1% hotel tax in Wayne County. State contributed $55M out of Michigan Strategic Fund. Tigers pay $145 million.	2000
Cincinnati	Great America (Reds)	1996	Passed (62%)	$270M¹	$334M	*General Sales Tax* – 0.5% on taxable goods sold in Hamilton County. (County sales tax increased from 5.5% to 6.0%.)	2003
Houston	Minute Maid Park (Astros)	1996	Passed (51%)	$169M	$248M	*Tourist Development Taxes* - 2% hotel-motel tax and 5% car rental tax in Harris County. County residents exempt from car tax.	2000
Seattle	Safeco Field (Mariners)	1995	Defeated (49%)	$372M	$534M	Voters rejected proposed 0.1% increase in county's sales tax. Legislature subsequently devised state and local government financing plan. State share from proceeds of two new sport lottery games. King County share from three "Soft" taxes: 2% car rental tax, 0.5% tax on restaurants and bars and 5% admission tax for ballpark events. Team contributed $150 million as a result of $100 in cost overruns.	2001
San Francisco	Pacific Bell Park (Giants)	1996	Passed (66%)	$10M	$330M	Public support limited to $15M in tax increment financing by City Redevelopment Agency. Team financed through $170M bank loan, $135M from naming rights, other sponsorships, concession rights, and sale of PSLs.	2000
Pittsburgh	PNC Park (Pirates)	1997	1997 Defeated (NA)	$222M	$262M	Voters in 11-county area rejected proposal to increase general sales tax 0.5% to fund new ballpark. Legislature agreed to provide $75M and County $100M. Primary source a tourist development tax from % increase in hotel-motel tax.	2001

National Football League

Market	Facility (Team)	Referendum Year	Referendum Result	Taxpayer Support	Total Cost	Public Sources of Facility Financing	Open
Cleveland	Browns Stadium (Browns)	1995	Passed (NA)	$293M	$314M	*Sin Tax extensions* - Continuation of alcohol and cigarette taxes used to finance Jacobs Field and Gund Arena. Team contributed $80 million.	2001
Detroit	Ford Field (Lions)	1996	Passed (59%)	$115M	$325M	*Tourist Development Taxes* – 2% car rental tax and 1% hotel-motel tax in Wayne County. Team contribution at least $120M.	2003
Cincinnati	Paul Brown Stadium (Bengals)	1996	Passed (62%)	$450M[1]	$450M	*General Sales Tax* – 0.5% on taxable goods sold in Hamilton County. Team contributed $50M.	2002
Nashville	Adelphia Stadium (Titans)	1996	Passed (5 9%)	$234M	$292M	*Tourist Development Tax* – City of Nashville financed $153M from hotel-motel tax. State contributed $55M from sales tax imposed on sale of goods at the stadium. Team contributed $75M from sale of 57,000 PSLs.	1999
Tampa	Raymond James Stadium (Buccaneers)	1996	Passed (NA)	$169M	$169M	*General Sales Tax* – 0.5% on taxable goods sold in Hillsborough County. Tax increase revenues shared with municipalities and School Board to finance jails, fire stations, school construction, along with the new stadium.	1998
Pittsburgh	Heinz Field (Steelers)	1996	None	$175.5M	$252M	New stadium part of state's $840M sports facilities development plan (Plan B) to build new stadiums for four of Pennsylvania's pro sports teams (Pirates, Phillies, Eagles, Steelers). Primary sources: tourist development taxes including a hotel room excise tax and car rental tax. Steelers contributed $123M.	2002
Seattle	Seahawk Stadium (Seahawks)	1998	1998 Passed (51%)	$300M	$400M	*Mix of Tourist Development Taxes and User Fees* including $75M from 2% increase of car rental tax and 2% increase of hotel-motel tax, $127M from 6 new sport-related lottery games, $56M from admission and parking fees, and $101M from sales tax collected in King County attributable to stadium. Team contributed $100M.	2003
Denver	Invesco Field at Mile High Stadium (Broncos)	1999	1999 Passed (57%)	$300M	$400M	*General Sales Tax* - $298M raised by extending a 0.1% sales tax previously used to finance the Rockies Coors Field. Team's share of costs came to $112M.	2001
Green Bay	Lambeau Field (Packers)	2000	Passed (53%)	$160M	$295M	*General Sales Tax* – 0.5% on taxable goods sold in Brown County raised $160M. One time user fee assessed on all season ticket holders (avg. $2000/seat) raised $112M.	2003

National Basketball Association

Market	Facility (Team)	Referendum Year	Referendum Result	Taxpayer Support	Total Cost	Public Sources of Facility Financing	Open
Miami	American Airlines Arena (Heat)	1996	Passed (NA)	$39.1M	$213M	*Tourist Development Taxes* – Hotel and car rental taxes imposed in Dade County contributes $6.4 million a year to cover annual arena operation and maintenance costs. Team financed construction through $185 million corporate bond sale.	1999
Dallas	American Airlines Center (Mavericks and Stars)	1998	Passed (50%)	$125M	$427M	*Tourist Development Taxes* – 5% car rental tax and 2% hotel-motel tax increases raised $125M. Teams (Arena Group) responsible for all expenses beyond $125 million.	2001
San Antonio	SBC Arena (Spurs)	2000	Passed (60%)	$147M	$175M	*Tourist Development Taxes* – Hotel tax increased from 15% to 16.75% and car rental tax increased from 10 to 15% in Bexar County. Team contributed $28.5M plus covers any cost overruns.	2003
Houston	NBA Arena (Rockets and Comets)	1999	Defeated (46%)	$80M	$160M	Voters rejected a proposal that have raised $80M in public funds (see below).	2003
Houston	NBA Arena (Rockets and Comets)	2001	Passed (61%)	$175M	$175M	*Tourist Development Taxes* – Voters approved a more extensive financing plan to the proposal rejected one year earlier. $175M public contribution from existing 2% hotel tax and 5% car rental tax.	2003

National Basketball Association

Market	Facility (Team)	Referendum Year	Referendum Result	Taxpayer Support	Total Cost	Public Sources of Facility Financing	Open
Nashville	Gaylord Entertainment Center (Predators)	1995	Passed (NA)	$144M	$144M	*Property Tax* – Voters approved sale of General Obligation bonds to fully fund new downtown arena.	1997
Tampa	Ice Palace (Lightening)	1996	None	$102M	$161.8M	Unspecified portion of 5% tourist development tax on hotel-motel stays in Hillsborough county used to finance arena.	1996
Broward Co.	National Car Rental (Panthers)	1997	None	$184.2M	$212M	*Tourist Development Tax* – an additional 2% hotel-motel tax imposed in Broward County.	1998

Sources: Compiled from *Sports Business Daily, Sports Business Journal,* and *RSV* and other journal sources published prior to July 7, 2002. In addition, information was drawn from Team Marketing Report's *2000 Inside the Ownership of Professional Sports Teams* and Mediaventure's *2002 Revenues from Sport Venues,* and Appendix 2 to the Sports Facilities Reports, Volume 2, Number 2, Major League Sport Stadium/Arena Referendum's prepared by National Sports Law Institute of the Marquette University Law School, 2001.

sociation of America (TIAA) has proclaimed "taxing travelers to pay for sport facilities is the rage" (p. 1).[13]

This source is politically attractive for three main reasons. First, it does not require voter approval in most states, whereas approval is often required at the local level for general sales tax increases. Second, it transfers the costs of building (and sometimes also operating) a major recreational facility to out-of-town visitors. They do not vote on tax increases and are unlikely even to realize that the tax is underwriting those facilities. Hence, proponents of a bed tax to fund a new arena proclaimed in a television advertisement, "Relax, tourists will pick up the tab" (p. 83).[22] Third, ostensibly those who appear most likely to oppose the tax are a community's hoteliers because they are required to add it to their guests' bills and collect it. However, a major sports facility is likely to help fill rooms; therefore, hoteliers frequently support such taxes.

Tourist development taxes have become the most expedient approach to financing new sports venues. One prominent public official in Houston, Texas, commented, "Fair or unfair, it's the easiest thing to do. Of course, the team ought to pay. But, the average citizen in Houston doesn't face the [car] rental tax every day, and the attitude toward the tax is very favorable" (p. 9).[23]

Although the approval rate of soft-tax proposals has been high to date, opposition to tourist taxes is building in the car rental and hotel industry sectors. The Travel and Tourism Government Affairs Council (1996), an affiliate of the TIAA, has voted to oppose formally all taxes placed on travelers to finance sport facilities.[13] The primary objection of the travel industry is that such taxes force every visitor to pay irrespective of their travel intentions. The TIAA estimates that only 5% of all trips include any kind of sporting event on the travelers' itinerary.[9]

| Debt Financing | The ability of cities and counties to finance the construction of sport facilities has depended on their ability to borrow substantial amounts of money over extended periods of time. Most public agencies finance major capital development projects in the same way individuals purchase new homes or cars. Rather than paying the entire purchase price in advance, or up-front, government agencies pay for the cost of a new facility over several years. The needed capital for home construction is borrowed from a lending institution, typically a bank, that then requires the borrower to repay or retire the debt in a series of scheduled payments that may stretch out over 30 years. In the case of publicly funded sports facilities, the revenues pledged to repay the debt obligation are derived from either hard or soft taxes imposed by government agencies. |

The downside to spreading out payments over a 20- to 30-year period is that substantial interest costs are incurred. For example, the city of San Antonio adopted an up-front payment approach to financing its Alamodome, which cost $174 million to build. Most of the money was raised by a 5-year surcharge of an additional 0.5¢ on the local sales tax, which was approved by the city's voters in a referendum.[24] The project director estimated that if long-term, 30-year, general obligation bonds had been used to finance the project, taxpayers would have paid a total of $435 million in principal and interest payments over the years of the bond issue. This would have required annual debt service payments of $17 million, which would have been equivalent to a 15% increase in the property tax.

Using taxes collected over a period of years to pay the debt charges emanating from major capital development projects like stadiums and arenas is usually preferred for several reasons. First, by spreading the payments over an extended period, the annual tax burden borne by taxpayers in any single year is less onerous. For example, in a county that imposed a half-cent general sales tax increase to fund a new stadium, a household that spent $15,000 a year on taxable goods and services in the county would pay an additional $75 in taxes. Hypothetically, if 200,000 households were to spend at the same level on average, the general sales tax would produce $15 million in new revenues. That amount, if perceived by lending institutions to be a stable stream of revenue, could secure a construction loan for as much as $150 million. This approach is likely to be more palatable than asking each of those 200,000 households to pay $750 in additional taxes in one year to pay for the facility, the amount that would be required if the $150 million facility were funded by a one-time, up-front payment. When the Denver Rockies' new ballpark was being financed by residents of the Denver metropolitan area, the following comment was made:

> What are we talking about here? We're not talking about big dollars. It's a twelve-pack of Coke. And people aren't putting that in perspective. You have the political motivators out there who are using these fifty-million-dollar numbers. It's a twelve-pack of Coca-Cola per taxpayer in the district, it's not a big deal. Is that worth the price of having major league baseball in Denver? I think your average person would say yes, that's worth it.[25] (p. 199)

Second, from a political perspective, debt financing is a desirable approach. For many elected officials, guided by their preeminent goal to be reelected, financing that shifts the cost of a new facility as far forward as possible is an attractive option. This extended-payment approach pushes most of the potential political penalties associated with increased taxes well into the future, so they become problems for political successors. Meanwhile, politicians responsible for the facility reap the benefits of creating a new community asset.

Third, from an equity perspective, the use of long-term debt financing makes good sense, particularly when hard taxes, such as property or general sales taxes, are used to retire the debt. When the burden is placed on local residents, a system that defrays taxpayer payments over many years accommodates the reality that population turnover is a constant. If cities used alternatives to borrowing, such as making a one-time payment in full, then some present residents would pay the full cost of the facility, but if they later left the community, they would receive only partial benefit from their investment. Conversely, others moving into the community would receive benefits from an asset to which they had made no financial contribution. With debt financing, some measure of equity is achieved, because all residents contribute tax dollars and pay their share of the amenity to which they have access.

The method by which government agencies borrow money to finance major capital development projects like stadiums and arenas is through the sale of bonds.

Table 6-5 A Comparison of Two Common Types of Bond Retirement Schedules

STRAIGHT SERIAL					GRADUATED SERIAL				
Maturity Date	Principal	Coupon Rate	Interest Payment	Total Annual Payment	Maturity Date	Principal	Coupon Rate	Interest Payment	Total Annual Payment
6/1/00 12/1/00	500,000	6.5%	$325,000 $325,000	$1,500,000	6/1/00 12/1/00	$200,000	6.5%	$325,000 $325,000	$850,000
6/1/01 12/1/01	$500,000	6.5%	$308,750 $308,750	$1,117,500	6/1/01 12/1/01	$200,000	6.5%	$318,500 $318,500	$837,000
6/1/02 12/1/02	$500,000	6.5%	$292,500 $292,500	$1,085,000	6/1/02 12/1/02	$250,000	6.5%	$312,000 $312,000	$874,000
6/1/03 12/1/03	$500,000	6.5%	$276,250 $276,250	$1,052,500	6/1/03 12/1/03	$250,000	6.5%	$303,875 $303,875	$857,750
6/1/04 12/1/04	$500,000	6.5%	$260,000 $260,000	$1,020,000	6/1/04 12/1/04	$300,000	6.5%	$295,750 $295,750	$891,500
6/1/05 12/1/05	$500,000	6.5%	$243,750 $243,750	$ 987,500	6/1/05 12/1/05	$300,000	6.5%	$286,000 $286,000	$872,000
6/1/06 12/1/06	$500,000	6.5%	$227,500 $227,500	$ 955,000	6/1/06 12/1/06	$350,000	6.5%	$276,450 $276,450	$902,500
6/1/07 12/1/07	$500,000	6.5%	$211,250 $211,250	$ 922,500	6/1/07 12/1/07	$350,000	6.5%	$264,875 $264,875	$879,750
6/1/08 12/1/08	$500,000	6.5%	$195,000 $195,000	$ 890,000	6/1/08 12/1/08	$400,000	6.5%	$253,500 $253,500	$907,000
6/1/09 12/1/09	$500,000	6.5%	$178,750 $178,500	$ 857,500	6/1/09 12/1/09	$400,000	6.5%	$240,500 $240,500	$881,000
6/1/10 12//10	$500,000	6.5%	$162,500 $162,500	$ 825,000	6/1/10 12/1/10	$500,000	6.5%	$227,500 $227,500	$955,000
6/1/11 12/1/11	$500,000	6.5%	$146,250 $146,250	$ 792,500	6/1/11 12/1/11	$500,000	6.5%	$211,250 $211,250	$922,500
6/1/12 12/1/12	$500,000	6.5%	$130,000 $130,000	$ 760,000	6/1/12 12/1/12	$600,000	6.5%	$195,000 $195,000	$990,000
6/1/13 12/1/13	$500,000	6.5%	$113,750 $113,750	$ 727,500	6/1/13 12/1/13	$600,000	6.5%	$156,000 $156,000	$912,000
6/1/14 12/1/14	$500,000	6.5%	$ 97,500 $ 97,500	$ 695,000	6/1/14 12/1/14	$700,000	6.5%	$132,250 $132,250	$966,500
6/1/15 12/1/15	$500,000	6.5%	$ 81,250 $ 81,250	$ 662,500	6/1/15 12/1/15	$700,000	6.5%	$110,500 $110,250	$921,000
6/1/16 12/1/16	$500,000	6.5%	$ 65,000 $ 65,000	$ 630,000	6/1/16 12/1/16	$800,000	6.5%	$ 84,500 $ 84,500	$969,000
6/1/17 12/1/17	$500,000	6.5%	$ 48,750 $ 48,750	$ 597,500	6/1/17 12/1/17	$800,000	6.5%	$ 58,500 $ 58,500	$917,000
6/1/18 12/1/18	$500,000	6.5%	$ 32,500 $ 32,500	$ 565,000	6/1/18 12/1/18	$900,000	6.5%	$ 29,250 $ 29,250	$958,000
6/1/19 12/1/19	$500,000	6.5%	$ 16,250 $ 16,250	$ 532,000	6/1/19 12/1/19	$900,000	6.5%	$ 0 $ 0	$900,000
TOTALS	$10,000,000		$6,825,500	$16,824,500		$10,000,000		$8,904,250	$18,904,250

Formally, bonds are defined as a promise by the borrower (the public jurisdiction) to pay back to the lender (the financial institution) a specified amount of money, with interest, within a specified period of time.

Bonds are issued as formal certificates on which three primary elements are commonly engraved: (a) the face value or principal amount of the bond, typically $5,000; (b) the rate of interest, fixed at a specified percentage for the life of the bond; and (c) the date of maturity, which identifies the specific date on which the face value of the bond must be repaid in full. The dollar amount of the interest owed by the borrower is easy to calculate. The annual interest payment is determined by multiplying the rate of interest, often referred to as the *coupon rate*, by the face amount of the bond. For example, a bond with a face value of $5,000 and an interest rate of 7% would pay the lender $350 per year. Commonly, the interest is paid in two semiannual installments, which in the case of this example would be $175 per payment.

In a bond transaction where a city borrows $10 million, it would issue two thousand $5,000 bond certificates to the lender. The lender would then hold the bond certificates until their maturity. In effect, the certificates represent interest-bearing IOUs. In most transactions, the maturity dates on the bonds are sequenced so that a prespecified number of certificates will mature or be payable each year. Under this arrangement, the public agency pays off a small portion of the total debt obligation each year. This gradual, sequenced payment is referred to as a *serial retirement schedule*.

Table 6-5 demonstrates two approaches commonly used by government agencies to repay long-term debt obligations. The left side of the table shows a *straight serial retirement* schedule, and the right side shows a graduated serial schedule. In both hypothetical examples, a $10 million bond transaction is being repaid over 20 years at a fixed rate of interest of 6.5%. The major difference between the payback schedules is the manner in which the principal amount borrowed is repaid on an annual basis. The straight serial approach retires the $10 million over 20 years in equal annual principal payments of $500,000. In effect, this means that each year, 100 of the $5,000 engraved bond certificates mature or become payable. In addition to the one yearly principal payment of $500,000, the borrower (e.g., city or county) must pay interest (split between two semiannual payments at a coupon rate of 6.5%). The interest costs are based on the amount of debt obligation still outstanding. Consequently, in a straight serial arrangement, as the borrower pays off an equal portion of the outstanding principal year after year, the annual interest payments decline correspondingly. In the example, the agency pays $650,000 in interest costs in Year 1 (.065 coupon rate x $10 million total outstanding principal = $650,000). When the interest payments are added to the principal payment ($650,000 + $500,000), the total debt service payment in the initial year of the repayment schedule comes to $1,150,000. Under the straight serial arrangement, by Year 20 (2019) interest payments have fallen to a total of only $32,500 (two semiannual payments at $16,250 each) because the agency only has to pay interest on the final one hundred $5,000 certificates that remain to be paid.

In contrast, with the *graduated serial retirement* schedule, annual principal payments increase progressively over the duration of the borrowing period. In the hypothetical example shown in Table 6-5, the principal payments grow from $200,000 in years 1 and 2 to $900,000 in the final 2 years. Two differences are evident from comparing the alternative approaches to debt retirement. First, the graduated schedule is considerably more expensive than the straight serial option. Even though the basic lending terms are exactly the same, $10 million for 20 years at 6.5% interest, an agency using the straight serial method would have "saved" over $2 million. Using the equal principal payment approach, the entire debt service totaled $16,824,500. In comparison, the total cost of borrowing the $10 million comes to almost $19 million using the graduated payoff approach. Clearly, the more rapidly the agency can pay down the principal, the less interest it has to pay.

Given the significant cost savings of the straight serial method, why would an agency use the more expensive graduated retirement schedule? The primary reason for its adoption is that the graduated approach allows the agency more flexibility in managing its debt retirement obligation. This greater flexibility may be necessary when an agency is concerned about how much revenue will be available to meet its annual debt requirements. As shown in the far right column of Table 6-5, the total yearly payments under the graduated schedule are relatively stable over the duration of the lending period. The annual debt service payment does not exceed $1,000,000 in any given year of the retirement schedule. In contrast, due to the heavy interest costs on the front end of the straight serial schedule, the first five annual payments all top $1,000,000. In the example used here, an agency using the straight serial option would pay $5.43 million in principal and interest costs over the first 5 years. On the other hand, if the public jurisdiction were to use the graduated schedule, its total costs over the same period would be considerably lower, at $4.31 million.

For an agency faced with some uncertainty about the amount of revenue a new soft tax (e.g., players' salary tax or car rental tax) may produce, the more conservative, albeit more expensive, graduated schedule would be the more prudent choice.

On the other hand, when an agency has obtained voter approval to secure a bond through a hard tax source (e.g., property tax or broad-based sales tax), virtually guaranteeing sufficient revenues, the least expensive borrowing option (in this case, the straight serial approach) would be the appropriate choice.

A fundamental rule associated with issuing long-term debt instruments is not to issue them for a maturity longer than the project's useful life. People should not be paying for a major sports facility after it is no longer in use: "If the debt life exceeds useful life, the project's true annual cost has been understated and people will continue to pay for the project after it has gone. If the useful life exceeds the debt period, the annual cost has been overstated and people will receive benefits without payment" (p. 408).[26] In the context of major sports facilities, if a facility is being built to accommodate a franchise, then *useful life* effectively may be defined as the period of time for which a franchise occupies the structure. Thus, this rule counsels that the length of a bond's maturity should coincide with the duration of the municipality's lease agreement with the franchise. The longer the maturity term, the higher the interest rate required to borrow for that period of time,

Figure 6-5 Types of Debt Financing

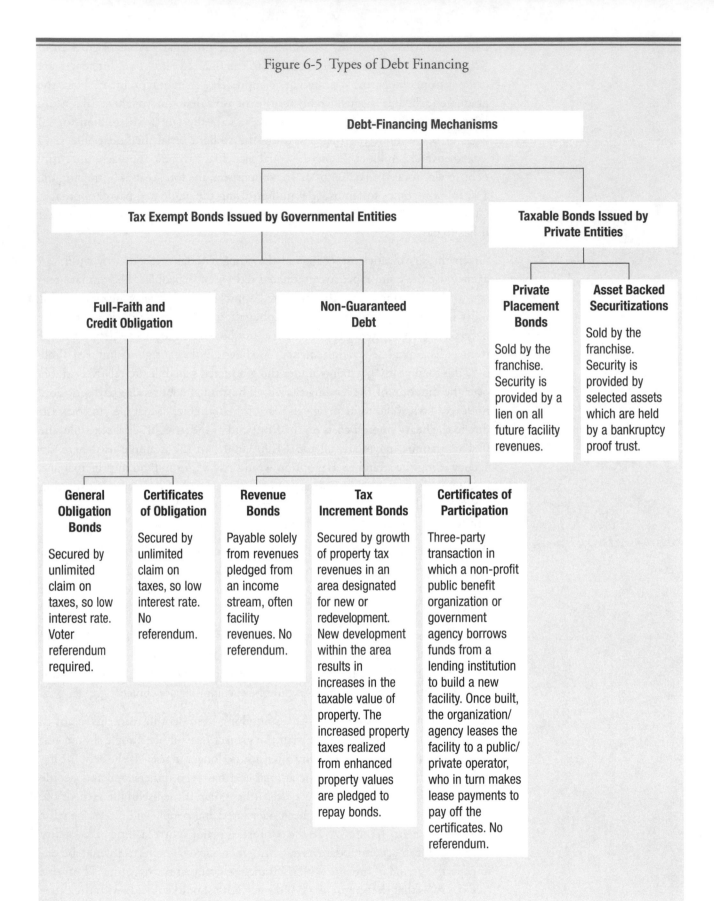

because borrowers have to compensate investors for locking up their resources for a longer time.

The main types of bonds that are issued to finance the acquisition or development of a sports facility are shown in Figure 6-5. The figure shows that the most fundamental differentiating quality among the various types of bonds is whether they are tax-exempt or taxable. Among those that are tax-exempt, a key differentiating quality is whether they constitute a *full-faith and credit* obligation of the government jurisdiction issuing them, which means that all taxpayers are responsible for their redemption; or whether their repayment is *nonguaranteed* by taxpayers, which means repayment is dependent only on revenues accruing from designated income sources. This section commences with a discussion of the differences between tax-exempt and taxable bonds and then proceeds to describe the characteristics of each of the types of bonds shown in Figure 6-5.

The Use of Tax-Exempt Bonds

Tax-exempt bonds can be issued only by governmental entities or by public benefit corporations serving as surrogates for government entities. The tax-exempt feature of these bonds means that the interest payments made to bondholders are free from all federal income taxes and usually from those in the state in which they are issued (if the state has an income tax). This results in substantial tax advantages for those in the highest income brackets. Thus, Table 6-6 indicates that an investor whose marginal tax rate is 39.1% (that is the rate on the last dollar earned, and this was the highest level of taxation paid to the federal government at the time this book was written) should be as willing to purchase a municipal bond offering 5% interest as a corporate bond offering 8.21%. Taking away the 39.1% federal income tax that would have to be paid on the 8.21% return would leave a taxable yield to the bond investor of 5%.

Table 6-6 The Yield Required on a Taxable Investment Equal to the Yield on a Tax-Exempt Investment for Four Different Tax Rates

Tax-exempt yields	Taxable yield equivalents			
	27.5%	30.5%	35.5%	39.1%
2.00%	2.76%	2.88%	3.10%	3.28%
2.50%	3.45%	3.60%	3.88%	4.10%
3.00%	4.14%	4.32%	4.66%	4.93%
3.50%	4.83%	5.04%	5.43%	5.80%
4.00%	5.52%	5.75%	6.20%	6.57%
5.00%	6.90%	7.20%	7.76%	8.21%
6.00%	8.28%	8.63%	9.30%	9.85%
7.00%	9.65%	10.07%	10.85%	11.49%

Table 6-6 illustrates that the higher a bondholder's tax rate, the more attractive tax-exempt bonds become. The taxable equivalent yield of a tax-exempt bond is calculated by using the following formula:

$$\text{Taxable equivalent yield} = \frac{\text{tax-free yield}}{100\% - \text{tax bracket \%}}$$

For example, an investor in the 30.5% tax bracket who invests in a 6% tax-exempt bond would receive a taxable equivalent yield of 8.63%:

$$\text{Tax equivalent yield} = \frac{6\%}{1 - 30.5} = 8.63\%$$

The tax-exempt provision allows governments to offer their bonds more cheaply than private firms can and to provide investors equivalent aftertax returns on their investment. In effect, this means that state and local public facilities funded by bonds receive a federal subsidy because their interest income is exempt from federal income taxes. Although the cost of borrowing differs widely depending on the fiscal strength of a public agency and its credit rating, that cost invariably will be lower than the cost of borrowing from a commercial organization.

If a government entity used taxable bonds to finance sports facilities, its costs would be substantially higher. Similarly, if a government entity can be persuaded to make its relatively inexpensive money available to a franchise or commercial operator, the private operator would receive a considerable subsidy. For example, over the past quarter-century, the interest-rate differential between long-term taxable corporate bonds and long-term tax-exempt state and local bonds has ranged between 2% and 4/5%. Assuming 1/30th of the bond principal is retired at the end of each year, it has been calculated that the savings (present value) as a percentage of construction cost at the 2% and 4% differential levels amount to 16.8% and 33.5%, respectively. Thus, on an arena costing $225 million, the savings at the 2% and 4% differential levels would be $37.7 million and $75.4 million, respectively.[27] This latter subsidy is $2.5 million per year over the life of the project.

From the outset of the first income tax law passed in the United States in 1913, the interest income of government bondholders was not taxable.[27] This enabled state and local government entities to issue bonds and use the proceeds to make loans to private businesses and individuals for any and every purpose. Typically, these bond issues were structured so that revenue in the form of lease fees from the private facility was used to fully pay the annual debt service, so state and local taxpayers saw no reason to oppose these arrangements. The government entity and private partner would sign an agreement under which the public agency built a facility with its capital to the commercial operator's specifications and leased it to the operator at a price that enabled bond repayments to be met. Leaseback arrangements of this type offered the lessee at least four advantages:

1) The lessee was freed from providing capital financing for the development.

2) The rental was tax deductible as an operating cost.

3) The rental amount was reduced because of the government owner's ability to finance the development with tax-exempt bonds.

4) The lessee did not have to pay property taxes on the development because it was municipally owned.

The tax-exempt status represents a subsidy by federal taxpayers who have foregone the federal tax revenues that would have been paid on the interest income that would have been forthcoming if taxable bonds had been used. Thus, in allowing these kinds of arrangements, the federal treasury was annually foregoing billions of dollars through not being able to tax investors' interest from these bonds. In 1968, Congress addressed this issue and imposed stringent conditions that tax-exempt bonds had to meet before they could be issued. However, sports facilities were among a limited list of uses that were exempted from most of these conditions.

Despite these conditions, these so-called private activity bonds continued to flourish. By the 1980s, they accounted for almost 80% of all government bonds issued and attracted so much capital from investors that there was relatively little left over for genuine public interest projects.[28]

In 1984, Congress made an attempt to curb tax-exempt financing for sports facilities in the Deficit Reduction Act by enacting that proceeds from these bonds could not be used to finance the construction of lucrative luxury boxes.[29] From 1984 onwards, it became obvious from Congressional hearings that there was strong sentiment among legislators to curtail the use of public tax-exempt bonds to develop facilities for private interests. Thus, many cities hustled either for their potential projects to be grandfathered into the legislation or to sell their bonds before such legislation was enacted. Some of the multitude of new sports buildings that were initiated in the 1980s (chapter 3) were the result of deals put together when the threat of changes in the federal tax law became apparent.

When the 1986 Tax Reform Act was passed, it was intended to terminate all tax-exempt funding of arenas and stadiums for franchise owners. It did impose more rigorous restrictions, but it contained some loopholes that subsequently have been exploited. Among them was a provision for the favorite projects of members of Congress to be grandfathered so that tax-exempt bonds for these specified projects could qualify under pre-1986 conditions.

The 1986 Tax Reform Act stated that states and local governments no longer had the right to issue tax-exempt bonds to finance the construction of sports facilities IF (a) more than 10% of the stadium's useful service was consumed by a private business entity OR (b) more than 10% of the principal and interest payments came directly or indirectly from sports franchise revenues. The first provision is called the *business use test*. This standard is difficult for most professional sports teams to meet because most clubs use or occupy more than 10% of a facility's schedule capacity over the course of a year. The intent of this test was to ensure that the primary beneficiary of the exemption is the general public, not a private entity such as a sports team. If one organization has preferential treatment that exceeds 10% of the facility's use, then the business use test is violated and the bonds do not qualify for an exemption.

However, the Tax Reform Act stipulated that government agencies could still issue tax-exempt bonds by meeting only one of the two tests. As a result, those attempting to secure tax-free bonds have concentrated on meeting the second provision, called the *private payment test*. To avoid exceeding the restriction imposed by this test, the bond repayment must be structured so that no more than 10% of the debt service is paid from revenues generated from stadium operations.[27] This precludes paying off the bonds from standard contractually obligated sources such as luxury suite leases, naming rights, and ticket-tax revenues. As shown in Table 6-7, dollars generated from parking, signage, and concession sales also count as private payment revenues. In general, any form of rent paid by private tenants, such as teams, to use the facility is applied to the 10% limit.

One potentially important source of facility-generated revenue, however, is not subject to the 10% limitation. The Act allows monies derived from permanent seat license (PSLs) sales to secure the issuance of tax-exempt bonds (a discussion of PSLs follows in chapter 7). Despite the controversy over the sale of these seat reservation programs, the government agency and/or team attempting to build a new stadium or arena may find the interest cost savings realized from their sale a compelling reason to use PSLs. Hence, it has been pointed out that "cities prefer to use PSLs in order to preserve [their] tax exemption" (p. 23).[30]

The 1986 Act has had two unanticipated effects.[27] First, if a facility is leased to a team that contributes less than 10% of revenues towards the debt payments, then the private payments test is met and tax-exempt bonds can be used. There was no anticipation among the sponsors of the 1986 Act that local officials would capitulate to team owners by signing agreements that repaid *less than* 10% of the debt charges. However, that is what has happened! In essence, this provision has resulted in government entities' providing highly favorable leases to franchises and has palpably weakened their government's bargaining position.

Table 6-7 Facility Revenue Sources That Can Be Used to Retire Taxable and Tax-exempt Bonds Under the Terms of the Tax Reform Act's "Private Activity Test"

Taxable Only	Tax-Exempt
• Luxury suite	• PSL sales
• Club seats	
• Ticket sales	
• Parking	
• Naming Rights	
• Concessions	

A second effect has been that because the owners are prohibited from pledging more than 10% of the debt payments from their franchises' revenues, more of the debt service burden has to be borne by general taxpayers. Effectively, general revenue sources, such as sales taxes, hotel-motel taxes, car rental taxes, and sin taxes, are substituted for stadium-related revenues.

The result of these unanticipated effects has been that "the owners reap a windfall as they rent the stadium for a minimal sum, collect the ticket and concession revenues, and are relieved of having to pay any of the interest on the construction debt" (p. 150).[29] There have been subsequent legislative efforts to further curtail the use of tax-exempt bonds for sports facilities, but none have yet been enacted. Most prominent among these was the proposed Stop Tax-Exempt Arena Debt Issuance Act (STADIA) in 1996. The Senate sponsor of this legislation stated "The legislation I am introducing will do what we intended to do, and thought we did, in 1986. This legislation makes clear that professional sports facilities may not be financed with tax-exempt bonds" (p. 151).[29] However, the bill attracted few sponsors, and to this point, such legislation has not been passed.

Full-Faith and Credit Obligations

Debts that are full-faith and credit obligations of a government entity have an unlimited claim on the taxes and other revenues of the jurisdiction borrowing the funds. The burden of paying these debts is spread over all taxable property within the issuing government's geographical boundaries. Figure 6-5 identifies the two most common forms of full-faith and credit obligations: general obligation bonds and certificates of obligation. They are discussed in this section.

General Obligation Bonds

When it issues general obligation bonds, a government unit makes an unconditional promise to the bondholder (usually a commercial bank) to pay back the principal and interest it owes through its authority to levy taxes. When general obligation bonds are issued by local governments (e.g., cities, counties, school districts), payment is usually secured by property taxes. State governments, which rely on nonproperty tax sources, usually pledge revenue streams from sales or income taxes to repay general obligation bonds.

State statutes impose limits on the total amount of general obligation debt a local government agency can assume. These limitations vary widely from one state to another. This restriction is generally referred to as the *statutory debt ceiling*. In almost all cases, the debt ceiling is expressed as a percentage of the total assessed value of property within a jurisdiction. For example, in the State of Oregon, local governments cannot issue general obligation debt that exceeds 3% of the aggregate value of taxable property within their jurisdictions.

General obligation bonds offer a number of advantages. Because of their full-faith and credit backing, they are the most secure of any of the available long-term debt instruments. Consequently, the borrowing costs associated with general obligation debt are considerably cheaper than any of the other debt financing options. The difference in interest rates between general obligation bonds and nonguaranteed tax-exempt bonds may be as much as 1% or 2%. In other words, it may cost 7% to finance a project using nonguaranteed bonds as opposed to 5% if general obligation bonds are used. The additional interest cost over the full period of the loan may be substantial. The difference between paying 5% and 7% on a 20-year, $5 million dollar issue is almost $1,500,000.

The government body's unconditional pledge of full tax support makes general obligation bonds easier to sell. The reduced risk associated with the almost certain probability of reimbursement increases the attractiveness of general obligation bonds to a greater range of potential lenders.

Because the sale of general obligation bonds represents an obligation that all taxpayers must meet, the government body desiring to issue them must first obtain voter approval. This has become increasingly difficult for financing new sports facilities. The growing unwillingness of taxpayers to wholly fund expensive sports projects was discussed earlier in this chapter. This has deterred many teams from pressuring communities to bring general obligation or hard-tax proposals before voters. As a result, in recent years, there has been a pronounced shift toward the issuance of bonds that do not require voter approval, such as revenue bonds, or of bonds secured by soft taxes, such as tourism development charges, where voter approval has been much easier to obtain. The pros and cons of general obligation bonds are summarized in Table 6-8.

Conducting a bond campaign. Although the challenge of convincing voters to raise their property taxes in support of new sports facilities may be daunting, a well-orchestrated campaign to educate residents as to the actual costs and benefits associated with the project can lead to a favorable outcome. This is particularly true for smaller projects that are perceived to provide widespread public benefit. Sports facilities that are good prospects for general obligation bond support include youth sport complexes, community swimming pools, and action or skate parks (e.g., skateboarding, in-line skating).

Presenting voters with a multimillion-dollar bond proposal for the acquisition and development of sports facilities is likely to be intimidating to many voters and result in a negative reaction from them. Such large aggregate figures are misleading because they represent the amount that all taxpayers are being asked to contribute. Thus, it is important to present bond costs in terms of their impact on an individual taxpayer. Table 6-9 illustrates how this may be done. The owners of property assessed by this particular jurisdiction at $75,000 will be required to pay an additional $5.25 per year, or approximately 50¢ per month, to pay the debt charges on a $4 million bond for an athletic complex.

Table 6-8 Summary of the Pros and Cons of General Obligation Bonds

Advantages	Disadvantages
1. Lower interest rates than nonguaranteed debt options 2. Full faith and credit backing virtually eliminating risk of default	1. Obtaining voter approval is required 2. All taxpayers pay regardless of any direct benefits they may receive 3. Borrowing capacity constrained by debt ceiling

Table 6-9 The Effect of a $4 Million Bond Issue on Individual Homeowners' Taxes in a Hypothetical Jurisdiction

Property Value	Annual Tax Increase	Monthly Approximate Tax Increase
$50,000	$3.50	$0.25
$75,000	$5.25	$0.50
$100,000	$7.00	$0.75
$125,000	$8.75	$1.00
$150,000	$10.50	$1.25

In addition to the cost of servicing the bond repayments, residents also need to be informed of how operating and maintaining the new facilities will affect their taxes. Thus, if it is estimated that operating expenses are $200,000, then residents should be informed that the ongoing tax implication for a home assessed at

$100,000 is likely to be (for example) 35¢ per year. Presenting costs in terms of their implications for individual taxpayers gives voters a perspective that, for "less than the equivalent of a cup of coffee a week," they can enjoy the benefits of the athletic complex.

Marketing theory offers three key concepts that are central for an effective campaign to pass a bond referendum. The first is *market segmentation*, which recognizes that residents are likely to have heterogeneous perceptions, attitudes, and interests toward sports facilities. Thus, there will be some residents who will not support any proposals that they are asked to consider because, as a matter of principle, they are opposed to increases in taxation. Investment of resources directed at changing their minds is likely to be wasted. Rather, efforts should be targeted at those segments of the population likely to be most supportive; that is, those who are likely to benefit most from the proposal.

In Dubuque, Iowa, authors of a bond referendum for a softball and baseball complex compared voter registration lists with softball rosters and determined that a large number of softball players were not registered to vote. A small group of enlisted softball players established voter registration booths at all softball fields. Finally, they mailed postcards to softball players prior to the election indicating the impact on softball should the referendum fail.[31]

In Waterloo, Iowa, volunteers staffed a bank of 14 telephones from 10:00 a.m. until 9:00 p.m. for 4 weeks before the bond referendum. They called individuals who had participated in the city's sports programs and activities. Using a prepared script and asking if people knew about the bond election and if they would vote "yes," the volunteers spent less than 1 minute on average for each call. They also answered questions that were later compiled and distributed as most frequently asked questions and answers. A second call made on election day reminded individuals to vote and arranged for rides. The bond election passed with an 85% "yes" vote.[31]

The second central marketing idea focuses on the *benefit principle*. This involves addressing the question "What's in it for them?" This question is relatively easy to answer for the groups who will use the proposed facilities, but there is also a need to identify benefits that may accrue to nonusers. Some of these nonusers may not have recognized that they were beneficiaries, and identifying the benefits they would receive may persuade them to support the proposal. Those nonuser benefits were discussed in detail in chapters 4 and 5 and may include

- economic impact on the community created by nonresidents using the new facilities and spending money in the area while doing so;

- increased community visibility;

- enhanced community image;

- stimulation of other development; and

- psychic income.

The third central marketing idea is *development of a strategic plan*. Passing a referendum requires much more than developing some promotional pieces and then hoping that enough sympathetic residents will turn out to vote on election day. It calls for a carefully organized campaign. Formulation of the plan should be based on research that identifies which segments of the community are likely to be responsive and unresponsive, which facets of the bond proposal are controversial, and which benefit appeals are likely to be most effective. The plan should address issues such as how to disseminate information, how to contact prospective voters, how to involve the media, how to raise funds to support the campaign, and how to organize the bond's supporters to maximize their effectiveness.

The campaign should build momentum steadily toward reaching a peak in the week of the actual referendum. It should begin 6 to 8 weeks before the referendum day. This allows sufficient time to generate the necessary support and still maintain the enthusiastic commitment of campaign volunteers. A good way to start the campaign is to hold a press conference to which representatives from all media are invited. Press packets containing prepared articles about the bond issue, illustrations, statistical data, and fact sheets would be made available to the media at this meeting. Media support is likely to be critical in the bond referendum, and close liaison should be maintained with the media throughout the campaign.

Brochures, posters, telephone calls, newsletters, lightweight display boards, door-to-door solicitations, television and radio shows, videotapes, slide shows, electronic messages, media advertisements, bumper stickers, buttons, and pins may all play a role in disseminating information. Some jurisdictions give details of the bond proposal by directly mailing literature to every resident or taxpayer, by paying for an insert in local newspapers, or by placing the material in retail stores and public buildings.

In addition to the written materials, every civic and community organization should be contacted, and an offer made to present information about the bond issue at their meetings. Some of the individuals in these groups are likely to be important opinion leaders in the community. For this purpose, presentations of 5, 10, and 20 minutes should be prepared so that different time slots can be accommodated. Endorsements from these groups and from prominent community residents should be solicited and then publicized. When these endorsements are made public through advertising materials, many voters are likely to be reassured that the bond proposal has merit.

Convincing more people to vote "yes" than "no" in a bond referendum is likely to be a substantial undertaking. When the referendum outcome is known, it is important that all of the people who were involved in supporting it be recognized and publicly thanked for their efforts.

Certificates of Obligation

In contrast to general obligation bonds, certificates of obligation do not require approval of the voters at a referendum, but they are still backed by the full faith and credit of a jurisdiction's tax base. The legislative body is required to publish a legal notice announcing a public hearing of their proposed use. The electorate can then petition the council requesting a public referendum on their use, but this rarely occurs.

These certificates usually are sold to local, rather than to regional or national, investors, and as with general obligation bonds, the debt is retired over a given period of years with property tax revenues. In the context of sports facilities, these instruments typically are used in one of the following circumstances:

- If the capital investment is not made quickly, then the opportunity will be lost. There is insufficient time to go through the lengthy process of obtaining voter approval for the investment.

- The legislative body has doubts that voters would approve the purchase, but its members are convinced strongly that the project is in the community's best long-term interest.

- They can be redeemed by designated income streams without recourse to property tax revenues.

Nonguaranteed Debt

The resistance to full-faith and credit obligations has caused most public sector investment in major sports facilities in recent years to use nonguaranteed funding mechanisms. These are not backed by the full-faith and credit of the government entity. Rather, they are sold on the basis that repayment will be forthcoming from other designated revenue sources. If revenue from the designated sources falls short of what is required to make the debt payments, the government entity is not obligated to make up the difference.

Nonguaranteed debt instruments have three major advantages. First, in most states, direct voter approval is not required because the general taxpayers are not being asked to pay these debts. Second, they are not considered statutory debts, so they do not count against the government entity's debt ceiling capacity. Third, if the revenue accrues directly from the project, then the people who most benefit from the facility pay for it.

It was noted earlier that investors who buy these nonguaranteed instruments incur more risk, which means that the government borrowers have to pay higher interest rates to lenders than they would pay on full-faith and credit obligations. However, cities often seek to reduce this risk by accepting either a real or a moral obligation to secure the loan. Accepting this obligation requires the jurisdiction to pledge either legally or orally that it will appropriate money from its annual revenues to meet full debt service on the bonds if the designated revenue source does not provide it. The jurisdiction does this for two reasons. First, it reduces risk and, hence, rate of interest that investors charge for the bonds. Second, even though a jurisdiction has no legal obligation to support nonguaranteed debt, a default would damage its reputation in the investment markets and make securing capital funds in the future more difficult and expensive for the jurisdiction.

A wide array of nonguaranteed funding mechanisms have been created, but the three that are likely to be most pertinent for development of major sports facilities are revenue bonds, tax-increment bonds, and certificates of participation (see Figure 6-5).

Figure 6-6 Developing a Softball Complex With Revenue Bonds

Johnson County, Kansas, used revenue bonds to develop an 80-acre, seven-field softball complex with three additional multipurpose fields for soccer and for flag and touch football (all irrigated) and with a 2.5-acre lake for fishing and ice skating, a jogging trail, a playground area, a concession stand, a restroom area, picnic shelters, and a parking lot. A federal Land and Water Conservation Fund grant of $246,000 was matched with $260,000 or revenue bonds to develop the complex. The county already owned the land but they had no capital money with which to develop it. They would not back the bonds with a cross-pledge of tax revenues, so the revenue bonds had to be sold at full risk on the commercial market.

The Johnson County Softball Players Association was approached. They contacted their 4,500 members who agreed to pay a surcharge of $5 per player to provide the funds needed to repay the revenue bonds. This surcharge was in addition to the normal fee paid to Johnson County that covered all operating, maintenance, utility, minor improvement, and overhead costs. The athletic associations were pleased to cooperate because it meant that they would have additional facilities available for their use. The district had turned away more than 240 softball teams, and the park and recreation agencies in the Kansas metropolitan area had turned away 1,000 teams due to a lack of facilities. This was evidence of a substantial demand for new ball fields.

The bonds were redeemable from the revenues received from players and teams playing in the softball and soccer leagues and tournaments scheduled through Johnson County. Table A illustrates that revenues from this source were projected on a yearly average of 1.95 times the necessary income to cover the average yearly principal and interest payments required, along with operation and maintenance costs. This income was derived from the approximately 6,000 players (3,000 in each of two seasons) whom the county projected were likely to use the facility. A second source of security was unencumbered recreation fees derived from other recreational programs scheduled through the Johnson County Park and Recreation District. Because these had historically exceeded $100,000, this latter provision enabled the bonds to be rated AA instead of A.

The surcharge was imposed for one year before the county sold the bonds in order to demonstrate to the banks that the scheme was feasible. In that year, officials collected $36,000 from the $5 surcharge. This convinced a consortium of local banks to buy the bonds, which had a 15-year payback period at 8.5% interest. The park and recreation district agreed to place the $36,000 in a special reserve account as an additional source of security to the lending banks. This amount exceeded the highest yearly payment for interest and principal (see Table A) and was meant to be used only to prevent default of payment of principal and interest on the bond.

The complex proved to be a financial and recreational success. It generated substantial surplus revenues that the county reinvested in further capital improvements on the project.

Revenue Bonds

Revenue bonds are particularly appropriate when a new facility is capable of generating enough revenue to pay for its own operations and any debt obligations incurred in its construction. Because revenue bonds are repaid from income produced by the facility and not from property or sales taxes, no referendum is required. They are secured by the revenues of the project being financed. In the case of stadiums and arenas, the bonds would be payable solely from income generated from venue operations such as ticket sales, parking, and the sale of in-

Table A Financial Feasibility of Revenue Bonds

Year	# Annual seasonal softball teams	# Annual seasonal soccer/ football teams	Total teams	Team annual special assessment maintenance fee	Total gross revenue	Annual (1) facility maintenance expenses	Available for debt service	Bond issuance debt service	Annual (2) debt coverage
1	470	77	547	$84	$45,948	$5,000	$40,948	--	--
2	800	77	877	85	74,545	15,000	59,545	31,212.50	1.90
3	800	77	877	86	75,422	16,500	58,922	30,387.50	1.93
4	800	77	877	87	76,299	18,150	58,149	29,562.50	1.96
5	800	77	877	88	77,176	19,965	57,211	28,737.50	1.99
6	800	77	877	102	89,454	21,961	67,493	27,912.50	2.41
7	800	77	877	103	90,331	24,157	66,174	32,112.50	2.06
8	800	77	877	103	90,331	26,572	63,759	30,912.50	2.06
9	800	77	877	103	90,331	29,229	61,102	29,712.50	2.05
10	800	77	877	103	90,331	32,151	58,180	33,512.50	1.73
11	800	77	877	111	97,734	35,366	62,368	31,912.50	1.95
12	800	77	877	111	97,734	38,902	58,832	30,312.50	1.94
13	800	77	877	111	97,734	42,792	54,942	33,662.50	1.63
14	800	77	877	111	97,734	47,071	50,663	31,600.00	1.60
15	800	77	877	111	97,734	51,778	45,956	29,537.50	1.55
16	800	77	877	111	97,734	56,955	40,779	32,475.00	2.27*
							$905,020	$463,562.50	

Average annual debt coverage 1.95

(1) Total gross revenues and annual facility maintenance expenses require
an increase in annual team assessments to cover anticipated increased in annual costs.

(2) Actual debt service.

*Coverage for Year 16 includes $33,000 in Bond Reserve

venue advertising. If no general fund pledge is provided as security, revenue bonds will typically have to pay higher interest charges.

Sport facility developers have attempted to make revenue bond financing a more attractive option to lending institutions by issuing *lease revenue bonds*. In an effort to enhance the security of the bond transaction, the borrower (the city or county issuing the bonds) pledges repayment from stadium or arena revenue sources that are specified in a long-term facility lease. Venue revenues frequently pledged as repayment for lease revenue bonds include

- Facility naming rights (15-25 years),
- Luxury suites/club seats (3-9 years),
- Food/Beverage concession contracts (5+ years), and
- Corporate sponsorship agreements (3-5 years).

Figure 6-7 Financing Golf Facilities With Revenue Bonds

The Fairfax County Park Authority (FCPA) in Virginia financed a substantial expansion of their golf facilities with a revenue bond issue of $13,870,000. The bond funds were used to develop new golf facilities at the Authority's existing Twin Lakes Golf Course and Oak Marr Park, as well as the renovation of the clubhouse at its Greendale Golf Course.

The Twin Lakes Golf Course was an existing 18-hole course that was 28 years old. Other than a small clubhouse (2,000 square feet) there were no practice facilities or other amenities associated with the existing golf course. A portion of the bond funds were used to construct a new 18-hole regulation length golf course, a new 4,000-5,000 square foot clubhouse, a 50 station practice range, croquet courts, and entrance road and parking improvements. There were also extensive renovations to the existing golf club, the removal of the existing maintenance facility, and the construction of a new maintenance facility. The cost of these improvements at Twin Lakes was $7,995,715.

The 137 acres of Oak Marr Park contained a recreation center, two soccer fields, a baseball field, and parking facilities. A portion of the bond funds was used to develop a golf teaching and practice center, with a 60 station driving range, a par 3 golf course, practice greens, a small clubhouse/control building, a maintenance building, a miniature golf course, and parking. Also included was improvement of the two existing soccer fields and elimination of the baseball field. These improvements cost $3,101,000.

The Greendale Golf Course was an existing 18-hole regulation length course with an 1,800 square foot clubhouse. The bond funds were used to remodel and enlarge the existing clubhouse to include an array of new amenities, such as proshop, snack bar, dining area, and secured storage area for 60 golf carts. The cost was $490,000.

The total investment at these three facilities was $11.586 million. Revenue bonds were sold to the value of $13.870 million and total **funding** for the project consisted of

Revenue Bonds	$13,870,000
Investment Earnings on the Bonds	$ 1,394,000
Total Available Funding	$15,264,000

This available funding **was spent** in the following ways:

Capital Investment in the 3 Golf Facilities	$ 11,586,000
Capitalized Interest	$ 2,145,000
Debt Service Reserve Fund	$ 1,166,000
Costs of Insurance	$ 367,000
	$15,264,000

N.B. *Capitalized Interest* is the fund used to pay the interest on the revenue bonds in the first three years. During this period, the improvements in the three facilities are being constructed and the revenue stream from them that is used to cover the bond's principal and interest payments cannot start until construction is finished.

Debt Service Reserve Fund will be used to make the principal and interest payments in any year in which the revenue stream from the golf project is inadequate to cover these payments. As an alternative to es-

Table A Annual Principal and Interest Payments

Year	Principal	Interest	Total Debt Service
1	00	375,000	375,000
2	00	900,000	900,000
3	265,000	900,000	1,165,000
4	280,000	886,000	1,166,000
5	295,000	870,000	1,165,000
6	310,000	852,000	1,162,000
7	330,000	834,000	1,164,000
8	350,000	814,000	1,164,000
9	370,000	793,000	1,163,000
10	395,000	770,000	1,165,000
11	420,000	745,000	1,165,000
12	445,000	719,000	1,164,000
13	475,000	690,000	1,165,000
14	505,000	658,000	1,163,000
15	540,000	625,000	1,165,000
16	575,000	589,000	1,164,000
17	610,000	551,000	1,161,000
18	655,000	510,000	1,165,000
19	695,000	467,000	1,162,000
20	745,000	421,000	1,166,000
21	790,000	372,000	1,162,000
22	845,000	319,000	1,164,000
23	900,000	263,000	1,163,000
24	960,000	204,000	1,164,000
25	1,025,000	140,000	1,165,000
26	1,090,000	72,000	1,162,000

[1] The FCPA Bond Years end on July 15. Hence, years 1 and 26 are approximate half years.

tablishing this fund, which gives some added protection to the buyer of the bonds, FCPA could have provided them with an insurance policy guaranteeing that deficits would be covered, or a letter of credit guaranteeing to meet any deficit out of the FCPA's general fund.

Costs of Insurance include legal fees, underwriters' discount, and other fees and costs of issuing the bonds. The bond schedule showing yearly payments of principal and interest is set forth in table A. The coverage ratio projections shown in Table B were not extended beyond

Table B. Coverage Ratios

Year	Projected Revenues	Projected Operating Expenses	Excess of Revenues Coverage	Over Expenditures Ratio
1	—	—	—	—
2	—	—	—	—
3	1,515,000	1,077,000	438,000	—
4	2,976,000	1,759,000	1,217,000	1.04
5	4,174,000	1,869,000	2,305,000	1.99
6	4,379,000	1,927,000	2,452,000	2.11
7	4,576,000	1,984,000	2,592,000	2.23
8	4,645,000	2,042,000	2,603,000	2.24
9	4,846,000	2,102,000	2,744,000	2.36
10	4,920,000	2,164,000	2,756,000	2.36
11	5,134,000	2,229,000	2,905,000	2.49
12	5,211,000	2,295,000	2,916,000	2.50
13	5,422,000	2,363,000	3,059,000	2.62
14	5,505,000	2,431,000	3,092,000	2.66

year 14 for two reasons. First, the consistent upward trend line from year 3 to year 14 of the coverage ratio was likely to continue since net revenues continued to increase while total debt service remained constant. Second, projection of what demand and prices are likely to be become increasingly speculative as the time frame of the projection is extended, so they serve little purpose.

FCPA already operated five courses (including Twin Lakes and Greendale) and the average ratio of revenues to expenditures across these facilities was 1.55. Thus, the agency had a strong track record of profitably operating golf courses that would give prospective investors added confidence in purchasing the bonds.

The debt service on the bonds was to be repaid from fees and charges generated by the facilities they funded. The operational revenues and expenditures of the facilities were derived from a feasibility study that FCPA commissioned from a respected outside consultancy firm. Their complete feasibility study was incorporated as part of the bond prospectus, so prospective investors in the bonds could see how these protections were derived and evaluate their likely level of accuracy. The bond prospectus stated in bold, capital letters, "**POTENTIAL PURCHASERS OF THE BONDS SHOULD READ THE FEASIBILITY STUDY IN ITS ENTIRETY.**"

The bond prospectus also carefully identified the risk factors associated with investment in the bonds. These included (1) the construction bids for the projects may substantially exceed the amounts available from the bonds; (2) completion data of the projects may be delayed substantially by the uncertainties inherent in construction; (3) demand for golf in the area may decline; (4) other new courses may provide competition that reduces the expected demand at these facilities; and (5) prolonged periods of inclement weather could adversely affect the demand and revenue projections.

This example is based on a Fairfax County Park Authority bond issue. It has been adapted here for illustrative purposes. The authors have omitted and changed some details in order to facilitate an easier understanding of the general procedure that was used.

All of these contractually obligated income (COI) streams are secured by long-term contracts of varying lengths and, as a result, are considered relatively stable and credit worthy.

What makes lease revenue bonds attractive to lenders is that the revenue streams pledged to repay the debt are contractually obligated *prior* to executing the bond agreement. The lender is assured in advance that a significant share of the facility's revenues will be committed to repaying the bonds, thereby reducing the risk of default.

The COI pledged to debt retirement should correspond with the length of the bond transaction and be sufficient to service the entire debt obligation. Achieving this standard of coverage, however, may be problematic for some of the venue revenue streams commonly obligated to retire lease revenue bonds. For example, most tenants (usually corporations) of skyboxes or luxury suites sign lease agreements averaging 3 to 5 years. This means that over the course of a long-term bond agreement of 20 to 25 years, suites in a typical venue would have to be resold 4-8 different times. For a struggling team, this could be a substantial challenge. Consequently, venue operators planning to pledge all of the revenues derived from suite contracts can provide lenders with no assurance of 100% occupancy beyond the length of the initial suite-lease agreements. In preparing for negotiations with prospective lending institutions to secure lease-revenue bond financing, those agencies seeking borrowed capital usually forecast suite revenues based on a more realistic occupancy rate of 60 to 70%. This provides sufficient slack to accommodate the ebb and flow of team performance and fan support, as well as fluctuations in economic cycles over a 20-year period.

In contrast, naming rights agreements, which typically extend over 15 or more years, are viewed as a stronger source of COI. The lender has more assurance that the contracted payments will be available to service the debt over the duration of the borrowing agreement.

Table 6-10 Summary of the Pros and Cons of Revenue Bonds

Advantages	Disadvantages
1. Reflects a "user pay" philosophy.	1. Higher interest rates due to their non-guaranteed status.
2. Voter approval not required.	2. Restricted to facilities with "profit-making" ability.
3. Do not count against the statutory debt ceiling.	3. High coverage rate requirements.
	4. May restrict participation because of higher user fees.

Revenue bonds have become a popular approach to financing the construction of a range of revenue-generating sports facilities, including golf courses, indoor tennis centers, athletic fields, and marinas. For these kinds of facilities, the revenue usually is generated from a variety of non-contractually obligated sources such as admission fees, concession income, and user fees. The fundamental requirement for the use of revenue bonds is that the facility has the means to generate sufficient income to cover both operating and maintenance costs as well as annual principal and interest payments. If the project has the ability to operate on a financially self-supporting basis, then revenue bonds are likely to be the preferred debt instrument for a number of reasons. Their use shifts the burden of facility financing from taxpayers to users who receive the direct benefit; it avoids the cost and uncertainty of voter referendums that are required for general obligations bonds; and it circumvents debt ceiling restrictions that are imposed on general obligation borrowing. (States do not place statutory limits on the amount of money a government agency can borrow through the sale of revenue bonds.) An illustration of how a softball complex was funded through the use of revenue bonds is provided in Figure 6-6 (see p. 34). The example shows how the imposition of a modest user surcharge resulted in the development of an 80-acre sports park.

The financial feasibility analysis shown in Figure 6-6 demonstrates that over the 16-year borrowing period, the revenues available from fees charged to teams using the complex would almost double the amount needed to repay annual debt service costs. By Year 16, aggregate user-fee revenues total $905,020, whereas the total principal and interest costs amount to $463,562. The relationship between revenues available for debt service and the total cost of the debt obligation is expressed as the *coverage rate*. The far right column of Figure 6-6 lists the coverage rates for each year of the lending agreement. In no single year is there less than $1.55 of available revenue for every $1 of debt obligation owed. The average annual debt coverage for the issue is a substantial 1.95. Most financial institutions will require a minimum coverage rate of 1.5 for revenue bonds.

In addition to substantial coverage rates, lenders usually require that borrowers create a debt-service reserve fund as additional security. The size of the debt-service reserve fund is usually equal to the maximum annual debt payment. The fund may be established from the proceeds of the bond when it is issued or as an up-front capital contribution from another source. In Figure 6-6, the reserve fund consisted of $36,000 derived from a one-year collection of a $5 surcharge fee on softball players before the revenue bonds were issued. A more complex example of the use of revenue bonds is described in Figure 6-7. The pros and cons of revenue bonds are summarized in Table 6-10.

Certificates of Participation

The certificate of participation (COP) is a financing vehicle that utilizes the leasing authority of local governments. Four entities are involved in the COP process. Their roles and the relationships between them are described in Figure 6-8.

The process starts with an *intermediary organization*, which may be a governmental agency or a public-benefit nonprofit organization, selling COPs to a financial institution to raise the money to build the facility (flow 1, Figure 6-8). The COPs are tax-exempt. The *financial institution* holds title to the facility as security for its loan, but confers "possessory interest" rights to the intermediary through a long-term agreement. After receiving funds from the financial institution (flow 2), the intermediary contracts with a *builder* (flow 3), who constructs the facility (flow 4). The intermediary leases the facility to a *facility operator* (flow 5), for a lease fee (flow 6) that is sufficient to pay the annual debt charges on the COPs (flow 7). When the COPs are paid off, the title for the facility passes to the facility operator.

Figure 6-8 Steps in the Issuance of Certificates of Participation

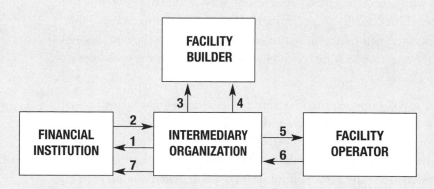

1. Intermediary sells COPs to a Financial Institution to raise the money to build the facility.

2. The Financial Institution delivers the funds to the Intermediary.

3. Intermediary pays a builder to construct the facility using the COP funds.

4. Builder delivers the facility to the Intermediary who holds title to it for the benefits of the investors.

5. Intermediary signs an annual renewable lease with a Facility Operator to run the facility.

6. Facility Operator pays a lease fee to the Intermediary that is sufficient to meet the annual debt charges on the COPs.

7. Intermediary pays the annual debt charges on the COPs to the Financial Institution.

Frequently, the commercial bank or trust company, in order to reduce any potential risk associated with the lending agreement, engages a municipal securities dealer to underwrite the resale of the certificates to individual investors. Rather than assuming the entire risk by holding all of the COPs, the lender spreads the risk across a number of investors who hold "participation shares" in the project. Certain investors find purchasing the certificates attractive because the income they receive from the leasing payments (passed through the intermediary) is tax-exempt since the project serves a government purpose.

The use of COPs is growing rapidly, and the increase appears likely to continue. Such certificates are a means of surmounting legal and political impediments of the use of traditional bonds, so their growth has been particularly prominent in states severely constrained in their ability to borrow funds by tax limits or expenditure limitation statutes:

> For instance, California local governments can borrow only after receiving approval from two thirds of the voters in a special referendum. In that environment, one vote over a one-third minority could prevent projects from having the support, including the willingness to pay a tax to finance the project, of the remaining voters. The COPs provide easier access to capital markets without the referendum test; given the size of the state, the pressures on state and local governments there to provide services, and the rigidity of the debt constraint, it is no surprise that California has the largest share of the COP market.[33]

The ability to enter into these arrangements without voter approval is a controversial feature of COPs.[34] In some jurisdictions, voters have opposed their use because they are not subject to citizen review and they dilute the government's general resources. This concern is particularly relevant in relation to the public trust model (described below), because under this arrangement the city assumes the role of facility operator so lease payments could come from the jurisdiction's general operating fund.

A referendum is usually not required because the lease agreement is not backed by the full-faith and credit of the city, and certificates of participation do not count against the jurisdiction's debt ceiling. There is a moral, rather than a legal, obligation for the jurisdiction to pay the lease fee to the lender annually either from appropriations from the general fund or from a designated income stream. Hence, certificates tend to be viewed as higher risk than traditional bonds and so tend to have higher interest rates. Typically, COPs are rated approximately one letter grade lower than general obligation bonds (the meanings of these ratings are discussed in the next section of this chapter). As a result, interest rates on COPs commonly run as much as 1% higher than borrowing rates for general obligation bonds. Lending rates for COPs are often equivalent to rates charged for revenue bonds.

Two models of COPs have emerged: the *public trust model* and the *public-private partnership model*. The essential difference between them is that in the former arrangement, the facility operator is a public entity, whereas in the latter model, the intermediary leases the facility to a private company.

The public trust model. In the public trust model, if the lease fees are a revenue stream from a facility, such as a sports arena or golf course, and smaller than anticipated revenues accrue, then the public agencies' general fund guarantees the debt service. The intermediary is usually a nonprofit organization acting as a public-benefit corporation, but in some circumstances, it may be a different government entity. If a public-benefit corporation is used, its directors are likely to be publicly spirited citizens deemed acceptable to the government entity. When the debt is paid in full, then the sports facility becomes the jurisdiction's property. COPs tend to be used as alternatives to bonds and, thus, possess relatively long maturities (more than 20 years).

In the city of North Augusta, South Carolina, for example, the Riverview Park Activity Center was funded by $2.4 million from the city's capital projects fund and $3.12 million in COPs. A corporation named Riverview Park Facilities Incorporated was established, and its directors constituted the five members of the North Augusta Parks and Recreation Advisory Board. The North Augusta City Ordinance No. 92-02 reads as follows:

> Whereas, in order to finance the cost of the project, the City has determined to enter into a Base Lease Agreement whereby the City will lease the existing site whereon the Project will be constructed (the "Land") to RIVERVIEW PARK FACILITIES, INC. (the "Corporation"), and contemporaneously with the execution of such Base Lease, the city will enter into a Project Lease Agreement whereby the Corporation will lease back the Project together with the land, as improved in the manner discussed

above (the "Facilities") to the City; and WHEREAS, the Corporation will assign its interest in the Project Lease Agreement to FIRST UNION NATIONAL BANK OF SOUTH CAROLINA, as Trustee for holders of Certificates of Participation in the Project Lease Agreement, which will provide the financing source for the project.[32] (p. 1)

The public-private partnership model. In this alternative approach to using COPs, the local government agency assumes the role of intermediary. Rather than taking direct operational responsibility for the new facility as in the previous model, under this arrangement, the city or county engages a private company to manage the day-to-day operation of a new building. Using the services of a private operator is most appropriate when the project requires specialized know-how beyond the customary expertise of the local government unit. In the context of sports facilities, such amenities as golf courses, marinas, ice rinks, and stadiums are good candidates for this type of public-private collaboration. A particularly innovative use of COPs is demonstrated in Figure 6-9, which describes the financing of Anaheim's Arrowhead Pond Arena.

In its role as broker of the development project, the city or county first procures the services of a qualified operator with a successful track record of managing the kind of facility the agency believes would be a community asset, such as a new ice rink, baseball stadium, or municipal golf course. The intent is to create a needed

---

Figure 6-9 Anaheim's Arrowhead Pond

The Arrowhead Pond arena was a joint venture between the City of Anaheim and Ogden Facility Management Corporation. The project to construct the Arrowhead Pond was funded by Certificates of Participation. However, all of the debt service payments associated with the COPs are paid by Ogden Management Corporation in return for which Ogden received a 30-year contract to manage the arena during which period the company retained all arena revenues excluding those associated with the Mighty Ducks. Ogden also received 7.5% of gross gate revenues from the Mighty Ducks. At the end of the 30-year period, when the bonds are paid off, the arena is turned over to the City of Anaheim. The city paid for the land, infrastructure improvements, and legal documentation, while Ogden's total cost was $126 million (including cost of debt service). Ogden anticipated losses in the first 12 years of operation, but they projected the profits in the last 18 years would be more than the first 12 years of losses. Apart from the naming rights to the facility and approval of the annual budget, the City gave Ogden almost complete autonomy to operate the arena. The financing arrangement is unique in that Ogden is solely responsible for guaranteeing payment of the facility's debt service.

Ogden's facility manager at Arrowhead Pond:

As far as the way this was financed, you'll probably never see one like it again. When you're a publicly traded company, everybody's looking for an immediate return. On the other hand, 15 years from now, when the people who put this deal together no longer work for the company, someone else is going to see the fruit of their labor.[a] (p. 59)

In addition to the Mighty Ducks, the arena is the home of the Anaheim Bullfrogs, a franchise of the Roller Hockey International League. Arrowhead Pond also hosts indoor soccer, tennis events, and many concerts. The aggregate number of annual visitors exceeds 2 million.

[a] Cohen, A. (1995). Webbed feet first. *Athletic Business,* April, 57-59.

resource for the community. The inducement for the private operator such as a hotel management company or owner of a minor league baseball team is that the city can borrow the construction capital to build the new asset at a much more favorable rate of interest through the use of COPs. Because of their tax-exempt status, COPs can be issued at significantly lower rates, as much as 3.5% lower, than the cost charged to private companies for standard commercial bank loans. Access to such relatively inexpensive development capital by partnering with a government agency is a powerful inducement for a private company to seek collaboration.

Tax-Increment Bonds

In 1952, California became the first state to authorize tax-increment financing (TIF).[35] It was initially viewed as a mechanism local communities could use to generate their share of matching revenues that were required to secure federal urban renewal grants and loans. Today, almost all states have passed enabling legislation authorizing TIF, and it is used by over 5,000 agencies. The original intent was that it should be used to stop the growth of urban decay and blight, but its subsequent uses have broadened so it is now perceived as a tool for facilitating economic development in any context rather than only in decaying urban areas.

TIF has contributed to the financing of a number of sports venues, for example, Akron, Ohio; Peoria, Illinois; Fresno, California; Memphis, Tennessee; and San Francisco. Although specific regulations for administering TIF programs vary from state to state, the basic concept is the same. In every state, the legislation allows cities and other local jurisdictions to create TIF districts to subsidize the cost of redeveloping designated areas in a community. Typically, the tax-increment process involves two phases. The first stage requires designating the area to be developed or revitalized as a TIF district. Usually, a specific agency is established to plan and oversee the redevelopment process. For example, in Florida, the administrative designation of TIF districts is *redevelopment agencies*, and in Oregon they are referred to as *urban renewal agencies*. In the second stage, the local development authority issues tax-increment bonds and uses the proceeds to demolish substandard buildings, clear land, or prepare land for development by installing infrastructure improvements such as utilities or roads.

The idea behind tax-increment financing is that new development in the TIF district will generate additional property taxes sufficient to pay for retirement of the bonds used to enact the improvements. With tax-increment financing, the development agency "captures" the increased property taxes produced by the new development and uses the "tax increment" to pay all or a portion of the development costs. Typically, tax-increment bonds are secured only by projected increases in property tax revenues in the TIF district. The future revenue flow from the tax increment is formally committed to pay off the bonds with interest.

Figure 6-10 illustrates how TIF works. It is important to understand that from the time the TIF district is formed, two sets of property tax records are maintained. The first set of records reflects the value of property at the time the district is created, and the second set reflects the growth in assessed property value *after* the improvements have been made. At the time the district is created, property tax rates imposed by government jurisdictions are "frozen" on all properties within the TIF district. The frozen tax base reflects the assessed value of property at the time the district was formed. Typically, the county tax assessor determines the predevelopment value of property within the TIF district. Every year after the district is formed, each taxing jurisdiction (city, county, school district, etc.) first applies its tax rate to the frozen value of the property within the district and then applies the same tax rate to the enhanced or incremental value of district property.

Under the first part of this arrangement, public jurisdictions continue to receive revenue from the predevelopment tax base, so there is no reduction in the revenues realized by them. The second part of the arrangement uses the incremental portion of the tax revenues to pay the annual debt charges on the bonds that paid

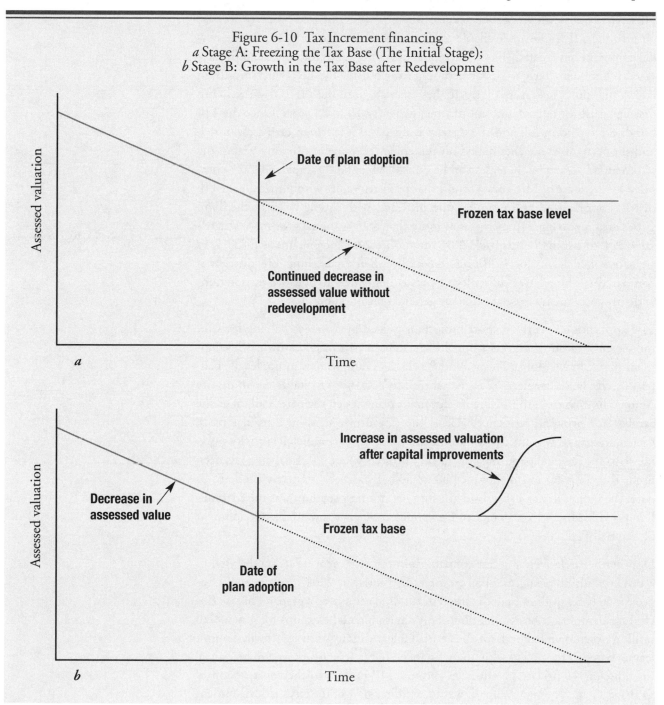

Figure 6-10 Tax Increment financing
a Stage A: Freezing the Tax Base (The Initial Stage);
b Stage B: Growth in the Tax Base after Redevelopment

for the improvements. Property owners within the TIF district pay only the additional property values created by the increase in the value of their property—there is no surcharge on them.

Most state laws require all taxing entities affected by the formation of the TIF district, such as cities, schools, and counties, to agree to its establishment. Each taxing unit can choose to dedicate all, a portion of, or none of the tax revenue that is attributable to the increase in property values due to the improvements within the TIF zone. Most taxing entities agree to dedicate the revenues to the TIF because in the short term, TIF districts assure continued tax collections, whereas in the long term, they promise significant future gains. The expectation is that the development or rejuvenation of the district will lead to enhanced property values.

However, because all property taxes accruing from the enhanced property tax base go into the TIF, none are available to pay for the increased services that the new development has created. Thus, additional operating funds for police and fire services, schools, etc. have to be forthcoming from outside the TIF, which means, in effect, that other taxpayers subsidize these services until the TIF is dissolved. TIF districts exist for a fixed amount of time, generally 10 to 25 years. Once the TIF bonds are repaid in full and the district is dissolved, the frozen tax base is lifted, and property taxes are then based on the enhanced value of property within the redeveloped area. The increases can be considerable. For example, a report compiled by the State of Minnesota found that property values within metro-area TIF districts appreciated at an annual rate of 7.8%, with several cities in the Twin Cities area reporting TIF increases of more than a 25% annual growth.[36] The relative ease of issuing bonds backed by the property tax increment has made TIFs attractive vehicles to local officials, especially when establishing TIF districts is compared to the relative difficulty of persuading voters to approve jurisdiction-wide property tax increases to finance general obligation bonds.

The application of TIF to sport projects is guided by a state's enabling laws. In most cases, stadium projects using TIF have been part of downtown redevelopment plans. In Memphis, Fresno, and Peoria, for example, new minor league ballparks were the centerpieces of each community's efforts to revitalize declining city centers. In each case, the TIF redevelopment plan viewed the new stadium as the catalyst for bringing residents back to the downtown areas on a regular basis, which, in turn, it was anticipated would stimulate other commercial activity proximate to the new ballpark. In sport facility projects where TIF financing has been used, the contribution of tax-increment dollars has been relatively modest. To date, the largest direct TIF subsidy in support of a new stadium was the $10 million provided by the San Francisco Development Agency toward the development of Pac Bell Park.

Despite their relatively modest contribution, tax-increment funds can be vital to a project's ultimate success. For example, in Peoria, in 2001, the city spent approximately $3 million in tax-increment funds to acquire and prepare the site (including demolition of old buildings and environmental cleanup) for a new $20 million downtown ballpark for the Peoria Chiefs, the city's privately owned minor league baseball team. These publicly financed improvements proved to be crucial to inducing 41 private investors to commit $17 million to the construction of O'Brien Field. The new ballpark was located in a part of the city's redevelopment

Figure 6-11 Using TIF to Fund an Arena

A 192-acre site of rolling farmland and scattered trees was designated a TIF district. The undeveloped land was located on the edge of the city. It was owned by two developers who petitioned the city to designate the area a TIF district. The developers planned a 315-bedroom, up-market hotel and a 250,000 square foot office development, whereas the remaining acreage was designated for office, high-density residential, and commercial use. The projected value of the development was $153.35 million.

The city saw an opportunity to capture the property tax revenues from this development to build a 60,000 square foot arena and encouraged the developers to submit their petition to the city council. The TIF district was established for 20 years. It was also approved by the county commissioners who, like the city, authorized the incremental tax the county would have received from the development to be used for constructing the arena. A board of directors to oversee the TIF district was established comprising six representatives appointed by the city council and three by the county commissioners. All the appointees by state law either must own property in the TIF district or be an employee or agent of a person who owns property in the district.

A schedule showing the annual tax increments that were projected to accrue from the development is given in Table X. The Base Value shown in column 2 is the total appraised value of all property in the TIF district at the time it was created; that is, $3.444 million. The table indicates that the first increment from development was to accrue in 2005 with the completion of the hotel, which was valued at $31.675 million (column 3). In the first 3 years of the district, the plans would be produced and construction initiated, but no development would be completed in this period, so there is no annual capture of property taxes in those years. The 2005 hotel development was followed by the large office development in the following year ($36.675 million). By year 2015, the development would be completed and its cumulative value was estimated at $153.35 million (column 4).

The city and county tax rates were 0.4777 and 0.4244, respectively, per $100 assessed valuation. Thus, the total tax rate available was 0.9021 (column 5). In 2005, when the tax rate of 0.9021 is levied on the new value of $31.675 million it generates $285,741 in property taxes towards redeeming the TIF debt (column 6). Column 7 shows that during the life of the district, the cumulative amount of property taxes accruing is $20.149 million (column 7).

To pay for the arena, the city issued $18 million of certificates of obligation (COs). In this case, they served as the tax-increment financing bond mechanism. These were a full-faith and credit obligation of the city. Thus, their redemption was not solely dependent on project revenues. If the projections were wrong, the city was required to pay the annual debt charges to redeem the COs.

The schedule of debt repayments is shown in Table Y. The annual debt payments on the COs are shown in column 2. The city and county used three revenue streams to pay the annual debt. First, hotel/motel taxes generated by the 315-bedroom hotel were pledged to the TIF and were estimated at $550,000 per year when the hotel was fully operational (column 3). Property taxes from the development increments are shown in column 4. Because these were inadequate in the first few years, the city also loaned the TIF $300,000 in 2004 and a total of $1.175 million in the first 6 years from its existing hotel-motel tax fund. This was to be repaid after the year 2015, when the TIF started showing positive cumulative balances. Column 6 shows the aggregate funds from these three sources to meet the debt charges (column 2). Column 7 shows that in every year up to 2009, the annual revenue streams are inadequate to meet the debt charges, but after 2009 the development reaches a threshold level generating sufficient resources to make the annual cash flow positive. By the end of the 20-year life of the district, a cumulative positive balance of over $4 million is projected.

Table X Schedule of Annual Tax Increments from the Development

1	2	3	4	5	6	7
Year	Base	Annual Capture	Cumulative Captured	Tax Rate	Annual Tax Increment Generated	Cumul. Tax Increment Generated
2002	$3,444,610	$0	$0	.9021	$0	$0
2003	$3,444,610	$0	$0	.9021	$0	$0
2004	$3,444,610	$0	$0	.9021	$0	$0
2005	$3,444,610	$31,675,000	$31,675,000	.9021	$285,741	$285,741
2006	$3,444,610	$36,675,000	$68,350,000	.9021	$616,585	$902,326
2007	$3,444,610	$10,000,000	$78,350,000	.9021	$706,795	$1,609,121
2008	$3,444,610	$10,000,000	$88,350,000	.9021	$797,005	$2,406,126
2009	$3,444,610	$10,000,000	$98,350,000	.9021	$887,215	$3,293,341
2010	$3,444,610	$10,000,000	$108,350,000	.9021	$977,425	$4,270,766
2011	$3,444,610	$10,000,000	$118,350,000	.9021	$1,067,635	$5,338,401
2012	$3,444,610	$10,000,000	$128,350,000	.9021	$1,157,845	$6,496,246
2013	$3,444,610	$10,000,000	$138,350,000	.9021	$1,248,055	$7,744,301
2014	$3,444,610	$10,000,000	$148,350,000	.9021	$1,338,265	$9,082,566
2015	$3,444,610	$5,000,000	$153,350,000	.9021	$1,383,370	$10,465,936
2016-2022	$3,444,610	$0	$153,350,000	.9021	$1,383,370	$20,149,526

If all debts of the TIF district are paid off before the end of its 20-year life, then the district will be dissolved at that point and its pledged tax revenues will revert to the general funds of the city and the county. The tables assume no increase in either the tax rate or the tax base beyond their 2002 values. It would be politically unwise for an elected official to suggest that these will increase in the future—tantamount to acknowledging that an increase in taxes is inevitable! However, such increases are inevitable. The result is that, if the development occurs as projected, then the annual tax increments will be bigger than shown so the COs will be redeemed in a shorter period than shown in Table Y.

The biggest winner from this arrangement is likely to be the school district. It did not contribute to the TIF district, so revenues from the development started flowing into the school district's general fund in 2005. The school district will receive $1 million in tax revenues in 2007, increasing to $2.5 million annually when the development is built-out in 2015.

There are two other upsides for the community. First, the city receives a "free" arena from the development, in the sense that existing taxpayers do not have to pay for it through higher property taxes. Second, when the TIF district is dissolved, the city and county will receive an additional $1.383 million per year (column 6, Table X) in tax revenue from the developments.

The major downside to the community is that because all the property tax funds in the new development are designated to retire the capital debt, the development contributes nothing to pay for the city services it will require until the TIF district is dissolved. Roads, water, wastewater, and utility improvements were not funded through the TIF, and no property taxes are available from it to pay for police, fire, street repair, public transportation, park maintenance, or any of the other services the area will require. The rest of the community will effectively be subsidizing the development with these until the district is dissolved.

Table Y Schedule of Debt Repayments

1	2	3	4	5	6	7
Year	Annual Debt Payments	Hotel-Motel Tax Revenues	TIF Revenues	Hotel-Motel Tax Transfer	Total Available Revenues	Cumulative Balance
2002	$0	$0	$0	$0	$0	$0
2003	$0	$0	$0	$0	$0	$0
2004	$465,055	$62,500	$0	$300,000	$362,500	$102,555
2005	$1,719,790	$400,000	$285,741	$250,000	$935,740	$886,605
2006	$1,513,123	$450,000	$616,585	$250,000	$1,316,585	$1,083,142
2007	$1,515,680	$500,000	$706,795	$150,000	$1,356,795	$1,242,027
2008	$1,517,258	$550,000	$797,005	$150,000	$1,497,005	$1,262,280
2009	$1,512,948	$550,000	$887,215	$75,000	$1,512,215	$1,263,012
2010	$1,517,598	$550,000	$977,425	$0	$1,527,425	$1,253,185
2011	$1,516,139	$550,000	$1,067,635	$0	$1,617,635	$1,151,689
2012	$1,513,755	$550,000	$1,157,845	$0	$1,707,845	$957,598
2013	$1,515,395	$550,000	$1,248,055	$0	$1,798,055	$674,938
2014	$1,515,918	$550,000	$1,338,265	$0	$1,888,265	$302,591
2015	$1,653,618	$550,000	$1,383,370	$0	$1,933,370	$22,838
2016	$1,688,580	$550,000	$1,383,370	$0	$1,933,370	$221,952
2017	$1,686,630	$550,000	$1,383,370	$0	$1,933,370	$468,692
2018	$1,222,641	$550,000	$1,383,370	$0	$1,933,370	$1,179,423
2019	$1,224,940	$550,000	$1,383,370	$0	$1,933,370	$1,887,853
2020	$1,226,690	$550,000	$1,383,370	$0	$1,933,370	$2,594,533
2021	$1,227,890	$550,000	$1,383,370	$0	$1,933,370	$3,300,014
2022	$1,223,680	$550,000	$1,383,370	$0	$1,933,370	$4,009,704

Another downside is the risk that the development will not be built-out in the time frame shown in the schedule or that its appraised value will be lower than that anticipated in the schedule. If either of these situations occurs, it would adversely affect the revenue flow from the development, and the city's taxpayers would be required to provide the compensatory funding necessary to meet the debt payments.

district, which the local newspaper had declared prior to the project's initiation as "a hardcore hangout for the city's underclass, a gathering place for the homeless and the hopelessly addicted."[37] Within the first year of the park's opening, significant benefits for the neighborhood were apparent. Capacity crowds consistently filled the 7,500-seat stadium, stimulating new business activity in the area that locals were beginning to refer to as "O'Brienville." A detailed case study describing the central role of TIF in the financing of an arena is shown in Figure 6-11.

With the trend toward cities requiring teams and owners to pay a greater share of the cost of building new facilities, TIF may be an effective way for franchises to attract at least some level of pubic financial support. The arrangement allows for a mutually beneficial relationship to be forged between the local government entity and the sports property.

If a facility can be built in a TIF-eligible district, the franchise operator has the opportunity for site preparation and infrastructure costs to be borne by the authority's issuance of TIF bonds, so the team can focus its capital acquisition efforts on securing funds necessary to cover only the "brick and mortar" expenses. This multimillion-dollar savings to the team can be crucial to making a project financially feasible. On the other hand, for a relatively small investment, the community stands to receive a significant economic return. The underlying promise of TIF investments in redevelopment contexts is that they leverage private spending in a part of the city that needs new attractions and infrastructure development.

Taxable Bonds

Faced with growing taxpayer resistance to large-scale public subsidies for new sports facilities and the difficulty of meeting either of the eligibility tests (10% limits) for issuing tax-exempt bonds, an increasing number of franchises have opted to issue taxable bonds. These have taken two main forms: private-placement bonds and asset-backed securitizations.

Private-Placement Bonds

Facilities built in the mid-1990s that were financed primarily with private-placement bonds include the Fleet Center in Boston, the First Union Center in Philadelphia, and the Rose Garden in Portland. With private placements, the organization developing the facility issues long-term, fixed-interest-rate bond certificates to private lenders. Typically, the parties interested in private placements are large institutional investors such as insurance companies and employee pension funds. Because the bonds are taxable, the interest rates the lenders receive are equivalent to alternate investments that they could make such as corporate bonds.

Private-placement bonds are secured by revenues generated by the facility, so in effect, they represent a form of revenue bond financing. The difference is that unlike traditional revenue bonds, which can only be issued by government agencies, private-placement bonds are issued by private companies (e.g., teams, facility development firms) or individuals (e.g., owners). With most private placements, the borrower pledges most, if not all, of the revenues produced by the facility to pay off the debt obligation. In addition, in some cases, these agreements are backed by a guarantee from a financially responsible party, usually the owner. Generally, investors will require that at least 60% of the revenue generated by the new facility comes from sources that have multiyear contracts.[38] This means that COI sources such as luxury-suite lease contracts (typically 3 to 10 years in length), and long-term naming rights agreements are particularly attractive collateral assets for private-placement bonds. Firms selling private placements on behalf of teams have found that institutional investors look for projects that show a coverage rate of at least 1.5,[39] which is similar to their requirements for revenue bonds. In other words, the facility's net earnings should exceed annual debt-service obligations by at least 1.5 times.

Portland's Rose Garden provides an illustration of how private-placement deals are arranged. The arena was one of the first major sports facilities to be almost entirely privately financed, and it has served as a model for subsequent private bond issues in Boston and Philadelphia. The Portland Trailblazers basketball team

(NBA) established the Oregon Arena Corporation for the purpose of raising private capital to fund the construction of a 20,350-seat multipurpose sports and entertainment center. The Oregon Arena Corporation enlisted the services of a national firm experienced in underwriting large bond transactions to first advise the team on how to structure the private debt offering and, then, to place the bonds with institutional investors. The firm received more than $215 million in orders for the $155 million arena debt offering. Nine insurance companies bought the taxable private-placement bonds at 8.99% interest for 27 years. As security, the Oregon Arena Corporation pledged almost all of the new facility's contract-guaranteed revenues such as suite sales, rent from the Trailblazers' 30-year lease, advertising, and rent by the team and other tenants of an adjacent office building.[40]

Although borrowing costs at 8.99%, when compared to tax-exempt bond rates, were expensive, the arrangement made good business sense to the Trailblazers' organization for a number of reasons. First, significant public support for building the arena was not available. The City of Portland had already committed a substantial portion of the local hotel-motel tax to building a new convention center. Therefore, the City limited its financial contribution to $34.5 million for the provision of plazas, improved access, and some parking around the arena. Given the absence of large-scale public subsidies (construction costs of the new arena were projected to exceed $200 million), securing private financing was the only option available to the team. Second, the 8.99% fixed rate was much lower than the interest rate the team or Oregon Arena Corporation would have had to pay to obtain a conventional loan from a commercial bank.[41] Banks were reluctant to lend for longer than 10 years. In addition, banks would have insisted on a much higher level of security by imposing a lien not only on the revenues of the facility but also on the franchise itself. Conversely, under the private-placement arrangement, the 27-year fixed rate was made without recourse to the basketball team or to the owner of the Oregon Arena Corporation (who was also the sole owner of the Portland Trailblazers).

Following the successful Rose Garden financing, the Boston Bruins (NHL) and Celtics (NBA) sold $160 million of private-placement bonds to build the Fleet Center. The owner of the NHL Philadelphia Flyers used a $142 million private placement to finance a new arena that opened as the new home of the Flyers and NBA 76ers. According to a spokesperson, "The deal worked out because the 22-year life of the bonds frees up more cash each year to go towards the teams . . . of an estimated $35 million in annual revenues coming from premium seating, advertising, and concessions, $14.5 million goes to debt service" (p. 59).[3]

Asset-Backed Securitizations

A variation on private-placement bonds called asset-backed securitizations (ABS) has emerged as an attractive approach to sport facility financing. ABS financing was first used to capitalize the construction of the Pepsi Center Arena in Denver. The developer of the new arena raised $139.8 million to underwrite a significant share of the construction costs. Shortly thereafter, the Los Angeles Arena Corporation used ABS financing to borrow $315 million to build the Staples Center. To date, securitizations have been used to build at least 12 major sport facilities, totaling more than $1 billion.[42]

With ABS, the most creditworthy revenue streams are bundled into a financial security and sold to private, usually institutional, investors. The major difference between ABS financing and standard private-placement debt agreements is that the asset-backed approach does not require that all revenue produced by a facility be pledged to debt repayment. For example, the Pepsi Center deal required that only 4 of the 10 multimillion, multiyear Founding Partners sponsorships and the facility's suite leases be pledged as security for the ABS bonds.[43] Typically, in private-placement arrangements, the team or facility operator is required to commit all future venue income as collateral for construction loans. The attraction of the ABS option is that only a portion of a new facility's revenues must be pledged as security.

To date, ABS bonds have been secured from such contractually obligated income sources as long-term naming rights agreements, luxury suite leases, concession contracts, and long-term corporate sponsorship deals. In the latest generation of sports facilities, the revenue produced from these contractually binding sources can be considerable. The Staples Arena is a prime example. The downtown Los Angeles arena is one of the biggest revenue generators of all the state-of-the-art facilities built over the last decade. The facility contains 160 suites that lease from $197,500 to $307,500 annually; the 10 "founding" corporate sponsorship agreements net $50 million, and the naming rights contract is worth $105 million.[44] These three assets alone produce an estimated $40 to $45 million annually. The ability of facilities like the Staples Center to generate such substantial cash flows makes them attractive candidates for ABS.

With ABS transactions, the future cash flow from these facility "assets" is sold to investors. In this respect, ABS is similar to traditional revenue bond and private-placement agreements. What makes ABS financings different and more complex is that the contractual ownership of the specific revenues is first sold into a trust that, in turn, issues notes to investors. The trust structure is created to make the possibility of bankruptcy more remote, so that if the arena or stadium owner should declare bankruptcy, the assets of the trust remain inviolable. This "bankruptcy remote" feature of the ABS transaction makes it more attractive to prospective institutional investors. Typically, an established financial institution will establish and administer the trust. The trust sells investors the ABS bonds secured by the future income from contracted revenue streams, together with the renewal rights to any of the selected revenue streams. The commitment of renewal rights is an important feature of ABS transactions because it means that investors have a long-term claim on revenue sources that are often short-term in nature. For example, the initial contract term for many luxury suites and corporate sponsorships does not extend beyond 3 to 5 years. By conveying the right to access revenues from subsequent contract renewals of suite leases, concession contracts, etc., investors have greater assurance of timely repayment.

With an asset-backed transaction, the independent trust acts as the transaction agent. The trust first collects the promised facility revenues pledged by the facility operator and then redistributes them to each investor on a pro rata basis to meet guaranteed principal and interest payment obligations.

Asset-backed bonds for both the Pepsi Center and Staples Center sold out quickly. In the case of the Pepsi Center, the $139.8 million ABS notes were sold at a 6.94% rate of interest for 21 years to five institutional investors. The bonds were secured by revenues produced from three contracted asset sources: luxury suites, concessionaire contracts, and 4 of 10 corporate sponsor packages. The interest rate was one percent above the 10-year U.S. Treasury Note rate at the time of the transaction. The company developing the arena proclaimed that the lower interest rate saved up to $3 million annually (approximately 10% to 15% of the Denver Nuggets' and Colorado Avalanche's annual operating revenues) compared to the cost of traditional financing. In addition, the facility operator and its principal tenants (the Nuggets and Avalanche) have unrestricted rights to all revenues not dedicated to repaying the ABS bonds.

The Spanish soccer club, Real Madrid, one of the world's elite teams, sold $70 million worth of bonds secured solely by its membership fees (Real has 75,000 fans who pay to be official club members) and ticket sales that typically amount to $40 million a year. The team used the proceeds to acquire top players. The ABS is perceived to initiate a circle of events; that is, the club uses the money to buy players who help the club become more successful. This, in turn, means the team gets more people in the stadium and more television revenue, so there is additional income to pay the bonds. Previously, Real Madrid had securitized the team's $10 million annual footwear and apparel sponsorship agreement with Adidas, which enabled the club to sell $50 million of bonds to investors, and in the summer of 2003 they added the most pre-eminent player in all of soccer, David Beckham, to their roster.[45]

Perhaps the largest ABS bond was proposed by the U.K.-based Formula One, which manages the international grand prix automobile-racing circuit. The $2 billion worth of bonds were to be secured by Formula One's lucrative broadcasting and sponsorship revenue.[46]

Despite the great promise of ABS financing, its application may be limited by the legal complexities and, therefore, greater costs associated with its use. The expertise needed to set up the trust and to place the bonds requires the use of experienced investment banking specialists and legal counsel. The law firm handling the Pepsi Center ABS transaction produced 15 two-inch-thick bound notebooks containing the materials needed to complete the Denver arena arrangement.[43] Although actual transaction costs associated with any of the ABS arrangements have not been publicly disclosed, the likelihood is that they are substantial.

A preliminary step to determining the viability of using the asset-backed approach in preference to other options would be to conduct a benefit-cost analysis. Such an analysis would weigh such factors as the following:

- Extent of the collateral pledge (dedication of all rather than only selected income sources as collateral)
- Favorability of the interest rate (actual percentage as well as whether fixed or variable terms)
- Restrictions imposed by the lender (e.g., some banks require budget approvals, quarterly reports, etc.)
- Length of borrowing period (a longer lending period generally reduces the annual principal and interest payments)

- Magnitude of costs to establish the funding vehicles (legal fees and other transaction expenses)

Mechanics of Selling Bonds

After a sports facility bond proposal has been approved, a jurisdiction's officials will hire bond consultant specialists and work with them to develop the financial, legal, and technical details that are required before the bonds can be offered for sale. Three tasks must be accomplished when preparing the bonds for sale: obtain a bond rating, ensure the financial transactions are completed efficiently, and ensure the legal contractual language in the bond sale agreement is accurate. Jurisdictions usually hire bond-specialist lawyers and financial consultants to complete the latter two tasks.

Bond Ratings

The level of risk that investors incur strongly influences the interest rate that government entities will pay on their bonds. Full-faith and credit bonds remain among the safest investments available; however, very occasionally, defaults do occur. The largest default was on $2.25 billion of bonds issued by the Washington Public Power Supply System in 1983. Although it was many years ago, the memory of this large default reminds investors that investments in government bonds are not entirely risk free.

To provide potential investors with information regarding the degree of risk involved in a bond issue, two major rating agencies—Moody's Investor Service, Inc., and Standard & Poor's—analyze an issue's risk of default and assign a credit rating to the bonds. The bond issuer pays for the rating. The rating agencies prepare an opinion of the borrower's credit quality (for full-faith and credit issues) or of the particular bond issue (for nonguaranteed bonds). Credit quality depends on the ability of the tax base or revenue source to generate the required debt service payments while financing regular current expenditures. The agencies' ratings are distributed widely to the investment community and have a major influence on borrowing costs. An issue without a rating seldom will sell on national markets, but issues may not be rated if banks in local markets will buy them, such as in the Johnson County, Kansas, sports complex example.

The alphabetical rating systems used by the two agencies are generally considered to be equivalent, and the characteristics of a government entity that they consider when determining bond ratings are similar. An issue is assigned one of the ratings shown in Table 6-11. To illustrate the impact of these ratings in one community, the difference between AA and AA+ ratings, which are only marginally differentiated for a bond of $11.8 million over 20 years, was 0.5%, which amounted to over $850,000 over the life of the bond.[47] Table 6-12 shows bond ratings for selected cities in which sports franchises are located.

In recent years, the influence of ratings on borrowing costs has been altered with the evolution of insurance for new municipal bond issues. In the early 1980s, less than 4% of new municipal bond issues were insured, but this percentage now has increased to more than 50%. Typically, an insurer agrees to guarantee the timely payment of principal and interest to investors in return for a one-time premium

Table 6-11 Credit Ratings by Moody's and Standard & Poor's

Moody's Ratings	Symbol	Symbol	Standard & Poor's Ratings
INVESTMENT GRADE Best quality, smallest degree of investment risk; referred to as "gilt edge."	**Aaa**	**AAA**	The highest rating. Capacity to meet debt payments is extremely strong.
High quality; smaller margin of protection or larger fluctuation of protective elements than Aaa.	**Aa**	**AA**	Strong capacity to meet debt payments; differ from the highest rated issues only in small degree.
Upper medium grade, many favorable investment attributes; but elements may be present which suggest some susceptibility to future risk.	**A**	**A**	Strong, but more susceptible to adverse effects in circumstances and economic conditions than in debt in higher rated categories.
Medium grade: neither highly protected nor poorly secured; adequate present security that debt payments will be met but may be unreliable over any great length of time.	**Baa**	**BBB**	Adequate capacity to meet debt payments, but adverse economic conditions or changing circumstances are more likely to weaken this capacity than in higher rated categories.
SPECULATIVE GRADE Judged to have speculative elements; not well safeguarded; very moderate protection of principal and interest, payments over both good and bad times. Element of uncertainty.	**Ba**	**BB**	Less near-term vulnerability to default than other speculative issues, but faces major ongoing uncertainties or exposure to adverse economic conditions which could lead to inadequate capacity to meet debt payments.
Lack characteristics of desirable investment. Assurance of debt payments over the long term may be small.	**B**	**B**	Greater vulnerability to default, but currently has the capacity to meet payments.
Poor standing; may be in default or may be elements of danger to meeting debt payments.	**Caa**	**CCC**	Has current identifiable vulnerability to default. Is dependent on favorable economic conditions to meet debt payments. If these conditions deteriorate, it is not likely to have the capacity to meet debt payments.
Speculative in high degree; in default or other marked shortcomings.	**Ca**	**CC**	Economic conditions are deteriorating, making bankruptcy a likely option.
Lowest rated class; extremely poor prospects of ever attaining any real investment standing.	**C**	**C**	Bankruptcy petition has been filed, but debt service payments are continued.
		D	Default. Debt payments are not made on the date due.

Moody's rating may be modified by the addition of a plus or minus sign to show relative standing within the major rating categories. In Standard & Poor's ratings, numerical modifiers 1, 2 and 3 are added to letter ratings.

Sources: Standard & Poor's *Municipal Finance Criteria.* New York: Standard and Poor's 1994, p. 4.
Moody's Investors Service, *An Issuers Guide to the Rating Process.* New York: Moody's Investors Service, 1994.

paid on the issue date of the bonds. The insurance enables a lower-rated issue to be sold at the level of a AAA rating. Fees for insurance fall somewhere between the interest payment that would be due on a bond issued with the jurisdiction's credit rating and the interest payments on a bond with the insurance company guaranteeing it as a AAA rating. The insurance allows the jurisdiction to harvest some of the interest-rate savings that the higher credit rating may confer. Typically, borrowers seek competitive bids on the insurance premium and have investors interested in their bond offerings bid on both an insured and uninsured basis. This allows the market to determine the cheaper way to borrow.

Table 6-12 Bond Ratings for Selected Cities with Sports Franchises

City	Standard & Poor's	Moody's
New York	A	A2
Los Angeles	AA	Aa2
Chicago	A+	A1
Houston	AA-	Aa3
Philadelphia	BBB	Baa1
San Diego	AA	Aa1
Phoenix	AA+	Aa1
San Antonio	AA+	Aa2
Dallas	AAA	Aaa
Detroit	A-	Baa1
Washington, D.C.	BBB+	Baa1
New Orleans	BBB+	Baa2
Miami	BB	Baa3
Minneapolis	AAA	Aaa
Anaheim	AA	Aa2

Source: U.S. Census Bureau (2001). "Bond Ratings for City Governments by Largest Cities: 2000," in *Statistical Abstract of the United States,* (p.176), by U.S Census Bureau, 2001, Washington, D.C.: Superintendent of Documents.

Financial and Legal Advisors

If employed, financial advisors serve as a jurisdiction's impartial consultants on structuring and selling the bonds. Their primary responsibilities are to advise on the most feasible timetable for retiring the debt (this includes a maturity schedule and interest payment dates), the fee structure and methods necessary for supplying enough money to pay the principal and interest, and the relative acceptability of bids when sealed bids are opened. All states have laws that require general obligation bonds to be sold to the bidder offering the lowest net-interest cost at an advertised public sale. The bond consultants also assist in distributing the official notice of sale to potential lenders. Financial periodicals generally are used to ensure broad exposure. Prospective lenders (e.g., banks, investment houses, insurance companies) are invited to submit bids to the government entity detailing the terms under which they will lend the money.

Bond counsel play a critical role in an agency's attempt to attract the interest of potential investors in its bond issue. Bond buyers place great confidence in nationally recognized bond counsel. They are lawyers who have proven records in working with bonds, and investors expect the bond counsel to help screen out unacceptable risks. Legal restrictions are prone to new interpretations and tests. It is the job of bond counsel to monitor and incorporate these changes in the advice and documents prepared for their clients' jurisdictions. Bond counsel will be called on to make numerous interpretations of federal laws and regulations, state constitutions and statues, and local charters and ordinances. Even the smallest technical or legal error may result in invalidating an entire issue. There have been many unfortunate examples of jurisdictions' having to resubmit their bond proposal to the voters because of inappropriate legal advice.

Summary

State and local governments play a major role in financing and operating a wide spectrum of sports facilities. Property and general sales taxes have been the traditional revenue sources used by government entities to fund sports venues. In the past decade, there has been a dramatic shift away from these hard taxes, where the burden of payment falls on all taxpayers, toward soft taxes. These include hotel-motel, car rental, sin taxes, and player taxes, where the burden of payment is borne only by those staying in hotels, renting cars, and/or buying alcoholic beverages and cigarettes. Some of these soft taxes are categorized as tourist development taxes because, in the case of the hotel and car rental taxes, the majority of those paying are likely to be visitors from outside the local area.

Cities, counties, and school districts rely heavily on property taxes. Property tax values are determined by an assessor, and the aggregate value of all the assessed values within a particular jurisdiction is referred to as the tax base. After the tax base has been determined by assessment, the government entity sets a tax rate to meet its revenue needs. Property taxes may be increased annually by raising the value of the tax base, by increasing the tax rate, or by raising both elements. Although property taxes are a stable source of revenues, most states and/or local governments require at least a simple majority of voters to use property tax monies to construct sports facilities. Some states now require double or super majorities to pass a property tax increase. As a result, over the past decade, property tax-financed sport facilities have been less common.

The second largest source of revenues for state and local governments is the general sales tax. When they have been used to fund major sports facilities, sales taxes have usually been adopted over a regional or county-wide area. Imposing a sales tax on selected purchases has become a favored approach in the field. Thus, some three-fourths of the major sport venues built between 1997 and 2001 were financed at least in part by either a bed tax on hotel guests or a car rental tax. Despite growing opposition from the hotel and car rental industries, these soft taxes continue to be the most popular approach to securing public tax support for building or renovating sport facilities.

Despite a number of legal challenges, a tax on players' salaries has become an established revenue source for state and local governments. Most states and a growing number of cities have passed laws that allow them to collect taxes on the portion of a visiting player's salary earned in their jurisdictions. Typically, the tax is determined by calculating the number of "duty days" a player accumulates in a particular state or city. To date, the nonresident-player tax has not been widely used as a source of revenue for facility development. However, based on the benefit principle of taxation, a strong case could be made for it to be applied in this way.

Debt financing is the most common way local governments raise money to pay for major capital development projects like sports complexes and stadiums. Cities and counties borrow money from lending institutions and private investors through the sale of bonds. Bonds are defined as a promise by the local government agency borrowing the money to pay back the principal and interest amount within a specified period of time. The source of funds used to repay or "secure" the debt comes from either tax sources (e.g., property, sales) or from revenues produced by the facility itself. The major types of bonds are named by the source of revenue used to repay them.

The 1986 Tax Reform Act was intended to severely curtail the issuance of tax-exempt bonds for the construction of stadiums and arenas. The loss of the tax exemption can result in an increase in debt service costs of as much as 2%. Under the Act, a city or county loses its tax-exempt eligibility if (a) more than 10% of the debt service is paid from stadium revenues or (b) more than 10% of the stadium or arena's utilization is consumed by a single private tenant, such as a professional sports team. Revenue derived from the sale of personal seat licenses (PSLs) and tourist development taxes still qualify as tax-exempt under the Act. Given the difficulty of meeting the 10% limits and growing taxpayer resistance to any form of tax support for sport facility construction, teams and owners have pursued other borrowing alternatives.

General obligation bonds are full-faith and credit obligations backed by the local government's authority to levy taxes. Typically, general obligation bonds are secured by an increase in either property or general sales taxes. These bonds are very secure, and as a result, the interest rates charged by lenders are relatively low compared to other bond options. Before state and local governments are authorized to issue general obligation bonds, they must have voter approval.

In contrast, revenue bonds rely on revenue produced by a facility designated or other revenue streams to redeem them. With revenue bonds, the burden of facility financing shifts from general taxpayers to users who receive direct benefit. Admission fees and concession and parking revenues are user-generated revenues that are typically used to secure revenue bonds. With expensive arenas and stadiums, contractually obligated income (COI) sources have been pledged as primary security for revenue-bond-financed projects. Prominent COI sources include revenue derived from naming rights agreements, luxury suite leases, and concession contracts. Certificates of Participation (COPs) use the leasing power of local governments to secure long-term debt financing. COPs require a third party to act as an intermediary. With the public trust model, a public benefit corporation borrows money through the issuance of COPs to build the facility and then leases it back to the city. The public corporation repays the debt obligation from the lease fees it receives from the government entity. In the public-private participation model, the city acts as the intermediary by recruiting a private operator for the proposed facility. The city issues COPs to a local bank to raise money to build the new facility. The city then leases the facility to a private operator and uses the lease payments to repay the debt. No referendum is necessary with COPs.

Used primarily as a tool to revitalize blighted neighborhoods or underdeveloped areas, tax–increment bonds (TIF) are repaid by incremental property tax collections resulting from the infrastructure and amenity improvements paid for by the bonds. Although the application of tax-increment financing to sport projects is limited, TIF has often have been used to subsidize expensive up-front infrastructure costs associated with facility development.

Two private debt-financing options have become prominent: private-placement bonds and asset-backed securitization bonds. Both are taxable debt options, so the interest rates associated with their issue are typically higher than the rates charged for tax-exempt bonds. Both types of bonds are sold by a private entity, commonly the team, its owner, or a development corporation representing the team's interests. In each case, the bonds are secured by revenues generated by the facility being financed. With private placements, security for the bonds is provided by a lien on all of the future facility revenues, particularly from contractually obligated sources. Asset-backed securitization bonds have emerged as an attractive alternative to private placements because the former impose less stringent collateral requirements. With asset-backed transactions, the revenues of selected assets (naming rights, luxury suites, etc.) are bundled into a financial security and sold first to a "bankruptcy-proof" trust, which in turn issues the notes to private investors.

The selection of the most appropriate debt-financing mechanism among those discussed in this chapter is determined by the situational contract of a proposed facility. For example, replacement of a city swimming pool that has long been perceived as a well-used community resource might be best achieved by using straight serial general obligation bond financing. Obtaining voter support for such a project may have a high probability of success. On the other hand, the user-pay philosophy demonstrated in the Johnson County, Kansas, sports complex and Fairfax County golf course examples was the optimal financing decision for developing those facilities. Using revenue bonds, paid for by those who directly benefited from the creation of the softball and golf amenities, to finance the projects made a great deal of sense. In a growing number of communities, taxpayer support for major sport facilities is not widespread. Under such circumstances, perhaps, tax-increment financing may be the only public source of financing available to a sports property hoping to develop a new ballpark or arena. Finally, for those projects that have the capability of generating substantial amounts of income, private-placement bonds and, more recently, asset-backed securitizations may be legitimate alternatives.

An agency intending to sell a bond must procure the expertise of a number of specialized consultants. The process may involve retaining a bond counsel to ensure that all aspects of the bond process, including the contractual language in the bond documents, are legal and accurate; and hiring a financial consultant to structure the debt retirement schedule, sell the bonds, and in some cases, obtain a bond rating.

References

1. Standard & Poor's. (1994). *Municipal criteria.* New York: Standard & Poor's Rating Group.
2. U.S. Census Bureau (2001). *Statistical Abstract of the United States.* Washington, DC: Superintendent of Documents.
3. O'Sullivan, A., & Sheffrin, S. M. (1995). *Property taxes and tax revolts: The legacy of Proposition 13.* Cambridge, England: Cambridge University Press.
4. Mikesell, J.L. (1991). *Fiscal administration: Analysis and applications for the public sector* (3rd ed.). Pacific Grove, CA: Brooks/Cole.
5. Kozlowski, J.C. (1995). Private property bill more demanding than Constitution. *Parks and Recreation, 30* (5), 16-24.

6. O'Sullivan, A. (2001). Limits on local property taxation: The United States' experience. In W.E. Oates (Ed.), *Property Taxation and Local Government Finance* (pp. 177-207). Cambridge, MA: Lincoln Institute of Land Policy.

7. Danielson, M.N. (1997). *Hometeam: Professional sports and the American metropolis.* Princeton, NJ: Princeton University Press.

8. Mukherjee, S. (1997b, April 25). U.S. cities are taxing tourists to fund new stadiums. *Boston Business Journal,* p. 1-4

9. Mukherjee, S. (1997a, March 31). An all-American game: Taxing travelers to fund sports arenas. *Houston Business Journal,* 1.

10. Wade, B. (2000, June 18). Need an arena? Tax a tourist. *New York Times,* D2.

11. Baldo, A. (1991, November 26). Edifice complex. *Financial World, 160* (21), 34-37.

12. Rafool, M. (1997). Playing the stadium game. *Legislative Finance Paper, #106,* Denver, CO: National Conference of State Legislatures.

13. The Travel and Tourism Government Affairs Council. (1996, December 4). 17 cities sock it to travelers to pay for stadiums [Travel Industry Association of America press release].

14. Weiss, S. (1999, October 18-24). Car-rental tax for Spurs' home is drawing fire. *Sports Business,* 8.

15. Brown, M. (2002, July 9). Squeeze play: Athletes are challenging Illinois' income tax system. Retrieved from niu.edu/ipo/ii000631.html

16. Comptroller of Maryland. (2001). *Nonresident professional athletes and entertainers* [Administrative release No. 24].Retrieved from www.marylandtaxes.com/publications/bulletins/it/ar_it24.pdf

17. Cohen, A. (2001, October). Thanks, and come again. *Athletic Business,* 9-10.

18. Lombardo, J. (2001, May 21-27). Taxmen target visiting teams. *SportsBusiness Journal,* 1, 56.

19. Wharnsby, T. (2002, June 4). NHLPA files grievance over Alberta's proposed players' tax. *Toronto Globe & Mail,* D4.

20. DiRienzo, D. (2002, May 31). Officials seek wage taxes from Steelers player. *Pittsburgh Tribune-Review,* C3.

21. Coates, D., & Humphreys, B. (2002, March). *Voting on stadium and arena subsidies.* Paper presented in the Spring Seminar Series, Department of Economics, University of Maryland, Baltimore County. Retrieved from www.umbc.edu/economic/seminar_papers/brown_new.pdf

22. Howard, D. R. (1999). The changing fanscape for big-league sports: Implications for sport managers. *Journal of Sport Management, 13* (1), 78-91.

23. Sanders, L. (1997, September 23). To subsidize or not subsidize? First ask who benefits. *Stadium & Arena Financing,* 9.

24. Kormon, R. (1989, February 20). A matter of pride. *Sports Inc.,* 34.

25. Quirk, J., & Fort, R.D. (1999). *Hardball: The abuse of power in pro sports teams.* Princeton, NJ: Princeton University Press.

26. Mikesell, J.L. (1991). *Fiscal administration: Analysis and applications for the public sector* (3rd ed.). Pacific Grove, CA: Brooks/Cole.

27. Zimmerman, D. (1997). Subsidizing stadiums: Who benefits, who pays? In R. Noll & A. Zimbalist (Eds.), *Sports, jobs and taxes* (pp. 119-145). Washington DC: The Brookings Institution.

28. Cagan, J., & DeMause, N. (1998). *Field of schemes: How the great stadium swindle turns public money into private profit.* Monroe, ME: Common Courage Press.

29. Burke, D. (1997). The Stop Tax-Exempt Arena Debt Issuance Act. *Journal of Legislation, 23,* 149-157.

30. Noll, R., & Zimbalist, A. (1997). Build the stadium—create the jobs! In R. Noll & A. Zimbalist (Eds.), *Sports, jobs and taxes* (pp. 1-54).Washington DC: The Brookings Institution.

31. McLean, D.D., & Martin, W.D. (1991). Blueprints for successful bond referendums. *Journal of Physical Education, Recreation and Dance, 62*(10), 40-44.

32. Gladwell, N., Sellers, J., & Brooks, J. (1997). Certificates of participation as an alternative funding source for capital projects: A case study. *Journal of Park and Recreation Administration, 15* (4), 23-37.

33. Johnson, C., & Mikesell, J. (1994). Certificates of participation and capital markets: Lessons from Brevard County and Richmond Union School District. *Public Budgeting and Finance, 14* (3), 41-54.

34. Joseph, J. (1994). *Debt issuance and management: A guide for smaller governments.* Chicago: Government Finance Officers Association.

35. Chapman, J.I. (1998). Tax increment financing as a tool of redevelopment. In Helen F. Ladd (Ed.), *Local government tax and land use policies in the United States.* Northampton, MA: Edwood Elgar.

36. Citizens League. (2001). TIF by the numbers. Retrieved from www.citizensleague.net/mj/2001/07

37. Reynolds, D. (2002, May 22). Stadium might be neighborhood's springboard [Electronic version]. Peoria Journal Star, Special section ("Guide to O'Brien Field"). Retrieved from www.pjstar.com/services/special/2002obrienfield/stories.html

38. Fischl, J. (1997, June 17). Private Parts. *Financial World*, 58-60.

39. Prudential Securities. Statement of qualifications: Guide to sport facility finance, Using public and private funds to build sport facilities. Presented at Bond Buyer Conference, September 8, 1996.

40. Stephens, K. (1994). The new arena. *Dallas Morning News,* June 24, D5.

41. Personal interview with Jim Kotchik, Chief Financial Officer, Portland Trailblazers, June 3, 2001.

42. Kaplan, D. (1998). New strategy creates buzz around bear. *SportsBusiness Journal,* November 2-8, 8.

43. Mitchell, E. (1999). Developers financed with securities, saving millions. *SportsBusiness Journal,* August 30-September 5, 8.

44. Kaplan, D. (1999, February 22-28). Rating agency backs private arena bonds. *SportsBusiness Journal,* 26.

45. Kaplan, D. (1998, May 3-9). Real Madrid soccer team will sell $70 million in bonds. *Sports Business,* 10.

46. Kaplan, D. (1998, October 12-18). Bond offer may pave way for Formula One IPO. *Sports Business,* 9.

47. Lee, R., & Johnson, R.W. (1989). *Public budgeting systems.* Rockville, MD: Aspen Publications.

Photo courtesy of University Oregon Athletic Department.

Chapter Seven

Sources of Revenue for Sport Enterprises

Over the last decade, the revenue model for sports organizations at all levels of professional sport, and at a growing number of colleges, has changed dramatically. With the advent of fully loaded sport facilities that characterized the construction boom of the 1990s and early 2000s, sport managers have been able to develop new sources of revenue. This chapter examines three major innovations in venue development that have transformed the revenue status of sports teams and leagues: (a) premium seating (the sale of luxury suites and club seats), (b) the sale of venue naming rights, and (c) the sale of personal seat licenses, or PSLs.

Operators of an increasing number of sports enterprises have been able to "grow" their operational revenues to unprecedented levels by exploiting the desire of corporations to use new state-of-the-art facilities to increase their visibility and create new business opportunities. In the last decade, companies have committed over $3 billion to place their company (or brand) names on an arena or stadium. During the same period, over 10,000 luxury suites have been built, primarily to accommodate the entertainment demands of corporations that have found sports venues an effective place to extend hospitality to key clients.

In addition to describing these new revenue sources, this chapter also discusses the changing economic circumstances and marketplace conditions that have encouraged the evolution of these sources. Sustaining the current levels of revenue that these income streams produced in the early years of their development may not be possible. Circumstances have changed substantially since 1989 when the Palace at Auburn Hills was built, setting off the luxury-suite phenomenon that has characterized nearly all subsequent sport facility construction. In a number of cities (e.g., Phoenix, Denver, Minneapolis), multiple teams have built new fully loaded facilities, and there is concern that these markets are oversaturated, with more luxury suites available than there are companies to lease them. This situation was aggravated by the economic recession of the early 2000s and the resultant corporate belt-tightening that ensued. Coaxing current corporate suite holders to renew and finding new corporate prospects to fill an ever-expanding inventory of available suites are formidable challenges.

Similar challenges exist with the sale of naming rights, because by the early years of the new century, over 100 major and minor league venues had been corporately named. Thus, the novelty effect and the ability of a company to clearly differentiate itself in the marketplace by taking title to an arena or stadium have diminished.

Perhaps no single development in the last several decades has had more of a transformational effect on major team sports than luxury seating. Luxury suites (originally called skyboxes) are a universal and dominant feature of every new stadium or arena built since the early 1990s. The executive director of the Association of Luxury Suite Directors noted, "Ten years ago, only about 3% of seating in stadiums and arenas was designated as premium and club seating. That figure now is approaching 20%"(p. 24).[1] The average NBA arena now contains 82 luxury suites and 2,152 club seats.[2]

Although the physical features of luxury suites may vary from one venue to another, they all are likely to include amenities such as carpeting, wet bar, restroom, and seating ranging from 12 to 24 seats. The picture (see Figure 7-1) of a premium suite in Cleveland's Jacobs Field displays the deluxe features typical of luxury suites.

Figure 7-1 Luxury Suite

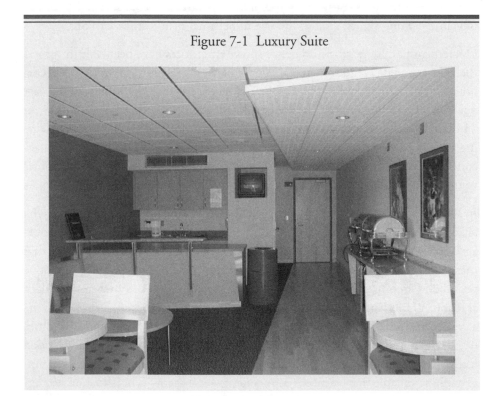

The Houston Astrodome is credited with being the first facility to introduce the modern concept of luxury suites in sport venues. Ordered by Judge Roy Hofheinz, the original owner of the Houston Astros, who was also the visionary builder of the Astrodome, the facility incorporated a lavish suite for the judge that included a bowling alley, movie theater, and gilded toilet seats.[3] Billed as the "Eighth Wonder of the World" when it opened in 1965, the Astrodome was the world's first air-conditioned, domed, all-purpose stadium. Along with luxurious skyboxes, the Astrodome introduced other facility "firsts," such as artificial grass named "Astroturf," in-stadium restaurants, and air-conditioned baseball.

However, the concept of luxury suites as revenue producers did not materialize until two decades later. The Association of Luxury Suite Directors noted, "In the 1970s, a few stadiums got suites, but nothing much happened until the late 1980s" (p. 3C).[4] It took the development of two privately financed facilities in the late 1980s—The Palace at Auburn Hills and Joe Robbie Stadium (which was subsequently renamed Pro Player)—to ignite the sport facility boom of the 1990s. In both instances, the new facilities were financed largely from luxury suite sales. As discussed in chapter 3, once other team owners saw the abundant revenue that the Detroit Pistons could generate from the new arena's 180 luxury suites, the "Palace Revolt" was underway. The $12-million-a-year income that the facility produced from suite rentals (the highest priced suites sold for $120,000 per season) allowed the owner to pay off the entire $70 million construction debt within 6 years. Similarly, the Miami Dolphins realized gross revenues of close to $20 million per year from leasing 216 luxury suites in their new stadium, which in 1990 represented more than half of the team's gross revenues. Ever since, the income from selling or leasing luxury suites (and, more recently, other premium seating options like club seats) has become a wellspring for new sport-facility financing.

The venues in which teams in the four major leagues played contained close to 12,000 luxury suites by 2001. Table 7-1 shows that from 1997 to 2001, almost 2,700 new suites were added to the total major league inventory. NFL stadiums led the way, with an average of 139 suites per venue.

Figure 7-1 Luxury Suites

League	# of Suites 1997 / (# of Teams)	# of Suites 2001 / (# of Teams)
MLB	2,258 (30)	2,286 (30)
NBA	1,531 (29)	2,533 (29)
NFL	3,575 (30)	4,294 (31)
NHL	1,920 (26)	2,813 (30)
Total	**9,824 (115)**	**11,926 (120)**

Source: Dorsey, B. (2001). Premium Seating: The Next Ten Years. Summer 2001, Available: *www.alsd.com.*

Luxury suites have now become a common feature at all types of sport venues in North America. Suites have opened at major automobile race tracks, PGA Tour sites, tennis stadiums, and even at rodeo grounds. The Mesquite (Texas) Championship Rodeo facility has 78 luxury suites. At least 66 minor league baseball parks were built in the 1990s, and one analyst commented, "I don't think there's been a minor league park in the last 10 years that hasn't had them put in" (3C).[4]

A number of college athletic programs also have reaped great financial benefit from the sale of luxury seating. The University of Texas Athletic Department receives $3.2 million a year from leasing 66 suites in its Royal-Memorial Stadium.[5] Similarly, Auburn University incorporated 71 executive suites into a $15.5 million stadium renovation project. The 68 revenue-producing suites sold for as much as $862,865 each, completely offsetting the $1-million-plus annual debt incurred by the expansion project. When the debt is retired, Auburn will realize an annual profit of $1,776,000.[6] Other notable examples of schools that have financed stadium expansions from luxury-suite proceeds are Boston College, Clemson University, the University of Florida, and the University of Oregon.

The Revenue Impetus

The rapid growth and development of luxury suites are attributable to the substantial revenue they produce. The Palace at Auburn Hills initiated the trend, but more recent adaptations have taken the concept of premium seating to much higher levels. Nowhere is the enormous revenue-generating capacity of luxury seating more apparent than at the Staples Center. The $400 million arena in downtown Los Angeles, home to the NBA Lakers and Clippers and the NHL Kings, generates an estimated $68 million per season from the sale of 160 suites (ranging in price from $307,000 to $188,278) and 2,476 club seats (selling at an average of $14,000).[7] To provide some perspective of the magnitude of this income, the revenue produced from premium seating alone at the Staples Center exceeded the *total* operating revenues of an average NHL franchise in 2000.

Table 7-2 shows the average suite prices in facilities used by the four major leagues. Arenas that offer fans luxurious accommodations for watching both NBA and NHL teams (e.g., the American Airlines Arena in Dallas, the Pepsi Center in Denver) charge the highest rates, at an average of $199,000 per suite. The price charged by NFL teams is slightly lower than the NBA average of $113,000, but when the much smaller game inventory of the NFL compared to those of the NHL and NBA is taken into account (8 versus 41 regular-season home games), it is evident that football teams realize significantly more revenue from luxury suite sales on a per-game basis. The NFL's advantage is a function of the classic supply and demand relationship:

Table 7-2 Average Annual Luxury Suite Prices by League

League	Annual Lease Price
NBA/NHL Share Arena	$199,000
NBA Only	$113,000
NFL Only	$100,000
MLB Only	$ 85,000
NHL Only	$ 77,000

Sources: Street & Smith's *Sports Business Journal, Team Marketing Report,* and individual team data

> The less supply (defined as the total number of suites times the total number of games), the greater the demand. Although the NFL has the most suites per venue, it has by far the fewest events (10 per season). Because the demand for suites is higher, the price is correspondingly higher. The average (per game) price of a suite in the NFL ranges from $5,250 to $16,940. Average (per game) price of a MLB suite is $962 to $1,993.[8] (p. 6)

The gross annual income produced by the almost 12,000 luxury suites in major league venues in North America is approximately $600,000,000.

NFL owners have a particular incentive to incorporate as much premium seating as possible into their stadiums, because revenues derived from the sale or rental of luxury suites and club seats, unlike gate receipts and television money, are not shared with the rest of the league. The NFL's generous revenue-sharing arrangement, which was discussed in chapter 2, does not apply to venue-generated income streams like premium seating and naming-rights sales.

The Washington Redskins have been particularly adroit at maximizing *unshared* revenues. Following the purchase of the NFL Redskins for a record $800 million in 1999, the new owner immediately implemented an aggressive strategy to grow nonshared income. This included entering into a $205 million (over 27 years) naming-rights agreement with Federal Express and boosting the number (to 15,000) and average price (from $995 to $1,995) of club seats. A year after the new owner's acquisition, the Redskins had generated nearly $100 million in unshared stadium revenue, an increase of almost $20 million over the previous season.[9]

Marketing Premium Seating

Figure 7-2 describes the development and execution of the type of carefully planned marketing strategy needed to sell luxury suites. Despite considerable competition in the Cleveland marketplace from the NBA Cavaliers and MLB Indians, the Browns were able to sell over two thirds of their suites (74 of 108) in the first 2 weeks of their sales campaign. The club's success was attributable in large part to an extensive investment in customer research. Before launching their suite program, the Cleveland Stadium marketing group conducted focus groups and detailed interviews with corporate executives whose companies were the most likely prospects for buying suites. The intent of the customer research was to determine what specific elements of a suite program (amenities, price, etc.) were most important to their company. Their feedback allowed the Browns organization to incorporate into their new stadium the most attractive amenity features and offer price options that best fit the market.

Note the variation in both price and terms. The annual lease prices, ranging from $125,000 to $60,000, varied according to location (with the highest prices for suites on the 50-yard line), size, and number of amenity features. Equally important, suite contracts were offered on a long-term, staggered basis, with payment terms designed to encourage clients to select extended lease agreements. Suite holders who elected the 10-year lease paid considerably less on an annual basis than did those choosing the 5-year term. Staggering the length of suite contracts at 5-, 7-, and 10-year intervals ensured the team would not be overwhelmed by the need to renew or replace all current suite holders at the same time.

It is clear that good market research is the key to the successful sale of luxury suites and club seats. Sports properties like the Cleveland Browns that have conducted field research ranging from mail surveys and telephone interviews with current season-ticket holders, to focus groups with corporate decision makers, can implement their sales program confidently because they know what people want and what they are willing to pay.

In its first two weeks of sales, Cleveland Stadium Marketing sold 74 of the 108 suites available for the Cleveland Browns' future stadium. An agreement with the NFL dictates that the group must generate at least $9,422,000 in sales by January 31, 1997, for the league to contribute to stadium construction costs. The suite lease prices and terms were as follows:

Pricing

$125,000/year	.........33 suites
$100,000/year	.........27 suites
$80,000/year	..........37 suites
$60,000/year	..........11 suites

Payment terms

10-year lease: no increase first 5 years; 2% escalator next 5 years

7-year lease: no increase first 3 years; 3% escalator next 4 years

5-year lease: 2.5% escalator years 2 through 5.

The Managing Partner of Cleveland Stadium Marketing was asked to explain the group's suite marketing strategy.

The Cleveland Indians and Cavaliers have marketed premium seats for new buildings in only the last three years. Is the market ready for more new luxury suites?

We know there is a lot of good product out there. The Indians and Cavaliers have done a very good job of selling their product… and they've had the team performance to go along with it, so we knew it would be tough to sell luxury suites for football.

On the other hand, the Indians and Cavaliers have conditioned the market to a new level of new entertainment opportunities and amenities these facilities can offer.

Cleveland is now a very sophisticated premium seat market. And people's experiences have helped with suite sales and will help with club seat sales.

What guided you in deciding how to market the suites?

We did a lot of homework on what has happened… in Jacksonville, St. Louis, Charlotte, Oakland, Washington, and Baltimore. And we went to our strong base of support [from fans of the old Browns].

At Cleveland Stadium, 77 loges [small boxes] were leased and 74 were paid for in 1996 when the Browns left. That's where we are today, with 74 suites leased.

I would say most of the people we've sold to were loge holders at the stadium, and virtually all of them have or share a suite at one of the other facilities [Gund Arena and Jacobs Field]. We've done two weeks of presentations so far and now our calendar is fully scheduled with companies that aren't in that category.

We also took a lot of time to talk to a focus group of senior-level executives under the aegis of Cleveland Tomorrow [a coalition of top companies in Cleveland]. They were very helpful in letting us discuss configurations, locations, sizes, amenities, and prices of the suites.

What did you learn?

First, customers just wanted amenities on par with the other facilities in town.

Also, after talking to the executives, we changed our thinking. We had been looking at a greater number of price categories. We want to reach the goal

In 2003, the University of Oregon completed an almost $100 million expansion of its football stadium. Crucial to the successful financing of the project was the sale of 30 new and upgraded luxury suites. The athletic department's market research produced a surprising result, but one that ultimately saved tens of thousands of dollars. On the basis of a series of focus group interviews with current suite holders and major donors, the University of Oregon discovered that including private bathrooms in suites, an almost universal feature in both collegiate and professional venues, was not important. Indeed, it was considered undesirable by most of their prospective suite purchasers. As long as these suite holders had convenient access to a bathroom in the concourse lobby area, they felt there was no need for a private bathroom inside their suite.

Club seats are a less extravagant premium seating option to luxury suites. Table 7-3 illustrates the growing prominence of club seating, and the substantial prices charged by teams for club seats across the various leagues. Typically, this preferred seating arrangement provides fans with chair-back, wide-bottom, cushioned seats and immediate access to a variety of specialty services and amenities. In Wash-

set by the NFL and make this team prosperous for the new owner so the team can compete—but there are a lot of different ways to get to that revenue goal.

The number of suites and the prices are the key variables. We were looking at larger suites, but not a lot of them.

But because of the demand, there would have been too much sharing of the larger suites, and we would have been cannibalizing our own sales. As it is, I think we have two companies that are buying two suites.

How did the plan change?

We went from nine price levels to four, and our total revenue stayed the same. We went from 120 or 130 suites to 108 now, with the opportunity to expand if the demand is there.

How did you structure the contract length for suite leases?

Both the Cavs and the Indians have long-term leases. The Cavs have 5-, 8-, and 10-year leases, and the Indians have 3-, 5-, and 10-year leases.

Ours are 5-, 7-, and 10-year leases, and part of the program was that the average lease term would be eight years.

But the average of the leases we've signed is almost nine-and-a-half years. Most customers are going for the 10-year lease, which is a pleasant surprise.

We are offering a pre-payment option, which gives a discount if you pay in advance for the amount of the lease and the tickets.

How did you target and reach viable customers?

We have a database of about 500 companies and we rated them on a sliding scale and priority basis— although we have already had companies from our "least likely" group buy.

Companies in our highest priority group were loge buyers at Cleveland Stadium, are in the Cleveland Tomorrow organization, and have suites at Jacobs Field or Gund Arena.

Virtually all of those companies were invited to a kickoff party for the sales drive, and we ended up with a standing-room only crowd of about 350 people.

We asked for reply cards from attendees, and we prioritized our level of follow-up based on those responses.

What materials do you use to sell the suites once you have a potential customer?

We have a model suite that was designed by HOK and a local design firm. And we have a great video presentation that shows the legacy of the Browns and includes computer animation on the future of the new team.

We bring people in for one-hour appointments. Very few people who have come in so far have left without a commitment.

Source: *Team Marketing Report* (1996)

ington, D.C., FedEx Field, home of the NFL Redskins, offers its 15,000 club-seat fans private, carpeted concourses, lounges, and bar facilities, as well as in-seat wait service.

Figure 7-3 provides an example of the leasing options offered by the Cleveland Indians for the 2,000 club seats available at Jacobs Field. The prepaid provision in the 10-year membership alternative is common among preferred or luxury seating plans. The intent is to generate cash up-front to meet the financing maxim that a dollar received immediately is preferable to a dollar received at some future date.

Challenges

Periodic economic recessions and saturation of available luxury suites in some markets are the major challenges confronting those charged with selling premium seating. In the 1990s, the United States enjoyed the longest period of sustained growth in its history. Sports organizations were beneficiaries of this, and during this period, major league teams more than doubled their ticket prices and induced

Table 7-3 Sampling of the Number of Club Seats at Various Venues and the Prices Charged by Teams for their Occupancy

Team	Facility	Number of Club Seats	Price Range Per Year
Los Angeles Lakers (NBA)	Staples Center	4,500	$12,995 to $14,995/season
Portland T'Blazers (NBA)	Rose Garden	2,500	$ 7,500 to $11,500/pair midcourt $11,000 to $32,500/pair courtside
Denver Nuggets (NBA)	Pepsi Center	1,854	$65 to $100 per game
New York Knicks (NBA)	Madison Square	3,000	$175 to $1,350 per game
Calgary Flames (NHL)	Saddledome	1,600	$2,500 membership fee for 5 years + $3,500 annual fee
Phoenix Coyotes (NHL)	America West	1,651	$72 per game; $3250 per season
Toronto Maple Leafs (NHL)	Air Canada Ctr.	3,700	$2,000 to $2,500
Cincinnati Bengals (NFL)	Paul Brown	7,700	$ 995 to $1,900
Tampa Bay Bucs (NFL)	Raymond James	12,000	$950 to $2,500
Baltimore Ravens (NFL)	PSINet	3,196	$108 to $298 per game
Cleveland Indians (MLB)	Jacobs Field	2,064	$32 per game; $1,905 per season
Colorado Rockies (MLB)	Coors Field	4,400	$30 to $32 per game
Texas Rangers (MLB)	Arlington	5,700	$2,000 to $3,000

Source: Stadiums & Arenas: Club Seat Breakdowns. Street & Smith's *Sports Business Journal,* July 17-23, 10-11.

Figure 7-3 Club Seat Leasing Options at Cleveland's Jacobs Field

Three-Year Membership-Lease	Three-Year Membership-Lease	Three-Year Membership-Lease
• Initial lease payment of $1,215 for first year, excluding the cost of tickets.*	• Initial lease payment of $1,215 for first year, excluding the cost of tickets.*	• Priority seat selection • One-time lease payment of $13,770, excluding the cost of tickets.*
• Locked in at seven percent annual lease escalator in years two and three.	• Locked in at only a five percent annual lease escalator in subsequent years.	• Avoid annual lease price escalators for life of lease.
• Guarantee your personally selected seat for three years.	• Guarantee your personally selected seat for five years.	• Guarantee your personally selected seat for 10 years.
• Optional on-site parking available for term of lease.	• Optional on-site parking available for term of lease.	• Optional on-site parking available for term of lease.

*Tickets are not included in lease price, and will be billed to you annually. The Club Seat ticket price will not exceed field level box seat price.

Note: Information provided by the Cleveland Indians.

corporations to invest billions of dollars in premium seating, naming rights, and sponsorships. However, the U.S. economy experienced a recession in 2001-02, demonstrating that sports teams are not recession-proof. The chief financial officer of an NHL franchise noted, "Fear and uncertainty regarding the economy had a significant impact on both corporate and individual season ticket and suite renewals. Even our most loyal fans had some trepidations about committing to us in this economy" (p. 385).[10] During this recession, the occupancy rates of suites declined and prices remained static.[8] An NHL executive explained the conundrum faced by companies in the recession:

> In the case of a corporate suite at the arena, you're not talking about a company representative taking one or two clients out to dinner, you're taking 10-14 out to dinner, if you give away all your seats. That can run the firm $2500 for a night in the suite—not to mention the lease payment itself—how can a firm justify that when, in some cases, they just laid people off?[10] (p. 389)

Over the last half-century, the U.S. economy has proven to be extremely resilient. Despite cyclical downturns, most slumps have been relatively short—of the 10 recessions between 1948 and 2002, the average lasted 11 months—and the economy bounced back relatively quickly. However, it would be imprudent for sport managers to presume that the U.S. economy will recapture its exuberance of the 1990s. The 2001-02 recession served as a warning to sport managers, especially to those responsible for selling premium seating. Offering incentives to corporate clients to lock in on long-term deals, as in Cleveland (Figure 7-2) and making sure that suite expiration dates are carefully staggered so only a limited number must be renewed from year to year are prudent hedges against periodic and often unpredictable economic downturns.

The second challenge that in some markets may be more difficult to address than planning for periodic economic slowdowns is the growing inventory of luxury suites in many cities across the United States. Several markets have become saturated with luxury seating so that there are not enough companies or affluent fans to purchase them. In such circumstances, "ten-year leases become five-year leases, and five-year leases become three-year leases" (p. 24).[1]

The NBA's Golden State Warriors faced this situation when they offered 72 suites in the newly renovated Oakland Coliseum. In the crowded San Francisco Bay Area marketplace, with six major league teams selling 564 luxury suites, corporate response to the Warriors' suite program was disappointing. In the first 2 months, only 20 of the 72 suites offered at $125,000 were leased.[11] The tepid reaction was partially attributable to the team's poor performance over much of the 1990s, but a more fundamental problem facing the franchise was that even in a market as large as the San Francisco-Oakland-San Jose metro area, fewer than 400 corporations produced annual sales in excess of $100 million,[12] and these are the prime corporate prospects for luxury suites.[13]

The slow sales prompted dramatic adjustments in the price and terms the Warriors offered corporate clients. Annual lease rates for center court suites were reduced from $125,000 to $89,000; and instead of requiring 5- and 7-year lease agreements, companies were allowed leases as short as 1 to 2 years in length.[14] Other cities that may have reached the saturation point with respect to luxury seating include Atlanta, Denver, Seattle, and Dallas. In each case, the supply of suites may now exceed the number of corporations that can afford full-price suite leases.[8]

Responding to the Challenge

It is clear that successful premium-seating sales programs will have to become more creative and flexible to respond to the challenges of periodic economic downturns and saturated markets. Suite sharing and suite reselling are among the strategies emerging to address these challenges.

Based on the real estate maxim "location, location, location," the best suites—those at the lower level or center court—command ultrapremiums. However, it has been found that there is substantial elasticity in pricing these preferred suites.[15] Thus, in order to maintain current suite prices, often at around $100,000 per year, more franchises or venue operators are offering suite leases on a shared basis. Rather than perpetuating the traditional leasing model of one corporation per luxury suite, the intent is to spread the cost (as well as the benefits) across two or more suite holders, so, for example, over half the suites leased for NHL games are now shared.[15]

Suite-sharing benefits teams in many ways. By selling half or even one-third shares, those who are charged with marketing suites are likely to find many more companies receptive to proposals that substantially reduce their entry costs. This approach may be particularly appealing to company executives wary of committing to a full season of major league baseball (81 home games) or NBA or NHL home games (41 dates in each case). Given the volume of dates and attendant service costs related to entertaining guests on each occasion—on top of the expensive lease fee—many firms are likely to be more comfortable with a smaller, more manageable set of games at a more affordable price.

Suite reselling is also becoming commonplace.[8] The concept enables teams to establish a long-term partnership with corporate suite holders who do not want to share a suite. When suite tenants are allowed to sublet the suite any time it is not in use, then "the suiteholders realize the best of both worlds: they can keep their suite and great location, and resell it when not in use" (p. 9).[8] These resale arrangements are sometimes called *suite adoption programs*. It seems probable that partnerships will emerge between teams and their best corporate suite tenants, in which the teams agree to resell the suite on a per-event or game basis on those dates when the company chooses not to use its suite. This arrangement could compensate the corporate suite holder for the resale, or alternatively, "One of the more intriguing ways is to provide the suiteholder a credit for use of its suite on the next renewal contract. This allows an added incentive for the suiteholder to renew come contract time"(p. 9).[8]

Professional Sports Venues

Naming Rights

The corporate naming of major sports facilities is a relatively recent phenomenon. The first reputed naming-rights agreement dates back to 1971, when Schaefer Brewing Company paid $150,000 to name the Patriots' stadium Schaefer Field. Two years later, the Buffalo Bills renamed War Memorial Stadium Rich Stadium, after signing a $1.5 million, 20-year agreement with Rich Products, a local frozen-food supplier,[16] whereas in the mid-1970s, Busch Stadium was named in St. Louis.

These early naming-rights agreements did not stimulate a trend in sport facility entitlements in other regions of the United States. From the early 1970s through the mid-1980s, few sports facilities were corporately named. During this period, major sports venues, all of which were publicly financed, typically maintained the tradition of being named either to honor prominent civic leaders such as the Hubert H. Humphrey Dome in Minneapolis (1982) and Brandon Byrne Arena (1981) in New Jersey or to provide local or civic identity such as the Louisiana Superdome (1975) and Pontiac Stadium (1978).

The naming rights of the Los Angeles Forum were sold to Great Western Bank in 1987, Arco Arena was named in Sacramento in 1988, and the Target Center in Minneapolis in 1990, but it was not until the last half of the 1990s that naming-rights agreements became prominent. From 1995 through 2000, the number and financial magnitude of venue sponsorships grew exponentially. By 1997, one third (41 of 113) of the venues used by teams in the four major leagues had been named for corporations,[16] but by 2002 the number of corporately named venues had increased to almost 70%, with 80 of 121 teams playing in facilities named after major companies.[17] In part, this growth was stimulated by the large number of new sports facilities that were constructed in the late 1990s. The availability of these new facilities created an unprecedented inventory of entitlement opportunities for corporations seeking to exploit the commercial benefit of placing their names on prominent sports venues.

In some instances there has been public resistance to the sale of naming rights. Opponents of selling naming rights to public facilities in which professional teams play argue there is a civic cost to having a public building named after a corporation:

> The airport doesn't have a corporate name. Parks don't have corporate names. Bridges don't have corporate names. If, as political leaders and sports boosters claim, stadiums and arenas are components of our social and cultural infrastructure, then why not honor public heroes and heroines by naming our sports venues after them?[18] (p. 482)

An example of public opposition occurred when the computer software developer 3Com acquired the naming rights for Candlestick Park in San Francisco. Although the official name became 3Com Park at Candlestick Point, the majority of fans and media continued to call it Candlestick. Indeed, residents of San Francisco vigorously protested the city's decision to selling the naming rights. When the agreement ended in 2002, the Giants did not seek to extend it. When a corporate name is attached to something that already has a strong identity, then it is not "top of the mind" or "on the tip of the tongue" of stakeholders.[19] It does not become part of the community conversation; hence, it is ignored. When a franchise moves to a new facility, a new identity may be established and the corporate name may be accepted as that identity. However, if the new facility retains too many features of the old facility, this will not occur. For example, it was noted earlier in Figure 5-5 that residents of Denver continued to call their new stadium Mile High Stadium rather than Invesco Field at Mile High because Mile High (over 5,000 feet above sea level) is part of the City's national identity, and there is a strong community emotional attachment to it. The Denver situation was further exacerbated by the stadium's being primarily financed with public money, so the public believed it should be "their" stadium—not some company's stadium.

The exponential growth in entitlement opportunities created by new facilities was accompanied by quantum increases in the prices paid by corporations for these rights. As shown in Table 7-4, the average annual price of a naming rights agreement almost quadrupled, from $1.28 million in 1995 to $4.8 million a year in 1999. Between 1995 and 2002, the aggregate amount corporations had committed to place their company's name on sports venues exceeded $3.5 billion. Table 7-5 shows the largest sports-venue naming rights that have been signed.

Table 7-4 shows that the average price paid for naming rights increased annually from 1995 to 1999 and then plateaued at a little over $4 million per year. This significant increase in the number and financial magnitude of agreements coincided with the peak years of the sport facility construction boom of the 1990s. During 1999, 10 major naming-rights agreements were reached with corporate sponsors committing more than $1 billion to secure entitlement rights. Three times that year, a new record was set for the total cost of the naming rights agreement, culminating with Federal Express eclipsing the $200 million barrier when the package delivery company paid $205 million ($7.6 million per year on average over 27 years) to the Washington Redskins to name the NFL team's football stadium FedEx Field.

Substantial naming-rights activity occurred through 2000, with eight new agreements, including the single largest deal, which was Reliant Energy's purchase of the naming rights for the new Houston Texans' football stadium for $300 million over 30 years. The Texans were able to secure their record price for three primary reasons.[20] First, the 69,500–seat, retractable-roof stadium also is the permanent site of the Houston Livestock Show and Rodeo, which attracts 2 million visitors during its 2 weeks of operation. Second, the Texans' stadium was selected to host the 2004 Super Bowl and was expected to become a part of the Super Bowl rota-

Table 7-4 Average Price of Naming Rights Agreements for Major Sports Venues from 1995 to 2002

Year	No. of Venues Corporately Named	Aggregate Amount Committed	Average Total Price	Average Length	Average Annual Price
2002	5	$ 441.0 M	$ 88.2 M	20.6 years	$4.28 M
2001	3	$ 265.5 M	$ 88.5 M	21 years	$4.01 M
2000	8	$ 793.2 M	$ 92.9 M	20 years	$4.26 M
1999	10	$1,020 M	$102.0 M	20.2 years	$4.80 M
1998	9	$ 468 M	$ 52.0 M	18.1 years	$2.75 M
1997	8	$ 418.4 M	$ 52.3 M	24.3 years	$2.24 M
1996	2	$ 62.4 M	$ 31.2 M	17.5 years	$1.75 M
1995	5	$ 107.5 M	$ 21.5 M	17.5 years	$1.28 M

Source: Street & Smith's (2002). By the numbers. *Sports Business Journal* (4)37, 10-11.

Table 7-5 The Largest Sports Venue Naming Rights Agreements

Venue Name	Team	Value/Years	Average Annual
Reliant Stadium	Houston Texans (NFL)	$300 M/30	$10.0 M
Philips Arena	Atlanta Hawks (NBA) Atlanta Thrashers (NHL)	$185 M/20	$ 9.3 M
CMGI Stadium	New England Patriots (NFL)	$ 114 M/15	$ 7.6 M
FedEx Field	Washington Redskins (NFL)	$205 M/27	$ 7.6 M
Lincoln Financial Field	Philadelphia Eagles (NFL)	$139.6 M/20	$ 6.98 M
American Airlines Center	Dallas Mavericks (NBA)	$195 M/30	$ 6.5 M
Invesco at Mile High	Denver Broncos (NFL)	$120 M/20	$ 6.0 M
Staples Center	Los Angeles Lakers (NBA) Los Angeles Kings (NBA)	$116 M/20	$ 5.8 M
PSINet Stadium	Baltimore Ravens (NFL)	$105.5 M/20	$ 5.3 M
Saavis Center	St. Louis Blues (NHL)	$ 83 M/20	$ 4.2 M
Minute Maid Field	Houston Astros (MLB)	$100 M/28	$ 3.58 M

Source: Street & Smith's (2002). By the numbers. *Sports Business Journal* (4)37, 10-11.

tion. Finally, the agreement permitted Reliant also to have its name on the Astrodome complex, which includes the Astrodome, the Astroarena, and a new convention center. These "added-value" elements substantially increased the company's willingness to pay a premium for the naming rights.

Other notable naming rights arrangements occurred in 2002 when the Lincoln Financial Group pledged $139.6 million for naming rights to the NFL Eagles' new stadium for 20 years. This ranked as the fourth most lucrative NFL naming-rights deal ever. It was quickly followed by the largest ever naming-rights payment in MLB when Minute Maid agreed to pay $100 million to the Houston Astros over 28 years. However, the total Minute Maid sponsorship package was $170 million, which included pouring rights and other entitlements as well as the naming rights. It is significant that both these companies are "hometown players;" that is, Minute Maid has been based in Houston for 35 years whereas Lincoln Financial moved its headquarters to Philadelphia from Fort Wayne, Indiana, in 1999.[21]

These high payments for naming rights did not prevail in all markets. At the other end of the spectrum in a smaller market, for example, was the agreement signed with the H. J. Heinz Company and the Pittsburgh Steelers in 2001. Heinz is also a hometown player, but they agreed to pay $57 million over 20 years for the title rights to the NFL Steelers' new stadium. The price of the agreement was less than half that received by the Philadelphia Eagles from the Lincoln Group. A spokesperson for the company advising the Heinz Corporation during the negotiations indicated, "The Steelers wanted the deal in the range of $90 to $100 million" (p. 1C).[22] An analyst commented that the rights fee paid by Heinz "reflects

. . . a leveling off. We're starting to see a little more sanity in the value of these deals"(1C).[22]

The selling of facility naming rights exists outside the four major league sports. For example, Charlotte Motor Speedway, one of the most famous motor sports tracks, changed its name to Lowe's Motor Speedway as part of a 10-year, $35 million arrangement with Lowe's home improvement stores.

The Rose Garden in Portland offered a variation on traditional naming rights when it sold "media totems" at the four corners of the building. These give a sponsor a major exclusive exposure with perceived ownership of the corner of the building in the concourses. The totems act as landmarks and meeting places for patrons to help orient them in the large arena. The Rose Garden believed that these generated a similar income to that which would have been received if they had sold the building naming rights, and they kept the name, which reflects the city of Portland's motto, the City of Roses. Rose Garden officials also viewed this as a way of reducing the risk of negative associations if a sponsor declared bankruptcy or was embroiled in a major scandal.[23]

The Rose Garden's lead has subsequently been followed by others. For example, the North Texas Ford Association signed a 10-year, $39 million agreement that grants Ford naming rights and use of a lobby in the American Airlines Center in Dallas. The Center has two lobbies so "fans could go to the American Airlines lobby and see the airline's history and then go to the Ford lobby and build tomorrow's concept car"(p. 3).[26]

College Sports Venues

Table 7-6 shows that a growing number of colleges and universities also have sold naming rights to stadiums and arenas on their campuses. Although most of the early collegiate naming-rights agreements were modest in comparison to those negotiated by major league teams, agreements signed since 2000 have approximated values realized by big league venues. The single largest agreement was the $40 million agreement Pepsi signed with Fresno State University. After acquiring the naming rights to the university's proposed sports and entertainment center, the soft drink company passed along the opportunity to one of its key retail suppliers in central California, Save Mart Supermarkets. The joint sponsorship agreement resulted in the new facility's being called the Save Mart Center, with PepsiCo retaining exclusive pouring rights across the entire Fresno State campus.

Colleges frequently name sports facilities after major donors. The requirement at most universities to qualify for naming status is that the lead donor contribute 50% of the cost of the construction or renovation.[25] However, this is not a rigid criterion, and in some cases it may be as low as 30%. In addition, an increasing number of colleges are requiring a maintenance endowment to accompany the 30% to 50% capital contribution before they will offer naming rights. Again the magnitude of the maintenance endowment varies, but 30% of the total maintenance costs appears to be a fairly typical figure.

Naming rights extend beyond the building to particular facilities within the building.[24] These may include plazas, auditoriums, halls of fame, natatoriums, gymnasiums, weight rooms, and locker rooms. Thus, Ohio State University sold

Table 7-6 College Corporate Naming Rights

Venue	School	Total Value	Average Annual	Length	Years
Save Mart Center	Fresno State University	$40 million	$1.74 million	23 years	2000-2022
Comcast Center	University of Maryland	$20 million	$800,000*	25 years	2002-2026
Value City Arena at the Schottenstein Center	Ohio State University	$12.5 million	NA	Indefinite	1998-indef.
Cox Arena	San Diego State University	$12 million	NA	Indefinite	1998-indef.
United Spirit Center	Texas Tech University	$10 million	$500,000	20 years	1996-2015
Bank of America Arena	University of Washington	$5.1 million	$510,000	10 years	1999-2008
Cox Pavilion	Nevada-Las Vegas	$5 million	$500,000	10 years	2000-2009
Wells Fargo Arena	Arizona State Univ.	$5 million	NA	Indefinite	1998-Indef.
Papa John's Cardinal Stadium.	University of Louisville	$5 million	$333,333	15 years	1998-2012
Coors Event Center	University of Colorado	$5 million	NA	Indefinite	1991-Indef.
Carrier Dome	Syracuse University	$2.75 million	NA	Indefinite	1980-Indef.
Alltel Arena	Virginia Commonwealth	$2 million	$200,000	10 years	1998-2008
Rawlings Stadium	Georgetown (Ky.) College	$200,000**	$50,000	4 years	1997-2003
Midwest Wireless Center at Mankato	University of Minnesota-Mankato	$6 million	$300,000	20 years	NA
U.S. Cellular Arena	Marquette University	$2 million	$333,000	6 years	1999-2005
First National Bank Center	North Dakota University	$7.2 million	$360,000	20 years	NA
Reser Stadium	Oregon State University	$5 million	$500,000	10 years	1999-2009
Ryder Center	University of Miami (FL)	$9 million	NA	NA	NA

*Total amount paid over first 10 years of agreement
**The amount is an annual deal for equipment and apparel
Sources: Street & Smith's (2001). *Sports Business Journal.*
National Sports Law Institute. Marquette University (2002).

its naming rights to the gymnasium inside its new event center to Value City Department Stores for $12.5 million, so the university's basketball and hockey teams play at the Value City Arena in the Jerome Schottenstein Center. Similarly, Georgia Institute of Technology signed a 6-year agreement with McDonald's restaurants. In return for $5.5 million and a percentage of gross revenues, McDonald's received the rights to operate restaurants at two campus locations, and Georgia Tech agreed to rename a square-block area of the campus containing its basketball arena and other athletics facilities. The area was known as the McDonald's Center at Alexander Memorial Coliseum.[26]

When dealing with donors, naming rights are made in perpetuity. This is an important difference from naming rights at professional facilities that are in force only for as long as they are paid for or until the agreement terminates. When a college needs to renovate a facility 20 years after its construction, it cannot jettison the original owner's name and replace it with the name of the lead donor of the renovation. A way has to be found to incorporate both donors' names. For example, the original Smith Pool, when renovated, may become the Smith Pool in the Jones Natatorium to accommodate both the original and the renovation lead donors.

Although the number and value of agreements have increased, there is resistance among some schools that are wary of increasing commercialism on campuses. Some on college campuses view the selling of corporate exposure as "an invasion of the sacred realm of academe," arguing that educational programs "should not be in the business of promoting commercial products" (p. 13).[27]

Thus, the athletic department at Stanford University reacted to criticism of growing commercialism by removing all large corporate signs and banners from its football, basketball, and baseball venues. This corporate "cleansing" cost the athletic department approximately $2.5 million per year.[28] The athletic director at Stanford commented, "I see this as the right decision for Stanford, but I'm not sure we're a national model for anybody else. Only the rich can afford to be moral. If the choice had been either to have advertising or drop sports, we might have come to another decision" (p.3).[29] Although few schools may follow Stanford's lead, it is clear that many will struggle with finding an appropriate balance between maintaining the ideals of amateurism and academic integrity and the ever-increasing expense of sustaining big-time collegiate athletic programs.

Perhaps the compromise reached by the University of Iowa offers a model for future collegiate naming-rights agreements. To address both institutional concerns regarding academic mission and the athletic department's pragmatic need for financial support, Iowa named its on-campus arena Carver-Hawkeye Arena. Roy J. Carver, chair and founder of a tire manufacturing company, gave $25 million to the university. The university "insisted that Hawkeye be part of the name so you'd know where the thing is" (p. C12).[30]

Given the growing sensitivity about the overcommercialization of college sports, negotiations involving the sale of naming rights are especially complicated in the college sector. One experienced naming-rights negotiator commented,

> There are many more folks in the mix on the college-side than on the professional side. On the pro side, you're dealing with single ownership. But, on the college side you're dealing with an AD (Athletic Director), a president, a board of regents or trustees, and then sometimes there's also a state public works division involved. There are just more hoops to go through.[31]
> (p. 14)

Why Companies Buy Naming Rights

There are two fundamental reasons corporations seek the naming rights on sports facilities. Initially, these decisions were driven by a corporation's desire to take advantage of the *exposure* afforded the company by taking the name of a conspicuous public attraction. Consider the following example:

> America West Airlines purchased the naming rights for the Phoenix Suns arena at a cost of $550,000 per year. When the Suns hosted the NBA Finals, a single 30-second commercial on NBC cost $300,000. Because the company purchased the naming rights to the facility, America West's name and logo were seen countless times throughout the series even though the annual fee was less than the cost of two 30-second commercials.[32]

More recently, an increasingly prominent driving force behind corporate naming agreements has been sponsors' desire to use the facility as a platform for *increasing sales*. The price of such deals is determined by the company's assessment of the business-building opportunities the entitlement offers, either indirectly (e.g., entertaining key clients in "their" building) or directly by becoming the exclusive product supplier (e.g., beer, soft drinks) at the venue.

From an exposure perspective, naming rights agreements offer companies several significant advantages over traditional advertising alternatives:

> You can't bypass a name on a stadium the way you zap through a commercial—its tougher to ignore. While each sponsorship needs to be measured for its effectiveness, a lot of marketers are looking for a less cluttered, high impact way to get a brand in front of the public eye. Associating with marquee properties is one great way to accomplish this.[33] (p. 14)

This kind of "24-7" brand exposure is especially appealing to companies with little or no brand recognition. Swedish telecommunications giant Ericsson, Inc. was virtually unknown in the United States when it paid $20 million in 1995 for the naming rights to the NFL Carolina Panthers' new football stadium in Charlotte, North Carolina. From 1996 to 1998, the number of impressions (the times the company name and/or logo was used) Ericsson received in the national media increased by almost 400%, mostly in connection with the stadium. The effect of such exposure had a remarkable impact on Ericsson's brand awareness, both regionally and nationally. Market research conducted in 1998 found that in less than 3 years, the Ericsson brand grew from almost no public presence prior to signing the naming rights agreement to being recognized by 50% of adults in the Carolinas and by 44% nationally.[34] The owner of the Carolina Panthers observed that the naming rights deal has all but "eliminated the 'Who is Ericsson?' question" (p. 14).[33]

In addition to rapidly enhancing the recognition of a new product or company in a cluttered marketplace, established consumer product companies have been attracted to naming rights deals because of the long-term, national exposure benefits they offer. After RCA Corporation paid $10 million in 1995 to name the former Hoosier Dome in Indianapolis the RCA Dome, the RCA executive who negotiated the agreement declared, "The Dome has become the cornerstone of our getting broad exposure, with nationally televised Indianapolis Colts games and our products throughout. There's not a better way to put a footprint on the marketplace" (p. 24).[34]

In the late 1990s, naming rights agreements evolved from being one-dimensional signage deals, albeit on a grand new scale, to multidimensional, integrated packages that provide corporate naming partners with a range of hospitality, media, and "business-building" benefits in addition to exposure. As venues built extensive premium seating, a standard element of a naming rights agreement was access to a luxury suite so naming rights sponsors had the opportunity to entertain key clients in their "own building." The summary of benefits received by Corel Corporation in its 1995 agreement with the NHL Ottawa Senators shows the expanded rights that were extended to naming sponsors (see Figure 7-4). For C$26 million over a 20-year period, the software company received exclusive entitlement to the new arena. In addition to the arena's being named the Corel Center, return on the company's investment included premium seating options (two suites and two box seats), exclusive access to the facility for an annual computer-industry trade show, and a day on the ice for company employees.

Corporate sponsors invariably seek to exploit the business-building potential of the naming relationship: "While naming rights partners enjoyed the many tangible elements provided in the newer agreements, the critical addition was the op-

---

Figure 7-4 Benefits Received by Corel Corporation From Naming Rights Agreement

Corel Corporation agreed to pay C$26 million over 20 years to the Corel Center, the home of the NHL Ottawa Senators. In addition to venue entitlement, the software marketing firm receives the following:

Premium Seating: . . . . One luxury suite
One lower level suite
Two box seats

Other Tickets: . . . . Tickets to every event

Advertising/Signage: . . . . 18-ft backlit sign on front of arena
Advertising on playing surface
Scoreboard signage
Marquee sign in front of arena
Stadium-owned vehicles
Employee uniforms
Cups, plates, napkins at concession stands
Letterhead, stationary,
and employee business cards
Tickets

Other: . . . . Use of arena for annual computer
industry meeting
Parking passes
One internal marketing promotion
annually
Use of ice rink one day a year
for employees

---

portunity for the naming rights partner to derive 'business-back'" (p. 40).[35] Deriving business back from an agreement can occur in a variety of ways, such as receiving exclusive pouring rights at the Pepsi Center in Denver, the strategic placement of ATMs by Bank One in and around Bank One Ballpark in Phoenix, and ticket booths for purchasing airline tickets at facilities named for airlines.

The quintessential business-back naming rights agreement is that between Philips Electronics North America and Time Warner Inc.'s Turner Broadcast System, owner of Atlanta's 20,000-seat arena built in 1999. The European-based electronic products manufacturer (television sets, lighting, home telephone products, and electric shavers) agreed to pay $185 million over 20 years for the naming rights. Not only did Philips obtain the usual arena rights described in Figure 7-4, but the sponsor also was granted premium retail space in the arena. The agreement provided Philips with a 10,000-square-foot consumer products display area, the Philips Experience, where the company can showcase its state-of-the-art video, audio, and entertainment products. The showcase area is strategically located to ensure maximum exposure to fans attending arena events and to the hundreds of thousands of conventioneers who must pass through the Philips Arena foyer on their way to and from the adjacent Georgia World Congress Center, one of the country's busiest convention centers. The agreement also required the $213 million arena to be completely fitted with Philips' equipment, including state-of-the-art turnstiles at the arena's 22 entrances and hundreds of big-screen television monitors located throughout the facility's main concourse.

Key Elements of Naming Rights Agreements

The standard naming-rights agreement is typically a 15- to 25-page contract that stipulates the terms and conditions in explicit terms. Typically, the primary elements of a naming rights agreement address:

1. *Term or Length of Contract*

2. *Consideration* (amount and schedule of payments)

3. *Signage Rights and Limitations* (number, size, placement, and type of signs; and design approval process)

4. *Installation Costs* (responsibility for expenses related to preparation, installation, and maintenance of signage)

5. *Marketing Rights* (number and location of luxury suites, boxes, club seats, and on-site exhibit space, ATMs, etc.)

6. *Termination Upon Default* (provision to terminate contract if either party fails to perform obligations of the agreement with no more than 90 days notice)

7. *Reimbursement* (naming sponsor compensation in event of incomplete season due to strike, lockout, weather)

8. *Renewal Option* (current sponsor given first right of refusal to extend agreement, generally 30 days to 6 months prior to expiration of contract)

The specific terms and conditions related to each of the major provisions vary, reflecting the negotiation process between the naming rights partners. Two central aspects of the agreement, which are discussed in the following subsections, are the manner in which the corporate sponsor will pay consideration for receiving the benefits of the title sponsorship and the length of the agreement.

Method of payment. Historically, naming rights fees have been paid either as an up-front cash payment or as annual payments over the length of the agreement. Although annual installment payments have been the most commonly used approach, a number of agreements have been consummated that have required a single up-front payment. When Marine Midland Bank purchased naming rights for 20 years to Buffalo's downtown arena in 1995, the financial institution made a single payment to the NHL Sabers of $6.73 million. When interest and inflation were taken into account, that figure was estimated to be equivalent to approximately $15 million over 20 years.[36]

The one-time, up-front payment provides the team or venue operator with an immediate infusion of cash. That approach is likely to be especially advantageous to a team having to make an up-front contribution to the construction of a new venue. By applying the rights fee to the team's share of financing the new facility, the team will reduce the amount of debt obligation it would otherwise incur. At the same time, the corporation paying the rights fee will pay considerably less in "actual" dollars. Further, unlike naming rights agreements based on annual payments, the company knows the exact cost of its investment. In contrast, estimating the present value of a stream of annual payments for as long as 30 years is difficult because the rates used to equate present values, such as the cost of capital and interest rates, are unpredictable.

Despite the benefits of greater certainty to the corporation buying the rights and immediate cash to the team, few naming rights transactions are paid in this way. It was noted in chapter 6 that almost all new facilities are debt financed. Typically, bonds are sold either by a government authority or privately, by the team, with the contractual obligation to repay the borrowed amount, with interest, over a specified period of time. A prominent potential source of debt repayment revenues is the money realized from the sale of naming rights. The magnitude of its role is illustrated in the example described in Figure 7-5. Lenders require projects they finance to produce significant and stable amounts of contractually obligated income (or COI). Naming rights transactions have been an excellent source of COI because of their financial magnitude and the long-term nature of the agreements. Thus, lenders have determined that naming rights contracts, along with luxury suite leases, club seat licenses, and concessionaire contracts, are acceptable security for venue financing.

Under such an arrangement, the team pledges the annual payment it receives from its naming rights partner (e.g., Bank One, PepsiCo, Ericsson) to the lender or bondholder. Thus, the agreement between the team and the naming rights holder must include a specific payment schedule spread over the length of the naming rights sponsorship. Typically, naming rights agreements are structured with an initial rights fee payment, followed by annual cash payments that increase by a predetermined percentage every year, usually between 2 and 5%.[16] The annual percentage increase, commonly referred to as an "escalator clause," is used as a hedge against rising operating costs and inflation.

In addition, the gradual annual increases reduce the potential "sticker shock" effect when the agreement is up for renewal. "Slight increases each year in the value of the deal are easier for sponsors to digest," said one team executive. "The idea is to avoid a major jump in price when it comes time for renewal" (p. 47).[16]

The naming rights agreement between the City of Seattle and Keycorp for the Key Arena, home of the NBA Supersonics, provides an example of a typical annual payment schedule. The 15-year agreement calls for an initial payment of $750,000 in the first year, and the escalator clause increases the annual payment at a rate of 4% each remaining year. The actual payment schedule:

Year 1	$750,000	Year 9	$1,022,000
Year 2	$780,000	Year 10	$1,062,000
Year 3	$811,000	Year 11	$1,105,000
Year 4	$843,000	Year 12	$1,149,000
Year 5	$878,000	Year 13	$1,194,000
Year 6	$913,000	Year 14	$1,241,000
Year 7	$950,000	Year 15	$1,290,000
Year 8	$988,000		

Teams have used naming rights revenues to meet their contribution to the upfront costs of a new facility. Thus, when the Seattle Mariners were lobbying the state legislature to fund a new stadium with public money, it was repeatedly pointed out that the team was investing $45 million of its "own" money into the stadium. However, in the stadium lease agreement, the team was given the naming rights to the stadium, that is, the rights to sell the name of the stadium to the highest bidder. These naming rights were the source of the team's contribution.[37]

In some cases, the value received by the team from the corporate naming partner comes in the form of in-kind benefits rather than cash. For example, Continental Airlines, in lieu of cash, provides $700,000 annually in complimentary air service as a part of its 12-year agreement with the New Jersey Sports & Exposition Authority. The arrangement enables the two anchor tenants of the Continental Arena, the NHL Devils and NBA Nets, to substantially reduce their annual travel expenses.

Sometimes naming rights are acquired as part of a larger business package. For example, Coors made an equity investment of $30 million for an ownership stake in the Colorado Rockies, but it is estimated that $7 to $8 million of this investment was attributable to naming rights.[32] Fleet Bank arranged the financing for the Boston arena that hosts the Boston Bruins and Celtics. It obtained the naming rights to the facility and uses the naming rights fee to reduce debt payments on the facility.[32]

Length of agreement. Table 7-4 showed that most naming rights agreements are long-term in nature, with a majority extending 15-20 years. The prevailing attitude of both parties throughout the 1990s was that longer contracts benefited both the corporate sponsor and the team. Teams favored long-term agreements because they ensured a stable income stream over an extended period of time. At the same time, the long-term relationship enabled the naming rights partner to develop an enduring identity with the sports facility and provided the opportunity to develop marketing programs to realize an acceptable return on investment. Further, with a long-term contract the corporation eliminated the risk of being outbid and replaced in a short period of time by a competitor, and received price stability and certainty over a long time period.

Recently, however, some corporate and team executives have questioned the desirability of committing to 15- or 20-year naming rights deals. Companies are concerned about committing major dollars so far into the future, whereas sports teams are also more cautious. Their caution is the result of several agreements that failed. The economic downturn and accounting scandals in 2001-02, which were especially severe in the high-tech, communication, and airline sectors, led seven companies with major facility naming-rights deals to file for bankruptcy: Enron Corp (Houston Astros); ANC Rental Group, parent company of National Rental Car (Florida Panthers); Adelphia (Tennessee Titans); Fruit of the Loom, Ltd., parent company of Pro Player (Miami Dolphins); Trans World Airlines (St. Louis Rams); WorldCom, parent company of MCI (Washington Capitals and Washington Wizards); and PSINet Inc. (Baltimore Ravens). It seems likely that future agreements will be much shorter. Rather than a 30-year agreement with no renewal option (e.g., America West Arena in Phoenix), increasingly contracts will be structured with shorter terms, say 3 to 7 years, with subsequent options to the agreement for 3- to 5-year increments. This kind of arrangement provides both parties with greater flexibility in managing their relationship over time.

The Impact of Naming Rights' Partner Failings

In some cases, the bankruptcy of corporate partners that prematurely terminates a naming rights contract may be a blessing if the franchise entered into a long-term agreement in the early 1990s, when naming rights prices were relatively low. For example, in 1995, TWA agreed to pay the St. Louis Rams $15 million a year over 20 years to put its name on their new domed stadium. When TWA declared bankruptcy, the Rams were able to negotiate a new agreement with Edward James company, a financial services firm headquartered in St. Louis. In return for naming the facility the Edward James Dome, the firm paid the Rams $31.8 million for 12 years ($2.85 million per year), with an option to extend the agreement another 11 years for an additional $35.2 million. Thus, the bankruptcy enabled the Rams to almost double their revenues from naming rights.

In other situations, bankruptcy can create a major public relations and image problem. Enron Corporation was America's seventh largest company when it signed a 30-year, $100 million agreement with the Houston Astros to name their new ballpark Enron Field. The name was on all exterior and interior signage, uniforms worn by game-day staff, cups, plates, napkins, and tickets. When Enron collapsed at the end of 2001 as a result of unethical accounting practices, tens of thousands of people experienced financial hardship through the loss of their jobs, pension funds, or stock. To the Houston and broader American public, Enron quickly became a pariah. The name became synonymous with unethical behavior, shame, and failure. The continued use of the name Enron Field stigmatized the Astros. Their spokesperson noted,

> The Enron logo displayed on the stadium wrongly suggests to the public that the Astros are associated with the alleged bad business practices of Enron. . . The current perception of Enron is incompatible with the honesty and integrity embodied in baseball as America's pastime and espoused by the Houston Astros.[38] (p. A5)

The trustees acting for Enron's creditors refused to surrender the naming rights because they regarded the rights as an asset that had value. Ultimately, the Astros paid $2.1 million to Enron to remove the company's name from the stadium. The team then regained this revenue stream by reselling the naming rights to Minute Maid Company for $100 million over 28 years, so the ballpark became Minute Maid Park.

Similar challenges may also confront colleges that accept naming rights. For example, John E. DuPont gave Villanova University $5 million to build a recreation center that was named the DuPont Pavilion. However, in a high-profile court case some years later, DuPont was convicted of murder.[25] Fortunately for Villanova, there was no formal written agreement requiring the school to retain the name, and it was able to simply call the center The Pavilion.

The potential of corporate partners' names becoming an embarrassment at some time in the future suggests that contracts should contain a clause that provides a disassociation option if a donor or corporate partner embarrasses a college or franchise, respectively. Companies commonly include such clauses in contracts with celebrity endorsers, and this appears to be an analogous situation.[26]

The corporate sponsor can also be a loser in naming rights deals. For example, in the 16 months after Lowe's home improvements chain invested $35 million for the naming rights to Charlotte Motor Speedway, the company became associated with a series of accidents and tragedies that took place at the track. First, during an event at the speedway, debris from a wreck flew into the crowd and killed three fans. Four months later, two Lowe's stores were pipe-bombed in apparent retaliation for the accident. Next, a pedestrian bridge at the speedway collapsed, killing

107 people. Finally, an explosion staged as part of a Memorial Day observance before a major race sent plywood into the crowd and injured four people. Lowe's misfortune has caused companies to add clauses to naming rights contracts enabling companies to terminate if anything occurs that has a negative impact on the company's image or reputation. One commentator noted, "When you pay to name a facility and then your name and image are part of such negative situations, it's almost like turning lemonade back into lemons" (p. 80).[39]

Shirt and Team Naming Rights

Although facility naming rights are widely accepted by the four major professional leagues, this acceptance has not been extended to shirt or apparel naming rights. The NFL uniforms do permit the manufacturer's name or logo to be discretely featured on footwear, apparel, and helmets. Similarly, the NBA uniform has the maker's insignia on it. Their regulations require manufacturers to pay the leagues a fee for the right to display these logos. Major League Soccer (MLS) players do sell shirt sponsorship. Uniform sponsorships are negotiated through the main MLS office, and the league charges $2.5 million annually to place a company logo on a team uniform as well as on sideline boards and television scoreboards. Even Olympic athletes wear the logos of competing apparel companies. However, none of the four major professional sports leagues—NFL, MLB, NBA, or the NHL—permit anything other than discrete manufacturers' logos and do not embrace shirt sponsorship wholeheartedly as has been done by European soccer teams.

The reticence of the American leagues to embrace shirt sponsorship was shared by the European soccer leagues a decade or so ago. Club uniforms were an integral part of a team's heritage and of the heritage of the sport. However, once a couple of pioneering teams braved the critics and accepted shirt sponsorship, others quickly followed, so within a decade it had become an accepted uncontroversial practice. For example, Arsenal and Manchester United, two of the leading English Premier League teams, recently signed shirt sponsorship agreements worth approximately $4 million per year for 4 and 2 years, respectively.

From a corporate sponsor's perspective, shirt naming rights are likely to be more preferable than facility naming rights, because the former have the added value not only of appearing in front of live crowds but also on television and in press action photographs. In addition, they appear on the replica uniforms purchased and worn by fans of the teams. Thus, shirt sponsorship creates thousands of "mobile billboards" displaying a company's name in every park and open space in the country where children seek to emulate the skills of their team idols, and these shirts are also worn by older people as casual leisure wear. In their ongoing search for new revenue sources, it seems likely that the major leagues ultimately will follow the European soccer precedent and embrace shirt naming rights.

Perhaps the ultimate naming-rights agreement from a corporate perspective is to have the franchise branded with the corporate name. Tau Ceramica is one of the best basketball teams in Europe, but it is also one of Spain's top producers of floor and wall tile.[40] The company bought the team name in exchange for an infusion of money and changed the team's existing name to the corporate name. The company does not own the team. If it did so, then it would be unable to withdraw its name if the team were chronic losers and would have to invest company funds in players and basketball, which is not its business. The team's name resonates among the young, active, sports-minded consumers who make up the company's desired demographic target market. There are other examples of this in Europe. For example, Caja San Fernando and Unicafa are named after Spanish banks. In the United States, major league franchises have remained linked to geography, not corporate entities. However, in 2001 Federal Express Corporation tried to buy the team name of the Vancouver Grizzlies franchise when it moved to Memphis. The NBA refused to allow this sort of naming, but it seems likely they will revisit this in the future because it is a potentially lucrative revenue source.

Personal Seat Licenses (PSLs)

Like premium seating and naming rights, selling seat licenses became a widespread practice with the extraordinary increase in new sports venues in the 1990s.

The concept requires an individual to make an advance payment to purchase the right to secure a particular seat in the venue. Buyers make a one-time payment that provides them with the opportunity to purchase a season ticket to that seat for a specified period of time, usually for as long as the team plays in the same venue.

Seat license programs are to individual fans what luxury suites are to corporations.[22] Both seating options are presold with the intention of raising considerable revenue, thereby reducing the amount of money either the owner and/or public entity would have to invest in building a venue. Although seat licenses targeted at individuals at an average of close to $1,000 sell for much less than luxury suites targeted at companies at $100,000 per season, their volume (50,000 on average for an NFL stadium) can produce large amounts of revenue. For example, the 62,000 seat licenses sold in Charlotte raised $125 million toward the construction of the Carolina Panthers' new football stadium.

Seat licenses are commonly referred to as PSLs, but there is no agreement as to the meaning of the "P" in the term PSL. Across North America, PSL programs have been characterized as private, personal, or permanent seat licenses. In Houston, the PSLs sold by the NFL Texans stood for *permanent* seat licenses, because the one-time payment gave the fan lifetime control over the seat purchased in the team's new Reliant Stadium. However, others use the term PSL to mean *personal* or *private* seat licenses, recognizing that many programs restrict licenses to a fixed period of time. Examples include the Seattle Mariners and Oakland Raiders, who limited their seat guarantees to 20 and 10 years, respectively.

Fans and media have sometimes objected to PSLs, asserting that, in effect, they hold fans hostage by forcing them to pay a large up-front fee for the privilege of buying tickets. To counter the assertion that PSL revenues were going directly into the owners' pockets, teams like the Pittsburgh Steelers labeled their seat licenses SBLs, or stadium builder licenses. This term explicitly conveys the Steelers' intention to apply all of the money raised through license sales to stadium construction.

The Growth and Magnitude of PSL Programs

The general notion that people would pay extra to buy tickets was recognized by colleges 30 years ago when they began linking the purchase of the better seats in their basketball and football facilities to annual contributions to their athletic departments. However, it is generally recognized that it was the Dallas Cowboys who introduced the concept of seat licenses in 1968, when the team offered 40-year "seat options" allowing fans to buy and sell their season-ticket rights to raise money to build Texas Stadium.[41] Despite the success of the Cowboys' program, the widespread application of PSLs did not emerge for another 25 years. The successful PSL program implemented by the Carolina Panthers in 1993 is generally accepted as the contemporary model for all subsequent seat licensing programs.[41] The developer of the idea sought to guarantee fans the opportunity to acquire the rights to scarce season tickets in exchange for a nonrefundable fee. He explained:

> Instead of the team dictating who could have your seat if you moved out of town or whatever—in some cities you couldn't give the seat to your buddy and in some cases couldn't transfer your tickets to a family member if there was a waiting list—we thought it would be nice to designate these as seat rights that could be held by the original ticket buyer.[42] (p. 55)

Table 7-7 Size, Price, and Economic Magnitude of Current PSL Programs

Team (League)	Total (Venue #of PSLs / Capacity)	Price Range	Total Revenue
Philadelphia Eagles (NFL)	29,000 / (66,000)	$1,760 - $3,617	$50 - $60 M
Seattle Seahawks (NFL)	8,300 / (67,000)	$2,000 - $3,000	$16 - $17 M
Pittsburgh Steelers (NFL)	48,000 / (65,000)	$ 250 - $2,700	$35 - $40 M
San Francisco Giants (MLB)	15,000 / (40,930)	$1,500 - $7,500	$40 - $45 M
Cincinnati Bengals (NFL)	50,000 / (65,600)	$ 300 - $1,500	$35 - $40 M
Pittsburgh Pirates (MLB)	NA / (38,127)	$2,000 - $6,000	NA
Houston Texans (NFL)	50,000 / (69,500)	$ 600 - $3,900	$50 M
Baltimore Ravens (NFL)	59,000 / (69,000)	$ 250 - $3,000	$65 - $70 M
Tennessee Titans (NFL)	57,000 / (67,000)	$ 450 - $4,500	$60 M
St. Louis Rams (NFL)	46,000 / (65,800)	$ 250 - $4,500	$74 M
Houston Astros (MLB)	2,300 / (40,950)	$2,000 - $20,000	$15 - $20 M
Cleveland Browns (NFL)	64,000 / (72,800)	$ 250 - $1,500	$60 M
Carolina Panthers (NFL)	62,000 / (72,685)	$ 600 - $5,400	$125 M
Tampa Bay Buccaneers (NFL)	40,000 / (65,647)	$ 190 - $2,450	NA
Seattle Mariners (MLB)	966 / (46,621)	$10,460 - $25,000	$15 - $20 M
Chicago Bears (NFL)	28,000 / (63,000)	$ 765 - $3,825	$65 - $76 M
Oakland Raiders (NFL)	29,000 / (63,026)	$ 250 - $3,600	$45 M
Columbus BlueJackets (NHL)	12,000 / (20,000)	$ 750 - $4,000	NA

Source: 2000 Inside the Ownership of Professional Sports Franchises, *Team Marketing Report,* Chicago, IL

The first day PSLs were placed on sale, the Panthers sold 41,632. The new NFL franchise's ability to raise $125 million from the sale of PSLs priced from $600 to $5,400 stimulated widespread interest in seat licenses.

By 2002, almost 30 professional teams, a growing number of colleges and several automobile racetracks had implemented PSL programs. Table 7-7 provides an overview of the magnitude, price range, and revenue return of seat license programs adopted by major league teams in the 10 years after they were introduced by the Carolina Panthers.

NFL franchises have been able to take the greatest advantage of PSL programs. Of the 16 NFL teams that have moved into new venues between 1993 and 2002, 14 sold seat licenses. Only the Detroit Lions and Green Bay Packers rejected the idea of selling PSLs in their new or renovated stadiums. The Lions vice-chairman stated, "I don't believe in them. I think it's asking a lot of fans to step up and [pay more]. I didn't think PSLs were the right thing to do" (p. 4E).[43] However, although the Lions ownership decided against PSLs, the team did raise the average cost of a ticket the first season in their new venue, Ford Field, by 22%, from $41 to $50. PSL programs have been most successful when they have been offered in markets with a substantial pent-up demand for professional sports, such as in NFL expansion cities like Charlotte and Nashville, or in existing markets with a particularly fervent fan base. The Cleveland Browns and Pittsburgh Steelers, for example, are two storied franchises with large, hard-core fan bases. Both teams' PSL programs were met with overwhelming demand. In the case of the Steelers, the original plan to sell 35,000 SBLs had to be quickly adjusted up to 48,000 to accommodate local interest.

Major League Baseball teams with a much greater inventory of games than the NFL (81 dates vs. 10) have approached PSL programs more conservatively. Because baseball offers both more opportunities to attend games and greater flexibility in buying tickets (day of game, mini-season ticket packages, etc.), the necessity of paying a premium to guarantee the right to purchase a ticket is not as compelling to fans. Consequently, the few MLB teams that have implemented seat license programs have offered only a limited inventory. The most successful Major League Baseball PSL offering was the San Francisco Giants' Charter Seat program. The club offered 13,700 seat licenses (approximately one third of the total seating capacity in the new PacBell Park) priced from $1,500 for an upper box seat location to $7,500 for a premium field seat. The one-time, up-front payment provided the purchaser with a "lifetime guarantee" to buy tickets to the Charter Seats they purchased. The Giants' entire seat license allocation sold out in less than six months. The club attributed the program's success to its ability to convince the public that all revenue raised from seat license sales would be used to finance the construction of the new ballpark and, according to a team representative, "not line the pockets of team owners" (p. 12).[44]

How PSLs Work

Although the prices and lengths of PSL programs vary widely from one team to another, the basic conditions and administration of seat license programs are similar. Fundamental to all PSL programs is the idea that once awarded a seat license, the seat holder must purchase season tickets to the assigned seat on an annual basis. Failure to renew season tickets results in forfeiture of the PSL. The guaranteed right of purchase is good only for as long as the rights holder continues to buy tickets.

Most PSL programs offer substantial price discounts to current season-ticket holders. The seat license discounts have proven to be very effective in those cities where an existing team is moving to a new venue and a PSL charge is being imposed for the first time. Clubs offer price discounts in an effort to reduce negative fan reaction to the prospect of having to pay substantially more to continue buying tickets. Some teams offer simple, straightforward discount rewards to their existing ticket holders. For example, the NFL Philadelphia Eagles extended an across-the-board 13% discount to all current ticket accounts. The Cleveland Browns, however, created a much more elaborate discount program targeted at rewarding current fans on the basis of their longstanding loyalty. Figure 7-6 shows the Browns' graduated discount program was based on the length of continuous season ticket ownership. Those fans who had demonstrated the greatest loyalty were rewarded with the deepest discounts, up to 50% off for those who had maintained season tickets for 30 or more consecutive years.

As an additional effort to reduce price resistance, teams typically allow fans the opportunity to pay for PSLs over time. The Houston Texans extended their fans the option of paying for their seat licenses at Reliant Stadium over three installment payments, interest free. The Texans sold $48 million worth of PSLs in 3 weeks, with one third of these being Internet sales. Before the stadium opened, the Texans sold their full complement of $74 million of PSLs. These PSLs were for 30 years (i.e., the projected life of the stadium) and were fully transferable.

In addition to discounts, most programs allow the rights holder to transfer the PSL by gift, bequest, or sale to any third party. The transfer feature is attractive in that it provides seat holders with the ability to pass their seats on to family members. In addition to establishing a family legacy, PSLs also have proven to be reasonable investments. In Charlotte, for example, the Carolina Panthers' fully transferable PSLs, which originally sold for between $600 to $5,400, are now being resold for as much as $975 to $12,000 in what is called the PSL "aftermarket."

Figure 7-6 The Cleveland Browns PSL Program

- No PSL – 10,000 Dawg Pound section seats and 5,580 other seats (21.9%)

- $250 PSL – 5,195 seats (7.3%)

- $500 PSL – 18,050 seats (25.5%)

- $750 PSL – 11,175 seats (15.8%)

- $1,000 PSL – 17,100 seats (24.1%)

- $1,500 PSL – 3,800 seats (5.4%)

Discounts: Season ticket holders 1-3 years (10%); 4-6 years (15%); 7-9 years (20%); 10-19 years (30%); 20-29 years (40%); 30 or more years (50%)

Seat licenses have provided multiple benefits to teams. They provide a sizable amount of money and the one-time, up-front payment means those dollars are immediately available to the sports property. The ability to presell seat licenses in advance of construction ensures that the team and/or government authorities responsible for financing the construction will not have to borrow as much money. Thus, PSLs reduce the financial requirements of teams and governments by pushing more of the financial burden on to sports fans who buy the licenses. For those subscribing to the benefit principle of taxation discussed in chapter 3, placing more of the cost on those who receive the most direct benefit is an eminently fair and supportable arrangement. With seat licenses, those who benefit the most pay the most. This rationale gains greater credence when the "user-pays" orientation of PSLs is compared against "soft taxes," which were discussed in chapter 6, where the primary burden of venue financing often is carried by tourist or business visitors paying higher hotel and/or car rental taxes.

Although PSLs are justifiable from the perspective of the tax benefit principle, their added cost per seat increases the probability that for many fans the cost of the PSL plus payment of season tickets may be prohibitive. A serious question facing sports properties using PSLs is "How much of a direct burden is it fair for their fans to assume?" For example, for an existing Chicago Bears season-ticket holder to gain access to one of the approximately 20,000 "nonclub" PSL seats offered in the newly renovated Soldier Field, the fan was required to pay at least $2,500 (the PSLs average $2,000, and season tickets range from $450 to $650). Thus, for a family of four with plans to renew season tickets, the total cost in the first year of the PSL program approximated $10,000.

A financial commitment of that magnitude places even the most loyal fans in a difficult position. Some might be forced to give up their tickets because they simply cannot afford to pay for one or more seat licenses. Others, who may be financially able to afford the payment, may harbor substantial resentment at being required to pay so much more for the privilege of buying tickets to seats they had held for many years. Further, the PSLs are useful only for as long as a franchise is in the facility. If the team moves, PSL owners are not compensated.

It is imperative, therefore, that teams planning to implement PSL programs give careful consideration to many of the features designed to reduce price barriers, such as installment payment plans and graduated discounts similar to the Cleveland Browns' successful fan loyalty initiative (Figure 7-2). In addition, PSL purchasers must be convinced that their payment is making a direct and meaningful contribution to facility construction. They need to believe they are being offered the "thrill of participating" in either attracting a new team to their city or enhancing the fortunes (literally and figuratively!) of their beloved sports team.

Summary

During the Fully Loaded Era (1994-present), many teams and venue operators have been able to exploit the abundant revenue-generating capability associated with the construction of new sport facilities. The development of three sources of income—premium seating, naming rights, and PSLs—has dramatically altered the revenue model of both professional sports teams and a growing number of other industry sectors (e.g., collegiate sports, auto racing).

The gross income produced by approximately 12,000 luxury suites in major league venues in North America is estimated at $600 million a year. During the 1990s, premium seating came to symbolize the meaning of fully loaded venues as sport facilities were fitted with large numbers of luxurious private suites and preferred club seats. The addition of more expensive premium seating options has physically, as well as fiscally, transformed the design and operation of modern sports venues. During the 1990s, the percentage of luxury and club seating increased from 3% to more than 20% of a venue's available capacity.

Given the average cost of approximately $50,000 per year, luxury suite sales typically are targeted at large corporations. Between 80% and 85% of the suites at arenas and stadiums are leased by companies that use the luxury accommodations to entertain key clients. In some cities, the supply of high-priced suites exceeds the available number of prime corporate prospects. When this situation is further aggravated by an economic slowdown such as that which occurred in 2001-2002, selling luxury suites is especially challenging. In such circumstances, sport managers have to implement more flexible and creative luxury-seating sales programs. Suite sharing, in which two or more corporations lease the same suite, is one such option. Suite subletting or reselling is another emerging innovation, whereas suite adoption programs allow corporate suite holders to resell their suites on a per-event basis when they choose not to use the suites.

Since 1995, many venues have taken the title of corporate sponsors that have paid substantial amounts for this right. Over 70% of the four major league sports facilities in North America have been corporately named, and the aggregate investment between 1995 and 2002 exceeded $3.55 billion. Reliant Energy, a Houston-based energy company, set the standard when it agreed to pay the Houston Texans $300 million over 30 years to name the new NFL franchise's stadium Reliant Field.

Corporations seek two major benefits from becoming naming rights sponsors: (a) 24/7 exposure and (b) the ability to increase sales. The remarkable visibility provided corporations through their alignment with prominent sports venues is especially attractive to companies with little or no brand recognition, such as Ericsson Inc., which was a virtual unknown brand until it took naming rights to the NFL Carolina Panthers' stadium. Increasingly, however, corporations have been attracted to naming agreements because of the substantial business-building opportunities they provide. Many agreements now include provisions that guarantee corporate naming partners opportunities to sell their products inside "their" venues.

Standard naming-rights contracts stipulate the terms and conditions by which the corporate naming sponsor and venue operator must abide. Two central features of a naming rights agreement are how the corporation will pay for the title sponsorship and the length of the deal. Sport managers have to weigh the relative benefits of accepting a cash-in-hand, lump-sum payment when the agreement is signed against annual payments, with escalator clauses, over the length of the contract. Both sports properties and corporations have become more cautious about entering into long-term, 25-30 year agreements, which were characteristic of the 1990s.

The third revenue development innovation that emerged in the 1990s was the concept of PSLs, most commonly referred to as personal seat licenses. PSLs require purchasers to make a one-time payment, which provides the seat license holder with the right to purchase a ticket to that seat either for the lifetime of that facility or for a fixed period of time, typically 10 or 20 years.

Although PSL programs have been successful, they also have been controversial. The most serious concern is that seat licenses hold fans hostage by requiring them to pay a substantial up-front fee (on average, around $1,000 per seat) for the privilege of being permitted to buy tickets. This is particularly contentious among long-time season-ticket holders.

Some teams have recently attempted to alter negative perceptions by assuring fans that all income derived from the sale of seat licenses will be applied to stadium construction. The Pittsburgh Steelers coined the phrase "stadium builder licenses" to convey the clear message that by purchasing an SBL, fans were making a meaningful contribution to building a new home for the Steelers. Teams can also reduce potential negative fan reaction by designing PSL programs that reduce price barriers and reward team loyalty through mechanisms such as installment payment plans and graduated discount programs that provide deep discounts for long-time season-ticket purchasers.

References

1. The making of the $213 billion sports business industry. (1999, December 20-26). *Sport Business Journal*, 24-25.
2. Bucking the trend in Milwaukee. (2000, April). *Stadium Insider, 3*, 5.
3. Custred, J. (1999, October 3). The wonder years. *Houston Chronicle*, 2, 27.
4. Heistand, M. (1999, May 26). Skyboxes gain mass appeal. *USA Today*, 3C.
5. Johnson, R. (1999, December 20). How one college program runs the business: Inside Longhorn, Inc., *Fortune, (140)*, 160-174.
6. Rosenblatt, R. (1988, July). Naming game. *Sports Inc.*, 13-14.
7. Simers, T.J., & Wharton, D. (1999, October 10). How the game was played. *Los Angeles Times Magazine*, 28-31, 128-131.
8. Dorsey, B. (2001, Summer). Premium seating: The next ten years. *SEAT Magazine*. Available: http://www.alsd.com/publications
9. Lombardo, J. (2000, September, 4-10). Reaching for the revenue sky. *SportsBusiness Journal*, 25.
10. Howard, D.R., & R. Burton (2002, March/April). Sports marketing in a recession. It's a brand new game. *International Journal of Sports Marketing & Sponsorship, 4* (1), 383-400.
11. Nevius, C.W. (1998, January 13). Warriors not under Cohan the barbarian. *San Francisco Chronicle*, C5.
12. Dunn and Bradstreet. (2001). *Business Rankings Annual.*
13. Howard, D.R. (1999). The changing fanscape of big league sports: Implications for sport managers. *Journal of Sport Management, 13* (4), 78-91
14. Del Vecchio, R. (1998, November 7). Arena polished, ready for fans. *San Francisco Chronicle*, A21.
15. Friedman, A. (1998, August 10-16). Luxury suites to get even pricier. *SportsBusiness Journal*, 39.
16. Team Marketing Report. (1997). *Naming rights deals*. Chicago, IL: pp 1-63.
17. Mahony, D., & Howard, D.R. (2001). Sports business in the next decade. *Journal of Sport Management, 15* (4), 275-296.
18. Weiner, J. (1999). *Stadium games: Fifty years of big league greed and bush league boondoggles.* Minneapolis: University of Minnesota Press.
19. Guzzo, G. (2001, September). The Mile High debate: Why the Denver Post decided against "Invesco Field at Mile High." *Team Marketing Report*, 8.
20. Lombardo, J. (2000, October 23-29). Only NYC, San Francisco have shot to beat Houston deal. *SportsBusiness Journal*, 1, 53.
21. Bernstein, A., & Brockington, L. (2002, June 10-16). Huge deals put spark in naming rights. *Sports Business Journal*, 1, 36.
22. Yeomans, M. (2001, June 16). Heinz' naming rights deal. *Pittsburgh Tribune Review*, p. 1C.
23. Rubel, C. (1996). Who needs corporate sponsor when you have a "media totem"? *Marketing New, 30*(9), 1, 7.
24. Teams search and fund new avenues of revenue from the naming rights of stadiums and arenas sections. (2001, January). *Team Marketing Report, 13*(4), 1-2.

25. Cohen, A. (1999, July). The naming game. *Athletic Business*, 37-43.

26. Blumenstyk, G. (1995). Georgia Tech and McDonald's sign $5.5 million deal. *Chronicle of Higher Education, XLI,* (21), A44.

27. Tucker, J. (2000, December 26). Schools for sale? *Oakland Tribune*, 1, 13.

28. Workman, B. (February 20, 1998). Stanford seeks way to reverse trend of commercial sponsors. *San Francisco Chronicle*, 1C.

29. Post now billboards. (2000, September/October). *Stanford Magazine*, 3.

30. Miller, A. (1995, November 17). It pays to play name game. *Columbus Dispatch*, C12.

31. Lee, J. (2001, August 8-13). Colleges feature fewer chances, more hassle. *SportsBusiness Journal*, 14.

32. Greenberg, M.J., & Gray, J.T. (1996). *The stadium game.* Marquette University Law School: National Sports Law Institute.

33. Zoghby, J. (1999, November 1-7). Ericsson makes name with N.C. stadium. *SportsBusiness Journal*, 14.

34. Friedman, A. (1997). *Naming rights deals.* Chicago, IL: Team Marketing Report.

35. Wallace, R., & J. Vogel (2000). The proliferation of naming rights and escalation of fees. In D. Gruen & M. Freedman (Eds.), *2000 Inside the ownership of professional sports teams.* Pp. 40-43. Chicago, IL: Team Marketing Report.

36. Bernstein, A. (2000, July 3-9). Arenas wrangle over new names. *SportsBusiness Journal*, 23.

37. Quirk, J. & Fort, R.D. (1999). *Hard ball: The abuse of power in pro sports teams.* Princeton, NJ: Princeton University Press.

38. Easton, P. (2002, February 8). Astros want Enron name off stadium. *The Bryan-College Station Eagle*, A1, A5.

39. Fleming, D. (2000, June 22). Lowe's can't catch a break. *Sports Illustrated*, 93, 80.

40. Schoenfeld, B. (2001, May 28-June 3). No city name, just a happy sponsor. *Sports Business Journal*, 1, 38.

41. Noll, R., & Zimbalist, A. (1997). Build the stadium—create the jobs! In R. Noll & A. Zimbalist (Eds.), *Sports, Jobs, & Taxes.* Washington DC: Brookings Institution Press.

42. Cagan, J., & DeMause, N. (*1998*). *Field of schemes: How the great stadium swindle turns public money into private profit.* Monroe, ME: Common Courage Press.

43. Walker, D. (1999, October 19). Seat licenses may be Packer's pass to future. *Milwaukee Journal Sentinel*, 4E.

44. Feurerstein, A. (1996, October 11). Giants take early lead in seat sales. *San Francisco Business Times*, 12.

Photo courtesy University of Oregon Athletic Department

Chapter Eight

Implementation of Public-Private Partnerships

Collaboration refers to the process of two or more stakeholders pooling resources to achieve a goal that no party can or will do alone. The collaborators share mutual aspirations and a commitment to work with others over time. Collaborations between the public and private sectors are almost endemic in the case of proposed major business developments. Private developers invariably seek assistance from public entities before bringing projects to fruition, especially for the footloose industries that many communities are trying to attract. Because they are not tied to a location that has specialist raw materials, natural resources, or energy supplies, such businesses are perceived to be less constrained and more flexible in their choice of location than are traditional manufacturing companies. There is considerable competition among public entities to attract these businesses, placing them in a strong position to negotiate assistance and incentives from public entities. These incentives complement and reduce development costs because jurisdictions seek the jobs and enhanced tax base businesses will bring. Many sports businesses, including professional sport franchises, can be conceptualized as being footloose.

This chapter discusses the challenges in facilitating public-private partnerships, reviews the complementary assets that public agencies and private sport businesses potentially could pool in collaborations to produce opportunities that neither sector could or would do alone, and gives examples of different types of joint venture models.

In chapter 3 it was noted that over the past 15 years, there has been substantial movement toward greater cooperation between government agencies and sports organizations in the financing of new sports facilities. The collaboration has resulted largely from economic necessity. The increased cost of building modern, fully loaded venues, coupled with growing taxpayer resistance to providing large-scale government subsidies for stadiums and arenas, has required sports organizations and government jurisdictions to forge close working partnerships. During the late 1980s, a number of effective public-private sport joint ventures emerged, notably in Phoenix and Cleveland, in which government agencies and team owners shared the cost of developing new sports facilities. These projects became development models for many venues built through the early 2000s. Over the past decade, only a small number of facilities were built without substantial public sector participation. In the case of the most notable example, the $314 million Pac Bell Park, home of the San Francisco Giants, the owner's decision to fund the ballpark from his own and team resources came only after voters rejected tax subsidies on four different occasions.

As documented in chapter 3, construction costs for stadiums and arenas over the last 30 years have increased dramatically. The abundant revenues emanating from modern facilities incorporating such features as luxury suites and corporate naming rights provide teams with the ability to fund a substantial portion of the development costs. However, owners have been reluctant to commit a significant share of the facility revenues toward facility construction, because the more dollars devoted to construction, the fewer there are for meeting team operating costs and for profit taking. The San Francisco Giants provide a good illustration of this point. The Giants must pay $20 million in debt service annually on a $155 million construction loan. The team took on the debt obligation as part of its effort to raise the $314 million needed to privately finance construction of its new ballpark. The balance of the funding came from corporate support through the sale of naming rights (Pac Bell Park) and long-term sponsorship agreements. However, the amount of "incremental income"—the amount of money the new ballpark generated annually after debt service and other operating expenses—available to the Giants totaled less than $5 million in 2001.[1] Clearly, the debt service obligation had a significant negative impact on the team's bottom line.

Consequently, teams continue to exert their leverage on local governments to finance a substantial share of new facility development costs. Despite owners' efforts to extract significant public subsidies from cities and counties, it was noted in chapter 3 that over the past decade there has been a dramatic shift toward franchise owners' assuming a greater share of the construction costs. Since 1995, owners have contributed approximately 40% of the capital to build new stadiums, up from just 15% in the mid-1980s. Similarly, owners paid 60% of the construction costs for new arenas. This is in stark contrast to earlier eras when facilities were financed entirely from public tax sources. It seems likely that public-private sector collaboration will continue to be the dominant model for sport facility construction.

Challenges in Facilitating Public-Private Partnerships

The initial challenge for both sides in a proposed public-private collaboration is to create a climate that is conducive to the partnerships' being successful. This section discusses the two most important facets involved in creating this nurturing climate for partnerships.

The spheres of business and government traditionally have been viewed as distinct in terms of philosophies, objectives, reward structures, and codes of conduct. Relations between the two spheres have not always been cordial. If any antipathy that prevails is not removed, then partnerships are unlikely. Hence, the first challenge is for both parties to understand, reconcile, and accept as legitimate the different value systems and constituent expectations that prevail in the two sectors.

It is useless to laud the benefits of partnerships if public agencies engage in activities that engender distrust and alienation among potential private-sector partners. Thus, a second task is to remove any suspicion that the public agency is competing unfairly with sports organizations in the services it delivers. A perception of unfair competition is likely to result in animosity from the sports community and to negate the possibility of partnerships with it.

Reconciling Value Systems

Agencies are mandated to serve the whole community, especially its most disadvantaged members. Hence, their traditional value systems are concerned with social outcomes and benefits that are relatively intangible and difficult to measure. In contrast, the value systems of private sports organizations focus on the tangible, easily measured outcomes of financial return on investment, and their mandate is to maximize return to stockholders. This means that their services tend to be targeted narrowly at those segments from which the sports business perceives the highest return on investment is likely to be realized. Clearly, there is inherent potential for frustration, friction, and conflict between those working in these two different value systems.

Tensions are heightened by the different environmental milieus in which the two sectors operate. Public agencies are constrained by bureaucratic procedures that are necessary to ensure accountability for their expenditure of public funds. Thus, although a sports organization may want to proceed with a project immediately, a public agency may be required to engage in an extensive planning process involving wide public participation, lengthy legislative approval procedures, extended budgetary hearings, and frequent consultation with elected officials. These checks and balances, which accountability necessitates, cause delays and may cause potential sports business partners who do not understand how government works to perceive a public agency as lacking commitment to the project, being slow moving, or being indecisive.

Synchronization of budgets may be a particularly frustrating problem when capital facilities are involved. A sports business probably can borrow funds quickly for a promising investment, but an agency interested in partnering with it may have to wait a long time for resources to be authorized by legislative authority or a bond referendum. If more than one public agency is involved in a partnership, the problem is compounded because city, county, state, and federal agencies may all have different fiscal years and budget-planning cycles.

These distinctive differences between the two sections sometimes lead to the formation of negative stereotypical attitudes that impede the development of partnerships. In the authors' experience, both popular perceptions of government inefficiency and private sector efficiency are exaggerated grossly. Media opportunities and media actions have helped build the view that public and private organizations represent opposite poles of the efficiency continuum.

There is a segment of the population, including some managers in the private sports sector, who perceive public agencies as being wasteful, unresponsive, tradition-bound, incompetent, and inefficient bureaucracies staffed by people who have never had to meet a payroll and who sometimes seek to frustrate the legitimate goals of business. Much of this perception is derived from public agencies' being required to operate openly and to give the media full access to all of their actions. Freedom of information acts and government-in-the-sunshine laws are deliberately written to guarantee public and media access to whatever is done by the officials who act in the public's name. These laws are designed to ensure that the public agencies are fully accountable to their taxpayer bosses for their actions.

In contrast, private organizations, for the most part, are entitled to keep their decision processes and actions confidential. Hence, media focus all of their investigative reporting efforts on public organizations because the rights of privacy that prevail in the private sector preclude public access.

The requirement that government decisions be transparent means that actions taken by public managers or elected officials that fail to achieve the projected positive outcome are likely to result in those responsible being subjected to public criticism, scorn, and ridicule when the failure is extensively reported in the media. This causes many in the public sector to pursue a course of action that is risk aversive:

> Agency officials often feel that they are on the front lines, encumbered by bureaucracy, politics, the press and insufficient resources. It is difficult to take risks in such an environment, whether real or perceived. Working cooperatively with private sector organizations is a risk outside of normal government operations.[2] (p. 164)

Much of the perceived risk is associated with giving up control. If a public agency commits to seeking partnerships, then an inherent corollary of that commitment is a willingness to compromise the degree of control it can exercise over the service delivered. Private sports organizations have to be able to demonstrate to investors and bankers that they have sufficient control to operate the venture successfully before they can acquire the capital necessary to develop it.

A key factor in control is the length of a contract or lease. When the length is short, for example, less than five years, control largely is retained because the arrangement is periodically evaluated to ensure that it remains in the public interest. Long leases mean surrendering control of a public resource for ten years or, more frequently, for 25 to 30 years. Such long leases are needed when the commercial sector invests substantially in capital assets in order for developers to have time to amortize successfully all of their capital improvements and secure an acceptable return on their investment. At the same time, a long-term lease provides the agency with evidence of the operator's long-term commitment to the project.

One manager who is widely experienced in developing partnerships observed that financial necessity alone does not ensure that successful partnerships will ensue:

> Partnerships can fail because the parties become too eager to close a deal before they have squared their visions (Why are we building a new facility?) and missions (Once we build it, what are we going to stand for?). Some people partner just because of financial reasons, but that is not the only reason to do it. The real reason is that you want to solve a community problem and create a better quality of life, and you want to find a

partner who can complement your strengths and improve on your weaknesses—and everybody has both.[3] (p. 35)

The success of partnerships depends on how the parties work together, but each partner also has to ensure that its own organization's objectives are met in the arrangement. Each entity's negotiators are responsible for meeting the expectations of its stakeholders about the outcome. Because the cooperating parties may have different outcome objectives, this frequently causes friction in partnership negotiations. A consequence is that partnerships often take longer than anticipated to come to fruition. The likelihood of acceptable compromise positions being agreed upon is likely to depend on the extent to which there are mutual trust and understanding and the effectiveness of communication. There are no generalizable formulas for forging partnerships because personalities, local conditions, state and local enabling laws, community values, and other factors vary widely. However, the two elements of mutual trust and effective communication appear to be common guiding principles that underlie successful partnerships.

Ultimately, the personalities of individuals involved in a partnership and the personal relationships they forge determine the effectiveness of the partnership. If attempts are made to consummate partnership arrangements without a genuine commitment from those who will be responsible for executing them, then the arrangements will be undermined and fail. Mutual trust and understanding usually grow over time. They stem from familiarity and successful experiences of working together. This suggests that partnerships are most likely to flourish in jurisdictions where leadership in key organizations in the public, nonprofit, and private sports sectors is relatively stable, enabling networks of trusting interpersonal relationships to evolve. Indeed, for this reason, development of partnerships in a community is best viewed not as a series of independent projects but as a continuous process.

With multiple parties involved, confusion and misunderstanding easily can emerge over goals, funding, timing, division of responsibilities, and a host of other issues. Effective communication alleviates these problems. Communication should start with clear articulation of the outcomes each partner seeks from an arrangement and the common vision and purpose the partners share for it. Sometimes this initial step is overlooked because it is assumed that each partner is aware of the others' goals and aspirations. Overlooking the first step may lead, for example, to a public agency's interpreting a partner's expectations in a manner that is consistent with the outcomes that the agency seeks, although this interpretation may be incorrect. Throughout the negotiation process, written documentation should be continued because points that were initially clear and agreed upon may not be recalled accurately 12 months later.

The Unfair Competition Issue

Let's say you own a small neighborhood grocery store. You have owned your store for many years, dutifully paying taxes and contributing to the community in a variety of ways. Suddenly, you find out that you will have new competition in six months. Another grocery store will open just down the road.

"Fair enough," you say. "My customers like my store because the prices are fair, the store is clean, and my employees are friendly. I may lose a few customers, but having good, clean competition is part of doing business. Besides, this may help me find new ways to appeal to my loyal customers." But wait a minute. . . . You find out that the new store will look exactly like yours (only newer). The new store claims that selling food is a service to the community and that it will sell healthy food which promotes a sound mind and body. Since the store will "benefit the community as a whole" and "promote health," the money to buy the land and build will come from tax-exempt bonds redeemed by public tax dollars. You pay thousands of dollars every year in interest on the money you borrowed to buy the land and build your store. The competition won't be paying for anything.

Not only does the new store avoid paying debt charges but because it "promotes health" and wants to encourage as many residents as possible to take advantage of its healthy foods, its annual operating costs are subsidized by taxpayers— it is not required to breakeven. Further, since it is owned and operated by the public sector, it does not have to pay property, sales, or income taxes which you are required to do. Finally, it receives free advertising and promotion from agency brochures, literature, and articles, and is signed on all the surrounding highways informing travelers of its existence and location. In contrast, you have to pay for all your promotional vehicles.[4]

Given these advantages, the new grocery store is able to price its food products at half the prices you are charging. How can you compete with it? This scenario occurs repeatedly in the world of sports when public sector and nonprofit organizations offer similar services in the same geographic area to those offered by commercial sports operators. Consider the following example:

> I operate two clubs, 4 miles apart. One club is a multi-sport facility with 4,000 foot square feet of the facility dedicated to swimming. The other club is a 16,000 square foot facility including a $500,000 addition for a swimming pool, also occupying 4,000 square feet of the total. The North Clackamas Parks and Recreation District, formed in November of 1990, will locate its 80 acre Regional Park complex, costing $16 million, precisely between my two clubs. The new indoor complex will be a 60,000 square foot aquatic center with five pools under one roof. My combined square footage for swimming is only 8,000 square feet. The projected costs to users of the huge regional complex who purchase monthly passes will be one-third to one-half the cost that my business charges. My business caters to middle class families, not upper income wealthy individuals. The regional complex will market their facility to this same group.

> Clackamas County orchestrated a sophisticated marketing and advertising campaign in order to sell this idea to the voters, with the assistance of three highly compensated, full-time staffs who worked on this project for 18 months prior to advancing the concept to the voters.[5]

The advantages of the public sector include paying no property, sales, or income taxes; being self-insured; financing improvements with tax-exempt funds rather than borrowing money at commercial rates; not being required to cover debt charges with operating revenues; not being required to cover operating expenses with revenues; being exempted from many regulations; and receiving free advertising from the agency. The potentially devastating impact of this competition is illustrated by the following examples:

- Lafayette, Colorado, has a population of 15,000. The city built a $4 million sports and fitness facility with three pools, steam rooms, a whirlpool, dry saunas, racquetball courts, a gymnasium, an indoor track, a fitness center with free weights and cardiovascular equipment, and babysitting services. When it opened, three private fitness clubs operated in Lafayette. After one year, one had gone out of business; a second saw its membership decline from 500 to 250; and the third, which was an aerobics studio, was unable to maintain the numbers it needed to justify proceeding with an expansion to which it had previously committed.[6]

Table 8-1 A Comparison of Costs Incurred by a Public Agency or Non-Profit Organization and a Private Athletic Club on a $3 Million Facility

Venue Name	Public/Nonprofit	Private Club
Annual Land Carrying Costs (assuming a land value of $100,000 per acre and a 15-year loan on $500,000 at 9% interest)	0	$60,856
Annual Building Mortgage (assuming a $2 million, 15-year loan at 9% interest)	0	$243,424
Furnishings and Equipment ($300,000 borrowed for five years at 11%)	0	$78,273
Postage (tax-exempt or public sector entitled to a 33% discount)	$13,400	$20,000
Real Estate Taxes (assuming a property value of $3,000,000 at 50% taxation rate of $4 per $100)	0	$37,800
Personal Property Taxes: State Income Taxes (state tax rate of 7% on profit of $200,000)	0	$14,000
Federal Income Taxes (federal rate of 22.25% on first $100,000 and 39% on next $100,000)	0	$61,250
Total Annual Costs	$13,400	$515,603
ANNUAL COST ADVANTAGE TO PUBLIC/TAX EXEMPT SECTOR		$502,203

* Prepared by Roger Ralph, President, Bel Air Athletic Club and Chairman, Harford County Coalition for Fair Competition. Reproduced in International Health. Racquet & Sportsclub Association (nd). *The Case for Fair Competition in the Fitness Industry.* Boston, MA: IHRSA

- Gore Mountain Ski Center, a public facility operated by the state of New York, received an annual tax subsidy of $50,000 each year and was constructed with tax-free bonds. It applied for $246,000 in federal grants to help fund a $2.87 million capital extension that involved installing snowmaking machinery and other equipment. The balance of the capital was raised by issuing tax-free bonds. With these advantages, Gore Mountain charged $400 for a family season pass. The four commercial resorts in the area charged an average of $1,125 for the same pass because they had to pay commercial prices for investment capital and received no assistance from federal grants. They also had to show a reasonable return on their investment. Thus, the publicly operated state project gradually forced the commercial operations out of business. An editorial in the *Wall Street Journal* commented, "By a sort of Gresham's law of competition, we have noticed that state enterprises in the mixed economy tend to drive out private enterprise."[7] (p. 4)

Table 8-1 documents the financial disadvantages faced by a private athletic club operator who is in competition with a public or nonprofit organization in the same area. The example assumes the private athletic club invested $3 million in acquiring five acres of land and is building the facility. In this example, the private club has to pass an additional $502,203 in annual costs on to its customers. If the club had 1,800 members, then each would pay $279 per year, or $23.25 extra per month. Because the public or nonprofit facility does not bear these costs, it can provide identical services at a substantially lower price than that of the private club. This egregious situation is exacerbated if the public agency's annual operations are also subsidized by tax funds.

Many private sports club managers allege that new public or nonprofit centers are often indistinguishable from their existing facilities and services and serve only to drive private clubs out of the marketplace. Some of their more extreme spokespeople ask, "Why should government build public sports centers when they don't build public food stores or pharmacies?" Others more reasonably ask, "Is the city going to build and operate its own movie theaters and bowling centers as well as sports centers, since they are also recreation facilities?"

Public agencies argue that because community sports centers usually are financed with general obligation bonds that have to be approved by a referendum, the public's willingness to finance these centers indicates that citizens do not perceive that the private sector is meeting their demands. Further, they note that municipalities, colleges, and YMCAs have had gyms, pools, weight rooms, and playing fields that predate the first commercial sports clubs by 75 years or more.[8] Finally, competing public sports centers generally are defended on the grounds that they aim at target markets in the community that do not have access to commercial facilities, such as families, seniors, and children, whereas commercial operators primarily target young adults ranging from 16 to 30 years of age. For example, a spokesman defending the decision of the city of North Richland Hills, Texas, to build a $7.8 million fun water park stated "The park is not meant to compete with the large commercial water parks that target teens with their high-adventure rides, but is for families, particularly those with young children. We wanted elements that mom and dad would get out with the kids and interact together" (p. 34).[9]

It has been suggested that the opposition of private sports and fitness club owners is short-sighted because

> it hurts facility owners—if not now, then later. Today's 14-year-old who is introduced to weights and stationary bikes in the community recreation center may well become an 18-year-old habitué of the college recreation center and then a 22-year-old or 30-, or 40-, or 50-year-old enthusiastic health or racquet-club member. Killing opportunities for recreation in an industry that knows it is not even reaching 20 percent of the country—well, that's just bad business.[8] (p. 11)

In Boise, Idaho, the West Family YMCA/Boise City Aquatic Center was the result of a three-way partnership between the city, which paid $5 million of the $9.4 million construction costs; the YMCA, which paid the rest of the construction cost and operates both the city's aquatic center portion and its own fitness center portion of the facility; and a research park, which donated the land. The facility's manager stated, "Part of the Y's mission is to help provide for those who would otherwise not be able to afford it." That closely conforms to what the city wanted to do by making sport facilities very affordable. However, the project was perceived differently by community health and fitness club owners in the area. One of them described it as "one of the most lavish health clubs in the area which has been responsible for putting four clubs out of business since it opened." Another club owner stated,

> It was presented as a place for our youth to learn solid values and strengthen body, mind and spirit, as a way to counteract the influence of gangs. Who can complain about that? . . . But in actual fact, they're catering to middle- and upper-class adults. From our point of view, what they are doing is using their special treatment through their tax exemptions, and the fact that they don't have a mortgage to pay. They were given this facility by the community, and are using these advantages to unfairly compete with the non-paying businesses in the fitness industry here in Boise.[10]

The funding for most public-agency sports facilities has to be approved by a public referendum. Because in most parts of the country there is no legal mechanism for stopping public agencies from constructing competing facilities if they wish to do so, private sports managers have to mount campaigns to stop facilities at the voting booth.

Figure 8-1 reports the response of sports and fitness club owners who led a successful campaign to defeat a $25 million bond proposal for a family recreational center in Southfield, Michigan. A similar campaign in Fairfax County, Virginia, was not successful, but it emphasized the convincing arguments that can be made by the sport and fitness industry against new public recreational centers. In the Fairfax County case, the private-sector recreation suppliers authored a 16-page report documenting how the county park authority was directly and unfairly competing with them when it proposed to build four new recreational centers. The report was entitled *Unfair, Unfair, Unfair Competition: How The Fairfax County*

Figure 8-1 Defeat of a $25 Million Bond Proposal for a Family Recreational Center

Proposal A on the ballot in Southfield, Michigan, sought a 20-year bond issue of up to $25 million to expand the existing civic center sports arena, which contained a 30-year-old ice rink, into a family recreational center and to renovate the existing space. This would have added a 1.09 mill tax to taxpayers' bills, so the owner of a $92,000 home (average for Southfield) would pay $50.14 each year. The proposed facilities included

- a three-court gymnasium;

- an elevated jogging track;

- an indoor-outdoor aquatic center with a leisure pool and a second pool for lap swimming;

- a second full-sized ice arena with 1,500 spectator seats and a studio ice facility for figure skating;

- a senior citizen center;

- a teen center; and

- meeting rooms, kitchen facilities, food services, and locker rooms.

Fitness businesses in the community quickly organized to oppose it. "We pay a lot of taxes and pay a lot of people and we will be hurt by this," said the general manager of Franklin Fitness & Racquet Club. "We've been a solid business operation in this community for 25 years," he said. "You don't want to start competing with the city which is using donated land and doesn't pay taxes to itself. If the measure passes, we and other clubs through the increased taxes we'd be paying, in effect, would be subsidizing a competitor. Is there a need to tax 100% of the people for what 5, 10, or even 15% are going to use?"

The city authorities argued that they had an obligation to provide recreational facilities for their citizens, to which the fitness club general managers responded, "Maybe, but to what degree? When does it stop? Sure cities provide recreational facilities, but at what level? Would they want to provide bowling? Should they build a movie house?"

"There's a misunderstanding that may be there," said the assistant parks and recreation director. "They feel we're being competitive, but we're not. We have a family atmosphere, not a club atmosphere. We feel we can bring in fun for young people, toddlers, and adults. There would be no full-blown fitness program or body-building facility . . . We don't think we compete for the same clientele. We offer an introduction to people to the things they do at the private clubs. In that regard, we may actually be helping them because people try something out and if they find out they like it, they might want to sign up with a club."

Franklin Racquet Club celebrated its 25th anniversary that year by dedicating a new $1 million basketball-volleyball floor. "Basketball leagues are flourishing here on weekends and in the evenings," the club's manager said, "but volleyball hasn't yet gotten so popular here. And if the city winds up with a new basketball/volleyball gym, what will that mean to places like Franklin? It definitely will affect our business. We can't grow like we want to. If someone could afford a league over here and get it at half-price over there—even if they could afford the higher price—why wouldn't they go there? We may not have made that $1 million investment if we knew we'd have been competing with the city."

At approximately the same time that this proposal was announced, the city, in conjunction with Providence Hospital, opened a new wellness center at its Beach Woods Recreation Center. They filled an existing 12,000 sq. ft. room with equipment. They charged $250 per year for membership and hoped to attract from 300 to 350 members. Four physiologists, who were not employed by the hospital, were available to members, each working 20 hours per week in the center.

The fitness clubs developed a brochure that emphasize reasons the bond proposal should be rejected (see figure 8-1A). This brochure gave no indication that the fitness clubs planned and funded the campaign. The group registered itself as Friends Opposed to Proposal A. This strategy was designed to ensure that the residents objectively reviewed the points raised. If this had not been done, some recipients may have dismissed the campaign as merely the disgruntled efforts of a narrowly vested commercial interest.

The fitness group invested approximately $20,000 in their opposition campaign that included the following:

- A brochure mailed to each household in Southfield (see figure 8-1A)—printing, postage, and mailing cost $6,500
- Brochure inserts in the *Detroit Free Press and News* for Southfield—$3,000
- A full-page advertisement in the *Free Press and News*—$4,200
- A full-page advertisement in the *Southfield Observer*—$2,500
- Individuals handing out a brochure outside voting areas on the day of balloting—$2,000

As a result of their efforts, Proposal A was defeated overwhelmingly by 5,582 votes to 2,055 votes.

Government and Fairfax County Park Authority Directly Compete Against Private Recreation.[11] The first paragraph of the report stated,

> We are optimistic this document will make governmental agencies aware of the unfair situation that occurs when non-taxpaying public facilities compete directly against private taxpaying facilities, and will encourage responsible public officials to pass legislation that would prohibit any government recreation facility from locating within a specific distance of an existing private facility. This type of legislation would give the Fairfax County Park Authority a clear guideline and prohibit the park system from competing unfairly or duplicating recreation that is already provided by a tax paying business. In Fairfax County there are numerous privately owned recreational facilities . . . Competition in the leisure/recreation field has become increasingly fierce due to many factors; however, when you consider normal business expenses and the additional burden created by trying to compete with the very government you pay taxes to, it is difficult to understand why any new recreational businesses would enter the market. It should be noted that hundreds of privately-owned recreation/leisure facilities are competing for the same recreation/leisure dollar. A large general public is needed to support and patronize these businesses for them to succeed. As the County continues to expand into the revenue-producing recreation field, the recreational dollar is further diluted, which eventually will bankrupt some businesses and certainly discourage others that hope to build additional facilities.[11]

Although competition with commercial sport operators may present significant philosophical, ethical, and political problems, agencies are not required legally to refrain from such competition. Under the general power authorizing them to provide park and recreational opportunities for citizens, agencies (if they choose to do so) legally can provide facilities and programs similar to those that private businesses offer. Thus, the courts generally have rejected suits brought by businesses alleging unfair competitions, confirming that agencies have no obligations to businesses that suffer from such actions.[12]

The state of Colorado responded to concerns that recreation special districts were developing facilities that were traditionally the domain of the private sector by passing a statute that stated,

> No district shall construct, own, or operate any bowling alley, roller skating rink, batting cage, golf course on which the game is played on an artificial surface, or an amusement park that has water recreation as its central theme, unless the board of such district receives approval for such project from the board of county commissioners of each county that has territory included in the district. The board of county commissioners shall disapprove the facility or service unless evidence satisfactory to the board of each of the following is presented:
>
> (I)   The facility or service is not adequately provided in the district by private providers;
>
> (II) There is sufficient existing and projected need for the facility or service within the district;
>
> (III) The existing facilities or services in the district are inadequate for present and projected needs;
>
> (IV) The district has or will have the financial ability to discharge any proposed indebtedness on a reasonable basis; and
>
> (V)   The facility or service will be in the best interests of the district and of the residents of the district.

This was designed to safeguard the interests of private recreation suppliers in the state.

In Pennsylvania, sports and fitness club managers worked through the state's strongest lobbying organization for small business and succeeded in getting legislation passed. The Pennsylvania Public Charities Act included the following language:

- Section 8A: "It is the policy of this act that institutions of purely public charity shall not use their tax-exempt status to compete unfairly with small business."

- Section 8B: "An institution of purely public charity may not fund, guarantee the indebtedness of, lease obligations of, or subsidize a commercial business that is unrelated to the institution's charitable purpose as stated in the institution's charter or governing legal documents."

- "Commercial Business" is defined as "the sale of products or services that are principally the same in those offered by an existing small business in the same community" (p. 88).[13]

This "fair competition" law has attracted considerable attention among private sports club operators, and it seems likely that efforts will be made to pass similar legislation in other states.

Regardless of the legal and ethical issues raised by unfair competition, there are two pragmatic reasons that public agencies should avoid it. First, the presence of fair competition by private suppliers may stimulate the agency to improve performance in terms both of responding to user demands and of minimizing costs. Second, most public agencies are unable to satisfy fully all of the demands expected of them. If some of these demands can be met by the private sector, then agency resources can be redirected to meet other needs.

Unfair competition from nonprofits. In the case of public agencies, allegations of unfair competitions are resolved through the political process because public agencies are legally authorized to engage in unfair competition if they elect to do so. However, when the unfair competition emanates from nonprofit organizations such as YMCAs or nonprofit hospitals, then private sports organizations can seek legal redress. The legal case has been articulated in the following terms:

> We argue that YMCA recreation and fitness centers are not tax-exempt by reason of what they do (providing such facilities), but rather by reason of whom they are serving. YMCA facilities, whose services are focused primarily on taking care of youth, the elderly, the poor, the handicapped, etc., deserve every tax break they receive. On the other hand, YMCA facilities whose services are primarily focused on providing recreational fitness services to affluent suburban communities or an upscale business and professional clientele are not public charities and ought not to be tax exempt.[14]

This fundamental principle has been accepted as the key factor by courts that have ruled in these cases. The argument points out that many YMCAs have changed from their traditional role of charitable, donation-driven organizations to commercial-style operations to generate a source of dependable operating revenue. Thus, only 15% of the YMCA's revenues come from donations, whereas 75% is commercial income from fees, and the remaining 10% comes from government support, investment income, etc. This contrasts with the Boys and Girls Clubs of America, in which 57% of revenues come from donations and only 15% come from fees.

Traditionally, YMCAs offered basic no-frills facilities in urban areas and targeted their programs at low-income youth. Hundreds of YMCAs continue to serve the poor, aged, underprivileged, those with disabilities, and youth, and these YMCAs are clearly public charities. However, in some areas, the YMCA has moved away from this model and has constructed modern fitness centers that cater to downtown businessmen or middle-class suburbanites. These are physically and operationally indistinguishable from commercially operated fitness and sports clubs. In the last decade, YMCAs in the United States have constructed over $1 billion worth of new buildings. These new facilities use commercial advertising that focuses on selling memberships and not on appealing for volunteer and financial help for the needy. In form and format, their advertisements are often no different from those of commercial facility operators.

When the YMCA built a $2 million facility in Salisbury, Maryland, the existing Merritt Athletic Club lost 33% of its members to the YMCA. In Saco, Maine, the New England Health and Racquet Club saw its sales fall 50% when the $2.6 million North York County Family YMCA opened within three miles. Executive Athletic Club had been in Oakland, California, for 50 years when the YMCA opened a $10 million facility around the corner and drove the taxpaying club out of business.[15]

The unfair competitive advantage that the YMCAs enjoy stems from a myriad of special privileges granted under federal, state, and local laws and regulations governing them. These include

> Exemption from federal income taxation under Section 501 of the Internal Revenue Code. Nonprofits also enjoy exemption from state and local income and property taxes, and many are exempt from state unemployment compensation regulations. They benefit from significantly lower nonprofit postal rates. In addition, a nonprofit organization enjoys a special status in the marketplace; tax-exempt status makes an organization especially attractive to prospective customers.[16]

The conceptual rationale for these exemptions is that the YMCAs are providing social services that would otherwise have to be provided by government, so it is appropriate that they be subsidized in this way. However, sport and fitness club owners argue that these new YMCAs render few, if any, charitable services; allocate only small proportions of their revenue toward financial assistance or subsidized programs targeted at low-income groups; and target their services at those who can pay substantive fees. The YMCA points out that it needs to have some profitable programs, even if such programs compete with private businesses, because they are a major revenue source for providing services to the needy. However, it is illegal for a tax-exempt organization to use profits to subsidize other services. If a charity makes money from a source unrelated to its exempt purpose, it is required to pay taxes on that revenue. In this context, the IRS has made it clear that colleges are required to pay taxes on income they receive from fees paid by the general public to use college facilities. For example, the IRS demanded that the University of Michigan pay $7.6 million in taxes for income received from the university's ice-rink, golf, and other sports facilities.[17] In the view of the IRS, this income falls outside the school's nonprofit exemption.

The focus of the court cases to this point has been the legitimacy of the YMCA's exemption from local property taxes. The most prominent case concerned the Columbia-Willamette YMCA's Metro Fitness Center located in Portland.[18] The Oregon Supreme Court ruled that this 4,400-member YMCA club should be placed on the tax rolls because too few of its services could be defined as charitable. Indeed, only 5% of its revenue went toward financial assistance. This ruling required the YMCA to pay $150,000 in annual property taxes from which it had previously been exempt. However, 2 years later, its property-tax exemption status was restored when it changed its name to Metro Family YMCA, expanded beyond its adult fitness focus by adding 20 new programs for youth, including drug and alcohol rehabilitation and alternative education, and increased the level of financial assistance so it was extended to 33% of its members.

Similar court rulings have been made against hospital health clubs that have claimed tax-exempt status. The Supreme Court of South Dakota found that Sioux Valley Hospital's $6 million wellness center was not a charitable organization because the court found only 0.5% of the club's 2,600 memberships were subsidized by the hospital. It rejected the argument that wellness centers are exempt as health care facilities:

> The Court noted that if it adopted such a broad definition of health care, all physical activity and all healthy activities would be exempt so that if the cafeteria provided health foods related to maintaining a state of soundness of the mind and body, the cafeteria would be tax exempt. Again, if the pro shop sold items used for general fitness, which related to maintain a state of soundness of the mind and body, the pro shop would be tax exempt.[19]

A similar decision was reached in *Middle Tennessee Medical Center v. Assessment of Appeals Commission of the State of Tennessee* (1994). In that case, the court found that the hospital fitness center was not exempt from state taxes for nonpatient use. The court noted,

> The great majority of those who use the. . . Center are not under a doctor's care. They have chosen the Center over competing health spas for reasons of their own, and it is not the role of this court to encourage that choice by according the. . . . Center a more favorable tax treatment than that permitted by its competitors.[20]

The court added, "We feel it would be a misuse of the tax exemption granted to charitable hospitals if every revenue-generating venture they embarked upon automatically benefited from the exemption, so long as that venture could be characterized as in some way promoting health."[20]

The Complementary Assets of Public Agency and Private Sports Enterprises

In the past, governments were active investors in the private economy, routinely using their assets to seed new businesses. For example, the federal government gave 9.3% of all land in the continental United States to the railroads as an inducement to build a transcontinental system.[21] Similarity, public jurisdictions today have assets that they use as incentives to stimulate investment by sports businesses that otherwise might not be forthcoming. These public assets can be used to prime the pump and leverage commercial investment by encouraging businesses to enter partnerships.

Critical to understanding the potential of partnerships is a recognition that each sector has resources of value to offer the other. The essence of forging a collaborative agreement is finding a way to fuse the complementary resources of each sector to the mutual advantage of all parties involved. Public sector organizations have access to a range of resources that can act as powerful enticements to private businesses. These resources include a substantial land bank, the ability to access low-cost developmental capital, the capacity to confer a number of tax incentives, and control over zoning and permit applications. On the other hand, the private sector offers an array of resources that have proven to be attractive stimulants for public sector cooperation. These inducements include specialized management expertise, reduced labor costs, adaptability to scale of service, and reduced liabil-

Figure 8-2 Agency Assets Can be Used to "Prime the Pump"

ity risks. The complementary resources that serve as the basis for public-private sector collaboration are summarized in Table 8-2.

Public Sector Assets

Land bank. Among the valuable assets that a public agency possesses are the land it owns and the mechanisms and vehicles it is authorized to use to acquire land for public purposes. It is not easy to find sites in urban areas for sports facilities, and the challenge has intensified as sports facilities have become larger, with higher capacities, more exclusive concessions areas, and more ancillary areas such as restaurants and hotels:

> Additional land is needed for parking lots, access roads, and expressway connections to accommodate the automobiles that bring most customers to games. Their size and nature make sports facilities unwelcome neighbors for most urban dwellers. Sports facilities bring crowds, litter, noise, and crime to an area, along with more traffic, air pollution, and parking problems. Residents fear that sports facilities, like other large developments, will inalterably change the character of their communities and reduce their property values, worries that are reinforced by the scheduling of most sporting events at night.[22] (p. 280)

It is common to find a substantial portion of a community's existing open space under the jurisdiction of a county or municipal park and recreation agency. Often, this inventory includes not only the largest tracts of potentially developable property, but also some of the most attractive parcels with respect to location, access, and commercial value. If such land is not available, then a public

Table 8-2 Complementary Assets that the Public and Private Sectors Can Contribute to Joint-Venture Collaborations

Public Sector Assets	Private Sector Assets
• Land Bank	• Management Expertise
• Low-Cost Capital	• Reduced Labor Costs
• Tax Waivers	• Adaptability to Scale of Service
• Control Over Permit and Zoning Processes	• Reduced Liability Risks

jurisdiction can use its extensive regulatory and financing powers to assemble a site. It is much more difficult for a private entity to do this, and it is inconceivable that a private entity would attempt it without support from a public agency.

Once land has been deemed by a public jurisdiction to be available for a sports project use, the jurisdiction may be prepared to offer a nominal lease (for example, $1 a year) in order to encourage development of a sports amenity that the public agency lacks the resources to develop on its own. Without this incentive, the high cost of land would make the project economically infeasible for a private organization. Before considering arrangements of this type, there should be a careful review of local and state enabling legislation to ensure that the agency has the authority and power to proceed in this way. In a few cases, passage of new legislation at the state level may be required to create the necessary authority. In addition, each piece of land considered for use in this way should be reviewed to ensure that it is free of restraints and covenants imposed when it was obtained because these could prevent such use. This is especially important if the agency land was purchased with federal funds, which often prohibit any change of use.

In order to attract private investment funds, it is likely that an agency will be required to offer a long lease of 15 to 20 years on the land to allow a developer sufficient time to obtain a reasonable return on the investment. Normally, these leases provide optional permit-renewal clauses allowing continued private operation for one or two additional 5-year periods, after which time the entire facility usually becomes the property of the public agency.

Development of the Joe Robbie Stadium (subsequently renamed the Pro Player Stadium) in Miami provides an example of how land can be used to prime the pump. The $90 million, 73,000-seat, open-air stadium on the northern edge of Dade County was financed almost entirely by Joe Robbie, owner of the Miami Dolphins. The project became financially feasible when the land was offered at no cost to Mr. Robbie, the owner at that time of the NFL team. The developer who owned the 100-acre parcel of land on which the stadium was built leased it to Dade County for 99 years at $1.00 per year. Dade County then offered it on a similar lease to the Dolphins. Freed from site acquisition costs that would have run into the millions and from paying sales taxes because it was on county property, the owner of the Dolphins was able to apply all of the revenues raised through the successful sale of luxury suites and club seats prior to construction. The revenue was used as security on a 30-year, revenue-bond issue by Dade County. Robbie pledged income from the leasing of 234 luxury boxes and 10,000 club seats. Leases on the luxury boxes averaged $45,000 to $50,000 per year for a period of 10 years. Club seats, also leased for 10 years, rented from $600 to $1,400 per year. Most of these exclusive seats were sold by the first year

Figure 8-3 Development of Disney Ice

The city of Anaheim joined with Disney to develop Disney Ice as a community ice skating center, which was a complementary facility to the Arrowhead Pond amenity described in Figure 7-5. There were three parties involved in the development:

1) The Anaheim Redevelopment Agency, which is charged by the city with leading its downtown redevelopment efforts;

2) DSCR Inc., which is a wholly owned subsidiary of The Walt Disney Corporation; and

3) Disney GOALS, Inc., a 501(c) (iii) organization.

The genesis for Disney Ice occurred when the Walt Disney Company purchased a National Hockey League franchise, the Mighty Ducks. City officials were enthusiastic about the idea of partnering with Disney to develop a high profile sports venue in Downtown Anaheim. Designed by architect Frank Ghery, the City envisaged this would create another focal point in Downtown Anaheim, which was only minutes away from Disneyland and the Anaheim Convention Center.

The project's four objectives were to provide:

1. a fully equipped training center for the Mighty Ducks of Anaheim, a National Hockey League franchise, which committed to use the ice-rink as its primary practice facility;

2. a focal point for local and regional hockey leagues and exhibition games;

3. community programs that offered free skating and other activities for seniors and youth; and

4. a resource for under-served youth in the area through the Disney GOALS program (Growth Opportunities through Athletics, Learning and Service).

The Redevelopment Agency conveyed the 3.2 acre site for Disney Ice to Disney GOALS. This land was valued at $4.3 million. Disney GOALS and DSCR Inc., constructed the facility. The glass enclosed en-

of the stadium's operation. The leases generated over $13 million a year, exceeding the $10 million annual debt charges on the stadium.

Similarly, the contribution of land by the city of Anaheim Re-development Agency was a key element in the partnership collaboration that led to the development of Disney Ice, a community ice-skating center adjacent to the Arrowhead Pond Arena, which is described in Figure 8-3.

Although land is a powerful pump-priming asset, any proposal to change the use of existing park land to accommodate sports activities is likely to stimulate vigorous opposition. This opposition is likely to be especially pronounced if the activities are offered by a private business. An illustration of the backlash that may occur when park land is used to encourage private investment is given in Figure 8-4.

There are multiple examples of public agencies contributing land to jointly develop golf courses. Typically, the private developer/operator leases the land for a nominal rent of $1 per year and pays a rent to the public agency. The rent usually includes a fixed minimum guarantee and a percentage of gross revenues from

trance fronts a large plaza designed for community functions and activities and painted in the Mighty Ducks' colors. A 3,000 square foot pro shop and Mighty Ducks superstore (where visitors can purchase top-of-the-line figure skating, ice hockey, and in-line hockey equipment and National Hockey League merchandise) are located to the right of the entrance. Rental skates are located on the left with plenty of seating room throughout the area. As visitors walk through the entrance hall, they see an 85 foot x 200 foot National Hockey League-size rink to the left, and a 100 foot x 200 foot Olympic-sized rink to the right.

The facility was leased by Disney GOALS to DSCR Inc. Thus, GOALS has income from the property, which is used for its ongoing programs. The primary purpose of the community programs provided through Disney GOALS and through DSCR's operation of the ice rink is to address the city's gang/drug problem by focusing on youth and families. The programs are required to provide a mix of activities that will attract Anaheim citizens of all ages; however, an emphasis will be on youth activities, ranging in age from preschool to senior high school; involving both boys and girls; and discouraging drug, alcohol, and tobacco use.

The agreement required Disney GOALS to provide services in the form of ice time, equipment, instruction, and services to the community on an annual basis for 30 years. The financial arrangements required the value of the public programs and services offered by Disney GOALS to be $375,000 annually. These contributions are made in lieu of cash payments for the land. The value of the annual services over the 30 years term of the agreement is $11.25 million. The net present value is $4.35 million. Thus, the services provided by Disney GOALS exceeded the cost to the city of providing the land by $50,000. In addition, the new property tax income derived from the facility was projected to provide $1.15 million (net present value) over the 30-year life of the contract.

The $375,000 annual in-kind contribution consists of 500 hours of ice-time, valued at $115,000; services, equipment rental, and/or vouchers/coupons to be redeemed at the Ice Rink, valued at $85,000; and the Disney GOALS program agreed to expend no less than $125,000 annually on salaries and services to the youth of Anaheim located in targeted neighborhoods. The GOALS programs include youth hockey, "learn to skate," and figure skating lessons, and their implementation is monitored and evaluated by the Anaheim Community Services Department.

the course's operations. When the lease expires, ownership of the course reverts in its entirety to the public agency. An example of this type of arrangement is the Mile Square Golf Course in Orange County, California, which was one of the earliest public-private joint ventures in the sports field.[23] This is described in Figure 8-5.

A review of a number of these kinds of joint venture golf courses indicated that the features of a typical lease included

- Thirty- to 50-year leases;

- Minimum fixed annual rent, which typically starts at under $100,000 and increases in steps over the early years of operation, depending on the income and expenses of the golf course;

- Percentage lease payments ranging from 5 to 15% of the gross golf revenues (green fees, golf car fees, use of the driving range, sales, and other fees);

Figure 8-4 A Backlash to the Commercialization of Parks

The Metropolitan Dade County Parks and Recreation Department is widely recognized as one of the nation's outstanding agencies. Like many others, it has been required to accept substantial additional responsibilities but has not been provided with additional tax funds commensurate with fulfilling those responsibilities. In the past decade, the land that the department managed increased more than 50%, from 8,700 to 13,500 acres, while its tax revenues actually shrunk when adjusted for inflation from $27 million to $24 million. Hence, the agency's managers had no alternative except to raise additional funds by encouraging private businesses to operate in some of the agency's parks.

This created a passionate backlash from park lovers and stimulated a campaign for a charter amendment that would have required county voters' specific approval before any commercial structure larger than a snack stand was placed in a park. The leader of this movement called what was happening to Dade parks an "ecological Chernobyl. This is a nightmare. I don't think the public has realized how much of this is going on." One of his associates observed:

> The county sees park property as a way to steal from the parks budget and invest in the tourism budget. They're leasing out our birthright. The tennis stadium may be the biggest example, and you know they've even rented space so used cars could be sold in a park, but my personal favorite is Santa's Enchanted Forest at Christmastime. This is in Tropical Park. They charge you $8 so you can see a drunken spider weaving up and down stringing the lights. This gaudy display is the tackiest thing I've ever seen in my life. The county has been shameless in this. Every time there's been the slightest bit of land available, they've had this urge to make money on it.

The agency's director responded that his department desperately needs the $165,000 that the Christmas attraction poured into the county coffers just as it needs the other concessions to help keep the parks going as the budgets continued to be squeezed. "I need money to pay for cutting the grass," he said.

The director pointed out that throughout the county, neighborhoods were crying out for more services in their parks from tot lots to ballfields. With no tax money available, new ways of securing financing had to be found. These included inviting bids from private companies to build ballfields on west Dade County park land. The selected company would get its money back by charging the teams that use the fields.

Working arrangements with private businesses that allowed them to operate in the parks resulted in substantial revenues accruing to the agency. For example, the Sundays on Key Biscayne, which was an expansion of what was once a little snack shop on park land, generated $350,000 each year to the agency. The restaurant at Haulover Beach in north Dade County netted the county $157,000. The beach grill managed by Christy's at Matheson Hammock earned the department $84,000.

From John Dorshner. Keep off the grass: Must Dade's parks be paved to be saved? *The Miami Herald.* July 29, 1992, pages 8-12. Reprinted with permission of *The Miami Herald.*

Figure 8-5 Using Land to Pump Prime a Golf Development

The Mile Square Golf Course was constructed on land owned by Orange County and leased to the developer/operator for 30 years. Orange County has been one of the fastest growing regions in the United States for many years, and there was a substantial demand for a new golf course. Mile Square is an 18 hole, par 72, 6,400 yard course. It accommodates over 100,000 annually and generates gross revenues in excess of $2 million. Orange County receives over $250,000 in lease payments, which were based on the following schedule:

| | | Percentage Rent | |
Year	Minimum Rent $	Green Fees Golf Car Rentals Range Fees %	Food & Beverage Sales Retail Sales %
1	12,000	7	3-4
2	12,000	8	3-4
3	12,000	9	3-4
4	12,000	10	3-4
5-10	12,000	12	3-4
11-30	12,000	14	3-4

Source: Muirhead, D. and Rando, G. L. (1994). *Golf course development and real estate.* Washington, DC: The Urban Land Institute.

- Percentage payments ranging from 3 to 5% of gross food and beverage sales and 5 to 10% of gross pro shop sales.

This approach has several advantages:

- It is the simplest approach, in structure, for a public-private joint venture.

- The risk to the public agency is relatively small as long as the developer's/operator's financial health is ensured.

- The developer receives the land at no initial cost, and the long-term lease allows sufficient time to generate a reasonable return on investment and to amortize invested capital.

- Lease payments are tied to gross revenues and generally held low in the first years of operation until play builds to above break-even levels.

- The discounted reversionary value of the course is relatively small and therefore does not play a major role in negotiations.

- The developer retains control over the design of the golf course and any associated real estate development, facilitating coordination between land planning and the golf operation and maximizing the value of both entities without seriously compromising either one.

It also has some disadvantages:

- The approach depends on a strong golf market that can generate sufficient revenues to cover operating expenses, the cost of capital, and a reasonable return on investment.

- The public agency loses some control over operations.[23]

Low-cost capital. It was pointed out in chapter 6 that the public sector is able to borrow money at a lower interest rate than a private organization can. If the public organization can make this relatively inexpensive money available to a business enterprise, it can contribute a substantial financial incentive. For example, in an assessment of financial arrangements for financing a domed stadium in St. Louis (now named the Edward Jones Dome), it was calculated that if $120 million of tax-free bonds were issued by the county, the bonds would

> sell at yields considerably less than what the bonds would have to pay if they were not tax-exempt and if they did not have county backing. A conservative estimate of the subsidy involved here is $4 million a year, assuming that county bonds will sell to yield 3.5 percent less than non tax-exempt bonds.[24] (p. SR 7)

Another commentator calculated that "a $225 million stadium built today and financed 100 percent with tax exempt bonds might receive a lifetime federal tax subsidy as high as $75 million, 34 percent of construction costs."[25] The lifetime federal subsidy represents the amount the federal treasury foregoes by allowing the business to benefit from tax-exempt bonds rather than requiring it to finance the venture with nonexempt bonds.

The 1986 Tax Reform Act made it more difficult for local jurisdictions to directly assist private sports facility developers with access to their low-cost capital. More frequently, governments now use their low-cost capital to assist projects by developing infrastructure such as roads, sewers, water, and utilities, which reduces the developer's total costs. Thus, for example, the city of Portland paid $34.5 million for streets, public plazas, and some of the parking around the Rose Garden. The city's obligations were paid over six years by a 6.5% ticket-user fee. Once their obligations were fulfilled, the city will continue to require the 6.5% user fee as a perpetual return on its investment.[26]

Tax waivers. The ability of the public sector to substantially reduce the property tax payments of private investors can be a powerful inducement to encouraging their participation in a partnership. These incentives most commonly take the form of tax abatements. A *tax abatement* is an agreement between a public jurisdiction and a commercial operator that the jurisdiction will waive at least some of the property taxes on a proposed new development for a given period of time. This incentive is used as a competitive strategy to encourage a business to locate in a community.

The terms of a tax abatement are negotiable and may range from a waiver of some proportion of taxes for a short period to absolution of all property taxes for an extended period. Abatement programs exist in almost all of the states. Typically, if a community has a policy to grant abatements, then abatements are awarded whenever they are requested and they routinely constitute part of a community's incentive package in negotiations with commercial enterprises. The length of the time period varies according to state enabling legislation. For example, the usual period in New York is ten years, whereas the period in Ohio is 20 years. The conceptual rationale for tax abatements is that the overall long-term economic benefits the sports project creates justify the tax relief extended to the private developer. At the same time, these concessions again reflect the ability of franchise owners to exert strong leverage on cities.

> The Cleveland Indians and Cavaliers, professional baseball and basketball franchises, respectively, were granted property tax exemptions as principal tenants of their new stadium and arena in downtown Cleveland. The Indians occupy a $175 million, 42,000-seat ballpark (Jacobs Field) with a 30-year lease agreement. Under the arrangement, the baseball team will be absolved of all property-tax obligations for both real property and the improvements made on the property (infrastructure, parking, stadium). The Cavaliers enjoy comparable property-tax relief as primary tenants of the new $152 million, 21,000-seat arena. The savings in forgiven tax payments to both clubs, although not publicly disclosed, will amount to millions of dollars over the life of the joint venture.

Although the use of tax abatements is widespread, some jurisdictions have discontinued them because they were perceived as discriminating unfairly against established businesses in the community. The unfair competition issue was discussed earlier in the chapter. Consider the following example:

> A new $3 million health and fitness club is granted a tax abatement for 10 years, meaning that it does not have to pay the property taxes of $50,000 each year for which it normally would be liable. Similar clubs that have been operating in the city for many years pay property taxes. The new facility is able to offer its services at a lower price than the long-established clubs, which threatens their survival, because the new facility pays no property taxes, making its costs of operation substantially lower.

Control over permit and zoning processes. Nowhere is the adage "Time is money" more relevant than with respect to development projects. Invariably, one of the most challenging, and often time-consuming, aspects of the development process is meeting the various preconstruction permit requirements.

The ability to expedite permit applications has become increasingly important. The impact of government legislation and regulations is felt by the private sector from the initial planning of a project through to its development and operation phases. The development of a sports facility by a private company is subject to myriad regulations and requirements that a great number of government agencies administer. The complexity of the situation for a large project is illustrated in Figure 8-6. It shows the steps that would have confronted the San Francisco professional baseball franchise if it had proceeded with a proposal to build a new baseball stadium in the China Basin, which it investigated in the 1990s. The site was owned by two public agencies, the state of California and the San Francisco Port Commission:[25]

> Imagine a private firm setting out to build a ballpark in China Basin on its own. Starting in the upper left corner, Figure 8-6 describes the steps with

which the firm would be confronted in simply acquiring a site. Initially, a tract of land (large by any measure) would have to be assembled. As Figure 8-6 indicates, once a site has been selected, elected government officials would be required to act. The colossal height of a coliseum would require a zoning variance by the zoning board, by the San Francisco Board of Supervisors, or by an initiative. Because the building of stadiums is controversial, local politicians prefer an initiative that provides approval by the voters through a referendum. Therefore, site assembly would probably involve a referendum.

If the ballot measure were approved, as Figure 8-6 illustrates, a host of further approvals from the city would be required to meet environmental remediation and traffic mitigation requirements, culminating once again with a vote of the Board of Supervisors. If that hurdle were passed, Figure 8-6 imagines what would have to happen next if this very large site were acquired. Many agencies would have to sign off, and once again the Board of Supervisors would have to give its assent. Getting environmental, safety, and traffic approvals and the acquisition of the state land definitely would be easier if an organ of government—for example, the Port of San Francisco—were the agency applying. Government agencies have credibility before other public agencies, and probably before the press and public also, that private firms do not have. It is hard to imagine a private firm working through the 28 steps indicated in Figure 8-6 without the prior agreement of the mayor and a majority of the board of supervisors.[25] (p. 328)

The San Francisco Giants persevered, and their privately financed ballpark opened in 2000, but obtaining all of the necessary permits and permissions to proceed frequently is a frustrating process that discourages many developers. A public jurisdiction is likely to be able to assist in expediting this process. The public agency working from within the government system can push much more effectively for rapid permit approval than can private firms operating outside the structure of government.

Control over land use through zoning is a basic asset that most local governments possess. Land-use zoning substantially impacts the value of land, and changes in it can greatly amend a project's viability. If a business purchases land that is zoned for agricultural purposes, then the land's cost and its value are likely to be much lower than if it were zoned for development because the income potential of agricultural land is significantly lower. If the zoning is changed after the land has been purchased at a price reflecting agricultural use, and if the land is then used to develop a sports project (so the operator does not use land already zoned for development), then the cost to the business will be much lower, making the purchase potentially more profitable. Hence, changes in zoning that increase the amount of development allowed on a piece of land are likely to increase its value.

After Sacramento voters rejected an initiative to construct a stadium on county land, private developers acquired 510 acres of rice farm land on the edge of the city that was zoned for agricultural use. In making this purchase, the developers gambled they could convince the city to rezone the site for commercial development. The developers purchased the Kansas City Kings NBA franchise and brought it to Sacramento. This mobilized

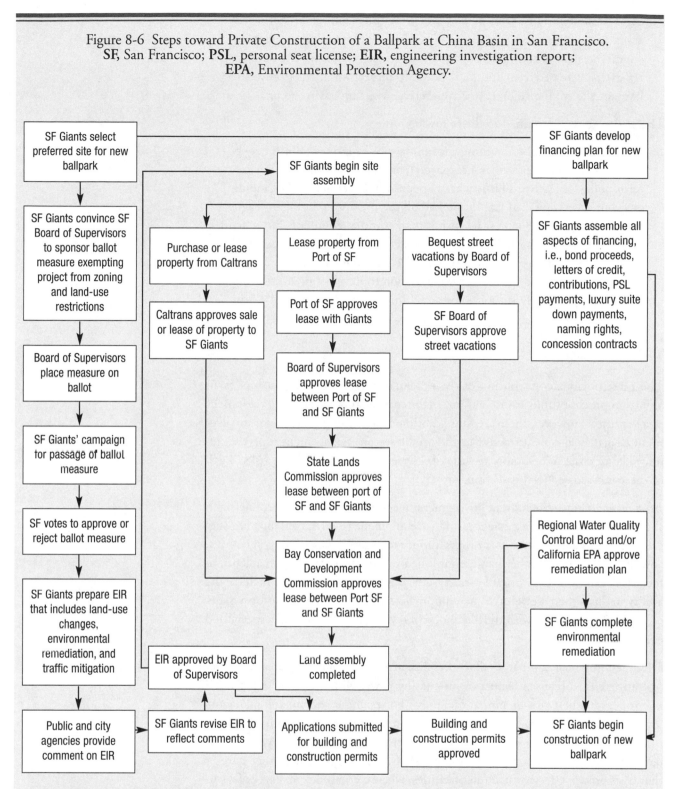

Figure 8-6 Steps toward Private Construction of a Ballpark at China Basin in San Francisco. **SF**, San Francisco; **PSL**, personal seat license; **EIR**, engineering investigation report; **EPA**, Environmental Protection Agency.

SF Giants select preferred site for new ballpark

SF Giants develop financing plan for new ballpark

SF Giants begin site assembly

SF Giants convince SF Board of Supervisors to sponsor ballot measure exempting project from zoning and land-use restrictions

Purchase or lease property from Caltrans

Lease property from Port of SF

Bequest street vacations by Board of Supervisors

SF Giants assemble all aspects of financing, i.e., bond proceeds, letters of credit, contributions, PSL payments, luxury suite down payments, naming rights, concession contracts

Caltrans approves sale or lease of property to SF Giants

Port of SF approves lease with Giants

SF Board of Supervisors approve street vacations

Board of Supervisors place measure on ballot

Board of Supervisors approves lease between Port of SF and SF Giants

SF Giants' campaign for passage of ballot measure

State Lands Commission approves lease between port of SF and SF Giants

SF votes to approve or reject ballot measure

Regional Water Quality Control Board and/or California EPA approve remediation plan

Bay Conservation and Development Commission approves lease between Port SF and SF Giants

SF Giants prepare EIR that includes land-use changes, environmental remediation, and traffic mitigation

SF Giants complete environmental remediation

EIR approved by Board of Supervisors

Land assembly completed

Public and city agencies provide comment on EIR

SF Giants revise EIR to reflect comments

Applications submitted for building and construction permits

Building and construction permits approved

SF Giants begin construction of new ballpark

Source: Agostini, S. J., Quigley, J. M. & Smolensky, E. (1997). Stickball in San Francisco. In R. G.Noll & A. Zimblast (ed.). *Sports, Jobs & Texas*. Washington D.C.: Brookings Institution, p.397

eager basketball fans, who helped lobby for the rezoning so that a new arena could be built for the team on this land. The rezoning was granted, which meant that the value of the rice farm land and hence the developers' assets increased dramatically. The sports project was used effectively to leverage the zoning change, which otherwise was unlikely to occur.[27]

The trade-out was described in the following terms:

> Sometimes the cost of obtaining a team may not be money (which may be put up by business leaders, not taxpayers), but rather the sacrifice of a long term policy objective. This is what happened in Sacramento. The rapidly growing state capital of California had all the makings of a major-league town (it was the 21st largest television market in the country.). But when local developer Gregg Lukenbill bought the Kansas City Kings basketball team, he and a few other landowners effectively traded their promise to bring the team to Sacramento for permission to develop an area the city voters had previously set aside for agriculture. The City Council—hungering for big-league status—eagerly went along with the deal.[28]

Private Sector Assets

The most obvious contribution of the private sector to joint partnerships is an ability to provide funds for operation, maintenance, and/or capital development of a venture. However, there are four additional aspects of private sector involvement that may also be attractive to the public sector: management expertise, reduced labor costs, adaptability to scale of service, and reduced liability risks. Each of these is discussed in this section.

Management expertise. Often, government agencies do not have personnel with the necessary training, experience, and/or equipment to effectively operate specialized sport facilities such as ice rinks, indoor tennis centers, arenas, golf courses, and ski areas. On the other hand, established private firms draw upon a depth of technical expertise that provides many advantages. These benefits include the ability to focus their work force and equipment more intensively to perform a specific function, coupled with the likelihood of owning more up-to-date, specialized equipment.

Often, commercial companies that specialize in a particular service area can lower operating costs because of superior purchasing power with suppliers, especially if they operate a network of similar facilities. For example, a company managing several arenas is likely to be more successful at attracting top entertainment talent than an agency manager responsible for only one facility would be. A large company may also have an array of marketing skills, cost controls, and other systems that have proven effective at similar facilities, whereas an agency manager of a single facility may have to reinvent the wheel. An experienced sports manager in charge of food and beverages at a facility highlighted the importance of such systems:

> I am not for one moment suggesting that people who work in food and beverage are one iota more dishonest than anyone else in this imperfect world. But these staff, and anyone who comes into contact with them in the course of their work, from delivery drivers to the customers, are deal-

ing in cash, food and drinks. I can't think of three more temptingly tradable or consumable commodities handled together!

It is for very good reasons that the best commercial vendors spend an enormous amount of time and money establishing effective and efficient control systems. When these are well monitored they ensure a tight grip on the business. I have looked at food and beverage operations where a 10% royalty from a good contractor would have far exceeded a presumed 30% profit from "our own people" for reasons of control alone.[29] (p. 21)

A large business with specialized expertise in a given service area may be better able to attract good managers to be responsible for the service than some public agencies are. Such an organization can offer that manager a career path with promotion to larger facilities and more responsibility, whereas a public agency frequently can offer promotion only to a relatively restricted level unless other duties outside the area of expertise are included. Further, the organization will have other trained managers with new ideas to replace the current manager when he or she resigns or is promoted, whereas an agency will have to invest effort and re-

---

Figure 8-7 The American Golf Edge

American Golf has been the world's leader in public golf course management for the past 20 years. We have provided excellence in every facet of our operations and continually strive to stay on the leading edge of all developments in the golf industry.

We are able to provide services like no other management company because of the expertise found in our corporate personnel and our management and operations techniques.

Some of our unique human resources are

- *the construction department.* This department supervises all designs and construction of new site facilities and renovation of existing buildings.

- *landfill construction.* One example is Mountain Gate Country Club, a 27-hole private country club located in Los Angeles.

- *drainage reconstruction.* Inadequate draining is a problem on many courses. We have had experience with every type of drainage problem across the country. One example of our redesign and construction can be found at Fullerton Golf Course in Fullerton, California.

- *agronomy expertise.* Our in-house agronomy expert supervises and advises all regional and course superintendents nationwide in the proper care of trees and turf.

- *training.* This department ensures that all new employees are thoroughly trained in American Golf procedures, policies, and philosophy.

- *employment opportunities.* Career opportunities and competitive wages are offered nationwide (based on nationally collected salary survey information).

- *the marketing department.* All corporate marketing, advertising, promotion, and public relations direction, as well as pro-shop merchandise coordination, falls under this umbrella. Where possible, central buying results in tremendous price savings for all American Golf pro shops.

Adapted from The American Golf Edge. Produced by American Golf Corporation, 1633 26th Street, Santa Monica, CA 90404.

sources in recruiting from outside or will have to promote an assistant who may not be as able.

The American Golf Corporation provides a good example of how one firm has parlayed its management expertise into becoming the world's leader in public golf course management. Figure 8-7 indicates that the company offers a public agency a range of specialist services designed to enhance both operating efficiencies and the quality of the golf experience. Rarely does a public agency responsible for operating a golf course have the resources or expertise to furnish such a complete array of specialized services.

American Golf Corporation has become the largest golf course management company in the world. The privately held corporation operates more than 250 golf courses. The company specializes in revitalizing golf courses for which governments do not have capital funds. American Golf's approach involves initial investment (sometimes reaching $1 million) to improve the course and related infrastructure, dramatically increasing rounds of play through enhanced service quality and vigorous marketing and reducing costs largely through more flexible and cost-effective use of personnel. The company's takeover of four municipally owned golf courses in Detroit illustrates the benefits of private sector expertise:

> American Golf Corporation entered into a 20-year lease agreement with the City of Detroit Recreation Department to operate four of the six city golf courses. The courses consistently had lost money for the city. Operating losses of close to $600,000 had to be covered by monies from Detroit's general fund. The contract required American Golf to spend close to $2 million for improvements, including clubhouse renovations, new irrigation systems, landscaping, bunker restoration, and drainage work. In addition, the terms of the agreement stipulated that American Golf pay the city $50,000 in the first year of the lease, increasing to $200,000 by the fifth year. In return, the possessory lease provided American Golf with exclusive operating rights to the four courses. American Golf's regional director acknowledged the risks for his firm: "We'll lose money for six years." However, American Golf's strategy was to recoup losses as the dramatic changes in the courses drew people back. The company's goal was to attract 10,000 more golfers per year to each of the courses. The use of its own employees, who were paid considerably less than unionized city workers; sales from concessions; and equipment rentals also helped create efficiencies.[30]

It is important to note that the city of Detroit excluded two of its six golf courses from the management agreement with the American Golf Corporation. Jurisdictions that encourage some level of competition among service providers produce substantial savings from contractors. In this case, the city induced competition between the courses that American Golf Corporation operated and those that the city maintained in-house; this action gave both service providers incentive to produce high levels of service.

Reduced labor costs. The labor-intensive nature of many sporting opportunities offered by governments makes the cost of personnel a major element in the cost of service delivery. The bargaining agreements that public employee unions negotiate, the longevity of many agency personnel, and the protection that civil service regulations afford the employees frequently mean that their wages are substantially higher than those that businesses pay. For example, when Indianapolis contracted out its 12 golf courses, the contractors hired staff at an average of $7 per hour, whereas the city's average cost for the same positions was $18 per hour plus an incremental amount per hour for overtime when employees worked more than 40 hours each week.

When agency and business wage rates are similar, agencies typically pay from 30% to 35% in fringe benefits to employees for things such as health insurance, retirement, sick leave, and maternity leave. Many businesses, in contrast, are not required to maintain such a high level of overhead. Federal and state laws may require commercial operators to pay Social Security and payroll taxes but not employee medical or pension benefits. As a result, payroll overhead costs for private firms may only be 12% to 15%. The approximately 20% savings advantage in overhead costs that many businesses enjoy allows them to provide the same level of service much more economically than a public organization can. In addition, their exemption from civil service requirements provides them with greater flexibility in determining level of pay, fringe-benefit payments, and a mix of full- and part-time personnel.

Even when businesses pay their employees as much as public agencies both in salary and fringe benefits, they are able to save in labor costs. One empirical study reported that these savings emerged because businesses

- used less labor,

- had about 5% less absenteeism,

- made managers responsible for equipment as well as labor,

- used younger workers (who tend to cost less),

- used more part-time labor,

- terminated more employees (which is probably why there was less absenteeism), and

- used more capital equipment (which may be why less labor was needed).[30]

The following example illustrates how one government agency overcame a difficult staffing cost problem by taking advantage of the flexibility afforded a private business:

A publicly managed golf course in Alameda County, California, operated on a 13-hour summer schedule, opening at 6:00 a.m. and closing at 7:00 p.m. All maintenance activities were performed by public employees of a regional park and recreation agency. The employees formed a bargaining unit, affiliating with the American Federation of State, County, and Municipal Employees, which is a public-employee labor union. The labor contract established between the federation and the park agency stipulated a standard workday of 8 hours for full-time employees. Compliance with the contract required the park agency to commit two separate 8-hour shifts of maintenance and operations personnel to the golf course. The park and recreation agency estimated that under this agreement, staffing costs at the golf course would increase as much as 21%.

Faced with an intractable situation, the agency made the decision to contract out the operation of the golf course to a specialized management firm. An advertisement placed in the *Wall Street Journal* produced several legitimate bidders. A long-term lease (5 years with four 5-year renewable options) was awarded to a private firm with a successful track record in operating and maintaining golf courses. The agreement called for the management company to provide more than $600,000 in capital improvements over the first 5 years of the lease. By applying a more flexible personnel schedule to accommodate actual work demands and, at the same time, not being obligated to pay as high an overhead (e.g., retirement, vacation, and hospitalization benefits), the park agency estimated that the private firm reduced labor expenses at the golf course by as much as 50%. The result was that the golfing public benefited from an enhanced resource. At the same time, the park agency freed approximately $400,000 each year in public monies, which previously were committed to paying golf course personnel, to apply to other service areas of concern.

Adaptability to scale of service. The commercial sector is often better equipped to deliver services that require large numbers of part-time employees for short time periods. The bureaucratic procedures required of government agencies to hire and pay part-time employees is sometimes lengthy, cumbersome, and onerous, whereas it is generally easy for businesses to do this. Thus, it may be efficient for an agency to partner with businesses for producing special events or highly seasonal services.

Partnerships with a commercial entity are also likely to be beneficial when an agency cannot take advantage of economies of scale. A business serving multiple organizations is likely to be able to purchase state-of-the-art equipment and materials at a lower price and is likely to be able to use them more efficiently than a single government agency can because the business services a larger number of units. An agency may not be able to justify purchasing equipment that will sit idle for much of the year. An example of gains accruing to public agencies as a result of partnering with businesses is illustrated by the economies of scale available to large companies like American Golf Corporation.

Each year American Golf Corporation may purchase more than 3,000 golf carts for the 250 golf courses it operates, and this volume enables the company to negotiate a substantially lower purchase price per cart than any single public agency can. This scenario is repeated for its purchase of all other types of golf course maintenance equipment and of clothing and supplies sold in pro shops.

A related advantage that sometimes accrues to large commercial companies is that they may be able to take advantage of federal business tax laws, which may permit rapid depreciation of new equipment and offer investment tax credits for its purchase. These types of regulations make it advantageous for companies to acquire new equipment, and this translates into greater operating efficiency (although, conversely, it should be noted that unlike public agencies, private companies are required to pay sales tax on equipment).

Reduced liability risks. An increasingly attractive incentive for public agencies to enter working partnerships with private organizations is that such a collaboration can substantially reduce the liability risks borne by government organizations. Most liability suits arise from careless or reckless acts (negligence) that result in unintentional harm to an injured party. The decline in the doctrine of sovereign immunity, which historically prohibited units of government from being sued, has resulted in cities, counties, and school districts being more vulnerable to negligence claims. Now there are many examples of multimillion-dollar liability awards that government agencies have paid. The increased threat of such catastrophic claims has necessitated that agencies purchase expensive insurance premiums.

A key question, then, for agency managers is how they can minimize the possibility of a financially catastrophic claim being made against their agency. Because liability insurance premiums largely are based on the estimated degree of risk facing an agency, any actions that it can take to reduce level of exposure to risk should lead to reduced premium costs. Government agencies have found joint ventures to be an effective strategy for minimizing their liability risks and, therefore, the costs associated with insurance protection. Increasingly, agencies are structuring partnership agreements in order to transfer as much of the risk and responsibility for liability as possible to the commercial or private operator. Typically, the transfer of liability risk is conferred in the lease agreement establishing a public-private partnership. The following sample is drawn from an actual lease agreement established between a municipality and a commercial operator for the maintenance and operation of a sports complex:

> CLAIMS. The contractor shall hold harmless the city and all of its agents, employees and officers from any and all damages or claims of any kind or nature, that may be made or may arise directly or indirectly from the performance of duties by the contractor, its agents and employees, including but not limited to any claims which may arise either directly or indirectly from the use of any equipment or tools which the city may lease or sell to the contractor. The contractor shall appear and defend any action or suit instituted against the city arising in any manner out of the acts or omissions defined herein above. The contractor's duty to indemnify hereunder shall include all costs or expenses arising out of all claims specified herein, including all court, and/or arbitration costs, filing fees, and attorney's fees and costs of settlement.

The excerpt identifies two provisions key to effective transfer of liability risks. The first element establishes that the public agency will be held harmless in the event of a negligence claim. The intent is to release the agency from all liability risks. However, although crucial, the hold-harmless clause alone may not provide ironclad protection. A standard provision is to add an indemnification clause stipulating that if the hold-harmless agreement is not completely adequate—for example, if the government agency is found liable of contributory negligence—the commercial operator would pay any damages that the agency owed. Thus, the private contractor exclusively bears responsibility and costs related to liability concerns.

In a well-conceived public-private partnership, the exclusive costs and responsibility for liability borne by the private contractor are offset by benefits derived from the agreement. The potential savings realized by the contractor, who has to pay only nominal lease consideration ($1.00 a year) for access to a prime site, otherwise unaffordable, compensate for the potential additional liability insurance costs.

It is evident that each sector has resources that could be of significant value to the other. In public-private partnership arrangements, public and private sector organizations agree from the outset to share mutual responsibility for development and/or expansion of a sport resource. Impetus for forming the working relationship can come from either sector. To provide a framework for understanding how these assets can be forged into effective public-private partnerships, examples of partnership arrangements are presented in this section. They have been classified into seven categories: (a) public sector leasing, (b) leaseback arrangements, (c) public sector takeovers, (d) private sector takeovers, (e) private sector pump-priming, (f) expansion of existing public facilities, and (g) multiparty arrangements. The latter category is a catchall classification that presents an array of different joint-funding models that have been used. There is no common thread among them except the desire on the part of multiple stakeholders to see a sports project come to fruition. The partnership examples described in this section illustrate the remarkably imaginative and creative funding arrangements that have characterized the financing of sports developments over the last decade.

Public Sector Leasing

The most common form of public-private sports partnership is the leasing of facilities to private entities in which public funds have been invested. Leases establish the fee a private entity will pay to a landlord (lessor) to use a facility over a given time period. Leases may include buyout clauses that enable the party renting the property (the lessee) to break the agreement by paying an amount specified in the lease agreement to the lessor. They may also include conditions that enable the lessee to be released from the contract if they are not met. Such conditions may include promised improvement to the facility by the lessor or failure to meet attendance expectations. For example, the Minnesota Twins' lease on the Metrodome permitted the team to opt out of the agreement if attendance fell below $1.4 million during three straight seasons.[22]

Most lease agreements involve much more than negotiating a fixed rent for use of a facility. Some indication of their complexity, versatility, and variety can be gleaned from the list of lease structure formats shown in Table 8-3. These 19 different structures were identified as being used in the four major leagues.[26] The array of revenue streams whose disposition may be negotiated in a lease includes ticket sales, concessions (food, beverages, retail, etc.), parking, advertising, naming rights, luxury suites, and nonteam use of the facility. In professional sports,

Table 8-3 Types of Lease Structures

1. Fixed rent	11. Either a minimum rental or a percentage, whichever is greater
2. Fixed rent plus additional stadium related payments	12. A floor and cap provision: where the rental is stated in a maximum amount and a minimum amount
3. Per game rent	
4. Minimum per game payment, percentage rent and seat use charge	13. Attendance based rent
5. Minimum rent plus attendance based rent	14. Percentage rent, attendance based rent, and revenue from hockey
6. Straight percentage-based formula	15. Base rent or fluctuating attendance based payments, whichever is greater
7. Fixed minimum rent combined with a percentage based formula	16. Rent as operating and maintenance costs
8. Fixed rent minus rental credits, plus additional rents	17. Payments in regard to luxury boxes with a rental off-set
9. Initial per-game rent followed by percentage rent	18. Combination of fee payments
10. Percentage rent, but if less than a specified amount, then a minimum rental	19. Nominal or rent free structure

Source: Greenberg, M. J. & Grey, J. T. (1996). *The Stadium Game.* Maryland: National Sports Law Institute, Marquette University Law School, p. 89.

these leases have become increasingly favorable to teams as franchises have exercised their leverage power, which was described in chapter 3.

Leaseback Arrangements

It is not unusual for government agencies to use facilities leased from the commercial sector. Indeed, it is standard federal government practice to lease commercial office space rather than to encourage agencies to purchase their own office space. The same principle can be used to extend the range of opportunities that a public agency can offer its clientele. Leaseback arrangements offer communities a way to fulfill equipment or facility needs without paying out large sums upfront. A common approach to applying this joint-development alternative is for the public agency and commercial operator to enter into a long-term development and facility management contract. Typically, cost of construction is borne entirely by the private developer. Upon completion, exclusive or partial utilization rights are leased to the public agency at a previously negotiated, fixed or graduated annual rent for an extended period of time (often as long as 20-30 years). This type of leaseback arrangement means that a public jurisdiction does not have to pay large sums initially or seek a bond issue for capital development costs. This type of arrangement was used by the Dallas Stars and the city of Euless in the construction of the Star Center Ice Arena, which is described in Figure 8-8.

Another example of this approach was the leaseback agreement established between the City of Dublin, Ohio, and Columbus Hockey, Inc., owners of the East Coast Hockey League franchise, the Columbus Chill:

Figure 8-8 The Euless Dr. Pepper Star Center

The Dallas Stars are one of several franchises that have located in the Sun Belt in the past decade. With the exception of some migrants from the north, the four million residents of the Dallas-Fort Worth Metroplex area have no long-standing heritage or tradition of playing or watching ice hockey. Thus, a major challenge confronting the franchise was to create a market for ice hockey. The Stars' strategy for doing this was comprised of two elements.

First, there was recognition of the importance of a winning team in arousing local interest, and the Stars experienced success relatively soon after locating in Dallas. In 1999 they won the NHL's Stanley Cup, and in 2000 they were defeated in the Stanley Cup finals in the last match of a seven game series.

The second element in the strategy was to stimulate long-term grassroots involvement in ice hockey by encouraging youth to play the game. The key to this being successful was the availability of ice hockey facilities. The Stars long-term goal was to cooperate with cities to build and operate ten ice hockey facilities across the Metroplex area. The case study presented here describes the public-private partnership between the Stars and the city of Euless. This was the second of the Stars' facilities to be opened. The first was the Star Center in Valley Ranch. A third facility is being constructed in Duncanville, and the Stars are negotiating for a fourth and fifth with the cities of Southlake and Plano.

The partnership arrangement between the Stars and the city of Euless is typical of the model the Stars are pursuing in the other communities. Euless has a population of approximately 50,000. The Euless Dr. Pepper Star Center stands on six acres of land owned by the city, which was leased to the Stars. The Stars built the facility, which is approximately 95,000 square feet and contains two NHL size ice-rinks, a proshop, skate rental service; a self-service grill, a number of meeting rooms, and 125 parking spaces. When construction was completed, the city bought the facility from the Stars for $10.29 million, which was the cost of construction. The city sold Certificates of Obligation to raise the needed capital. The city then leased the facility to the Stars for a 25-year period. The annual lease fee is equal to the amount of the annual amortization of the city's principal and interest payments on the Certificates of Obligation and other expenses incurred by the city in obtaining financing. The lease fee is paid to the city in monthly installments. The Stars have the option to extend the 25-year agreement for two successive five-year periods if they wish to do so. The city agreed not to assist or become involved in any other ice-skating facility during the term of the lease without the consent of the Stars. If the Stars withdraw from the agreement before the end of the 25-year period, they are required to give the city one year's notice, so the city can find another operator or organizer to operate the facility itself.

The Stars pay no property taxes because the city owns the land on which the building is situated, but they do pay all utility bills. The Stars have full and exclusive control of the management and operation of the leased facility. They own all revenues from all sources generated in the building, and have all sponsorship rights including those associated with naming the building. The Stars pay for all maintenance and repairs of the building, but the city pays for all maintenance and repairs to the parking areas adjacent to the building and for all landscaping maintenance. The city has 24 hours per year of free use of the meeting rooms at the facility and 24 hours of free ice time.

When the city initiated discussions with the Stars, it considered forming a quasi-public benefit company as an intermediary with authority to issue tax free bonds. However, their bond consultants subsequently reported this would be in breach of the 1986 Tax Reform Act, so the facility was paid for by the Stars using the more expensive taxable bonds. If the city had issued the bonds under the terms of the 1986 Act, the city would have had to operate it or to accept lease payments of no more than 10% of the facility's annual debt service.

The involvement of the Dallas Stars in the public-private partnership was a key factor in the city agreeing to participate because of the Stars' reputation for excellence. The Euless city manager said, "This is not just another ice arena run by some private group. It's an ice arena run by the Dallas Stars. If it had not been with the Dallas Stars, I don't think it would have occurred in our city."

It would be reasonable to ask: Why didn't the Stars organization borrow the money to build the facility from a financial institution and make annual repayments to that institution, which is the normal way businesses finance their capital development? Why did the Stars want to partner with the city when there was no "cheap money" from tax free bonds available? There were two reasons for involving the city:

1) The city's ownership of the building and the land means that the Stars do not pay property taxes.

2) The venture is too risky for a traditional financial institution to finance over 25 years. Recreation interests change, demand may wane, and the project may become non-viable. The partnership contract enables the Stars to withdraw from the agreement if they give one year's notice. These conditions would be unacceptable to financial institutions. Thus, the city of Euless essentially acts as guarantor and banker. The city carries the risk. If the Stars exercise their right to give one year's notice, then the city has to take over the facility and pay the annual amortization payments. This is not an untenable position for the city since many public recreation facilities are subsidized. Hence, the city can legitimately reposition the ice hockey facility as a merit good rather than a private good, whereas a traditional financial institution has to evaluate the project's financial feasibility on its merits as a private good.

The city and the hockey team agreed to collaborate on development of a $3.3 million indoor ice rink. The 60,000-square foot facility included two ice surfaces (one NHL size—190' x 85'—and one Olympic size—200' x 100'), a pro shop, skate rental area, video game room, public locker room, and a concession area. In addition, the ice arena housed offices for the Chill's management staff and a team locker room and training facility.

Impetus for establishing a new ice rink came from the Chill, who were finding it increasingly difficult to reserve adequate ice time for team practices at the one ice rink in the metropolitan area of 1.4 million residents. So great was the demand for ice at the single arena owned and operated by the local state university that the Chill were limited to one-hour practices, often at 5:00 or 6:00 a.m. Analysis of the area's imbalance between supply and demand led management of the hockey team to develop a proposal for creation of a permanent facility, which could be utilized beyond the team's practice needs to accommodate the apparent demand for youth and adult hockey, figure skating, and speed skating in central Ohio. The Chill approached the City of Dublin with a joint development proposal in which the hockey team would build and operate the ice arena but lease back initially up to 20% of the facility's ice time to the city. In return for utilization privileges, the city agreed to lease an eight-acre parcel of land (market value $400,000) to the Chill for 25 years at $1.00 per year. The reciprocal benefits from this partial leaseback arrangement are extensive. The city received (a) a state-of-the-art community resource that will serve the ice-skating needs of its residents year-round at minimal taxpayer expense and (b) a regional attraction that will lure thousands of overnight and day-use visitors each year to the city to attend tournaments and annual events. The project also was aided by the stadium developers' being able to finance the construction with tax-exempt bonds. This saved the project an estimated $17 million in interest payments over the 15-year life of the bonds.

It was noted in chapter 6 that tax-free bonds can no longer be used for many of these types of projects, which means that leaseback partnerships now effectively substitute private credit for public credit. Thus, a major disadvantage arising from this mechanism is that it is more expensive for commercial developers to borrow money than it is for public agencies. In addition, the costs to an agency have to include the investor's profit margin. Hence, this method of financing projects is likely to be more expensive than the direct use of public bond issues.

Perhaps the most common type of leaseback is lease/purchase financing involving a leasehold contract between a private developer and a public entity. The public entity will usually solicit bids for the project. Golf courses are particularly good candidates for this approach because the installment on lease payments may be funded from a course's net revenues. However, the public agency's general fund remains the ultimate guarantee if projected revenues are inadequate to meet the payments. Usually, revenue bonds are a superior option for public agencies for the reasons cited in the previous paragraph. However, if the revenue bonds are too high-risk or the political climate makes their use unadvisable, lease/purchase offers an alternative.

Public Sector Takeovers

The takeover of a faltering private sports facility should not necessarily be viewed as a public bailout. There are occasions when it should be viewed as an opportunity to retain an existing sport asset that will otherwise disappear. Takeovers may be an appropriate strategy if a private entity closes and the type of sport opportunity that it offers either is not offered by another supplier in the area or can be used to service a market segment that is presently not being reached with that opportunity. However, sometimes takeover opportunities have to be foregone because a public agency cannot respond quickly to market forces and the business or lending institution is unable to wait for the time-consuming referendum process necessary to authorize bonds for capital investment.

> The Minnesota Timberwolves contemplated moving to New Orleans because although the team itself was profitable, the Target Center, which was built with private funds, was costing the owners $6.25 million per year in debt charges. The owners could not see how the overall venture could be profitable while they were encumbered with these debt charges. The Minnesota community mobilized and forestalled the move by another local partnership group agreeing to purchase the franchise and, most important, a city agency agreeing to buy the Target Center. The facility purchase was undertaken with general obligation bonds backed by property taxes, tax-increment financing, dedicated revenues from the city's parking fund, a 3% citywide entertainment tax, and a $750,000 annual appropriation from the state.

The takeover of facilities such as golf courses, ski facilities, softball complexes, or ice rinks is likely to be much less controversial than taking over a facility for a professional sports franchise, because the former facilities are more consistent with the public's image of the types of facilities that are appropriate for government to provide. For example, the town of Eastchester on Long Island purchased the financially ailing Lake Isle Country Club with its 18-hole golf course, five pools, eight tennis courts, and large banquet hall. The wording of the referendum that approved the town's purchasing the facility required it to be a self-sufficient operation. It could not look to local tax revenues to support its $2.4 million budget. However, the complex did not have to yield a return on equity or meet debt charges associated with the purchase cost, so it was easier for the complex to be self-sufficient than for the previous private operator, who had to recover capital debt and equity costs.[31]

A further financial advantage that accrues to a public agency when it takes over a facility is that the facility may be eligible for grants for capital improvements from federal or state programs that are not available when the facility is operated privately. Thus, the Lake Isle complex received more than $750,000 in capital grants from the federal Land and Water Conservation Fund's matching grant program. The grant funds and the low interest rate of public debt mean that these improvements cost substantially less than half of what they would have cost a private operator.

> In Euless, Texas, which is centrally located between Dallas and Fort Worth, the city of Euless purchased Softball World from a private operator who could not pay the debt charges on the facility. The city renamed the park Softball World at Texas Star. It is a state-of-the art facility with plush, bermuda-grass outfields, finely groomed infields, 30-foot electronic scoreboards, professional lighting, the largest softball pro shop in Texas, and a full-line concession stand with sales that include alcohol. Annually, over 2,000 league and tournament teams played at the facility, and it was too important to the city's economy to allow it to fold and be used for other purposes.

A public agency may be able to operate a facility that commercially fails because the purchase price that an agency pays for a takeover may be substantially less than the original cost or the asset value of the operation as a going concern.

Consider the situation confronting a bank that is forced to foreclose on a specialized sport facility, such as a ski lift, because the operator is unable to make contributions toward the loan payments. The equipment has minimal resale value, and the bank is unlikely to have either the expertise or the inclination to operate the ski lift. Thus, the bank may be receptive to an offer from a public agency to purchase it for (say) 50% of its cost because this would enable the bank to recoup at least some of the capital it lent the operator to build the facility. In addition, by enabling the facility to continue to operate, the bank is contributing to maintenance of the area's economic health and quality of life, both of which are important to the bank's long-term profitability.

Private-Sector Takeovers

This category of partnerships refers to situations in which a private organization takes over responsibility for operation of a facility or service owned by the public sector. Toronto's Sky Dome offers an example of this principle. It was built with a combination of public and private funding. Thirty Canadian companies contributed $5 million each towards construction of the stadium, with city and provincial government paying the rest of the bill. The project ended up costing approximately $600 million, more than 2 times the original projected cost. The debt charges on the Sky Dome were $60,000 a day. The Blue Jays MLB team attracted 4 million baseball fans in a year and sold out consistently, so the franchise made impressive annual operating profits of $30 to $35 million. However, the stadium's onerous debt charges and business taxes resulted in annual net losses of over $30 million a year. This persuaded the provincial government to cut its losses and sell the Sky Dome for $151 million to a consortium of private investors.

Given the escalating costs of renovating sports facilities, some cities are effectively giving their stadiums to franchises without going through the controversial process of handing over title to a facility. For example, the city of Anaheim's arrangement with Disney Corporation when the company purchased the MLB Anaheim Angels effectively handed over the stadium to Disney:

> Anaheim stadium required a $100 million renovation. In exchange for financing $70 million of the restoration cost, Disney was allowed to retain all revenues derived from ticket sales below 2.6 million people and any revenues from stadium naming rights, concessions, and inside-stadium advertising. Disney was allowed to keep all baseball parking revenues below $4 million and all outside advertising revenues above $800,000.

> In return for its $30 million, the city of Anaheim had the team renamed the Anaheim Angels and received any revenues not retained by Disney. Because the Angels had only exceeded an attendance of 2.6 million four times in their history, these revenues seemed likely to be minimal. However, the city's mayor, in defense of what seemed a one-sided agreement, noted, "No longer will the citizens of Anaheim have to worry about the burden of overhead required to operate the stadium. For the past 30 years, it has been a burden to Anaheim. It is right and proper to shift the burden to the private sector."[26] (p. 29)

Most older cities throughout the United States and Canada have a large number of decaying, underused sports facilities desperately in need of rehabilitation. Given the fiscal constraints confronting most local governments, public funds are invariably inadequate or nonexistent for refurbishing tennis courts, athletic fields, ice rinks, and golf courses that have fallen into disrepair, so governments are often receptive to overtures from private sector investors.

Private Sector Pump-Priming

A business may use some of its assets to induce a public agency to make a major investment in a facility from which the enterprise also will gain. This type of partnership has occurred most frequently in golf course provision. Developers offer land and perhaps other resources such as cash, equipment, infrastructure preparation, or in-kind assistance to encourage a public agency to build and operate a public golf course. They do this because such a facility substantially increases the value of the property that the developer sells around the course; it releases the developer from an obligation to operate the golf course; and it removes the developer's liability for property taxes from the course acreage. Often the land dedicated to the public sector is unsuited for construction of buildings. For example, it is often flood plain or environmentally sensitive land.

From a public agency's perspective, the cost of land is a major element in building a golf course. If this is removed, then often it becomes feasible for a public course to be self-sufficient, including covering its debt charges. This enables revenue bonds to be issued to pay for course construction; therefore, a service can be provided to the community at no cost to the taxpayer.

- As part of a 1,600-unit residential development called Rancho Solano in Fairfield, California, the developer dedicated 200 acres for development of an 18-hole, par 72, 7,000-yard golf course. As part of the development agreement, the city built a championship golf course and provided partial funding for a clubhouse with restaurant, cocktail lounge, and pro shop. The city invested $1.25 million for one-quarter ownership of the clubhouse, with the developer putting up the remaining portion. The clubhouse was dedicated to the city, with food and beverage operations leased to an operator for a long term. The city shared 25% of the profit or loss from all operations. The city retained CCA-Silband to operate the course and clubhouse and contracted with Rancho Solano Country Club and Resort, Inc., to operate the food and beverage services. It issued $7 million in bonds to cover the construction of the course and one fourth of the clubhouse.[23]

- Richmond Bay Development Company developed Meadow Lakes, a master-planned residential community in North Richland Hills, a suburb located about ten miles north of Forth Worth. The developer, electing not to enter the golf course development business, was unsuccessful in attracting a private firm to develop the course. A number of apparent issues concerned these firms, including the tree cover, the terrain and other land features, cost and availability of water, and the limited amount of land area (the 120 acres available would not allow construction of a regulation golf course).

  Subsequently, the city of North Richland Hills reached an agreement with the developer to construct a golf course, with the understanding that the course would be high-quality design. The city assembled three parcels—the 120 acres dedicated at no cost by the developer, a 35-acre parcel acquired for the nominal price of $1.00 from the Federal Savings and Loan Insurance Corporation, and a five-acre parcel leased from an adjoining city—for construction of a regulation course. Most of the land was in a flood plain. The city retained a designer and an operator and acted as developer, coordinating design and construction.

Construction cost of the golf course was $2 million; total turnkey cost was $4.5 million. Tax-exempt bonds totaling $4.25 million were sold to finance the course. The developer contributed $100,000 toward construction, in addition to dedicating the land. The developer designed a subdivision with approximately 65 lots fronting on the golf course.[23]

Lee County, Florida, solicited a donation of 150 acres of land from developers and land speculators. The county intended to build a championship, 18-hole golf course on the land. Six offers were received. All of the proposals observed that a quality golf course could enhance residential developments being considered. For example, one corporation proposed that the city build its course on 150 acres of a 340-acre residential community that it was planning to build. Another corporation offered to contribute $100,000 for the planning and design of the course, in addition to the land, if it were built on its 1,800-acre residential area site.[32]

There are many examples of this strategy along the Front Range in Colorado. Developers in Westminster donated land to the city for a golf course, and the developers then built expensive homes overlooking the course. In the Denver suburb of Commerce City, land for an 18-hole golf course built close to the new Denver International Airport was donated by landowners who planned to develop around it. Other golf examples are the Coal Creek course in Louisville, Mariana Butte in Loveland, West Woods in Arvada, and Indian Peaks in Lafayette. A golf course architect in the area who was involved in designing several of these courses states: "The biggest rationale on all the courses is upscale housing. Developers are coming in and saying, 'I know the value of homes on golf courses. I'm willing to give the land to the tax entity so I can build around it'" (p. 42).[33] He added that many times the developer is giving up land that could not be built on anyway. Coal Creek, Indian Peaks, and Mariana Butte are on flood plains. Also located on flood plains is Fox Hollow, which is a prime championship course built in the Denver suburb, or Lakewood on land leased from the Corps of Engineers. Under the lease agreement, no homes can be built on the course.[33]

The pump-priming principle was used by a commercial developer in the context of the Salt Lake City Winter Olympic Games:

A real estate developer gave 386 acres of his mountainous tract to a Utah state agency as a site for a winter sports park that would include ski jumps and a bobsled and luge run. This became Utah Olympic Park—a central facility for the 2002 Salt Lake City Winter Olympic Games. In exchange, the agency agreed to build an access road to the sports park that would run through the remaining 750 acres of the developer's land, opening the area to the development of single-family homes and condos. In addition, the agency pledged to install "all necessary utilities including electrical power, natural gas, telephone, water system and sewer" to serve both the sports park and the 700 residences built on the remaining 750 acres. When the land was acquired, it was valued at $5 million. Ten years later, the land alone—excluding houses that had been built—was valued at $48 million, a 16-fold increase.[34]

Expansion of Existing Public Facilities

Expansion of an existing public facility may be achieved with the assistance of a sports business that is prepared to invest in improvements, renovations, or expansion of the facility in exchange for the authority to lease the facility or to operate it at off-peak times. Figure 8-9 illustrates how an existing facility may be adapted by additional investment to accommodate new activities. In this case, a velodrome was adapted so that go-cart racing could also take place there.

Figure 8-9 Expanding a Velodrome to Include Go-Carts

Indianapolis Parks and Recreation Department constructed and operated the Taylor Velodrome at the city's Lake Sullivan Recreational Area. The annual net operating loss for the Velodrome was more than $50,000, and its losses meant that it was in danger of being closed. The department entered into a partnership with Fast Masters, Inc., by which the company constructed, at its own expense of approximately $250,000, a permanent track for go-cart racing inside the velodrome. Go-cart racing was becoming popular in the area, and there was a shortage of facilities. The stands for spectators, concession areas, parking, and infrastructure at the velodrome were used only occasionally for bike racing, so go-cart racing was a complementary use. The partnership was for a three-year period, after which ownership of the track reverted to the city.

Before Fast Masters entered the partnership, the company and a television network, ESPN2, agreed that the network would transmit 12 races per year with each session lasting 3 hours. ESPN required Fast Masters to raise $75,000 in advertising for the network to pay for these transmissions. The television coverage was key to the company's ability to attract sponsors. Any sponsorship fees in excess of $75,000 remained with Fast Masters. Other revenue sources for Fast Masters were entry fees received from the go-cart racers (from 125 to 150 people raced at each meet) and admission fees received from spectators.

The city's return from the agreement comprised $25 from the entry fee of each go-cart, one-eighth of the gross receipts from spectator admissions, and all revenues from concessions that the city operated. Fast Masters paid utility and cleanup costs associated with the 12 events.

More commonly, this type of joint venture has occurred in northern states and has involved the commercial developer in converting an existing facility for winter use.

> The city of Oak Park, Michigan, leased land to a commercial operator for a 10-year period with the lessee having an additional two successive 5-year options to extend the lease. The lessee paid 5% of gross sales to the city for rent. The developer constructed and operated a five-court indoor tennis facility, including a permanent support building; five asphalt courts; and a five-court air-supported structure. The city provided all utilities to the site and prepared the site for contractors.
>
> The operator had exclusive use of the courts for a 32-week winter season and erected and dismantled the air-supported structure at the beginning and end of each season. The city had exclusive rights to the courts in the 20-week summer season without the air structure. At the end of the agree-

ment, ownership of all facilities, with the exception of the air-supported structure, passed to the city. To the satisfaction of both parties, the agreement worked successfully, and it was extended to cover an additional five courts. To safeguard the operator's investment, the city agreed not to construct, operate, or allow the construction or operation of any other indoor tennis facility on municipal property in Oak Park without first offering the rights for construction and operation to the lessee.

Similar partnerships to the tennis joint venture described at Oak Park have been forged for a wide range of activities. For example, a golf driving range under an inflatable dome was operated by a developer between November and May on a 2.5-acre park site in Oakland County, Michigan. A similar structure was used in Madison Heights, Michigan, for winter softball games. These structures were removed in the summer months. The agencies received an agreed percentage of the gross receipts and access for constituents to a facility that otherwise would not be available without incurring capital costs.

In this type of arrangement, it is important that the developer build facilities that meet the public agency' specifications. This is the only way in which quality control can be exerted. Without this condition, the developer may use lower quality materials that need replacement in a shorter period of time. Hence, when the public agency takes over the development at the end of the lease, which typically is negotiated in the contract, it may be faced with substantial renovation costs.

Multiparty Arrangements

It is increasingly common for large-scale public-private sports partnerships to be complex arrangements involving multiple financial partners. Often they are spearheaded by an independent quasi-governmental body to facilitate collaborative exchange between the various public and private entities involved with the project. Figure 8-10 offers an example of such an arrangement. The Hubert Humphrey Metrodome, Pilot Field in Buffalo, AAA baseball in Colorado Springs, a golf academy in Indianapolis, and adaptations of the principles of timesharing to build a sports center are all examples of this type of arrangement.

In the case of the Metrodome in Minneapolis, the Metro Sports Facilities Commission (the Commission), a special authority created by the state legislature, was established to assemble the necessary financing from various private and public sources and to oversee the operation of the facility.

Initially, the Commission negotiated with a group of Minneapolis land developers to have a 20-acre stadium site, valued at $9 million, donated to the Commission in return for the right to develop the surrounding real estate, which the developers owned. However, the key to success of the project was the Commission's ability to broker an agreement between the City of Minneapolis and the downtown business community for the sale of $55 million of revenue bonds. The tax-exempt bonds issued by the City were purchased by five local corporations. To secure bond repayment, the Commission entered an agreement with the City of Minneapolis to collect an annual hotel-motel tax (2%) and liquor tax (2%). The revenues collected from these taxes were used to pay all the debt-service costs (principal and interest) on the revenue bonds. In addition, the Commission as-

Figure 8-10 Developing the Chelsea Piers Complex in New York City

Piers 59 to 62 between the city of New York's 17th Street and 23rd Street are historic. Built in 1910 to serve the major passenger liners, the piers extend 0.75 miles along the Hudson River. Views from these four piers include the Statue of Liberty and the Verrazano-Narrows Bridge to the south and include the George Washington Bridge and New Jersey Palisades to the north. They contain magnificent two-story structures that were designed to accommodate the needs of departing ocean liner passengers. These structures are large indoor spaces (120 feet wide and 840 feet long) with no columns. However, by the early 1990s, these four piers were no longer used and were in danger of falling into disrepair.

A city-state agency, the Hudson River Park Conservancy, leased 30 acres containing the piers to a developer for 49 years for $157,000 each month, which was adjusted annually for inflation. The lease payments were used to maintain bike paths, gardens, playgrounds, promenades, and playing fields. The lease payments were expected to generate approximately $70 million in revenue for the Conservancy over the 20-year period.

The developers invested $90 million (of which $25 million in improvements was made by subtenants) in adapting the structures on the piers for leisure use. They estimated that constructing similar facilities from scratch would cost $250 million and noted that obtaining building permits would be impossible. The development was completed in four years from bidding to opening, which is remarkably fast for a project of this scale in New York. The absence of new construction was key because it reduced the number of community groups who had to be involved in the process. The elements of the complex included the following (see Figure A):

- Pier 59 included a 200-yard golf driving range with 52 weather-protected hitting stalls in four tiers, a proshop and training-center locker rooms, meeting rooms, a putting green, lounges, and a restaurant grill and lounge. This was one of the most technically advanced driving ranges and teaching centers in the world and could be used regardless of the weather conditions.

- Pier 60, which was covered with large structures, contained the 150,000 square foot Sports Center featuring a 0.5 mile indoor jogging track; a banked six-lane, 200-meter competition track with arena seating for 1,500 spectators; three basketball courts; volleyball courts; a 15,000 square foot rock-climbing wall that was the largest in the Northeast; a fully equipped locker room; six-lane, 25-yard swimming pool; boxing ring; steam and sauna rooms; a waterfront restaurant; and a sundeck. It was designated the Summer Games Sports Center.

- Pier 61 contained the Sky Rink that had two ice-skating rinks with seating for 1,600 spectators (including two heated sky boxes). Floor-to-ceiling windows in the two ice rinks offered spectacular views of the Hudson River.

- Pier 62 featured two outdoor, regulation-sized, in-line and roller skating rinks for roller hockey league play or, when the rinks were combined, for public skating. At the water's end of Pier 62 was a public park that the developer funded and managed.

- The headhouse associated with the piers stretched from 22nd Street to 18th Street and housed the Silver Screen Studios, which was a 300,000 square foot center for film and television production, and a 90,000 square foot field house containing an Olympic-quality gymnastics training facility, a 40-lane bowling facility, rock-climbing wall for children, two basketball courts, two artificial turf playing fields, and four batting cages.

(continued)

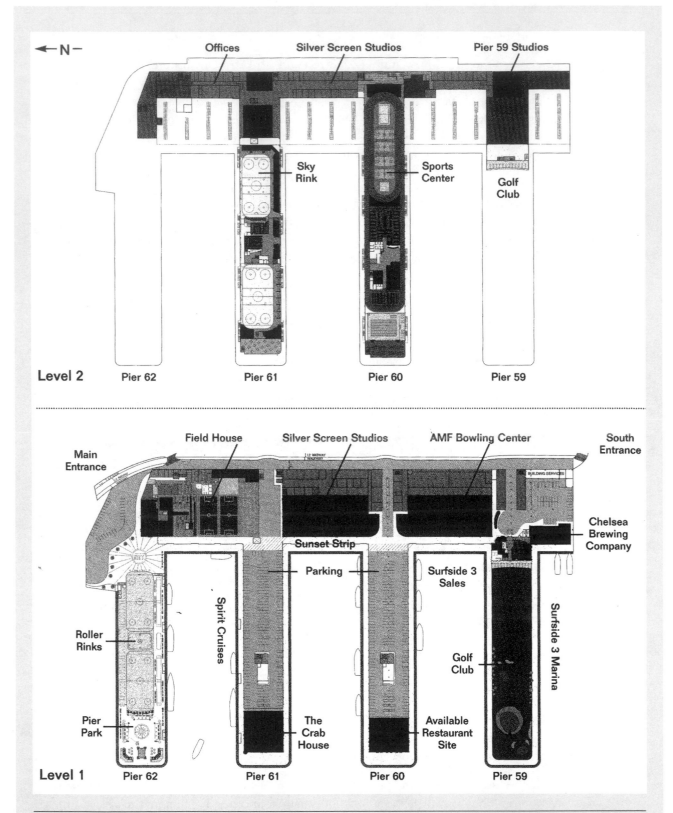

Level 2

N

Offices   Silver Screen Studios   Pier 59 Studios

Sky Rink

Sports Center

Golf Club

Pier 62   Pier 61   Pier 60   Pier 59

Level 1

Field House   Silver Screen Studios   AMF Bowling Center   South Entrance

Main Entrance

BUILDING SERVICES

Chelsea Brewing Company

Sunset Strip

Roller Rinks

Spirit Cruises

Parking

Surfside 3 Sales

Golf Club

Surfside 3 Marina

Pier Park

The Crab House

Available Restaurant Site

Pier 62   Pier 61   Pier 60   Pier 59

Figure A: Piers 60 and 61, the enclosed piers, primarily house the Sports Center and the Sky Rink. At the western end of Pier 62, Pier Park is open to the public, providing benches, picnic tables, and a wooden shade structure for visitors to take advantage of the spectacular river views. A five-block-long building called the headhouse connects the piers and houses to additional athletic facilities, retail stores, and restaurants, as well as film, television, and photography studios.

Along the 1.2 mile perimeter of the Chelsea Piers, dinner boats, charter boats, luxury yachts, and a sailing school were to be accommodated. Private marina facilities were planned. The development also featured two destination waterfront restaurants. The Crab House and Chelsea Brewing Company with seating capacities of 600 and 300, respectively, and 500 parking spaces.

Even without using the sports facilities, pedestrians could walk throughout the project along Sunset Strip, which was a walkway that ran parallel to the river. From there they could enter any of the commercial spaces: the stores, the café, the seafood house, and the microbrewery. They could watch the sports at the outdoor facilities, including the roller rink and the golf club; they could sit in the park at the end of Pier 62; and they could sit on any of the benches that dotted the esplanade. Chelsea Piers attracted from 8,000 to 10,000 visitors daily and became a stop on New York Apple Tours. The complex was kept immaculately clean, which was one of several management ideas that the developers freely admit they stole from Disney. Badges for all 600 employees (including owners, managers, and the 150 part-time employees) bore only a first name. Chelsea Piers had its own security force, but the limited entrances helped eliminate problems by providing natural checkpoints.

This imaginative, expanded use of a moribund public facility made productive use of the city's waterfront, stimulated economic development in the area, revitalized historically significant structures, and created a host of new sporting opportunities for New York residents at no cost to the taxpayer.

Adapted from Vilma Barr, The Chelsea Piers complex *Urban Land*, August 1994, pp. 38-41, and Alexander Garvin & Gayle Berian, *Urban Parks and Open Space*, The Urban Land Institute, Washington, D.C. 1997.

sessed a 10% admission tax on all events held at the Metrodome. Monies realized from this surcharge were used to cover annual operating expenses. The remaining $20 million was raised from $13 million in interest earned on the revenue bonds and $7 million from two of the Metrodome's principal tenants, the Minnesota Vikings and Twins football and baseball teams, respectively. The latter revenue came principally from the lease of luxury box suites.

Crucial to establishing financial stability was the Commission's effort to negotiate long-term tenant lease agreements with the Twins, the Vikings, and the University of Minnesota. These agreements confirmed a minimum of 100 dates per year for the next 20 to 30 years. The 30-year lease arrangement with the Vikings provided the Commission with 10% of the gross ticket sales. For 81 regular season games played in the Metrodome, the Twins surrendered 7.5% of their gross gate receipts. To date, these revenues, along with admission tax proceeds from other events, have allowed the Commission to operate the Metrodome free from public subsidy of any kind.

Pilot Field in Buffalo is the home of the AAA Buffalo Bisons, which is one of the most successful baseball minor league teams. It was constructed in the late 1980s and is another example of a complex multiparty agreement with a host of different organizations contributing to its financing. The stadium has been called "a minor league stadium with all the major league amenities," "the best ballpark in the minor leagues," and "the city's ticket to Glory Days" (p. 35).[35] The principal objectives of the project were to develop a facility designed to attract a major league baseball franchise and to act as a catalyst for downtown redevelopment. The arrangement is described in Figure 8-11.

Figure 8-11 The Financing of Pilot Field in Buffalo

Contributions of the financial partners in the construction of Pilot Field are shown below:

Contributions	Amount (in millions)
City of Buffalo	
General improvement serial bonds	5.32
Downpayment on bonds	0.28
Three-year operation and maintenance budget	<u>2.10</u>
	7.70
New York State	
State Urban Development Corporation funds	22.50
ECIDA	
Revenue bonds	4.20
Other Contributions	
Buffalo Development Companies	4.00
Buffalo Bisons	3.00
Buffalo Urban Renewal Agency (land credit)	2.00
Erie County legislature	<u>0.75</u>
	9.75
Total Cost of Pilot Field	**44.15**

The largest contributor to Pilot Field was the New York State legislature, which appropriated $22.5 million in state Urban Development Corporation funds for the project. When these funds were approved, tripartite agreements were signed that delineated the responsibilities of the state, the city, and the Erie County Industrial Development Agency (ECIDA), which was the developer of the project. The ECIDA was a public-benefit corporation created to foster economic prosperity in Buffalo and Erie County. Under these agreements, the state was repaid from any profits that may be realized after a

The owner of the AAA Pacific Coast League Hawaii Baseball team was interested in relocating the team to Colorado Springs. The city needed a stadium for the team, but voters had previously rejected proposals to spend public money for a stadium. The owner was referred to a major real estate development company that was developing a 2,000-acre site, 8.5 miles from downtown. Believing it would give visibility to their development, the company agreed to donate the land for a stadium. The city agreed to pay the owner who was developing the new stadium $500,000 as its share of the project. This pump-priming contribution was crucial to bringing the stadium to fruition: "City financial participation was critical to the owner and was perceived by city officials as a potential deal-breaker" (p. 238)[34]. Because the state's constitution forbade the use of public money for private interests, the city was required to receive something of value for its $500,000. Thus, a joint use agreement called for the stadium to be used by the city 180 days of each year.

maintenance reserve fund of up to $75,000 annually was established and after the debt service was paid on bonds issued by the ECIDA and the city. The agreements also required the city government to pay for all cost overruns. Under the terms of the tripartite agreement, the ECIDA was the owner of Pilot Field, and the city had a noncancelling, 15-year agreement with the agency. At the end of the lease, title to the stadium passes to the city.

The city was responsible for operation and maintenance of the facility. Its major source of revenue was a contract with the Buffalo Bisons, the principal tenant. The lease agreement was critical because it was the city's guarantee that it could operate and maintain the stadium without having to subsidize the operation with additional tax dollars. Since the project involved the construction of an expandable stadium so that it could accommodate major league baseball in the future, the council wanted an expandable lease to ensure the city would benefit from the future growth.

To forge this partnership, a lease was developed that linked the rent to paid admissions. That is, the percentage of ticket revenues that the Bisons paid to the city increased as gross receipts increased. Any profit the city realized from the operation of Pilot Field was to be applied toward the $800,135 it paid annually for principal and interest on the bonds issued by the ECIDA and the city for stadium construction. The term of these bonds was 15 years, corresponding to the term of the lease agreement the city had with the ECIDA. ECIDA's participation as project director was important because it had the ability to establish a construction price ceiling that the contractor was required to meet for the entire project. If the city had served as the developer, it would have been compelled by the city charter to bid each of the various aspects of the project and face the cost overruns that would occur with the inevitable change orders.

The city council authorized the sale of city bonds in the amount of $5.32 million to cover the city's share of the project. As Table 8-2 reports, several other groups also contributed. The Buffalo Development Companies, a consortium of local development agencies, contributed $4 million, including $150,000 in Urban Development Corporation handicapped-access funds. The Buffalo Urban Renewal Agency, an ancillary agency of city government, contributed the land. The Bisons contributed $3 million towards the purchase of the scoreboard and the construction of the concession areas, the restaurant, and team offices. The project also was aided by being included as a "grandfathered" project in the 1986 Tax Reform Act, enabling construction to be financed by tax-exempt bonds. This inclusion saved the project an estimated $17 million in interest payments over the 15-year life of the bonds.

This figure is adapted from Johnson, A.T. (1993). Minor league baseball and local economic development. Urbana, Illinois: University of Illinois Press.

However, given the weather conditions in Colorado Springs outside baseball season, this use was much less generous than it may at first appear to be.[34]

One of the most common approaches to developing tourism real estate has been time-sharing. Time-sharing enables individuals who desire to own property at a resort area to purchase a selected number of weeks per year at a condominium rather than having to purchase a whole condominium unit. This enables the purchase price to be shared by a number of buyers (52 of them if each buys one week), and maintenance of the unit is the responsibility of a management company. A county agency planned to use the time-sharing principle to finance the building of an indoor sports center that would have provided a new facility for residents at no cost to the sponsoring county agency:

Figure 8-12 Establishing a Golf Academy Through Multiple Partnerships

Indianapolis had no public facility for teaching golf and no course on which learners could practice. Thus, the Indianapolis Parks and Recreation Department envisaged creating a golf academy, which was to be a teaching facility incorporating six elements:

1. A clubhouse approximately 14,400 square foot in size that included a proshop, concession area, a covered 80 foot x 20 foot training area with 18 tee positions, a training video viewing area, a club fitting and repair area, a classroom, and two golf simulators.

2. An outdoor, lighted driving range with 40 outdoor tee positions.

3. A practice putting green.

4. A pitching practice area.

5. A sand-trap practice area.

6. A nine-hole, par three training golf course with greens built to Professional Golf Association standards but with holes not exceeding 150 yards in length. Regular courses intimidate learners because of the level of difficulty and their tendency to slow play, frustrating experienced golfers behind them. The nine-hole facility would alleviate this problem.

The golf academy's mission was to expand the exposure of golf to Indianapolis residents, particularly to young people. Total projected cost of the project was $1,750,000. To bring it to fruition, resources were pooled from four partners: the park department, a private golf course operator (R. N. Thompson & Associates), the United States Golf Association, and the Indianapolis corporate community.

The park department issued a request for proposals, inviting private operators to lease a 35-acre site for 15 years for the purpose of funding, constructing, and operating the golf academy. The site was located in Riverside Regional Park, which was a 680-acre park incorporating both a wide range of recreational facilities and extensive passive areas. The site was highly visible from major traffic arteries, and it was situated in a lower-income, racially diverse area with moderate gang activity. Within 1.5 miles of the site were three golf courses. There was no other driving range in the area, and this component of the academy was seen as the cash cow undergirding the financial viability of the venture.

The park department established a 501(c)(iii) organization, the Indianapolis Junior Golf Foundation, to own and govern the project for two reasons. First, the academy was intended to be a self-sufficient, but nonprofit, venture with any surplus funds being reinvested to fund capital improvements, improve promotion, and offer additional training opportunities for youth. To operate in this manner, it needed to be free of political interference from the city council. Second, if the city directly operated the academy, the city would likely have more difficulty persuading corporations to contribute to its construction.

In response to the request for proposals, R. N. Thompson & Associates were selected. The company was a major real estate developer in the Indianapolis area, had developed four residential golf courses, and owned and operated four other daily-fee golf courses and a private golf academy in the area. Thompson agreed to pay a lease fee to the park department of 10% of the first $500,000 gross receipts; 7%, between $500,000 and $750,000; and 5%, in excess of $750,000. This lease fee went into the park's golf enterprise fund and was reinvested in golf. Thompson also agreed to contribute $450,000 toward design and construction of the academy and to operate it for a management fee set at an amount necessary to reimburse actual maintenance and management expenses. R. N. Thompson & Associates were entitled to additional compensation if specified performance goals were exceeded.

R.N. Thompson & Associates were required to maintain a capital improvement fund of at least $40,000 each year to reinvest in the academy's operation and to appoint a full-time experienced general manager, who was acceptable to the park department and was a licensed, Class A, Professional Golf Association golf professional. The lessee could not sublet or assign the lease to anyone else under the contract terms because the city's long relationship and shared vision with Thompson were viewed as key to the venture's success.

The United States Golf Association contributed a grant of $300,000 to the golf academy. Additionally, it provided technical assistance with the design, construction, and operation of it. The Association recognized that much of the current boom in golf was attributable to the baby boomer cohort reaching the prime age for golfers. They believed that 7% of adults played golf. Given the smaller numbers of people in age cohorts following the baby boomers, a larger proportion of them would have to be players if the demand for golf was not to fall. The Association saw minority groups as a main target market because minorities were substantially under-represented among golfers and were the fastest growing demographic segments.

The golf academy site was easily accessible to minorities in Indianapolis. Prices and quality standards were controlled by the park department through the contract with Thompson, and a variety of measures were used to permit economically disadvantaged youth to earn green fee credit as an alternative to paying the academy's fees. The academy was available to all youth regardless of their access to funds. The United States Golf Association invested in similar programs targeted at minority youth in San Diego, Dallas, and New Orleans. If these pilot projects were successful in expanding the number of minority golfers, the Association was likely to increase substantially its investment by extending the program to other cities.

The final partner was the corporate community in Indianapolis from whom the park department solicited $1 million to raise the balance of the funds. The department did this by working with the Indianapolis Corporate Community Council, comprising major businesses that annually selected quality-of-life projects to support. Appeals to the corporate community were based on the belief that if golf is made available to inner-city youth, then acquisition of the skill to play golf and participation in junior tournaments will assist in building self-esteem, confidence, and good social characteristics. This involvement would provide an alternative to joining local gangs. The golf academy's development was phased so that the clubhouse's indoor components were constructed while corporate donations were solicited to complete the project.

A 501(c)(iii) organization is a non-profit, non-government corporation organized and operated for the benefit of the general public. The number refers to a paragraph in the IRS Code that defines this type of nonprofit organization.

Seven of a number of corporations who were invited to participate agreed to buy exclusive use of part or all of a proposed sport center for their employees at selected times on weekdays from 11:00 a.m. to 1:00 p.m. and from 5:00 p.m. to 8:00 p.m. At other weekday times and on weekends, the facility would be available for use by all residents of the county. The facility would be operated and managed by the county at all times.

The capital cost of the facility was approximately $3 million. Each corporation agreed to pay $100 per day per hour for the exclusive use of the facility's space. This space and time was purchased in advance for a 5-year period with an option under which it could be renewed for a further 5-year period. The presold space and time allocations from the seven corporations provided all of the initial finance needed to construct the building. The county had negotiated with a private developer to lease a park site to him for a 15-year period, and he agreed to build the facility.

He would then lease it back to the county in order to take advantage of depreciation on the structure. The county agreed to pay him a lease fee based on the debt charges on the building that were covered by the presold time shares purchased by the seven corporations.

Although the county commissioners were informed fully of the progress of the intended development, they refused to support it in the end because they were reluctant to grant the developer an exclusive 15-year lease on county property. The developer required an exclusive lease because, if for some reason the scheme failed, he had to be able to use the building for some other purpose in order to generate revenue to pay the annual debt charges on the building for which he would be liable. After being rebuffed by the commissioners, the developer took the feasibility data that the county staff had assembled and proceeded to build the facility elsewhere and manage it himself as a private venture.

A more complex joint development involved the city of Indianapolis, a commercial operator, the United States Golf Association, and philanthropic donations from civic-minded major businesses, coming together to establish a public golf academy. It is described in Figure 8-12.

Summary

Before entities from the public and private sectors enter into direct partnership and pool their resources to deliver a service or build a facility, a favorable supportive environment for such partnerships has to be present. The first challenge is for the potential partners to recognize and accept as legitimate their different value systems. Public agencies are mandated to serve the whole community, especially its disadvantaged members; are concerned with social outcomes and benefits that are relatively intangible and difficult to measure; and are constrained by bureaucratic procedures that are necessary to ensure accountability for their expenditure of public funds. Private organizations are mandated to serve their stockholders by maximizing their return on investment, which is frequently obtained by focusing on narrowly defined, responsive target markets, and they are relatively flexible with the ability to respond quickly to new opportunities. The different value systems may result in negative stereotypes and attitudes between those working in the different sectors. Removing these stereotypes and attitudes and building the mutual respect needed for partnerships to succeed require the establishment of forums to facilitate communication and liaison.

A second factor that may inhibit the formation of partnerships is allegations of the public sector's engaging in unfair competition with businesses. Public agencies have advantages that enable them to deliver services at a lower price than commercial enterprises can. The advantages include paying no property, sales, or income taxes; not being required to cover operating expenses with revenues; being exempt from many regulations; being self-insured; financing improvements with tax-exempt bonds; not being required to cover debt charges with operating revenues; and receiving free advertisements and promotion.

Because there is no legal mechanism for stopping public agencies from constructing competing facilities if they wish to do so, private sports managers have to mount campaigns at the ballot box to stop facilities from being built. However, at the same time in at least two states, private sports businesses have been successful in lobbying for legislation that makes it more difficult for the public sector to engage in unfair competition. In the case of unfair competition from nonprofit organizations such as YMCAs, private sports organizations have had some success in seeking legal redress to remove the tax-exempt states of those nonprofits that are serving affluent clienteles rather than underprivileged groups.

The potential for public-private partnerships stems from a recognition that each sector has resources of value to offer the other. A successful collaboration requires finding a way to fuse the complementary resources of each sector to the mutual advantage of all parties involved. Public sector organizations have four major assets to which the private sector is likely to seek access: (a) a substantial land bank and/or the regulatory authority to assemble land needed for a project, (b) ability to borrow money at a lower interest than a private organization, (c) authorization to waive a proportion of, or all, property and other local and/or state tax payments, and (d) control over permit and zoning processes enabling their processes to be expedited and, in some cases, even changed or waived. Public officials often can use these assets to negotiate with private sports organizations without being subjected to the scale of controversy and criticism that invariably surrounds proposals to use tax dollars for this purpose.

The private sector has five types of assets that it can contribute to a partnership arrangement with a public agency. First, it has the capacity to raise capital quickly and easily, provided it can be demonstrated that a project is likely to generate a satisfactory return on the investment. Second, it has management expertise in specialized areas that it may not be efficient for a public agency to acquire through hiring personnel with these skills. Third, labor costs often are lower in terms of both salaries and fringe benefits. Fourth, it often is much easier for a business than for an agency to hire and pay part-time workers who may be required to handle one-time services or short peak seasons. Further, businesses serving multiple organizations may be better able to take advantage of efficiencies associated with economies of scale. Fifth, the involvement of sport businesses may enable public agencies to reduce substantially their vulnerability to liability claims by passing such risks along to their business partners.

A remarkable array of imaginative and creative public-private partnerships has emerged in the financing of sports projects over the last decade. Their creativity and, in some cases, complexity make their classification into a comprehensive taxonomy somewhat arbitrary. Nevertheless, seven broad categories of partnerships have been identified: (a) public sector leasing, where a private sports business pays a fee to lease a public facility; (b) leaseback arrangements, where a private developer constructs a facility and leases exclusive or partial use rights to the public agency at a previously negotiated rent; (c) public sector takeover of a private sports business to preserve a sports opportunity that would otherwise become unavailable to a jurisdiction's residents; (d) private sector takeover of facilities whose ongoing costs have become an unacceptable burden to public agencies; (e) private sector pump-priming whereby a business uses some of its assets to induce a public agency to make a major investment in a sports facility from which the enterprise will also gain; (f) expansion of an existing public sports facility by an infusion of funds from a private organization; and (g) multiparty arrangements that involve multiple financial partners making contributions to a project.

References

1. Schalman, H. (2001, December 3). Giants predict red ink for 2002. Baer Foresees $5 million loss. *San Francisco Chronicle*, D 3.
2. Bendick, R. L. (1993). State partnerships to preserve open space: Lessons from Rhode Island and New York. In E. Endicott (Ed.), *Land conservation through public-private partnerships* (pp.149-171). Washington, DC: Island Press.
3. Cohen, A. (1996). Togetherness. *Athletic Business, 20*(10), 31-37.
4. International Health, Racquet & Sportsclub Association. (n.d.). *The case for fair competition*. Boston: Author.
5. *HB 3513: The Unfair Competition Bill*, which would have prohibited public sector organizations from providing goods and services that are already provided by private businesses: Hearings before the Oregon House of Representatives (testimony of Jennifer Harding).
6. Martinsons, J. (1994, May 20-26). The new kids on the block: Parks and rec departments. *Club Industry*, 20-23.
7. Mike Brandt's Competitors. (1975, September 12). *Wall Street Journal*, B3.
8. Cohen, A. (2002, June). Good business. *Athletic Business*, 11.
9. Schmid, S. (1995). Water world: It's water, water everywhere at a Texas water park. *Athletic Business, 20*(10), 31-37.
10. Cohen, A (1996). Togetherness: IRS forces university recreation departments to limit public access. *Athletic Business*, 18-20.
11. Weisiger, H. (1983, October). *Unfair, unfair, unfair competition: How the Fairfax County government and Fairfax County Park Authority directly compete against private recreation*. Unpublished manuscript.
12. Kozlowski, J. C. (1993). Authorized public recreation may legally compete with private facilities. *Park and Recreation, 28*(9), 36-44.
13. Ablondi, J. (1999, January). Law and order: Rewriting the rules for non-profits. *Club Business Industry*, 88.
14. McCarthy, J. (1990, February). Competition for the sports dollar–A response to Mr. Cousins. *Non-Profit Times*, 20-21.
15. International Health, Racquet & Sportsclub Association. (n.d.). *Non-profit Expansion of Impact* [Information sheet]. Boston: IHRSA.
16. De Marcus, R. (1985, November). Non-profit commercialism: A growing problem. *Club Business*, 57-58.
17. Cohen, A (1996, April). Audited: IRS forces university recreation departments to limit public access. *Athletic Business*, 18-20.
18. Young Men's Christian Association of Columbia-Willamette v. Department of Revenue, 308 Or. 644, 784 P.2d. 1086. (1990).
19. Sioux Valley Hospital Association v. South Dakota State Board of Equalization, 513 N.W. 2d 562 (1994).
20. Middle Tennessee Medical Center v. Assessment of Appeals Commission of the State of Tennessee, 1994 Tennessee App. LEXIS 43.
21. Osborne, D., & Gaebler, T. (1992). *Reinventing government*. Reading, PA: Addison-Wesley.
22. Danielson, M.N. (1997). *Hometeam: Professional sports and the American Metropolis*. Princeton, NJ: Princeton University Press.
23. Muirhead, D., & Rando, G. L. (1994). *Golf course development and real estate*. Washington, DC: The Urban Land Institute.
24. Quirk, J.P. (1987, January 18). The Quirk study: A close look at the two proposals. *St. Louis Post-Dispatch*, Special Report 8.
25. Agostini, S. J., Quigley, J.M., & Smolensky, E. (1997). Stickball in San Francisco. In R. G. Noll & A. Zimbalist (Eds.), *Sports, Jobs & Taxes* (pp. 385-426). Washington, DC: Brookings Institution.
26. Greenberg, M.J., & Gray, J.T. (1996). *The stadium game*. Milwaukee, WI: National Sports Law Institute.
27. Korman, R. (1989., February 20). A matter of pride. *Sports, Inc.*, 32-37.
28. Fulton, W. (1988, March). Politicians who chase after sports franchises may get less than they pay for. *Governing, 2*, 34-40.
29. Urquhart, J. (1986). Catering: To contract or not? *Leisure Management, 16*(5), 21-22.

30. Stevens, B. (1984). *Delivering municipal services efficiently: A comparison of municipal and private service delivery. Summary.* U.S. Department of Housing and Urban Development, New York: Ecodata.

31. Steinborg, J. (1993, August 13). Public park is too private to suit the government. *New York Times*, B1.

32. Winton, P. (1994, August 3). Developers scramble for shot at public golf course. *Fort Myers News-Press*, 1, 16.

33. Marchant, W. (1995). Open range: Municipalities and developers coordinate their respective interest to fuel a public golf boom in Colorado. *Golf Course Management, 63*(7), 41-42.

34. Bartlett, D.L., & Steele, J.B. (2001, December 10). Salt Lake money. *Sports Illustrated, 94*, 79-98.

35. Johnson, A.T. (1993). *Minor league baseball and local economic development.* Urbana, IL: University of Illinois Press.

SECTION III:
FINANCIAL RESOURCES ACCRUING DIRECTLY FROM SPORT ENTERPRISES

Photos courtesy of Robin Ammon, Jr.

Chapter Nine

Ticket Sales and Operations

This chapter examines a number of issues facing sport managers with respect to the selling and pricing of tickets for sporting events. First, the chapter provides a perspective on attendance trends for collegiate and professional sports and their implications for increasing revenues from charged admissions. Next, the opportunities and problems sport managers face in establishing a price for admission to a sporting event are discussed because pricing is one of the least understood aspects of sport management. The chapter also devotes considerable attention to the major impacts emerging technology is having on the sale and distribution of tickets, including web-based ticketing applications. The chapter concludes with an in-depth discussion of the organization and administration of ticket sales. The intent is to provide the reader with a basic understanding of various kinds of ticketing plans and methods. Accounting procedures as well as current ticketing systems are described.

It is estimated that U.S. consumers spend almost $12 billion a year on tickets to sporting events.[1] As shown in chapter 2, the importance of ticket sale revenue to professional sports varies considerably from one league to another. Whereas in the NHL and NBA gate receipts are the single greatest source of income, the media-rich NFL receives less than one third of its overall revenues from ticket sales. Gate receipts are the lifeblood of minor league baseball. A former general manager with the Class A Everett Giants notes, "The core of a (minor league) team's existence is the admission ticket"(p. 27).[2] Approximately half the total revenues generated by minor league teams comes from ticket sales, and it has been pointed out that

> high attendance is desirable not only for the ticket revenue, but also for the revenue from the sale of concessions and novelties. The size of the concession revenues greatly influences whether a team is profitable. In many cases, concessions account for more than 25% of a team's revenues.[3] (p. 25)

At the collegiate level, ticket sales are a primary source of revenue. NCAA studies on the financial condition of intercollegiate athletic programs show that in-

Table 9–1 Principal Revenue Sources for NCAA Athletic Programs by Division

Source of Revenue	Div. IA	Div. IAA	Div. II	Div. III
Ticket Sales	27%	10%	6%	(NA)
Student Fees	6%	22%	22%	(NA)
Donations	17%	9%	8%	11%
Bowls	4%	1%	0%	(NA)
Government Support	1%	6%	8%	(NA)
Institutional Support	9%	35%	45%	69%
NCAA/Conf. Distributions	8%	5%	1%	(NA)
Radio/TV	8%	1%	0%	(NA)
Signage/Sponsorship	4%	4%	1%	(NA)
Guarantees	4%	3%	1%	(NA)
Other				22%

Source: Revenues and Expenses of Divisions I/II and III Intercollegiate Athletics Programs: Financial Trends and Relationships – 1999. D. Fulks, Indianapolis, IN: National Collegiate Athletic Association.

Figure 9–1 Percentage of Seating Capacity Sold by League Over Past Several Years

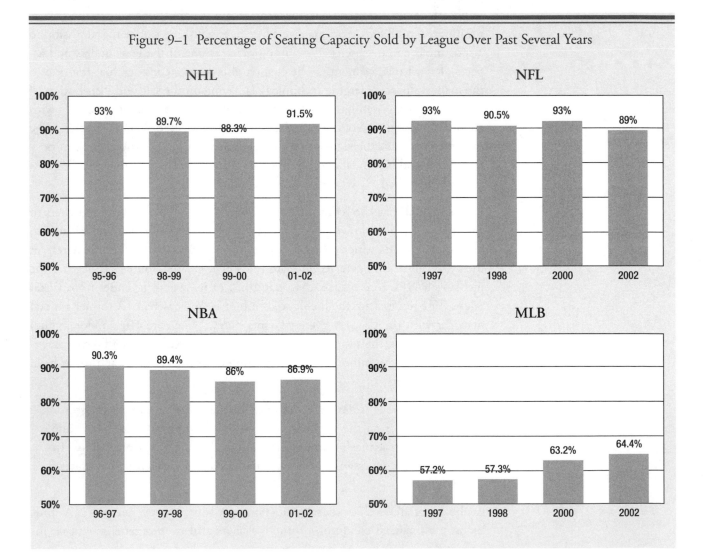

come from the sale of tickets constitutes a significant share of overall revenue (Table 9-1). At the Division I-A level, 27% of athletic departments' annual revenues are derived from ticket sales, the single largest revenue category. At Michigan and Ohio State, ticket sales to football games in 2002 earned each athletic department approximately $28 million.[4] When the University of Michigan raised the cost of a football ticket by $10 to an average of $41 per game, the increase brought Michigan's ticket prices in line with other Big Ten competitors such as Penn State and Ohio State, which charged on average $38 and $41, respectively.[5]

The prominence of ticket revenues diminishes for smaller collegiate programs. At the Division II and III levels, direct subsidies from the institution or student activity fees, or both, replace gate receipts as the most important sources of revenue. A concern for many of these schools is that when faced with a funding crisis in which support for sports has to be weighed against support for academic programs, support among students and administrations for athletic programs may diminish. It appears that managers at all levels will be faced with the challenge of sustaining and/or increasing revenues from ticket sales.

Admission Pricing

Professional Sports

Increasing gate receipts can result from either selling more tickets or raising the unit cost or price of tickets sold. Through the prosperous '90s, many organizations were able to accomplish both. From 1991 to 2000, ticket prices for all leagues grew at an annual rate of 8.4%, so that gate receipts more than doubled.[6] The economic recession that persisted in the early years of the new century, however, contributed to widespread attendance declines across all four major leagues. As discussed in chapter 2, almost half the teams in the NHL, NFL, MLB, and the NBA reported attendance losses in both 2001 and 2002.

Figure 9-1 shows the percentage of available seating capacity actually sold across the four major North American sports leagues from 1995 to 2001-02. The overall profile indicates a generally flat or stagnant attendance pattern during this period. The league demonstrating the most significant improvement was MLB, moving from selling 56% of its seating capacity in 1995 to over 64% in 2002. However, an inspection of individual team attendance records reveals that 10 MLB teams posted double-digit attendance losses during the 2002 season. In part, the inability of many MLB teams to sell a significant portion of their seating capacity is attributable to the MLB's 162 regular-season game schedule's being much longer than those of the other major professional sport leagues (NBA 82; NHL 82; and NFL 16 games). Given baseball's significantly larger inventory, it is more difficult to sell out the 81 home dates.

Clearly, the widespread erosion in fan attendance is attributable to several factors. In addition to the persistent economic slowdown of the early 2000s, other factors contributing to attendance losses include the increased competition from the entertainment industry, the availability of more sports programs on free or cable television than ever before, and the steady cost increases of attending major sporting events.

The impact of escalating prices was discussed at length in chapter 2. As shown in Figure 9-2, ticket prices to sporting events more than doubled from 1991-92 to 2002-03. The relatively high prices make it likely that potential spectators will substitute a host of other less expensive entertainment options for attending games. Although there is little empirical evidence on the type and extent of switching that occurs among entertainment options (such as renting a movie instead of attending an NBA game), the potential for cost-saving substitution is considerable and deserving of careful examination by sport managers. It is clear that the relatively high costs associated with attending major league sporting events place them in a particularly vulnerable price position (see Table 9-2).

Figure 9-2 Rising Cost of Attending Major League Sporting Events for "Famliy of Four"

League	'91-'92	'02-'03	% Change
MLB	$77.41	$145.21	+85%
NBA	$138.82	$254.88	+84%
NFL	$152.55	$290.41	+90%
NHL	$132.62	$240.43	+81%

Based on Fan Cost Index (FCI) calculated by *Team Marketing Report* to represent the average cost for family of four attending a major league game (2 adult and 2 child tickets, 4 sodas, 4 hot dogs, 2 beers, 2 programs, 2 caps).

Table 9–2 Price of Alternative Entertainment Options

Type of Entertainment	Estimated National Range of Cost per Engagement
Watch TV	$0.03 to $1.00 per day (1)
Internet Access	$0.75 to $1.25 per day (2)
Watch Cable TV	$1.75 to $2.00 per day (2)
Watch Satellite TV	$2.00 to $3.00 per day (2)
Rent a video tape	$3.00 to $5.00 for three-day use (2)
Rent a PlayStation 2 cartridge	$4.00 to $6.00 for three-day use (2)
Rent a DVD	$5.00 to $7.00 for three-day use (2)
Attend a movie	$5.00 to $10.00 for single viewing (3)
Purchase a CD	$9.00 to $20.00 (1, 2)
Go out to dinner	$5.00 to $40.00
Rock concert tickets	$45.00 (3)
Broadway Show	$56.00 (3)
Attend MLB	$11.13 to $36.08 ($18.30**)
Attend NFL	$37.50 to $81.99 ($50.02**)
Attend NBA	$33.16 to $91.15 ($43.65**)
Attend NHL	$32.79 to $75.91 ($41.56**)

(1) Based on cost of electricity. Sunk cost of purchasing TV is not included.
(2) Based on cost of monthly subscription fees or standard rental cost. Sunk cost of computer, VCR, DVD player, CD player, satellite dish, PlayStation2 unit is not included (e.g., consumer already Owns a TV or DVD player).
(3) Source: Newsweek, July 9, 2001. (Horn, 2001).
(**) Average Ticket Cost only. Does not include parking, food concessions, program, or souvenir.
Source: *Team Marketing Report* website, January 2003

Until recently, tickets to most major professional sport league games have not been price sensitive. Even during the 2001 recession, almost 7 out of every 10 major league teams raised their ticket prices. During this period the NFL and MLB increased their ticket prices on average by 12.9% and 8.7%, respectively. It appears the pricing approach of most sports teams is cost oriented. The overriding concern of this pricing strategy is recovering costs. It has been reported that most cost-oriented service providers do not lower prices during slower demand periods.[7] This finding is particularly relevant. Among the 23 MLB teams that increased ticket prices in 2001, 15 lost attendance during that season. Although a direct causal relationship between increased prices and declining attendance has yet to be established, given the increased price sensitivity in difficult economic times, switching from a cost-oriented to a more demand-oriented pricing strategy appears to be prudent. Empirical evidence indicates that the most effective price changes are based on anticipated reactions of customers, rather than on only a firm's own costs and circumstances.[8] Approaching the market with greater sensitivity to customers' price tolerance levels is crucial to sustaining fan support.

Recognizing the precarious position of sports properties, some in the industry have adopted a more price-sensitive approach to the market. The owner of the NBA Los Angeles Lakers proclaimed, "The league must do everything possible to slow rapidly escalating costs of tickets" (C 4).[9] There is evidence that teams are recognizing this because in 2002-03, 55% of teams across the four major sports leagues either reduced or did not increase the cost of a ticket during that season. In that year, over half the NBA teams *lowered* ticket costs—some significantly. For example, Portland and Seattle were reduced 36% and 32%, respectively. It appears that the widespread pattern of substantial, almost automatic annual increases that persisted through the decade of the 1990s came to an end by the 2002-03 season.

Collegiate Sports

Table 9-3 indicates there were steady attendance increases for college football over the last several years. Although there was relatively modest growth (about 5%) in the number of colleges fielding football teams in this period, total attendance in basketball and football over the same period grew by more than 3.5 million to more than 40 million spectators in 2001.

Given the dependence on football revenues, most schools competing in major conferences (Big 10, Big 12, Pac 10, SEC) have developed "priority seating" programs for football, which ties preferred seating locations to additional donations to the athletic program. To purchase the best seats in the stadium, fans have to make an extra contribution to the athletic department for the right to buy those seats. This "privilege" may cost a season-ticket purchaser at a major school as much as $5,000-10,000 for two season tickets. Generally, the larger the donation, the better the seat location. First introduced in the early 1980s, priority seating has become the norm at the Division I level, with about 90% of Division IA schools currently implementing the concept.

Table 9-3 Attendance Trends for Selected Sports
Full Season Totals by Year (in millions)

Sport	1997-1998	1998-1999	1999-2000	2000-2001	2001-2002
BASEBALL					
MLB					
Teams	28	30	30	30	30
Attendance	64,291	70,372	72,782	72,566	67,245
Minor Leagues					
Teams			(NA)	175	178
Attendance			37,601	38,808	38,639
BASKETBALL					
NBA					
Teams	29	29	29	29	29
Attendance	21,801	(NA)	20,057	19,950	20,182
NCAA Men's					
Teams	865	895	932	932	937
Attendance	27,738	28,032	29,025	29,025	28,949
NCAA Women's					
Teams	879	911	956	958	975
Attendance	6,734	7,387	8,698	8,285	9,533
FOOTBALL					
NFL					
Teams	31	31	32	32	32
Attendance	19,050	19,742	20,763	20,953	(NA)
NCAA College					
Teams	595	601	606	608	
Attendance	37,491	39,483	39,147	40,501	(NA)
HOCKEY					
NHL					
Teams	28	28	28	30	30
Attendance	17,641	18,057	18,800	20,372	20,614

Source: U.S. Census Bureau, Statistical Abstract of the United States, 2002.

Pricing Tickets for Sporting Events

When it comes to establishing ticket prices, it appears that most sport managers make decisions "by the seat of their pants." For example, it has been suggested that "ticket prices for professional sport teams are the best-informed *guesses* [italics added] of management" (p. 144).[10] Historically, sport managers have relied almost exclusively on their own judgment as to what ticket prices would be most acceptable to fans. The prevailing approach has been to raise prices incrementally by some arbitrary percentage or flat rate. Although prices have consistently increased for admission to most professional and collegiate events, pricing decisions seem to be based loosely on two considerations, either the estimated revenue needs of the organization or management's perception of what the market will bear.

In this section, we discuss some of the issues and concerns sport managers should consider in establishing prices for the services they provide. It is important to consider the price a fan pays for a ticket in a broad context. Normally, price is conceived of as simply the direct amount of money sacrificed to acquire access to a desired service or event. However, the monetary price of buying a ticket is only part of the overall direct monetary expenditure made by a fan. Fans pay considerably more—from 25 to 50 cents on every dollar—for such things as transportation to and from the game, parking, and ballpark concessions.[11] As chapter 11 illustrates, expenditures on concessions alone have grown substantially, with fans who attend major league games spending an average of $12 each on food and beverage concessions.

For many fans, transportation costs are a significant part of the total cost of attendance. These costs are a function of mode of transportation, travel distance, and fee for parking at a stadium, ballpark, or arena. The magnitude of these expenses varies widely. It is increasingly common, however, to find the fee for parking adjacent to a crowded sport venue almost as costly as the admission charge itself. In addition to these direct expenses, individuals may incur extensive non-monetary costs associated with traveling to and from sporting events. There are two types of nonmonetary time costs that sport managers should be cognizant of: travel time and waiting time. The amount of travel time that creates a barrier to attending events obviously varies according to the individual and the event, but apparently even small travel times will inhibit attendance. Substantial effects have been reported for travel times of 30 minutes and less.[12]

The cost of waiting time—for example, in long lines to purchase tickets prior to a game or to use a bathroom stall in the women's restroom—may be substantial. Substantial enough for some people to conclude that the non-monetary costs associated with attendance are too high even though the direct ticket charge may be acceptable. In these instances, fans not able to see a favorable balance between the nonmonetary and monetary costs associated with attendance are likely to seek alternate forms of entertainment. The investment that fans make includes not only the direct charge of purchasing a ticket, but also the monetary and nonmonetary opportunity costs (travel and waiting time) associated with attendance. For some people, these access costs may involve more personal sacrifice than money and, therefore, may be more influential than monetary costs in determining whether or not these individuals attend. The important point is that sport managers should consider all the costs of attending sporting events.

Psychology of Pricing

Establishing a price that will be accepted by sports attendees requires considering several psychological dimensions of pricing. The most important of these are discussed in the following paragraphs.

Expected price threshold. Research has shown that consumers have an expected range of prices they are willing to pay for a particular program or service and for various products.[13] People refrain from purchasing a product not only when the price is considered too high, but also when the price is perceived to be too low. If a price is set above a threshold price, people will find it too expensive. If a price is set below the expected level, potential consumers will be suspicious of the quality of the service. The upper and lower boundaries of this zone of acceptance may have been formed from an individual's recollection of prices asked or paid in the past.

An important factor in establishing the expected price threshold may be the initial price the organization charges for admission to an event or for a particular service. If consumers have not previously attended this type of sporting event or have no previous exposure to the service, the initial price is likely to become the reference price. This first price firmly establishes in the consumer's mind the fair price for the service. Hence, it becomes the reference price against which subsequent price revisions are compared. An organization is likely to have more flexibility in the first pricing decision than in any subsequent decisions, which will always be constrained by consumers' relating their sense of appropriateness and fairness back to the former price. The first pricing decision, therefore, usually has a strong determining impact on the level of price that can be charged for that service throughout its life.

The function of the initial pricing decision in formulating a reference price point emphasizes the risks involved in pricing an event or service too low when it is first offered, so that potential fans or patrons will be enticed to try it. This objective can best be achieved by offering a promotional price that is recognized by all potential users as temporary. A fixed, relatively short period during which the special, low promotional price will apply should be established. This should be communicated *together* with the regular price that will be charged for the service at the end of this "introductory" period.

Understanding sport consumers' expected price thresholds is important for athletic directors concerned with attempting to generate revenue from what have been commonly labeled "nonrevenue" sports. Although deriving substantial gate income from many of these sports may not be possible or even intended, some of these sports appear to have potential for expanded revenue production. Good prospects, for example, include many women's sports and men's baseball and hockey.

The challenge facing many programs is how to induce people to pay either at all, or more, for something that historically has been provided free or at a nominal cost. Currently, in the Big 10 Conference, for example, the general public can attend three fourths of all sporting events sponsored by the member institutions at no direct cost. This pattern of free admission is common among collegiate institutions across the United States and Canada.

Athletic directors hoping to generate more from nonrevenue sports face a challenging dilemma. Whereas establishing the first price is crucial to setting the standard for any subsequent price adjustments—therefore, the first price should not be artificially low—at the same time, any new or abrupt increase in price may exceed consumers' price thresholds. The existing price threshold may be low, because the reference price has been conditioned by years of free or nominal admission.

Increasing the sport consumer's willingness to pay. If a price is to be charged for the first time or if a relatively large price increase beyond the expected threshold is to be made, fans' resistance may be reduced by raising their perception of the value of the event or service. If consumers think that the value of the event they are purchasing is commensurate with the price being charged, then they are less likely to react adversely to the price increase.

Directly conveying the existing benefits or attributes of attending a sporting event may raise the consciousness of aspects of the overall experience that otherwise may have been ignored or taken for granted. Providing a detailed description of an event's primary attributes and the benefits it offers may assist in raising its perceived value. For example, it has been demonstrated that consumers' willingness to pay for selected recreation and sport activities could be raised substantially by offering information that directly communicated the personal benefits consumers would derive from the activity.[14]

Another way to produce changes in perceived value to increase an individual's willingness to pay is to use price comparisons with other substitutable events or services. Comparisons with competitors' activities or services may help convey the impression that although an increase in prices occurred, the new price is still reasonable. The intent is to communicate excellent value relative to competitive options. For example, "for $5, you get the best in college baseball at less than half the cost of attending a professional game in the area." Comparisons with non-substituted services may provide individuals with a point of reference with which to favorably compare a price: "For less than the cost of a hamburger and fries at your favorite fast-food outlet, you can spend an afternoon watching the best in college baseball."

Tolerance zone. The concept of a tolerance zone suggests that if price increases are within a sufficiently small range or zone, they will not adversely impact attendance at an event or the purchase of a service. For example, an increase in admission charge to a collegiate men's hockey game from $2.50 to $3.00 may be noticed by fans, but it is likely to be small enough that it will not alter their pattern of attendance. Perceptions of price increases and decreases are relative to the original price. An increase in the price of an event from $5.00 to $10.00 may arouse vigorous protests, whereas an increase in the price of a different service from $10.00 to $15.00 may raise no comment. Even though the increase in each case is $5.00, the first is a 100% change, whereas the second is perceived as "only" a 50% change and not resisted as vigorously.

A series of small incremental increases in price over a period of time—all of which fall within the tolerance zone—is less likely to meet consumer resistance than is a single major increase. Sport managers should consider increasing their prices regularly rather than holding back increases until a large relative change is required. However, any price change, no matter how necessary from the sport organization's standpoint, should be carefully considered. Too often, sport managers have failed to recognize that consumers ultimately decide how much they are willing to pay for a ticket or service. No matter how justifiable a price hike might be from the team's perspective, in the end all that matters is whether fans are willing to pay the higher amount. It is crucial, therefore, that prior to the initiation of any price hike, market surveys that assess consumers' levels of price tolerance be conducted to ensure that the new price falls within a potential target market's expected price threshold.

One effective approach to learning how consumers may react to a proposed price hike would be for the sport organization to conduct focus group interviews. Focus groups provide sport managers with the opportunity to probe representatives of key consumer segments (e.g., season-ticket holders) as to how they might respond to an organization's plan to raise ticket prices. The feedback would be crucial in determining how much, if any, price tolerance might exist among targeted consumers. The information retrieved from focus group participants would provide the organization with the ability to make pricing decisions with greater confidence. Beyond determining whether fans would be willing to pay more and at what level, the interactive nature of focus groups would allow sport managers to identify benefits that would enhance the perceived value of the purchase (e.g., free parking, admission to pregame tail-gating experience).

Tactics for Improving Ticket Sales

Ticket sales programs are designed to achieve a number of objectives. For profit-oriented sport organizations, such as private golf clubs and professional sports teams, the primary objective of pricing greens fees for admissions tickets is revenue production. Pricing decisions focus on cost recovery and profit maximization goals. On the other hand, for many sport organizations, pricing objectives may be based on achieving nonmonetary outcomes. For example, small college athletic programs may place greater emphasis on building academic community support and involvement. For this reason, students, faculty, and staff are charged zero or a nominal admission fee to athletic events. This encourages more fan support and a more stimulating atmosphere for student competition. Regardless of differing objectives, pricing should be based on a market orientation that allows consumers greater flexibility in choosing the time and specific seat location, as well as the price they are willing to pay to attend a sporting event.

Differential Pricing

At the core of a consumer-oriented approach is the concept of differential pricing. Sometimes referred to as dynamic or variable pricing, the practice involves charging different prices for essentially the same product or service, even though there is no directly corresponding difference in the cost of producing the service. A handful of major league teams, and a growing number of golf courses and ski resorts, have experimented with the demand-based pricing scheme in recent years. Differential pricing, however, has been standard practice in the airline and hotel industries for decades.

When sport organizations have instituted differential pricing programs, the method of selling different seats (or greens fees at golf courses or lift tickets at ski resorts) at different prices has been based on one of two variables:

1) *Time.* Prices vary by different times of day, week, or season of the year, or first-round versus championship game or match.

2) *Place.* Prices vary by different seating locations.

A growing number of teams sell tickets at different prices depending on the attractiveness of the opponent and the dates of play. The Colorado Rockies charge fans extra when the team plays the New York Yankees. The San Francisco Giants have added a surcharge for weekend games. The St. Louis Cardinals require fans to pay more for tickets in the summer months. In all three cases, teams used the pricing tactic to achieve a fuller and/or more balanced use of venue capacity. The intent is to encourage use of services at off-peak times and to maximize revenue production during peak demand times.

The St. Louis Cardinals reduced ticket prices in order to raise attendance during the traditionally slower months of the seven-month long major-league baseball season. According to a club spokesperson, "We reduced prices for those times of year when we'd had trouble. Basically, we're talking about April, May, and September, when kids are in school. It's a practice we're going to continue, because there's a definite benefit to having people in the ballpark even at a lower price"(p. 50).[15] On the other hand, the Cardinals compensate for the discounted portion of the season by raising every ticket $1 for games played in the high-demand period between May 31 and September 2, which was projected to net the team $750,000 in increased revenues annually.[16]

The San Francisco Giants charge $1 to $5 more for weekend games (Friday evening to Sunday afternoon). This decision produced the team an additional $1 million in net revenue.[16] According to one baseball executive, "Weekend summer games and certain matchups generate a different level of demand than other games. It only makes sense to price them differently" (p. 40).[17]

Although a growing number of teams have begun to apply differential pricing, according to one analyst, the jury is still out as to whether adjusting ticket prices by demand will work in every circumstance. As the accompanying vignette ("New Game To Play: Variable Pricing") implies, sport managers should carefully consider a number of factors (e.g., the reaction of core fans) before adopting variable pricing.

New Game to Play: Variable Pricing

The Colorado Rockies charge fans extra when the team plays the New York Yankees. The San Francisco Giants added a surcharge for weekend games. The St. Louis Cardinals fans pay more for tickets in the summer months.

And the Boston Bruins said this week that they'll set a maximum price for each seat, then adjust downward as demand reveals fans' preferences for opponents or days of the week.

Sports has started experimenting—somewhat tentatively—with variable pricing. Only a handful of teams are doing it, but the concept has generated a lot of buzz as teams look for ways to increase revenue and fill empty seats.

Variable pricing hasn't arrived in the Dallas-Fort Worth market, but local teams are keeping an eye on the trend. "You can never say never in this business," said Jeff Overton, executive vice-president for marketing for the Texas Rangers and Dallas Stars.

The Dallas Cowboys charge the same price for all regular-season games. So do the Mavericks, and team owner Mark Cuban says he's not yet sold on variable pricing. "I want to see how it goes for others," he said.

For airlines, hotels and, movie theaters, it's standard practice to adjust prices to reflect variations in demand—for time, day, destination, or other factors.

Most sports teams charge the same for all regular-season games, even though fans clearly have preferences for opponent, day of the week, or time of the year. "There are some events that you know are going to be sellouts, no matter what, and others that aren't," said University of San Francisco economist Dan Rascher, a sports business expert. "So why wouldn't you be charging premium prices for those top-demand games, the way it works in other businesses."

More Revenue

Higher prices will mean more revenue as long as teams don't lose customers. If the Giants continue to sell out weekend games, they will reap an additional $1 million from the variable pricing scheme.

The Cardinals, Giants, and Bruins are trying variable pricing for the first time this year, but the Rockies started it three years ago. The team wanted to increase revenue without giving season-ticket holders sticker shock.

This year, the Rockies selected nine games for premium pricing—Opening Day, three dates with the Yankees and Cleveland Indians, and two games around the Fourth of July. Aside from the cheap seats, ticket prices range from $17 to $43 for these games, up from $15 and $41 for the rest of the schedule.

A Rockies spokesman said fans aren't griping about variable prices, but at least one local fan doesn't like the idea. "Ticket prices are too high already," said Jimmy Williams, an Irving, TX, resident who attended a Rangers game at the Ballpark in Arlington last week.

Overton doubts variable pricing will catch on everywhere. "You have to start with a core product that is in high demand for it to work," he said. That's not the case at the Ballpark this year, where Rangers' attendance is running more that 20 percent behind last year, and sales are lagging, even for the top dates. Tickets are still available for the July 4 game, which usually sells out early.

Fair Play

The Dallas Stars are riding a long string of sellouts, which might make variable pricing an attractive strategy. Overton says the team might look at the issue, but it's not really considering changing its present policies.

Before going to work for the Rangers and Stars in November, Overton was marketing director for the Cleveland Indians. Once the team moved into Jacobs Field in 1994, it sold out every game for more than five seasons. The Indians could have charged more for games against attractive oppo-

Flexible Ticket Packaging

Until recently, most teams offered minimal flexibility to fans hoping to buy season tickets. A majority of teams offered potential customers only one or two options. College and pro football teams, with their relatively small inventory of
games (5 to 8 home games per season), typically offered only a full-season ticket
alternative (all home games). Basketball, hockey, and baseball, with their much
more extensive game inventory, historically provide fans with the option of either
buying a full-season or a half-season package (21 to 23 games for hockey and basketball and 41 to 43 dates for baseball). Under these traditional arrangements,
consumers were expected to make both a substantial monetary and time commitment for the privilege of reserving a more desirable seat location.

As ticket prices have increased over the past decade, the cost of purchasing full-
season ticket packages to major league sporting events has required an ever-in-
creasing financial commitment. The average cost of a full-season, 43-game (41
regular season, plus 2 preseason) ticket plan for NHL and NBA teams exceeded
$2,000 for the 2002-03 season. Given that relatively few households have the fi-
nancial capacity to make such a significant investment—according to the 2000
U.S. Census, only 12% of American households earned more than $100,000 an-
nually—teams and leagues have had to extend more affordable ticketing options
to consumers. Full-season ticket plans have been split into partial plans to accommodate individuals and companies who either could not afford the full package or
knew they would be unable to attend a majority of games.

Mini-ticket plans. One of the early successful efforts to create more flexible and
affordable ticket plan alternatives for fans was a "mini-plan" program implemented by the Milwaukee Brewers. In 1992, the team sold a total of 6,326 (full-
season equivalent) tickets, one of the lowest totals in Major League Baseball.[18] The
Brewers had struggled for wins and fan support for many years. Their trip to the
1982 World Series was the team's only appearance in the past 40 years.

However, in 1992 the team challenged for the division title, winning 92 games,
leaving fans upbeat at the end of the season. Team officials recognized that they
were facing the most positive selling environment they had seen in years. At the

same time, they realized that in order to take full advantage of the team's growing popularity, they would need to develop a more consumer-oriented approach to selling season tickets.

Their first action was to expand their understanding of the marketplace. The Brewers added a new computer system that enabled them to collect customer data. In addition to integrating a database management system with ticketing, the team conducted market research through surveys and focus groups to learn more about its customers, where they came from, why they purchased season tickets, and what benefits they valued most.

An important finding was that considerable potential existed for increased sales by converting customers from their individual-game buying pattern to buying mini-season packages. To encourage this, the Brewers developed a "product line" of 16- and 13-game packages based on themes that market research indicated would be attractive to customers in the Milwaukee market. Among the new lines of mini packages were

- Arch-Rival Pack (16 games): featuring the Brewers' most attractive opponents

- Hot Summer Nights (16 games): consisting of games between May 28 and September 10

- Game Day Pack (16 games): packaging all the day games

- Sunday Pack (13 games): focusing on attracting families to the ball-park.

This variety of customized ticket packages proved popular. In 1993, the Brewers achieved a franchise record by selling 9,018 full-season equivalent ticket packages, an increase of 43% in just one year. Most of the incremental sales were attributable to the mini packages. The vice president for ticket sales and operations stated, "The revamped approach to our mini season plans attracted many customers, both business and individual, who would have otherwise spent little or no money with us" (p. 9).[18]

Following the Milwaukee Brewers' successful model, most major and minor league teams across all sports, as well as a growing number of collegiate athletic programs, offered partial or mini-season ticket plans. For example, the NBA Phoenix Suns, after a disappointing 9% attendance decline the previous season, aggressively offered a half-dozen brand-new themed, partial ticket plans to their fans (p. 9).[19] The Suns created several six-ticket packages that allow fans, for $100, the opportunity to "sample" NBA games throughout the season. They also offered three 10-packs that focused on weekends, Western Conference ("West Coast"), and Eastern Conference ("East Coast") games, respectively. The team created a 20-game (half-season) package and a "family night" package that included, along with four Suns game tickets, four vouchers to a local movie theater chain, four sandwiches, and four sodas. The family package was offered at $75, with a face value of $125. The Suns found corporate sponsors for several of their partial ticket programs such as the "Budweiser 6 Packs" and the "AT&T Wireless Big 10 Packs" (see Figure 9-3). Not only did the team benefit from extending

Figure 9-3 Sample of Phoenix Sun's Mini-Ticket Package

AT&T Wireless Big Ten Packs

Maximize your free time and entertainment dollar with a flexible, affordable AT&T Wireless Big Ten Suns ticket package. Packages start at just $100 and you get an extra preseason game FREE!

- Same great seats for all 10 games!
- Save up to $50 off single-game prices!
- Buy playoff tickets BEFORE they go on sale to general public!

PICK THE PACK THAT FITS YOUR STYLE:

WEST COAST

DAY	DATE	OPPONENT
Friday	Nov. 8	Portland Trailblazers
Friday	Nov. 15	Houston Rockets
Monday	Dec. 23	Seattle Sonics
Sunday	Jan. 12	Utah Jazz
Weds.	Jan 29	L.A. Lakers
Tues.	Feb. 11	L.A. Clippers
Sunday	March 9	Minnesota Timberwolves
Thurs.	March 13	Sacramento Kings
Weds.	April 9	Dallas Mavericks
Sunday	April 13	San Antonio Spurs

EAST COAST

DAY	DATE	OPPONENT
Monday	Nov. 4	Cleveland Cavaliers
Monday	Nov. 25	Milwaukee Bucks
Weds.	Nov. 27	New Jersey Nets
Monday	Dec. 16	Orlando Magic
Thurs.	Jan 2	Philadelphia 76ers
Monday	Feb. 3	Chicago Bulls
Friday	Feb. 14	New York Knicks
Sunday	Feb. 16	Boston Celtics
Monday	March 17	Toronto Raptors
Friday	March 21	Washington Wizards

WEEKEND

DAY	DATE	OPPONENT
Friday	Nov. 1	Cleveland Cavaliers
Friday	Nov. 29	San Antonio Spurs
Friday	Dec. 6	Indiana Pacers
Saturday	Dec. 21	Sacramento Kings
Friday	Dec. 27	L.A. Clippers
Saturday	Jan. 4	L.A. Lakers
Friday	Jan. 17	Dallas Mavericks
Saturday	Feb. 1	Golden State Warriors
Saturday	March 1	New Orleans Hornets
Saturday	April 5	Minnesota Timberwolves

greater branding opportunities to its corporate partners, but also the sponsors in turn helped to promote the ticket plans through company TV, radio, and print advertisements throughout the season.

Although teams would rather sell full- and half-season packages, it has become evident that many fans look for more flexible and affordable ticketing options.   A senior vice-president of an NBA franchise noted, "Teams can no longer rely on a handful of traditional ticket plans as before." He stated that the future will be in "creating packages for distinct demographic groups and marketing them in a targeted way to appeal to those particular audiences" (p. 9).[20]

Money-Back Guarantees

In addition to making tickets easier to buy from both a convenience and affordability standpoint, some sport organizations have encouraged sales by reducing the potential risk fans incur in buying expensive ticket packages. Service guarantees, which are a promise to refund the purchase price to unsatisfied customers, have proven effective. Cost-conscious consumers are responsive to service guarantees that eliminate or reduce financial uncertainty.[21] The concept of service guarantees is not yet widespread in professional sports. The New Jersey Nets of the NBA provide an example of a team's use of a satisfaction guarantee tied to ticket sales. The Nets extended the offer to new corporate season-ticket buyers, promising that if the season tickets did not help ticket holders increase their company's sales, the Nets would refund the cost of tickets plus interest. According to the Nets' vice president for ticket operations, "Everybody we issued that money-back guarantee to renewed. . .The program helped the team generate $250,000 in new season ticket business" (p. 48).[21]

The University of Kansas athletic department adopted the service-guarantee concept in an attempt to induce fans to buy season tickets to KU football games. The program was targeted at "first-time" season-ticket buyers, who were offered a two-game "test drive" for the season. For $157, new buyers received tickets to the Jayhawks' six home games and, according to a personal communication between Rick Mullins and one of the authors, had an "option for a full refund if they were not satisfied after the first two games." The season-ticket promotion indicated that those who were dissatisfied or uninterested in attending the final four games would have 3 weeks—the interval between the next home game—to exercise their full money-back guarantee. Even though the Jayhawks football program struggled, Rick Mullins told one of the authors that the Director of Promotions stated, "You could count on one hand the number of people who exercised the guarantee, maybe five total."

Web-Based Ticketing Sales

As discussed in chapter 1, sport organizations use the Internet to enhance ticket sales. Web-based ticketing—applying Internet technology to selling and/or reselling tickets—is a prominent component of ticket operations. Major ski areas, for example, now offer consumers opportunities to prepurchase almost all of their services online. Those interested in skiing at Mt. Bachelor Ski Resort can go to the Central Oregon resort's website, click on the "e-center" and choose from an array of options including 22 different season passes, a variety of daily lift-ticket prices, lesson programs, and even gift certificates. The interactive "Season Pass Wizard" website feature helps users select the most suitable options by guiding them through a series of questions about the specific types of experiences they seek and the prices they are willing to pay. The Breckinridge Ski Resort website allows users to prebook every aspect of their visit to the Colorado Ski Resort, including choice of lodging, lift ticket packages, and entertainment options, complete with "early booking" discounts and a variety of other "web special inducements."

The NHL Washington Capitals recently reported that "60% of our season tickets and individual tickets are sold online—not by phone, not the salesmen, not

TicketMaster. . ." (p. 2).[23] In the early days of this technology, those buying tickets online were required to physically claim their reserved seats at a stadium or arena's will-call window. As more fans purchased tickets online, they found themselves waiting in long lines to pick up tickets. However, the advent of "print-at-home" options for ticket buyers enables them to print game tickets from their personal computers. The NBA entered into an arrangement with TicketMaster to equip 28 of its 29 arenas with bar code technology capable of reading print-at-home tickets, so NBA fans can print their own direct admission tickets online. Not only has this technology benefited consumers, but the ability of fans to bypass will-call windows also has enabled teams to reallocate staff from serving will-call clients to opening more windows for direct on-site sales.

Web-based ticketing's greatest contribution to enhancing the ticket distribution process is its ability to facilitate the resale of already-purchased tickets. The "secondary" ticketing market has long been a problem for many sport organizations. For fans unable to attend games, the available alternatives were either to sell their tickets to scalpers or to forfeit the use of the prepurchased tickets. Season-ticket holders either had to fend for themselves in the secondary market or accept the loss of expensive unused tickets. Both consumers and teams suffered. When consumers do not use their tickets, teams lose additional revenues that would have accrued from the ticket holder's expenditures on parking, food, beverage, and merchandise. As these on-site ancillary revenues typically amount to $15 per person at major sports venues, a 10 to 15% no-show rate translates into as many as 1,500 to 2,500 ticket-buying customers not attending NBA or NHL games. A no-show rate extended over 41 home games (41 x 1,500 = 61,500 no-shows) means that a team could forfeit almost $1 million in ancillary revenues over the course of the season ($15 x 61,500 = $922,500). Not only does the sport organization forfeit substantial income, but it also risks many of its season-ticket holders not renewing their season-ticket packages.

MLB, with the largest inventory of home games, has taken the lead in using web technology to alleviate the problem facing full-season ticket holders who cannot attend each of the team's 81 home games. The system was introduced by the San Francisco Giants in 2000, and now all MLB teams use the Internet to resell unused tickets of season-ticket holders through an online ticketing service. Available through either individual team websites or MLB.com, the service allows season-ticket holders both a convenient and safe outlet to sell tickets they are unable to use. Fans interested in attending games can access some of the most desirable seats in the venue by going to a website up to 48 hours before a game. The teams become ticket brokers, using their websites to match season-ticket holders unable to use their tickets to certain games with fans interested in purchasing choice seat locations.

The San Francisco Giants' "Double Play Ticket Window" allows season-ticket holders to sell their tickets online at any price above the face value of the ticket, ensuring that the ticket holder, not a scalper, is the recipient of any incremental benefit. When a ticket buyer agrees to pay the price designated by the ticket holder, the Giants process the order in which they make the tickets available to the purchaser either at the will-call window or at one of the team's many 24-hour "Automated Will Call" machines throughout PacBell Park. The team charges a

10% "convenience fee" that is added to the price of the ticket. Season-ticket holders can either have the money refunded to them at the end of the season or exchange the money for team merchandise.

All parties benefit from the web-based ticket program. The Giants not only reduced no-shows by 50% but also generated an additional half-million dollars from their 10% transaction fee.[25] Season-ticket holders are not left with a drawer full of unused tickets, and fans who may not have the time or resources to attend more than a few games a year have the ability to purchase some of the most desirable seats in the ballpark.

A number of vendors, most notably LiquidSeats and Season Tickets, now offer web-based secondary ticket programs similar to the Giants' ticket exchange. These software development companies design custom-tailored ticket resale programs that are built onto a sport organization's own branded website.

Types of Tickets

Sport organizations typically use one or more of five different types of tickets: (a) full season, (b) partial season, (c) individual game, (d) complimentary, and (e) student.

The specific circumstance of each team usually determines which ticket options are used. For example, established major and minor league professional teams are likely to offer all five options, with a priority on the sale of full and/or partial season-ticket plans. Their intent is to presell as many seats as possible prior to the start of the season to ensure greater financial stability. A brand-new team, however, without an established fan base, may find it necessary to distribute substantial numbers of complimentary tickets to introduce local residents to its team. Teams with a large inventory of games, such as MLB, may find it necessary to place greater emphasis on selling partial-season (or mini) ticket plans in order to generate greater attendance. A Division I athletic program may offer a full-season ticket option for its football team's five or six home games, while offering both full and partial ticket plans to increase demand for the 12-13 home games for its basketball team. Typically, the athletic department will designate a section of seats at both venues for the exclusive distribution of student tickets. Each of the ticketing options is discussed in greater detail below.

Full season. Season-ticket sales provide a guaranteed source of revenue before the season starts and are not dependent on variable factors such as weather, quality of a particular opponent, and team record. The money received from sales can be invested and begin earning interest. Season tickets can be distributed before the beginning of the season, and mailing tickets for 81 home MLB games at one time is less expensive than selling and distributing them for each of the 81 games individually.

Some NFL, NHL, NBA, and other sport organizations have been able to sell all their seats on a season basis. This may appear to be an ideal scenario, but there are some disadvantages, particularly for new teams. Fans who are never able to watch their team in person may lose interest. The interest of these fans may be needed to increase television and radio ratings, to buy tickets if support for the team declines, or to fill seats if the team moves to a larger facility. Also, season-ticket holders may spend less money on programs and merchandise on a per-game basis than would an occasional game attendee. Therefore, it may be advisable to sell at least 10% of the tickets on an individual basis, even in situations where a season sellout is possible.

One creative approach to this situation was used by the Columbus Chill minor league hockey team. The Chill played their games in a 5,700-seat facility. In the early 1990s, the team became popular and could easily sell all their seats on a season basis. Instead of confining its fan support to the first 5,700 to purchase season tickets, Chill management devised a strategy intended to expand its fan base. They set a limit for season-ticket packages of 2,500 seats. Another 2,500 seats were sold as part of two miniplan packages, one for 15 games and the other for 10. The organization still had 9 other games for which the 2,500 seats were available to the general public. The Chill also set up 700 floor seats for each game to be sold to the general public. This strategy was used to increase the number of fans who could come to games, without decreasing the amount of per-game ticket revenue. Rather than selling 5,700 full-season tickets, the ticketing strategy used by the Chill allowed them to maintain their consecutive sellout streak with a much larger fan base, which included 7,500 full or partial season-ticket holders and 25,000 single-game purchasers.

Season-ticket sales generally involve the sale of a particular seat in the stadium for an entire season for a one-time fee. Season tickets often are discounted compared to the individual game price. Both professional and college sport organizations focus effort on selling the best-seat season tickets first, because generally they are the most expensive. The organization will offer these premium seats to the existing holders first, then to season-ticket holders in "nonchoice" sections, and finally to new season-ticket holders. However, a ticket manager should never sell all of these tickets before the season. Some choice seats need to be kept for players' and coaches' families and special guests of the organization. Organization administrators expect ticket managers to have some choice seats available for "last-second emergencies."

At the college level, choice seats generally go to those who donate the most money to the athletic department. Donors generally are given first priority in seating, so donation club seating is an effective means for encouraging donations and increasing revenue.[26] Many fans would rather donate an additional amount of money than pay more for tickets, because donations offer tax advantages not available to ticket purchasers.

Partial season. As discussed earlier in the chapter, because most sport organizations cannot sell all their tickets on a season basis, many offer a variety of partial season-ticket options, often called miniplans, that allow fans to purchase tickets for a portion of the total season. Such plans offer a lower financial commitment to individual-game ticket holders who wish to become more active fans, but are not ready to purchase season tickets. Like season tickets, these plans are beneficial to the sport organization because they provide a source of revenue before the season and offer the efficiency of being sold and distributed at one time.

Figure 9-4 Example of Collegiate Mini-Season Ticket Plan

5 Ticket Plans to Choose From

Plan A
Full Season
All 13 games

College of Wooster
Mississippi Valley
Lamar
Tennessee State
Northern Illinois
Wisconsin-Green Bay
Western Illinois
Eastern Illinois
Youngstown State
Wright State
Valparaiso
Illinois-Chicago
Cleveland State

$78

Plan B
Conference Special
8 Conference Games

Northern Illinois
Wisconsin-Green Bay
Western Illinois
Eastern Illinois
Wright State
Valparaiso
Illinois-Chicago
Cleveland State

$48

Plan C
Saturday Night Special
All Saturday Games

Mississippi Valley
Lamar
Northern Illinois
Western Illinois
Wright State
Valparaiso

$36

Plan D
Faculty/Staff
(with Faculty I.D.)
Limit 2 Season Tickets

College of Wooster
Mississippi Valley
Lamar
Tennessee State
Northern Illinois
Wisconsin-Green Bay
Western Illinois
Eastern Illinois
Youngstown State
Wright State
Valparaiso
Illinois-Chicago
Cleveland State

$36

Plan E
Family Plan
Children 18 Years and
Under Get Free Ticket

College of Wooster
Mississippi Valley
Lamar
Tennessee State
Northern Illinois
Wisconsin-Green Bay
Western Illinois
Eastern Illinois
Youngstown State
Wright State
Valparaiso
Illinois-Chicago
Cleveland State

$156

Miniplans require tickets to be purchased for a specific number of games. One type of plan specifies exactly which games are being offered. Generally, when these "set" plans are being used, the organization will present a few different options from which the fan may choose. For example, the University of Akron offered two miniplan packages in addition to various season-ticket plans (see Figure 9-4). Plan B featured all the conference games, whereas Plan C included all Saturday games. A second type of miniplan is flexible and allows the fan to list which games he or she wishes to attend. Although it is better for the customer, this type of plan will be far more difficult for the ticket office and will not help to sell the less popular games. Also, flexible plans make it virtually impossible to guarantee the fan the same seat for every game.

A third plan involves a combination of a number of specified games and a number of games that are chosen by the fans. For example, an eight-game miniplan may specify four games and allow fans to choose the other four games. The fourth type of miniplan involves the sale of ticket books that include coupons that can be used for any games the fan chooses throughout the year. Ticket books are best suited for situations where sellouts are rare. The coupons may allow direct admittance to the sport facility or may have to be exchanged for a ticket.

Complimentary. Complimentary tickets (also known as "comps") are those given to individuals or groups at no cost. Most commonly, they are offered to VIPs (e.g., donors, key clients, politicians) with the goal of reaping future benefits. A number of comps are set aside to accommodate friends and/or family of players and coaches. Sometimes, complimentary tickets are distributed in large numbers by teams hoping to attract larger crowds. The team hopes the "free" experience will be so positive that fans will want to return as paying customers. However, careful consideration should be given to the distribution of complimentary tickets. As discussed previously in the Psychology of Pricing section, consumers often make a connection between price and the quality of the product or service. Teams that "give their product away" may be devaluing customers' perceptions of its worth. In the future, it may be difficult for a team to induce customers to pay fair value for a ticket they once received at no cost.

Complimentary tickets must be accounted for carefully. The documentation for these tickets will be audited. Because of strict NCAA rules regarding complimentary tickets, documentation is especially important at the college level. Schools have been penalized and placed on probation because of the improper use of complimentary tickets.

Student. Colleges and universities generally allocate seats for students. These tickets are usually discounted, but some larger schools with popular athletic teams require students to pay full price for tickets.   Schools that allocate student tickets may require students to pick up tickets before a game to control crowd size and to allow the athletic department to sell unclaimed student tickets. Many athletic departments receive money from student fees, and this is considered to be full or partial payment for the student tickets. Most schools require that students show their student ID when being admitted to prevent them from selling these tickets to scalpers.

Preseason Sales

The ticket sales campaign typically begins three months before the season. The ticket office is likely to need three months to ensure that orders are recorded, seats are assigned, all tickets are printed (if done by the office), and tickets are mailed at least two weeks before the season. However, at major sport organizations, ticket sales have become a year-round effort with preseason sales beginning soon after the prior season is completed. Sport organizations should try to take advantage of increases in fan enthusiasm. If a team completes an unusually successful season, the organization may begin selling tickets as soon as the season is completed. The signing of a superstar player or the hiring of a new coach also may lead to increases in optimism and sales. It would be a mistake to ignore such opportunities and wait until three months before the season to begin ticket sales.

Before the campaign begins, the ticket office needs to be prepared. First, all brochures should be ordered and received for the direct mail campaign. Second, the ticket stock or printed tickets should be ordered and received. Ticket office employees need to remember that state institutions must go through a bidding process before ordering these materials, which will take additional time. Third, open seats should be identified so that ticket office personnel can be knowledge-able when talking to potential ticket holders. Fourth, a schedule needs to be clearly outlined, including starting dates for the sale of each type of ticket (season, miniplans, individual games, etc.), deadlines for renewal, date on which final seat assignments will be made, and deadline for mailing tickets to fans.

The seat-assignments procedure is important to the ticket purchaser. Seat assignments may be based on a variety of criteria, including (a) longevity, (b) date the order was received, and (c) donation level. Some colleges use complex point systems that base seat assignments on a combination of the size of donations and the number of years of giving (See the Point System section in chapter 16 for more information about how some athletic ticket offices assign preferred seat locations on the basis of a point system). Although the method used may vary among teams, a clearly defined system for assignment should be documented and followed. Season-ticket holders want to be assured they are treated fairly and a rational system for assignment has been established.

Methods of Selling

Ticket offices can use a combination of methods to sell tickets. This section will describe a few of the most common: (a) direct mail, (b) follow-up phone calls, (c) telemarketing, (d) direct sales, (e) outlets, and (f) e-ticketing. All of these methods are most effective when combined with a targeted advertising campaign.

Many sport organizations use direct mail campaigns to sell tickets. Brochures are sent to current and past season-ticket holders presenting the various options available. Ticket office personnel add potential customer names to the database so that anyone who orders tickets will receive a brochure the following year. The ticket office identifies the team's trading radius and the groups it is targeting when determining to whom brochures will be mailed, because general mailings that are not targeted are costly and inefficient.

Sport organizations can use follow-up phone calls after the mailing. They call all season-ticket holders from the previous year who have not responded to the brochure solicitation after a reasonable period of time. These calls can be used to encourage renewals and to identify which seats will be open. In addition, the phone calls provide valuable customer feedback. If staff resources are available, the organization calls others who received the mailing. Colleges have access to an inexpensive source of labor in work-study students, and some professional organizations have used interns and volunteer fan groups to make these calls.

Telemarketing has been used by many sports organizations to encourage purchases by people who were not contacted during the direct mail campaign. Again, many organizations have inexpensive sources of labor that allow telemarketing campaigns to be cost-effective. However, the public's increasing distaste for such campaigns, the growing number of states with "no call" laws, and the use of answering machines to screen phone calls have decreased the effectiveness of telemarketing. Such campaigns will be less successful if the organization does not determine target groups in advance. For example, the Los Angeles Clippers found they achieved more success in telemarketing by targeting mostly business executives, who are likely to be able to afford season tickets.[27]

To compensate for the decreasing effectiveness of telemarketing, some organizations use aggressive direct sales campaigns. The Oakland A's employ a force of full-time, commissioned salespeople who "knock on doors in commercial buildings, industrial parks, and even dentists' offices" (p. El).[27] They work on straight commission, 10% of sales; thus, the campaign costs to the organization are minimal. The A's management believes "that it is easier to hang up a phone or toss a brochure in a wastebasket" than it is to get rid of a member of their sales force (p. El).[27]

Ticket outlets such as TicketMaster are used by many sport organizations to sell tickets. These outlets are convenient for the consumer. They have multiple locations and are open longer hours than the typical sport organization ticket office. The work by the outlets also decreases the amount of work for the ticket office and some of the costs of operation.[28] Finally, some of the outlets pay the sport organizations for the rights to sell their tickets. This provides the sport organization with an additional source of guaranteed revenue.

TicketMaster and similar ticket-distribution companies typically charge the fan and the sport organization various service fees. The fee paid by the organization is usually a small percentage of the ticket price, and the service fee paid by the fan is generally a few dollars per ticket. There is concern the service fees may decrease sales by raising the price of tickets beyond the fan's range. Moreover, if fans are willing to pay the additional amount for the tickets, it is possible that the increase could have been kept by the sport organization if it had sold the tickets. There is concern among some sport organizations that they lose control over customer service when they contract out the sale of their tickets to the outlets. Each sport organization should weigh the advantages and disadvantages when determining whether using ticket outlets is appropriate.

As discussed earlier in the chapter, the Internet offers sport organizations many advantages, and it is likely that in the future, most tickets will be sold on the Net.[29] Ordering online is more convenient and has a number of other customer service advantages, such as allowing fans to see a map of all seats in the facility and to pick the best seat for themselves. However, not all fans feel comfortable ordering online. Fears about the security of online orders exist, and sport organizations have to find a way to overcome this hesitation. Possibilities include providing a discount for the first online order, holding a sweepstakes for those who order online, and offering tickets online before they are available at the box office outlets.[30] Once fans order online once or twice, their fear of placing orders on the Internet will generally decrease, and the convenience of ordering online may encourage their repeated use.

A number of incentives can be used to encourage purchases. One of the most popular incentives is a tax deduction. Businesses can deduct 50% of the price of the tickets they purchase as a business expense. Individuals and businesses can also deduct 80% of a donation to the alumni association or athletic department that is related to the purchase of college tickets. The ticket office needs to be careful, however, to separate the cost of the tickets from the donation package. Payment for tickets is not a charitable donation, and deducting it as such is a violation of IRS regulations.

Some organizations guarantee that season-ticket holders can renew the same seat location for the rest of their lives. Even though a "seats-for-life" program can be effective in encouraging sales, the disadvantage is that once the tickets are promised to the holder for life, it inhibits the organization's future flexibility and revenue-generating potential.

In-Season Sales

The ticket sales campaign does not end with the mailing of season tickets and the beginning of the season. After the season starts, the ticket office knows how many tickets are available on an individual-game basis, and its personnel have a number of means available to try to sell the remaining seats. An advertising campaign can be used to encourage individual game sales. Similar to direct mail and telemarketing, the advertising campaign will be more successful if it is targeted. In addition to focusing on the general excitement of the game experience, advertising campaigns should attempt to promote aspects of individual games that may be unique, such as a star player on the opposing team, a player going for a record, or the impact of the game on the playoff race. In addition to general advertising, other methods for increasing sales and filling seats are (a) group sales, (b) consignment, (c) discounts, (d) complimentary admission, and (e) giveaways.

Group sales. Sport organizations that have excess capacity may offer group rates that allow the ticket office to sell a large number of tickets at one time and help to fill empty sections of the stands. Often, a group sales department actively solicits groups and may offer packages that include transportation and lodging. Sometimes these groups are sold seats in an empty and poorly located section, but this strategy is likely to hurt repeat business and decrease group sales over the long term.

Consignment. Tickets may be consigned to another group or organization, which then sells them. The most common groups to which tickets are consigned are the visiting team (especially common in intercollegiate athletics) and charitable organizations. Visiting teams often request a small consignment of tickets in order to ensure tickets are conveniently available for their loyal fans and/or large donors. Charitable organizations that sell tickets for the sport organization generally receive a portion of the ticket price as a donation to their organization. There are two items to remember when consigning tickets. First, the ticket office should maintain written documentation for all consignments and require someone from the other organization to sign for the tickets and accept responsibility for them. Second, a deadline for the return of unsold tickets by the other organization should be set and should be early enough to allow the ticket office to sell the remaining tickets.

Discounts. The sport organization may decide to discount tickets for specific games, but this should not be a last-minute decision because it may decrease the perceived value of the tickets and will make the organization look desperate. As discussed earlier in the section on psychology of pricing, for those attending for the first time, the heavily discounted price may become the fan's reference price. Organizations that deeply discount tickets risk the discounted price's becoming the reference price against which subsequent price revisions are compared. Thus a "quick fix" at the gate may unwittingly erode the long-term price tolerance of potential fans.

Fans are likely to wait longer to buy tickets in the future if they know the tickets will be discounted on game day. This increases the heavy workload on game day and may decrease the amount of revenue. Further, fans who have already purchased tickets may become upset and ask for refunds. One sport organization found that a late discount significantly increased its workload (they had to process numerous refunds), and the organization actually refunded more money than it made by selling the discount tickets.

An example of an effective discount system is that used by the Cincinnati Reds. The Reds sell the top six rows of the stadium at a discount on game day, if the seats are still available. This provides the team with the opportunity to sell the tickets at regular price, but allows them to discount unsold seats on game day. Because the discount is well publicized by the organization, the fans are not surprised and do not feel cheated if they paid the full price.

Complimentary. Ticket offices may give away more complimentary tickets in order to increase attendance. The advantage of this strategy is that a larger crowd will improve the game atmosphere, and the team will generate more money from concessions and parking. Also, the tickets can be given to charitable organizations, which is good for public relations. The disadvantage is that these giveaways may decrease the perceived value of the tickets. Many struggling leagues have tried to increase attendance by giving away complimentary tickets and selling tickets at a great discount. However, as discussed earlier, there is a danger that $0 may become the consumer's reference price. For that reason, complimentary tickets are most successful when they are given to charity or advertised as a special one-time-only deal.

Giveaways. Another method used by sport organizations to increase attendance is to give away something of value to those who attend the game. Many of the giveaways are related to the team or sport, such as baseball bats, hats, T-shirts, posters of the team or a star player, and player cards. Some giveaways are unrelated to sport. For example, many MLB teams gave away Beanie Babies at selected games, resulting in a significant increase in attendance.[31] The relationship between the giveaway and the team is not critical. As long as the giveaway has some value to the potential spectators, it has potential to increase attendance. Because sport organizations typically pay little or have the giveaways donated by a sponsor, even a small increase in attendance results in a financial benefit to the organization.

The sophistication of computerization in ticket offices has increased over the past 15 years. The days of shoe boxes full of season-ticket-holder cards, large handwritten seating charts, and multicolumn spreadsheets completed by hand are long over for sport organizations. With a personal computer, even a small sport organization can purchase relatively inexpensive programs to maintain a database of ticket holders and produce necessary documentation for accounting purposes such as spreadsheets and records of sales. TicketMaster and other outlets use computers to locate the best seats, maintain a record for each seat in the facility, and print all tickets. After the athletic venue is entered into the system, selling tickets for any event at the facility is relatively easy. Point-of-sale printers can be used to print the tickets as they are sold so there are no printed but unsold tickets (these tickets are referred to as "deadwood"), and reconciling tickets to receipts is facilitated by the use of daily printouts from the computer. The system allows the ticket office worker to view a "map" of the facility showing which seats are open, which are sold, and which are on hold for a particular reason. However, it was noted earlier that reliance on outside outlets has disadvantages.

Specialized computer systems such as Paciolan and Select-A-Seat allow ticket offices to store their ticket records in a computer memory. For example, Paciolan maintains perpetual records on everyone who purchases tickets, including their ticket orders, payment history, seat assignments, and donation levels. Computer systems can be used to assign seats more rapidly and to print all tickets in the office. Generally, point-of-sale printers also are available for sales at the ticket window. Although the ticket office still needs to keep some "paper" documentation for the annual audit and for investigations of any discrepancies, most of this can be disposed of after a few years. Although these computer systems have advantages, they are not the best option for all sport organizations. The hardware and software needed to run the systems is quite expensive and beyond the means of many smaller sport organizations.

Printing

Tickets may be printed by an outside company or by the ticket office. Even when the tickets are printed internally, the ticket stock has to be ordered. Each ticket that is printed externally must be counted and checked to assure that there are no duplications. When season tickets are mailed, each seat for each game must be pulled from the stacks, double-checked, and then placed into the envelope before mailing. Every ticket for every game must be printed before the season, even though many will not be sold for some games. This system is costly and time-consuming.

The ticket office has more control when its personnel order the ticket stock and print all their own tickets. Specialized computer systems allow the organization to print complete season-ticket packages (a ticket for each game for a specific seat) with mailing labels attached. Employees then separate each season order and place it into an envelope for mailing. Internal printing also enables the ticket manager to control how many tickets are printed for each game, which will decrease the amount of deadwood. Printing tickets internally is preferable for the organizations that can afford this type of system.

Accounting Procedures for Ticket Revenue

The ticket office receives payments throughout the year and has a system to maintain accurate records of receipts, deposits, and accounts receivable. Employees record both the amount received and the reason for the receipt. When deposits are recorded, every dollar is attributed to the game or event for which it was received. Money received for outstanding accounts is attributed to the paying customer. Although deposits should be made daily, the deposit is not ready to be sent to the cashier's office or the bank until the ticket manager is sure that everything has been accurately recorded. Mistakes are easier to locate on the day of the receipt than days or weeks later. The deposit is kept in a vault until it is taken to the bank.

Many ticket offices allow, and sometimes encourage, fans to order tickets without immediate payment. The ticket office maintains accurate records and pursues payments for these outstanding accounts. Although allowing customers to order now and pay later is temporarily good for customer relations, there are disadvantages. First, some of the money will be uncollectible. Second, the ticket office may have to become a pseudocollection agency. This unpleasant task can be time-consuming. Third, relations with customers may be damaged if they view the collection calls and letters as harassment. Because of these problems, some sport organizations have instituted policies that require payment to be received before tickets are mailed or distributed. This is similar to the policy used by many retail businesses and is not difficult for customers to comply with because of the availability of credit cards. Regardless of the type of approach chosen, the ticket office must have a documented policy that is clearly understood by customers and employees.

Ticket Records

The ticket office maintains records to account for every ticket. For each game, the organization knows the number of tickets that have been (a) sold at each price; (b) consigned, and the organizations that have them; and (c) distributed as complimentary with an explanation and approval for these giveaways. The ticket office maintains records that include signatures for consigned tickets and complimentary approvals. The records relating to tickets are audited at the end of the year, and the office has to account for every ticket and every dollar. If the records are accurate and detailed, the audit is easy for all parties involved. However, an audit is complex and stressful for a ticket office that is not prepared and does not have good records.

Game Day

Pregame preparations. Many preparations are done before the ticket windows are opened (usually 90 minutes before game time). First, the ticket office assigns a small "bank" to each ticket seller from the petty cash fund. Both the sellers' banks and the petty cash fund include the type of change needed for that event. For example, plenty of quarters should be available if the ticket price is $5.25.

Second, the ticket office assigns a sufficient number of tickets to each seller when preprinted tickets are going to be used. The tickets assigned to a seller should be easily accessed from his or her ticket-selling location. If there are ticket printers at the seller's station, plenty of ticket stock should be available. After counting assigned tickets and money, each seller signs an assignment sheet to acknowledge responsibility for both. Tickets also are assigned to the ticket manager so that he or she has them available for sellers if they sell their allotment.

Figure 9-5a Men's Basketball Game, Toledo vs. Topeka
March 4, 2003 at 7:30 PM

Part 1: Pregame Ticket Reconciliation

	Paciolan 11,500	TicketMaster 500	Student 3,000
Season Adult	5,000		
Season Youth	500		
Miniplan	250		
Individual Game			
$10	1,300	400	
$ 8	700	100	
$ 6	250		
Complimentary	1,500		
Visiting Team	200		
Student			2,000
Sellers:			
#1	300		150
#2	300		150
#3	300		150
#4	300		150
#5	300		200
Ticket Manager	200		125
Control	100		75
	11,500	500	3,000

Part 2: Deadwood (Seller Checkout)

Control	100		75
Seller #1	200		50
Seller #2	0		25
Seller #3	150		25
Seller #4	200		50
Seller #5	250		50
Ticket Manager	100		25
	1,000	0	300

Note: The ticket manager assigned 100 more Paciolan tickets to Seller #2 and 100 more Student tickets to Seller #1.

Third, a ticket office employee completes a pregame reconciliation to account for all tickets printed and pregame receipts (see Part 1 of Figure 9-5a and Part 1 of 9-5b). This reconciliation can be done early in the morning, or the night before, so the employee has time to investigate any discrepancies before the day becomes hectic.

The employee should start with Part 1 of Figure 9-5a. The amounts at the top of each column are equal to the number of tickets printed in each category. The

Figure 9-5b Mens' Basketball Game, Toledo vs. Topeka
March 4, 2003 at 7:30 PM

Part 1: Pregame Sales

	Tickets	Receipts
Season Adult ($8)	5,000	$ 40,000
Season Youth ($6)	500	3,000
Miniplan ($8)	250	2,000
Individual Game (TicketMaster)		
$10	400	4,000
$ 8	100	800
Individual Game (Paciolan)		
$10	1,300	13,000
$ 8	700	5,600
$ 6	250	1,500
Student	2,000	4,000
	10,500	$ 73,900
Visiting Team Sales ($10)	200	2,000
Total Pregame Sales	10,700	$ 75,900

Part 2: Game Day Sales (Seller Checkout)

	$10	$8	$6	Student	Total Receipts
Seller #1	50	20	30	200	$1,240
Seller #2	300	50	50	125	3,950
Seller #3	100	50	20	125	1,610
Seller #$	20	50	30	100	980
Seller #5	25	0	25	150	700
	495	150	155	700	$8,480

Pregame Sales	$ 75,900
Game Day Sales	8,480
Total Sales	$ 84,380

numbers for season tickets, miniplan tickets, individual-game tickets, complimentary tickets, visiting team tickets, and student tickets are available from a computer printout or daily sales log totals. The totals for each seller and the ticket manager are on the assignment sheets. The control tickets are generally assorted singles that probably will not be sold. If the total of each column is equal to the top (number of tickets printed), this part is complete. If these two figures are not equal, ticket office personnel re-count tickets assigned and control and recheck their logs or printouts to find the discrepancies.

After this section is complete, the employee completes Part 1 of Figure 9-5b. The number of tickets sold in each category is available in Part 1 of Figure 9-5a. These totals are then multiplied by their respective prices to determine the amount received. The total receipts should equal the ticket office records of the total game deposits plus the accounts receivable for that game. If this is not true, further investigation is needed. The pregame reconciliation will assure that tickets and receipts are balanced at that point, and problems with the postgame reconciliation can be attributed to a mistake made during game day.

During game. Although game day is invariably difficult for the ticket office, there are strategies to help the operation to run more smoothly. First, the organization should hire a sufficient number of experienced ticket sellers. Although a cheaper source of labor may be available (i.e., students), experienced sellers are generally quicker, more professional, and less likely to make mistakes. Although most fans will arrive close to game time, long lines and unhappy fans can be avoided if extra sellers are hired.

Second, the ticket office should have a clearly identified window(s) at which fans can pick up prepaid tickets, complimentary tickets, or tickets being held for someone (this is referred to as the will-call window). The ticket office should have enough workers to distribute these tickets quickly. Teams may separate the will-calls alphabetically and hire more workers to decrease the length of the lines. Some organizations require advance payment, so that time-consuming cash transactions are avoided at the will-call window. The ticket office should have a separate players' and coaches' will-call area so these special guests do not have to wait in long lines. Also, the NCAA rules regarding players' complimentary tickets require that an established procedure be followed that is different from the normal will-call policy. Third, the organization should have as many employees as possible without preassigned responsibilities to deal with situations that may arise. Even the best-prepared organization will have to cope with last-second problems.

Postgame. The ticket office's job is not done when the ticket sales are finished. The office checks the ticket sales and receipts for each seller to make sure his or her records are accurate. Proving a mistake is difficult after the seller has signed out. The sales figures for each seller are recorded on Part 2 of Figure 9-5b. The total receipts (in this case, $8,480) should equal the money received from the sellers minus the bank they received before the game. The number of unsold tickets, or deadwood, is recorded in Part 2 of Figure 9-5a. The total deadwood should equal the number of printed tickets left after the game (these tickets must be kept for auditing purposes).

Sometime before the game is completed, the ticket office gives an attendance figure to the media. Contrary to popular belief, this number is not generally arrived at "scientifically." In fact, teams and leagues report attendance figures in a number of different ways, ranging from (a) total tickets distributed (including both sold and complimentary), (b) turnstile count (sometimes referred to as the *drop count*), or (c) an estimate based on what the crowd size looks like ("eyeball count"). Using the number of tickets distributed to represent attendance often exaggerates the actual count because it fails to account for the number of no-shows, or individuals who, for whatever reasons, do not use their tickets.

Figure 9-6 Postgame Reconciliation, Men's Basketball Game
Toledo vs. Topeka, March 4, 2003 at 7:30 PM

	Total	Paciolan	TicketMaster	Student
Purchased Tickets	12,200	9,000	500	2,700
Complimentary	1,500	1,500	0	0
Deadwood	1,300	1,000	0	300
	15,000	11,500	500	3,000

	Tickets	Receipts
Season Adult ($8)	5,000	$ 40,000
Season Youth ($6)	500	3,000
Miniplan ($8)	250	2,000
Individual Game (TicketMaster)		
$10	400	4,000
$ 8	100	800
Individual Game (Paciolan)		
$10	1,995	19,950
$ 8	850	6,800
$ 6	405	2,430
Student ($2)	2,700	5,400
Total Sales	12,200	$ 84,340
Complimentary	1,500	
Total Tickets Distributed	13,700	
Turnstile Count (attached)	12,000	
Attendance to Press	12,500	

Weather: 45, Rain

Score: Topeka 88, Toledo 83

Comments: Bad weather, both team undefeated and nationally ranked, many students came to buy tickets the morning of the game, west ticket window #2 was very busy

Signature: _____

The office does a postgame reconciliation (see Figure 9-6), which is easy if the pregame reconciliation and seller checkouts have been done accurately. The middle section is completed by adding the pregame sales figures in Figure 9-5b (Part 1) with the game sales in Figure 9-5b (Part 2). The total is then compared with total receipts at the bottom of Figure 9-5b to ensure that all figures in Figure 9-6 are accurate. The complimentary-tickets total (from Figure 9-5a) is added to total sales to determine the total tickets distributed. In this case, this amount is used with the turnstile count to determine the attendance to the press. The last check is at the top of Figure 9-6. All the figures are available in Figure 9-6 or Figure 9-5a, except the total for Paciolan-purchased tickets. This amount is computed using the middle section by adding all Paciolan tickets sold.

The final game report includes the pre- and postgame reconciliations and information, such as turnstile counts, attendance to the press, weather, team records, and comments that will make this report more useful to the ticket office in future years. Reports from previous years can help determine the number of tickets to print and sellers to hire. The report is placed in a file that includes all documentation related to the game (signed consignment sheets, complimentary approval forms, etc.). Using the information in the game file, the ticket office can answer any questions an auditor may have regarding the tickets printed and the game receipts.

Summary

Consumers in the United States spend almost $12 billion a year buying tickets to sporting events. For many sport organizations, ticket sales are a key source of revenue; the NBA and NHL depend on gate receipts as their single greatest source of income. Admission charges and fees are the lifeblood of a range of other sport organizations. In collegiate sport, ticket sales are a vital source of revenue, comprising almost 30% of the total income generated by Division IA athletic departments.

The economic recession of the early 2000s contributed to a widespread decline in attendance and a corresponding decrease in gate receipts at many sport organizations. Erosion in ticket sales was aggravated by a sharp rise in the cost of attending many sporting events. Ticket prices for major professional league and collegiate football and basketball games more than doubled over the past decade.

Determining the cost of tickets to fall within fans' price tolerance is key to maintaining attendance. The prevailing approach has been to raise prices incrementally by an arbitrary percentage or flat rate. Historically, pricing decisions have been based on either the revenue needs of the organization or on management's perception of what the market will bear. Confronted with increased competition from other entertainment providers for consumers' discretionary dollars, faced with a "soft" economy and widespread attendance declines, sport organizations must adopt more price-sensitive approaches to setting admission and service prices.

Sport managers need an understanding of key psychological concepts of pricing such as reference price and price tolerance zones. Application of these concepts is likely to be important in increasing fans' willingness to pay.

A number of teams have adopted differential or variable pricing strategies, whereby different prices are charged for essentially the same product (attending a game) or service (using a ski lift). Prices are raised or lowered based on time of day or season and/or by seat location to either increase demand at off-peak times or to maximize revenue during peak-use times. Flexible ticket packaging or the use of mini-ticket plans has proven effective in stimulating demand by providing more flexible and affordable options. Although money-back guarantees have been used sparingly by sport organizations, evidence suggests that a promise to refund the purchase price (e.g., season-ticket package, season pass) to customers who are not satisfied can encourage sales.

Internet ticketing has become a prominent vehicle for the sale and resale of tickets to sporting events. The Internet's greatest contribution to the ticket distribution process may be its ability to facilitate the resale or exchange of prepurchased tickets. Organizations have created team websites with "secondary" ticket programs where season-ticket holders can sell tickets to games they are unable to attend. Fans are not left with expensive, unused tickets at the end of the season and are inclined to renew their season-ticket packages.

Effective ticket-sales offices share sound fundamentals. First, they are proactive, not reactive. Extensive preparation can lessen the number and severity of last-minute problems. Second, they maintain accurate and complete records, needed for the annual audit and for investigation of any discrepancies. Third, they are focused on customer service, crucial to building a positive image of the organization and sustaining a high level of repeat sales.

References

1. Dollars in sports: $194.6 spent in 2001. (2002, March 11-17). *SportsBusiness Journal*, 1, 25-29.
2. Pajak, M. (1990, March). Every fly ball is an adventure. *Athletic Business*, 26-28.
3. Johnson, A. T. (1993). *Minor league baseball and local economic development.* Urbana, IL: University of Illinois Press.
4. U-M athletics announce football ticket price increases. (2001, Winter). *Michigan Today Online.* Retrieved from http://www.umich.edu/newsinfo/MIT/html
5. Markiewicz, D. (2002, July 14). U-M upbeat despite more financial woes. *Detroit Free Press.*
6. Howard, D.R., & Burton, R. (2002). Sports marketing in a recession: It's a brand new game. *International Journal of Sport Marketing & Sponsorship, f(1), 23-40.*
7. Zeithaml, V., Parsuraman, A., & Berry, L. (1985). Problems and strategies in services marketing. *Journal of Marketing, 49*(1), 33-46.
8. Ross, E. (1984). Making money with proactive pricing. *Harvard Business Review, 84*(6), 145-155.
9. Beck, H. (2001, June). Laker owner says ticket prices must stop rising. *LA Daily News*, 8-9.
10. Fulks, D. (2000). *Revenues and expenses of Division I/II athletic programs – 1999.* Indianapolis, IN: National Collegiate Athletic Association.
11. Quirk, J., & Fort, R.D. (1992). *Pay dirt: The business of professional team sports.* Princeton, NJ: Princeton University Press.
12. TMR's fan cost index for MLB, NBA, NFL, NHL. (2002). *Team Marketing Report.* Retrieved from http://www.teammarketing.com/fci/cfm
13. Crompton, J., & Lamb, C. (1986). *Marketing government and social services.* New York: John Wiley & Sons.
14. Monroe, K. (1971, November). Measuring price thresholds and latitude of acceptance. *Journal of Marketing Research*, 460-464.
15. McCarville, R., Crompton, J.L., & Sell, J. (1993). The influence of outcome messages on references prices. *Leisure Sciences, 15*(2), 115-130.
16. Cameron, S. (2002. March 4-10). Bruins set prices hourly. *SportsBusiness Journal*, 1, 50.
17. Rovell, D. (2002, June 21). Sports fans feel pinch in seat (prices). *ESPN.com.* Retrieved from http://www.espn.go.com/sportsbusiness/s/2002/0621/1397693.html

18. King, B. (2002, April 1-7). Baseball tires variable pricing. *SportsBusiness Journal*, 1, 4.

19. Eisenberg, J. (1993, October). Small-market success: How the Milwaukee Brewers sold 43% more season tickets. *Team Marketing Report*, 9, 11.

20. Liberman, N. (2002, September 2-8). Suns try to rebound at gate with fistful of ticket pans. *SportsBusiness Journal*, 9.

21. Burton, R., & Howard, D.R. (2000). Recovery strategies for sports marketers. *Marketing Management, 9*(1), 42-50.

23. Web sales. (2002, January 21). *Sports Business Daily*. Retrieved from http://www.sportsbusinessdaily.com/tdi

24. On the rebound. (2001, July 9). *Team Marketing Report*, 9.

25. Dickey, G. (2000, June14). Giants new ticket plan a winner [Electronic version]. *San Francisco Chronicle*. Retrieved from http://www.sfgate.~cm/cgbin/artic~e.cgi?fi~=/chr~nic~e/archive/2~~~/~4/SP96~27DTL

26. Hall, J.S., & Mahony, D. F. (1997). Factors affecting methods used by annual giving programs: A qualitative study of NCAA Division I athletic departments. *Sport Marketing Quarterly, 6*(3), 21-30.

27. Mulligan, T.S. (1992, July 2). Sports teams pitch hard to generate ticket sales. *Los Angeles Times*, E1.

28. Miller, L., & Fielding, L. (1997). Ticket distribution agencies and professional sport franchises: The successful partnership. *Sport Marketing Quarterly, 6*(1), 47-60.

29. Swift, E.M. (2000, May 15). Hey fans—sit on it! *Sports Illustrated, 93*, 70-85.

30. Migala, D. (2000, June 5-11). Make online ticketing a winner with these 4 tips. *SportsBusiness Journal*, 22.

31. King, B. (1998, May 25-31). Teams add beanie babies to lineups. *SportsBusiness Journal*, 1, 49.

Photo courtesy of the Dominion Post. Photo taken by Dale Sparks.

Chapter Ten

Sale of Broadcast Rights

by Tim Ashwell and Mary A. Hums

Electronic media form the financial foundation of the sport industry. The Internet and world wide web are becoming more influential, but television remains the wealthiest medium for the sports industry, with radio following. Rights fees from television and radio broadcasts provide an important revenue source for major league and Division IA college sports teams. Publicity generated by the media is not directly measurable, but its value is undisputed.

Established, marketable sporting events mean guaranteed audiences, which translate into substantial revenues. The NFL averages $2.2 billion annually from its multinetwork contract that runs through 2005. The NBA hopes to average $756 million annually from Time-Warner's Turner Broadcasting and from Disney's ABC and ESPN for nationally broadcast and cable television games through 2008. Despite protests from the broadcast industry that increasing broadcast rights fees cannot continue indefinitely, the battle for sports programming and the escalation in rights fees show no signs of slowing. Days after losing television rights to important NASCAR events to rivals NBC, TBS, and Fox, CBS locked up the NCAA men's basketball tournament through 2013 with a $6 billion contract extension that will pay the NCAA an average of $545 million a year.[1]

Major league professional sports and a growing number of college athletic programs have become reliant on the revenue streams from networks, cable services, and local stations. Fortunately for sport managers, the broadcasting industry is as competitive as athletics. "There's an insatiable appetite among the American public for sports programming," stated a senior analyst at Paul Kagan Associates, a leading industry monitor. "There's still only one Super Bowl, one World Series, one NBA playoff, one Stanley Cup final." Premier sporting events bring audiences, revenue and prestige to broadcasting (p. 34).[2]

Table 10-1: Major Sports Television Deals

Property/Network	Package	Terms
National Football League ABC, CBS, ESPN and FOX	The nets are flipping the bill each year	$17.6B, 1998-2005
Major League Baseball Fox, ESPN	Playoffs, World Series, All-Star Game, Sat. GOTW Wednesday, Sunday telecasts	$2.5B, 2001-2006 $851M, 2000-2005
National Basketball Association ESPN, ABC, Turner (Time Warner)	Regular season, playoffs, finals	$4.6M, 2003-08
National Hockey League ABC, ESPN	Regular season, playoffs, finals	$600M, 1999-2004
NASCAR Fox (also FX, Fox Sports Net) NBC, TBS	First half of Winston Cup, Busch Series Split second half of season	$1.6B, 2001-08 $1.2B, 2001-06
NCAA Men's Basketball Tournament CBS	Every tournament game	$1.725B, 1996-2003, then $6B, 11-year ext.
NCAA Football ABC	Bowl Championship Series	$500M, through 2005
Professional Golf Association CBS, ABC, NBC, ESPN	PGA events, excluding U.S. Open, Masters, PGA championship and British Open	$107M, 2001-04

Source: Schlosser, J., & Carter, D. (2001, April 2). TV sports: A numbers game. *Broadcast & Cable*, 32-33.

The Business of Broadcasting

Television and radio broadcasters are businesspeople in search of profit. Like the medicine show operators of the Old West, broadcasters offer free entertainment to attract a crowd. Once broadcasters attract an audience, advertisers pay to make their pitch. The broadcasters' "product," then, is not programming; it is the audience that is sold to advertisers. Programming is merely a tool used to build audiences.

Because audiences are bought and sold, they must be measured. Nielsen Media Research provides audience estimates and demographics data to both television broadcasters and advertisers. Nielsen reports there are more than 105 million television households in the United States today, and Nielsen has divided the nation into 210 distinct designated market areas (DMAs). Television DMAs are not of equal size. The largest, New York, covers not only New York City but also adjacent counties in New York State, New Jersey, Connecticut, and Pennsylvania, a total of over 7.3 million households. The smallest, rural Glendive, Montana, encompasses just 3,900 homes in the northeastern corner of the state.[3] Through electronic meters, viewers' diaries and intensive surveying, Nielsen determines what people are watching. A similar market-based system is used by Arbitron to measure radio audiences.

Audience size in television is expressed most often in terms of ratings and shares. A program's *rating* represents the percentage of television households within the survey universe tuned to the program. For a network program shown in every market, then, a nationwide rating of 10 means 10% of the nation's 105.4 million households with television sets are tuned in, nearly 10.5 million households. A program's *share* represents the percentage of television households with *sets in use* tuned in to the program. As both research and common sense indicate, not every home is watching television all the time. Viewership gradually builds during the day, peaks in the evening at an average of 61.9% of the nation's television households, and then declines again. If 60 million households across the country were using televisions, the program being viewed in 10.5 million would have a 17.5 share—17.5% of the households using television. If only 30 million homes were using televisions, the program would boast a 35 share—10.5 million is 35% of 30 million.

Nielsen ratings are closely monitored in the industry and are published in many major newspapers. Ratings for sports broadcasts usually trail those of the more popular entertainment programs on television and are lower than most sports fans would suspect. They show that only marquee sports attractions approach the audience levels of leading entertainment programs, which routinely garner ratings in the teens. The Super Bowl and the Olympics are the great exception. Traditionally the most-watched telecast of the year, the NFL title game constantly draws ratings in the low to mid-40s. The Olympic Games usually average in the high teens and hold special attraction to advertisers because, unlike most sporting events, they attract a high percentage of female viewers. Most national sports broadcasts garner ratings in the single digits. Local professional and college sports events can reach double-digits for key contests, but they too usually finish well down the list of most-watched programs.

Table 10-2: TV Ratings for Major Sports Properties
From 1996-2000

League/Property	Avg. National Household Rating
National Football League	
Fox	10.8
CBS, NBC	10.1
Monday Night Football	12.7
Major League Baseball	
Fox	2.8
World Series	12.4
National Basketball Association	
NBC	4.4
TNT/TBS	1.1
National Hockey League	
Fox, ABC	1.6
ESPN	0.6
NASCAR	
Winston Cup	5.0

Source: Schlosser, J., & Carter, D. (2001, April 2). TV sports: A numbers game. *Broadcast & Cable*, 32-33.

Broadcasters and sports promoters argue the Nielsen numbers do not reveal the true size of the audience because they do not accurately count viewers at parties in private homes, in sports bars, or college residence halls. Because local teams' broadcasts draw larger audiences than out-of-town contestants, a so-so national rating may disguise a smash hit in local ratings. When, for example, Kentucky played Massachusetts in an NCAA men's basketball semifinal game, the broadcast received a 12.3 rating and 22 shares nationally. In the Boston market, however, the game drew a 23 rating and 38 share, whereas in the Cincinnati market, which includes portions of northern Kentucky, the game had a 26.2 rating and 47 share.

Ratings and shares tell only part of the story. We can determine that a program has a 10 rating and a 17.5 share—usually expressed as 10/17.5 in industry shorthand—but ratings and shares measure only households. Both advertisers and broadcasters want to know how many people are in front of those sets and, most critically, what kind of consumer those viewers may be. Are they rich or poor? Men or women? Old or young? Do they prefer to read books or ride bicycles in their free time?

Broadcasters, advertisers, and marketing research firms conduct elaborate surveys and sift through data to answer those questions in order to match the advertiser with the correct audience. Television is generally a women's medium. Nielsen studies indicate women aged 19-34 watch nearly 5 hours more television weekly than men. At any given time during the prime viewing hours of 8 to 11 p.m., when the television audience is largest, 62% of the audience is likely to be made up of women, teenagers, and children. In the morning and afternoon, the percentage of women, teens, and children exceeds 70%. In most households, women and teens decide which programs will be watched during the evening hours.[4]

Sports broadcasting offers advertisers an alternative: a predominantly male audience, one that is difficult to reach efficiently through other mass media. Although sports broadcasts often attract a smaller audience in absolute numbers than do popular prime-time entertainment shows, the demographics of the audience makes a difference. Most sporting events attract audiences dominated by adult men who, on average, are better educated and wealthier than the average television viewer or radio listener. Sports also offers a vehicle for reaching minority men, a difficult market to address through mass media. Though audience surveys ranked WTEM, the all-sports radio station in Washington, DC, 25th in total audience size among the city's stations, 80% of the station's audience was men, and 58% were men aged 25-54. The station ranked first among men aged 25-54 who had graduated from college and second among men with annual household incomes of $150,000 or more.[5] ESPN, citing Nielson survey data, claims its typical audience is well over 60% adult men. The all-sports cable network calculated that for every 1,000 households tuned in during prime time, its audience includes 850 men over age 18.[6] The Boston Celtics' local television outlet reported that 70% of the audience for the typical game was men aged 25-54.[7] For advertisers targeting a male demographic, sports can be a highly desirable media buy.

Typically, advertisers purchase audiences by the thousand. Advertisers calculate the number of *impressions*—the number of people who will see or hear their message—and compare that number with the price of the advertisement. The calculation yields the *cost per thousand,* or CPM (M = 1,000 in Roman numerals). CPM allows advertisers to compare the efficiency of different media. Depending on the time of day, the total size and demographics of the audience, advertisers on the major television networks expect to pay about $10 to $30 for every thousand viewers they reach.[4] CPM is sometimes translated into a related concept: *cost per point,* or CPP. This compares the price of an advertisement with a program's rating to determine the cost of reaching one rating point—1.5 million homes nationally—with a sponsor's message.

Marketing and sales research is both a science and an art. Broadcasters and advertisers use advanced statistical theories and sophisticated technology to crunch the numbers, but the results then must be interpreted. Advertisers seek the most efficient means of reaching their targeted audience, whereas broadcasters look for programming that attracts the kind of audiences advertisers covet. There is no such thing as a bad audience. It is simply a question of matching the right advertiser with the desired audience.

Total Return

Although the dollar amounts involving major sports broadcasts are truly mind-boggling—CBS, for example, claimed $2.3 million for a single 30-second commercial during the 2002 Super Bowl—broadcasters and sport managers must look beyond the bottom line when they calculate the worth of sports. They need to consider the *total return* they are likely to enjoy from their partnership.[8]

Teams and leagues profit from rights payments. However, there are a variety of noncash benefits accruing from television and radio exposure. Televised games play a critical role in establishing a fan base. A new franchise or professional league gains credibility if its games are on television. New fans, unfamiliar with the team, its players, or the sport, are introduced to the game and perhaps persuaded to attend future events. Television gives a team a platform for promoting upcoming contests and special events, selling team merchandise, and cultivating its public image. Many college television contracts, for example, explicitly include requirements that the broadcaster set aside time for promotional announcements extolling the college's academic and public service achievements. The NFL uses its network broadcasts to promote the league's charitable activities with United Way. The NBA promotes a similar "Stay in School" campaign.

Broadcasters, too, rely on high-profile sporting events to raise their public image. ABC used its sport programming in the 1960s to shed its image as the "Almost Broadcasting Company," a pale imitation of CBS and NBC, and become a major player in the broadcast business. The meteoric rise of the cable industry in the 1970s and the 1980s owes a great deal to ESPN, the all-sport network. ESPN's 24-hour sports coverage motivated millions of suburban viewers to sign up for cable. Skeptics said Fox would lose millions when it signed a $1.58 billion contract to broadcast NFC games, and subsequent write-offs by News Corporation, Fox's parent company, proved the critics right. The daring move, however, yielded a variety of indirect benefits to the then-fledgling network. Fox immediately became a major network in the eyes of viewers, advertisers, and television stations owners across the country. In Detroit, Jacksonville, Dallas, Atlanta, and several other key markets, established stations signed up with Fox to gain access to the games, giving the network's entire programming lineup more viewers. The games offered Fox the opportunity to promote its prime-time programs to millions of fans who had yet to find their local Fox affiliate, resulting in larger audiences and higher advertising revenue. CBS, on the other hand, lost key affiliates and viewers when it lost the NFL to Fox and was eager to recapture NFL rights when the contract came up for renewal. Broadcasters are every bit as competitive as football teams, and they will bid for high-profile sports events to gain the edge over a rival.

Sport Media Outlets

The commercial broadcasting system links audience size and revenue. The larger the audience, the higher the revenue from advertising sales. Broadcasters seek programming that will appeal to larger, more valuable audiences. Not every sports organization can hope to land a billion-dollar contract with a national television network, but every team or league can find a niche somewhere in the hierarchy of broadcasting.

National Broadcasters

Atop the pyramid are the major national television networks: ABC, CBS, NBC, and Fox. Each boasts affiliated stations that beam the network's programming into 105 million homes with television.

National basic cable service such as ESPN, Fox Sports Network, USA, and Turner outlets TBS and TNT are available in households with cable or direct satellite access. Only about four fifths of the nation's television homes subscribe to cable or satellite programming services. Therefore, ESPN and similar services are limited to an audience roughly 80% of the size of the national networks, and because cable and satellite homes receive scores of different programming services, the viewing audience is fragmented. Many choices are available to cable viewers, resulting in cable services becoming "niche broadcasters" and tailoring their programming to tightly targeted segments of the public. Sports services such as ESPN and Fox Sports are willing to devote hours to sports coverage that major networks would not consider carrying.

The basic cable services enjoy a second revenue stream denied to over-the-air broadcasters that helps offset their smaller audience numbers: subscriber fees. ESPN charges cable and satellite companies a monthly fee for each subscriber. ESPN, the most expensive basic service, averages 72¢ per subscriber per month in fees, a $60 million annual windfall that is reflected in consumer bills and provides more cash for rights fees. The advantage to receiving these earnings was evident when in 2002

> along with ABC, a sister unit of Walt Disney Co., ESPN had outbid NBC for six years of NBA games. The price tag: $2.4 billion. . . NBC, which had held the contract for the past twelve years, refused to shell out more than $1.3 billion.[9]

National radio networks still offer coast-to-coast broadcasts of major sports events, but because of television, they no longer produce the audience or the revenue they once did. Westwood One/CBS Radio Sports and ESPN Radio are the leading sports providers today. Westwood One carries NFL football, the NCAA basketball tournament, Notre Dame football, and the Olympics, whereas ESPN offers affiliates Major League Baseball and NBA broadcasts.

Regional Cable Networks

Regional cable sports networks occupy a niche in the market between the national service providers and local stations and traditionally specialize in covering sports with strong regional appeal. The regional sports network picture shifted radically in 1999 as News Corporation, the multinational parent company of Fox, assumed full control of 21 regional sports networks and launched the Fox Sports Networks. The Fox family of regional sports networks is available in more than 70 million households and combines regional coverage, the traditional strength of regional channels, with a nationwide platform for programming. Taken together, the Fox Sports Networks control local television rights of 73 major league baseball, basketball, and hockey teams as well as numerous college sports conferences. In addition, each regional network produces highlight shows and feature programs tailored to local fans. Fox also produces national highlight shows and programs shown coast to coast. The creation of Fox Sports Network marks an escalation in News Corporation's declared "ongoing effort to dominate the market in sports broadcasting."[10]

The evolution of regional sports channels demonstrates how conventional wisdom in the broadcasting industry changes over time. Many regional sports cable networks were launched in the 1970s and 1980s as premium services. Borrowing the business plan of HBO, which charges subscribers a monthly fee for programming not available on other channels, network managers bet that fans would pay about $10 a month over and above their basic cable bill to watch the local team. Many did, but many more did not. Today, most regional sports channels are included in a package of cable services available to subscribers for a flat monthly fee. By expanding the size of their potential audience, the regional sports channels realized higher advertising revenue.

Syndicators

Syndicators are independent producers who purchase the rights to events or create programs, produce the programs, and then seek to place them on stations or cable services across the country. TVS was the pioneer in the field, and it scored a major coup when it obtained national rights to the UCLA-Houston basketball game in 1968. TVS created a coast-to-coast web of affiliates that delivered a huge national audience. Creative Sports, Raycom, and other syndicators do the same today, but the growth of regional cable channels has changed the business landscape. Today, much syndicated sports programming appears on cable rather than on over-the-air television.

Syndication remains an important tool for sports producers. Whether on radio, television, or cable, a syndicator takes responsibility for producing an air-ready broadcast, then offers the complete package to the broadcaster for little or no direct cost. The programs are either sold outright to interested stations or, more frequently, bartered. In a barter arrangement, the station agrees to air the program in exchange for the right to sell a predetermined amount of local advertising time. The syndicator makes its money by selling the remaining advertising in the broadcast to national advertisers. Syndicators of some programs, especially popular entertainment shows, use a hybrid system called *cash-barter* in which a station pays a fee to air the program and also makes advertising time available to the syndicator. The size of the fee is usually determined by an auction among the stations seeking the program.

Local Television and Radio

There are 1,600 VHF and UHF television stations and nearly 13,000 AM and FM radio stations currently on the air in the United States. Each is scrambling for an audience, and many see sports as a proven audience favorite. Because local stations by definition serve limited local audiences, they cannot generate the advertising revenue to bid on national events such as the World Series or the NCAA men's basketball tournament. Local stations can and do, however, actively pursue contracts to cover individual teams and typically establish regional networks of affiliates to broaden their audience and advertising base.

In a major market, rights fees can be impressive. The New York Yankees commanded an annual local television and radio rights fee of more than $50 million before creating YES, their in-house network in hopes of generating even greater profits. In smaller markets, teams earn substantially less. As always, the size of the potential audience and competition among potential broadcasters dictates the price paid.

In smaller markets where college and minor league franchises often flourish, a team's game may generate no guaranteed rights fee at all. The team may accept a portion of the advertising revenue or help a local station meet the cost of production simply to gain the total-return benefits of having its schedule broadcast to local fans.

Marketing and Managing Broadcast Rights

Sports producers and broadcasters are partners. The relationship between a team and a radio or television station or network can survive and prosper only if both parties are satisfied they are receiving a fair return, either in immediate profit or in long-term gains such as promotions, competitive advantage, or improved public image.

Broadcast rights may be assigned in several ways, but in all cases, the sports producer and broadcaster work together, and nearly everything is negotiable. For example, a sports organization may want to reserve advertising time during a broadcast to promote upcoming games and season-ticket packages. This request reduces the broadcaster's inventory of commercial air time and limits potential profit. Therefore, the broadcaster may argue for a lower rights fee or seek advantages such as free tickets, venue signage, advertising space in the team's game program, personal appearances by players, or similar benefits.

Broadcast contracts routinely reveal tradeoffs. Rather than maximizing the amount of cash they can realize through rights fees, many sports teams instead ask for commercial time to promote themselves or their corporate sponsors, authority to determine the announcers for the game, time for a weekly coach's show, or use of the broadcaster's facilities to produce advertisements or promotional videos. Broadcasters will agree to pay more for rights to a team's game if they can freely use the team's marks (e.g., name, logo) and personnel for on-air or in-person promotions, if they can be guaranteed choice seats for clients and friends of the station, or if they can have a say in the team's scheduling to ensure the game fits in the station's broadcast lineup. In order to accommodate television, for example, many major athletic contests are scheduled to start eight minutes after the hour or half-hour. Many major college basketball and football teams willingly agree to schedule certain opponents and adjust game times in accordance to their broadcaster's wishes.

Within this partnership framework, however, sports broadcast deals are almost always arranged in one of three ways: (a) direct sales of rights from a team to a broadcaster for a guaranteed right fee, (b) in-house production of games by the team or league that then syndicates the broadcast, or (c) a cooperative or revenue-sharing agreement in which both the teams or league share the potential profit and, in some cases, the loss.

Direct Sales of Rights

If a sports producer's product is a proven commodity in the marketplace, broadcasters will be eager to bid for rights. Major professional leagues and teams and major colleges frequently choose between rival stations or networks seeking the rights to broadcast their games.

Usually, the rights go to the highest bidder, but that is not always the case. In the 1994 negotiations for NFL broadcast rights, the league jumped from CBS to Fox for the National Football Conference games when Fox topped the older network's bid. When the league assigned rights to the American Football Conference games, the NFL rejected a higher bid by CBS in favor of a lower, earlier bid from NBC, the long-time rights holder. The National Hockey League apparently blundered when it accepted a $17 million-a-year bid from SportsChannel America in 1988, turning its back on ESPN. Although ESPN offered less cash, it would have brought NHL games into four times as many homes and provided a far greater promotional boost to the league. Most experts agree the four-season hiatus with SportsChannel dealt the NHL a severe public relations setback.

Both rights holders and broadcasters consider many variables as they bargain over rights fees. Broadcasters look at production and distribution costs, but they also consider audience demographics and how the games will affect their overall broadcast schedule, and they frequently agree to carry less attractive games to gain access to key events. Traditionally, regular-season MLB games of the week attract small viewing audiences because fans follow their local franchises and show little interest in battles between out-of-town clubs. Fox agreed to baseball's demands for regular-season coverage in order to gain the rights to the All-Star Game, League Championship Series, and World Series.

On the other hand, sport organizations will sometimes leave money on the bargaining table to ensure greater exposure and broadcast services. The NCAA's original 1989 contract with CBS for men's basketball tournament telecasts required CBS to air selected games from the women's basketball tournament as well as NCAA championships in baseball, track, swimming, and a dozen other low-profile sports. CBS executives actually offered to pay the NCAA a higher rights fee if they did not have to carry the additional telecasts, but the NCAA accepted less money in order to get the additional exposure. When the tournament contract was renegotiated in 1994, the NCAA was able to sell the women's basketball tournament to ESPN as part of a separate contract. The value of the women's tournament had been increased significantly by the network exposure on CBS.

When a sport organization sells rights to a broadcaster, it should maintain as much control over the product as possible. Teams and leagues regularly demand and receive permission to veto a station's choice of announcers. Rights holders may also negotiate advertising restrictions that can benefit corporate sponsors by keeping the competition off the air. These points are, of course, negotiable and will usually require give and take with the broadcaster.

In-House Production

Despite the proliferation of outlets for televising sporting events, it is difficult for all but major sport properties to succeed in having their games or events aired regularly on network or cable outlets. In deciding to air sporting events, broadcasters consider a range of factors, including the size of the potential audience, the cost of producing the event, and the attractiveness of the event to commercial sponsors. The demand for many sporting events in terms of both audience and commercial appeal may be insufficient initially to attract a broadcast partner, particularly one eager to pay a rights fee to the sports organization to air the event and absorb all production costs.

Sport managers who hope to benefit from television exposure may be able to change the calculus by producing their own broadcast and syndicating the finished program.

World Wrestling Entertainment (WWE) is the classic example of the benefit of in-house production. Pro wrestling's popularity has ebbed and flowed. Titan Sports of Stamford, Connecticut, the parent company of WWE, arranged matches, hired announcers and technical crew, and offered finished programs to stations around the country at no cost. All the WWE demanded in return was the right to sell a portion of advertising time. Station operators who would not have considered telecasting a wrestling program if they had to produce and pay for it themselves gladly accepted the offer. Broadcasters received professionally produced programs that appealed to a younger demographic, especially teens, and any advertising revenue the station's sales corps generated was theirs to keep. The WWE used the programs as promotional platforms for upcoming pay-per-view and live shows and covered the cost of production and distribution by selling its allotment of commercial time to fast food chains, video-game manufacturers, candy makers, and others who wanted to make their pitch to a teen audience.

As the WWE surged in popularity throughout the 1990s, broadcasters began to battle for the right to carry the wrestling programs. The WWE signed a national distribution deal with the USA cable network and in 1999 struck an even better deal with Viacom networks MTV and TNN.

Baseball's New York Yankees followed the WWE's script when they created YES—Yankee Entertainment & Sports—to produce and distribute Yankee games. With the dual revenue stream of subscriber fees and advertising revenue, the Yankees hoped to double or triple their annual broadcast income and produce more than enough to offset the costs of production, promotion, and administration.

Many college sports networks are also self-produced. Brigham Young University beams coverage of BYU sports to stations throughout the mountain states on the Blue & White Network, using staff and equipment from the school's radio and television facility. West Virginia University's Mountaineer Sports Network produces games as well as coaches' shows and a weekly sports magazine in WVU's on-campus broadcast center and distributes the programs to stations around the state. The Big East Conference produced and syndicated its own regional football and basketball network with freelance talent coordinated by the league office. Ultimately, the network became so successful the league hired Creative Sports of

Charlotte to run the operation. More individual colleges and universities have turned to production companies to package radio and television broadcasts of their games.

By controlling production themselves, sport organizations maintain complete control of the broadcast and can ensure their product is presented and promoted in a positive manner. Because they do not have to bear the cost of production, many stations, especially in smaller markets, find games and related programs a means of filling airtime with impressive programming they could not otherwise afford to air. Ideally, in-house networks sell enough advertising to cover the cost of production and turn a profit. Colleges and pro teams frequently include broadcast advertising on their in-house network in sponsorship packages. At West Virginia, for example, United National Bank is a major athletic sponsor. The bank receives stadium signage, game program, team yearbook and website advertising, and sponsorship of West Virginia radio and television broadcasts for one price. Even if an in-house radio or television network operates at a loss, sport managers should consider the value of game broadcasts as an advertising and promotion vehicle.

Revenue-Sharing Cooperation Productions

As the cost of broadcast rights has risen and the inventory of sports advertising time has increased, many broadcasters have grown leery of guaranteeing large rights payments. At all levels of sports, revenue-sharing agreements have become increasingly common as a means of ensuring against losses. Under revenue-sharing agreements, sports properties split revenues generated from a broadcast with their media partner.

The NHL and the NBA were among the first to incorporate revenue sharing in their national network television contracts. The NHL received a $250 million deal with Fox and ESPN by assuring the broadcasters that league sponsors such as Anheuser-Busch and VISA would purchase television advertising as part of their sponsorship. When NBC and the NBA agreed to a 4-year, $868 million contract in 1994, the league agreed to forego guaranteed rights payments over a certain level in exchange for a share of advertising revenue. The NBA's $4.6 billion deal with AOL Time Warner and Disney took cooperation a step farther. A portion of the NBA's revenue is tied to projected income from a proposed cable television service that will be co-owned by the league and AOL Time Warner. A growing number of local radio and television sports contracts contain similar revenue-sharing provisions.

Broadcasters endorse revenue sharing because it protects them from downturns in advertising sales or the team's on-field fortunes. If a team slumps and advertising sales decline, the broadcaster is not required to pay a lump sum. Because the team benefits if advertising sales increase, broadcasters find teams are eager to become active broadcast-time sellers rather than passive partners. Revenue sharing is beneficial for teams and leagues, because by becoming financial partners in broadcasts with a stake in the program's success, they exercise more control over the production and promotion of their games. Teams also use advertising sales for game broadcasts to enhance their corporate sponsorship package.

Revenue-sharing partnerships are also becoming more common in collegiate athletics. The following section, provided by Rick Burton, Executive Director of the University of Oregon's Sports Marketing Center, describes how and why the University of Oregon Athletic Department partnered with ESPN Regional Television to manage the department's radio and television network, the Oregon Sports Network. The "OSN Story" illustrates the considerable benefits that can be realized when an athletic department *outsources* (also known as "contracting out") its broadcast sales and production functions to a private company. In just 3 years, the University of Oregon's partnership with ESPN Plus (the brand name for ESPN Regional TV) resulted in a fourfold increase in revenues from the Oregon Sports Network. Under the revenue-sharing agreement, which guarantees the athletic department a minimum of $800,000 a year, the University of Oregon receives 55% and ESPN Plus 45% of the net revenues realized from annual OSN sales. With gross revenues close to $4 million in 2003, both parties received substantial benefit, with the University of Oregon netting approximately $1,045,000 and ESPN Plus, $850,000.

The Oregon Sports Network

As shown previously in this chapter, regional cable networks emerged dramatically in the late 1990s when both Fox Sports and ESPN realized free-to-air networks (FTAs) and even all sports cable channels could not provide enough regional coverage for avid sports fans.

Most interesting to these big broadcast players was the American college sports scene where huge football- and basketball-playing conferences, notably the Big East, Big Ten, Big 12, ACC, SEC, and Pac 10, held considerable sway with alumni and devout supporters. Big schools like Michigan, Ohio State, Florida, Tennessee, Florida State, North Carolina, Duke, Miami, Syracuse, Texas, Oklahoma, Kansas, Nebraska, UCLA, Oregon, and Washington generated significant avidity among their fans.

It was easy to see that with overlapping schedules—NCAA football begins in late August and runs until the four BCS bowl games (Orange, Sugar, Rose, and Fiesta) are finished in early January, whereas men's and women's college basketball starts in early November and concludes with NCAA tournaments in March and April—the college sports window extended beyond what even the NFL, the NBA, or MLB offered.

In addition, if regional college sports such as hockey in Minnesota, wrestling in Iowa and Oklahoma, lacrosse in New York and Maryland, track and field in Oregon, and softball in California and Texas were considered, the NCAA sports calendar was stretched well into May. Given the advent of coaches' shows, recruiting news, and special events, there was consumer demand for a collegiate programming for nearly nine months of the year.

"The idea to create ESPN Regional Television and ESPN-Plus came about in 1995 and was actually formed in 1997," said Tim Roberts, regional manager of ESPN-Plus for the University of Oregon. "We realized the insatiable appetite the public had for college sports and recognized there was tremendous opportunity in delivering regionalized or local sports telecasts."

Ultimately, groups like ESPN realized they could assist universities such as Kansas or Oregon by offering a full-service approach to the Jayhawks' or Ducks' media needs. Both schools were located in states where college athletics provided pride for state residents in big cities and rural counties. Prior to the agreement, the University of Oregon was only realizing $450,000 in revenues from the sale of its broadcast rights (for the Oregon Sports Network – OSN) and netting approximately $200,000 in profits.

At one time, that might have been acceptable, but Oregon, like other athletic departments around the country, faced issues of increased costs for athletic recruitment, facilities management, and the addition of women's sports to secure compliance with Title IX. Given that reality, revenue generation from sports became increasingly important.

By selling the marketing rights to an organization such as ESPN Regional, the University of Oregon Athletic Department could better attempt to balance the goals of its student athletes within the broader academic institution. In addition, ESPN's expertise in selling advertising and marketing their broadcasts made them a natural to handle multiple aspects of Oregon's growing sports marketing needs.

Prior to the start of the 1999 season, ESPN broke the Ducks' assets down on a number of levels. With radio, the Ducks offered three high-profile properties in football, men's basketball, and women's basketball for more than 70 distinct game broadcasts.

In addition, *Duck Sports Rap*, a weekly one-hour "insider" sports talk show hosted by the "Voice of the Ducks" announcer Jerry Allen, aired for 30 consecutive weeks. This type of programming allowed Oregon to feature its coaches talking about their respective seasons from contemporary restaurants or pubs around Eugene. ESPN also designed "Mallard Minutes" as one-minute historical filler that ran daily during morning or afternoon drive time from August to March.

From a distribution standpoint, ESPN was able to take this programming and provide the Ducks with coverage that stretched into four other states (Washington, California, Idaho, and Alaska) and 20 significant Oregon markets. Most significant was the opportunity for an electronic blanketing of the entire state of Oregon. This was relevant to Oregon's athletic department because one of Oregon's in-state Pac-10 athletic rivals was Oregon State, and recruiting fans and student-athletes by both schools was intense.

Management of the radio content was just the beginning. ESPN also built a mini-network to assist the Ducks in televising football or basketball games that were not already contractually assigned to ABC Sports or Fox due to the Pac Ten's conference agreement. In that complex scenario, ABC Sports, the *primary rights holder,* received the first pick of major Pac Ten football games during the regular season. Once their pick was announced, Fox Sports Net, the *secondary rights holder*, could select two games for regular season games.

In the late '80s and early '90s, when schools such as UCLA, USC, or Washington frequently overshadowed Duck football teams, a game featuring the Ducks on TV might not have warranted regional or national visibility; but by the late 90s, under successful football coach Mike Bellotti, the Ducks were regularly ranked and frequently showcased Heisman Trophy candidate quarterbacks such as Akili Smith or Joey Harrington (both of whom were taken third in the NFL Draft following their final season). This meant almost all of the Duck games were featured on television. In addition, as the Ducks' fortunes swelled on the football field (with visits to the Rose Bowl, Cotton Bowl, and Fiesta Bowl between 1995 and 2002), more Duck fans emerged.

However, on rare occasions, the Oregon Sports Network (OSN), *the tertiary rights holder*, found itself in a position to broadcast a nonconference game or early-season matchup that had slipped under the radar.

"The benefit for ESPN in that situation was additional programming and the benefit of being involved with a Pac-10 school, which was nice given that ESPN didn't own any Pac-10 conference television rights," said Roberts. "And the benefit to the Oregon Athletic Department was increased exposure."

The concept of increasing exposure was, at one time, relatively unknown in college sports. Athletic directors frequently came into their positions having served successfully as coaches. Their background was in teaching and motivating young athletes, not in breaking down market demographics and developing brand equities. When the NCAA "Arms Race" heated up in the '90s, a time when universities increased athletic department spending dramatically, athletic directors found they needed to bring more fans and more revenue to their programs in order to successfully compete for the best student athletes and upgrade on-campus facilities such as stadiums, arenas, weight rooms, study halls, and indoor workout centers.

"Our work with schools like Oregon and Kansas meant both parties could enhance their position in the marketplace," said Roberts. "Another key value was obviously incremental revenue to the athletic department."

The regional network did not stop just with broadcasts. As ESPN's skills grew at assisting the athletic department, they also grew at creating events for television. In fact, in 2000, in the same time frame ESPN was creating events like the X Games and Winter X Games, the regional network arm also helped create or stage the UAB Classic in Birmingham, Alabama; the Pape Group Portland Jam in Portland's Rose Garden (home of the Portland Trail Blazers); the Dodge Shootout in Tampa Sun Dome (for the University of South Florida); the Las Vegas Showdown; Fort Worth Classic (for TCU); Gatorade Rock-N-Roll Shootout (at Cleveland's Gund Arena) and the Sprint Shootout in Kansas City.

As the above list of events shows, ESPN realized the value of attracting national consumer product sponsors like Sprint, Dodge, and Gatorade or regional sponsors like the Pape Group to underwrite special events that continued the win-win combination of the property (the university and its athletic department) and the media partner (i.e., ESPN Regional or Fox Sports Northwest).

Sponsorship elements could include floor decals, basketball stanchion signage, ticket mailings, pre-event promotions and hospitality, VIP event tickets, event gifts, in-game promotions and PA announcements, TV advertising, courtside signage, chair-back advertising, golf tournament invitations, radio advertising and corporate presence at press conferences or media events.

The potentially negative side of these increased marketing efforts was whether any particular university might lose sight of its need to balance the goals of student-athletes with the academic mission of the institution. In addition, where men's sports were historically developed during the entire 20th century, the advent of women's sports did not start to take place until the 1972 passage of the federal government's Title IX legislation, which mandated equal opportunities for both genders from institutions receiving federal aid. If an athletic director were to mix in the expectations of his or her multiple constituencies (the university's administration, faculty, regional media, students, alumni, boosters, and local charities), the challenge of delivering or outsourcing elements of the marketing mix was significant.

All in all, however, regional networks like ESPN Regional were able to suggest to athletic directors at Oregon, UNLV, TCU, USF, Alabama-Birmingham, and Kansas that working with a comprehensive media partner with integrated marketing capabilities could be "a great investment."

Rick Burton is the executive director of the University of Oregon's Warsaw Sports Marketing Center. Special thanks to ESPN Regional's Tim Roberts for his review of this work and assistance in providing review materials.

Barter agreements are another form of revenue sharing used most commonly by minor league teams and colleges in smaller markets. Typically, under such an arrangement, the local television or radio station that agrees to air the game pays no rights fee. Instead, the sports property offers all or a portion of the game's commercial inventory to the broadcaster, who in turn sells this air time to local or regional advertisers. For example, for a football broadcast with 50 minutes of available commercial airtime, the barter agreement might stipulate that 40 minutes (or eighty 30-second commercial units) be controlled by the broadcaster and 10 minutes (or 20 commercial units) by the sports property.

The barter-agreement approach may be well suited to a sports property trying to build fan interest in a new market. A broadcaster interested in finding new programming may be willing to take a chance on an unproven commodity, such as a new minor league baseball team, if the broadcaster does not have to make a financial commitment in advance of the first broadcast. In this circumstance, a team primarily interested in increasing its exposure to local fans may assign the entire inventory of commercials to the local broadcaster. The goal is to achieve a win-win outcome for both the broadcaster and the new team. Eventually, if the broadcasts are successful in building a substantial audience, it is likely the team could renegotiate a more favorable revenue-sharing arrangement with its media partner.

Sports Broadcasting Contracts

Each major sports property is unique in the way it handles its broadcast contracts. The following section provides an historical perspective and description of the nature and scope of each property's current broadcast agreements.

All regular and postseason television rights rest with the league, and revenues are divided equally among all franchises. This unique policy of all-for-one, one-for-all "league-think" was advocated by former commissioner Pete Rozelle and made legal by the Sports Broadcast Act of 1961, which granted an antitrust exemption to the four major professional sports for pooled broadcast contracts. Rozelle understood the broadcasting industry, knew the value of expanding the bidding pool, and involved as many outlets as possible for NFL games. He expanded the NFL's inventory by introducing *Monday Night Football* on ABC in 1970 and Sunday night cable games on ESPN and TNT.

The NFL's revenue-sharing policy allowed small-market teams such as the Green Bay Packers to survive. Individual teams retain local radio and preseason TV rights, but earnings from these local contracts are relativity insignificant, approximately $3-5 million per year, as opposed to the approximately $75 million per year each franchise receives from the sale of national rights.

Rozelle's policy of league think also helped boost the popularity of the NFL as an entity. Because the league was presented and promoted as a package and viewers saw games involving many teams over the course of a season, the NFL developed a national fan base. Although hometown loyalties remained strong, because of television, many viewers became fans of teams representing other cities.

Major League Baseball

Because baseball was a mainstay on the radio by the mid-1920s and on television by the late 1940s, local contracts were in place long before national television networks became well established in the 1950s. Major-market teams in New York and Chicago prospered under the system of "localism" and had little incentive to share the wealth with smaller market teams. When network games of the week debuted on television in the 1950s, the contract blacked out games in the major

Table 10-3 Major League Baseball 2001 Local Broadcast Revenues (in thousands)

Teams	Revenues
Anaheim	$10,927
Arizona	14,174
Atlanta	19,988
Baltimore	20,994
Boston	33,353
Chicago Cubs	23,559
Chicago White Sox	30,092
Cincinnati	7,861
Cleveland	21,076
Colorado	18,200
Detroit	19,073
Florida	15,353
Houston	13,722
Kansas City	6,505
Los Angeles	27,342
Milwaukee	5,918
Minnesota	7,273
Montreal	536
NY Mets	46,251
NY Yankees	56,750
Oakland	9,458
Philadelphia	18,940
Pittsburgh	9,097
St. Louis	11,905
San Diego	12,436
San Francisco	17,197
Seattle	37,860
Tampa Bay	15,511
Texas	25,284
Toronto	14,460
Total	571,095

Source: Associated Press. (2001, December 6). 2001 broadcast money and gate receipts. Retrieved 7 November 2002 from http://www.canoe.com/ BaseballMoneyMatters/broadcast_gate-ap.html

league cities when the home team's games were on local TV. Baseball fans developed intense local loyalties and had little opportunity to become familiar with other major league teams. As a result, baseball does not enjoy a national fan base similar to the NFL's. In addition, critics say baseball has suffered in television ratings because it is not a "made-for-television" sport. The rhythm and flow of baseball does not fit the fast pace required by today's television audiences.

The fans' fixation with their local teams has led to a sharp financial division between the media "haves" and "have-nots." Major-market teams such as the Yankees and Dodgers, and clubs that enjoy large regional fan bases such as the Rangers and Red Sox, command local media contracts worth $50 million a year or more. Small-market clubs such as Milwaukee and Kansas City are lucky to claim one tenth of that. With few exceptions, the income gap has been reflected in payrolls and on-field performance. Table 10-3 illustrates local broadcast revenues for MLB teams in 2001.

Despite the game's well-documented problems and a history of sagging television ratings, baseball remains an important element in sports broadcasting. It is the only major team sport that plays throughout the summer months and provides hours of warm-weather programming. ESPN pays Major League Baseball $815 million for cable rights to games through 2005 in order to fill those summer hours. Fox surprised many analysts by snapping up exclusive network rights for $2.5 billion through 2006. The contract gives Fox, which already controls local television rights to most big league teams, exclusive rights to the World Series. It also provides a powerful platform for cross-promotion between the national Fox network and the regional Fox Sports Networks.

National Basketball Association

The NBA is a relative newcomer among major sports and combines aspects of football's and baseball's broadcasting policies. The NBA has a national presence with regular season and playoff games on ABC, ESPN, and Turner and a $756 million annual package, but the lion's share of each team's broadcast revenue comes from local radio and television packages. The NBA was a pioneer in mixing over-the-air and cable television coverage, and NBA games remain a major selling point for many regional sports channels. Basketball fans can follow their local teams throughout the season, but because of the league's national contract, they can watch other teams dozens of times each season as well.

Played on a brightly illuminated indoor court just 30 yards long, basketball is a television-friendly sport. From the beginning, cameras could give viewers an intimate look at the action. Technological advances such as slow-motion replay and extreme close-ups emphasize the grace, physical skill, and emotion of the players.

National Hockey League

Although NFL and NBA games are particularly telegenic, often enhancing the viewing experience, hockey has not fared nearly as well as a televised sport. Network contracts with CBS, NBC, and Fox came and went because of low ratings. Critics argued that fans unfamiliar with the game could not follow the puck during telecasts. NBC tried to correct this by teaching newcomers the fine points with the cartoon icon Peter Puck, and Fox experimented with computer enhancement that turned the puck into a colorful computer streak. To date, nothing has enabled hockey to break out as a truly national sport. Although clubs in major markets with established hockey traditions flourish, the league's national television agreement is by far the weakest among major team sports. ABC and ESPN hold national television rights through 2004, paying an average of $120 million a year, less than one sixth of the NBA's annual national television income.

NASCAR

Long seen as a regional sport, NASCAR has become an acknowledged leader in sports marketing and promotion. In 1999, NASCAR convinced racetrack owners across the country to relinquish their television rights and signed a $2.4 billion, 6-year deal with Fox, NBC, and Turner to broadcast Winston Cup and Busch Series races.

Winston Cup races, the most popular stock-car events, have in recent years drawn higher ratings than regular season NBA, NHL, or MLB contests and are especially popular among young men. NASCAR's multinetwork deal provides unusual cross-promotional and marketing challenges and opportunities.

NCAA

Because it is not covered by the antitrust provision of the Sports Broadcast Act, the NCAA owns rights only to its own championship events. The universities of Georgia and Oklahoma went to court to break the longstanding NCAA football cartel in 1983. Since then, each school has the authority to make its own broadcast deals. As a result, the airwaves have been flooded by literally thousands of football and basketball games, fragmenting the viewing audience, increasing the inventory of advertising availability, and reducing the market value of any one game.

The only university with its own network-television football contract is Notre Dame. For the rest of the collegiate sports world, conference agreements are the rule. It is not considered an antitrust violation if conference members voluntarily pool their broadcast rights, and both broadcasters and advertisers find regional conference packages a desirable way to reach advertisers. The Big East Conference, for example, includes schools in markets that encompass 35% of the nation's homes. The league has conference-wide deals with CBS and ESPN and shares revenue. It also operates its own network in the east, again sharing revenue equally. Some individual schools also have local radio and, in some cases, TV deals. The University of Connecticut, for example, places football and men's and women's basketball games on WTNH in New Haven as well as the statewide Connecticut Public Television Network. UConn radio broadcasts are assigned to WTIC radio in Hartford, which places the games on affiliate stations across the state. UConn keeps its local broadcast revenue and also receives a share of the leaguewide purse.

Because of the proliferation of college games on television, ratings and advertising revenues have declined for regular season contests. Colleges, however, see television exposure as an important public relations marketing tool, a valuable asset in recruiting student-athletes and nonathlete undergraduates, for rallying alumni, and for increasing public support.

The NCAA's television "gold mine" is the Division I men's basketball tournament. The NCAA signed an 11-year, $6 billion contract with CBS that hiked the NCAA's "March Madness" revenue from $237 million to $545 million per year. The NCAA/CBS agreement is innovative and elevates broadcast partnerships to a new level. In exchange for $6 billion, CBS received exclusive rights to tournament television, radio, and Internet broadcasts as well as to most marketing, licensing, and promotional opportunities. Because the agreement reaches across media boundaries and extends beyond traditional game-day programming to include the right to publish game programs and stage on-site "fan festivals," both sport organizations and broadcasters will be watching the new experiment closely.

The Olympic Games

The Olympic Games are unique among major sporting events because they attract a predominantly female audience. As a major international event, the Olympics can command huge audiences for two consecutive weeks, and the networks will pay lavish sums for broadcast rights. NBC purchased rights for all winter and summer games from 2000 through 2008. The network paid $456 million for rights to the 1996 Atlanta games and was rewarded with record ratings and public visibility. The 2000 summer games in Sydney, however, were a ratings disappointment, if not an outright disaster. TV ratings were down 36% from Atlanta, the lowest for any Olympics since 1968, averaging a 13.8 rating and a 24 share. Observers blamed the decline on NBC's reliance on pretaped events and a lack of compelling characters and stories, but as NBC pointed out, the Olympics allowed NBC to attract a larger audience than any of its competitors and turn a profit on the games. Ratings rebounded sharply for the 2002 winter games in Salt Lake City, even though many of the prime-time offerings had been taped hours before.

Roone Arledge of ABC Sports pioneered modern coverage of the Olympics. He emphasized the stories of the athletes, bringing viewers "up close and personal" and giving them a reason to become emotionally involved in "the thrill of victory and the agony of defeat." NBC's Atlanta and Sydney coverage was often criticized for devoting too much time to the stories and not enough to the competition, but this was the network's intent in order to attract the broadest possible audience. NBC conducted exhaustive audience research and determined viewers wanted "not sports but stories about sports, stories that focused on patriotism, triumph over adversity, interesting personalities and the like, a continuing narrative which, like any drama would draw them in" (p. 27).[11]

Because the Olympic audience closely resembled the typical television audience dominated by women and included a large percentage of teenagers, NBC devoted many hours to sports such as gymnastics, swimming, and equestrian events, which appealed to younger, suburban women, the prototypical "soccer mom" who is seen as a key consumer and decision maker. NBC's coverage of Salt Lake City made a bid for younger viewers by giving plenty of time to extreme sports such as free-style skiing and snowboard events.

Golf and Tennis

Golf and tennis are regularly seen on television, but they rarely draw large audiences. The relatively small audiences, however, include a high proportion of difficult-to-reach upper-income men and are highly desirable to certain advertisers. Tennis and golf tournament advertising frequently includes sports equipment chosen to appeal to this distinct audience as well as luxury cars, business-travel-related products such as hotels, airlines and credit cards, and financial planning instruments. The Masters golf tournament, for example, is presented by CBS and the Augusta National Golf Club as a "prestige" event with low-key, limited advertising telecast. The Masters sponsors are Cadillac and Citigroup, companies that seek a "prestige" audience and sell primarily to affluent, older males. Tennis is attempting to cultivate a younger and more diverse television audience, but the sport's bedrock viewers remain older and more affluent than the typical television audience.

Boxing

Boxing was omnipresent on television in the 1940s and 1950s, but it has largely faded from the network television scene. Boxing boasts an intensely loyal audience of older men, but many women and younger men find the sport offensive. The sport suffers from an image of violence and corruption, and this discourages many advertisers. In recent years, younger boxing fans have been siphoned away from boxing by professional wrestling and "tough man" competitions that provide fast-paced action without the subtlety or the potential for serious injury that is ever present in the "sweet science."

Several lessons can be learned from boxing's problematic relationship with broadcasting. The sport was popular in the early days of television because it was easy to telecast. The figure of two fighters in a confined, well-lighted ring could be seen on early television sets. The media, however, changed fans' perceptions of the sport. The subtlety of the sport—slipping punches, feint and blocks—did not show well on the small screen. Viewers wanted big punchers, knockout artists whose ring work was easily visible. The nearly nightly telecasts also rapidly drained the available talent pool. Boxing clubs suffered because fans chose to stay home and watch the fights on TV. In addition, fans wanted to see winners, so a boxer who lost several fights was no longer welcome on TV, and new talent had no local club system to use to develop their craft. Boxing received an initial boost from television, but the sport became overexposed and eventually disappeared from regular network broadcasts.

Because boxing retains a loyal core of fans, it is popular on cable and has been a leader in pay-per-view telecasts. Major fights are sold to viewers on a per-event basis, with the payout usually divided equally between the promoter and the local cable system or satellite distributor. Boxer Oscar De la Hoya may attract a pay-per-view "buy rate" of 3-4% of potential homes, small in terms of mass media, but in dollar terms, the income can be enormous. Important fights have grossed $40 million or more in pay-per-view revenue for the cable company.

International Sports

On April 2, 1965, the first commercial communication satellite—Intelsat I— was launched into the earth's orbit. Today, dozens of satellites circle the globe, orbiting in time with the earth's rotation so they remain fixed at a constant point in the sky. These geosynchronous satellites enable television signals to be flashed to viewers around the world at the speed of light. The international television audience is growing rapidly, and sports remain a favorite programming source. ESPN, through its international services and worldwide affiliates, now has more viewers overseas than in the United States. Direct satellite services are making multichannel television programming available to hundreds of millions of viewers in Asia, Africa, and Latin America. Channels like EUROSPORT provide 24-hour sports coverage, similar to ESPN, across Europe.

Sports with international appeal stand to profit in this new environment. The Olympics are a worldwide attraction. The 2002 FIFA Soccer World Cup in Japan and South Korea attracted a large worldwide television audience. A combined total of approximately 1.5 billion people watched the 2002 World Cup in the 18 markets measured by Nielsen Media Research. The final between Germany and Brazil was the most watched match, with nearly 63 million viewers tuning in.[12] Formula 1 auto racing, international test cricket, and professional soccer and rugby now play before worldwide audiences. The growing interrelation among the world's broadcast systems may also lead to plush times for some sports. Rupert Murdoch's News Corporation controls the Fox network in the United States, the Seven networks in Australia, B-Sky-B satellite television in Great Britain, and similar services around the world. Murdoch organized an international rugby league, dubbed "Super League," that is telecast worldwide. International programmers with hours of airtime to fill will look to sports, and events that can travel across international borders will be at a premium.

New Technology

Communication technologies are converging. Video, audio, and textual information is flashed around the world at the speed of light and recorded in flawless digital media. Radio, television, and computers are becoming one medium. Digitalization and streaming media are enabling fans around the world to watch, listen to, and interact with their favorite sporting events.

Sports remain a driving force behind much of the new technology. Radio broadcasters used heavyweight title fights and World Series broadcasts to publicize their medium and lure new purchasers. Television used sports to convince families to buy their first television set. Promoters of the new digital technologies, too, rely on sports to sell their products. Computers have made virtually anything possible in video today, but the fundamental rules still apply: Will the market support the product? Will consumers pay for the services? Will they attract audiences large enough to attract advertisers?

Both team owners and broadcasters hoped that pay-per-view would be highly profitable. Technology allows viewers to choose a game and be billed a fee, a system similar to that used for a long-distance telephone call. Attempts to package games on a pay-per-view basis have not fared well. Major boxing matches have been successful, but pay-per-view experiments involving MLB, college sports, and hockey have failed.

Consumers are reluctant to embrace pay-per-view. They want a predetermined product at a predetermined price. ABC has offered pay-per-view college football with modest success, but because the network already produces the game for regional over-the-air distribution, the additional cost of providing the broadcasts on a pay-per-view basis to audiences in the rest of the country is minimal. Several professional leagues have eschewed pay-per-view in favor of season-long packages of out-of-market games. Digital cable television and multichannel direct-to-home satellites provide fans with access to games never before available. An NBA fan in Boston, for example, previously limited to the local Celtics broadcast and the NBA's NBC and TNT national games, can purchase NBA League Pass, comprising locally produced games from around the league. Because the games are already produced for viewers in local markets, the production cost is minimal. Similar packages are available from the NFL, NHL, and MLB.

Although direct-to-home satellites are a fast-growing technology, only about 15 million of the nation's 105 million television homes subscribe to these services. The potential market for hundreds of basketball, baseball, football, and hockey games, over and above the local and network games already available, remains undetermined.

Technology has reached the point where almost anything is possible, yet the question remains: Do consumers want it enough to pay for it? As one industry observer suggested, the only way to find out is to build it and hope they will come.[13]

Summary

The sale of broadcast rights is a major source of revenue for many sports properties. The magnitude of television and radio broadcast deals is particularly evident at the major league level, with the Big Four (MLB, NHL, NFL, and NBA) receiving almost $4 billion from national broadcast and regional cable networks in 2002. In 1998, the NFL signed a $17.6 billion, 8-year deal with its broadcast partners CBS, Fox, ABC, and ESPN, providing the league with an average of $2.2 billion annually through 2005. College athletics has also been a major beneficiary of growing broadcast rights deals. In 2002, the NCAA signed a $6 billion contract with CBS to televise the men's basketball tournament, also known as March Madness, through 2013.

Television and radio broadcasters are in search of sporting events that produce large audiences or attract viewers who are desirable targets for commercial advertisers. Many sporting events are attractive programming options for broadcasters because their audiences are often dominated by adult men with above-average education and income. Particularly for advertisers seeking to reach a male demographic, sports can be a very desirable media buy.

Broadcasts are provided free to consumers, so radio and television networks must sell advertising during the broadcasts to cover their expenses and to realize a profit. On average, college football games provide 50 minutes of commercial inventory for advertisers. Commercials, or "spots," are typically sold in 30- or 60-

second units. How much the commercial units can be sold for depends largely on the size and makeup of the broadcast audience. Nielsen media research and Arbitron provide audience estimates and demographic data for television and radio broadcasts, respectively. Audience size in television is measured in terms of ratings and shares. Generally, the higher the rating, the more expensive the commercial unit.

The commercial broadcasting system links audience size and revenue. The larger the audience, the higher the revenue from advertising sales. Broadcasters seek programming that will appeal to larger, more valuable audiences. The four national television networks, ABC, CBS, NBC, and Fox, have affiliate stations to carry their programming into 105 million homes with television sets. National basic cable services such as ESPN, Fox Sports Network, USA, and Turner outlets TBS and TNT are available in households with cable or direct satellite access, and these services reach roughly 80% of the national networks' audience.

Cable services are becoming "niche broadcasters" that target their programming to specific segments of the public. The basic cable services offset their smaller audience with subscriber fees. ESPN, the most expensive basic service, averages 72 cents per subscriber per month in fees, resulting in approximately $60 million annually. The increased earnings enable ESPN to compete successfully for lucrative sporting event contracts, as it did in 2002 when it outbid NBC to attain 6 years of NBA games at a price of $2.4 billion.

National radio networks still offer coast-to-coast broadcasts of major sports events, but television has cut into their revenue production. Westwood One/CBS Radio Sports and ESPN Radio are the leading sports providers today.

Regional cable sports networks occupy a market niche between the national service providers and local stations and traditionally specialize in covering sports with strong regional appeal.

The evolution of regional sports channels demonstrates how the broadcasting industry has adapted to the marketplace. Regional cable sports networks progressed from being premium services in the 1970s and 1980s, a failed attempt to generate sufficient profit, to being included in a package of cable services available to subscribers for a flat monthly fee. By making this change, regional cable sports networks expanded the size of their audience and realized greater advertising revenue.

Syndicators are independent producers that purchase the rights to events or create and produce programs, then seek to place them on stations or cable services across the country. TVS was the pioneer in the field and created a coast-to-coast web of affiliates that delivered a huge national audience. Today, much syndicated sports programming appears on cable rather than over-the-air television. Syndication remains an important tool for sports producers. The station airs the program in exchange for the right to sell a predetermined amount of advertising time. The syndicator makes its money by selling the remaining advertising in the broadcast to national advertisers.

There are 1,600 VHS and UHF television stations and nearly 13,000 AM and FM radio stations currently on the air in the United States. Because local stations serve limited local audiences, they cannot generate the advertising revenue to bid on national events. Local stations can and do actively pursue contracts to cover individual teams, and such stations typically establish regional networks of affiliates to broaden their audience and advertising base.

In a major market, rights fees can be impressive. The New York Yankees commanded an annual local television and radio rights fee of more than $50 million before creating YES, their own in-house network. In smaller markets, teams earn substantially less. Size of audience and competition among broadcasters dictates the price paid. In smaller markets where college and minor league franchises often flourish, a team's game may generate no guaranteed rights fee at all.

Sports producers and broadcasters are partners. Both parties must be satisfied they are receiving a fair return on each transaction, either in immediate profit or in long-term gains such as promotions, competitive advantage, or improved public image.

Broadcast rights may be assigned in several ways, but in all cases the sports producer and broadcaster work together and nearly everything is negotiable. Even with the many options that are open to negotiation, within the partnership framework sports broadcast deals are usually arranged in one of three ways: (a) direct sales of rights from a team to a broadcaster for a guaranteed rights fee; (b) in-house production of games by the team or league, which then syndicates the broadcast; or 3) cooperative or revenue-sharing agreement in which both the teams or the league share the potential profit and, in some cases, the loss.

Escalating broadcast rights fees and an expanding inventory of sports advertising time has led to a proliferation of revenue-sharing agreements at all levels of sport. Each of the professional sports properties manages its broadcast contracts differently and has its own unique relationship with the broadcast media. In the NFL, all regular and postseason television rights rest with the league, and revenues are divided equally among all franchises. Individual teams retain local radio and preseason television rights and also share in the approximately $75 million per year each franchise receives from the sale of national rights. The league is presented and promoted as a package, and viewers see many teams over the course of a season, so the NFL has developed a national fan base. MLB was a mainstay on the radio by the mid-1920s and on television by the late 1940s, and local contracts were in place long before national television networks became well established in the 1950s. Fans developed fierce team loyalties, and the sport did not develop a national fan base. Fans' fixation with local teams has led to a sharp financial division between media haves and have-nots, resulting in prosperity for major-market teams whereas small-market teams continue to struggle. Yet baseball remains an important element in sports broadcasting, as it is the only major team sport that plays throughout the summer months and provides hours of programming.

The NBA combines aspects of football's and baseball's broadcasting policies. It has a national presence with regular season and playoff games on ABC, ESPN, and Turner, but the lion's share of each team's broadcast revenue comes from local radio and television packages. The NBA was a pioneer in mixing over-the-air and cable television coverage. NBA games remain a major selling point for many regional sport channels.

The NHL has not fared well as a televised sport. Although clubs in major markets with established hockey traditions flourish, the league's national television agreement is by far the weakest among major team sports. ABC and ESPN hold national television rights through 2004, paying an average of $120 million annually, less than one sixth of the NBA's annual national television income.

NASCAR has become an acknowledged leader in sports marketing and promotion. In 1999, NASCAR signed a $2.4 billion, 6-year deal with Fox, NBC, and Turner to broadcast Winston Cup and Busch series races. NASCAR's multinetwork deal provides cross-promotional marketing challenges and opportunities.

The NCAA owns rights only to its own championship events, and each school has the authority to make its own broadcast deals. This has resulted in fragmenting the viewing audience, increasing the inventory of advertising availability, and reducing the market value of any one game. In the collegiate sports world, conference agreements are the norm, with the exception of Notre Dame, which has its own network television football contract. Both broadcasters and advertisers use regional conference packages to reach advertisers. Some individual schools have local radio and television deals. Though advertising revenues have declined for the regular season, colleges still see television exposure as important for public relations, recruiting, and alumni relations.

The Olympic Games are unique in that they attract a predominantly female audience, are a major international event, and are televised for two weeks. For these reasons, networks will pay huge sums for broadcast rights. NBC paid $456 million for rights to the 1996 Atlanta games and has purchased the rights for all winter and summer games through 2008.

Golf and tennis are regularly seen on television, but rarely draw large audiences unless a high-profile player is present. However, the audience for these sports tends to include upper-income men who are difficult for advertisers to reach and are considered a highly desirable target market.

Boxing, popular in the 1940s and 1950s on network television, is now seen primarily on cable or pay-per-view, where major bouts are capable of generating huge sums of revenue for the cable company. Although it still boasts a loyal core of fans, primarily older men, the sport is seen as too violent by many women and younger men, and this discourages many advertisers.

The international television audience is growing rapidly, and sport remains a preferred programming option. ESPN now has more viewers overseas than in the United States, and channels like EUROSPORT provide 24-hour sports coverage across Europe. Programmers realize that sports has appeal across international borders and look to sport programming to fill airtime.

Sports remain a driving force behind much of today's emerging technology. Just as radio and television manufacturers and broadcasters used sporting events to market their media, current promoters of innovative new technologies rely on sports to sell their products.

1. Hiestand, M. (1999, November 19). CBS keeps NCAA men's tournament [Electronic version]. *USA Today*. Retrieved http://www.usatoday.com/sports/sfri12.htm
2. TV sports: The $3.5 billion ticket. (1996, May 13). *Broadcasting & Cable*, 34-46.
3. Neilsen Media Research. (2001). Who we are & what we do. Retrieved from http://www.neilsenmedia.com
4. Television Bureau of Advertising. (2001, March 13). *Online TV facts*. Retrieved http://www.tvb./tvfacts/index.html
5. WTEM Washington. (1995). *Sports Talk 570*. Promotional material citing Scarborough 1995 Washington metro radio survey.
6. ESPN. (1992). *ESPN delivers the right viewers!* Unpaginated promotional material from ESPN citing 1992 Neilsen quarterly reports. In author's files.
7. WSBK Boston. (1993). *Celtics Basketball*. Promotional material citing Nov. 1992-May 1993. Nielsen survey of metro Boston.
8. Klatell, D.A., & Marcus N. (1996). *Inside big time sports: Television, money & the fans*. New York: Mastermedia.
9. Weiner, J. (2002, February 11). ESPN's full court press. *Business Week, 3805,* 60-61.
10. News Corporation (1999). *Annual report*. Retrieved from http://www.newscorp.com /report99
11. Remnick, D. (1996, August 5). Inside-Out Olympics. *The New Yorker, 74,* 26-28.
12. Nielsen Media Report: Nearly 1.5 billion TV viewers watch 2002 World Cup. (2002, July 31). Retrieved from http:www.businesswire.com
13. Auletta, K. (1994, April 11). The magic box. *The New Yorker, 72,* 40-45.

Tim Ashwell, PhD, teaches at the University of New Hampshire and has extensive experience working in the broadcasting industry.

Mary A. Hums, PhD, is a professor of sport administration at the University of Louisville and a leading authority on policy development in sport organizations as it pertains to increasing sport management opportunities for women, people with disabilities, and racial/ethnic minorities.

Photos courtesy of Robin Ammon, Jr. and Richard M. Southall.

Chapter Eleven

Sales of Foodservice and Souvenir Concessions

by Chris Bigelow, FCSI, President

Although the concession industry has long played an integral role in sports, it has historically been relegated to back-room, behind-the-scenes dealings rarely known to the public. Team owners offered concessionaires long-term, low-commission contracts in return for large cash grants, loans, and advances. One team executive commented that without the concessionaires' loans, Major League Baseball may have never survived the '30s, '40s, or '50s.

Today that financing source is still available, but there are few secret deals, spur-of-the-moment handshake agreements, or one-sided contracts. Sports team owners have teams of accountants, lawyers, and consultants who assist them in structuring contracts that make financial sense for both parties and that comply with the complicated regulations of their facility leases and with overall banking and IRS financing mandates.

Stadiums and their foodservices entered a new era in 1987, when Joe Robbie (now Pro Player) Stadium opened in Miami. Privately financed through the pre-opening sale of luxury suites and previously unheard-of club seats, Joe Robbie Stadium offered its customers a new level of service never before available in a sports facility: valet parking, private stadium entrances and elevators, wait-staff service at their seats, and a fully air-conditioned and carpeted private concourse featuring bountiful buffets with gourmet sandwiches, homemade pasta, and freshly carved prime rib.

This new level of stadium amenities prompted team owners to speak in terms of a fan's *entertainment experience,* not just the team's win/loss record. A new level of culinary expertise would now be required of the concessionaire, and the concessionaire's skill would be instrumental in the success of the customers' total entertainment experience at the sports venue. This trend of highlighting the role of foodservice in modern sports venues has continued. Between 1998 and 2002, more than 1.8 million new seats were added in 28 new arenas, 26 stadiums, and 12 multipurpose university venues.[1] In addition to the inclusion of more premium seats (club seats and luxury suites), these new facilities invariably included more elaborate and strategically located foodservice areas to maximize food and beverage purchase opportunities for fans. The intent was to significantly increase the per capita spending of patrons during the sporting event.

The concession industry is a North American phenomenon. Even today in Europe, Asia, Africa, and Central and South America, foodservice and merchandise sales play a minor, albeit growing, role in sports. Big international sports like soccer and cricket are a concessionaire's nightmare, because there are no time-outs during competition, therefore fewer uninterrupted opportunities for spectators to purchase concessions.

Although street vendors selling their wares and foods have been prevalent in all cultures for centuries, the sports concessions industry traces its roots to 1887. That was the year a young man decided to print a program for a baseball game in Columbus, Ohio—because "you can't tell the players without a scorecard." From that venture, young Harry M. Stevens expanded to other venues, selling soft drinks and sausages to enthusiastic sports crowds. A local New York cartoonist, observing Stevens selling red hots in a bun at New York's Polo Grounds, drew a cartoon showing the sausage styled with a face and legs and Stevens barking the sales. The cartoonist coined the phrase "hot dog." Those events ushered in the beginning of the concession industry and the start of the H. M. Stevens Concession Company.

Around the same time, three brothers named Jacobs began popping popcorn during intermissions at a theater in upstate New York. They soon expanded into more theaters and shortly thereafter into a minor league baseball park. That marked the beginning of the Sportservice Company. Other local and regional companies entered the field, but few survived. It was not until the early 1960s that most of today's major competitors of H. M. Stevens and Sportservice entered the marketplace.

Leading Concession Service Companies

It is difficult to quantify the concessions industry because there are so many components. Souvenirs and foodservice, licensed merchandise and nonlicensed merchandise, professional sports facilities, community civic centers, arenas, college, university and other amateur sports venues, even amusement parks, fairs, and convention centers are all a part of the so-called concession industry.

Managers of sports facilities generally have two primary options with respect to the delivery of food and beverage services. Either they can hire or "contract out" to established companies specializing in the sale of food service and souvenirs, or they can assume in-house responsibility for concessions by selling food and beverage items on their own.

Under the contracting-out option, concessionaires typically pay a commission to the team or venue that contracts for their services. The commission generally is based on a revenue-sharing arrangement in which the concessionaire and team split gross sales after taxes, according to a prenegotiated agreement. Typically, concessions sales commissions at stadiums and arenas range from 35% to 50% of the gross net of sales (total sales revenue after taxes). The following example illustrates how revenues are shared between a team and concessionaire under a 50-50 commission split. Assume that a beer sells for $3.50 and produces a gross net of $3.32. Under a 50% commission split, the team and the vendor each make $1.66. Of that $1.66, the concessionaire will spend approximately 31 cents on labor, and the beer itself costs around 60 cents. The remaining 75 cents would be available to meet the concessionaire's overhead, which includes management costs and profit. The benefits of contracting out concessions sales versus doing them in-house will be discussed later in the chapter.

There are six companies that dominate the concession industry in North America. Known as the Big 6, these companies include

- *Aramark, Inc.*, Philadelphia, PA. Purchased H. M. Stevens. Owns 50% of SMG (Spectacor Management Group), which manages public assembly facilities. Major accounts: The First Union Center in Philadelphia, Oriole Park at Camden Yards, the Meadowlands in New Jersey, and Fenway Park in Boston.

- *Boston Concessions*, Cambridge, MA. Large regional provider in ski resorts and theaters now moving into college and professional accounts such as National Car Rental Arena and the World Arena in Colorado Springs.

- *Fine Host Corporation*, Greenwich, CT. Major accounts: Pro Player Stadium, Ravens Stadium in Baltimore, and Raymond James Stadium in Tampa.

- *Levy*, Chicago, IL. Pioneers of premium suite and club level services. Major accounts: Jacobs Field in Cleveland, MCI Center in Washington, D.C., and the Staples Center in Los Angeles.

- *Ogden Entertainment Services*, New York, NY. Parent company manages public assembly facilities. Major accounts: Staples Center in Los Angeles, Wrigley Field in Chicago, and Philadelphia Veterans Stadium.

- *Restaura*, Phoenix, AZ. Major accounts: America West Arena and Bank One Ballpark. Both in Phoenix.

- *Restaurant Associates*, New York, NY. New to the industry and looking to share in the premium services market. Major account: USTA National Tennis Center, New York City.

- *Sodexho-Marriott*, Washington, D.C. Major player in the college arena and stadium market. Major accounts: Husky Stadium (University of Washington), Schottenstein Center (Ohio State University), Reunion Arena in Dallas, and The Orlando Arena.

- *Sportservice Corporation*, Buffalo, NY. Parent company owns the Boston Bruins and Fleet Center. Major accounts: The Fleet Center in Boston, New Comiskey Park in Chicago, Busch Stadium in St. Louis, and the Ice Palace in Tampa.

- *Swanson*, Omaha, NE. Specializes in college and smaller accounts including Arkansas State, Iowa State, and Beaumont Arena in Texas.

- *Volume Services America*, Spartanburg, SC. Servomation in Canada. Formed in 1998 with merger of Volume Services and Service America. Major Accounts: Qualcom Stadium in San Diego, BC Place (Vancouver, B.C.), Yankee Stadium, and the Truman Sports Complex in Kansas City.

An annual poll of arenas, stadiums, amphitheaters, and amusement parks conducted by a leading industry publication, *Amusement Business,* included the following highlights:[1]

Economic Contribution of Concessions

1.	Average facility attendance	947,080
2.	Average facility foodservice revenues	$3,105,154
3.	Weighted average facility per cap	$3.28
4.	Average facility event per cap reported	$4.58
5.	Facilities experiencing increased per caps over previous year	84%

Concession revenues play a larger role in some facilities than others. For an NFL team that receives millions of dollars from network television or a convention center that receives revenues from a large hotel-bed tax, concession revenues may represent only 10% of total receipts. However, for many sports franchises, stadiums, and arenas, concession income is one of the top three sources of revenue, along with ticket sales and advertising income. Just as important is the fact that in-stadium revenues such as concessions may not be subject to revenue sharing with other teams or the players in some leagues.

In minor league sports such as minor league baseball, in which the major league team pays the players' salaries and ticket prices are relatively low, concessions profits are often the difference between a profitable and an unprofitable team. For years, the theater industry has publicized that it breaks even on film costs through ticket sales, but makes its profits from the concession stands. Those same economics are in place at many sports venues and at hundreds of stock-car tracks throughout the United States, where the owners break even on ticket sales and advertising, requiring foodservice and souvenirs to produce the profits.

Creative facility managers at all types of venues now review all of their revenue sources, including concessions and parking, before negotiating leases or facility rental agreements with a sports team or promoters. By knowing their potential profits from concessions as well as their operating costs for such items as security, ushers, ticket takers, parking lot attendants, and cleanup crew, they can establish an equitable rental structure for the building.

One of the best illustrations of the value of the concession operation to a facility is the Charlotte Coliseum's original lease with the NBA Hornets. The Hornets paid the facility rent of one dollar per year and retained all revenue sources, *except concessions,* which the facility retained. Although that arrangement appeared to be a favorable deal for the team, within a year the team was also asking for a piece of the concessions to remain profitable.

Many teams have formed their own concession companies to maximize their revenues as well as control the level of services. The Wirtz family, owners of the Chicago Blackhawks and co-owners of the United Center, own Bismarck Foods, a Chicago concessionaire. Michael Ilitch, owner of the Detroit Tigers, Detroit Red Wings, and Little Caesar's Pizza, formed a concessions division, as did the Utah Jazz and Madison Square Garden, to operate the foodservice in the arenas where their teams play. The Portland Trailblazers, St. Louis Blues, and Atlanta Hawks manage their own concessions while contracting their upscale restaurant and club foodservice to private foodservice companies.

Table 11-1 provides perspective on the extent to which the four primary professional sports leagues and major college athletic programs either use an outside contractor or manage their own concessions. The chart also reflects the trend of hiring multiple contractors, a concessionaire for general concessions, a restaurateur for premium club and suite services, and a merchandiser to handle the sale of team souvenirs.

Table 11-1 Contracted Versus Self-Operated Services

Sport Property	Self-Operated	Combination Self-Operation and Contracted	Single Contractors	Multiple Contractors
Major League Baseball	0%	6.7%	60%	33.3%
National Basketball Association	24.1%	6.9%	55.2%	13.8%
National Football League	9.7%	3.2%	61.3%	25.8%
National Hockey League	23.3%	3.3%	60%	13.3%

Note: Data compiled by The Bigelow Companies, Inc. Kansas City, MO. February 16,1999.

The Sale of Alcohol at Amateur Sporting Events

In amateur sports, foodservice and merchandise play a smaller financial role than in professional sports for two primary reasons: (a) the disposable income of the fan and (b) the lack of beer sales. Beer sales often account for 35 to 55% of a concessionaire's sales, depending on the event. Because most colleges do not allow beer sales at their facilities, and no high schools allow alcoholic beverage sales, concession volumes are at a minimum 35% less than at professional sports.

The NCAA has no authority over alcohol sales during regular season play and can ban the sale of alcoholic beverages only in postseason and postconference play.

The individual schools and sometimes the conference dictate alcoholic beverage sales policies during regular season events. Many colleges do not allow beer to be sold to the general public, but do have private clubs, alumni rooms, and athletic booster rooms where beer and liquor are readily available.

The value of beer sales to a concessionaire was best illustrated when one concessionaire established a scholarship fund in exchange for allowing beer sales at a conference postseason tournament. The colleges most willing to allow beer sales tend to attract a large alumni and community following. The alumni and community are both of age and are used to a higher level of service at other professional sporting events. Also, universities that are business oriented and interested in maximizing their revenues often allow sales of alcoholic beverages.

Colleges often allow suite holders to bring in their own alcohol, thereby losing a major revenue source. Most college football programs encourage pre- and postgame tail-gating as well as "pass outs" (readmission tickets) to the parking lot during halftime. Although the schools feel that tail-gating adds to the excitement and tradition of college sports, they also acknowledge this allows the customer an opportunity to obtain an alcoholic beverage without the institution's officially sanctioning its sale.

A growing number of colleges are realizing that by providing a service their customers want and by controlling the sale of alcohol through the use of trained and well-supervised employees, they can decrease public rowdiness and, at the same time, dramatically increase revenues.

Concession Industry Standards

Per capita sales are the primary standard that a concessionaire uses to analyze an event. "Per caps," or the average purchase per person for one visit, are the common measure of concession sales. Per capita sales are determined by dividing the actual turnstile attendance into the gross (total receipts less sales tax) concession sales. This number indicates the average expenditure per customer.

It is important to know the actual turnstile attendance for an accurate per capita sales count rather than use the announced attendance, estimated attendance, or even the number of tickets sold. Many colleges and minor league sports will publicize an announced attendance that they use for public relations purposes. In baseball, the American League announces paid ticket sales, whereas the National League announces turnstile attendance. Paid ticket sales do not reflect no-shows, or comps.

All facility managers should maintain an accurate turnstile count. This confidential information can be used by concessionaires to derive authentic per cap estimates for food and beverage and merchandise sales. Accurate per caps allow a facility manager and a concessionaire to measure the concessionaire's performance against industry standards and against their own past performance.

Table 11-2 offers a range of per caps that can be considered industry standards. The variation within and between leagues is a result of many differences, including the number of concession service lines at a venue, menu pricing, geographic spending habits, and whether the event is played indoors or outdoors (domed stadiums traditionally have lower per capita sales than do outdoor stadiums in the summer).

Table 11-2 Foodservice Per Capita Spending - Industry Ranges

Sports League or Event	Low	High
High School Basketball & Football (without Beer)	$0.25	$2.00
College Basketball (without beer)	1.00	2.00
College Football (without Beer)	1.50	3.50
Minor League Baseball	2.75	6.25
NBA Basketball	4.50	10.00
NHL Hockey	5.00	12.00
MLB Baseball	5.50	12.00
NFL Football	6.00	15.00
Championships/Super Bowls	12.00	30.00

Note: Data compiled by The Bigelow Companies, Inc. Kansas City, MO. February 16, 1999.

Table 11-3 Merchandise Per Capita Spending- Industry Standards

Event	Low	High
High School Basketball and Football	N/A	
College Basketball	$0.50	$1.75
College Football	0.50	1.75
Minor League Baseball	0.50	3.00
NBA Basketball	1.00	3.00
NHL Hockey	8.00	25.00
MLB Baseball	0.25	$0.50
NFL Football	0.25	0.75
Championship/ Super Bowl, etc.	0.25	1.50

Note: Data compiled by The Bigelow Companies, Inc. Kansas City, MO. February 16, 1999.

Many concessionaires will break down their sales even further with a beer per cap or a per cap by seating level. In the premium seating section, offering wait-staff service and more upscale concessions, per capita spending is often 50% to 100% greater than in the traditional concession levels. In stadium/arena club restaurants and luxury suites, food and beverage per caps can range from $20 to $35.

Concessionaires will monitor the spending for merchandise and programs as well. Table 11-3 indicates the ranges that are more affected by the win/loss record of the team and the popularity of the team colors, designs, and fashions than actual attendance.

Operating Costs

To anticipate what a team owner or facility manager can expect financially from a concessionaire, it is important to understand the concessionaire's operations in terms of both sales and expenses. A popular misconception, even on the part of experienced facility directors, is that concessionaires earn huge profits from their operations. This belief stems from the appearance of product markups that are much greater than those of traditional retailers or restaurants. Facility managers also reflect on stories of profit levels of concessionaires in the 1950s, 1960s, and early 1970s and at the concessionaires' ability to pay large commissions. Most concessionaires, in fact, operate on razor-thin margins.

There are two major controllable costs in a concession operation, product cost and payroll, which combined account for 40% to 50% of the concessionaires' overall costs. The other expenses, such as repairs, maintenance, office supplies, licenses, telephone, and marketing, although partially variable and partially fixed, rarely exceed 10% of gross sales. Likewise, depreciation and commissions, which will be discussed later in the chapter, are fixed by contract. Therefore, a successful concessions manager must concentrate on maximizing sales while properly managing the two major controllable cost areas, product and payroll.

Product cost is the total cost of the item sold. This includes the souvenir or food item (e.g., hot dog, buns), condiments, wrappers, napkins, serving implements, and containers. A concessionaire can control the product cost, first, by purchasing the proper quality product at the best available price. Next, a weighted product cost must be established, projecting unit sales and individual product cost. Finally, selling prices are set to provide an overall or weighted product cost based on the concessionaire's budget.

Typical concession food costs range from 15% to 25% of actual sale prices. In effect, menu items are marked up 4 to 7 times above the product cost. The cost of catered foods typically ranges from 28% to 38% of cash register prices. The markup of traditional souvenirs is similar to that of catered foods, ranging from 2 1/2 to 4 times the cost of novelty items.

Payroll costs are divided into two categories: salaried and hourly. Salaries are fixed costs that the concessionaire can change only by permanently hiring or firing employees. The hourly wages, however, can and should be managed for each event.

The concessionaire projects an event's concession sales by multiplying the expected per capita sales times the estimated attendance. Once gross sales are estimated for each area such as food and beverage, catering/restaurant workers, and souvenir vendors, it is possible to determine the approximate payroll dollars a concessionaire will spend on the event by applying the following budget standards:

Employee Group	Percentage of Sales Allocated to Payroll Costs
Concession-stand Workers	8-12% of concession sales
Food and Beverage Vendors	15-20% of vending sales
Catering/Restaurant Workers	18-30% of catering/restaurant sales
Sports Souvenir Vendors	12-17% of sports souvenir sales

A conflict may arise when a facility manager wants a higher level of customer service than the concessionaire's budget allows. This is often the case when concessionaires are paying extremely high commissions and need to minimize all of their operating expenses to produce a profit. The result can be too few concession stands open, slow customer service, long lines, and financial losses. It is important that the concessionaire and the facility manager meet regularly to discuss reasonable payroll costs and staffing levels to avoid this outcome. Payroll costs and staffing information should be shared by facility management and concessionaire prior to contracting with any foodservice concessionaire.

Concession Revenues

The concessions department in any facility exists equally as a customer-service function and as a major revenue center for the facility. The most successful venues find the proper balance between those two functions. The recommended strength of each function is most dependent on the type of facility and the types of events that the facility hosts.

The majority of sports venues do view the revenue production of their concessions department as the most critical issue. However, many team owners now view the quality of catering for their premium seating areas as a tool for enticing suite and club seat holders to renew their seating contracts. Satisfied customers are much more likely to continue their high-priced relationship with the team.

In estimating the amount of concession revenues a facility can generate, a manager will typically prepare an operating pro forma. The level of revenues that concessions generate for a facility depends on five factors:

1. Attendance at each event.

2. Event types and degree of risk of sports franchises.

3. Investment made by the concessions department.

4. Contract term (if services are contracted).

5. The initial capital costs (the greater these costs, the smaller the commissions).

If the concessions are operated in-house, in other words, solely by the team or venue operator, there may be no minimum acceptable profit level. However, for contracted accounts, those in which a private company contracts to provide concessions services, concessionaires rarely will operate an account unless it can generate a minimum of $100,000 profit after all on-site expenses, including commissions. That number can be reduced if the concessionaire has a large base of operations already existing in the market area. If one assumes that at the $100,000 profit level the concessionaire is earning 10% of the gross sales, it follows that a concessionaire would not be interested in serving an account grossing less than $1,000,000 annually. Smaller accounts should consider either self-operation or contracts with a smaller regional firm.

Typical Facility Commissions Range

Sales Category
Concession Sales
Catering/Suite Sales
Restaurant Sales
Sports/Souvenir Sales

Commissions Range
35% to 55%
15% to 35%
0% to 15%
30% to 45%

Design Programming

To ensure a facility has the potential to maximize both services and revenues, a foodservice and merchandise specialist is an integral part of the architect's team from the time the venue's space is being allocated and the operational program is being developed. The specialist's goal in this process is to ensure the optimal location of concession points of sale.

Several facilities have set the blueprint for what a state-of-the-art sports complex must have. The simple and efficient twin design of the sports complex in Kansas City of Arrowhead Stadium for football and Kauffman Stadium for baseball is still the basic infrastructure used for most modern stadiums. Pro Player Stadium in Miami and the SkyDome in Toronto illustrate the importance of luxury services such as club seats, destination restaurants (e.g., Hard Rock Cafe), and multievent capabilities. The Palace at Auburn Hills outside of Detroit and, more recently, the Staples Center in Los Angeles clearly show the capacity of luxury suites and concessions in an indoor arena. Finally, Oriole Park at Camden Yards in Baltimore illustrates the success a new facility can enjoy when all of the functional elements of high levels of customer service are combined and surrounded by a unique building facade that creates a nostalgic baseball feeling and adds to the customer's overall entertainment experience.

The common theme of all these facilities is a high level of customer service. The services available allow the concessions department and the team to maximize revenues. In order to achieve high-quality customer service, the facility must be designed to operate efficiently. Conveniences such as restrooms, information booths, and security must fit the typical patron's needs. More important, the income producers, such as concessions, vending rooms, suites, retail souvenir stores, portable stands, club wait-staff kitchens, dining rooms, parking, and ticket offices, must be placed in the proper quantity and location to maximize potential operating revenues.

The following guidelines are used by foodservice consultants and architects in today's newest stadiums and arenas.

Design and Program Criteria

- Concession Stands With Beer in Stadium

    - 1 point of service per 150 seats (Locate by seating patterns)

- Concession Stands Without Beer in Stadium

    - 1 point of service per 350 seats

- Vending Rooms

    - 2 food and soft drink vendors per 1,000 seats

    - 3 beer vendors per 1,000 seats

    - 1 vending room per 8,000 seats

- Club Seats

    - 1 server or combination of server and runner per 40 seats

    - 1 service kitchen/bar per 1,500 seats

    - 1 concession point of service per 100-150 seats

- Suites

    - 1 service steward/captain per 5-8 suites

- Restaurant/Lounge

    - Requirements vary by facility. Restaurant should not be less than 150 seats, or more that 600 seats, depending on facility size. Lounge not less than 25 seats, no maximum size. Banquet facilities are advisable.

- Picnic/Group Sales Area

    - Multipurpose rooms or tents capable of serving banquets from a remote kitchen or picnic areas with commercial grills and preparation equipment are essential for expanding group-sales business.

- Souvenir Stands

    - Portable or permanent one point of service per 1,000 to 1,500 seats for professional sports, one point of service per 1,500 to 5,000 for amateur and minor league sports. Locate by exits and entrances.

- Souvenir Retail Stores

    - Number and size vary by team's popularity. Locate centrally and adjacent to advance ticket window if planning to be open on both event and nonevent days. In larger outdoor stadiums, locate one per level or multiple smaller stores.

Contracting Versus Self-Orientation

Most of this chapter has made reference to services provided by an outside concessionaire, because the majority of larger professional sports venues do contract food and beverage services. However, the majority of smaller professional and collegiate venues either operate concessions in-house or use a local concessionaire. There is a trend developing in which team owners generate their own concessions division.

The primary reason facility directors operate their own concessions is to maintain control. They want to decide if prices are too low or too high, or if a concession stand should be open for an event even though ticket sales are light. They want to be able to determine the quality of products purchased without having every decision become a negotiating session with the concessionaire.

Self-operators also feel they are maximizing their revenues by not having to share a significant portion of their sales revenue with the concessionaire. Facility managers will admit that the decision to self-operate does mean a time commitment on their part of up to 40% of the day devoted to foodservice issues, but they feel the potential extra 3% to 6% profit is worthwhile.

Contracting proponents point out that they use a concessionaire because they do not want the headaches and hassles that a foodservice and souvenir operation brings. Scheduling hourly part-time employees; purchasing perishable foodstuffs or imported souvenirs; determining what stands are open, whether or not the sanitation policies are enforced, and who might be pilfering cash are all issues these managers do not want to oversee, even with a qualified concessions manager on staff. In addition, many of these facility managers do not have the necessary resources (e.g., budget and personnel) to run a concessions department effectively and do not have the freedom to establish autonomous purchasing and personnel offices.

Of course, both of these perspectives are correct. There are advantages and disadvantages to both systems. A good concessionaire working with a fair contract acts as though it were a department within the facility manager's organization. At the same time, a well-qualified in-house concessions manager can operate just as efficiently as a large corporation and act with greater flexibility when local events require it.

Concessionaires do provide proven systems of operations and a network of resources to help each other with new menu ideas, management trends, and training techniques. As mentioned earlier, a concessionaire can provide its own capital, thereby freeing the facility's money for other projects.

In large venues that generate high-volume foodservice and souvenir sales, an in-house operation can compete effectively on price with a national concessionaire. Locally bid products, such as soft drinks, meat, and bread, can often be obtained at or below a concessionaire's national price in a large venue; and beer, the single largest product purchased, is typically priced by state law; consequently, everyone buys at the same price. Although concessionaires do have national purchasing contracts for equipment, which helps when replacing a single item, their price will not be significantly different from that of an in-house operator that develops a public bid for any major purchases such as new construction or major remodeling.

The real key to the successful concession operation, whether contracted or self-operated, is the on-site concessions manager. The concessionaire can offer that manager a career path of promotion to larger and larger facilities, whereas the in-house operator must find other duties for the manager or risk stagnation if he or she stays in the job too long. Likewise, a concessionaire has other trained managers with new ideas to replace the current manager when he or she is ready for a promotion, whereas an in-house operator will have to recruit outside the facility or promote an assistant when replacing the manager. However, even the best concessionaire can assign a bad manager or one who does not fit into a facility's culture. A bad manager negates the benefits of either system and needs to be replaced immediately.

The decision to contract or self-operate needs to be evaluated both quantitatively and qualitatively. The answer will be dependent on the facility's unique requirement and on the management staff's capabilities and desires.

Contract Negotiations

One reason many facility directors self-operate today is that they had a bad experience with a concessionaire in the past. "They were uncooperative, they were penny pinchers, they were too interested in their own bottom line and not the good of the facility" are phrases overheard in the sports facility industry. Investigation of the problem often shows the concessionaire was as unhappy as the facility director, and the reason was a concessions contract.

Although facility-concessionaire agreements do not give equal rights to both parties, they should clearly establish the parameters by which concessionaires will operate and should provide concessionaires with an equitable return for their work. For this reason, it is recommended that sport managers understand a concessionaire's financial objectives (pricing strategies, product, payroll, operating costs, and profit projections) before entering into an agreement. They should make sure the vendor's expectations are reasonable and obtainable, based on the facility's event and attendance schedule. A knowledgeable source such as a consultant should be used to evaluate the information that prospective concessionaires say they will provide. In fact, most facilities are now employing a consultant who can assist in the development of the request-for-proposal (RFP) document, into the evaluation and selection process, and right through to the final contract negotiations.

Sport managers are in a "buyer's market." Concessionaires are eager to expand and often are willing to meet a team's demands in order to secure the contract. The facility manager or team operator considering offering a contract should complete a thorough reference check of potential concessionaires. This process involves contacting other facility operators who are currently employing the services of the company under consideration. Basic questions would include the following: Does this concessionaire live up to marketing promises? Does the company exceed service expectations?

The following issues should be addressed in a concessions contract:

- Foodservice Contract Demands
- Exclusions—Itemize Potential Exclusions
- Community Festivals
- Religious Conventions
- Ringling Brothers Circus
- Disney on Ice
- Luxury Suites
- Open Catering
- Definitions—Gross versus Net
- Gross Sales
- Gratuities
- Off-Premise Sales
- Subcontracted Sales
- Novelty Sales
- Product Control—Capitalize on Advertising
- Branding
- Variety
- Quality
- Portion
- Pricing
- Management Control—Treat Contractor as Department Head
- Interviews with Management Candidates
- Authority to Dismiss Management
- Staffing levels
- Training Involvement
- Investment—Leasehold, Equipment, Smallwares

- Approval of All Investments
- Approval of Depreciation/Amortization
- Buyout Provisions
- Insurance—Insulate Your Liability
- Hold Harmless
- Product Liability
- Audit Controls—Constant Supervision
- Daily Event Summaries
- Monthly Profit and Loss
- Annual Audit
- Unannounced Audits
- Miscellaneous
- Computerization
- Cash Registers
- Operational Audits
- Repairs and Renovations
- Marketing
- Utilities
- Default
- Bankruptcy
- Mechanic's Liens
- Investment—Leasehold, Equipment, Smallwares
- Approval of All Investments
- Approval of Depreciation/Amortization
- Quality Assurance
- Management
- Staffing
- Product
- Service

There are two basic contract types: the traditional commission agreement and the management fee agreement, which has been growing in acceptance in recent years. Each contract type offers some benefits and some risks.

The *commission agreement* provides for the concessionaire to pay the venue operator a percentage of the concessionaire's gross receipts. The concessionaire supplies and pays all costs for payroll, product, and operating supplies; and the concessionaire retains all profits after the above costs are deducted.

The *management fee agreement* provides for the concessionaire to receive a management fee, typically stated as a percentage of gross receipts and a profit incentive, which is likely to be stated as a percentage of *net* profits. The concessionaire supplies all personnel, product, and operating supplies; and the facility operator reimburses the concessionaire for those costs. The facility retains all profits after the above costs are deducted.

Advantages of the Commission Agreement:

- Eliminates the risk of financial loss to the facility.

- Simplifies the auditing of the concessionaire's operation.

- Insulates the facility from daily operating decision.

Advantages of the Management Fee Agreement:

- Develops a partnership of mutual interest between concessionaire and facility.

- Provides the potential for increased revenues to the facility.

- Provides the facility with greater control and flexibility for foodservice operating decisions.

The management fee arrangement eliminates the typical adversarial relationships found in so many foodservice contracts. Many times, the facility makes demands that cost the concessionaire additional payroll or product cost. The client makes these decisions for the overall good of the facility, but the concessionaire sees it as a negative financial influence to its profits while having to pay the same commissions to the facility.

Under the management fee agreement, both contractor and facility share the costs of operation and the profits. The management fee arrangement reduces the risk a concessionaire may have on low-volume events to provide quality service, but rewards the facility even more for high-volume sales and efficient operations.

The management fee arrangement encourages regular input from the facility manager on items such as product quality, staffing levels, and special pricing for unique events. Management fees typically range from 0 to 7.5%, depending on sales volume and profit. Splits of net profits range from 3 to 25%. The RCA Dome is an example of a facility that switched to a management fee arrangement after 20 years under a commission agreement. RCA Dome management felt the change benefited them by allowing staff more input into concession operations and by increasing revenues to the facility as sales increased.

Financial and Operational Quality Assurance

The successful sport concessions operation is one in which the facility and concessionaire function as partners. Each party is aware of the other's requirements, and each party understands the other's financial constraints. To maintain this mutual respect, it is important for the facility to know that the concessions department is maintaining the highest level of financial and operational integrity.

Annual financial audits and regularly scheduled operational audits provide a facility director with the confidence that the concessionaire is maximizing concession revenues. The use of secret shoppers, comment cards, focus groups, season-ticket-holder surveys, direct mailings, a fan accommodation booth, and even regular appearances on the local sports call-in radio show help facility managers evaluate the concessions and other customer service departments from the customer's point of view. Although every comment is important, if a complaint is repeated several times by several customers, chances are a problem exists that must be corrected immediately. Some large venues are developing quality assurance managers whose sole function is to identify potential problems before customers experience them.

It is recommended that managers of sport venues act as customers for a day each month. In this role, they drive to the facility during rush hour, wait in line to pay to park, wait in line to purchase tickets, ask lots of questions of the service employees, wait in line to purchase concessions, and even to go the restrooms. They sit in the cheap seats. How is the view? Are there any vendors up there? One manager did all of this in a wheelchair to check his ADA compliance and accessibility. The closer sport managers get to their customers, the higher the level of services they can provide, and the more time and money customers will want to spend at their stadiums and arenas.

Summary

Developing a concessions department or contracting with a concessionaire is one of the most important decisions a sport manager makes to ensure the highest level of customer service and maximum operating revenues for the venue. This chapter has detailed many of the critical issues a manager must analyze before initiating a concession program and while overseeing a concessions department or contract.

For sport managers to maximize both customer service and revenues, their concession managers must capitalize on the customers' impulse-spending habits. When managers design the correct facilities and deal with a flexible concessions department, new menu items can be introduced, slow-moving items repackaged or showcased, and new services tried, and all for very little investment.

If an item does not sell, it should be taken off the menu. To find out how high a per cap can be generated without decreasing profits due to excessive payroll, managers should keep adding portable carts and service lines. If a local restaurateur is getting all of the facility's pre-event business, that operator should be brought into the building as a subcontractor, or the facility should produce its product better than the original restaurateur. In other words, managers must keep experimenting and analyzing those per capita spending trends and operating costs.

Currently, customers want higher levels of service and products, and they are willing to pay a premium for such amenities. Managers might package the first ten rows of seats with VIP parking and charge a premium or package a pregame meal, VIP seats, and valet parking and charge a premium. The in-seat wait-staff should use computerized handheld order terminals. Customers are impressed by the fast service. The facility can feature the city's native products, foods, and services. Managers should offer valet parking and a season-ticket-holders' lounge. A premium can be charged for parking spaces closest to the building. Managers can develop a sponsor's lounge where the building sponsors can entertain their customers.

None of these ideas is new. They have all worked at other facilities, and those facility managers all agree: Customers are willing to spend more when they are offered a higher level of service, when their expectations are exceeded, and when they can purchase an exclusive service or be part of an exclusive club.

References

1. Market boom for new venues. (1998, April 27). *Amusement Business*, 3.

Chris Bigelow, FCSI, is president of the Bigelow Companies, Inc., Kansas City, Missouri, and foodservice and merchandise consultant offering management, advisory, and design services to stadiums, arenas, and convention centers.

SECTION IV:
SOLICITING FINANCIAL SUPPORT FROM CORPORATE AND PRIVATE SOURCES

Photo courtesy University of Oregon Athletic Department.

Chapter Twelve

Nature of the Sponsorship Exchange

As we developed this book, some argued with us that sponsorship belongs in a sport marketing rather than a sport financing text. We disagree. From the perspective of a sport manager, sponsorship is viewed primarily as a source of additional financial support. For the most part, sport managers do not enter into sponsorship agreements with companies for the purpose of advertising their event or product to a target audience (media tie-ins may be exceptions to this generalization). In contrast, the primary reason that many companies become sponsors with sport organizations is to communicate with their target audiences by linking with a sports event or facility. The sport manager's role is to understand how companies use sponsorship in their marketing programs, to be responsive to their needs, and then to charge them the maximum fee they are prepared to pay for providing them with these communication opportunities.

The discussion of financing sport through sponsorship is divided into four chapters. This chapter considers the nature of the sponsorship exchange. Chapter 13 views a sponsorship partnership from the perspective of investing companies, while chapter 14 discusses the process sport organizations use to solicit sponsorships from businesses. Finally, in chapter 15, techniques for measuring the impact of sponsorships are presented.

This chapter starts by differentiating between sponsorship and donations, which are discussed later in chapter 16. The evolution of sport sponsorship to its current ubiquitous presence in major professional and elite sport is briefly traced, and its penetration into colleges and high schools is noted. The major factors contributing to sponsorship's current high profile are discussed.

The essence of successful sponsorship is the exchange of mutual benefits, which occurs between the business and sport organization. It is a reciprocal relationship. The organization is likely to seek financial, in-kind, and media benefits, while the benefits that may be sought by businesses can be classified into five categories: increased awareness, image enhancement, demonstration platform, hospitality opportunities, product trial, or sales opportunities. The potential positive and negative consequences of this exchange relationship are discussed.

Exchange theory is the central concept underlying both sponsorship and donations. This theory is one of the most prominent theoretical perspectives in the social sciences and has been used to explain a wide range of phenomena. It has two main precepts: (i) two or more parties exchange resources and (ii) the resources offered by each party must be equally valued by the reciprocating parties.

In the context of this book, sponsorship is defined as a business relationship between a provider of funds, resources, or services and a sport event or organization, which offers in return specific rights that may be used for commercial advantage. The terms in this definition that differentiate sponsorship from philanthropy are *business relationship* and *commercial advantage*.[1]

In response to the first precept of exchange theory, sport organizations and businesses have multiple resources that they may use as "currency" to facilitate an exchange. The sport facility or event may offer businesses increased awareness, image enhancement, a demonstration platform, hospitality opportunities, or product trial or sales opportunities. Companies in return may offer support through investments of money, media exposure, or in-kind services.

The second precept of exchange theory suggests that a corporate partner will ask two questions, "What's in it for me?" and "How much will it cost me?" The trade-off is weighed between what will be gained and what will have to be given up. A decision to invest will only be forthcoming if the trade-off is perceived to be positive and if the benefits accruing cannot be secured more effectively or efficiently from another vehicle. A key feature of this second precept is that the exchange is perceived to be fair by both sides. Fairness is judged by two criteria: (i) the level of benefits received compared to those that were expected and (ii) the level of benefits received compared to those received by other sponsors.[2] If these two criteria are not met, then a sponsor is likely to be dissatisfied and unlikely to invest in the

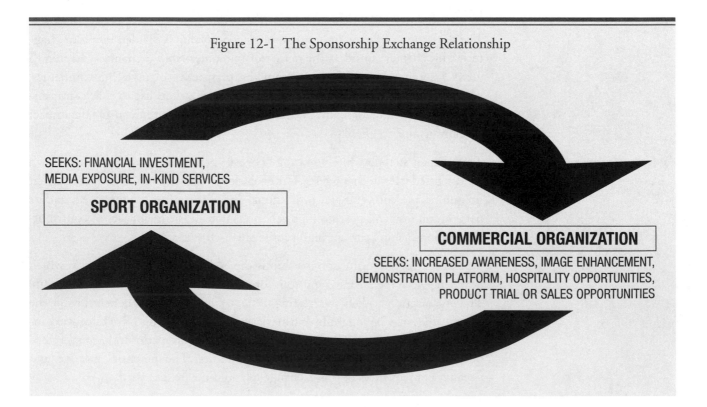

Figure 12-1 The Sponsorship Exchange Relationship

SEEKS: FINANCIAL INVESTMENT, MEDIA EXPOSURE, IN-KIND SERVICES

SPORT ORGANIZATION

COMMERCIAL ORGANIZATION

SEEKS: INCREASED AWARENESS, IMAGE ENHANCEMENT, DEMONSTRATION PLATFORM, HOSPITALITY OPPORTUNITIES, PRODUCT TRIAL OR SALES OPPORTUNITIES

future. In such situations, "rain checks" or future discounts will be required to restore balance to the exchange and remove the sponsor's dissatisfaction.

Both sponsorship and philanthropy offer sources of funds, resources, and in-kind services to sport organizations, but they differ in the nature of the benefits they seek in the exchange. The central benefit sought in philanthropy is the satisfaction of knowing that good is being done with the donated resources. There is no expectation of a more tangible return. The motives underlying philanthropic donations are altruistic rather than commercial. They are concerned with humanistic or community concerns, rather than a commercial return on the investment.

In the early days of sponsorship, it was not often differentiated from philanthropy. Decisions to support a particular sport or sporting event frequently reflected the personal interests of senior management, rather than a careful assessment of the benefits that were likely to accrue to the company from its investment. Today, decisions made in this way are unusual, but they are not unknown. One commentator insists that ego-driven, rather than rational, decisions by senior managers are evident in sponsorship of the men's professional golf tour:

> Between 1989 and 1999, despite the emergence of Tiger Woods, television ratings of PGA events dropped by 19%, while the cost of reaching 1000 households rose 71%. The rationale for golf sponsorships is that they facilitate communication with an upscale audience of consumers and they provide a hospitality forum for hosting important potential and actual business customers. However, many golf sponsorships are purchased by brands that are not targeted at affluent consumers or hosting key business customers. "Let's be honest here. Many companies are in the sport primarily because the CEO is dying to be in the Pro-Am with Tiger Woods."[3] (p. 5)

However, the corporate scandals that emerged in the early years of this century focused attention on corporate governance. As a result, there is now more pressure on senior managers to demonstrate accountability for sponsorship investments by showing their potential for increasing a company's profitability.

Nevertheless, sponsoring sports, like many other corporate innovations, is more likely to come to fruition if it is championed by a senior level decision-maker and the champion's commitment may be stimulated by personal interest. For example, a title sponsor of one of the tournaments on the Ladies Professional Golf Association tour became involved because the company president played golf with the LPGA Commissioner at another event. At the end of the round, the president had committed to hosting a tournament.[4] One executive responsible for sport sponsorships observed,

> There certainly must be corporate interest. It may be employee interest that precipitates the event interest. It may of course be a key executive, an agency recommendation, or the outcome of a marketing plan. To make the event work, there must be a champion. The champion must have the interest, authority, and single minded vision to make the event work.[5] (p. 212)

Executives and directors of a sport property are likely to have strong social networks, and there is evidence that these resources are key to sponsorship decisions. Interlocking directorships and high ranking friendships among senior managers are a primary asset when seeking sponsor partners. Decision makers are likely to invest in those ventures managed by those whom they know and trust. A public relations manager explained that if the president knows someone who sends a proposal, "It'll get a lot more attention than it would at our level if it had come in to us" (p.131).[6] In the context of sponsorship, friendship and trust are key resources because it may take several years for a sponsorship to generate the returns a company seeks.

> The first sponsor of sport was probably a Roman patrician currying favor with his Emperor by underwriting a day of blood-letting in the Coliseum. He would have regarded himself as the patron of the games but since he was seeking a return on investment, he was being no more philanthropic than any of today's commercial sponsors.[7] (p. 157)

Evolution of Sport Sponsorship

The first businesses in the United States to be associated with and invest in sport events were in the transportation industry.[8] In 1852 a New England railroad transported the Harvard and Yale teams to a crew competition and vigorously promoted it. The company profited from the rail tickets sold to thousands of fans who traveled to the site. By the late 1890s, in many cities streetcar and rail companies had developed close links with baseball teams, and other attractions such as amusement parks and public parks, in order to generate traffic from downtown areas to the ballparks.

Similar pioneering sponsorship arrangements were instigated elsewhere. For example, two expatriate Englishmen, Felix Spiers and Christopher Pond, who had established a substantial catering business in supplying refreshments to the Melbourne and Ballarate Railway in Australia, underwrote the cost of the first tour of an English cricket team to Australia in 1861. Referring to this investment, a commentator noted, "It might be stretching the definition to classify as a sponsor a company who walked away with $11,000 in profit" (p. 157).[7] Spiers and Pond capitalized on the publicity they received from this very successful venture by returning to Britain to establish a famous catering company. Similarly, in France the magazine *Velocipide* sponsored an early automobile race in 1887.[9]

In marked contrast to these early isolated examples, sponsorship in the past two decades has emerged as a primary communication vehicle for many thousands of corporations. In 1987 sponsorship spending in North America amounted to $1.35 billion, but by 2003 it had escalated to over $10.5 billion.[10] The top ten U.S. sponsors, each of which invests over $75 million in sponsorship, are shown in Table 12-1. Worldwide spending on sponsorship exceeds $26 billion.[10]

Over two-thirds of this sponsorship ($7.21 billion) was invested in sports (Figure 12-2). Among sports, professional baseball attracts a larger number of sponsoring companies than any other sport. There are at least four reasons for this. First, there are more major and minor league teams than in any other professional sport, and teams play more games in a season. Second, "it's a product that is aligned with some of the peak selling seasons of products like soft drinks and beer, which are

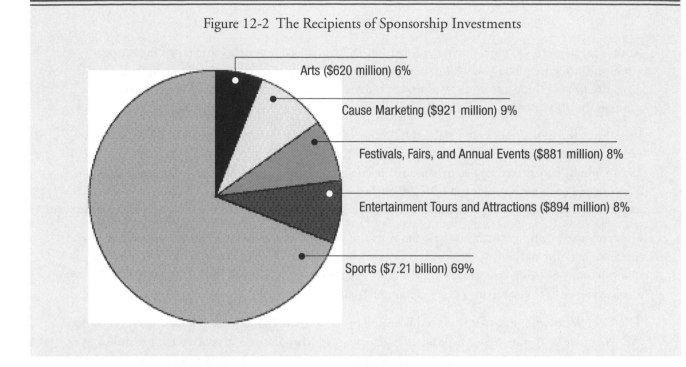

Figure 12-2 The Recipients of Sponsorship Investments

Arts ($620 million) 6%

Cause Marketing ($921 million) 9%

Festivals, Fairs, and Annual Events ($881 million) 8%

Entertainment Tours and Attractions ($894 million) 8%

Sports ($7.21 billion) 69%

Table 12-1 Top 10 U.S. Sponsors: Companies Spending More Than $75 Million

Amount	Company	2001 Rank
$215M-$220M	Anheuser-Busch Cos.	1
$190M-$195M	Philip Morris Cos.	2
	PepsiCo, Inc.	3
$165M-$170M	General Motors Corp.	4
$130M-$135M	The Coca-Cola Co.	5
$105M-$110M	DaimlerChrysler Corp.	6
	Nike, Inc	7
$90M-$95M	Eastman Kodak Co.	8
$75M-$80M	Ford Motor Co.	9
	McDonald's Corp.	10

*These figures represent fees paid for sponsorship rights. They do not include additional expenditures for advertising, promotion, client entertainment, or philanthropic contributions.

Source: IEG. (2001). *Sponsorship Report,* December 25.

probably the two biggest categories putting money into professional sports" (p. 16).[11] Third, the natural breaks between innings offer opportunities for sponsors to communicate their messages. Fourth, the slow pace of the game enables spectators to look around: "The action doesn't move quite as quickly as it does in the other sports and your eye wanders, making the signs in the outfield or on the scoreboard that much more visible" (p.16).[11]

The evolution of sponsorship at the early Olympic Games is briefly described in Figure 12-3. In more contemporary times, increases in Olympic Games sponsorship fees offer perhaps the most dramatic indication of sponsorship growth over the past two decades. The 1976 Olympics had 628 sponsors who attached themselves to the Games for a total of $4.18 million.[12] In 1984, the Los Angeles Olympic Organizing Committee conceived the idea of acquiring a substantial proportion of funding for the Games from corporate sponsorship. They persuaded 32 companies to each pay between $4 million and $13 million in cash, goods, and services. As a result, the 1984 Games reported a net profit of $222 million.

After the Los Angeles Games, the International Olympic Committee (IOC) established The Olympic Program (TOP) that was run by the IOC, not the host

Figure 12-3 The Evolution of Sponsorship at the Olympic Games

At the first modern Olympic Games in Athens in 1896, financial pressures caused the Organizing Committee to raise money by selling souvenir stamps and medals as well as advertising in the souvenir program. One of those advertisers was Kodak and the company is committed as a TOP sponsor through the 2008 Beijing Games. Thus, from the beginning, the Olympics had a commercial presence.

In 1912 at the Stockholm Games, the IOC commenced selling broader commercial rights to corporations: several Swedish companies were permitted to take photographs and sell memorabilia. At the 1924 Games, two advertising signs appeared inside the Olympic Stadium adjacent to the scoreboard. This created such a furor that the IOC established a new rule in the Olympic Charter: "Commercial installations and advertising signs shall not be allowed in the stadia, nor in the other sports grounds."

However, the Olympics had to be paid for, so at the 1928 Amsterdam Games on-site concessions were solicited, and one of the first vendors was Coca-Cola. Coca-Cola was perhaps the first company to extend the value of being associated with the games by claiming the title of Official Olympic Supplier as a consequence of the company's contribution of 1,000 cases of the soft drink to the American Team.

The Oslo Winter Olympics introduced licensing in 1952 when 135 agreements were signed mostly for decorative souvenirs; value-in-kind arrangements with corporations supported the Helsinki Games that summer and delivered food to the athletes. The first full showing of sponsorship surfaced eight years later in Rome, when 46 companies paid to become "official sponsors/suppliers" of non-sports related products. This was the start of a flood of commercial support that reached its crest in Montreal with 628 sponsors.

Source: Adopted from Rozin, S. (1996). Olympic Partnership, *Sports Illustrated*, Special Advertising Section.

Table 12-2 TOPs Lead Sponsorships in the Olympic Games 1988 through 2000

		Number of Companies	Total Revenue (US $)
1988	Calgary/Seoul	9	$95M
1992	Albertville/Barcelona	12	$175M
1996	Lillehammer/Atlanta	10	$350M
2000	Nagano/Sydney	11	$550M

Source: Brown, G. (2002). Taking the pulse of Olympic sponsorship. *Event Management*, 7, 187-196.

Olympic organizing committee. Under TOP, companies sign on for a four-year period, embracing both Summer and Winter Games. They gain the right to promote their Olympic affiliation in every participating country and gain worldwide exclusivity within their product category.[12]

TOP led to an exponential increase in the fee for sponsorship but added value through substantially reducing "clutter" by having fewer sponsors. The trend is shown in Table 12-2. At the Sydney Olympics, the 11 TOP sponsors each invested $50 million, so total sponsorship from this source amounted to $550 million.[13] In addition, most corporations invested at least twice that amount to

Table 12-3 Companies Involved in the IOC's "TOP" Sponsorship

Sponsor	Exclusive product or service category	First Olympic involvement	First Olympics as a top sponsor	Current sponsorship ends
Coca-Cola	Nonalcoholic beverages	1928	1988	2008
IBM	Information technology	1960	1994	2000
John Hancock	Life insurance/annuities	1994	1994	2004
Kodak	Film/photographics and imaging	1896	1988	2008
Matsushita (Panasonic)	Audio/TV/video equipment	1988	1998	2000
McDonald's	Retail food services	1976	1998	2004
Samsung	Wireless communication	1998	1998	2000
Sema Group	Systems integration, operations management, and application delivery	1998	2002	2008
Sports Illustrated/Time	Periodicals/newspapers/ magazines	1980	1988	2004
UPS	Express mail/package delivery service	1994	1996	2000
Visa	Consumer payment systems	1988	1988	2004
Xerox	Document publishing, processing, and supplies	1964	1994	2004

Source: Woodward, S. (2000). Going for the corporate gold. *Sports Business*. September 11-17, 4 & 34.

leverage benefits from their sponsorship. Nevertheless, most claimed to have received a good return. Indeed, 9 of the 11 partners had signed agreements for the subsequent quadrennium embracing the Salt Lake City and Athens' Games before the Sydney Games were held! Table 12-3 shows that most of the major contemporary Olympic sponsors have had an enduring relationship with the Games since the IOC established TOP in 1988. The TOP sponsorship fee for the 2008 Beijing Olympics will be approximately $70 million. The benefits corporations accrued from previous Olympics will be boosted at the Beijing Games by the unparalleled platform it offers for establishing a relationship with the emerging Chinese market of 1.3 billion people.

In addition to TOP sponsorship, the host organizing committee offers sponsorship opportunities. These rights permit corporations to associate themselves domestically with the Games. Thus, the Sydney Organizing Committee of the Olympic Games generated $492 million in sponsorships, which was equivalent to more than $25 for every Australian citizen. Finally, a third category of sponsors are licensees whose rights are most narrowly defined. In all cases, the rights are exclusive within specific categories.

In addition to increased recognition of sponsorship's marketing value as a communication vehicle and the concomitant increase in magnitude of corporate investment, two other trends have emerged in the evolution of sponsorship in recent years. First has been its widespread extension from professional and elite sport to collegiate and high school sport. In a 1989 article in the *Chronicle of Higher Education*, corporate sponsorship was characterized as having made "relatively limited inroads into college athletics."[14] That has changed. Almost all NCAA Division I and II colleges and universities have some form of corporate sponsorship. For example, Texas A&M and the University of Texas partnered with AT&T and renamed their annual Thanksgiving football game "The AT&T Lone Star Showdown." In addition to the title, there were banners at the gate and in the stadium; public address announcements; and inclusion of the title in publicity, advertisements for the game, and on the program. Each team received $125,000 from the sponsorship. Similarly, the annual football game between Texas and Oklahoma in Dallas became the "Dr. Pepper Red River Shootout." Facility sponsorship now is common on campuses, and it goes beyond the sale of naming rights that was discussed in chapter 7.

For example, at Ohio State University's Jerome Schottenstein Center, sponsors can buy in at three different levels ranging in price from $75,000 to $250,000 per year. In exchange, sponsors receive a combination of signage, tickets, and access to luxury suites—but no television, radio, or program advertising. The Center's 15 sponsors generate $2.5 million per year for Ohio State. Signage is located on the main scoreboard, on the facia in the inner bowl, on the scorer's table, and on the four giant matrix boards that occupy each of the arena's four corners. Because they are guaranteed to appear when games are televised, the scoreboard and the scorer's table invariably are the most attractive signage options to potential sponsors. To minimize the adverse visual impact of signage, like most schools, Ohio State uses rotating signage. Each rotating panel contains multiple faces, which means a school can meet the needs of many sponsors in a single, compact space. Sponsors also tend to prefer this approach because their message does not get lost in a mass of competing messages in the arena.

Sponsorship is now percolating from varsity level to intramural sports on campus. The corporate goal is to raise brand awareness among college students who are an influential, but relatively difficult to access, consumer group. While only 2% of college students are varsity athletes, it is claimed that 80% of them participate in recreational sports.[15] An illustration of intramural sponsorship is given in Figure 12-4.

At the high school level, an increasing number of school districts are unable to provide the funds needed to offer a full range of high school athletic programs. More high schools are moving to a "pay to play" system in which athletes pay a fee for each sport in which they participate. There are more than 18,000 high school programs across the United States managing over 6.5 million athletic participants. Approximately one-fourth collect participation fees from students.[14] High school tournaments are becoming more expensive to organize and gate receipts in those sports for which there is a charge are insufficient to cover the costs of many tournaments. These conditions have created interest in soliciting sponsors. The trend began in the mid 1980s with corporate sponsored regional and state athletic championships. The companies have carefully segmented the high school market into ever smaller niches. For example, apparel manufacturers initially associated their name with statewide tournaments, then moved to targeting specific school districts with larger or wealthier populations of potential buyers, and then to specific athletic programs (those that won frequently!). It has become relatively common for comprehensive partner agreements to be signed with schools offering sponsorship of their entire athletic department or even their entire school population to corporations. Agreements of this nature with soft-drink companies are particularly prevalent.[15] For example, the Metropolitan School District in Madison, Wisconsin, contracted exclusive pouring rights on its campuses to Coca-Cola for more than $1.5 million.[16]

Most of the high school sponsorship agreements are with governing bodies rather than individual schools:

- Wendy's International Inc., and its North Carolina franchises acquired a five-year, $2 million sponsorship with the North Carolina High School Athletic Association. The company receives presenting status at all NCHSAA's championships and all-star summer events and couponing opportunities with member high schools in the state.

Figure 12-4 Sponsorship of Intramural Flag Football

Flag football is a popular intramural program that has attracted sponsorship. Recent sponsors were Target (title sponsor), Nestlé Crunch (presenting sponsor), and Mentadent (presenting sponsor). The sponsors enjoy near year-round visibility on campuses that offer intramural flag football. Their banners encircle playing fields. Their names appear on cones that mark boundaries, and on flag belts. They distribute product samples and award prizes to the winners of sideline competitions. And they award expenses-paid trips to New Orleans to regional-winning teams in men's, women's, and co-ed divisions.

Regional hosts have welcomed as many as 58 teams to their campuses for three days of competition. "It is quite a sight," noted the intramural director at a regional tournament host institution. "If you drive by the fields during that weekend, you know who the sponsors are. It's very visible, almost a party atmosphere."

Another regional tournament host director observed that the advent of corporate sponsorship generated more interest in the tournament from local media, the campus community, and visiting participants. He said, "With corporate sponsorship, you have things like windbreakers, and you can do a lot of the niceties that you normally wouldn't have the money to do."

The director of marketing at Nestlé said that students surveyed three months after participating in the flag football tournament were twice as likely to list Nestlé Crunch among their five favorite brands of candy bars as they were upon their tournament registration. "What the sponsorship program allows us to do is to have continued brand presence throughout the year, via the Web sites that students access to look at calendars and the standings and via the message boards that are in the intramural facilities. Most important, we have a chance to participate in a relevant way in the consumers' lives by sponsoring an activity that is very near and dear to them."

Source: Adapted from Steinback, P. (2000). Intramarketing, *Athletic Business*, January, 26-28.

AT&T provided telephones, PBX switches, wiring and cabling for venues, video phones, desktop video teleconference equipment, AT&T Language Line translation services, voice mail, and international calling centers for Olympic athletes, officials, and spectators.

Eastman Kodak provided imaging equipment and supplies.

Xerox provided document-processing equipment, including laser printers, fax machines, copiers, electronic scanners, engineering reprographic products, document creation supplies, and networked and stand-alone systems reprographics.

IBM computers supported virtually every aspect of the Olympic Games from the results system to the design of Olympic venues prior to construction.

Sensormatic Electronics provided closed-circuit video surveillance systems, access control and electronic article surveillance during the Games and high-tech electronic security systems for USOC headquarters and Olympic training centers.

Randstad Staffing Services addressed the Organizing Committee's staffing needs through recruiting, screening, training, and placing people to fill administrative positions.

Bell South provided a wide spectrum of communications services including wireline video and data transmission, cellular, local, and nationwide paging.

Blue Cross and Blue Shield provided health insurance coverage for employees of ACOG and the USOC.

Borg-Warner Security provided a wide range of security personnel and services at ACOG headquarters, ACOG-hosted events and the Games, including uniformed security officers and armored transport.

UPS met the logistical needs of the Games with distribution services between Atlanta and the almost 200 participating countries.

There are 186 Wendy's and 326 high schools in the state, which is almost a one-to-two relationship between stores and high schools.

To increase restaurant traffic, Wendy's distributed more than 3.75 million tickets to NCHSAA schools. Schools may use the blank tickets, which feature coupon offers for a free hamburger with a fries and drink purchase, rather than printing their own tickets to athletic events or other activities. About 80 percent of the state's high schools used the Wendy's tickets. Besides increasing sales, Wendy's hoped visibility from the tie would lead to enhanced student interest in employment opportunities.[17]

• US West Communications Group agreed on a ten-year, $2 million sponsorship with the Jefferson County (Colorado) School District to be its "strategic supplier" of telecommunications services. This included naming rights to the District's football stadium.[18]

A second emerging trend in the evolution of sponsorship in sports is the emergence of affinity cards. These are used both by colleges and professional teams. The team links with a bank that issues credit cards. Each time someone uses the card, the team receives a contribution—typically 1%—of the amount charged. A team challenges its supporters to ask the question, "Why use a bank card that just gives money to the bank, when you can use one that gives money to the team you support?" By tapping people's loyalty to a team in this way, banks have an opportunity to encourage card-switching and to increase their market share. The cost to the banks is relatively small because these payments reflect a small portion of what they earn from annual fees and the interest that they charge card holders. It is also a small part of the percentage of each transaction that they charge their participating merchants, which ranges from 1.5% to 6%:

> Manchester United, England's leading soccer club, has a Visa affinity card. It is promoted through direct mail and game program advertising. The club has a database of over 150,000 adult supporters who are targeted. The club's marketing manager said, "We find the card is a good way for fans to support the club without paying any extra. This service gives fans the opportunity to support Manchester United."[19]

Factors Stimulating Sponsorship Growth

In the past decade, the rate of growth in sponsorship has far outpaced that of investment in any other form of marketing communication or promotion vehicle. We noted earlier that the 1984 Los Angeles Olympic Games was a watershed event that demonstrated to the corporate sector that sponsorship could be a highly effective promotional medium. It created substantial impetus, but there were several factors that undergirded it and continue to stimulate contemporary corporate involvement in sponsorship.

One strength of sponsorship is that it is able to efficiently communicate with specific target audiences. Thus, widespread acceptance of the concept of market segmentation, which emerged in the 1970s and 1980s, enhanced corporate interest in sponsorship. Market segmentation is the process of partitioning large markets into smaller homogenous subsets of people with similar characteristics who are likely to exhibit similar purchasing behavior. In the 1960s, most companies were moving products by mass marketing. By the 1980s, successful companies recognized that a mass market did not exist, but rather the marketplace consisted of segments or clusters of potential customers with a different propensity to purchase particular products and services. Acceptance of segmentation was accelerated by the high profile documentation provided by demographers of the fragmentation of society into yuppies, single parent families, dual-income households with children, "empty nesters," and so on. This fragmentation made a company's potential consumer more elusive and difficult to reach.

Sports fans are spread widely across the full range of demographic and psychographic types, so sponsors can target specific audiences by their choice of sport. This has been reflected in the growth of more narrowly focused outlets that cater to special interests both in the broadcast and print media. For example, 40 years ago sports magazines were dominated by generic publications such as *Sports Illustrated* and were relatively few in number. Today, there are likely to be between two and six magazines catering to each individual sport such as golf, running, or base-ball. Their readership profiles offer the potential for sponsors to reach a large pro-portion of their target market through association with events conveyed as news by these media. The advent of cable and satellite dishes has created similar target-ing opportunities for sponsors in the television media. It has been noted that "sponsorship works because it fulfills the most important criterion of a commu-nications medium—it allows a particular audience to be targeted with a particu-lar set of messages" (p. 42).[1]

The proliferation of television channels, of subscription services via cable and satellite, and of pay-per-view special events has led to a substantial increase in the amount of televised sport produced. Sport attracts a relatively high percentage of television air time since much of it is relatively inexpensive to produce, and it is widely popular compared to shows, documentaries, etc. The use of television to expand a sponsorship's impact beyond those attending an event is highly valued by sponsors, so the increased opportunities to do this stimulated sponsorship.

The growth of sponsorship has been inextricably linked with increasing accep-tance of the commercialization of sport by the public and by organizing bodies. One of the authors recalls participating in a meeting with the chairman of a lead-ing English professional soccer club in the early 1970s, who was also chairman of the Football League, professional soccer's organizing body in England. The chair-man was genuinely outraged and scornful of the idea of sponsorship, saying, "You'd have all our players running around with Texaco on their shirts." Ten years later, all major British soccer clubs were doing just that! We noted earlier that a similar "acceptance curve" of sports sponsorship is moving down from profes-sional sports organizations, to colleges, and even to the high school level in the United States.

The proliferation of products and services and the increased competition that have characterized the marketplace in the past decade have been accompanied by a consolidation of companies through mergers and take-overs. Thus, in many in-dustries, fewer but larger companies exercise more control and influence in distri-bution channels. This has made it more critical for producers to enhance relations with distributors. Sponsorships offer communication opportunities through sport entertainment and hospitality. A related stimulus has been the evolution of large national food and drug chains who stock their own "No Name" and house brands. This has persuaded some consumer goods companies to invest more heav-ily in sponsorship promotional tie-ins that offer incentives for the trade and "push" volume through trade channels to consumers.[20]

The influence of two other factors that provided the initial impetus for sponsor-ship in the early 1980s and early 1990s has waned in recent years. In 1971, Con-gress passed legislation banning tobacco advertisements on television, so companies making these products sought alternative promotion avenues. Spon-sorship partnerships with sports were appealing for three main reasons. First, the association gave these potentially harmful products an aura of public respectabil-ity. Second, the extensive television coverage of sport provided them with access to a medium from which they were technically banned, even tough their messages had to be indirect. Third, it enabled them to access the youth market, and re-cruiting adolescents to smoke is crucial to the future viability of the tobacco industry. However, legal restraints were imposed on tobacco sponsorship of sporting events in 2001, which substantially reduced the sponsorship activity of tobacco companies.

In the 1980s and early 1990s, when the number of television channels increased fourfold, the number of advertising messages vying for attention made it difficult for a particular message to make an impact. The clutter problem arising from the proliferation of advertisements was accentuated by an increase in the growth of 15-second spots and in the amount of commercial time inserted into programs by the television companies: "The constant clutter of traditional media is like a roomful of people talking. If you cannot separate your voice, then you are wasting your money " (p. 4).[21] The reduced ability to communicate effectively with a target audience was negatively reinforced by the introduction and widespread use of the "zapper," which enabled people to tune out commercials without leaving their arm chair, and of the videocassette recorder, which enabled them to fast-forward commercials. In this environment, sponsorship was perceived to be a cost-efficient means of communicating that avoided this clutter. However, this initial sponsorship stimulus has waned. The profusion of sponsorships associated with televised sport has created clutter, and this now is among the reasons cited by companies for terminating their involvement with sponsorship of sport. For example, the marketing director of a company who did not renew a sponsorship agreement with the NFL observed,

> The NBA went from selling just eight major sponsorships a few years ago to selling 30 or more today. It's very hard to stand out in that crowd. There are so many sponsors that your brand's presence there is simply ignored, and the millions you paid to be involved are thoroughly wasted.[3] (p. 73)

This situation arose because of the extraordinarily large fees the television networks paid for major sports properties. For example, in 1998, Disney, CBS, and Fox together paid $17.6 billion to televise NFL games through 2005.[3] In chapter 2, we noted the net worth of the NBA in 2002 was $6.55 billion. This suggests that the networks could have bought the entire NFL for less than they paid for the television rights! To recoup the investment on these fees, the networks had to add more commercial spots, so now there are 59 in each NFL game, which creates substantial clutter.

Sponsorship has three special strengths that have sustained its growth. First, positioning has become a central concept in marketing strategy, and corporate and brand image development are key factors in positioning. Image is used to differentiate and position products that are essentially similar, and sponsorship is particularly suited to image enhancement.

A second strength is that companies can use sponsorship for both integrating a promotion strategy (this is discussed in chapter 13) and as a platform for furthering objectives with employees, distributors, and customers. Among employees, it may be used to create a sense of pride and commitment to the company:

- The Home Depot, Inc., has 200,000 employees. The company's vice-president of marketing and communications noted that a goal of all their sponsorships, whether it was the Olympics, NASCAR, or a community event, was to enhance employee morale. "At the end of the day, it's the person in that orange apron who smiles and walks you to your product who will be the difference. . . There aren't a lot of companies where you can wear an apron with Olympic team emblems. . . It's a real powerful emotional platform. . . They get used to it and feel good about it."

The company takes the association with the Olympics one step further by hiring Olympic contenders through its Olympic Job Opportunity Program. A spokesperson said, "It's our piece of the Olympics; we have Olympic hopefuls working side by side with our associates. They're great role models, goal oriented, dedicated, and have a great work ethic."[22] (p. 1)

Among distributors and salesmen, sponsorship can be used as an incentive for them to increase sales:

- Kodak offered packages to the Sydney Olympics to distributors who achieved sales targets, and hospitality and travel costs were more than offset by the incremental sales that were gained.[23]

- Nabisco was a major sponsor of the men's professional golf tour. Most of the buyers at the supermarket chains liked to play golf. In the words of a former Nabisco manager, "They bribed them. 'Stock Oreos, Premium Saltines, Chips Ahoy and we'll go golf!' And it worked—at least until scanners came along and stores were able to determine exactly how well these items sold compared to their competitors."[24]

The third, and perhaps the defining, strength of sponsorship is that it offers opportunities for a company to establish a more intimate and emotionally involved relationship with its target audience than is feasible with traditional advertising. Unlike advertising, the activity in which a sponsor invests is not part of the company's central commercial function. Advertising asks consumers to pay attention to the company's message and to buy the products, but gives them nothing in return.[3] However, sponsorship offers a more balanced exchange in that in return for accepting a company's commercial presence, consumers are offered a sporting event in which they are interested that might not have taken place without the sponsor. This may reinforce their interest and respect.

A company's relationship with most of its audiences is usually rather distant and obviously commercial, while sponsorship enables a target market to be approached through activities in which they are personally interested. The intent is to communicate with audiences through their interests and lifestyle activities and, thus, create an emotional attachment between the audience and the sponsoring organization. The marketing director of a food service business observed in explaining his company's shift from advertising to sponsorship,

The food service business traditionally advertises to people via radio, TV, and coupons—things most of us are bombarded with in our daily life. What feels right to us is a need to be more passionate and intimate because that's how we treat customers in our stores.[25] (p. 1)

One of the pioneers of sponsorship stated,

> Sponsorship gives products value in the social and moral sense. It tells the consumer what a company believes, so the consumer may choose the product for its affinity with the realities of the consumer's life. Products don't borrow equity from sponsorship; they express equity through sponsorship.

> Companies that treat sponsorship simply as a channel for broadcasting messages, distributing products, and processing transactions fail to gain the medium's real benefits. Sponsorship's power lies in its ability to draw an individual customer into conversation with the company. Sponsorship is not just a means to communicate a message. It is the message.[26] (p. 2)

The commercial intent of establishing an emotional relationship is to persuade consumers that "the sponsor supports sports events they care about, so they should patronize the sponsor."[27] Evidence of this reciprocity occurs when consumers make a conscious decision to go out of their way to support the brands that support the events they care about.

Sport matters to people, and for this reason it is an invaluable conduit for any message that a company might wish to convey. Sport sponsorship enables a company to deliver its message to potential purchasers who are relaxed and in a state of mind and an environment that makes them likely to be receptive. Sponsorship has the capacity to touch the hearts and minds of people. If it achieves this, then it is likely to facilitate potential purchasers spending quality time with a company and its products: "When you reach prospects who are interested in or are attending an event, they are yours. They are there because they want to be. They're part of the event and in a receptive mood" (p. 4).[28]

When Visa decided to sponsor the decathlon in the 1990s, it was not an obvious choice. The sport was in sorry shape in America. Visa's sponsorship meant that athletes could quit their day jobs and focus on the event. Almost single-handedly, Visa returned the U.S. to the top in the sport, wrapped itself in the flag, linked itself in its customers' minds with some of the bravest athletes in the world and generated considerable publicity, goodwill, and admiration for its brand among Americans. All this for about the same price as a single prime-time 30-second television commercial.[3]

However, the onset of sponsorship clutter has made the establishment of this emotional connection more difficult. In the 1980s and early 1990s, the novelty of companies making major investments in sporting events made audiences more receptive to emotionally bonding with them. Now the profusion of sponsorship partnerships has led many to take them for granted. The CEO of a prominent sponsor company noted, "We have to work a lot harder now to get consumers to transfer the warm feelings they have about a property to its sponsors" (p. 4).[29] He went on to articulate the importance of sponsorship's emotional relationship to his company's business:

> I've been at John Hancock for 17 years. I have yet to meet the broker, financial advisor, or insurance agent who would ever admit that he or she wrote a piece of business because of our Olympic sponsorship. They, of course, believe it's the genius of their salesmanship that does the job. Yet

we know the Olympics are a factor. In our business, where people are basically paying us to collect something they aren't going to live to collect, they are not about to give money to a stranger. They entrust it to someone with whom they have a relationship, a company about which they feel strongly. If they associate your brand with an American winning a gold medal at an Olympic event, that goes a long way toward building that trust. When the sponsorship precedes the sales pitch, it softens that consumer and creates a certain receptivity that makes a sale more likely.[29] (p. 4)

Benefits Sought from Sponsorship by Sport Organizations

A sport manager is likely to solicit three types of sponsorship benefits: financial, media, and in-kind. Often, the first question asked by a potential sponsor relates to how much media promotion will be forthcoming. Thus, if media sponsorship is secured early, it is likely to make it easier to attract other sponsors. Alternatively, the sport organization can ask the major sponsor with which media the company would prefer to be associated or with whom it has worked effectively in the past, and then it can approach these media. The downside of having a prominent media sponsor is that its competitors are unlikely to give the event significant coverage.

In-kind sponsorship with media is more difficult to obtain than it used to be. The amount of space available has shrunk considerably. Media realized that many sport managers, after negotiating the in-kind media assistance, were collecting revenues from it by selling the in-kind space to other co-sponsors. Instead of allowing events to broker this space, the media now do it themselves, or else write into agreements that mention of co-sponsors in that space is precluded.

There are five main types of in-kind benefits that a business sponsor may provide: (i) product support, which could include equipment and food and beverages; (ii) personnel support, such as assistance from staff who may have computing expertise the sport organization needs; (iii) communication resources and expertise to increase awareness and interest; (iv) prizes such as merchandise and gift certificates that can be used by both the event organizers and event cosponsors; (v) website exposure that provides exposure to the sport organization and its event. Figure 12-5 shows a sample of the in-kind benefits provided by companies that sponsored the Atlanta Olympic Games. The sponsorship fee they paid was comprised of some combination of money and the value of in-kind services the companies provided.

If a sponsor invests in extending the promotion accompanying a sports event because of a desire to increase awareness of the sponsor's linkage to it, this widens the market for the event. Sponsoring corporations sometimes have more expertise and funds available for promotion than the sport organization responsible for an event:

> Every sports property, no matter how large, is in the midst of a ferocious battle for the attention of consumers. If the properties are honest, most will tell you they don't have the marketing expertise or dollars to make themselves unforgettable. But, we sponsors do have those dollars, and unfortunately most event organizers—*most*—don't want sponsors to behave

like marketing partners, regardless of what their agents tell us in the sales pitch.

If we were smart, event organizers would end up in a situation where it doesn't cost you money to promote your property. Instead, other people—your sponsors—would actually pay you to promote it. MLB leverages its sponsors' dollars by requiring them to promote the game. Sponsors have to build sweepstakes and promotions around baseball, they have to buy commercial time on national games, and a certain percentage of that commercial time must be spent on baseball-themed ads. When you add up these commitments, baseball has an extra advertising budget of millions of dollars that we sponsors are paying for.[29] (p. 5)

It is easier for companies to invest in in-kind sponsorship because it can be "hidden" from shareholders or employees who may be skeptical of the value of sponsorship. Thus, an executive from Target commenting on his company's sponsorship of the NBA Minnesota Timberwolves' basketball arena observed, "We were concerned about negative reaction from the press, public, and employees. Try telling your employees you can afford to put the company's name on an arena when they are receiving only minimal raises" (p. 4).[30] One of the most widely cited sponsor successes in sport was the Cornhill Insurance Company's sponsorship of English international cricket games, but one commentator recalls,

One retains the memory of Cornhill staff pickets parading outside the Oval Cricket Ground in London during a Test [international] match. Their banners pointed out that, while the company was spending £400,000 a year on cricket, it was, so they alleged, being less than generous in current wage negotiations with its own employees. The fact that sponsorship funds, even if diverted into wage packets, would have little effect on them, or that, as part of a marketing campaign, the money is better spent in promoting business and thus underpinning salaries in the long term, is an esoteric argument that cannot compete with emotive banners, especially at a time of rising unemployment.[31] (p. 77)

Associated Costs

These investments may require the sport organization to accept some costs. Four of these types of costs may not immediately be apparent, but have the potential to be controversial. First, in return for their support, sponsors may insist on changing the sporting event, altering the very nature of the sport. There is a well-known aphorism that says he who pays the piper calls the tune. Often, changes may be implemented to make the sporting event more exciting, entertaining, and attractive to television, or to better fit the media's programming format so the sponsor's audience is expanded. Tennis is an example of this type of influence. The method of scoring was changed by the introduction of sudden death tie breakers to shorten the length of matches, and the traditional white apparel was replaced by multi-colored outfits. There are many other examples:

- The growth of one-day cricket matches in national and international competitions was, in part, a result of television audiences wanting to see an immediate and definite outcome, rather than waiting up to six days for a result which, even then, was not guaranteed to produce a winner. In amateur sport, field hockey has experienced a number of rule changes aimed at making the game faster and therefore more attractive to spectators. The sport of lacrosse witnessed another form of development through the formation of the Major Indoor Lacrosse League in the United States. In order to increase goal-scoring opportunities, the net was widened by six inches and the number of penalties reduced, as compared to traditional box style lacrosse.[32] (p. 334)

- Seed money from AT&T helped launch the Women's Pro Fastpitch League, but that capital came at a price—the sponsor hand-picked the cities where the league would play, placing teams in new markets AT&T was looking to crack open. That kept the league out of some cities with a strong amateur and college softball tradition.[33]

A second type of cost is a perception that the ancillary commercial needs of a sponsor become more important than the intrinsic merit of the sporting event itself. The Olympic Games is perhaps the forum in which this debate reaches its epitome, but the issue is debated in many other contexts at lower levels of sport. The central role of U.S. television companies and sponsors in financing the Olympic Games, for example, has resulted in the schedule of track and field events being arranged so they can be shown live on prime time television in the United States. Thus, on occasions, for example, marathoners have been required to race during the hottest part of the day. In such cases, the welfare of the athletes and focus on the event become subservient to commercial interests.

Commercial ties to the Olympic Games date from the beginning of the century. One writer described the early Olympics as "nothing more than 'sporting sideshows' for the Universial Exhibition in Paris (1890), the Great Exhibition and Fair in St. Louis (1904), and the Anglo-French Exhibition in London (1908). The Exhibitions promoted the products of industrial capital and provided venues for the seduction of new custom" (p.205).[34] However, such commercial linkages were subtle—far removed from the ostentatious sponsorship links that first emerged in the Los Angeles Games that led one writer to conclude, "Who won the L.A. Olympics? It is clear from this analysis that commercialism ran away with the Gold" (p. 204).[34]

Such criticism tends to emerge when sponsorship is invested in an event for the first time if it transgresses a long established precedent of not having commercial involvement. Over time the criticism typically wanes as it becomes accepted as the new norm. Consider the case of the Olympic flame:

> The Major of Olympia threatened to prevent the Olympic flame leaving his city when the Los Angeles Olympic Organizing Committee announced that it had sold sections of the flame's path across the U.S. for $3000 per kilometer. It is interesting to note that no similar objection was raised in 1988 when Petro-Canada sponsored the Olympic Torch relay across Canada prior to the Calgary Winter Olympic Games.[32] (p. 335)

In the context of college athletics, Georgia Tech's decision to solicit sponsorships for each of its seven home games brought forth the following comment:

After selling games, what's next? How long before we hear Georgia Tech's stadium announcer say, "Wake Forest's Bell South extra-point try was blocked by Tech's Coca-Cola linebacker Wood Woodson, and now the Georgia-Pacific scoreboard shows Wake Forest with 20 Marriott points to Georgia Tech's 17 Domino's Pizza Points"? (p. 96)[35]

In an attempt to ameliorate the impact of this type of backlash, many sports organizations, including the NCAA, NFL, and NBA, have imposed rules limiting the size of corporate logos that can be displayed on team uniforms. For example, the NCAA's Rule 43 limits the size and number of manufacturers' logos on team uniforms and equipment to "a single manufacturer's logo not to exceed 1 inch square."

The concern that sponsorship's commercial needs impinge on the intrinsic merits of sport and its associated values is particularly prominent in the high school context. When soft drink companies provide free scoreboards in exchange for their advertisements being placed on the scoreboards, questions arise: "Should high school sports events be used to promote consumption of a product that the U.S. Department of Agriculture and all reputable health and nutrition texts urge students to avoid?" and "Does it make sense for the school to be teaching avoidance in the classroom and to encourage use on the sports field?" There appears to be an ethical issue with schools embracing a set of values they probably should be against:

> The fast food industry is under attack from a growing army of lawyers, doctors and otherwise ordinary citizens. Elected officials are coming under pressure to pass laws limiting the junk food sold in schools. "Big Food" is becoming a target of protest just as "Big Tobacco" was in the 1990s. Protestors are campaigning for fast-food companies to put cigarette-style warning labels on their food. Junk-food makers have to appeal to children to sell their products. They need to create their customer to service, but is this something that sport managers should support through accepting sponsorship from such companies? Everyone can get excited at the revenues these sponsors bring to the organization, school, or association, but don't sport managers have an obligation to ask whether these products are good for the people being targeted before accepting them as sponsors?[36]

Chapter 7 noted the potential negative consequences to a team's image of its naming rights sponsor going bankrupt. The potential of negative repercussions to a property also exists if the sponsor engages in actions that are perceived to be antisocial, which generate adverse publicity. This is a third potential cost properties may incur in sponsorship partnerships.

- The IOC prohibited the Salt Lake Organizing Committee from naming an official gun sponsor of the 2002 Games, saying that handguns do not mesh with the Olympics' mission of peace, even though the Olympic Games includes shooting as one of its summer sports. The company SIG Saver had agreed to provide $150,000 in funding and commemorative sidearms to police officers who volunteered during the Olympics.[37]

- Edison International power company was a major sponsor of the MLB Anaheim Angels. Its sponsorship included naming rights to Edison International Field. Its subsidiary, Southern California Edison, was in financial difficulty and unable to make payments to suppliers. Hence, the suppliers threatened to refuse to deliver power to the company for distribution, making it likely that Edison would have to impose blackouts in the Southern California area. Edison, nevertheless, paid the Angels its annual sponsorship fee, electing to do this rather than allocate those funds for its supplies. This caused some to protest, "They are giving a higher priority to sponsoring the Angels than to keeping the lights on in Southern California." There was concern among executives at Disney Corporation, which owned the Angels, that some of people's anger at suffering blackouts would be directed at the Angels and Disney for encouraging what they perceived to be inappropriate priorities.[38]

Obviously, no sport organization would enter a partnership when the sponsor could damage the image of the event, but there are occasions when this may occur inadvertently. The following vignette illustrates the nuances involved in potential relationships that could result in negative costs to the property:

> Women's professional tennis rejected a $10 million offer by Tampax tampons to become the sport's global sponsor because the tour feared the affiliation would adversely affect the image and marketability of women's tennis. Local tournament sponsors didn't want to be associated with a WTA Tour presented by Tampax. The Tour spokesman commented, "No doubt it would have been great to work with a top flight company like Tambrands, but whether the offer was $3 million or $10 million, image is image, and we received a tremendous backlash for even considering the proposal." A local tournament director added, "I see complications in it. It didn't make me feel comfortable, and I sensed it might not be perceived as positive by my title sponsors and by the public in general. You could almost hear the Letterman jokes and, if you want to deal with reality, the hecklers."[39] (p.136)

Another cost that was of concern to nonprofit organizations throughout the 1990s was monetary costs payable to the Internal Revenue Service (IRS). The IRS had ruled that since sponsoring companies' funds were being used for commercial purposes not directly related to the prime function of the nonprofit organization, they were subject to paying the unrelated business income tax (UBIT). It considered sponsorship payments to be advertising, which has long been subjected to UBIT. In 1997, Congress passed the Taxpayer Relief Act. One of its clauses amended the Internal Revenue Code by adding Section 513(i) to address corporate sponsorship payments. The law exempted qualified corporate sponsorship payments from tax, but it defined the safe harbor for these payments in such a way that the payments were protected from tax only if the corporate sponsor had no expectation of a substantial return benefit, other than use of the sponsor's name, logo, or established slogan. Any advertising would still generate UBIT for the exempt organization. Thus, payments for most traditional sponsorship benefits were exempted from tax.[40]

In 2002, the IRS issued its final regulations on the UBIT issue to clarify contentious points of the 1997 Act. The result of these rules is that a large majority of sponsorships will not be subjected to UBIT and that in cases where it does apply a carefully drafted contract will be able to minimize any tax.

Benefits Sought From Sponsorship by Business Organizations and the Consumer's Purchase Decision

It was noted earlier that companies could use sponsorship to further their goals with employees and distributors, but in this section the discussion is focused primarily on how businesses use sponsorship to communicate with customer publics, since this is likely to be the predominant concern when sponsorship decisions are made. A large number of relatively narrowly focused benefits may be sought by businesses from sponsorship, but they can be classified into five broad categories: increased awareness, enhanced image, demonstration platform, hospitality opportunities, and product trial or sales opportunities (Figure 12-6).

As sponsorship has matured, there has been a progression in the benefits companies prioritize, moving from the top to the bottom of those shown in Figure 12-6. In the 1980s and early 1990s, sponsorship was viewed primarily as an alternative to advertising and as a way of getting media exposure. The primary benefits sought often were limited to visibility and image. This has changed. Today it is the latter three benefits in Figure 12-6 that are prioritized, and the emphasis is on sales. A Kodak executive noted,

> As a sponsor, I look to the promoter to come to us with ideas on how the property can, in our case, sell film. Like most other companies today, we are no longer satisfied with enhanced image; give us opportunities for on-site sales, well-developed hospitality packages, dealer tie-ins, etc., and we'll listen.[41] (p. 5)

Similarly, a Sony executive reported,

> We can't afford to do image and awareness. Our sponsorships will be completely dealer-based, including a complete selling environment on site with dealer signage, a dealer's model mix, pricing, and cash registers. People are going to be scrutinizing proposals even further to look for those benefits.[24] (p. 2)

However, the emphasis on short-term sales generation may be misplaced in many cases because most sponsorships do not serve as "mega-promotions" designed to create a large immediate increase in sales. Like other elements in the promotion mix, they are more likely to contribute to the overall impression of a brand over time.[42] Most sponsorships are not designed to generate immediate short-term sales, so it is unrealistic to expect them to do this.

A sponsorship is likely to have the potential to yield multiple benefits involving all, or some combination of, the five categories. For example, sponsorship of a single sports event may lead to increased awareness of the sponsor's product; stronger bonding by extending hospitality to existing key clients, potential clients, distributors and decision-makers; demonstration of a superior technology; use of hospitality privileges to create staff and dealer incentives; and product trial by potential customers. A corporate sponsor is likely to devise as many benefit opportunities as possible from a sponsorship in order to optimize return on the investment.

Figure 12-6 Benefits that May Be Sought by Businesses from Sponsorship

1. **INCREASE AWARENESS:**

   a) Create awareness of a new product

   b) Increase awareness of an existing product in new target markets

   c) By-pass legal prohibition on television advertising imposed upon tobacco and liquor products

2. **IMAGE ENHANCEMENT:**

   a) Create an image for a new product

   b) Reinforce the image of an existing product

   c) Change public perceptions of an existing product

   d) Counter negative or adverse publicity

   e) Build pride among employees and distributors for the product

   f) Assist employee recruitment

3. **DEMONSTRATION PLATFORM:**

   a) Showcase products and services

   b) Reinforce the image of an existing product

4. **HOSPITALITY OPPORTUNITIES:**

   a) Develop bonding with key customers, distributors, and employees

   b) Develop in-house incentive opportunities

5. **PRODUCT TRIAL OR SALES OPPORTUNITIES:**

   a) Offer product trial to potential new customers

   b) Induce incremental sales increases through promotional give-aways, couponing tie-ins, sweepstakes, and point of purchase displays

   c) Create on-site sales opportunities

   d) Promote a different use of an existing product

A variety of decision-making paradigms that model the stages through which potential consumers pass before purchasing a product have been proposed. A review of their similarities, differences, and relative merits is provided elsewhere.[43] The most widely accepted of these models is the AIDA concept. The acronym stands for Awareness-Interest-Desire-Action. In the model of the product adoption process shown in Figure 12-7, an additional stage, Reinforcement, has been added to the end of the AIDA sequence. It has been noted that

> What the company does to nurture the relationship with the customer, to build it, to strengthen it, is crucial to the company's marketing effective-

ness and efficiency. To work hard to attract new customers and then to be complacent in strengthening the relationship makes little sense.[44] (p. 132)

Hence, customer retention as well as attraction of new customers is likely to be a primary objective of some businesses sponsoring sport. This involves reinforcing, reassuring, and confirming to customers that they made a wise decision in purchasing the company's product.

The product adoption model shown on the left side of Figure 12-7 suggests that potential purchasers of a product pass through a process that consists of five stages from initial awareness to committed loyalty. They are defined as follows:

Awareness: an individual becomes aware of the existence of a particular product and acquires some limited knowledge of its attributes.

Interest: more detailed knowledge of the product's benefits is acquired. Interest in it and a preference for it develop as a favorable attitude emerges. A distinctive image of it evolves.

Desire: an appraisal of the product's merits is made. If it is perceived to meet an individual's needs better than alternative offerings, then there is a desire or intent to purchase.

Purchase Action: this is the culmination of all that has gone before and the product is purchased or rejected.

Reinforcement: to reassure and confirm to purchasers that a wise decision was made, and to consolidate loyalty to the product.

The product adoption model emphasizes that a purchase decision is usually the culmination of a process that starts long before an actual purchase takes place, and continues long after an initial purchase is made. A company's challenge is to design sponsorship benefits that will move potential customers from their present stage in the adoption process toward the next stage of committed loyalty.

The biggest challenge with this model from the perspective of sponsors is that it is a relatively long-term "drip-feed" association process that relies on creating a positive image for a brand or product, leading to desire and ultimately to purchase. The most frequent breakdown point in the progression is between the desire and purchase stages. What has been missing is the ability of targeted audiences to act quickly when they reach the desire stage. For most brands and products, consumers have to be in a given location before they can make a purchase, which is a major constraint on the movement from desire to purchase. One of the rapid changes emerging in information technology is mobile phone companies' efforts to replace the personal computer as the main access point to the Internet. When this occurs, it is likely to provide a further boost for sponsorship activity because purchases could be made instantly on-site, eroding the gap between the desire and purchase stages:

As people become more familiar with the new technology available and in particular as the mobile phone becomes more widely used as a means for all forms of communication, so the link in the chain where probably 80% of potential sales breakdown will be strengthened considerably.[45] (p. 166)

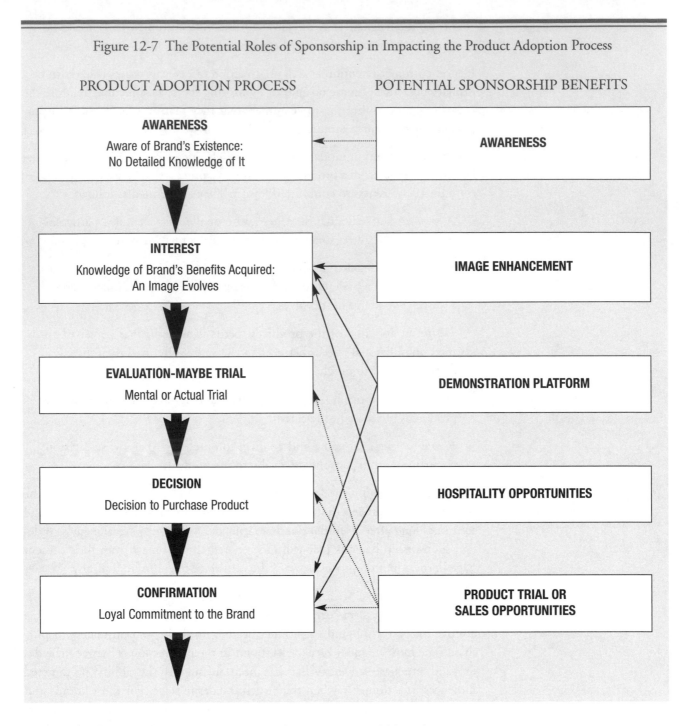

Figure 12-7 The Potential Roles of Sponsorship in Impacting the Product Adoption Process

Figure 12-7 illustrates how the five main benefit categories available to businesses from sponsorship may be used to facilitate the product adoption process. The broken, dotted, and continuous lines in Figure 12-7 indicate the stage in the adoption process at which each of the sponsorship benefits may be targeted. For example, the two solid lines emanating from hospitality opportunities indicate that this benefit may be targeted at two groups: to reinforce and consolidate links with existing customers and suppliers; and/or to nurture the interest in the company and its products of those individuals who have been identified as strong future prospects. In the following sub-sections, the potential role in facilitating the product adoption process of each of the five categories of sponsorship benefits is described and illustrated.

Increased Awareness

Sponsors who seek awareness benefits are trying to move potential consumers on to the first stage of the adoption process (Figure 12-7). All else equal, repeated exposure is likely to lead to positive affect among potential customers. The more frequently a sponsor's name is encountered by consumers in the context of an event, the more positive feelings they are likely to have towards the brand. Further, the increase in positive feelings from this kind of exposure is likely to be greater for less familiar brands than for more familiar brands.[27] However, the context in which exposure to the brand occurs is critical. For example, a Coca-Cola sign displayed prominently at a corner grocery store or on the side of a building is likely to be passively received and not register in the mind. The same sign displayed in a sports arena when spectators are cognitively involved and mentally alert is much more likely to register.

If a sponsor is a well-known company whose products already have high levels of awareness, then the awareness benefit will not be sought, because sponsorship could only marginally increase awareness. For this reason, most major sponsors who have a high profile with their target markets tend to use sponsorship to affect other stages of the product adoption process (Figure 12-7). However, in cases where the awareness level is low, sponsorship can expand the number of potential consumers, which provides a broader base for targeting communication strategies aimed at more advanced stages of the adoption process.

The merger of two companies and the subsequent creation of a new name for the new entity is one of the relatively rare conditions where awareness may be the primary goal of a sponsorship:

- Verizon was formed by the merger of Bell Atlantic and Vodopone and invested in widespread sponsorship designed to "generate mass awareness of the newly formed company."[46]

- Cornhill Insurance Company is located in the United Kingdom. It was ranked 12th in size among UK insurance companies. It invested $5 million in a five-year sponsorship of England's international cricket games. Public recognition of the company's name rose from 2% to 21%, a feat which would have cost an estimated $75 million in conventional advertising. Sales increased by over $25 million.[47]

- Danka was an office equipment company with annual revenues exceeding $3 billion, but its profile in Europe was low compared to rivals such as Xerox and Cannon. Lack of awareness was inhibiting its expansion. To strengthen brand awareness, Danka sponsored the Arrows Formula I racing team, rowing regattas, and horse racing stables. Research showed that "total awareness of Danka doubled in 12 months across Europe among its target audiences of printing professionals, information managers, IT directors, and the like. However, the company's marketing director emphasized that this was only the first part of a long campaign, saying, "It is one thing to make people familiar with the name, it's another to get them to associate it with the right area of business."[48]

- SEGA was a Japanese company specializing in the production of computer games. It planned to launch a major new product called Dreamcast. To assist its launch, the company invested $4 million a year for four years to sponsor the shirts of the Arsenal soccer team. Arsenal is consistently among the two or three best soccer teams in the English Premier League and their success entitles them to play regularly in the European Championship League. Arsenal's red and white shirts had the Dreamcast brand emblazoned on the front. The CEO of SEGA Europe stated, "There are two reasons why we made a deliberate choice to become involved with Arsenal FC . . . They are a European club with European players . . . This was an opportunity we could not miss. The chance to be associated with one of the best clubs in the world . . . The main Arsenal fan profile is ages 16 to 30, and this matches SEGA Europe's customer base". The SEGA European Marketing Director added, "We're bringing a new product with a new name to the market and the association with one of the world's leading clubs brings instant fame."[49] (p. 126)

Image Enhancement

Image is the sum of beliefs, ideas, and impressions that a person has of a business or its products. It may formally be defined as the mental construct developed by an individual on the basis of a few selected impressions. Images are ordered wholes built from scraps of information, much of which may be inferred rather than directly observed or experienced, and these inferences may have only a tenuous and indirect relationship to fact.

Sponsorship activities transmit implicit rather than explicit messages, so image association is of central importance. Brand image has been defined as "perceptions about a brand as reflected by the brand associations held in memory" (p. 3).[50] This definition recognizes that a brand's image is based upon linkages that individuals hold in their memory structure regarding the brand. By linking their brands with a sport event through sponsorship, businesses hope to "borrow" the image of the sport event and transfer it to enhance a brand's image with its target audience (Figure 12-7).

Image benefits are most frequently sought by companies that are striving to create interest and a favorable attitude towards their products. The intent is to "transfer" the positive feelings a target audience has towards a sport event to the sponsor's brand through the sponsorship association, so the audience at some cognitive level believes "this brand is like the event."[27] In crude terms, the company says, "We want to be known as a company that has this set of image attributes." The sports event says, "We will lend this set of image attributes to you."

This approach is likely to be particularly effective when a relatively new product or one with a low awareness profile is involved. In these cases, the challenge is to create an image rather than change an image. Because few or no competing impressions of the product currently exist, the company hopes that by associating with a sport, the sport's image attributes will be associated with its product. The John Hancock Insurance Company had a relatively low profile and was unknown to most Americans before it invested in sponsorship. The CEO stated, "What we sell is trust. People give us money for a policy and someday we give their loved ones more money back. The credibility of the Olympics is very important to a company like ours" (p. 103).[3] He explained how the company used the Olympics to create an image of size, strength, and credibility:

> The Olympic rings help John Hancock reinforce certain essential things about our brand over and over, in every line of business and in every market: that we are willing to support something our customers consider a good cause and that we are a big player. In truth, the rings suggest that we are a much bigger player than we actually are, given the company they put us in. The 10 other top Olympic sponsors include corporations like Coca-Cola and McDonald's, whose market capitalization dwarfs ours.[3] (p. 103)

The message to prospective consumers is that the company could not afford to sponsor the Olympics unless it was a large, stable company. Credibility is an important quality that companies seek to establish in consumers' minds, especially following the spate of corporate corruption scandals that were exposed in the early years of the new millennium. One way this can be obtained is by borrowing the halo/associative imagery of integrity and authenticity inherent in selective sport properties.

The product adoption process shown in Figure 12-7 shows that the ultimate purpose of seeking an enhanced image is to increase sales. The experience of a John Hancock salesman illustrates this linkage:

> The salesman was sitting in his John Hancock booth at a gymnastics championship, and young children were dragging their parents over to meet him. *To talk to the life-insurance salesman!* The attraction was the Olympic rings embellishing his booth and the Olympic pins and paraphernalia he was handing out. He collected a list of 700 appreciative families who might need a whole-life policy. By the time he finished his follow-up calls he had made 35 sales. He observed, "The Olympic rings break down barriers that are naturally there in our business." John Hancock believes the five-ring symbol is more valuable than the intangible symbols of its rivals: Prudential's rock or Met Life's Snoopy. The CEO said, "In an industry with a fair amount of scandal and shakeout, we're looking for market insulation."[51]

Sports do have distinctive images. For example, cricket is English, baseball is American, polo is upper-class, basketball has mass appeal, tennis is clean, and motor racing is dirty and dangerous.[52] Consider the image enhancement products gained from the following linkages with sports:

- In England, Gillette, an American company, was in competition with Wilkinson, a British company that makes razor blades. Through its involvement with cricket, a traditional English sport, Gillette effectively erased its American image in the U.K. market.[52]

- The banning of tobacco advertising on television in the United States and many other countries caused tobacco companies to invest more heavily in sponsorship as an alternative means of gaining media exposure until this was curtailed in 2001. Marlboro cigarettes elected to sponsor Formula 1 auto racing. The key factors in this decision were: (1) the glamorous image associated with the sport in terms of the color, personality, impact, and excitement associated with the Grand Prix circuit; (2) its "winning identity," showing Marlboro as being "ahead of all the others"; and (3) its provision of an internationally glamorous, yet masculine platform for the brand.[9]

Image is not static. It is amended by information received from the environment. However, it is unlikely to change easily. Once people develop a set of beliefs and impressions about a product, it is difficult to change them. This relative permanency exists because once people have a certain image of a product, they tend to be selective perceivers of further data. Their perceptions are oriented towards seeing what they expect to see. Hence, it is difficult for sponsorship to effectively change image. Thus, in addition to affecting the interest stage of the adoption process by borrowing a sport's image, many companies use image enhancement to reinforce existing product image, give existing purchasers good feelings about purchasing it, and to encourage their loyalty towards it (Figure 12-7). Cadillac, for example, has an established image and the company's sponsorship objective is "to reinforce and enhance Cadillac's image among the general public—to use our name as a metaphor for excellence: 'The Cadillac of its class.'"[53] (p. 4)

Demonstration Platform

Some companies use sport events as vehicles for demonstrating the excellence of their products. Especially with new technology, potential clients may be reluctant to pioneer untested systems because they either fear technology will not perform as expected, or they are not convinced that the gains will be worth its cost. Setting up and running the logistical technology/communications for a major sporting event is a way of addressing these concerns:

> By inviting key contacts to the nerve centers and hospitality facilities at events such as Wimbledon, the Olympics, Formula 1, or the FIFA World Cup, firms can demonstrate their products in the most exclusive and sought-after environments with absolutely no worries about competitor activity. They can also ask the question, "If it's good enough for the demands of this organization, will it be good enough for your business?"[54] (p. 451)

One of the benefits such companies invariably receive is that when viewers see a score, statistic, or graphic related to the sporting activity they are watching, they also see the name of the company whose technology provided the data.

Figure 12-8 illustrates how Hewlett-Packard used the Soccer World Cup as a demonstration platform. Among the sponsor companies doing this at the Salt Lake City Winter Olympic Games were York International and Seiko:

- York International planned the refrigeration systems for all six of the ice venues. The ice at the Utah Olympic Park bobsled and luge track was the fastest in the world. This was accomplished by installing sensors all over the track to closely monitor ice temperatures and adjust the refrigeration system to fluctuations and ambient sun loads.[55]

- Seiko provided the official timers. Its technology determined who won and who lost, and by how much. The different sports federations set the standards for how exact the timing was, and Seiko provided the equipment to meet those standards. Most of the timing was done to an accuracy of one hundredth of a second; some, like luge, to one thousandth. Every event presented its own challenges. For instance, biathlon combined rifle shooting and cross-country skiing, with sprints, relays, and pursuits. In some events, competitors started at 30-second intervals, thus eliminating the need for photo-finish cameras at the end.

"We now have transponders on the competitors' shins, and as they cross an antenna buried under the snow at the intermediate and finish points, the time is automatically measured," said Seiko's Salt Lake project manager. "We have a clever little system whereby the TV producer can select competitors that he wants to look at, and we can pull up their information and that data will be displayed on the TV screen before, during, and after they cross the intermediate point so we can see how they're doing compared to the rest of the field." For every

---

Figure 12-8 The Soccer World Cup: A Demonstration Platform For Hewlett-Packard

The Soccer World Cup was held in France and the 32 finalist countries played the games in 10 different cities. Hewlett-Packard (HP) was one of the event's information technology sponsors. As well as providing statistics and graphics for a combined television audience of 37 billion, nearly double that of the Olympics, the World Cup information network handled ticketing for 2.5 million spectators, accreditation of 50,000 staff, volunteers, and players, and the information and transportation needs of 10,000 journalists. The World Cup website handled 20 million Internet hits a day.

HP agreed to the sponsorship because it believed the tournament would be a showcase for its concept of the "extended enterprise"—a networked organisation using Internet technologies at every level of its operations: an 'intranet' to manage internal management processes, an 'extranet' to handle relations with customers and supplier, and the Internet itself, for a massive global communications exercise.

HP likened the exercise to the wiring from scratch of a medium-sized company. Each stadium had 10 Local Area Networks (LANs) linked to a Wide Area Network (WAN) covering the whole of France. They fed into the World Cup database, which contained over 1,000 web pages, a compendium of statistics, schedules, results, player biographies, and weather forecasts.

Every ground had its own complex ticketing arrangements, which were virtually managed. To avoid fraud, tickets were not printed and sent to holders until one month before the event.

HP installed 100 networks and servers, 500 networked printers, 1,900 PCs, 400 workstations for the media as well as analytic and measuring instruments and medical equipment. Internet traffic was handled at locations in Texas and France. The company needed 20,000 IT professionals to support and maintain the systems.

For the sponsors, the pay-off for this costly effort was their corporate logo flashing before a global audience every time a goal was scored.

Source: Adapted from Caulkin, S. (1997). Net set to bulge at the World Cup, *The Observer,* June 8, 16.

event, at least two timing systems worked simultaneously, independent of one another. The backup kicked in if a problem occurred.[55]

There is an implied endorsement of these sponsors' products whose message is, "This brand must be excellent or it would not be allowed to be a sponsor." The consumer is likely to infer that the event is endorsing the quality of the brand. The official status of a sponsor implies some measure of quality.[27]

In addition to being a showcase for its existing technology, a company's involvement may stimulate it to improve that technology. Manufacturers that sponsor cars in Formula 1 motor racing report it extends their research and development work. Lessons learned in the extreme environment of Formula 1 can help them with their roadgoing automobiles. A sponsor of tires for these cars said, "Our engineers have really pushed their knowledge of rubber and compounds in conditions that only the pressure of Formula 1 can create" (p. 9).[56]

Hospitality Opportunities

Hospitality opportunities may be used either to interest targeted individuals in a product or to strengthen bonds with existing customers and reinforce their commitment to the company and/or its products (Figure 12-7). "Guest hospitality refers to those opportunities whereby the company can make face-to-face contact with select publics in a prestigious social context, thereby strengthening and personalizing relationships with decision-makers, trade channels, and business associates" (p. 37).[52] There appear to be six specific reasons that companies identify for investing in corporate hospitality:

- The opportunity to develop relationships

- Thanks for business received

- Encouragement for staff, especially in an environment where skilled staff are at a premium

- To create the impression of a successful firm, which can afford to treat its clients to excellent hospitality

- Building new business

- Gifts and apologies for mishaps[57]

All of these specific reasons are dimensions of relationship marketing, indicating that hospitality is a key facet of the relationship marketing strategy of many companies. Relationship marketing is defined as attracting, developing, and retaining customer relationships. Its central tenet is

> The creation of "true customers"—customers who are glad they selected a firm, who perceived they are receiving value and feel valued, who are likely to buy additional services from the firm, and who are unlikely to defect to a competitor. True customers are the most profitable of all customers. They spend more money with the firm on a per-year basis and they stay with the firm for more years. They spread favorable word-of-mouth information about the firm, and they may even be willing to pay a premium price for the benefits the service offers.[44] (p. 133)

Establishing this kind of relationship requires the building of social bonds with customers, "staying in touch with them, learning about their wants and needs, customizing the relationships based on what is learned, and continually reselling the benefits of the relationship" (p. 138).[44] The objective of offering hospitality at a sport event to existing or prospective customers is not to conduct business, but rather to use a relaxed informal context outside the normal business environment to create a personal interactive chemistry that will be conducive to doing business later. The role of hospitality opportunities at the interest stage of the product adoption process (Figure 12-7) in facilitating sales is articulated below:

> An invitation to discuss trade is often counter-productive because the target audience is wary that acceptance of the invitation to discuss trade will be interpreted as a commitment to actually trade. Moreover, in the case of a meeting which has as its sole objective the investigation of opportunities for trade, embarrassment is the only result where one party wishes to trade but the other does not. This contrasts with a situation where any non-professional common interest—stamp collecting, social drinking or sporting event—is either the pretext for a meeting, the real object of which is to investigate opportunities for trade, or is the main attraction where trade is discussed only incidentally. In these cases both parties can avoid loss of dignity in the event that they are unable to reach agreement about prospects for trade, and can meet again in the future to discuss other projects without rancor.[58] (p. 176)

Hospitality can be facilitated without sponsorship, and this occurs at most major sport events through the scale of boxes, suites, and similar options. However, guests are likely to be more impressed and feel more important if they are invited to a sporting occasion for which their host is a sponsor. Hospitality linked with sponsorship is differentiating. When one sponsor was asked why his company invested in an eight-figure sponsorship of a NASCAR team rather than purchasing hospitality only, he said, "Anyone can throw tickets at buyers, but not everyone can give them time with the team and a behind-the-scenes tour" (p. 8).[59] United Parcel Services (UPS) also sponsors NASCAR. The company is well-known to the public and does not need NASCAR for exposure. The value of the sponsorship comes not from visibility but from interaction. A UPS spokesperson noted, "Having the shield on the hood of the car doesn't get us market share. But when you take customers to the track and that leads to relationships that can get us market share" (p. 30):[60]

> UPS marketers believe that a NASCAR team sponsorship will give them the ideal place to entertain customers—meaning companies that ship thousands of packages a year, not grandmas sending holiday cookies. While other sports offer similar chances through tickets and suites, football, baseball, and basketball games rarely give UPS a full day with its clients, the way a race does. And they don't offer the sort of up-close access of a NASCAR race, where drivers will shake hands and pose for pictures an hour before the race.[60]

Indeed, at the North Carolina Speedway, sponsors' guests have attended the NASCAR drivers' meetings, participated in pace car rides, met the NASCAR drivers onstage as part of driver introductions prior to the event, given the famous command "Gentlemen start your engines!" and presented the trophies to race winners.[61] This kind of access provided to sponsors enables a company to differentiate itself from other companies offering hospitality by conferring on the business the added value of being seen as a part of the event. The uniqueness of the hospitality opportunity is becoming more important. One sport marketer observed,

> The average trade manager now receives five invitations to NASCAR events. Five years ago, he would only get one. Obviously, he will look for the best package, the one that takes care of his kids and spouse. . . People want to do more than just attend an event, it has to be made special.[62] (p. 4)

Most major sport events receive large revenues from selling space for hospitality, but there is a potential downside to this: "The fight for tickets needed by the hospitality operators reduces those available to true sports fans and pushes up the black-market price. The sight of row after row of identical hospitality marquees disfigures many major sports venues" (p. 166).[1] Further, if hospitality opportunities are offered that are not tied to sponsorship, companies that have paid the more expensive fee to be a sponsor see their presence ambushed or diluted by hospitality buyers. All of these concerns suggest that the nature and capacity of the hospitality package is likely to form a key part of a sponsorship agreement.

The magnitude of investment in hospitality at the Olympics is illustrated in Figures 12-9 and 12-10. It may add substantially to the cost of a sponsorship, but the pay-offs are potentially valuable.

- The lavish hospitality provided by Nabisco as title sponsor of the French Open tennis tournament enabled the company to successfully court a major French grocery chain that had previously rejected its products.[63]

- A spokesperson for GCE that sponsors numerous sports events stated, "We use these events to entertain key customers. At the events we throw parties specifically for our sales reps to take their account to. . . . Snagging one $150 million customer is enough to pay for an event many times over. . . . Our events have brought about many positive changes in major customers relationships."[64]

- DeWalt Industrial Tool Co., as title sponsor for a NASCAR Winston Cup team, reported that the sponsorship generated enough profit to recoup its annul $14 million investment. For example, DeWalt generated $500,000 in new business from an industrial equipment distributor after hosting its buyers at a race. A spokesperson said, "Before the race, they were buying power generators from Honda. We got all of their business after the race." The spokesperson reported that DeWalt experienced similar responses at most Winston Cup races.[59]

In addition to fostering closer links with customers, hospitality opportunities can be used to perform the same function with other important publics. For example, Mazda Motors of America invested $3 million in sponsoring the Ladies Profes-

Figure 12-9 Hospitality at the Sydney Olympics

Hospitality opportunities were a central benefit received by the Olympic TOP sponsors, but in addition to their $50 million sponsorship commitment to the IOC these companies had to pay for the hospitality of their guests. The average business-class air ticket to Sydney from the United States cost $7,000. Additional costs for event tickets, hotel rooms, food and beverage, excursions et al., increased the total cost to approximately $30,000 per guest. Since the TOP sponsors each brought between 1,000 and 1,500 guests to the Games, their hospitality bills typically ranged from $30 million to $45 million. Given the magnitude of cost incurred, "Companies are far more deliberate because there is a lot more accountability. It's not any longer the chairman and 50 of his closest family and friends."

The Olympic hospitality programs typically are organized into four or five "waves." For example, Visa flew in 1,200 guests in four waves of 300 to Sydney for the Games. Each wave is likely to be of between 3 and 5 days' duration with transition days occurring when one group of guests departed and the next group arrived. Some guests were regarded as being more important than others in terms of benefits that accrued to a sponsor as a result of a long-term relationship between the sponsor and the guest. The most important guests received invitations to take part in either the first wave, that coincided with the Opening Ceremony, or the final wave, that included many of the gold medal events and the Closing Ceremony.

The sponsor hospitality department of the Sydney Organising Committee of the Olympic Games was responsible for meeting the needs of approximately 40,000 guests. Priority room allocations in the city's leading hotels were made available as part of the contractual agreement signed with each sponsor.

Source: Adapted from Woodward, S. (2000). Going for the corporate gold. *Sports Business*, September 11-17, pp.1 and 54; and Brown, G. (2000). Taking the pulse of Olympic sponsorship. *Event Management*, 7, 187-196.

Figure 12-10 The Pay-off from Hospitality at the Olympic Games for the John Hancock Company

Part of John Hancock's platform for leveraging its Winter Olympics sponsorship was to generate additional sales by using hospitality as an incentive for staff and to generate new business from potential clients. During the Games, Hancock rented a luxurious 15th century estate and guest house close to the Games' city. There it entertained its top sales people and pitched group insurance and pension plans to corporate clients. In all, John Hancock brought 650 people to the games. "Our program incorporated a number of different groups" said a spokesperson. "Over 50 percent were our top salespeople, what we call our 'President's Cabinet.' About 35 percent were the guests of a couple of divisions that brought over top prospects for a seminar wrapped around the Olympics. The rest were non-sales employees who had done well the previous year. We had a little business and had a little fun. It was basically used for incentive delivery, client entertainment and client prospecting."

Did John Hancock's Olympic mega-dollars pay off? While the company spent $1.4 million on its internal incentive program, several hundred thousand dollars more than normal, their spokesperson said that over 128 agents qualified for the trip, compared to the usual 50 or 60. Better yet, the Olympic program generated approximately $50 million in revenue from new policies, a 20-percent increase over last year. "We've already closed some deals with prospective clients we brought to the Games," he said.

Source: Adapted from Alonzo, V. (1994). The wide would of sports marketing. *Incentive, 168*(5), 44-50.

sional Golf Association Championship at Bethesda, Maryland. The area has a high percentage of professional women who constitute a big part of Mazda's market. However, there was another important target group. By holding it in the Washington area, Mazda was in a position to entertain and lobby politicians with its pro-am event, which preceded the championship.[65]

There is an emerging trend to extend the hospitality benefit of sponsorships to off-site locations:

> Xerox developed a program tied to its sponsorship of the Salt Lake City Olympics called Bringing the Olympics Home, which it offered to its 35 North American sales offices. The January-through-March program featured Olympic-themed overlays for customer events hosted by the offices, which held talks by former Olympians, showed videos highlighting Xerox's support of the Games, and distributed Olympic merchandise and Game-themed magazines printed using Xerox technology. One of the program's objectives was to jump-start the company's annual sales cycle and spur prospects to think about office equipment purchases early in the year. The sales offices embraced the program; more than 90% participated, holding 119 events. A spokesperson commented, "Our sales managers were very strong in praise of this program. They said the Olympics were a powerful tool in gaining customers' attention and getting them to attend the event. It helped accelerate sales. It was more effective than most of Xerox's trade show activities and direct mail campaigns.[66] (p. 6)

As corporate hospitality has matured, it has evolved to incorporate sponsorship of events in which guests can participate rather than only spectate. This has long been a feature of golf where executives of sponsoring companies are able to play with professional players on a day preceding the tournament. However, it has extended into other sporting areas:

> A Day in the Country was established in the U.K. by partners seeking to make use of their respective assets: a country location and hospitality experience gained in the hotel business. The organization now organizes hospitality events for companies' guests that include clay shooting, fly fishing, field archery, a range of four-wheel drives, Honda Pilots (small, 'sand buggy' vehicles), pistol shooting, and balloon flights. All the activities are guided by experienced leaders and supported by indoor catering in a country house style of the highest standards.[67]

Product Trial and Sales Opportunities

Product trial or sales opportunities may be used to affect the desire, purchase action, or reinforcement stages of the adoption process (Figure 12-7). Product trial opportunities are particularly valuable because moving people from interest in a product to the desire stage, which involves seriously evaluating its merits to determine whether a purchase should be made, is a difficult communications task (Figure 12-7). There are likely to be many products in which individuals have an interest and are favorably disposed towards but that they have never tried, especially products for which the cost of trial is high in terms of money, time, potential embarrassment, or whatever. Sponsorship offers a vehicle for encouraging trial, which frequently is the most effective method for potential customers to assess a product's merits:

- Palm, Inc., invested in a seven-figure-per-year sponsorship agreement with the PGA. One of the benefits that Palm obtained was the right to install Palm Pavilions at each course. From these pavilions, they distributed a few hundred handheld elements for tournament attendees to borrow for a day. The devices were loaded with software that let users monitor leader boards via Palm's link to the web. Users were also able to locate individual players on the course and access a list of the Tour's top money winners and live scoring for five players they chose. Users had to sign out the units, so Palm was able to follow up for sales leads after the event. The company also sold Palms at the pavilions.[68]

- Samsung was a latecomer to the wireless market, trying to catch up with brands like Nokia and Motorola. At the Sydney Olympic Games, Samsung flooded the games with thousands of new small Samsung-branded Olympic phones. Every reporter, Olympic official, and sponsor's guest received one. One recipient related the outcome, "The previous Christmas, I had given my two older teenage sons another company's phones. When they came back from Sydney, they started complaining about their phones: They were too clunky compared with Samsungs, and the reception wasn't as good. Needless to say, they now have two new Samsungs."[29]

- PopSecret was a NASCAR sponsor. The brand set up microwave ovens at every track entrance, treating fans to free samples. When the winner of the PopSecret Microwave Popcorn 400 drove into the victory lane, the driver and crew were showered with popcorn—a photograph that was transmitted around the world.

- Lowe's sponsors auto racing and BASS fishing events. At each site the company creates Lowe's How-To Village, where visitors can test tools and other products sold at the chain. The village also invites the product manufacturers to participate. In addition to facilitating trial, the village's objective is to inform consumers who are not familiar with Lowe's that it is in the do-it-yourself business. A spokesperson pointed out, "Our name is also synonymous with companies in other industries—like Lowe's Theaters."[69]

A similar strategy to Lowe's was adopted by Fleetwood Enterprises, the leading marketer of recreation vehicles, as part of its NASCAR sponsorship. Its on-site RV maintenance program provided attendees, including non-Fleetwood owners, with minor service repairs. The company's spokesperson noted that if a fan was able to enjoy the weekend because Fleetwood repaired her air-conditioning, "We couldn't pay the customer not to buy our product."[70]

Product trial may also be used to reinforce the favorable feelings that existing users have towards the product (Figure 12-7). When a beverage company or its distributors sponsor races, the availability of complimentary beverages at the end is intended to remind runners of their refreshing, recuperative qualities and to consolidate loyalty towards them.

The ultimate goal of a company's sponsorship is to increase sales of its product. However, in most cases, product sales on site alone are unlikely to be sufficient to justify a sponsorship investment. Often the sponsor's on-site activities are designed to generate targeted leads for subsequent selling efforts. Nevertheless, the right to incorporate on-site sales at sport events is a desirable component of many sponsorships, and such sales are no longer confined to categories like soft drinks and bottled water. For example, banks can negotiate ATM placements in their agreements, while retailers might erect temporary sales outlets.[71]

Given the pressure for companies to justify sponsorship in terms of actual sales, greater focus is being given to creating vehicles for accomplishing this end. Consider the following:

- The National Thoroughbred Racing Association established a subsidiary company, NTRA Purchasing, whose mission was to sell sponsors' products. For example, John Deere & Co. agreed on seven-figure deals with NTRA for presenting sponsorship of the Great State Challenge series of races and title of the Breeder's Cup Turf and associated races. The NTRA Purchasing subsidiary offered discounts on Deere products to the group's members, including 80 tracks and 200,000 horsemen, and "supporters," including 475,000 industry employees. The sponsorship payment increased when Deere equipment sales through NTRA Purchasing reached given targets. Deere's market share in the horse racing industry was 30% before the sponsorship. Two years after the sponsorship it was 80%, and NTRA members spent $12 million on Deere products.[72]

- Sprint, a long-distance and wireless phone provider, sponsored a PGA Tour stop and signed an agreement with PGA of America designed to encourage the group's 10,000 affiliated courses to use Sprint long-distance services. If PGA pros convinced their home courses to switch to Sprint, then Sprint contributed 3% - 6% of long-distance revenue from the course to the pro's 401K retirement plan.[73]

- A NASCAR Busch Series team paid the University of Tennessee $100,000 to become its prime sponsor for three races in Tennessee. The University's logo was painted on the car. In return, the team received the right to sell licensed merchandise, such as T-shirts, hats, jackets and die cast cars, both trackside and through the Home Shopping Network (the in-car camera showed an 800-number for HSN and tagline promoting the merchandise). The University thought it a good promotion vehicle and a mechanism for raising revenue. Their spokesperson commented, "There's a lot of crossover between NASCAR fans and football fans." The team and UT split a 15% royalty on merchandise sales. At the first race, 2,400 individual apparel sales were reported. The team also gained support from UT fans by identifying with the University.[73]

Risks Associated With Business

Sponsors enter partnerships with sports organizations to secure benefits, but there are risks associated with such investments beyond a company not receiving the benefits it anticipated. Sport events are unscripted and uncontrollable, so unexpected and unpredictable outcomes occur periodically. As a consequence, there are occasions when sponsors are confronted with a calamitous negative situation. Given sport's high profile, such outcomes frequently receive prominent and widespread coverage in the media. In these cases, the sponsorship could worsen a company's existing image and reputation. The effect may be enduring and take years to overcome. These types of risks can be classified into five categories: (i) risk of poor presentation of an event; (ii) risk of poor performance at an event; (iii) risk of disreputable behavior at an event; (iv) risk of community backlash from charges of overcommercialization; and (v) liability risk.

An example of the risk associated with poor presentation of an event was given by the public relations manager of Labatt Brewery, Canada's biggest sponsor of sport events:

> The brewery sponsored an ice skating event and paid for advertisements that stated a number of well-known Canadian skaters would appear. Many of the skaters never showed. Not only was the event unsuccessful, the brewery bore the brunt of some hostile consumer reaction. In these instances the backlash was against the major corporation sponsoring the event, not the promoter that nobody ever heard about.[74]

Risk of poor performance is inherent in sponsorships that focus on teams or individuals within a sports event, rather than the overall event itself, because a central tenet of sports is that there are winners and losers. If a product is associated with a loser, it may convey failure and inferiority to a target market:

- A race car or racehorse that consistently finishes "down the field" or crashes/falls hardly projects a winning image. An analyst of Formula 1 motor racing observed, "Coming second, third, or worse can be an embarrassment. There is even a drawback in winning as the only way forward is the same again or down. . . . If you are not going to win, you get a bad press. It is a huge risk" (p. C9).[56]

- Virgin Group founder Richard Branson made several attempts to be the first person to circle the globe in a hot-air balloon with a giant Virgin logo on it. Among the Virgin Group's most prominent companies are Virgin Atlantic Airlines, Virgin Express Airlines, and Virgin Trains. Branson's multiple attempts ended with him bailing into icy water off Scotland, crash-landing on a frozen lake in the Canadian wilderness, and nearly plummeting into the Saharan Atlas Mountains. Given the Virgin Group's prominence in air and train transportation, it is difficult to see how the company benefited by prominently sponsoring a balloon that kept crashing! One commentator observed, "After all, if you can't fly a balloon, what's the confidence that you can fly an airplane?" (p.76).[3]

- The Cartoon Network sponsored a NASCAR Series race car that it termed its "Wacky Racing" car. The intent was to capitalize on the famous loyalty of NASCAR fans to NASCAR brands. The car was var-

Figure 12-11 The IOC Corruption Scandal

Three years before the Salt Lake City Winter Olympics were held, the world learned that some members of the IOC were taking gifts from cities bidding for the Olympics. Despite widespread adverse publicity, the IOC made no effort to enact structural changes that would prevent such a scandal from reoccurring. John Hancock, one of the TOP sponsors, was especially concerned that the absence of reform and the public's distaste for the corruption would corrode the image of the Olympics and devalue the company's sponsorship investment. Their CEO commented, "We believe that if the scandal had gone on too long without a resolution, it might very well have hurt our brand."

The company insisted on structural reforms and threatened to lead a withdrawal of sponsors if the IOC failed to do so. Under pressure, the IOC called a special session and did reform. For an organization steeped in a hundred years of secrecy and self-regard, it reformed to a remarkable degree. It agreed to eliminate its members' visits to bid cities, to require them to regularly stand for reelection, to create financial transparency, and to change the composition of the IOC so that active athletes, national Olympic committees, and international sports federations are all represented on it. Finally, at a later session, under continuing pressure, the IOC agreed to the "Hancock clause," which was an ethics clause in the Olympic sponsorship agreement that allows sponsors to pull out if it ever again engages in unethical conduct. Now the sponsors, who contribute more than half a billion dollars to the IOC every four years, have half a billion dollars' worth of leverage that they didn't have before. The CEO of John Hancock offered the following advice based on this experience:

> Make sure that when you give the other players in a sponsorship your marketing dollars, you demand some influence in return. Down the road, because of scandal or overcommercialization, you may find yourself having to protect not just your brand, but also the event itself—and you want to have the power to do that.

Source: Adapted from D'Alessandro, D. F. (2001). *Brand warfare.* New York: McGraw Hill.

iously painted with Scooby-Doo, the Powerpuff Girls, and the Flintstones. However, what would be the impact on the Cartoon Network if children saw their favorite cartoon character on the charred and crumpled hood of a car in which the driver had died a violent death?[3]

Similarly, if a sponsorship is intended to provide a demonstration platform, and the demonstration fails, a company suffers public humiliation and negative promotion, which is likely to reduce its sales:

IBM's sponsorship of the Atlanta Olympic Games was intended to provide a demonstration platform to showcase its technology to the world. However, glitches appeared in the worst possible places in the IBM system that was supposed to deliver instant information to international newswire services, which would then disseminate it to the world. And, unfortunately, those glitches had an air of absurdity that reporters found irresistible. One boxer was described as being 2 feet tall; another was 21 feet tall. The system failed to yield results for contests that had taken place, but claimed that a Dane and an Australian set new world records in a bicycle race that hadn't yet occurred.

Eventually, IBM was reduced to faxing the results to the media center and running them to the news agencies. High tech had become humiliatingly low tech. And for the estimated $80 million it had spent in Atlanta, IBM got little except a beating in the world press that made every marketer in America wince in sympathy.[3] (p. 107)

If spectators engage in violence, which has frequently occurred among soccer crowds in Europe, or if players at an event use foul language, fight on the field, abuse officials, are caught taking drugs, or whatever, then sponsorship may damage a product's image:

> This downside can be huge, especially if you marry your brand to one of pro sports' seemingly endless supply of tabloid-friendly dunces. Make no mistake, consumers will judge your brand by the company it keeps. Yet, incredibly, brand builders still walk straight into dysfunctional relationships with their eyes open. Converse Shoes, for example, signed Dennis Rodman to a multi-year endorsement deal just two weeks after he kicked a courtside photographer in the groin during a Chicago Bulls game. The problem was, after that little performance, what mother in her right mind would buy her son a pair of shoes that made him feel like Dennis Rodman? Needless to say, Converse's All-Star Rodman shoe was not a success.[3] (p. 88)

> • Credit Suisse Bank terminated its 22 year-old sponsorship with cycling's Tour de Suisse. When asked which sports they believed had a drug problem, 83% of Swiss respondents cited cycling. This was more than double the number naming track and field, which was mentioned by 39%. Only 39% believed that companies should support the race, so Credit Suisse withdrew.[75]

The IOC corruption scandal preceding the Salt Lake City Olympics threatened to negatively affect sponsors. Figure 12-11 describes the incident and the safeguard that a major sponsor advised others to take so they could extricate themselves from a similar situation.

Community backlash is most likely to occur if the sponsors' products are considered to be a threat to the public welfare or if the sponsorship is perceived to be "over-commercialization." Backlash from the public used to be confined primarily to tobacco and alcohol products, but more recently sponsorship by other product categories has been challenged. In the case of soft drink and fast food companies, objections may involve the nutritional value of foods or beverages that are high in sugar, fat, calories, or caffeine. Sponsorship by shoe or clothing companies has provoked some backlash related to labor practices at some overseas manufacturing sites.

The likelihood of over-commercialization backlash is most prominent at the high school level. The following vignette illustrates the issue:

> Fila USA and Footlocker invested $1.5 million over 3 years to remove or refurbish dilapidated basketball backboards on 825 New York City elementary and junior high school playgrounds, and to maintain them. In exchange, the companies' logos appeared on the backboards above a moti-

vational message such as "Stay in school." A segment of the community protested vigorously at the "corporate takeover of classrooms, gyms, and arenas to sell kids products they don't need or can't afford."[76]

The death of legendary NASCAR driver Dale Earnhardt after a crash on the final lap of the Daytona 500 created a dilemma for Coca-Cola. The company had hundreds of vending machines around the country covered with his picture and tens of thousands of beverage packages that featured the driver. The conundrum:

> If Coke immediately began removing Earnhardt's likeness from machines and store shelves, some fans might interpret the move as an insult to the racer's memory. Others might see a decision to continue marketing Earnhardt's name and face as an effort to exploit a tragedy.[77] (p. E1)

Coca-Cola resolved the dilemma by meeting with Earnhardt's family and following their wishes on the issue.

Figure 12-12 Sponsorship and Negligence Liability: A Sample Case

In the case of Vogel v. West Mountain Corp., 470 N.Y.S.2d 475 (A.D. 3 Dept. 1983), the plaintiff, an experienced recreational skier, was injured when she struck a ski tower during a slalom race. In addition to the ski slope operator, Vogel sued the corporate sponsor (Miller) and local sponsor of the race which had been advertised as the "Miller Ski Club Slalom." In her complaint, Vogel argued "Miller was negligent in failing to properly arrange the race course and in failing to warn of the dangers inherent in slalom ski racing." In particular, Vogel maintained that promotional materials indicating Miller's sponsorship of a race "open to all skiers regardless of ability… allayed her apprehension and induced her to enter the race." The specific issue before the court was, therefore, "whether the sponsor of an athletic event, absent control, may be held liable in negligence for an injury to a participant."

As a general principle, the court found that mere sponsorship, absent control, does not render the sponsor of an athletic event legally responsible. According to the court, an important criterion in determining possible liability is "whether the realities of every day experience demonstrate that the party to be made responsible could have prevented the negligent conduct." In particular, the court found a legal duty pre-supposes that the organization sponsoring physical activity programs "had sufficient control over the event to be in a position to prevent the negligence." In this case, the court found Miller was never held to be in control, but was merely advertised as a 'sponsor.' Specifically, the court found the corporate sponsor had not "actually designed, supervised and controlled the event." Similarly, the court found the organizers of the race had no direct oral or written communication with Miller concerning the racing series. On the contrary, the court found the design of the slope and supervision and control over the race was handled exclusively by employees of the ski slope.

As a practical matter, the court noted that extending "legal liability over a sponsor of an athletic event would prove an undue expansion of the sponsorship relationship." According to the court, the net result of imposing a legal duty and potential negligence liability on mere sponsors would "discourage further participation" in promoting events. In general, the court noted that "a sponsor benefits by the promotion of its product." The court, however, concluded that "financial gain does not of itself give rise to a legal obligation."

Source: Kozlowski, J. C. (1995). Mere program sponsorship promoting physical activity insufficient control to trigger liability. *Parks and Recreation*, December, 24-29.

Some sponsors have been concerned about incurring liability risk but, for the most part, their fear of negligence liability is misplaced, "As a general rule, negligence liability presupposes that the responsible individual or agency had control over the condition that caused the injury. Conversely, there is no legal duty and subsequent negligence liability where control is lacking" (p. 25).[78] Typical of the case law in this area is the Vogel v. West Mountain Corp. case summarized in Figure 12-12.

Summary

Exchange theory is the central concept underlying both sponsorship and donations, but the distinctive features that differentiate sponsorship from philanthropy are that it is a business relationship, and it is seen by companies as a means of securing a commercial advantage. Sponsorship has grown exponentially in the past decade. In 1987, sponsorship spending in North America amounted to $1.35 billion, but by 2002 it has escalated to over $9.5 billion, over two-thirds of which was invested in sports.

The factors that stimulated this extraordinary growth were (i) the high profile success of sponsorship's marketing value demonstrated at the 1984 Los Angeles Olympic Games; (ii) its widespread extension from professional and elite sport to collegiate and high school sport, and the emergence of affinity cards; (iii) the emergence of market segmentation as a guiding principle and a focus on niche markets, which sponsorship is particularly suited to reach; (iv) a proliferation of television channels creating a need for more programming; (v) increasing acceptance of commercialization of sport by the public and organizing bodies; and (vi) the need to enhance relations with distributors, because fewer but larger companies exercise increasingly more control in distribution channels. Two other factors that provided initial impetus for sponsorship in the 1980s and early 1990s were the banning of tobacco advertisements on television and the "clutter" produced by the proliferation of advertisements on television and emergence of the "zapper." The stimulus influence of these two factors on sponsorship has waned in recent years.

Sponsorship has three special strengths that have sustained its growth. These are its role in contributing to a company's positioning strategy aimed at differentiating one brand from another; its ability to serve as a platform for both integrating a promotion strategy and furthering objectives with employees and distributors as well as customers; and the opportunities it offers companies to establish a more intimate and emotionally involved relationship with its target audience than is possible with advertising.

Three types of sponsorship benefits may be solicited by sport managers: financial, media, and in-kind. The in-kind benefits may be in the form of product support, personnel support, or communication resources and expertise. Sponsorship investment by companies may require a sport organization to accept some costs. Three of these may not be immediately apparent, but they have the potential to be controversial. First, in return for their support, sponsors may insist on changing the sporting event. Second, existing clientele may perceive the ancillary commercial needs of a sponsor as more important than the intrinsic merit of the sporting event itself. Third, if a sponsor engages in antisocial actions that receive wide publicity, there could be negative repercussions for the property.

A large number of relatively narrowly focused benefits may be sought by businesses from sponsorship, but those directed at their customers can be classified into five broad categories: increased awareness, enhanced image, demonstration platform, hospitality opportunities, and sales opportunities. These benefits are linked to the five stages of customers' product adoption process: awareness, interest, evaluation, decision, and confirmation. A company's challenge is to design sponsorship benefits that will move customers from their present stage in the adoption process on to the next stage toward committed loyalty.

If products already have high levels of awareness, as most major sponsors' products do, then this benefit will not be of interest. Image enhancement is more frequently sought. It is likely to be most effective when a relatively new product or one with a low awareness profile is involved. In those cases, the challenge is to create an image rather than change an image. Once people develop a set of beliefs and impressions about a product, it is difficult to change them.

Sponsorship may provide companies with a demonstration platform where they can use sport events as vehicles to showcase the excellence of their products. A sponsor's objective in creating hospitality opportunities is not likely to be to conduct business, rather the intent is likely to be to use a relaxed informal atmosphere to create a personal interactive chemistry that will be conducive to doing business later. Hospitality can be used to foster closer links, not only with customers, but also with other important publics such as distributors and retailers. Sponsorship may offer a vehicle for product trial. This is particularly valuable because until individuals try a product, they are unlikely to purchase it, especially if it is relatively expensive. The ultimate goal of sponsorship is to increase sales. Thus, on-site sales are a desirable component of a sponsorship agreement, but in most cases such sales alone are unlikely to be sufficient to justify a sponsorship investment.

Where companies engage in sponsorship, they also incur some risks that could worsen their existing image and reputation. These are (i) risk of poor presentation of an event, (ii) risk of poor performance by the sponsored organization; (iii) risk of disreputable behavior by those attending or participating; (iv) risk of community backlash from charges of overcommercialization; and (v) liability risk.

References

1. Sleight, S. (1989). *Sponsorship: What it is and how to use it.* Maidenhead, Berkshire, England: McGraw Hill.
2. McCarville, R. E. & Copeland, R. P. (1994). Understanding sport sponsorship through exchange theory. *Journal of Sport Management, 8*, 102-114.
3. D'Alessandro, D. F. (2001). *Brand warfare: 10 rules for building the killer brand.* New York: McGraw Hill.
4. Williams, J. (1998). Sponsorship evaluation practices of Ladies Professional Golf Association title sponsors. DPE thesis, Springfield, MA: Springfield College.
5. Copeland, R.P. (1991). *Sport sponsorship in Canada: A study of exchange between corporate sponsors and sport groups.* MA thesis, University of Waterloo, Waterloo, Canada.
6. Berrett, T., & Slack, T. (1999). An analysis of the influence of competitive and institutional pressures on corporate sponsorship decisions. *Journal of Sport Management*, 13, 114-138.
7. Wilson, N. (1988). *The Sports Business.* London: Piatkus.
8. Brooks, C. (1990). Sponsorship: Strictly business. *Athletic Business,* October: 59-62.

9. International Advertising Association. (1988). *Sponsorship: Its role and effects.* The Global Media Commission of the International Advertising Association, Madison Avenue, New York, September.

10. IEG. (2002). 2003 spending to rise as sponsors ask for, receive more for their money. *Sponsorship Report, 21*(24), 1, 4-5.

11. Cohen, A. (1993). Our unrelenting thirst for baseball. *Athletic Business*, April, 16.

12. Rozin, S. (1995). Olympic partnership. *Newsweek*, July 18, Special Advertising Section.

13. Brown, G. (2002). Taking the pulse of Olympic sponsorship. *Event Management 7*, 187-196.

14. Lederman, D. (1989). 60 colleges that play big-time sports debate forming a consortium to lure corporate sponsors. *The Chronicle of Higher Education*, February 22, A37.

15. Steinbach, P. (2000). Intramarketing. *Athletic Business*, January, 26-28.

16. Kelly, D. (2000). Sponsors pay so students can play. *Sports Business Journal*, December 11-17, 51.

17. IEG. (1998). Fast food chain cooks up high school sponsorship. *Sponsorship Report, 17*(9), 11, 1-2.

18. Cohen, A. (1999). Schools for sale. *Athletic Business*, July, 32-33.

19. Clough, A. (1995). Football cards. *Leisure Opportunities*, February 22, 6.

20. Cunningham, P., Taylor, S. & Reeder, C. (1992). *Event marketing: The evolution of sponsorship from philanthropy to strategic promotion.* Unpublished paper, School of Business, Queen's University, Kingston, Ontario, Canada.

21. Morse, J. (1989). Sponsorship from a small business perspective… or why a regional ice-cream company has high event content. *Special Events Report, 8*(14), 4-5.

22. IEG. (2000). Companies tap sponsorship to reach employees. *Sponsorship Report, 19*(7), 1.

23. IEG. (2000). Using sponsorship for B2B: Incenting business customers, trade channels. *Sponsorship Report, 19*(15), 1, 4-5.

24. IEG. (1996). Trends: New models for sponsorship profits. *Sponsorship Report*, May 6, 2-4.

25. IEG. (2000). Juice chain shifts spending from advertising to sponsorship. *Sponsorship Report, 19*(14), 1.

26. Ukman, L. (1996). Assertions. *Sponsorship Report*, May 6, 2.

27. Pracejus, J. W. (1998). *Seven psychological mechanisms through which sponsorship impacts consumers.* Paper presented at the 17th Annual Advertising and Consumer Psychology Conference, Portland, Oregon.

28. McCabe, J. (1989). Integrating sponsorship into the advertising and marketing mix. *Special Events Report, 8*(7), 4-5.

29. IEG. (2001). Companies focus on sponsorship's core of genetic connection. *Sponsorship Repor,t 20*(6), 1, 4, 5.

30. Eaton, R. (1991). Inside Target Stores' sponsorship philosophy. *Special Events Report, 10*(17), 4-5.

31. Head, V. (1981). *Sponsorship: The newest marketing skill.* Maidenhead, Berkshire, England: Woodhead-Faulkner.

32. Berrett, T. (1993). The sponsorship of amateur sport – government, national sport organization, and corporate perspectives. *Society and Leisure. 16*(2), 323-246.

33. Bernstein, A. (1999). Sponsor on deck for women's softball. *Sports Business*, December 6-12, 11.

34. Lawrence, G. (1986). In the race for profit: Commercialism and the Los Angeles Olympics. In Lawrence, G. and Rowe, D. (editors), *Essays in the Sociology of Australian Sport*, Sydney, Australia: Hale and Iremonger, 204-214.

35. Kindred, D. (1989). Pass the gravy, please. *Sports Illustrated, 70*(21), 96.

36. Tyre, P. (2002). Fighting 'Big Fat.' *Newsweek*, August 5, 38-40.

37. Romero, H. (2000). Dispatches. *Sports Illustrated*, January 17, 102.

38. Rope, T. & Mullen, L. (2001). Wounded Edison says it will still pay Angels. *Sports Business*, January 29-February 4, 3.

39. Finn, R. (1993). Sensitivity over image sinks a women's tennis sponsor. *New York Times*, March 16, B6.

40. Jacobs, J.A. (2000). Corporate sponsorship regulations. *Association Management*, August, 149-152.

41. Diggelman, R. (1992). The bottom line on sponsorship. *Sponsorship Report, 11*(24), 4-5.

42. Horn, M., & Baker, K. (1999). Measuring the impact of sponsorship. *International Journal of Sports Marketing & Sponsorship*, September/October, 296-301.

43. Reid, I. S. & Crompton, J. L. (1993). A taxonomy of leisure purchase decision paradigms based on level of involvement. *Journal of Leisure Research, 25*(2), 182-202.

44. Berry, L.L., & Parasuraman, A. (1991). *Marketing services: Competing through quality.* New York: The Free Press.

45. Currie, N. (2000). Maximizing sport sponsorship investments: A perspective on new and existing opportunities. *Sports Marketing & Sponsorship*, June/July, 159-166.

46. IEG. (2000). Venue title signals new round of ties for top wireless provider. *Sponsorship Report, 19*(10), 1-2.

47. Howard, D. R. & Crompton, J. L. (1995). *Financing Sport.* Morgantown, WV: Fitness Information Technology.

48. Trapp, R. (1998). The race to build awareness. *Independent on Sunday*, July 12, 6.

49. Rosen, P. (2001). Football shirt sponsorships: SEGA Europe and Arsenal F.C. *International Journal of Sport Marketing & Sponsorship,* June/July, 157-183.

50. Keller, K.L. (1993). Conceptualizing, measuring and managing customer-based brand equity. *Journal of Marketing, 57*(1), 1-22.

51. Starr, M. & Springen, K. (1996). A piece of the Olympic action. *Newsweek*, January 15, 58-59.

52. Meenaghan, J.A. (1983). Commercial sponsorship. *European Journal of Marketing, 17*(7), 5-73.

53. Perelli, S. & Levin, P. (1988). Getting results from sponsorship. *Special Events Report, 7*(22), 4-5.

54. Rines, S. (2002). Guiness Rugby World Cup sponsorship: A global platform for meeting business objectives. *International Journal of Sports Marketing & Sponsorship.* December/January, 399-464.

55. Rozin, S. (2001). The team behind the teams: How corporate sponsors support the Olympic Games. *Sports Illustrated*, Feb. 12, Special Advertising Section.

56. Steiner, R. (2001). Corporate fear that drives the F1 circus. *The Sunday Times*, July 15, C9.

57. Thomas, M. (1999). Hosts with the most. *The Leisure Manager*, January, 24-25.

58. Bentick, B. L. (1986). The role of the Grand Prix in promoting South Australian entrepreneurship; exports and the terms of trade. In J.P.A. Burns, J.H. Hatch and T.J. Mules, *The Adelaide Grand Prix: The Impact of a Special Event.* Adelaide: The Centre for South Australian Economic Studies, 169-185.

59. IEG. (2002). DeWalt strategy ensures eight-figure motorsports team title pays for itself. *Sponsorship Report, 21*(20), 8.

60. King, B. (2001). Perfect timing delivers UPS to Yates team. *Sports Business Journal*, February 5-11, 1 & 30.

61. NASCAR marketing 101: How to leverage a racing sponsorship. (2001). *Sports Business,* June 18-24, 20-21.

62. The changing role of hospitality in sponsorship. (1990a). *Special Events Report, 9*(14), 4-5.

63. Lowenstein, R. & Lancaster, H. (1986). Nation's businesses are scrambling to sponsor the nation's pastimes. *Wall Street Journal*, June 25, 33.

64. Penzer, E. (1990). And now a word from our sponsor. *Incentive*, May, 49-56.

65. Potter, J. (1993). Automakers target buyers with golf. *USA Today*, June 16, 9C.

66. IEG. (2002). Xerox documents ROI from expanded Olympic leveraging. *Sponsorship Report, 21*(9), 6.

67. Playing the field. (1999). *The Leisure Manager*, January, 19.

68. IEG. (2000). Tee is for tech: Palm sets activation for PGA tour tie. *Sponsorship Report, 19*(24), 1 & 7.

69. IEG. (2000). Lowe's test waters with title of new angling series. *Sponsorship Report, 19*(12), 7.

70. IEG. (2000). With sales increasing, Fleetwood RV plans to boost motorsports involvement *Sponsorship Report, 19*(12), 1-2.

71. IEG. (1998). Integrating sales rights into sponsorship. *Sponsorship Report, 17*(9), 4-5.

72. IEG. (2002). Paying Deerely. *Sponsorship Report, 21*(19), 3.

73. IEG. (1999). Innovative deal structures *Sponsorship Report, 18*(7), 4-5.

74. Brewery forms event production company. (1986). *Special Events Report, 5*(11), 7.

75. IEG. (2000). Assertions. *Sponsorship Report, 19*(21), 2.

76. Davis, R. A. (1994). Playground backboard idea nets advertisers, critics. *Advertising Age, 65*(23), 12.

77. Stern, C. (2001). His sponsor's dilemma. *The Washington Post*, February 24, E1.

78. Kozlowski, J. C. (1995). Mere program sponsorship promoting physical activity insufficient control to trigger liability. *Parks and Recreation*, December, 24-29.

Photo courtesy University of Oregon Athletic Department.

Chapter Thirteen

Corporate Concerns in Sponsorship Partnerships

Sport managers are most likely to succeed in soliciting sponsorship partners if a marketing approach is adopted, which means that they look at their sponsorship opportunities through the eyes of the businesses from which they seek to attract investment. This approach is illustrated by the well-known marketing aphorism, "To sell Jack Jones what Jack Jones buys, you have to see Jack Jones through Jack Jones' eyes." The extent to which sport managers are able to see their opportunities through the eyes of potential sponsors and tailor a proposal to meet the needs of businesses and the potential sponsors is likely to determine their success. For this reason, this chapter focuses on understanding the concerns of business organizations relating to sponsorship. Once these have been recognized, the discussion in chapter 14 shifts to explaining the process of soliciting sponsorships from corporate entities.

Businesses are likely to have five major concerns when considering sport sponsorships. Sport managers have to be cognizant of these concerns and be prepared to respond to them during the solicitation process. The concerns are shown in Figure 13-1. To simplify the explanation, they are shown and discussed in a linear sequence, but in reality, there is likely to be overlap in the time frames.

A company's first concern is to frame the benefits it seeks (which were discussed in chapter 12) in specific objectives. After specifying the objectives, attention will shift to identifying sports and entertainment properties that are a good "fit" for the company in terms of both its image and its target markets. A sponsorship is likely to be effective only if it is integrated with other communication vehicles, so a third concern is its potential for providing a platform or unifying theme upon which other promotional actions can be focused to reinforce the desired message. Sponsorship ambushing occurs when a company that is not an official sponsor promotes a sport event in a way that gives the false impression that it is a sponsor. The extent to which a property can offer protection from ambushing is a fourth concern. The final section of the chapter reviews the time a company needs to achieve its objectives from a sponsorship. The model in Figure 13-1 shows that evaluation of each of these elements is on-going and likely to result in amendments and fine tuning during the life of the sponsorship.

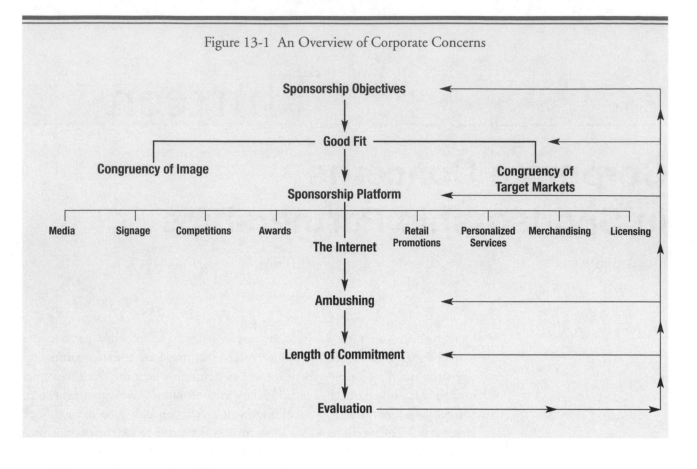

Figure 13-1 An Overview of Corporate Concerns

Many times sponsors' objectives indicate only what the sponsor would like an investment to accomplish in general terms. For example, consider the following statement by a Kodak executive:

> Kodak's event marketing objectives for film products include encouraging people to buy more film, to purchase more than one roll at a time, to try different speeds of film, to get excited about taking pictures, and to have the film processed by a Kodak Colorwatch dealer.[1] (p. 4)

The problem with these objectives is that they fail to meet the key criteria for effective objectives—they should be SMART—specific, measurable, achievable, results-oriented, and time-bounded. If the benefits sought are discussed in *specific* terms, then it removes the fuzziness and lack of operational focus that accompanies generalizations such as those espoused by the Kodak executive. *Measurable* objectives facilitate evaluation and accountability. Items that sponsors may seek to measure include the following:

Sales figures
Sales growth
Quantity and quality of media coverage
Number of attendees
Customer opinion and satisfaction
Sponsorship awareness
Brand awareness
Prompted and unprompted brand recall

Propensity to purchase data
Number of events held
Number of sponsors
Number of new names in the database
Number of sales leads generated
Target profit or revenue
Advance ticket sales
Wholesale ticket sales
Number and quality of cross promotions
Audience propensity to attend next sponsored event[2]

The *achievable* and *results-oriented* criteria serve to crystallize executive thinking, since managers are forced to consider the limitations of a sponsorship and carefully examine whether or not it is the best vehicle for achieving the specified objective. Finally, *time-boundedness* influences decisions related to the optimum length of commitment for a sponsorship.

Most sport sponsors have an intuitive feeling for what their investment might deliver. Unfortunately, relatively few express their expectations in SMART terms, but their numbers are increasing as the demands for accountability accentuate. There is a big difference between "The objective of our sports sponsorship is to increase consumer awareness of Brand X," and "The objective is to increase awareness of Brand X by 10% among professional working females ages 25 to 40 in the Houston metropolitan area in the next 6 months." Further examples of the difference between SMART and non-SMART objectives are given in Figure 13-2.

It was noted in chapter 12 that emphasis is moving away from awareness and interest to an expectation that sponsorships will contribute to sales. If the goal is to increase sales, the development of SMART objectives will require the following questions to be addressed:

- What type of sales—new customers, incremental, loyalty, up-selling?

- Through what distribution channels—retail, web, catalogue, telephone?

- To which target markets?

- During what time frame—length of the sponsorship or further?

- From what benchmark?

- How to be measured and determined—critical success factors?[2]

Sponsorship objectives have to fit within the broader goals of a company's overall communications strategy. At Cadillac, for example, a specific sport sponsorship investment's objectives must specifically contribute to one of two broad goals:

Two goals dominate our marketing strategy at Cadillac. A specific sport sponsorship investment's objectives must specifically contribute to one of these broad goals. One is to impact our narrow and demographically specific target market with direct product exposure that will result in immediate sales. The second goal, though more abstract, is equally

Figure 13-2 Non-SMART and SMART Objectives

Non-SMART	SMART
Increase Sales	Create incremental sales of 12 percent over the benchmark of $400,000 per week during the six weeks promotional period as determined by retailer returns.
Develop database	Develop a database of no less than 2,000 qualified prospects as determined by salary level, age range, professional and family status, and current life insurance products held.
Gain media coverage	Achieve a minimum of 10 news announcements in national, local, and regional media. Awareness of the sponsors linkage to the event will increase by 15% when pre-event recall is compared to past-event recall measured 4 weeks after the event is over.
Demonstrate good corporate citizenship	Increase positive public opinion about the organization's commitment to the local community from 45% to over 65% as determined by an annual public opinion survey.

Source: Adapted from Kolah, A. (2001). *How to Develop an Effective Sponsorship Programme*. London: Sport Business Information Resources.

important—to reinforce and enhance Cadillac's image among the general public—to use our name as a metaphor for excellence: "The Cadillac of its class."[3] (p. 4)

Answers to the following series of questions offer a basis for formulating a set of SMART objectives for a sponsorship investment:

- How are we trying to influence? Raise brand awareness, build trial, enhance corporate image, etc.?

- Who are we trying to influence? What is/are the specific target audiences we are trying to influence?

- What is the nature and size of the event? How and where can the target audience be reached?

- What is the brand usage level, corporate image, brand awareness, etc. prior to the event? What is the level at which we are starting?

- What levels of effect, increase, change, etc. are desired/necessary in order to proceed with sponsorship or consider the event to be successful?

- What are specific ways in which the event would be promoted? How extensive would this promotion be and how will prospects be reached?

- What would be done to merchandize the brand following the event and over what period of time?[4]

The Fit Between Sports Property and a Sponsor's Brand

A company will require that any property it considers be a good "fit" with the company's brand. The fit is determined by two elements. First, the sport property's image should be compatible with the desired image of the brand. Second, the target markets of the property and the brand should match.

Figure 13-3 displays these two elements on vertical and horizontal axes, which creates a grid. Those properties whose audience is similar in demographic and lifestyle profile to the brand's target market *and* whose image is congruent with the brand are likely to be considered "Viable" (cell 1). Those with a dissimilar target profile and non-congruent image are "Non-Viable" (cell 3). If the property's image is congruent with that of the brand but the audience profile is not, then it is an "Unlikely" candidate (cell 2). In cell 4, the target audiences are compatible but the image is non-congruent. In some cases, sponsors may see "Some Potential" in the property if there is an opportunity to upgrade a brand's image in the eyes of its target audience by associating with a property's strong positive image.

The tobacco companies offer an example of a cell 4 partnership. For decades they used the positive image of sport to obscure the substantial hazards of their products. For almost 20 years, Philip Morris' Virginia Slims brand was the title sponsor of the women's professional tennis tour. The target audiences were compatible. The images were non-congruent but Virginia Slims effectively transferred to the brand the positive image of female tennis players, "Quick speak the words 'Virginia Slims' and what do you see? A) Chris Evert or B) the cancer ward? If you answered A)–and most people do–then Philip Morris has you right where it wants you" (p. 36).[5] There is a link between the word "slim" and the activity of tennis as a means of becoming slim. Tennis champions are in peak physical condition, and since endurance is important, their hearts and lungs are particularly strong and healthy. The obvious implications of the linkage are that sport and smoking are both acceptable activities, and that smoking is acceptable, not harmful, and even desirable for women. A former Secretary of Health and Human Services observed, "When the tobacco industry sponsors an event in order to push their deadly product, they are trading on the health, the prestige and the image of the athlete to barter a product that will kill the user" (p. A23).[6] Another commentator stated, "When the pitchmen of Philip Morris say, 'You've come a long way baby,' they could very well be congratulating themselves; their success in co-opting the nation's health elite to promote a product that leads to an array of fatal diseases is extraordinary" (p. 35).[5] These associations with sport conferred on the tobacco products an unfortunate aura of respectability.

Congruency of Image

It was noted in chapter 12 that because sponsorship activities transmit implicit rather than explicit messages, image association is of central importance. The image and meanings associated with the sport event are derived from (i) the type of event; (ii) the event's characteristics (e.g., professional status, venue, size, etc.); and (iii) factors emanating from individual consumers, such as their past experience with the event or similar events.[7] It is possible that the image transfer could be from brand to event rather than from event to brand; sometimes this "reverse association" is deliberately sought from a sponsor. For example, a few years ago professional soccer in England was engulfed by a continuous flow of bad public-

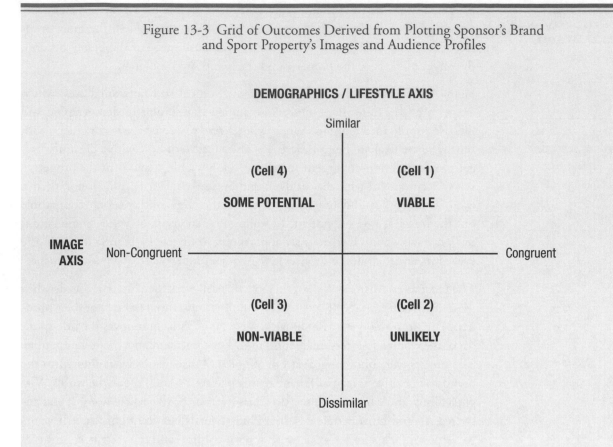

Figure 13-3 Grid of Outcomes Derived from Plotting Sponsor's Brand and Sport Property's Images and Audience Profiles

ity caused by hooligans and gangs fighting at the games. The Premier Soccer League attracted sponsorship from Barclays Bank, one of the country's premier companies and a symbol of propriety. The intent was to transfer "stability and order" from Barclays, without transferring "rowdiness" to Barclays.[8] These kinds of "reverse associations" are likely to be problematic if the event has a strong established image. Further, since the focus of spectators is on the event, its image is likely to be much more salient in their minds than that of the event.

Figure 13-4 suggests that the congruent/non-congruent continuum, which constitutes the horizontal image axis in Figure 13-3, is comprised of four categories of image linkages. The most congruent type of image fit occurs in situations where there is *direct functional based similarity*.[9] This means that a sponsoring company's brand could be used directly in the event. The level of investment needed to establish the image association between the brand and the sport event is likely to be small because the association is likely to be self-evident to a target audience. Shoe, clothing, and equipment products often fall into this category. Examples include companies that

- design and construct sport venues—architects, engineers, contractors and sub-contractors;

- develop, fabricate, and install sport lighting systems, indoors and out;

- make and market sports medical supplies—tape, wraps, ice packs, taping tables, whirlpools, and so on;

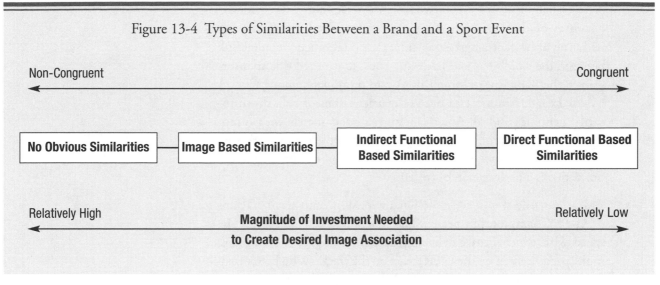

Figure 13-4 Types of Similarities Between a Brand and a Sport Event

Non-Congruent | Congruent

| No Obvious Similarities | Image Based Similarities | Indirect Functional Based Similarities | Direct Functional Based Similarities |

Relatively High — Magnitude of Investment Needed to Create Desired Image Association — Relatively Low

- manufacture and install sport surfaces—gym floors, tracks, aerobic floors, weight room floors, and rinks;

- develop and install equipment for heating, ventilating, dehumidifying, air conditioning, and acoustically treating sport venues;

- design and print tickets, programs, and other visual materials;

- manufacture and install the seats to accommodate spectators; and

- make, distribute, and service the implements of sports—the balls, sticks, bats, pucks, and nets.[10]

Indirect functional based similarity means there is a logical functional link between the use of a product (Figure 13-3) when spectating or participating, but that the product is not an essential requirement for the sport event to take place. It is likely to require more investment than products that have a direct role in production of the event to establish a desired level of association. The most pervasive sport sponsors of this type are the beverage and fast food suppliers, but, as the following two cases illustrate, the potential is much broader than that:

- Pharmacia Corp makes Celebrex, which is used to treat arthritis. It became a sponsor of the PGA tour when the company learned from Tour physicians that several of the players used the drug. This was supported by sponsorship of some of those players who were able to endorse the effectiveness of the drug .[11]

- Chicken of the Sea International is best known for its canned tuna. The company sponsored U.S. Synchronized Swimming, saying, "The tie made a lot of sense: Young athletes are the mermaids of the Olympics. The athletes often sit on the pool deck eating tuna—it is high protein and quick to eat" (p. 8).[12]

Image based similarity (Figure 13-3) means that a target audience perceives a natural and "comfortable" relationship between the brand's image and the sport event's image,[9] even though in some cases there may be no obvious product link. Consider the following examples:

- Nestlé's Baby Ruth candy bar was named after Ruth Cleveland, the daughter of then-President Grover Cleveland, but the association with one of baseball's biggest all-time stars established a natural link between the candy bar and baseball. Thus, it acquired title sponsorship to the Baby Ruth Home Run Award prominent among Class A Minor League Teams. The brand's characteristics of real, down-to-earth, genuine, and all-American were a good match with minor league baseball's family-oriented, grass roots approach in marketing to its fans. Their spokesperson stated, "Based on our brand perceptions, this is a perfect match" (p. 10).[13]

- FedEx was title sponsor for the Championship Auto Racing Teams (CART) Championship Series. The link was "Feel the speed: The speed with which FedEx delivers parcels is exemplified by the 230 mph speed reached by the CART cars on the track. Who better than FedEx to be the proud sponsor of CART? After all, they both share the same values: speed, technology, precision, and reliability. And like the champion drivers themselves, FedEx offers expert handling, shipping everything from car parts to the cars themselves".[14] (p. 3)

- A spokesperson for Visa Card explained the company's rationale for becoming the Olympic Program sponsor of the Olympic Games: "Since we came in as a worldwide sponsor of the Games following American Express' decision not to renew its commitment, our vision has been of a marriage between the world's No. 1 payment system and the world's No. 1 sporting event. To begin, the Olympics fit neatly within—and build upon—the brand's, It's Everywhere You Want to Be, positioning. The Olympics are everywhere you want to be: they are desirable and aspirational. The Games bring a bigness as well as international and travel elements that heighten and expand the meaning of the positioning. And because of that bigness, the Olympics provide a multi-faceted platform for a focused, fully integrated communications program."[15] (p. 30)

- Gillette's Dry Idea deodorant invested in sponsorship of the Mighty Marcy, a yacht which contested the America's Cup with an almost entirely all-female crew. The deodorant's tagline was "Working to Keep Up with Women," and this theme was consistent with the image of women pushing the frontier in sailing.

This type of image matching may be facilitated by sport managers listing a set of descriptors that best describe their event, then seeking products whose existing or defined image fits with those descriptors. Typical words:

accuracy	health	masculinity
strength	aggression	uniqueness
perseverance	thirst	reliability
speed	femininity	softness
risk	excellence	creativity
danger	co-operation	versatility
problem solving	teamwork	innovation

Thus, Ernst & Young, a large international professional services consulting firm, looked for a sponsorship that would convey speed, teamwork, innovation, aggression, and reliability. They signed a three-year agreement with the US Ski & Snowboard Association and used their sponsorship as a platform to communicate these values—associating them with the sport and then associating the same attributes to Ernst & Young. In addition, it fit the company's tagline, which was "from thought to finish" (p. 30).[16]

The following process has been suggested for distilling descriptors that best describe an event:

> On a whiteboard or large piece of paper, draw a large circle in the center of it. In the outside circle, write down every word that describes the personality of the event or property (fun, youthful, challenging, etc). From brainstorming this with a team, the sponsor seeker will arrive at the point where it is able to distill the personality of the event or property into two or three words that truly encompass what the property or event is all about, what it stands for to the target audience and how it makes them feel. Write this in the inner circle. One or more of the same words may appear among the attributes but do not worry—this is perfectly acceptable. It really is that easy![12] (p. 26)

If there are no obvious similarities (Figure 13-4) between a brand and a sport event in the target audience's mind, then it is unlikely that the company will receive commensurate return on its investment. For example, Southland Corporation, the former owner of 4,000 7-Eleven convenience stores, sponsored cycling. However, there was no obvious link between the stores and cycling. "They never figured out a way to use it to get people in the stores" (p. 33).[17] The lack of a natural link between sponsor and event means a target audience is likely to subconsciously filter out the relationship because it seems irrelevant.

There are examples of successes where there is no obvious linkage. It was noted earlier that cigarette brands that have forged strong image links with particular sports fall into this category. The magnitude of investment in direct and indirect expenditures needed to achieve such successes is likely to be relatively high (Figure 13-4). However, as tobacco companies have demonstrated, the benefits accruing to sponsors in image terms are also likely to be relatively high, since more added value will have been "borrowed" from the sport by the product.

Congruency of Target Markets

After image compatibility has been explored, the second key condition that characterizes a good fit is that the target market of the company and target market of the sport event must match. It is important to be able to say to a company, "Your clients are our clients." The most common type of match is based on sociodemographics. For example, the U.S. women's soccer team successfully attracts sponsors that are seeking to establish a relationship with children and their mothers. A spokesperson for Toys 'R' Us, Inc., explained, "If you saw any of the World Cup games, it was substantially kids and families at the stadiums. When the event has that sort of appeal, and we are the nation's top toy retailer, it's one of those things that makes way too much sense not to happen" (p. 7).[18] Similarly, the California

Dried Plum Board invested $1.5 million in sponsoring the U.S. women's team because the Board's target was females ages 30 to 49, who are the primary grocery shoppers for children: "We want the sponsorships to build awareness of the health and nutrition benefits of dried plums and build relevance with grocery shopping moms. This audience is interested in health, sports, and associated activities. Because many WUSA players are moms, our audience can relate to them" (p. 7).[19] The following examples further illustrate the idea of a sociodemographic fit:

- Subaru's Baja automobile was aimed at 25-34-year-olds, which was a younger cohort than Subaru's traditional 50-year-old professionals market. The company's spokesperson stated, "We're trying to push a bit younger and bring new consumers into the brand." This undergirded the company's sponsorship of the Pro Surfing of America series of events. Surfing attracts this younger audience, and the Baja name fits with the beach and ocean.[20]

- The hair salon chain, Supercuts, invested over $1 million in sponsoring a NASCAR Busch Series team to reach its male-skewed 18-to 49-year-old customer. The company "wanted to align with an aspirational sport that would resonate with our target."[21]

- Jaguar Cars sponsored the Grand Prix Show Jumping Series because it attracts upper-income spectators who are younger than spectators at other upscale events, like yachting. The $40,000 plus automobile targets consumers in their mid-40s, with a household income of over $150,000.[22]

An increasing number of companies are concluding that the availability of sociodemographic data relating to a sport event is not sufficient for them to make good decisions about the degree of fit. One respected commentator observed, "The information that sponsors generally gather—age, gender, marital status, education level, and income—is not what matters in determining what to sponsor. Does knowing your customer is a 32-year-old female tell you that she's passionate about skiing?" (p. 2).[23] Sponsors want to know the lifestyles and buying habits of those attending the event and those watching it in the media.

The basic premise of investigating lifestyles is the more that is known and understood about them, the more effectively a company can communicate with them. Lifestyle research seeks to draw more recognizable "live" human portraits of an audience than is possible with sociodemographics. A spokesperson for the Lincoln Financial Group, which invested in a sponsorship of the America's Cup, the most prestigious yachting event, explained, "We look at sports as a key aspect of the 'lifestyle segment' of our marketing program, and we associate with shows and events that appeal to their interests. The marketing strategy is really a lifestyle-oriented strategic view where you understand the lifestyle of your target audience" (p. 12).[24]

- An executive responsible for Toyota's luxury car model, Lexus, explained why they competed so strongly with Cadillac for title sponsorship of the Senior PGA Tour Series: "We did a lot of research on what our potential customers do in their leisure time. They go to art, they go to theaters, they play golf. We want Lexus to be there as part of their environment" (p. 16).[25]

- Globalstar USA was a start-up satellite phone company that invested $50,000 in sponsoring the Iditarod Trail Dog Sled Race. It used the race to promote its high-end handsets and service because "people interested in adventure travel are one of the biggest markets we're targeting" (p. 6). The event's remote location gave Globlestar a chance to demonstrate its capabilities outside of cellular calling areas.[26]

- The US Marine Corps paid $600,000 for an associate sponsorship of ESPN's X Games, because it viewed the event as an effective vehicle for targeting 17-24 year old males who enjoy physical challenges.[27]

The emphasis placed on compatibility of target audiences makes it imperative for sport managers to initiate research that delineates the audience profile of their event. Thus, the main reason Bausch & Lomb's Lens Division became a sponsor

---

Figure 13-5 How Bassing America Identified Potential Sponsors for Its Amateur Fishing Tournaments

Drawing from its 55,000 members, Bassing conducts an annual survey at its spring events. In a typical survey, 75 percent of participants in its amateur fishing tournaments completed the four-page questionnaire that included questions about product usage. Bassing used the results to target new sponsors.

In the survey, they discovered, for example, that 67 percent drank liquor and 61 percent cited bourbon as their liquor of choice. After analyzing brand preference and researching the industry, Bassing targeted two bourbons for proposals. Neither brand was a category leader; they were brands that Bassing felt could gain market share by sponsoring their events.

Within a few weeks, favorable responses were received from both. Bassing met with one and held the other on the sidelines. After two successful meetings, they were thrown a curve. The company's management wanted to use the tournaments to promote their rye brand instead. Bassing reminded them that the research showed only 8 percent of their liquor drinking members chose rye, but they were determined. Bassing declined the offer and broke off talks because they believed the sponsorship was doomed to fail. They contacted the other bourbon brand, George Dickel Tennessee Sippin' Whiskey, and signed a contract and promotional package at the first meeting.

Another question on the survey that helped Bassing obtain a sponsor was, "Do you eat while fishing?" It was followed by: "If yes, what?" Seventy-eight percent of respondents said they ate while fishing and 38% wrote in Vienna sausage. Bassing researched Vienna sausage makers and found only one brand had ample distribution within their tournament territory. They made a presentation to that brand, Amour Star Canned Meats, but were turned down because they missed the company's budget cycle. The following year an agreement was signed.

This type of survey can be conducted by all sport organizations. They could conduct on-site interviews themselves or hire a research firm. After two or three surveys, a definite mainstream customer lifestyle is likely to emerge. The organization is then in a strong position to systematically approach a prospective sponsor with a niche or target for its product or service.

*This case was adapted from John H. Brett, executive vice-president, Bassing America Corp. (1990).Evaluation: Measuring Return on Investment. *Special Events Report, 9(7)*, 3-6.

of the NBA was because research identified sports usage as the primary motivation for contact lens purchases.[28]

- The Pilot Pen tennis tournament is a stop on the WTA tour in New Haven, Connecticut. Pilot Pen surveyed 1,400 spectators at the tournament to identify their demographic profile and characteristics of their purchase behavior. Among the purchase behavior findings were that 80% had traveled by air in the previous year; 76% owned a cellular phone; 68% accessed the Internet at least twice a week; 78% invested in mutual funds; and 55% planned to make a purchase over the Internet in the next year. This information was used to court sponsors in those industries.[29]

Another example of the benefits of investigating purchasing behavior is given in Figure 13-5.

Leveraging the Sponsorship Platform

The term "platform" means that a sport event offers a central theme around which a sponsor can focus and integrate a consistent promotional message through an array of different communication vehicles. The sponsorship is simply a payment that gives a company the right to exploit the sport event—i.e., it buys the platform. Leveraging the platform involves developing an integrated promotion plan that specifies the role that each of the potential promotional tools will play and the extent to which each will be used.

The awareness, image, and emotional association benefits of sport sponsorship accrue by providing implicit messages generated by the linkage between the event and a brand. Unlike advertising or sales promotions, sponsorship does not offer direct messages that indicate why a brand should be purchased. If the target audience is aware of the name, but has no idea what the brand is or does, then awareness and image benefits are not delivered. Thus, there is no point in using sponsorship to create name awareness and to develop an image based on association with an event if supporting explicit information is not available to the audience of the sponsorship. In itself, the sponsorship is likely to have little impact on generating sales, it needs to be supplemented by an array of promotional tools that amplify the implied message. The purchase of sponsorship rights is the beginning of a promotion process, not the end. Unless a company invests resources to exploit the sponsorship platform, it is likely to have wasted its investment. Indeed, as sponsorship has matured, there has been a tendency for companies to commit to fewer sponsorships but to spend more in support of activities that leverage those sponsorships.

Sponsorship has emerged as a fifth element in the promotion mix, complementing the traditional four promotional vehicles of personal selling (which in the context of sponsorship is facilitated through hospitality), advertising, publicity, and incentives (sometimes termed sales promotions). The question often posed is, "Which of these five vehicles is the best to use?", but this is the wrong question to ask. The correct question is, "How can each of these vehicles link with the others to achieve our communication objectives?" Sponsorship offers a "hook"—a unifying theme—that can be used to focus on a specific target market, which can then be accessed by the full range of a company's communication tools.

Leveraging a sponsorship platform has cost implications. The *direct* sponsorship investment represents only part of a company's total investment. The associated *indirect activation* costs incurred in mobilizing other promotional vehicles to optimize a sponsorship's impacts are likely to be substantial. One way this is often overlooked in costing sponsorships is staff time. It is likely to take substantial amounts of staff time to leverage a sponsorship platform well. A decade ago, a 1:1 ratio was most frequently cited in the literature, but today conventional wisdom gleaned from the anecdotal experiences reported by industry experts is that there should be $3 invested in activation for every $1 spent to acquire a sponsorship. Despite this expert conventional wisdom, over 70% of companies still report spending $1 or less on activation for every rights fee dollar, suggesting they are not fully leveraging their investment.[30] If the fit is good, it makes sense to spend extensively to extract all possible leverage from the sponsorship.

However, the assertion that there is a single optimum ratio is an oversimplification. The ratio is likely to vary according to the dynamics of the sponsored event and its relationship to the sponsor's product category. That is, it will differ across sponsorship opportunity and industry sector. Further, it is likely that longevity of the sponsorship will cause the ratio to vary. For example, if the sponsorship is for one year, it may take a 5:1 ratio to establish a message with a target audience, but if it is for three years or five years, then the ratios needed to establish a message, loyalty, or strong association may only be 2:1 or 1:1, respectively, because there is more available time to achieve the desired objectives.

The activation investment required to support a sponsorship is substantial, but in many cases it does not require a company to make additional investment. If many of the promotional tools are already being used, the sponsorship platform provides the opportunity to refocus, redirect, and better integrate the use of existing resources in which the company has already invested. Thus, sponsorship may be regarded as an expeditious way of making more effective use of existing funds.

Some companies have concluded that they can better control the platform and maximize leverage if they create an event rather than sponsor an existing event. For example, the Standard Federal Bank 10K Series of running races was launched by the bank in four cities in Michigan. The goal of the sponsorship was to raise awareness of the bank's full-service capabilities after its merger with another bank. Previously it had been confined to serving retail clients and had not catered to commercial clients. The bank concluded that it was easier to initiate and own a running series than try to bundle existing events under the Standard Federal banner. A spokesperson said, "We wanted the series to have its own look and feel."[31]

In chapter 12, the product demonstration, hospitality, and product trial and sales elements of a sponsorship platform were discussed. Another major element in every platform is involvement of the media since companies invariably seek to extend the reach of their sponsorship beyond an on-site audience. The media's role in the platform is discussed in the following sub-section, and it is followed by an overview of the roles of other potential platform elements.

Media Involvement

One of the central issues in negotiations between a potential sponsor and a sport manager is likely to be the probable extent of the event's media coverage. This is a major component in the leverage of a sponsorship platform. If a sponsor is seeking increased awareness or image enhancement benefits, then a key to receiving them is the extent of visibility and the quality of that visibility in terms of its compatibility with the intended projected product image that can be achieved with the target audience. It is likely that a sponsor will require an estimate of the extent of media coverage before committing to an investment.

There are three avenues through which sport properties may pursue media exposure. The most traditional approach has been to negotiate trade-outs with a television station, radio station, or newspaper. The media provide some combination of advertising time or space that the property can use to promote the event and its other sponsors' roles in it; a commitment to an agreed amount of editorial coverage of the event; and provision of graphic, promotional, and production expertise for the property's promotion efforts. In return, the media receive some combination of identification; rights to transmit the event; event merchandise that they can give away as prizes to their audiences; tickets and VIP packages to give to their advertisers; and a portion of the property's paid advertising. A common arrangement is for the amount of free space to be equal to the property's paid advertisement commitment to the medium.

Loosened restrictions on the ownership of multiple media outlets have resulted in major consolidations among media companies. Whereas a decade ago there were perhaps a dozen radio companies competing in a local market, now there may be only two or three. This has resulted in companies being less interested in enhancing their visibility and image in a community. Thus, traditional trade-out agreements have become less appealing, and there is an insistence that sponsorships should lead directly to increasing a company's revenues.

This change in emphasis has resulted in a shift to a second avenue for securing media exposure. This requires the media to pay cash to sponsor the event in exchange for the right to sell others sponsorships. The media have strong relationships with many advertisers and for this reason are often in a stronger position to attract them as sponsors than the property itself. This arrangement is a non-traditional source of revenue for the media that directly enhances their bottom line. Typically, if the arrangement is limited to selling sponsorships in designated categories, then the media will buy all the rights and retain all revenues. If they take responsibility for all sponsorship sales, then the fees are likely to be divided between the media and the property on a commission basis. An executive in charge of a radio company's sponsorship observed,

> In general, the more properties want from their radio partners, the more they will have to give. You can hire us to put a marketing plan together and sell sponsorships and we'll split that revenue 50/50. Or if you want a joint venture partner where we support the downside, then we'll need to share in gate revenues, booth sales and concessions.[32] (p. 4)

When the media are involved in selling sponsorships, they have a vested interest in the event's success, which is likely to reinforce their efforts to effectively promote it.

The third avenue for obtaining media involvement is to secure editorial coverage. Some sponsors think of the media only as a conduit to a wider audience. However, in addition to extending the audience coverage, the media have a second important function in that their coverage takes the form of news, which engenders greater credibility than exposure gained through advertising. Sport is a particularly valuable sponsorship vehicle because it is especially newsworthy. In an editorial context, there is no exchange of benefits, and the media are interested in satisfying their audiences, not sponsors. Hence, sponsor visibility may be important to the sponsor, but it is not important to the media. To achieve exposure, the sponsor and sport manager have to start from a position of satisfying the media's needs by providing interesting and informative stories.

The media often are reluctant to accept and acknowledge the role of sponsors at a sport event. Many newspapers and television stations believe that to credit sponsors of sporting events in editorial coverage could potentially harm their advertising revenue, since companies are spending their communications money on the sponsorship rather than on advertising. The philosophy is, "When you are in the business of selling media time or space, you don't want to give away time or space." This explains why one company received so little television news coverage in its sponsorship of a major marathon:

> In more than three hours of coverage, our logo never appeared recognizably, even though it was on runner's bibs, start and finish line banners, and signs along the route. In fact, although pre-race interviews were conducted beneath the starting banner, shots were kept tight to frame our logo out of the picture.[33] (p. 16)

One of the ways in which events responded was by renaming their events or venues so editors could not omit the title sponsor. For example, they could omit the sponsor's name for the Rose, Cotton, Fiesta, and Citrus Bowls but were forced to incorporate it in the Outback Bowl.

The most common practice in the early 1990s was not to credit title sponsors at all. However, there was a realization that some events wouldn't happen without sponsors, which would remove a popular source of news for the media. Hence, a compromise position now appears to be the norm, whereby a majority of the print media (including The Associated Press wire service, which feeds hundreds of newspapers nationwide) mention title sponsors in the first reference to an event but not in subsequent references or headlines.[34] This industry practice typically pertains only to title sponsors; most newspapers ignore presenting and lower-level sponsors.

As a general rule, broadcast media will not credit title sponsors unless the event or sponsor purchases advertising time during the broadcast. There are two approaches to formulating this type of agreement.

First, properties can buy a block of time from the network—say 30 minutes—to broadcast an event. This fee includes the cost of the ten 30-second advertising spots that typically accompany a 30-minute show. In most cases, the property wants to sell advertising space to recoup the cost of purchasing the air time. The property can then produce the show itself or have the broadcaster do it. This approach enables the property to provide a fully integrated sponsorship/advertising package, including pictures and mentions of the sponsor on the air, in graphics, and in advertisements. Many PGA tournaments use this approach. However, the risk is that properties may not be able to sell all the advertising spots and thus have to absorb the cost. For example, the Women's Professional Volleyball Association purchased air time for five events from ABC, but had to absorb $1 million because it could not sell all the time.[34]

The alternative approach is for the property to purchase advertising time from the network in return for receiving title credits in mentions in pre-promotion of the event, graphics, and on-the-air pictures and mentions. Contracts will often specify such details as the number of mentions a company receives on the air and when its sign is to show on camera. Typically, broadcasters require title sponsors to purchase between 15% and 25% of the total inventory.[34]

Other Potential Platform Elements

The sport event platform usually should include ties with the athletes as well as the event since it is their performances that capture most of the attention. Such ties enable athletes to be used for endorsements and public appearances where people can meet them, which are likely to be important in drawing attention to the product. A host of other platform elements are available, including signage, competitions, awards, the Internet, retail promotions, personalized service, and licensing. The selection of vehicles used and the emphasis placed on them will vary in every sponsorship, depending on the target market a company is trying to reach, the attributes of the sport event, and the company's sponsorship goals.

Signage and sponsor identification at the venue is a standard element of most sponsorships. Negotiations with media are likely to determine the extent to which such signage would be included in television transmissions.

- North Carolina Speedway attracts 100,000 people to a NASCAR race, with 13 million watching on television. The Speedway's trackside main title sponsor sign is 16' x 40'; regional billboards in the area contain the title sponsor's name, as does the Winner's Circle backdrop (again, for television and print media), and a huge branded presence is painted on the infield grass in front of the pit lane in full view of the packed grandstands.[35]

There is widespread recognition that awareness of a company's sponsorship role is strengthened considerably if an interactive presence is established with a target market. This does not necessarily require substantial additional investment:

- Managers of a sponsor of the PGA tour stop in Phoenix could not understand why one of the other sponsors consistently emerged as the number one sponsor in studies measuring unaided recall and passion. They assumed this company was spending considerable amounts to leverage its platform. However, they found its leverage was limited to $500! They put water coolers with free water at every hole. On them it said, "Refreshment provided by America West Airlines." They provided something meaningful for fans in the hot desert sun, and people remembered. The event's major sponsors who used added value events like long drive contests all had lower recall.[36]

The most common form of establishing an interactive presence is to involve people in a sweepstakes or other form of *competition*. Thus, AT&T's sponsorship of MLB's Detroit Tigers included competitions for the chance to throw out a ceremonial first pitch at a Tigers game; a trip with the team to an away game; and a clinic for children with a Tigers player.[37]

- McDonald's was a team sponsor of the New York Yankees. The company held a six week instant-win promotion at 650 area restaurants, offering 15,000 prizes ranging from Yankees tickets and merchandise to spring training vacations and chances to meet Yankee legends.

Often, the sponsorship arrangement requires the event to provide tickets to the sponsor, which become the prizes for sponsor organized competitions.

Awards can be used as incentives for staff to generate extra sales. Employees may perceive the award as a gesture of appreciation from management. This may remove the skepticism and cynicism with which they sometimes view sponsorships—as ego-boosters for senior managers rather than legitimate promotional tools for the company.

The *Internet* provides sponsors with a platform for interacting directly with their target market. It also enables them to position their brand in an environment that is conducive to e-commerce.[2]

Retail promotions are often expedited by coupons that companies distribute at events they sponsor, but they also may be exploited by offering event tickets to retailers who provide especially favorable point-of-purchase displays for the brand in their stores:

- Gatorade was a sponsor of the NASCAR Daytona 500 race. A central goal of the sports drink maker was to gain better placement and additional store display. Their spokesperson said, "For us, getting display is 90% of the battle." The company visited the headquarters of one of the largest grocery chains in the U.S. Its executives arrived there in the Daytona event's pace car. Their spokesperson commented, "You would be amazed what happens when you tell the buyer you're looking for a certain level of merchandising in the stores for the summer and in return you'll give him a pace car he can use for consumer promotion."[38] (p. 6)

Sponsorship provides opportunities for *personalized service* that can reinforce an emotional attachment relationship with customers:

- Coleman sponsored eight NASCAR events, selecting the tracks with the largest campgrounds. It created a mobile Coleman Cares repair and sales center that visited each of the sites, providing free repairs to campers. The company's spokesperson said, "People are bringing products their parents gave them, and we're bringing them back to life. They're walking away with a family heirloom. That's the ultimate one-on-one connection" (p. 6). The company received letters, calls, and emails thanking Coleman for the repairs.[39]

Licensing merchandise is a major source of revenue to sport event owners, and in some cases, sponsors also participate in these programs. Hats, uniforms, jugs, pennants, balls, and an array of other paraphernalia that can be imprinted with a logo can be licensed by sport properties. Merchandise sales that incorporate a sponsor's message effectively extend the life of a sponsorship because they endure long after the company has formally exited from a partnership. The merchandising can also help a company make its sponsorship self-liquidating.[2]

- Coca-Cola produced a 32-page sales catalog featuring items emblazoned with the images and logos of some of its licensors such as the NFL, NBA, and Olympics, as well as the ubiquitous Coca-Cola symbol.[2]

Figure 13-6 offers a good example of how a major international company used its sponsorship as a platform using a plethora of different vehicles to leverage its investment.

Ambush Marketing

Ambush marketing is defined as "a company's intentional efforts to weaken—or ambush—its competitor's 'official' sponsorship by engaging in promotions and advertising that trade off the event or property's goodwill while seeking to confuse the buying public as to which company really holds official sponsorship rights" (p. 20).[40] It occurs when a company that has no formal rights as an official sponsor associates its own brand with a sport event with the intent of communicating the false impression that it is a sponsor. Ambushing has also been termed "parasitic marketing" because detractors argue that ambushers are obtaining nourishment from the host event without giving anything in return.

Ambushing has two complementary goals. The first is to weaken the public's perceptions of a competitor's official association with an event so these official sponsors derive less benefit from that association than anticipated. The second goal is to associate indirectly with the sports event in order to gain some of the recognition and benefits that are associated with being an official sponsor.

The term appears to have emerged at the 1984 Olympic Games when Kodak announced itself as the proud sponsor of ABC's broadcast of the Games and became the provider of the official film of the U.S. track team. This strategy was aimed at undermining and reducing any gains that accrued to Fuji, which had paid to be an official sponsor of the Games.

The opportunity for ambush arises because there are usually multiple entities involved in the staging of a sport event. These may include a sports federation or league; individual countries or teams; individual athletes; the media; and merchandise licensees with authorization to produce books, videos, records, toys, photographic collections etc., all of which offer sponsorship opportunities. Each of these entities has the right to sell sponsorship. This makes it almost inevitable that there will be conflict between competing companies, all of which have legitimately paid for sponsorship rights with one of these entities. This proliferation of

Figure 13-6 Developing a Sponsorship Platform to Leverage an Investment

Guinness is the world's leading stout brand of beer and market leader in every major territory in the world. The company considered itself to have an 80/20 market in which 80% of sales are accounted for from 20 percent of its customers. While there was room for growth within this section of the market, the company was keen to increase consumption within the 80 percent group of occasional stout drinkers as well as grow the stout market by attracting customers from drinkers of other types of beer.

Guinness became the first of eight companies to sign as a global sponsor of the Rugby World Cup (RWC), which also gave it the status of "Official Beer" of the RWC. This was the first truly global sponsorship undertaken by Guinness.

There were several reasons for Guinness' choice of the RWC. The company wanted to reinforce its image as a "world-class brand" and felt that this could be achieved through an association with a world-class event. The market for the brand and the RWC also provided a good match. Guinness was available in 150 countries worldwide; the RWC was broadcast to 135 countries with a television audience of three billion. Priority markets for Guinness also had a keen playing interest in the RWC, providing a strong communication platform for the brand to its target audience. Guinness and rugby were a good fit with a similar target audience and image and were inextricably linked through social drinking. Rugby was perceived as being good, clean, industrious, strong, virile, masculine and exciting. These descriptors were consistent with the image the brand wanted to project.

Objectives

Guinness allowed individual markets to prioritise objectives but the following were identified centrally:

- to increase consumption in priority markets (e.g., Great Britain, Ireland, France, Australia, New Zealand, South Africa and Canada) in both on and off trade in the lead up to, and during, the RWC;

- to achieve top-of-mind awareness linked to the RWC in priority markets and to be perceived as the dominant sponsor;

- to use the sponsorship as a vehicle to reinforce and build on the Guinness "brand essence" and to inject energy, promote newsworthiness and contemporise the brand;

- to create one, consistent global identity in terms of message, image and activity;

- to motivate and facilitate employees and business partners in all markets to exploit the sponsorship.

The Target Market

The external and internal target markets for the sponsorship programme were clearly defined:

External

- current consumers;

- young male beer drinkers (18 to 34);

- secondary – all male adults;

- on and off trade retail partners.

Internal

- employees;
- joint venture partners;
- agents.

Broadcast Sponsorship

The total investment by Guinness was approximately $24 million. The sponsorship fee was $4 million, broadcast sponsorship in the UK was $7.5 million, and broadcast sponsorship was also acquired in Ireland, South Africa, Canada, and on the European cable/satellite channel Eurosport. Television coverage in the UK included: (i) a preview program; (ii) 41 live matches; and (iii) 16 highlight programs. For each live match Guinness received one 15- second introduction; eight 5- second identification breaks; and one 10- second exit break, in which the company was recognized as the sponsor. Over the entire tournament this provided 512 slots. The context of the recognition spots was varied to reflect elements of the contestants in each game and their linkage to Guinness.

Advertising

Advertising was purchased in many of the broadcasts, and themed press and radio campaigns were organized. The press advertising campaign was initiated several months before the RWC and featured numbers on players' shirts as a countdown reference to the number of weeks before the competition began. The company purchased a one-page advertisement in the official souvenir brochure and in individual matchday programs.

Promotions

Guinness packs included a competition that had numbers on each pack. Numbers were featured on the broadcast sponsor spots and those with winning numbers were awarded vacations to rugby playing nations and an array of different merchandise with RWC and Guinness logos. Merchandise was also offered for sale and as gifts with the purchase of a 24-can case of Guinness.

Over 5,000 pubs posted an exterior "Official Banner" to encourage traffic to those pubs. Pubs also offered three drinks for the price of two one hour before key home matches, which encouraged early arrival at the pubs and encouraged trade support. Distinctive hats in the shape of a Guinness glass were given free for every four pints purchased at pubs close to stadiums.

Public Relations

Tickets were given to newspapers and radio stations to offer as prizes in competitions. Public relations coverage had to focus on fans and be fan based, because it would be inappropriate for an alcohol brand to focus on players. Streakers (fans who run on the pitch naked) have become a tradition, so a collapsible streaker prevention tube of material was issued to all stewards. When placed over a streaker, the tube resembled a pint glass of Guinness. This generated substantial interest and front page stories and pictures when it was demonstrated to the national press. Several other public relations gimmicks of this nature were also developed.

Journalists were invited to a briefing dinner at a London club and were given press packs, photographs and merchandise. Key speakers at the function were legendary players. Diary columns were produced and sent regularly to journalists. They featured humorous stories and off-the-wall statistics such as the amount of Guinness consumed in pubs and stadia during the event. Picture stories were created with the aim of placement in the news, rather than the sports pages of the press. One hundred thousand copies of the RWC Guide were produced and distributed by Guinness to journalists, employees, bars, and overseas markets for onward distribution. The guides were also used as premiums in Guinness promotions.

Guinness hired double-decker buses painted in black and white corporate livery to attend matches. The highly-visible vehicles had teams of singers who encouraged the crowds to sing rugby songs and handed out song sheets, and vouchers for free pints of Guinness from bar facilities inside the grounds. The company produced 23 million limited edition cans worldwide that were RWC themed. Guinness worms were animated characters created to feature in the broadcast sponsorship. They also featured in radio and press advertising and were brought to life on match days as "life-size" characters that took to the streets and mingled with the crowd.

Hospitality

Guinness used its hospitality rights to entertain key trade contacts, staff and competition winners. There was, for example, access to ticket/hospitality packages for all markets for trade incentives as far afield as Spain, South Africa and Dubai. In Dubai hospitality/ticket packages were used in pub promotions targeting ex-patriots. Similar promotions were organized in Malaysia, the Netherlands and Argentina.

Guinness RWC Ambassadors

Guinness used the services of some of rugby's best-known ex-players to be RWC ambassadors during the tournament. The ambassadors were used for both internal and external purposes. Internal use included the ambassadors attending staff and trade events. The ex-players attended various RWC campaign launches across the world. The ambassadors were present in Guinness hospitality suites during the tournament and mingled with the guests and employees of Guinness.

Trade loaders

A series of incentives was produced for the trade to encourage increased Guinness stocking levels and upgrades to larger packs. This included merchandise-based incentives as well as the opportunity to win match-day tickets.

Signage

The sponsorship arrangement with RWC gave Guinness perimeter boards at all matches, except those staged in France where the Loi Evin law prohibits alcohol sponsorship. Guinness was also able to negotiate additional signage opportunities including first and second tier sites, concourses, official training grounds, media centres, press conferences and official functions.

Website

Apart from the official RWC website, Guinness created its own site for the event. This was considered a success as the Daily Star newspaper voted it "Megasite of the Month" and it received a score of 72/100 in New Media Age. A survey suggested that 96 percent of visitors considered it to be "good fun" and the average visit duration was nine minutes.

Additional rugby sponsorship

Guinness sponsored minor rugby competitions in Italy, the Netherlands, Kenya, Malaysia and Spain to enhance the relevance between the brand and the sport and to increase sampling opportunities. In the Netherlands, the company sponsored a series of coaching clinics for local teams and used a famous player to launch the initiative. The training sponsorship was arranged in tandem with a campaign to ensure that all clubs promoted television viewing of the RWC in the rugby clubs, and this was, in turn, linked to Guinness promotional activity.

Source: Adapted from Rines, S. (2002). Guinness Rugby World Cup sponsorship: A global platform for meeting business objectives. *International Journal of Sports Marketing & Sponsorship*, December/January, 449-464.

entity sponsorships has been described as "the biggest challenge facing sponsorship as a medium, and indeed perhaps the major contributor to sponsor confusion, an environment in which ambush marketing is able to thrive" (p. 309).[41]

The proliferation of sponsorship opportunities makes it unlikely that one company would invest the resources to purchase the rights to all avenues for association with a property or to "buy the rights to the entire thematic space in which the purchased property is usually only one resident. . . When you own and license Kermit, you sell only the rights you own to one specific frog—not all frogs—and maybe not even all green ones" (p. 4).[42] Competitors that are not official sponsors have to ask the question, "What promotional efforts or programs can I do within this thematic space to get marketing benefits that are not part of the official sponsorship agreement?" (p. 4).[42]

Two key points about ambush marketing should be emphasized. First, it is a well-planned effort, not a one-shot commercial or *ad-hoc* decision. It may be costly to get people to perceive the ambushing company as being a sponsor, involving prime-time advertising and expensive tie-in promotions. Thus, the popular perception that ambushing may capture the benefits of a sponsor at a fraction of the official sponsor's costs often is fallacious. Second, the main objective is not exposure *per se* since this could be achieved by regular advertising independent of the sports event. Rather the intent is "to create miscomprehension in the consumer's mind about who the sponsor is and therefore gain the benefits associated with being a sponsor or weaken the impact of a main competitor being the exclusive sponsor of an event" (p. 11).[43]

Ambush Strategies

Seven potential ambush strategies are discussed in this section. Often some combination of all of them will be used in an ambush campaign.

Sponsorship of the broadcast of the event occurs when television rights holders create and offer to non-sponsors the right to be "a proud sponsor of the (for example) NCAA Final Four Championship broadcast." The sponsor pays a rights fee to the broadcast company, not to the NCAA, which is likely to cost much less than sponsoring the event itself. The sponsor's expectation is that the general public will not recognize this distinction:

- NBC facilitated this strategy when it paired its logo with the Olympic rings and used it on advertisements that thanked and promoted a variety of network advertisers, many of whom were not Olympic sponsors. This access to the corporate logo was intended to provide advertisers with "value added" assistance and was available to competitors seeking to ambush official sponsors.

Purchasing advertising time in and around event broadcasts. It was noted in the earlier discussion of the role of media in leveraging a platform that title sponsors typically are required to purchase 15% - 25% of commercial advertising time associated with the event in order for the media to recognize their title sponsorship. This leaves 75% - 85% of this time available for competitors. If most or all of it was purchased by a competitor, the saturation effect could overwhelm and negate association with the official sponsor.

- At the 1998 World Cup, Nike was not an official sponsor but did have an endorsement contract with the favorites, Brazil. Nike bought advertising slots world-wide in the breaks in the games and featured the Brazilian team in the adverts. Nike also built a football village near the World Cup's main stadium in Paris and paraded its star teams there, including Brazil, and the Brazilian team was featured as a major attraction of the village. The campaign was backed by a major poster campaign. Nike achieved a slightly higher awareness rating for the World Cup than Adidas, its main rival and official sponsor of the event. After this experience, Adidas announced it would review its decision to remain a major sponsor unless it could be assured that its investment could be better protected.[44]

Unless their agreement with the event or the sponsor specifically prohibits them from doing so, the media are likely to aggressively solicit competitors and point out the ambush potential of the opportunity. One experienced sponsor commented:

> Presumably, since your competitors haven't already spent many millions of dollars to be the official sponsor, they'll have the cash to buy in. And the truth is, the average American on his or her couch lazily watching these competing commercials is unlikely to notice who's "official" and who is not.[45] (p. 85)

Sponsor entities other than the organizing body, such as individual teams or individual athletes.

- The NFL had a sponsorship agreement with Coca-Cola, but the Dallas Cowboys sold "pouring rights" at their home stadium to Pepsi.

- The seminal event of the Atlanta Olympics was Michael Johnson's victories in both the 200 and 400 meter races and the remarkable world record he established in the 200 meters. Reebok was the official shoe sponsor, but Nike shoed many of the most prominent athletes, including Johnson, who wore distinctive gold Nike running shoes. The cameras, commentators, and other media made frequent mention of the shoes, and Johnson waved them prominently and frequently for the cameras. Johnson presented the shoes to his parents in tribute after his world record performances, prompting one analyst to assert, "It was a highly emotional moment, pure catnip to broadcasters who proceeded to spend the next 24 hours flashing close-ups of Johnson's gold Nikes in living rooms across the globe" (p. 87).[45] As a result, Nike usurped much of Reebok's association with the Games. Indeed, surveys after the Games reported higher numbers credited nonsponsor Nike with Olympic sponsorship than Reebok.

- At the Olympics in Sydney, Ian Thorpe dominated the swimming events in his home country. The official clothing supplier for the Australian Olympic Team was Nike, but Thorpe was sponsored by

Adidas. At the medal presentations, the swimmer draped his towel over the Nike logo on his official team tracksuit so it did not show in the photographs of him that appeared around the world.[46]

Purchase advertising space in close proximity to the event venue. The official clothing sponsor of the European Soccer Championships was Umbro, but Nike billboards saturated the entire road infrastructure leading to the major stadiums where the games were played, eclipsing Umbro's presence. In the case of the Olympic Games, the IOC rendered this strategy ineffective by requiring that any city bidding for the Games must secure all advertising space within the city limits for the entire month in which the Games are to be held. This includes billboards, posters, advertisements on buses, paintings on buildings, etc. The city of Athens, host of the 2004 Games, did this at a cost of $10 million.[46]

However, this solution is unique to the Games and not feasible in most other contexts. Thus, smaller events are confronted with competitors to their sponsors offering product trials immediately outside the event gates and comprehensive advertising and signage around the external periphery of the venue. In situations where the sponsor and/or sport organization is unable to control access to an event—for example, a marathon race using public thoroughfares—they are particularly vulnerable to this form of ambushing. Figure 13-7 illustrates the potential of this strategy.

Figure 13-7 Dueling Sponsors

Home Depot and Lowe's are the two largest do-it-yourself retailers in the US, but they are also major sponsors of two of NASCAR's top drivers, and Lowe's is the sponsor of Lowe's Motor Speedway in Charlotte. Home Depot displaced Lowe's as the official home improvement warehouse sponsor of NASCAR.

When the Coca-Cola 600 was held at Lowe's Motor Speedway, Home Depot put up a giant billboard that fans saw as they entered the speedway. It featured the driver Home Depot sponsored and the message: "We'll see who really owns the track." Home Depot also gave away about 75,000 orange glow sticks to fans so its corporate color would bathe the stands at dusk.

At another meet in Alabama, when the Home Depot driver called the fans "obnoxious," Lowe's put up billboards throughout Alabama that read: "We love all fans." Souvenirs featuring Home Depot's driver in raceway gift shops were removed at the six tracks operated by Speedway Motorsports, Inc., the owner of Lowe's Motor Speedway.

Source: Adapted from Markiewicz, D.A. (2003). Dueling sponsors. *The Bryan-College Station Eagle,* January 23, C2.

Thematic advertising and implied allusion. Themes, symbols, and images associated with the event may not carry direct reference to it because this is a sponsor's prerogative, but they may be sufficient to generate the association that competitors are seeking. Protected symbols aren't used, but the advertising is developed in such a way to give the impression that it is officially related to the event. A variation of this approach is given in Figure 13-8.

Figure 13-8 Ambushing the Sponsor of a Bicycle Race

The six-day Redlands Bicycle Classic race began in Redlands, California, and drew more than 50,000 spectators. The race's official sponsor was the dominant newspaper in the area, *the San Bernardino County Sun.* It's neighboring rival from Riverside, *The Press Enterprise*, was expanding into San Bernardino County. It had failed in repeated attempts to replace *the Sun* as the race's official sponsor, but viewed such sponsorship as an important promotional vehicle for building its circulation in the new area. Frustrated *Press Enterprise* executives decided to launch an ambush to try and become the public's perceived newspaper sponsor of the event. Among other things *The Press Enterprise*:

- Published editions with special wrap-around covers about the race, and had hawkers sell them.

- Expanded race coverage by increasing the sports section with two added full-color pages and a blizzard of race photographs.

- Published a 20-page race guide, and deployed 30 to 40 college students to hand out 4,000 copies of the free guide.

- Rented a lot within sight of the race starting line and parked a big delivery truck with a 28-foot-long ad for the paper on the side facing the crowd.

- Set up a booth at the first turn in the race to give away guides, sell the paper, and sign up subscribers.

The Press Enterprise vice-president for marketing concluded, "We were successful in creating the impression that we were the official newspaper sponsor, which, of course, we weren't."

Source: Adapted from Nicholson, J. (2000). Guerrilla promos' in the Golden state. *Editor & Publisher, 133*(40), 38-39.

- *The Sun*, a national daily tabloid newspaper in the UK, positioned booths outside the main stadium for the final of the European Soccer Championships held in England and handed out hats emblazoned with their logo to the fans. Their logo dominated the stadium at the event. Most people probably assumed *The Sun* was an official sponsor, when in reality it had no sponsorship role.[47]

- The official sponsor to the Rugby World Cup was Steinlager, a beer company. Fosters, a competing brand, ran an advertising campaign around the theme "Swing Low, Sweet Carryout" in the United Kingdom. "Swing Low, Sweet Chariot" is the rugby anthem of the English rugby team who were finalists in this tournament, which was held in England.[46]

- Wendy's used this approach as an element in their strategy to repeatedly ambush McDonald's, which was a consistent TOP official Olympic sponsor. Wendy's associated itself with the Games for a fraction of the cost by featuring posters announcing "We'll be there!"; by printing Olympic stories on its tray liners; and by being "A proud sponsor of ABC's broadcast of the Olympics." Their advertisements frequently were set in Olympic venues with Olympic stars. As one critic observed, "They looked, smelled and tasted like Olympic sponsors, but they weren't."[48]

An alternative version of this strategy is for an ambusher to organize a contest relating to the event and to give away as prizes licensed souvenirs, free tickets, or free trips to it, suggesting sponsorship involvement.[49]

- Coors organized a "Tourney Time" promotion featuring Dick Vitale, "the voice of college basketball." The grand prize was a "Trip for two to New Orleans, LA, April 4-8, 2003." The NCAA Final Four Basketball tournament was being held at that time. The average viewer probably assumed the company was an official sponsor as a result of this promotion, but it was not.[50]

Historical allusion may be an effective ambush strategy if a competitor previously was an official sponsor of an event, but no longer holds those rights. Their historical ties may be used to continue the association with the team or event in the public's mind:

- The New Zealand Rugby Team is know as the "All Blacks." The All Blacks have always been one of the world's top teams and are a source of great pride to New Zealanders. The team's official clothing sponsors from 1918 to 1999 were Canterbury International Ltd. (CIL). When they were pre-empted in 1999 by Adidas, CIL developed a range of clothing known as Invincibles, which was the name given to a legendary All Black team from a previous era that had worn CIL-made uniforms. The promotional campaign was dominated by photographs featuring members of the original Invincibles team. The illusion CIL attempted to create was that this clothing range was officially sanctioned by the New Zealand Rugby Football Union.[51]

Creation of a counter attraction could serve to mitigate the official sponsor's positive impact:

- Anheuser-Busch was prohibited from bringing its Clydesdales into a Miller sponsored rodeo. Thus, Anheuser-Bush siphoned people and media attention away by scheduling the horses' visit to the city on the same day as the rodeo.[52]

An *accidental ambush* may be created inadvertently by an event owner not being aware of the potential of third parties to innocently introduce competition. Examples include

- Inviting an attraction—for example, skydivers sponsored by a competitor;

- Not controlling merchandising rights and having a competitor's brands sold by fast food outlets—for example, the competitor's beer getting pouring rights at the event;

- Beverage vending machines and fast food trailers advertising competitor's products; and

- Competitor equipment sponsored by the opposition—for example, timing clocks, radar guns, and referees' attire.[2]

Does Ambushing Work?

The few studies that have investigated the issue and published their results in the public domain have been limited to assessing recall and recognition of official sponsors and ambushers. For example, a national advertising agency that has surveyed public recall of Olympic sponsors after every Olympic Games since 1984 has consistently found that non-sponsors that advertised were perceived by most as being official sponsors.[53] There is widespread anecdotal belief that ambushing is effective, but perhaps the most convincing evidence that it works is that it has persisted for over 20 years. Companies would not continue to invest large amounts of money in this strategy if they doubted its effectiveness.

A key issue that appears to be unresolved is the extent to which consumers harbor negative feelings towards ambushers for "hitching a free ride." It is possible that to some extent ambushing may be counterproductive because it might alienate some of those who are loyal to an event. Work undertaken by the IOC suggests that companies ambushing Olympic sponsors are not held in high regard, but other research has reported that consumers were generally indifferent to the issue, showing little support for the contention that the practice is unfair or unethical.[41] This may reflect a lack of awareness among respondents of the potential adverse financial impacts of ambushing on an event. On the other hand, there may be some who admire and applaud ambushing as the imaginative attempt by an underdog to match a market leader:

> It's a David and Goliath situation, where you've got the establishment spending a fortune on sponsorship. If you can find an imaginative way of hijacking the event, it's a very compelling thing to do. It's got this slightly subversive, guerrilla marketing feel about it.[47] (p. 34)

Strategies to Counter Ambushing

Official sponsors can pursue both legal and market avenues to defend their rights. Both are discussed in this section.

Legal remedies are pursued when it is believed that ambushers have appropriated property rights that they do not own. For example, if the logo or symbol of a team or event was used without official authorization, this would be an infringement of the entity's intellectual property rights. Similarly, it would be an obvious breach of the law to claim an official relationship with an event when none existed. However, the discussion of ambush strategies in the previous section showed that ambushers rely on implication and allusion rather than directly affronting the legal rights of properties. The issue then becomes one of degree—how far can they push the allusion before it infringes on an event's property rights?

Few cases have reached the courts because (i) this process is costly, so there is incentive to settle disputes privately; and (ii) the courts' decisions typically have favored ambushers, refusing to find a violation of existing law unless there has been a clear "trademark and trade name infringement" and this infringement is part of an overall marketing campaign.[46] The most prominent case, which was heard in a Canadian court, is summarized in Figure 13-9. The case related to Pepsi-Cola's ambushing of the National Hockey League and Coca-Cola, which had paid $2.6 million to be the league's official soft drink sponsor. In effect, the court confirmed

Pepsi had the right to associate with professional hockey by using a promotion based upon professional hockey players even though Coca-Cola had purchased exclusive sponsorship rights from the NHL.

After Sydney was awarded the 2000 Olympic Games, the Australian government passed the Sydney 2000 Games (Indicia and Images) Protection Act, which was intended to protect official sponsors against ambushing. However, a retrospective review of the Act's effectiveness concluded

> The Sydney 2000 Act, aimed as it was at rectifying the situations of most concern to official corporate sponsors, did not achieve that which its proponents had hoped for. As such, it does not stand out as an acceptable alternative for those charged with organizing future events and raises the question as to whether more can indeed be done to ensure better protection.[46] (p. 29)

More could be done and was done in the US when in 1998 the government passed amendments to the Olympic and Amateur Sports Act of 1978. These were

---

Figure 13-9 NHL VS. PEPSI-COLA CANADA: Overview of a Sports Ambushing Case

Pepsi-Cola Canada conducted a widely publicized consumer contest called the "Diet Pepsi $4,000,000 Pro Hockey Playoff Pool," whereby fans matching information under bottle caps with actual NHL Playoff results became eligible for prizes. The NHL (probably under pressure from Coca-Cola) filed a lawsuit, alleging that Pepsi-Cola Canada, which had no rights to NHL trademarks, had engaged in misappropriation and unfair competition by using marks "confusingly similar" to those owned by the NHL, had infringed on the NHL's trademarks and unlawfully interfered with the NHL's business associations.

The Supreme Court of British Columbia ruled against the NHL. The Court found that Pepsi-Cola Canada had used three techniques that effectively defended them from this charge. First, they generically referred to the promotion as the "Pro Playoff Hockey Pool" instead of the NHL Playoff Pool. Second, in all their promotion material relating to the contest they included a disclaimer that the contest "is neither associated with nor sponsored by the National Hockey League." Third, under the bottle caps and scratch cards were city names of NHL playoff participants, not the full trade marketed team names.

Pepsi's commercial spots advertised the promotion during NHL broadcasts and they featured former NHL coach Don Cherry, a regular on the television program "Hockey Night in Canada" who was viewed by many as the voice of the NHL. The NHL argued that the defendant's advertising by using a personality clearly identified with the NHL games and by causing the commercials to appear during and in conjunction with the broadcasting of NHL playoff games was "likely to convey to the public a false impression that the NHL and its member teams approved, authorized, endorsed or were in some manner associated with the contest, and thereby, Pepsi's products. The NHL states this was "clearly designed to tie into and trade upon the goodwill and regulation of the NHL and to thereby misrepresent or create confusion with the public as to Pepsi-Cola Canada's relationship with the NHL." This argument was rejected by the Court, who indicated that by purchasing advertising within the playoff broadcast, Pepsi had a legitimate connection with the games.

Source: Adapted from McKelvey, S. (1992). NHL v. Pepsi-Cola Canada, Uh-huh! Legal parameters of sports ambush marketing. *The Entertainment and Sports Lawyer,* Fall, 5-17; and McKelvey, S. (1993). *Corporate bushwhackers. Athletic Business,* March, 14.

---

designed to provide special legal protections for the Salt Lake City Winter Olympics. They entitled the USOC to sue companies that created even the appearance of an Olympics sponsorship. They were effective in substantially reducing ambush activity at those Games.[50] However, these wide-embracing protections were confined only to the Olympics and not available to any other organizations.

For the most part, events and official sponsors receive little legal protection from ambushing, so they have to develop *market remedies* to protect the value of their rights investment. Laws alone are unlikely to be equal to the task of responding to the imaginative ambushing strategies of marketers. Three types of market remedies are available. The first is comprehensive use of the platform the event provides, which was discussed earlier in the chapter. If sponsorship of an event is used to integrate and provide focus for an extensive set of marketing activities, which are pursued for an extended period both before and after the event, then the potential impact of an ambusher is minimized.

The second pre-emptive tool for combating ambushing is the contract. In the past, it was facilitated by poorly written contracts, but many previous loopholes are no longer there. Thus, greater coordination between event owners and broadcasters has reduced the likelihood that official sponsors will be ambushed by competitors claiming "official broadcast sponsor" status. Similarly, event sponsorship and advertising sales now are frequently linked. Media now tend to offer first option to the official sponsors to buy up remaining advertising time.

> In the case of the Soccer World Cup, all advertising time surrounding broadcast of the event in the U.S. market on ABC and ESPN, the official broadcasting networks for this event, was pre-sold to a selection of official sponsors, such as Coca-Cola, MasterCard, and General Motors, at the time of purchasing sponsorship rights to the event itself.[49]

The downside of this approach is that sponsors may be required to purchase large amounts of advertising they don't want. This can be addressed contractually either by sponsors being given first right of refusal, which preserves their chance to reconsider if a competitor seeks to buy time, or by not allowing media to sell advertising time around the event to any competing brand.

Other ambushing loopholes that can be closed through a contract include (i) specifying how tickets will be dispersed to avoid a competitor accessing blocks of tickets and awarding them as prizes;[54] (ii) web links to and from the event site to the sponsor's site and to cosponsors' sites; (iii) protection against ambush through technological detection, which puts video insertions into a television broadcast to create advertising messages when none existed and delete ones where they do exist;[55] (iv) event owners prohibiting broadcast partners from "sub-letting" the event's trademark rights to non-official sponsors through the use of composite logos and titles that convey an official association between the non-sponsor and the event; and (v) having a host city and/or event site ban advertising that directly competes with official sponsors:

- The NCAA creates a "clean zone" for its Final Four, whereby it imposes a ban on advertising in the area surrounding the facility hosting the event and at official Final Four hotels. To create the clean zone at the 1999 men's Final Four in St. Petersburg, 30 signs surrounding

Tropicana Field that would be visible from the basketball court were covered up. Non-sponsors' promotional items were also banned from the area outside the arena and the official hotels.[54]

If all else fails, a final strategy to forestall ambushing is to "name and shame" the ambushers. This involves publicizing the ambush and embarrassing the competitor.

- Opel Ireland (General Motors) was the long-time major sponsor of the Irish national soccer team. They had initiated sponsorship at a time when the team was not doing well. Some years later the team's fortunes changed. They succeeded on a world stage and the players were feted as national celebrities. At that point, a financial services company tried to ambush Opel using sponsorship of the players as its platform. Opel responded with an advertising campaign featuring the first team they had sponsored many years earlier, with the caption line, "We sponsored the band before the bandwagon." The financial services company was chastised by committed Irish soccer fans who expressed unbridled hostility towards it, terming it a "bandwagon supporter." As a result of the outcry, the company quickly ceased its involvement with Irish soccer.[41]

The US Olympic Committee threatens to "name and shame" ambushers with campaigns, which would consist of half or full page advertisements in many of the country's major newspapers featuring a photograph of an ambushing company's CEO under the headline, "Thief!" It is possible that other entities, especially the NCAA or individual colleges, could mount a "Don't hurt our Athletes" campaign against ambushers that might persuade them to "cease and desist."[50]

Is Ambushing Ethical?

Is ambushing unethical, or is it an example of imaginative, creative, ethical marketing? The issue has been extensively discussed, with the debaters predictably espousing views that reflect their self-interest.

Among property owners and official sponsors, the consensus is that it is unethical. They perceive ambushers are appropriating something that does not belong to them, usurping benefits from it for which they have not paid, and in so doing jeopardizing the financial standing of the property. Their pejorative rhetoric is robust and emotionally charged: "Like leaches they suck the lifeblood and goodwill out of the institution" (p. 353).[55] "It is a form of theft practiced by corporate pariahs" (p. 356),[55] or from the marketing director of Visa, "Ambush marketing implies a connection to an event for which you have not compensated the owner. There's another word for it: stealing" (p. 353).[55]

Those who engage in ambushing resent the suggestion that it is unethical and state that such changes represent only "self-serving pleading in the guise of intellectual commentary"(p. 4).[42] They consider it to be a healthy business practice consistent with the American tradition of encouraging competition in the marketplace. Indeed, it has been argued that such healthy competition has the long-range effect of "making sponsorship properties more valuable, not less, in that successful ambushes, over time, help to weed out inferior sponsorship properties"

(p. 4).[42] There is no doubt that ambushing has resulted in more extensive and creative use of the platform that sponsorship provides for integrated promotion, and to much cleaner, tighter contracts between properties and sponsors.

The U.S. economic system is designed to encourage companies to compete vigorously, but honestly. Managers have a moral obligation to maximize returns to the stockholders for whom they work. Provided actions are lawful and in the company's best long-term interest, they should be pursued. Thus, "the argument that if I'm an inventive non-sponsor mining the sponsored thematic space in a clever way, the public may come to think of me as an Olympic sponsor is not an argument supporting non-pursuit of ambushing activities, but is rather a possible testament to the marketing skills of a non-sponsoring competitor"(p. 4).[42]

A sponsor's investment does not operate in a vacuum, free of the competitive pressures that are inherent in the economic system. Sponsors and properties have an obligation to identify the parameters of what they are purchasing, including an understanding of what they can and cannot control. These are key factors in determining the price/value of a sponsorship. Competitors have no ethical obligation to make sure an official sponsor's investment is successful. The obligation lies with sponsors and event owners to remove or minimize ambushing opportunities.

Length of Commitment

There is a general consensus that for sponsorship to be effective, there should be a relatively long-term commitment, with three years often being suggested as the minimum desirable period. Short-term commitments do not provide adequate time to exploit and leverage a sponsorship. It usually takes longer to establish a linkage between the sport event and a sponsor's brand in a target market's mind, and this linkage is key to achieving the benefits being sought. A one-off or short-term commitment could hope to establish only a tentative linkage, which is likely to dissipate quickly. The typical evolution of a sponsorship has been described in the following terms:

> The first year will be spent learning about the event or activity, making contacts (and probably quite a few mistakes) and finding your way in this new area. The second will start to show the potential you are hoping for, while the third should, if you have done your work correctly, see the benefits accrue, the audience accept your presence and motives, and the media to be comfortable with linking you with the activity.[56] (p. 124)

In contrast to a short-term linkage, a long-term commitment may leave an enduring legacy, i.e., create value that endures beyond the actual sponsorship. Tracking studies have repeatedly reported instances where past long-term sponsors are credited with an association with an event that they ceased to sponsor many years previously. For example, Philip Morris' Virginia Slims brand was the title sponsor for the Women's Professional Tennis Tour from its controversial inception in the early 1970s until 1989, by which time it had become an established international event. People still associate Virginia Slims with tennis, even though Philip Morris exited its sponsorship over a decade ago! Similarly, when Lipton Tea ended its sponsorship of the ATP tournament in South Florida after 15 years, expunging the relationship in favor of one with Ericsson Mobile Phones proved difficult. Indeed, the tournament founder admitted, "We're creatures of habit, even the Ericsson people sometimes call it the Lipton."[57]

- Carling, a brand of beer, was a long-time sponsor of the English Premier League, and it used the sponsorship as a platform for its entire promotional campaign. Given the strong associative links it forged in the minds of the English population when it exited its sponsorship, it could still use football as its marketing platform without being the sponsor of the Premiership. This could involve sponsorship agreements with individual teams, major media links with print and broadcast outlets, and public relations activities.[58]

Thus, a corollary of a long sponsorship tenure is that a subsequent sponsor will need to make a long-term commitment to supplant the previous relationship in people's minds.

Although long-term relationships have advantages, it is likely that companies will initially commit for three years, review the results, and then decide whether or not to renew. There are two reasons why there may be no renewal, even if the results have met expectations. First, market conditions or a company's management may change, leading to changes in its communications strategy:

- Ford Motor Co. of Canada dropped its sponsorship of the MLB Toronto Blue Jays after ten years because its corporate marketing objectives changed. While the property continued to deliver plenty of impressions, good awareness scores, and desirable hospitality opportunities, the company had shifted its overall marketing focus to women and younger buyers. A spokesman said, "There was value there, but with a more youthful skew to our models, and with women buying 52 percent of our cars, it no longer made sense to spend a lot of money on a property that speaks to older men" (p. 4).[57]

A second reason why investment in a successful sponsorship may not be renewed is a reduction in impact or loss of conscious association of a sponsor with the event. For example, long-term sponsors for whom hospitality is an important benefit often feel obligated to invite most of the same customers to avoid offending them, which reduces its impact and makes it difficult for a company to realize incremental benefits.

Public consciousness of a company's sponsorship at some point may cease to be cumulative, as it comes to be taken for granted. A spokesperson for the RJ Reynolds tobacco company noted that after 30 years of continuous title sponsorship, "We have to constantly work to remind adult smokers who are NASCAR Winston Cup fans that we are the 'Winston' in Winston Cup" (p. 4).[57] They try to keep the sponsorship fresh by changing the activities associated with the platform. For example, a consumer sweepstakes is centered around Winston Cup races, and the components with it and the payout structures are periodically revised "Just to create constant buzz" (p. 4).[57] Thus, the challenge is to retain the equity in the association created by long-term sponsorship but to consistently amend the platform so the relationship does not become boring to the target audience.

Summary

Too frequently, sponsors' objectives are expressed only in general terms, which results in a lack of operational focus. Objectives should be SMART—specific, measurable, achievable, results-oriented, and time-bounded. These kinds of specific objectives remove fuzziness from what is being sought from a sponsorship and meet the increased pressures for demonstrating accountability.

The "fit" between a sport property and a company's brand is determined by compatibility of the images of the two entities and the congruency of their target markets. By linking their brands with a sport event through sponsorship, businesses hope to "borrow" the image of the event and transfer it to enhance a brand's image with its target audience. There are four categories of image linkage: (i) direct functional based similarity, indicating that a company's brand could be used directly in the event; (ii) indirect functional based similarity means that there is a logical functional link between use of a product when spectating or participating, but that the product is not an essential requirement for the sport event to take place; (iii) image based similarity recognizing that a target audience perceives a natural and "comfortable" relationship between the brand's image and the sport event's image; and (iv) no obvious similarity between a brand and the event.

The most common target market match is on the basis of sociodemographics. However, an increasing number of companies are concluding this is an insufficient basis for them to make good decisions about the degree of fit. They want to know about the lifestyles and buying habits of those attending and watching an event. Such lifestyle research draws more recognizable "live" human portraits of an audience than is possible with sociodemographics.

A sponsorship provides a promotional platform—a central theme around which a focused, integrated, consistent message can be communicated through an array of different conduits. The purchase of sponsorship rights is the beginning of a promotion process, not the end. If a company does not invest resources to exploit the platform a sponsorship provides, it is likely to have wasted its investment. Conventional wisdom suggests that $3 should be invested for every $1 spent to acquire a sponsorship. Given the substantial costs associated with sponsorships, some companies are focusing on investments that have the potential to be self-liquidating, while others have elected to create their own events rather than sponsor existing events.

Media involvement is a key component in leveraging a sponsorship agreement. There are three avenues through which sport properties may pursue media exposure. The most traditional approach has been to negotiate trade-outs, but the emerging trend is for the media to pay cash to sponsor the event in exchange for the right to sell sponsorship to it. The third avenue is to secure editorial coverage in the form of the property becoming a news event, which engenders greater credibility than exposure gained through advertising.

Media are reluctant to acknowledge the role of sponsors in editorial coverage because companies are spending their communications money on sponsoring the event rather than on advertising their products in the media. The policy of most print media is to mention title sponsors in the first reference to an event but not in subsequent references or headlines. As a general rule, broadcast media will not credit title sponsors unless the property or sponsor purchases advertising time during the broadcast.

The media element of the platform can be complemented by an array of other elements including signage, competitions, awards, the internet, retail promotions, personalized service, merchandising, and licensing.

Ambushing occurs when a company that has no formal rights as an official sponsor associates its own brand with a sport event with the intent of communicating the false impression that it is a sponsor. Seven potential ambush strategies have been identified: (i) sponsorship of the broadcast of the event; (ii) purchasing advertising in and around an event broadcast; (iii) sponsoring entities other than the organizing body; (iv) purchasing advertising space in close proximity to the event venue; (v) thematic advertising and implied allusion; (vi) creation of a counter attraction; and (vii) accidental ambushes.

There is widespread belief that ambushing is effective, but perhaps the most convincing evidence that it works is that it has persisted for over 20 years. For the most part, official sponsors receive little legal protection from ambushing so they have to develop market remedies. Three market remedies are available: (i) comprehensive use of the leveraging potential of the sponsorship platform; (ii) carefully written contracts; and (iii) "naming and shaming" ambushers by publicizing the ambush and embarrassing the competitor. Discussions of the ethics of ambushing predictably reflect the self-interest of the debaters, so invariably it is perceived as unethical by official sponsors and ethical by ambushers.

There is a general consensus that for sponsorship to be effective, there should be a relatively long-term commitment—three years is usually the minimum desirable period. Long-term commitments frequently create a level of association that endures beyond the actual sponsorship.

References

1. Barr, J. (1988). Boosting sales through sponsorship. *Special Events Report, 7*(8), 4-5.
2. Kolah, A. (2001). *How to develop an effective sponsorship programme.* London: Sport Business Information Resources.
3. Perelli, S. & Levin, P. (1988). Getting results from sponsorship. *Special Events Report, 7*(22), 4-5.
4. Dixon, D.R. (1985). Research in sports marketing. *Marketing Communications,* September, 79-82.
5. DeParle, J. (1989). Warning: Sports stars may be hazardous to your health. *The Washington Monthly,* September, 34-48.
6. Cimons, M. (1990). Tobacco firms' sports ties assailed. *Los Angeles Times,* February 24, 23.
7. Gwinner, K. P. & Eaton, J. (1999). Building brand image through event sponsorship: The role of image transfer. *Journal of Advertising, 28*(4), 47-57.
8. Pracejus, J. W. (1998). *Seven psychological mechanisms through which sponsorship impacts consumers.* Paper presented at the 17th Annual Advertising and Consumer Psychology Conference, Portland, Oregon.
9. Gwinner, K. P. (1997). A model of image creation and image transfer in event sponsorship. *International Marketing Review, 14*(3), 145-158.
10. Meagher, J. W. (1992). And now a word from our sponsor. *Athletic Business,* May 14.
11. IEG. (2000). Doctor referrals lead Celebrex to add golf title. *Sponsorship Report, 19*(18), 8.
12. IEG. (1999). Chicken of the Sea catches first tie with synchro swimming. *Sponsorship Report, 18*(23), 8.
13. Team Marketing (2001). Minor league baseball teams chow on new deal with natural sponsor. *Team Marketing Report, 13*(9), 10.
14. *Man + machine: A look inside champ car racing.* (1999). Chicago: CART.

15. Kronengold, R. (2000). For all the criticism, Olympic Games still the place to be. *Brandweek, 41*(39), 30.

16. Lefton, T. (2000). Forget golf, Ernst & Young hooks dot-coms on skis, snowboards. *Brandweek, 41*(20), 9.

17. Lowenstein, R. & Lancaster, H. (1986). Nation's businesses are scrambling to sponsor the nation's pastimes. *Wall Street Journal*, June 25, 33.

18. Bernstein, A. (1999). Toys 'R' Us makes play for soccer kids. *Sports Business Journal*, August 9-15, 7.

19. IEG. (2002). No pruning here: Growers group increases sponsorship spend. *Sponsorship Report, 21*(17), 7.

20. IEG. (2002). New models, new target signal new deals for Subaru. *Sponsorship Report, 21*(18), 1, 6.

21. IEG. (2002). Supercuts restores sponsorship to marketing unit. *Sponsorship Report, 21*(10), 6.

22. IEG. (1999). Jaguar pounces on new sponsorship campaign. *Sponsorship Report, 18*(11), 3.

23. Ukman, L. (2002). Assertions. *Sponsorship Report, 21*(16), 2.

24. Brockington, L. (1999). Lincoln's upscale drive leads to Cup. *Sports Business Journal*, August 9-15, 12.

25. Serafin, R. (1989). Caddy goes for golf: Luxury cars vie for sponsorship. *Advertising Age*, August 21, 16.

26. IEG. (2001). Globalstar stakes out adventure with Iditarod tie. *Sponsorship Report, 20*(5), 7.

27. Ostrowski, J. (2000). Corporate America cozies up to the tattooed extreme world. *Sports Business Journal*, September 18-24, 24.

28. IEG. (1992). Bausch & Lomb to contact men, teens through NBA. *Sponsorship Report, 11*(21), 2.

29. Sack, A. L. & Fried, G. (2001). Pitching women's tennis to corporate sponsors: A case study of Pilot Pen tennis. *Sport Marketing Quarterly, 19*(2), 68-76.

30. IEG. (2000). Performance Research/IEG study highlights what sponsors want. *Sponsorship Report*, Sample Issue.

31. IEG. (2002). Success with Chicago marathon leads to more deals for ABN AMRO banks. *Sponsorship Report, 21*(17), 8.

32. IEG. (2002). Radio/event partnerships grow more sophisticated. *Sponsorship Report, 21*(17), 1, 4-5.

33. Eaton, R. (1991). Inside Target Stores' sponsorship philosophy. *Special Events Report, 19*(17), 4-5.

34. IEG. (1998). Media standards for crediting title sponsors. *Sponsorship Report, 17*(5), 4-5.

35. NASCAR marketing 101: How to leverage a racing sponsorship. (2001). *Sports Business*, June 18-24, 30-31.

36. IEG. (1999). Sponsor loyalty –It's not just for NASCAR any more. *Sponsorship Report, 18*(6), 3

37. IEG. (2000). Eschewing branding as top goal. AT&T wireless seeks store traffic. *Sponsorship Report, 19*(12), 1, 3.

38. IEG. (2000). Using sponsorship for B2B: Incenting business customers, trade channels. *Sponsorship Report, 19*(15), 6.

39. IEG. (2000). Coleman expands sponsorship portfolio, increases focus on sales overlays. *Sponsorship Report, 19*(12), 6.

40. McKelvey, S. (1994). Sans legal restraint, no stopping brash, creative ambush marketers. *Brandweek*, April 18, 20.

41. Meenaghan, T. (1998). Ambush marketing: Corporate strategy and consumer reaction. *Psychology & Marketing, 15*(4), 305-322.

42. Welsh, J. (2002). In defense of ambush marketing. *Sponsorship Report, 21*(11), 1, 4-5.

43. Sandler, D. M. & Shani, D. (1989). Olympic sponsorship vs. ambush marketing: Who gets the gold. *Journal of Advertising Research*, August/September, 9-14.

44. Gratton, C. & Taylor, P. (2000). *Economics of sports and recreation*. New York: E & FN Spon.

45. D'Alessandro, D. F. (2001). *Brand warfare*. New York: McGraw Hill.

46. Kendall, C. & Curthoys, J. (2001). Ambush marketing and the Sydney 2000 Games Protection Act: A retrospective. *Murdoch University Electronic Journal of Law, 8*(2), 1-29.

47. Staheli, P. (1998). Rebel advertisers who are ready to ambush. *The Times*, February 6, 34.

48. Roskin, S. (1995). Olympic partnership. *Newsweek*, July 18, Special Advertising Section.

49. Meenaghan, T. (1994). Point of view: Ambush Marketing: Immoral or innovative practice. *Journal of Advertising Research*, September/October, 77-88.

50. McKelvey, S. (2002). Ambush threat the real madness in Manoh. *Sports Business*, April 22-28, 33.

51. Haek, J. & Gendall, P. (2002). When do ex-sponsors become ambush marketers? *International Journal of Sports Marketing & Sponsorship*, December/January, 383-401.

52. IEG. (1996). Negotiating smarter: Opportunistic chances for sponsors. *Sponsorship Report, 15*(15), 1-2.

53. Ukman, L. (1998). Assertions. *Sponsorship Report, 17*(4), 2.

54. Mullin, B. J. Hardy S. & Sutton, W. S. (2000). *Sport Marketing*. Second edition. Champaign, IL: Human Kinetics.

55. O'Sullivan, P. & Murphy, P. (1998). Ambush marketing: The ethical issues. *Psychology & Marketing, 15*(4), 349-366.

56. Sleight, S. (1989). *Sponsorship: What it is and how to use it*. McGraw Hill, Maidenhead, Berkshire, England.

57. IEG. (2000). How to keep long-term sponsorships fresh and productive. *Sponsorship Report, 19*(20), 1, 4-5.

58. Currie, N. (2000). Maximizing sport sponsorship investment: A perspective on new and existing opportunities. *Sports Marketing & Sponsorship*, June/July, 159-166.

Photos courtesy of Robin Ammon, Jr.

Chapter Fourteen

Soliciting Sponsorships From Business Organizations

The efficiency and effectiveness of efforts to solicit corporate sponsorship are likely to be a function of (i) the philosophy that underlies a sport organization's approach; and (ii) the extent to which the approach is systematically organized. A marketing approach to solicitation involves carefully targeting specific companies or types of companies, identifying their motivations for investing, and designing sponsorship programs that will bring about mutually satisfying exchanges over an extended period of time. Sport managers who accept this philosophy and use it to guide their actions are likely to view themselves as brokers concerned with furthering the welfare of the potential sponsor companies by encouraging them to "buy into" the organization's services. They seek situations in which both the business and agency win.

The marketing approach requires a sport organization to identify what companies are likely to want in return for investing their resources. This information forms the basis for developing a presentation for each prospect. Too often, sport organizations spend too much time thinking about their own needs and not enough time considering what their prospect—the potential investor—wants.

A primary reason for sponsors rejecting what appear to be good investment opportunities relates to budget cycles and amount of lead-time. Budgets are planning documents that operationalize what a company is committed to doing for the next 12 months. Most of the sponsorship budget will be allocated to projects in that budget. However, it is usual to leave a small amount (typically 20-25%) unallocated, which gives companies flexibility both to shift some of their sponsorship focus during a year to reflect changes in their competitive environments, or to take advantage of unusually desirable sponsorship opportunities that may emerge during the year. Nevertheless, if a sponsorship is not included in the annual budget, then it is more difficult for a company to support it. This means it is critical for sport organizations to be familiar with their target companies' budget cycles and to bring a sponsorship opportunity to a company's attention before the budget is formulated.

There are other constraints that reinforce the need for a long lead-time. After there is agreement in principle, detailed contract negotiations will take time. In the previous chapter, it was noted that a sponsorship provides a platform from which a company is likely to launch an integrated promotion and advertising campaign that also must be included in its budget. Implementing an integrative approach will require company manpower, which has to be planned and allotted so it is available at the time it is needed. Advertising is one of the major determinants of lead-time due to the time required to prepare and place advertising in the media. For these reasons, it is unlikely that companies will consider sponsorship proposals that are not part of their regular budgetary planning process.

It has been suggested that the process of courting a sponsor is somewhat analogous to courting a marriage partner:

- Attraction – chemical, physical, emotional, rational.

- The Approach – someone needs to make the first move.

- Courtship – get to know each other and exchange vital statistics.

- Engagement – it could take six weeks, six months, or even six years. . . but do not rush into this.

- Marriage – provided engagement has gone according to plan, the big day is when everything is signed, sealed, and delivered to the satisfaction of all sides. Now the hard work begins. As in marriage, it takes effort to make sponsorship work—and lots of effort from both sides.

When the sponsorship breaks down and ends in divorce, it is usually attributable to the communication between the parties, managing expectations, promises made and then broken, or 'infidelity,' where a better offer came along and broke the relationship.[1]

Developing a Set of Potential Company Investors

The chapter commences with a discussion of how to identify and nurture a set of companies whose images and target markets are compatible with the sport event. Special attention is given to the appropriateness of tobacco and alcohol companies as sponsors. Traditionally, they have been major investors in sport, but their participation has become increasingly contentious.

Before approaching targeted companies, sponsorship benefits have to be packaged and priced, and a proposal must be developed. Communicating the proposal involves finding out who in a company should be contacted, delivering the presentation, addressing negative reactions to points included in it, and facilitating the closing, during which a specific sponsorship commitment is sought. The criteria used by companies to screen and evaluate proposals are described. The chapter concludes with a discussion of the contract, ways of fostering a close working relationship between a sport organization and its sponsors, and follow-up actions to be taken when an event is completed.

Before any selling takes place, a sport organization has to identify a set of companies whose customers have demographic/lifestyle profiles consistent with those of the event audience/participants and whose image is compatible with that of the event. The Internet makes sponsorship prospecting relatively efficient, since from websites it is possible to find out information on a company's products, its mission and goals, location, target markets, whether it sponsors other sport events, and so on. Further, Internet services such as Hoovers.com, BusinesscreditUSA.com, and Dunn and Bradstreet provide extensive background on companies.[2] Annual reports of publicly owned corporations are also available online.

The effective development and nurturing of sponsors requires that a computerized system be established to facilitate networking and scheduling with this set of prospect companies. The system should enable an agency to scan corporate interests and characteristics quickly to compile a list of likely prospective corporations for a particular event. Thus, the agency can make the right contact with the right potential sponsor at the right time.

The geographic scope of a service's audience, including any media audience, will dictate whether the search for sponsors (i) should be limited to companies located within a community; (ii) should be extended to regional companies and regional offices of larger companies; or (iii) should include a national or international set of companies. Geographic location may be important even at events seeking national level sponsors. If major companies are headquartered in the host community, they are likely to be prime prospects because the event provides a particularly strong platform that could facilitate client visits to the headquarters and interaction with multiple company personnel, demonstration of the companies' support for the community, and extensive employee access and involvement with the event. The geographic scope decision guides the types of reference sources that will be used to develop an initial list of potential sponsors whose images and target markets are compatible to those of the sport event.

To test the efficacy of the initial set of prospect companies, sport managers should put themselves in the shoes of the prospective sponsor's managers. If they cannot see why the sponsor's representative would become excited about being a partner in the event, then they should discard the company from the list of prospects. If "the shoe doesn't fit," the sport organization might succeed in attracting a sponsor the first year, but the sponsor is then likely to withdraw with some level of bad feeling and the organization will have to replicate the effort to attract another company in the subsequent year.

Information related to each potential corporate investor should extend into a system that facilitates easy access and retrieval. A typical system, which was developed by an organization in the Kansas City area, is described in Figure 14-1. Each potential sponsor is issued an account code of 0 through 6 using the following classification:

0: fewer than 100 employees
1: from 101 to 250 employees
2: from 251 to 500 employees
3: from 501 to 1,000 employees
4: National Headquarters (regardless of size)
5: more than 1,000 employees
6: civic, social, and service organizations

Figure 14-1 A Sample Sponsorship Tracking System

Account type:	4
Prospect corporation:	Jones Manufacturing
Mailing address:	P.O. Box 1000
Mailing city:	Kansas City
Mailing state:	Missouri
Mailing zip code:	64141
Location:	31st and Southwest Trafficway
Location city:	Kansas City
Location state:	Missouri
Location zip:	64141
Telephone:	(816) 968-1234
I. Contact and title:	Frank Jones, chief executive officer
II. Contact and title:	Bill East, president
Type of company:	Headquarters of building systems manufacturing
Number of employees:	500
Product service:	1) Engineering, manufacturing, marketing of building systems for nonresidential construction, grain-storage bins, and farm buildings and 2) under-the-floor electrical distribution systems, agricultural products, and energy-management systems.
Budget month:	October
Advertising budget:	$3,000,000
Advertising media:	Newspapers, consumer magazines, business publications, direct mail to consumers and business establishments, and network and spot radio
Investment A:	
Date A:	00/00/00
Project A:	
Investment B:	
Date B:	00/00/00
Project B:	
Investment C:	
Date C:	00/00/00
Project C:	
Reason declined:	

Figure 14-2 A Sample Follow-Up File

Company:	Jones Manufacturing
Contact:	Bill East
Project:	Sponsorship of temporary building for hospitality purposes at LPGA Golf Tournament
Date:	07/09/04
Explain:	Mailed plans and schematics
Date:	07/17/04
Explain:	Received letter asking to set up time for a presentation. Set meeting for August 1, 9:00 A.M.
Date:	08/01/04
Explain:	Had meeting with Mr. East and Mr. Jones. Explained the project and the concepts. They will be in touch with us after they make a decision.
Date:	09/01/04
Explain:	Mr. Smith telephoned. Jones Manufacturing accepted our proposal.
Conclusion:	Will construct structure on site.

Each record contained the account number, the company name, address, telephone number, contact person and title, type of company product or service provided, advertising budget, budget cycle, advertising media, and space to record any investment that a company has made.

The budget cycle of each company's promotion budget was identified. Each week the computer printed out a list of corporations whose promotional budget cycle was due to begin in eight weeks. This eight-week lead period gave staff the time to re-establish contact with the corporation's decision makers and to prepare a proposal for possible inclusion in next year's promotion budget.

A second follow-up file maintained a record of all contacts made with prospective sponsors or contributors by telephone, mail, or in person. Each record contained the company name, the person contacted, and the project with which the contact was concerned. Files were provided for the dates and descriptions of contacts, their decisions to accept or decline a proposition, and comments that they made about the association that might be helpful at a later date. In this file, staff also kept a log of the companies to which a proposal was sent, the date it was mailed, and all follow-up contacts concerning that project. This type of system is valuable in preventing duplication so that companies are not invited by different people from the sport organization to support different programs without internal coordination of these requests.

One of the decisions likely to arise in the development of the list of prospect companies is whether alcohol or cigarette companies should be included on the list.

Traditionally, they have been major sponsors of sport events, but managers have to be careful that support from companies in these industries does not tarnish their own organization's image. The debate over the appropriateness of partnering with such businesses is likely to be contentious, and for that reason the issues surrounding such sponsorships are discussed in the following sub-section.

Sponsorship by Tobacco and Alcohol Companies

Traditionally, tobacco and alcohol companies have been major sponsors of sport. Indeed, at the end of the 1990s, they ranked second and third behind the automobile industry as the primary investors in sport.[3] To many people, it appears incongruous that sport, which exemplifies a healthy, fit lifestyle, should be used as a promotional vehicle for products that appear to be the antithesis of this. In short, these linkages, which are consummated for financial purposes, seem to defeat the broader *raison d'être* for sport. Some sport managers have chosen to remain indifferent to this incongruity because they believe their sports would not be financially viable without sponsorship from tobacco and alcohol companies. They are concerned that loss of these revenues would mean either that events would be eliminated or that ticket prices would be commensurately increased. The former outcome is likely to occur in some contexts, but an economist is likely to argue that the latter outcome is improbable. Both of these outcomes assume that costs would remain fixed if sponsorship revenues declined, but in many instances it is likely that efforts would be made to reduce costs. It is naive to believe that ticket prices would be increased. Most sport managers are charged with setting ticket prices at a level that will garner maximal revenues for their organization, so the current price of tickets is likely to be the highest price the market will bear. If patrons could pay more, then sport organizations would charge more. Thus, ticket prices could not be increased if sponsorship was withdrawn. The only way to retain viability or profit margin would be to reduce costs, which would involve reducing players' salaries, prize money, administrative overhead, etc.

In this section, the substantial changes in both public opinion and legislation that have occurred in recent years are discussed. These changes have adversely affected the potential of these two industries to provide sponsorship for sport, but they have not foreclosed it.

Tobacco Sponsorship

The tobacco industry is dominated by four companies (Philip Morris, R. J. Reynolds, Brown & Williamson, and Lorilland) who produce over 98% of cigarettes smoked in the U.S. It is a highly profitable industry with profits at approximately 38% of revenue.[4] The impetus that stimulated tobacco companies to emerge as major sponsors of sports events was the closure of television to the industry's products in 1971. This ban encouraged the companies to turn to sponsorship as a new medium through which they could promote their products. Thus, for example, in 1971 the Virginia Slims ladies' professional tennis circuit and the Winston Cup motor racing sponsorships were launched, while Philip Morris' 15-year sponsorship of the Marlboro Cup horse race was launched dramatically in 1973, with a stellar winning performance by the legendary horse Secretariat.

The controversy over permitting tobacco companies to link with sport events by sponsoring them revolves around three central issues. First, the linkage obscures the connection between tobacco products and disease. This is evident in the Virginia Slims case shown in Figure 14-3, where the product was associated with the vibrant health of tennis players, rather than with lung cancer. The U.S. Center for Disease Control consistently reports that annual deaths in the United States from causes attributable to smoking exceed 400,000, which is one in five of all deaths. Paralleling this enormous health toll is the economic burden of tobacco use: more than $50 billion in medical expenditures and another $50 billion in indirect costs. This makes the association of tobacco companies with sport objectionable to many.

A second central issue in the tobacco sponsorship controversy is the belief that the sport linkage enables tobacco companies to penetrate the youth market. More than 90% of people who will ever smoke on a regular basis begin doing so prior to the age of nineteen.[5] Each day some 3,000 children take up the habit, and the average age at which they begin is between twelve and thirteen. Since tobacco kills over 400,000 people each year, and other smokers die from other causes or quit, replenishing the pool of customers has to be a primary goal of the industry. It must either persuade children to start smoking, or it goes out of business. The failure of a generation of young people to start smoking would devastate the tobacco industry.

A third central issue is the contention that such sponsorship circumvents the ban on cigarette advertising and promotion in broadcast media. Critics argue that the inclusion of brand names and logos in broadcasts of events is a blatant breach of the spirit of the legislation against cigarette advertising. Indeed sport sponsorship offers one feature not available to tobacco companies in their advertising. That is, it enables cigarette brand names to be shown or mentioned on television and radio without being accompanied by the Surgeon General's health warnings that are required on print advertisements.

As a result of a series of Congressional hearings and judicial concerns in the 1990s, the tobacco companies were forced to open their files to public scrutiny. For almost half a century the tobacco industry had denied that their products were harmful to health and that they targeted children, despite extensive scientific data demonstrating these outcomes. Their confidential files revealed they had known of these outcomes for many decades, but had embarked on a policy of public denial. These disclosures created public and political momentum for further restrictions to be placed on the promotion of tobacco products. Additional pressure on the tobacco companies came from a plethora of lawsuits by states seeking large damages to reimburse them for the Medicaid costs they had incurred to treat health problems created by smoking.

In addition, there was growing momentum in the 1990s for the Federal Drug Administration agency to regulate nicotine and tobacco products. This would give it the authority to treat tobacco products as drugs and medical devices. That momentum is dependent on a sympathetic, politically supportive, regulatory environment, and this existed in the 1990s. It was not sustained in the new decade, but inevitably will return at some time in the future.

Figure 14-3 Virginia Slims: Benefits and Criticisms*

In 1971 Philip Morris brought out its first cigarette for women, called Virginia Slims. At the same time, Joseph Cullman III, who was a lifelong tennis fan and chairman of the board of Philip Morris, was approached by his friend Gladys Heldman and asked to support the fledgling women's tennis tour. He initially contributed $2,500, but it emerged as a fortuitous opportunity to combine a historic breakthrough for women with promotion of the new women's cigarette. From these small beginnings, players on the Women's Tennis Tour now compete for more than $20 million in prize money.

Cullman's personal and financial support for women's tennis—particularly after the women were expelled from the United States Tennis Association for forming their own tour—led to extraordinary player loyalty toward his corporation. Nearly all the top women tennis players supported maintaining a relationship with Virginia Slims, even when other corporations such as Proctor & Gamble offered more lucrative sponsorships.

As Cullman explained it, "With growing anti-cigarette publicity, a number of players are under pressure to reduce the dependence on Virginia Slims. But then there is great loyalty because we helped make the women's tour."

Virginia Slims underwrote the women's tour for over 15 years in return for worldwide publicity, access to audiences whose demographics matched the consumers of Virginia Slims, and opportunities for retail spin-offs. However, in response to criticism, the Women's International Professional Tennis Council, which oversees the tour and sanctions tournaments, ultimately yielded to the public press not to renew the Virginia Slims contract.

Tennis players are the epitome of physical fitness and vitality and to use them to legitimize smoking led to some scathing criticism of the tennis authorities for their continued linkage with Virginia Slims. One critic used top player Hana Mandlikova, who was featured in one of the annual press guides for the circuit, to illustrate his criticisms:

> Those of us less physically gifted than Hana Mandlikova can't help but envy the strength in her legs, power in her arms, and stamina in her lungs as she pauses, racket poised, before exploding

---

This series of events led to the Master Settlement Agreement (MSA) by which 11 tobacco companies executed a legal settlement with 46 states, the District of Columbia, and five commonwealths and territories. In the settlement, the companies agreed to pay these entities $246 billion over 25 years, which was approximately 45 cents per pack of cigarettes. Given the price inelasticity of the industry, it is likely this extra cost will be passed through to the customers as a price increase without damage to the companies' profits.[4]

In addition, the settlement agreement contained a number of important public health provisions, including several relating to sponsorship. Under the terms, tobacco companies are limited to one brand name sponsorship per year. However, this sponsorship is not necessarily confined to a single event; rather, it can be applied to a series of related events. This "series" clause allowed the R. J. Reynolds company, for example, to retain its Winston brand's sponsorship of NASCAR's Winston Cup Series, providing a presence at 34 events. This provision caused one researcher to conclude that the dollar value of television exposure would probably amount to over 70% of what tobacco companies achieved before the MSA came

into her backhand. It's precisely the rareness of these qualities that brings us to admire her so, and to pause a moment when looking at her picture. Because as Hana Mandlikova intently awaits a return, she does so in front of a big sign that says "Virginia Slims"—a product now known for promoting the powers of heart and lung that lie at the center of her trade. In fact, throughout the guide—not to mention the nation's sports pages and television broadcasts—we find these stars showcasing their enviable talents in front of cigarette ads. The bold corporate logo of the Virginia Slims series emphasizes the bond: a woman, sassy and sleek, holds a racket in one hand and a cigarette in the other.

This is odd. Tennis champions, after all, are models of health, particularly the health of heart and lungs, where endurance is essential. And cigarette smoking, as the Surgeon General reminds, "is the chief avoidable cause of death in our society"—death, more precisely, from heart and lung disease.

A leading tennis authority, Pam Shriver, said, "Virginia Slims doesn't mean cigarettes to me. To me it is people, it's a relationship, it's tennis. You don't see anyone wearing a Virginia Slim's patch on their shirt, and we would never be asked. Philip Morris is very sensitive to us and tries to make us comfortable... I don't feel bad at all about looking somebody in the eye and saying, 'Virginia Slims is our sponsor,' because they're a great sponsor. Too bad they're a cigarette."

Shriver's comments mirrored those by Billie Jean King, who was the major driving force behind the successful launching of the women's tennis circuit. King commented, "Personally I hate cigarette smoking. I hate cigarettes. Ninety-five percent of the girls do."

Critics respond to these types of comments by saying that this private view does not excuse the prominent role of tennis players in the very successful promotion of this brand of cigarettes over a period of two decades. They suggest this type of response means, Let someone else get lung cancer, it won't be me; and I'll get rich and famous in the process. These types of responses illustrate one of the main advantages of sports sponsorship to the tobacco companies, which is that it tends to build a constituency of thankful and financially dependent recipients who can be relied upon to support the industry.

*Note: This case was derived from information provided by James DeParle, "Warning Sports Stars May Be Hazardous to Your Health," Aloson Muscatine, "Where There's Smoke There's Ire: Tobacco Sponsorship Sparks Debate," and Elizabeth Comte, "Women's Tennis Replaces Slims."

into effect.[6] Another implication of the "one brand-name annually" provision was the amount invested in that sponsorship was likely to be substantial because all a brand's sponsorship funds now would be focused on a single event or series rather than being dissipated among multiple sponsorships.

The MSA expressly forbids brand sponsorship of (i) any event in which young people make up a significant percentage of the intended audience; (ii) any event in which any young people are paid participants or contestants; and (iii) any athletic event between opposing teams in any football, basketball, baseball, soccer, or hockey league. However, there are no limitations on sponsoring events in other sports held in adult-only facilities. Thus, for example, Camel was able to retain its $1.5 million sponsorship of the American Pool Players Association because its events were held in taverns in which youth are not admitted. This provided Camel with exposure in 9,000 taverns nationwide.

The MSA does not limit the number of *corporate* sponsorships a tobacco company may enter into each year, provided the corporate name does not include any brand name of tobacco products. Thus, for example, Philip Morris could continue as an official sponsor of the Kentucky Derby, R. J. Reynolds as a sponsor of Altamont Raceway Park, and Brown & Williamson as a sponsor of the Gateway International Raceway.

The annual brand sponsorships that are permitted cannot be used as a platform to explicitly promote tobacco products, since companies are prohibited from referring to a brand name sponsorship event or to a celebrity or other person in such an event in their advertising of a tobacco product. The MSA included some advertising restrictions, including the removal of billboard advertising for cigarettes and a ban on using cartoon characters in advertisements. Other clauses in the MSA prohibit brands from acquiring naming rights agreements for a stadium or arena; sponsoring a football, basketball, baseball, soccer, or hockey league (or any team involved in such a league); or selling/licensing/marketing any apparel or other merchandise that bears a tobacco brand name.

These restrictions on tobacco sponsorship of sport are consistent with actions taken in many other countries throughout the world.[7] In the mid-1990s, almost 90 countries had regulations that restricted tobacco advertising, but fewer than 30 of those limited or prohibited tobacco sponsorship. Tobacco companies took advantage of this legislative imbalance and became one of the largest investors in sport sponsorship globally. The MSA sponsorship restrictions in the U.S., and the banning of tobacco sponsorship of sport in the UK and elsewhere soon after, indicated that this imbalance was being rectified. Among the countries with an absolute ban on tobacco sponsorship (as opposed to the partial MSA prohibitions) are France, Belgium, Finland, Norway, Denmark, New Zealand, and Ireland.

Alcohol Sponsorship

Breweries are major sponsors of sport in North America, especially Anheuser-Busch, whose Budweiser brand name appears in 84% of US professional stadiums and arenas, Miller, Coors, and Labatt in Canada. The substantial investment by beer companies in sport sponsorship has been explained in these terms: "Beer drinkers and sports fans are one and the same—indivisible, inseparable, identical! No one drinks more beer than a sports fan, and no one likes sports better than a beer drinker" (p. 74).[8] The ages of maximum beer consumption and maximum sports involvement are the same, both for men and for women. The peak beer consuming years are from 18 to 29, which are the peak years for sports' participants and spectators. Males in the 18 to 34 age group constitute only 20% of the beer drinking population, but they consume 70% of all beer. Breweries have sought tie-ins with sport because this offers them a "macho" vehicle, which appeals to their core young adult male target audience. These heavy users are the most critical market segment for beer companies, and it is easy to communicate with them through sports associated events.

As the magnitude of sports sponsorship by breweries has increased, it has been accompanied by a commensurate increase in criticism from those concerned about alcohol abuse. There has been heightened awareness in recent years that alcohol is a drug with the potential to become addictive. The concern is that there are about 18.5 million Americans who abuse alcohol,[9] and beer companies promote that it is natural for this intoxicating drug to be consumed while watching or after participating in a pleasant sporting activity. Sponsorship and advertising by beer companies promotes the image that beer is not very different from soft drinks, and its negative consequences, such as traffic deaths, domestic violence, physical deterioration from cirrhosis, hypertension and stroke, and pregnancy risks, are ignored. Women's bodies react to alcohol differently from men's, and they are subject to other risks. For example, one well-regarded study reported that the risk of dying from breast cancer was 30% higher among women who drank at least once a day.[10]

It has been noted that "beer comes to share the luster of healthy athleticism," and that "It's really paradoxic that alcohol and all it stands for should be associated with excellent athletic performance. You cannot have one and the other at the same time. If you're going to perform as a top-grade athlete, you have to cut out alcohol" (p. 78).[8] The close relationship between beer and sport has caused some "to wonder just what kind of cultural hypocrisy is going on when Americans relentlessly insist on immersing sport—our most wholesome, most admired, even (sometimes) most heroic institution—in a sea of intoxicating drink" (p. 70).[8]

In response to their social critics, the beer companies point out that when used in moderation, beer has been shown to have positive effects on health. As recently as 1990, the U.S. Department of Health and Human Services' publication, *Dietary Guidelines for America*, indicated that "drinking has no health benefit" and "is not recommended." However, by 1995 these same guidelines stated, "Current evidence suggests that moderate drinking is associated with a lower risk for coronary heart disease in some individuals."[11] This conclusion has been reinforced by an abundance of evidence suggesting that regular, moderate consumption of beer, wine, and even hard liquor might be good for people. For example, a longitudinal study conducted by researchers at Harvard University followed almost 40,000 men and found that those who drank a glass or two, three to seven times a week, cut their risk of a heart attack by a third. This is probably because all kinds of alcohol raise levels of HDL, or "good cholesterol," and lower levels of a blood-clotting protein offering benefits similar to a daily dose of aspirin.[10]

Hence, the decision confronting sport managers as to whether or not they should solicit or accept sponsorship from beer companies is more difficult than that associated with tobacco companies because, unlike tobacco, the problem is not the consumption of beer, rather it is the abuse of beer. This makes it tempting for sport managers to rationalize that there does not appear to be a strong enough case to ban beer companies from sponsorship opportunities. Certainly, the case for a ban ostensibly appears to be much less compelling than the case that can be made to ban sponsorship by tobacco companies. However, the alcohol dilemma is compounded by the widespread abuse of alcohol and the consequences of that abuse. A reviewer of a paper written by one of the authors on this issue articulated the conundrum in the following terms:

> There is the contradiction of physical fitness being closely tied to drug uses. The advertising is aimed at youth and minorities. And, alcohol is a huge social problem in the U.S. (125,000 deaths yearly; indirect deaths from fires, traffic accidents, and drowning; $150 billion lost to job absenteeism, lost production, medical expenses, and work-related accidents; and the unmeasurable negative costs such as spouse and child abuse, de-

sertion, emotional problems, and fetal alcohol syndrome). Should sport be at all connected with a drug that is responsible for such problems?

In the United States, most universities have banned beer companies and their distributors from sponsoring events on campus. The evolution of the thinking process in recent years is captured in the following anecdote:

- In the mid-1990s, the director of men's athletics at the University of Minnesota negotiated a contract with Miller Brewing Company worth $150,000. Subsequently, he was promoted to vice-president for student development and intercollegiate athletics of the university system. When the contract expired, a new contract for $225,000 was offered. This time he declined explaining, "Being in a new position, I was able to get a big-picture view of what was happening . . . I felt like we were sending students a mixed message." That big picture had included the need for 14 students from the university to enter alcohol-rehabilitation programs and an increase in alcohol-related assaults on that campus, which constituted part of his new responsibilities.[12]

Packaging Sponsorships

There are a variety of different ways and levels at which companies can become associated with a sport event. Thus, it is normal practice to create different levels of benefit packages so a wide range of investment opportunities can be offered. The number of levels is likely to vary with the size of the event, but the standard structure that has emerged in recent years consists of four categories of sponsorship: title sponsorship, presenting sponsorship, official sponsorship, and official supplier status. Each higher level of sponsorship builds on the benefits package offered at the previous level. It has been noted that there is no established list of rights for each of the categories. Indeed, these sponsorship categories have no legal meaning other than what is agreed upon when the sponsorship is designed. There is, however, a general pattern that distinguishes the four sponsorship categories from each other.[13]

Title sponsorship means that the sponsor's name becomes integrated into the event title or team name. This is the highest form of association with an event and offers a sponsor maximum leverage for borrowing the image of the sport event to improve its brand's (or corporate) image. The major risk is that if unexpected costs occur, then the title sponsor may have to increase its financial commitment in order to avoid the risk of being closely linked to an inferior event. The title sponsor is likely to insist on the right to veto unsuitable co-sponsors, and to have substantive input into how the event is managed and organized.

Presenting sponsors of a sport event typically pay about one-half to one-fourth of what the title sponsor pays. They are given exclusive rights to associate with an event within a product category. Thus, a company may be the only life insurance, automobile, soft drink, or shoe company associated with the event. Since this association is not available to competitive brands, it can be exploited to strengthen a brand's position in the market place. The more money a sport organization needs to raise from sponsorships, the more narrowly it's tempted to define these categories. An Olympic official observed, "The more pressure there is for us to make money, the thinner we slice the apple" (p. 80).[14] Thus, an exclusive category may be defined as "soft drinks" or as "carbonated soft drinks." This latter, more narrow definition enables the organization to sell another exclusive category sponsorship to a non-carbonated soft drink brand. However, the added "clutter" is likely to mean the price that can be charged for each category will be lower. In major event sponsorship agreements, these categories are carefully negotiated and meticulously defined. This is illustrated in Table 14-1, which defines the scope of the exclusive product category negotiated by the Mars brand in its sponsorship of the World Cup Soccer competition.

Official sponsors typically are charged about ten percent of the title fee. Their benefit package is substantially smaller than that of presentation sponsors. They will only be allowed to invest in product categories that have not been reserved by presenting sponsors. This level offers smaller companies an opportunity to associate with relatively little financial risk but, given the commensurably small benefit package, they are likely to have to work hard to obtain their marketing objectives.

The brands of *official suppliers* generally are not directly linked to the sport event itself and have little obvious connection to it. They offer their goods or services to the sport organization staging it, or to the participants or spectators who are part of it. Typical of such sponsors would be food and beverage suppliers, credit card companies, and equipment suppliers.

Table 14-1   Categories Reserved by Mars as an Official Sponsor of the World Cup Soccer Tournament

Candy & confections	Tortilla chips
Block chocolate, cocoa	Corn chips
Chocolate covered snack bars, bisquits, mints	Nuts
	Pretzels
Chocolate covered granola snacks, hard candies	Popcorn
	Puffs, curls, balls
Potato chips	

Pricing Sponsorships

There are multiple variations of the four-category taxonomy of sponsorship categories described in the previous section, but all of them will incorporate a hierarchical structure of benefits and associated prices. The use of different levels allows companies who might not otherwise be able to afford the investment to choose a lower level of sponsorship. If this is not done, a sport manager may offer a $100,000 proposal to a company that has only $40,000 to invest and, therefore, may lose the opportunity to secure $40,000 of support. However, an organization should probably start by presenting the top-level package that contains all of the benefit components, while also letting the prospect know that smaller packages are available, because if the sport manager starts at a low level it is rare for the sponsor to suggest increasing it. The importance of this kind of flexibility is that it enables managers to work with a company to customize a package. Examples of hierarchical sponsorship categories used by the PGA tour and by the World Cup Soccer Tournament when it was held in the United States are given in Figures 14-4 and 14-5.

Developing, soliciting, and implementing sponsorships involves expense to a sport organization in the form of staff time, opportunity cost, and financial cost. Hence, the starting point for ascertaining a price for a package of sponsorship

Figure 14-4 Sponsorship Categories Used at a PGA Tournament

The average professional golf tournament receives about 75% of its revenues via corporate sponsorships. Among the typical categories of corporate involvement available for a PGA Tournament:

Title sponsor: Corporate name used in tournament title, with other benefits, including hospitality tent, on-site signs, 300-500 event tickets, 48 entries in the professional-amateur tournament. Cost: $750,000, plus a guarantee to buy $1 million in network TV advertising time.

Presenting sponsor: Comparable benefits to title sponsorship, but corporate name won't be in event title. Cost: $300,000, plus a $500,000 requirement to buy network TV advertising.

Associate sponsor: As many as seven sponsors at this level, which includes signs and/or on-site entertainment. Cost: $30,000-$35,000.

Smaller sponsorships: Costs: $16,500 for four participant spots in pro-am; $4,000-$16,000 for hospitality tent; $3,000-$10,000 for signs.

benefits is to list these expenses to ensure sponsorship agreements generate more revenue than they cost to implement. A typical sheet for explicating these costs is shown in Table 14-2. Staff time is notoriously difficult to calculate, but often it is likely to be the major cost center. For example, assume "Evaluation research" involves developing measures, collecting data, analyzing it, and producing a report, and that it takes two staff members a month to do this. If their annual salary and benefit package costs the company $60,000 for each of them, then the cost of staff time on this item is $10,000 [($60,000/12)]. Accurate measurement of staff time requires staff to keep time diaries.

In addition to staff time, costs listed on the cost sheet should include the face value of tickets, marketing costs (including advertising) associated with promoting the sponsor's involvement, the value of media time, the costs associated with organizing the hospitality opportunities, and so on. The total costs shown at the foot of Table 14-2 constitute the minimum sale price of a sponsorship. If it is sold for less than this amount, then the sport organization will lose money on the agreement.

Market acceptance of a sponsorship price will be determined by the sponsorship opportunities available in the market place. An event's price will be compared by companies to that of other events of similar stature and incrementally increased or decreased according to how well it is perceived to compare. An example of how this is applied is given in Figure 14-6. An indication of the prices of comparable events can be gleaned from publications such as *Sponsorship Report* and *Sport Business Journal,* which report on these issues.

Market value is strongly influenced by geographic reach and impact, which refers to the number, size, and value of the target market with which a sponsor is seeking to communicate. Part of the comparative assessment of value will be to investigate the equivalent opportunity cost for a company's investment, that is, what the company could have purchased in the regular media for the same amount of money. This involves comparing the cost of advertising in an event's program or

Figure 14-5 Sponsorship Packages at the World Cup Soccer Tournament

When the World Cup Soccer Tournament was played for the first time in its 64-year history (it is held every four years) in the United States, a worldwide television audience of 3 billion different people was expected to see the games held between June 17 and July 17. This increased to a cumulative 32 billion viewing audience during the month period, with 1.1 billion watching the final game alone. A three-tier sponsorship package was developed, although the third tier was divided into three levels.

Official Sponsor was the first tier, which was sold for an average of $15 million. It included worldwide rights to all works related to the World Cup, category exclusivity, and two to four sign boards per venue. The ten official sponsor opportunities were sold to Canon, Coca-Cola, Fuji, Gillette, JVC, Mars, MasterCard, McDonald's, Philips, and General Motors.

Official Marketing Partners paid $7 million and received worldwide rights to all marks, category exclusivity and one signboard per venue. These were purchased by American Airlines, Sprint Communication, Adidas, Upper Deck, ITT Sheraton, Anheuser-Busch, and Electronic Data Systems.

The third-tier consisted of three levels:

(i) Official Product/Service Company, which was the only third-tier level that offered unrestricted logo use. These opportunities were priced from $1 million to $2.5 million, depending on the product category, number of brands involved, and whether the purchaser wanted U.S. or worldwide rights.

(ii) Equipment Suppliers were given worldwide or U.S. rights to World Cup in print only, were not permitted use of the term "official" in their designation, and were not promised category exclusivity. These were sold for between $300,000 and $1 million, plus the in-kind provision of needed equipment.

(iii) Regional Supporters were granted exclusivity and marketing rights to one of the Cup's nine venues and its surrounding ADI. Sponsors were required to purchase all the games played at a particular site (which ranged between four and eight) at a cost of $40,000 per game.

Source: Materials provided by World Cup USA 1994 Inc. and a report in IEG *Sponsorship Reports, 12*(6) March 22, 1993: 1-3.

of signage on billboards, lightpoles, concourses, scoreboards, fence posts, etc. with the cost of advertising in the press. Similarly, the price of public announcements made at an event may be compared with the cost of radio advertising. The price per head reached that is charged by a sport property can usually be higher than that in other media because the communications are likely to be more tightly focused on a company's target market. Being able to demonstrate the superior value of a sponsorship in this way makes the sales process easier. If the total costs (listed in Table 14-2) are close to the market price so the net revenue accruing to the sport organization is relatively small, then consideration should be given as to how the costs can be reduced.

A package of benefits should be priced as a holistic entity. A single price should not be attached to each component in a package. If components of packages are individually priced, then a sponsor is likely to look for items to cut. If sponsors want to negotiate certain elements to reduce the price, then they will raise the issue. The sport manager should not invite this action by individually pricing

Table 14-2 Cost Sheet for the Sport Manager Seeking Sponsorship

ITEM AND QUANTITY All items that will incur either financial expenditure or person hours	REAL COST
Tickets	$
Hospitality, food, beverages	$
VIP parking passes	$
Event programmes	$
Additional printing	$
Signage printing	$
Signage production	$
Signage erection	$
Support advertising	$
Apparel for competitors, officials, media, etc. featuring the sponsor	$
Evaluation research	$
Media monitoring	$
Faxes, phone calls, emails, internet	$
Public relations support	$
Marketing costs	$
Advertising costs	$
Legal and accountancy costs	$
(Other items)	$
Cost of selling sponsorship staff time and expenses based on x hours at $ per hour multiplied by 1.5 for salary plus benefits	$
Cost of servicing sponsorship in staff time based on x hours over the season $ multiplied by 1.5 for salary plus benefits	$
Total costs	$

Source: Adapted from Kolah, A. (2001). *How to develop an effective sponsorship programme.* London: Sport Business Group, p.57.

components in the initial proposal. An alternative approach to quoting an initial price is for a company to specify its budget and sponsorship objectives, and for the sport organization to negotiate a customized set of benefits that best fits these parameters.

The bulk of a sponsorship fee (at least 65%) should be paid when contracts are signed because costs associated with obligations to the sponsor, such as exposure in collateral materials, are likely to be incurred for a period of time before the event takes place. A sport organization should offer discounts for multi-year commitments because they save time, labor, and legal fees compared to negotiating an equivalent number of one-year contracts.

Figure 14-6 Pricing Auto Racing Sponsorships

The Championship Auto Racing Team (CART) and Indy Racing League (IRL) circuits competed with the NASCAR circuit. Racing teams on all three circuits were dependent on sponsorship for their financial viability. NASCAR races were televised on the Fox, NBC, and Turner channels and averaged a national rating of 4 points. When multiplied by 36 events, the Winston Cup Series generated 144 accumulated national television rating points.

A NASCAR team needed about $10 million from a major sponsor to compete successfully week-to-week in the Winston Cup Series. Plenty of teams were funded at or near that level by sponsors. Therefore, the market determined that motorsports sponsors were willing to spend about $70,000 in rights fees for each domestic TV rating point. Motorsports sponsors believed that TV viewers of NASCAR, CART, and IRL were the same demographic group.

CART and IRL did not attract anywhere near the number of viewers as NASCAR. IRL had 15 races on its regular circuit, and each race on ABC and ESPN attracted a 1.0 rating, while its showcase event the Indianapolis 500 achieved a 5.0, so its cumulative national TV rating was 19 points.

CART has 20 races. The seven on CBS generated 1 point while the other 13 on Speed Channel generated 0.4 national rating points each, so CART's cumulative national rating was 12 points.

Applying sponsors' valuation of motorsports at the rate of $70,000 per rating point made an IRL car worth $1.3 million in rights fees and a CART team $840,000. Unfortunately, it took about $5 million and $9 million to operate a competitive IRL and CART team, respectively. These data suggest that the prices IRL and CART could charge for sponsorship were too low to sustain the viability of race teams on those circuits. Existing sponsors were paying much higher than the market rate in anticipation of higher TV ratings. Their failure to materialize caused many of the IRL and CART sponsors not to renew their investments.

Adapted from Poole, M. (2001). Sponsorship wheels coming off the CART. *Sports Business Journal,* November 19-25, 29.

Many companies prefer to support an event with in-kind services rather than cash, and this is equally valuable if the services are budget relieving. To ascertain the level of benefits a sponsor should receive in exchange for in-kind services, a valuation of the services has to be made. For example, if a company provides computing systems software and advice, in-house printing, or courier service, how is the real value of these services determined? The following procedure has been suggested:

> Treat in-kind deals the same as cash deals if they are substitutes for line items in your budget. For example, if you have no need for a car, do not let an auto company offset its cash payment by throwing in a car. However, if you require air travel, treat the airline as a cash sponsor. Clarify how you will calculate the value of its payment. For example, is it based on the value of the lowest discounted air fare or the retail rate.[15] (p. 5)

Given the substantial costs involved, there is a growing trend for major sponsors to seek to self-liquidate the cost of their sponsorship by involving many of their suppliers in the event. This might be achieved by a title sponsor sub-contracting product category rights to product manufacturers or distributors with which it has close ties, through direct merchandising sales, or through the sale of television rights fees (which was discussed in the previous chapter). For example, a sport manager may approach a grocery chain and offer it title sponsorship of a golf tournament for $90,000. The organization may suggest to the chain that it offer $5,000-per-hole packages to 18 of its vendors. In return for their sponsorship, the vendors may be offered special in-store promotions and the highly sought-after end-aisle location for a given period of time. Each hole on the course would have the sponsor's banner on it. This enables the grocery chain to receive all the visibility, image, and goodwill benefits associated with title sponsorship at no direct cost to itself.

- Mervyn's is a mid-market department store chain in California. To change its staid image to a place where younger shoppers find hip, relevant fashions, it sponsored Beach Bash at California's Hermosa Beach, which included AVP-sanctioned men's and women's pro beach volleyball, inline skating, skateboarding, stunt cycling, and alternative bands. Its lead sponsorship gave it the rights to sell cosponsorship to vendors. The company sold cosponsorships to several of its vendors including Side Out, a maker of volleyball apparel, and Lee Company's Pipes line, geared for bikers and skateboarders. Vendors received on-site benefits, identification in Mervyn's ad campaign, and an enhanced, event-themed presence in its stores. These cosponsorships enabled Mervyn's to come close to liquidating its rights fee. In addition, by parterning with brands already relevant to youths, Mervyn's reduced the risk that it would seem out of place at the youth-oriented event—i.e., it borrowed it's cosponsors' images as well as the event's image.[16]

Preparation of Proposals

Company managers are unlikely to review anything extensive initially. They are more likely to scan quickly rather than to read the material, so the first two paragraphs are particularly critical. The most common complaint from company managers is that sponsorship proposals are too long, too descriptive, and not tailored to their needs. A typical comment is, "Most of the requests that I get are too descriptive and do not outline the key features of the proposal, particularly the benefit that the request can provide to our company" (p. 196).[17] Hence, the first approach should be limited either to one or two pages or should comprise a full proposal with a brief executive overview at the front. The central concern should be to specify the potential benefits to the company. Too often, proposals make the mistake of describing the merits of a program, its level of excellence, or its economic impact. Sponsors do not buy programs; they buy the expectation of benefits. They buy promotional platforms that help them sell products or services. Hence, proposals should address the sponsor's need, not those of the agency.

If interest is forthcoming after receiving the one- or two-page proposal, then the remaining material and perhaps a short video can be used to offer more details. A video is useful to demonstrate such elements as the signage, promotional opportunities, and hospitality facilities, and to give a "feeling" of the event's atmosphere, but it should not exceed five minutes in length.

A complete proposal should incorporate the elements shown in Figure 14-7. The proposal specifies benefits that can be made available to the company, and under the 'Sponsorship Investment' heading it identifies the packages (with prices) that the sport event is offering. Sometimes, if a company is interested, it may respond by sending the sport organization a standard questionnaire to complete. This can be used to evaluate the investment's potential in terms of the company's objectives and other investment opportunities.

The sport organization may be requested to provide a detailed budget of the event's costs. This allows companies to understand the role of their investment in the context of the overall budget, and to reassure them that the event is adequately funded. Sponsors may also be able to identify areas where they can help reduce costs. For example, companies can often obtain better prices on printing, advertising, or other items than can sport organizations.

At the end of the short proposal, the sport manager should indicate an intention to call in a week to ten days to see if the company is interested and, if so, to arrange a meeting. This prevents the problem of companies taking weeks to respond and means that, if the response is negative, the organization can focus its efforts on more likely prospects.

Attention to detail and customizing proposals is key. Many potential sponsors are inundated with proposals and the simplest oversight can result in a proposal being discarded. Consider the following vignette:

- A Busch Grand National NASCAR team was in the process of negotiating a high six-figure sponsorship agreement with a well-known overnight package handler. The team and the company had reached the point where drafts of contracts were flowing back and forth, and both sides were optimistic that a deal would be signed shortly. The overnight package provider sent the final draft of the contract to the team for their review and signature. Several weeks after returning the agreement, the team owner contacted the new sponsor to discuss implementation plans. To his shock, he was informed that someone in his office had sent the signed contract back to the sponsor using a competitor's overnight service. Just like that, the deal was off, and the potential sponsor refused invitations to reopen negotiations.[18]

| Communicating the Proposal | There are four elements to consider in communicating a proposal. First is the preparation effort that requires a sport organization to determine who in the targeted company should be approached with the sponsorship proposal and then to seek out information about these contact people that will aid communication with them. The presentation element itself incorporates two other considerations: handling negative reactions and closing. |

Preparation

After a list of the most probable corporate investors has been derived and packages have been delivered and priced, the next stage is to prepare an approach tailored to each of these prospects. The preparation commitment is time consuming, but

Figure 14-7 Elements Incorporated into a Sponsorship Proposal

1. Concise description of the opportunity and why the prospect should sponsor the event/team

2. Mission statement of your organization and event/team history

   - Where is your event headed? Is it a one-time opportunity for the sponsor, or will there be an opportunity for a long-term relationship?

   - Describe the prestige of your event and your event's history or track record of success/importance.

   - Inventory your property's assets. Translate these assets into sponsor benefits.

3. Venue location, dates and times, staffing, estimated attendance, exposure

4. Product distribution

   - If the event doesn't move the sponsor's product, why should they become involved?

   - If the target is a food/beverage distributor, who will handle concessions?

   - If the target is a car/rental company, who will handle transportation?

5. Philosophical issues

   - What types of value-added deals are there for a long-term commitment by the target? Be explicit here.

   - What are the rights holder's long-term goals with the event?

6. Expected results if the target signs up with your organization

   - Will the event drive sales volume?

   - What are the long-term benefits of an extended relationship with your event?

   - Will the relationship help the company's image? Why? With whom?

7. Strategic fit

   - How will this sponsorship help the company communicate with its key markets?

     - e.g., a sponsorship with Coca-Cola: Classic Coke is more appropriate with a younger market, whereas Diet Coke is a better fit with an older market

8. Advertising & promotional opportunities

   - Analyze past sponsor exposure and how they benefited (e.g., include a small case study).

9. Customer promotion opportunities

   - How can the property (i.e., event) work for the target's customers?

10. Hospitality benefits and product category exclusivity issues

    - How will you defend the company against ambush?

11. Signage

    - Diagram where signs will be on-site.

    - Will there be broadcast visibility?

12. Cosponsors

    - Address the issue of sponsor clutter.

- Are there ways for cosponsors to cooperate in joint promotions? Give examples.

13. Cost and level of sponsorship

- How much will each level of sponsorship cost the target?

Source: Madrigal, R. Department of Marketing, University of Oregon.

it is essential. Success in soliciting support is more likely to result from good preparation than from good presentation techniques. Key questions in the preparation phase are, "Who in the company should be contacted?" and "What is their role?"

In companies that are extensively involved in sponsorship, it is likely to be the responsibility of a specialist executive or of a sponsorship department. In other companies, however, sponsorship decisions may be made by the chief executive if the business is relatively small, or by individuals with titles such as marketing, sales, or advertising vice-president, or by the public relations department. In large companies with multiple brands, if brand rather than corporate sponsorship is being solicited, then it is likely that brand managers rather than senior corporate officials will be the relevant contact. Finally, sales managers of regional offices should not be overlooked since an increasing number of companies are decentralizing marketing functions and funds.

The worst sort of approach is to send a proposal to the Vice-President of Marketing or to the Chief Executive Officer. It should be addressed personally to the contact person. The relevant individual can be tracked by checking the company's website or by phoning the company's public relations or press office, the company's receptionist, or the secretary or assistant of the vice-president of marketing.

Proposals should be directed to the highest accessible level. This recognizes the adage that top level managers are paid to say yes, while middle-managers are paid to say no. Too often there is a mistaken tendency to contact employees at a lower level and hope that the request will filter up to the key decision makers because sport managers feel less intimidated and more comfortable with them. Despite all that has been said about companies objectively evaluating proposals, there are still instances when the egos and personal interests of senior executives or marketing directors may be a consideration in the decision.

Once the contact person has been identified, that individual's role in the decision-making process has to be ascertained. Several corporate actors probably play a role in the decision process, and they fall into three categories: gatekeepers, influencers, and decision makers. However, one person may fill more than one of the roles.

It is most probable that the contact person in a large company will be a *gatekeeper*. This person may simply receive the sponsorship proposal and forward it to others who make the decisions. Alternatively, the gatekeeper may be assigned the role of a "first screener" who evaluates whether a proposal meets a company's objectives and if there are sufficient funds to support it. On these bases, the gatekeeper eliminates some proposals and forwards a selective list to the decision makers. A rule of thumb is that the gatekeeper can say no, but he or she cannot say yes. The manner in which a gatekeeper passes along a request may be critical. If he or she is not personally supportive, the information may be relayed less favorably and with fairly evident disapproval. Thus, gatekeepers are key people in determining the success of a proposal, and their support must be secured. Sport managers should try and persuade gatekeepers to permit them to present their case directly to the decision makers. This will ensure that the proposal is presented in its best light and that there is an opportunity to answer any questions or objections the decision makers may have.

An *influencer* is a person whose views or advice help shape the attitudes of decision makers and, thus, who exerts some influence on the final decisions. The third type of actor is the *decision maker,* who decides whether to support the proposal. In this preparation stage, it is important to identify who will have final decision authority.

For these reasons, it is useful to ask who will be representing the company at the meeting, and what is their position, status, and role in the decision process. This will influence who attends from the sport organization. One sport manager who is experienced in sponsorship solicitations suggests always taking one more person to the meeting than the sponsor will have there. He believes that one additional nodding head is always an advantage in any sales situation. Certainly it is important to have more than one person present because others can often catch verbal and non-verbal cues from the prospective contributor that one person working alone may miss.

An important adage in soliciting sponsorships is that people invest in people first and organizations second. This is true of corporate executives. A valid aphorism in soliciting sponsorship is, "It is not what you know, but who you know." Sport managers are not only selling sponsorship investments, they are also selling relationships. Success is likely to be as attributable to positive personal chemistry as to the worthiness of the investment. The optimum scenario for a sport manager is to have a well-known track record of successful sponsorship partnerships, and a network that enables him or her to personally call the decision maker in a targeted company, brief the individual on the proposal, and then follow-up with a comprehensive document.

The importance of personal chemistry makes it imperative that a sport organization search for linkages between its personnel and the gatekeepers, influencers, and decision makers in a targeted company. The key questions are, "Who in the organization knows any of the key corporate actors?" and "Who can we enlist as an ally?" The best type of linkages are personal acquaintances, but if these links are weak, then it becomes important to seek referrals. Are there any mutual contacts who could introduce organization personnel to key company officials?

The organization's task is to learn as much as possible about the individuals who are gatekeepers, influencers, and decision makers and to match their backgrounds with senior personnel from the organization who have similar backgrounds. A substantial body of empirical research demonstrates that positive interaction between the potential contributor and agency representatives is more likely to be facilitated greatly if their backgrounds, personalities, interests, and lifestyles are compatible. Greater perceived similarities result in stronger mutual attraction and affinity. This matching process necessitates finding out background information relating to interests, hobbies, families, and goals. The contact person's secretary or receptionist may be willing to give this type of information.

Presentation

An effective presentation explains all aspects of the organization's proposition as it relates to the benefits sought by the prospective sponsor. The first minute of a presentation can be the most critical part of it even though it represents only a minuscule percentage of the total presentation time. The first impression often determines receptivity in the mind of the potential sponsor to the central substance of the presentation.

Although there are many ways of making a presentation, the best approach is facilitating interaction with the prospect's representatives and encouraging them to be active participants in the communication. Rather than talking to the prospective sponsors, strive to enter into a dialogue with them. This approach begins by exploring the company's needs: What benefits do you want to see from a sponsorship in which you invest? And what criteria are most important in your evaluation of sponsorship proposals? The primary task of the sport manager during this stage is to listen and to suppress premature tendencies to talk about what the organization has to offer. The key is to build a sponsorship proposal around the company's priorities, which means asking questions to derive this information and not guessing. When the company personnel hear the proposal, they should believe that they are listening to an echo of their views. During the listening phase, the sport manager should be considering the features, advantages, and benefits of the organization's event that are relevant to the potential sponsor's needs.

After the company's representatives have explained their needs, the sport manager is in a position to organize and tailor the presentation to show how the event is able to meet them. The presentation should be careful not to promise more than can be delivered. In the interests of developing a long term, on-going relationship with a company, it is always better to under-promise and deliver more. Indeed, if it becomes apparent after listening to the company's expectations that the event cannot deliver them, in the interest of a long-term relationship, the organization should articulate that view and gracefully withdraw.

Using the features, advantages, and benefits approach, the sport manager begins by explaining the organization's credentials and the distinctive features of the event. The advantages portion of the presentation addresses ways in which the opportunity is superior to other investment options available to the company. The benefits section translates features and advantages into benefits and addresses the central question of how the event can help the company achieve its objectives. For example, if the company's primary aim is to increase sales in a market that the event can reach, then the presentation may concentrate on packaging trade incentives that can be presented to dealers, retailers, franchises, or wholesalers to encourage them to sell more products. Alternatively, if awareness is the major objective, then the presentation will identify ways that the event could extend the brand's audience reach, gain more publicity, or link with a media co-sponsor. The benefit packages that the sport manager has in mind will need to be customized and amended to obtain the best fit with a company's objectives.

It may be beneficial to demonstrate how the sport organization would work with the company's advertising agency, since the company may rely on its agency's advice. Such agencies frequently are not supportive of sponsorship investments since they take dollars from the advertising budget and agencies work on a fixed percentage commission of that budget. Thus, if the agency can see a useful role for advertising as part of the sponsorship program, the proposal is more likely to gain its support.

By the end of the presentation, company executives must feel comfortable with the sport manager's attitude toward the proposed arrangement and with the organization as a partner. They must believe that the organization is willing and able to fulfill its commitments and that it has an understanding of the company's commercial needs.

Handling Negative Reactions

If the presentation is to yield the anticipated result, it is necessary to draw out any negative reactions that the company may have. These should not be dreaded; they should be welcomed. They provide valuable feedback and are the prospect's way of communicating how to make the presentation successful. Responding to negative reactions removes barriers and the objections provide clues as to the best tack to take for the remainder of the presentation. Guidelines for dealing with negative reactions include the following:

- Never argue.

- Respond with facts.

- Avoid inflating the objection (i.e., if it is weak, try to ignore it).

- Show respect for honest objections.

- Find some common ground (e.g., "I know what you mean. I agree.").

- Turn the objection into a reason for investing (e.g., "Actually, this is exactly why this investment will work for you.").

- Address it as a positive addition to the dialogue (e.g., "I'm glad you brought that up.").

- Remember, the prospective investor is always right.

Quiet prospects who hold questions and reservations in their minds and give few clues about their inward resistances are likely to be least influenced by the presentation. If no negative reactions are raised, then it suggests either that the company representatives were prepared to respond positively at the start, or that they were not sufficiently interested to raise an objection.

Over a period of time a sport manager is likely to hear all of the various objections that can be raised and will not be surprised by them. The manager should "keep track of flack" by documenting the objections received and determining the best way to handle them so that he or she is prepared to respond when they arise again in the future.

Closing

At the closing stage, the sport manager typically summarizes the major benefits on which there has been agreement, addresses anticipated objections or reservations concerning the sponsorship, and requests that the company take specific affirmative action. Many people find closing to be the most difficult part of a presentation. They feel guilty or lack the self-confidence to ask for a commitment, or they have not thought through ahead of time how they will orchestrate the closing to obtain a commitment from the company.

There are many approaches to closing that could be used. Three of the most common are illustrated below:

- Obtain agreement on a major benefit and then build upon it: "If I understand you correctly, Mr. Smith, you are most interested in increased visibility from your investments." "Yes." "An investment of $50,000 would enable us to. . ."

- Ask an open question and pause: "Mr. Smith, you've seen the benefits this investment could provide. What are your reactions?" Or "How should we now move ahead?"

- Use the "based-on" technique that refers to a major point that was agreed previously and builds upon it: "Based on your desire for maximum visibility, I would like to suggest an investment of $50,000, which would give you high visibility with the new target you are trying to reach."

Often when the question is asked at closing, a company may not be prepared to invest in a project at the level the organization seeks. However, there may be a willingness to invest at a lower level. Thus, it reaffirms the desirability of the organization having more than one investment level in mind, so if the main investment opportunity is rejected, other options can be presented. In addition to asking for money, be prepared to seek contributions of in-kind materials; volunteer time; names of other potential contributors; and, perhaps, a commitment to solicit others on behalf of the event.

At the end of the meeting, the sport manager should have a clear idea of what happens next. The company representatives should be asked whether they require any further information from the organization, or whether a more comprehensive proposal for presentation to a committee or board should be prepared. Finally, there should be clarification of who will contact whom and when.

Criteria Used by Companies to Screen Proposals

The number of sponsorship opportunities offered to companies can be overwhelming. As sponsorship has grown, companies have developed approaches for sifting through the multiple opportunities that they are offered to identify those likely to yield the highest return on their investment. The criteria and screening procedures that they use are intended to ensure that the benefits specified in a company's sponsorship objectives are delivered.

The screening criteria likely to be most pertinent to businesses engaged in sponsorship can be summarized under eight headings from which the mnemonic acronym CEDAR SEE is derived: customer audience, exposure potential, distribution channel support, advantage over competitors, resource investment level required, sport organization's reputation, entertainment and hospitality, and event's characteristics. A set of screening criteria that make these eight major concerns operational are shown in Table 14-3.

A company is unlikely to consider all of the criteria listed in Table 14-3 in its screening process. To do so would create an unwieldy and unmanageable system that would defeat the objective of clarifying the process. Further, a common set is unlikely to be appropriate for all companies because the benefits sought from sponsorship are different. Rather, each company is likely to select from this comprehensive list the 12 to 15 criteria that are deemed to be most salient to its objectives.

Table 14-3 Items Contributing to the Total Cost of a Sponsorship Fee

1. **Customer Audience** - Questions such as Is the demographic, attitude, and lifestyle profile of the target audience congruent with the product's target market?

2. **Exposure Reach** - Questions such as What is the inherent news value of the event? and Can the event be tied into other media advertising?

3. **Distribution Channel Support** - Questions such as Are the sponsorship's advantages apparent to wholesalers, retailers, or franchises?

4. **Competitive Advantage** - Questions such as Is the event unique or distinctive? and Does the event need co-sponsors?

5. **Level of Resource Investment Required** - Questions such as Will it be unwieldy and difficult to manage the sponsorship investment? and What are the levels of barter, in-kind, and cash investments?

6. **Sport Organization's Reputation** - Questions such as Does it have a history of honoring its obligations? and Does the organization have a proven track record in this or comparable events?

7. **Event Characteristics** - Questions such as Does it have a "clean" image? and What is the perceived stature of the event?

8. **Entertainment or Hospitality Opportunities** - Questions such as Are tickets to the event included in the sponsorship? and Will celebrities be available to serve as spokespeople for the product?

Handling Rejections

Sponsorship may be conceptualized as a program that an organization is selling. From this perspective, it is reasonable to anticipate that the development of a corporate investment program may follow a typical program life-cycle curve that progresses from introduction through take-off and maturation to saturation. The introduction stage may last two or three years before the sponsorship program gathers momentum and enters the take-off stage. During this period, a sport organization may experience a large number of rejections to its proposals.

The success or failure of an initial personal communication interaction with a prospect should not be viewed in the immediate context of whether support was forthcoming. Rather, the contact should be regarded as the beginning of a long-term relationship. A period of time may be needed to consolidate personal relationships that have been established before sponsorship support emerges. Early efforts may yield relatively little, but they are made in the anticipation of increased return in the future as personal relationships and confidence in the sport organization are nurtured.

When a targeted company rejects a sponsorship proposal, there should always be an effort to find out why. This involves asking questions, such as *Was the package wrong?*, *Did we fail to deliver enough benefits?*; *Was the return on the company's projected investment inadequate?*; *Did we ask for too much of an investment?*; *Did we misread the company's target market?*; *Did we send the wrong person?*; and *Was the presentation ineffective?*

It is essential to follow-up. The objective is not to challenge the decision but rather to ascertain why the proposal was not accepted and if the company would be interested in working with the sport organization in the future. When proposals are turned down, it is often not because a business cannot benefit from them, but rather because the timing was not right for the company. Polite persistence pays off. Thus, immediately after an unsuccessful effort, a letter of thanks should be sent to let a prospect know that the time spent visiting with the organization's representatives was appreciated. Contact should be maintained with the targeted company on the assumption that it may be a prime prospect for support in the future.

The Contract

The notion of an exchange relationship is the conceptual underpinning of all marketing transactions. However, in the context of sponsorship, a fluent exchange is especially challenging to transact because it involves a business relationship between, at best, organizations with widely different aims, and, at worst, a commercial company and an inexperienced sport organization with different needs and expectations.[19] The two parties often operate in totally different environments, do not understand each others' businesses, have dissimilar reasons for their involvement, and seek different ends from the arrangement.

For these reasons, once general agreement has been reached with a company, some form of written document should be developed to ensure that both sides' interests are protected. Initially, this should be drafted by representatives from both sides without input from lawyers so that the issues are freely discussed. When a draft has been completed, then legal advisers may be used to ensure that the intent is expressed accurately.

Agreements may be documented by a letter of confirmation, a letter of agreement, or a formal contract. The magnitude of resources being exchanged and the expectations of the sponsor will guide the appropriate format. A confirming letter is not a contract per se since it is not signed by both parties. The letter agreement is a contract signed by both parties but is less formal, less expensive, and often less intimidating than a standard contract. The formal contract is no more enforceable than a letter of agreement, but it does commit the parties to giving greater attention to the details involved. The central purposes of the written agreement:

- Denote the rights of the sponsor (acquiring).

- Denote the rights of the sport organization (retaining).

- Delineate exclusivity.

- Protect the parties from unwanted liability.

- Protect the parties' reputations and trademarks, logos, and symbols.

- Protect the parties' respective proprietary and other interests in the event (to avoid sponsor theft of the event and/or to preserve the sponsor's long-term benefit).[19]

Figure 14-8 Issues to Address in a Sponsorship Agreement

- Official status:

  What is the sponsorship category? Are there veto rights with this category? That is, does a sponsor in this category have a say in who else can be a sponsor? Does the sponsorship extend to other sites or related events?

- Sponsorship fee:

  What is the fee? How and when is the fee to be paid? Is the fee refundable for any reason? Secured by letter of credit or escrow (e.g., if television ratings or other performance indicators are poor)?

- Title rights:

  Will the sponsor's name appear in the title? How will trophies be named? Who will present the trophy or prizes?

- Television exposure:

  Who owns and controls TV rights? Does the sponsor have rights of first refusal on television advertising spots? Is there a ratings guarantee? Will there be a rebate if ratings fall below this guarantee? Can the sponsor use TV video footage in its regular advertising? Does the sponsor need to obtain permission prior to using video clips for commercial reasons? Who is responsible for negotiating television time? Is a portion of the sponsorship fee credited to the TV coverage? Will the property obtain all the rights necessary from participants to allow use of clips in commercials without further compensation?

- Public relations and media exposure:

  Will key athletes mention the sponsor's name when being interviewed by the media? Will the sponsor's name be included in media releases? Who is responsible for media releases? Can the sponsor develop its own media marketing campaign?

- Logo use:

  Under what conditions can the sponsor use the organization's logos or trademarks? If special logos are developed, who owns them? Can the sponsor use the logo to promote its own image and products? Does the sponsor have merchandising rights? That is, can it make and sell souvenir items?

- Signage:

  How many banners, athlete patches, placards, arena boards, or flags can the sponsor use? What size? Where can banners be placed and what can appear on them? Who is responsible for making and paying for signage? Who is responsible for placing the signage on-site? Distance from others' signs? Signs on vehicles? Any conflicts with existing permanent signage at the venue?

It has been observed that

> Misunderstandings usually arise when the parties to the agreement have different views as to who will do what to exploit the sponsorship. The way to avoid this is to go through every possible element of the project beforehand and agree to the areas of responsibility. These details should be included in the contract so that in the event of any disagreements the original arrangement can be referred to.[19] (p. 192)

- Advertising rights:

    In what manner can the sponsor use the organization or event for advertising purposes? Will the sponsor's name be on stationery or in the program? On television billboards? On merchandise? Where will it be placed? Can the sponsor use photographs related to the sponsorship for product promotion and advertising? Who is responsible for individual consent to the use of the photographs in advertising? What limitations are placed on the use of photographs?

- Athlete use:

    Will athletes make personal appearances on behalf of the sponsor? Will key athletes or coaches attend pre- or postcompetition parties? Will athletes wear the sponsor's name during competition?

- Hospitality rights;

    Does the sponsor have the right to a hospitality tent? Does the sponsor get free tickets for tie-in contests to give to key clients or for other use?

- Point of sale promotion:

    Can the sponsor's products be sold on-site? What type: cigarettes, alcohol? Can the sponsor run on-site or off-site promotions associated with the sponsorship? Can the sponsor team up with other companies to form cooperative promotions? Who receives the profits from merchandising?

- Direct mail lists:

    Will mailing lists of ticket holders or athletes be made available to the sponsor? What form of promotions can the sponsor undertake with these mailing lists?

- Product sampling:

    Will a place be made available for product display and sampling? What types of products can be made available for sampling? Will you accept cigarettes and beer?

- Legal liabilities:

    Who is responsible for injuries to spectators, participants, or officials? For infringement of trademarks? What if it rains or there are problems with television transmissions? Who pays existing expenses?

- Future options:

    How many years does the sponsorship last? Does the sponsor have renewal options? How many years does the option last? How are sponsorship fee increases to be determined next year? After that?

This list is adapted from Christine Brooks. (1990). *Athletic Business,* December, 61-62.

A comprehensive list of the types of issues to be covered in contract agreement discussions is shown in Figure 14-8. However, given the element of unpredictability associated with sporting events (e.g., weather, injury, etc.) And the large number of facets involved in a sponsorship partnership, both parties should recognize the need for some degree of flexibility in interpreting their contracted agreement.

When a partnership agreement is reached, this should not be regarded as the terminal consummation of a relationship. From a company's perspective, it may be a trial offer only from which the business will withdraw if returns are not satisfactory. The sport organization also should view it from this perspective and recognize that the agreement offer is a tentative initial step. Sometimes all efforts are directed to securing a sponsorship and little thought is given to servicing it. A long-term association and commitment will evolve only if a company's objectives are met.

Working Together to Make It Happen

Sponsors add another dimension of responsibility for the sport organization. Additional efforts must be made to coordinate the sponsors' desires—they become a second audience who must be satisfied. A key to a successful on-going sponsor support effort is the marketing adage: your best customers are your best prospects. If companies are pleased with the results accruing from their expenditure, then they are likely to be receptive to future support requests. They are also likely to be valuable sources of testimonials and referrals to others. It is much less costly in time and effort to sustain an existing sponsorship arrangement than it is to find a new partner. This means the short-term perspective (we need the checks from sponsors so we can go about our business) is likely to be costly in the long term. There should be a consistent effort to add value:

- More than 20% of Major League Baseball players were born in Hispanic countries. So MLB decided to enhance its value to sponsors by energetically creating opportunities for them to connect with Hispanic fans. Baseball partnered with ESPN to offer Spanish-language simulcasts. It also created a newspaper insert called Major League Baseball in Español that allowed sponsors to target hundreds of thousands of Hispanic fans in key local markets.[20]

There should be an agreed upon plan and timetable with each sponsor for implementing all the promotional activities expected by each company. These activities should be carefully coordinated with the promotional platform the company uses to support and extend the impact of its sponsorship. Coordinating interactions with the media is particularly important to ensure that sponsors and sport event are communicating consistent and complementary messages at appropriate times. If a sport organization does not have the level of expertise in media relationships that is available to its major sponsor, then it should consider inviting the sponsor to coordinate this function.

A key to nurturing a close working relationship and to building goodwill is constant communication between the parties and a total commitment to meeting the company's needs. The sport organization should assign each sponsor a staff member as a contact liaison, who serves as a conduit for all communications. This individual should be positioned as an advocate within the organization, charged with seeking to further the sponsor's goals. If multiple sponsors are involved, regularly scheduled meetings that all attend will facilitate an interchange of promotional ideas and make sponsors feel part of the event:

Many organizers are nervous about bringing sponsors together and avoid it at all costs, but this route is fraught with dangers. Far better to get everybody to state their objectives in advance and to work together to satisfy them. Since the aims for each sponsor should be different there need be no conflict between them and there are many cross-sponsorship promotions that can be done when all parties cooperate.[19] (p. 229)

The organizers of the Olympic Festival in Minneapolis called their sponsors a Patron Advisory Group and used this regular meetings approach to good effect.

The Patron Advisory meetings were really a selling point for some smaller companies who wanted to get next to the big guys. Company representatives really looked forward to networking among themselves, to be able to create new business. We used the meetings to invite potential sponsors and show them how many sponsors were already on board and to show that this was a real live event. Also, it was a chance to tell all the sponsors the same thing at the same time. It gave them the perception that every one was getting equal treatment and were on an equal level.

The advisory meetings were also a way for the partners to gain publicity and to show off to each other. Many of the meetings were held at the corporate headquarters of the respective hosts. "3M gave out its corporate pin and Post-it Notes that announced its association with the Festival during one of the first meetings. That set the stage for the other sponsors. Some got really carried away and took it to the extremes. Dayton's and Target held an elaborate ceremony in the Metrodome where they set-up Greek architecture and had chariots riding around" (np).[21]

These types of meetings can also facilitate development of cross-promotion opportunities. These are cooperative arrangements among sponsors that enable the sponsors involved to obtain greater leverage—either from the sponsorship or from other business arrangements that evolve out of the sponsorship. Cross-promotions can extend a sponsor's visibility, place the company's product in new distribution outlets, and generate merchandise for use in sweepstakes and trade incentives programs:

- Two telecommunications companies were being courted by different properties. The companies agreed to invest only if the properties introduced them to other sponsors, and they won new contracts. One company refused to pay a flat sponsorship fee up front. Instead, it wanted to give the property a percentage of its profits from resulting deals.[20]

An example of cross-promotion that focused on better leveraging sponsorship of a sport event is given in Figure 14-9.

The more that executives and employees of a sponsoring business can be involved and can feel ownership in planning and implementing the sport event, the more likely they are to make a long-term commitment. As part of this process, key decision makers should be given access to celebrity sports people, behind-the-scenes areas where ordinary spectators are not permitted, and excellent seats from which to view the event. If there is extensive involvement by company managers, then when companies restructure or go through mergers, it reduces the chance that changes in personnel may leave a sport property without its company advocates.[2] Having multiple managers involved may help make the event "merger proof": "If

Figure 14-9 Naturite and Seven-Up Cross-Promotion at the Los Angeles Marathon

Naturite and the Seven-Up/RC Bottling Companies of Southern California implemented a successful cross-promotion at the Los Angeles marathon race. Naturite gave Seven-Up 200,000 marathon-themed bottle collars, some with vitamin samples, and Naturite inserted Seven-Up coupons in its packages.

"This was the most successful of our marathon promotions," said the director of marketing for vitamin-maker Naturite Inc. "Our objective with any event is to provide retailers with a promotional opportunity and to have them put money into reaching the consumer. Selling vitamins to retailers doesn't have the intensity of selling soft drinks, so our Seven-Up tie-in gives us access to a well established sales force that is in the stores practically seven days a week."

As an example of the power of the cross-promotion, the marketing director pointed to a Thrifty Drug and Discount Stores full-page advertisement in the Sunday *Los Angeles Times* promoting Naturite and Seven-Up.

"The bottom line is how much new business we generate. Naturite is now in three chains and several independent stores that we had never been in before. We also are a solid part of the promotional plans of our existing customers, many of whom called me to make sure we'd repeat the promotion," the marketing director said.

Note: Adapted from "Using Events for Cross-Promotions," December 12, 1988, *IEG Sponsorship Report*, p. 5.

you have a program with a company whose employees actively support your cause, if a new branch manager or CEO comes in, it's hard to throw the program away without angering a lot of people" (p. B-25).[1]

Post-Event Follow-up

The way in which the follow-up is addressed will influence the likelihood of receiving future support from investing companies. The intent in the follow-up stage is to enhance relationships that have been established. A prime objective should be to make the individual in the company who made the decision to invest look good to senior management and throughout the entire organization. The follow-up should consist of three actions. The first task is to evaluate (in association with, rather than for, the contributor) the extent to which a contributor's objectives were achieved to be sure it meets their needs. Evaluation measures relating to the impact of sponsorships will be discussed in chapter 15. This evaluation is critical in soliciting corporate sponsorship because executives need a scorecard to justify to stockholders and superiors their investment of company resources.

As well as a formal quantitative evaluation of how well objectives were met, the sport organization should compile and report the following to key sponsors:

- Number of participants/attendees, demographics, lifestyle information, purchasing habits and trends

- Local/regional/national/international news media print coverage and trends

- Television viewership, ratings, and demographics where possible and a VHS copy of the telecast, plus clips of local affiliates' coverage of the event

- Radio coverage with a broadcast signal overlay on the sponsors' sales areas (number of ads, promotional spots, and on-air mentions—compared to the stations' rate cards so value of exposure can be estimated)

- Complete list of associate sponsors/hospitality suite customers and trends

- Information on merchandising, product displays, sampling, and signage with photographs

- On-site sampling and merchandising report (number of coupons redeemed or number of people sampled)

- Samples of coupons generated by all sponsors and the event itself

- Clip book of advertisements and property-generated promotional activities relating to the event

- Clip book of news releases and news clips tracking back to event public relations

- Public-address system announcement log with sponsor scripts

- A copy of the event program and posters

- Samples of tickets, especially if the tickets included the sponsors' marks

- Samples of media sponsor promotional tie-ins with comments on their effectiveness

- A personal letter of thanks to the sponsor signed jointly by the property's senior managers[22]

The final follow-up task is to initiate discussions about future investments in the program. These will be guided by the timespan and arrangements for renewing or canceling that were included in the contract. The discussions should be held soon after the event is completed so that maximum time is available to make changes in any future partnership or to find other sponsors if necessary.

Summary

Adopting a marketing approach is key to successfully soliciting corporate sponsorship. This requires that proposals focus on the potential for delivering what companies are likely to want in return for contributing their resources. Sport managers should perceive themselves as brokers who are concerned with furthering the welfare of potential sponsor companies by offering opportunities in which both they and the organization win.

A primary reason why companies reflect proposals is because they are submitted too late to be included in the annual budget or to be leveraged extensively by associated advertising. This implies that a 15-18 month lead time is likely to be needed for most proposals if they are to receive serious consideration.

The first stage in soliciting sponsors is to identify a set of companies in the appropriate geographic area whose customers have demographic/lifestyle profiles consistent with those of the sport event's audience/participants and whose image is compatible with that of the event. Using these guidelines, a list of potential sponsors and a profile of each company on the list can be developed and entered into an information retrieval system.

Tobacco and alcohol companies traditionally have been major sponsors of sport. However, recent shifts in public opinion and legislation have adversely affected their level of involvement. Tobacco companies derive three major benefits from this association. First, links to sports confer upon them a positive image and an aura of respectability that obscures their role in causing an array of fatal diseases. Second, it enables them to penetrate the youth market. Third, sponsorship of sport offers a means by which the tobacco companies can circumvent the ban on cigarette advertising and promotion in broadcast media. However, their involvement in sponsorship was severely constrained by the Master Settlement Agreement, a legal agreement the tobacco companies signed with the states' attorneys general.

Breweries have a long history of associating with sport because the ages of maximal beer consumption and maximal sport interest are the same. Public sentiment to inhibit beer company sponsorship has been less strident than feelings toward tobacco sponsorship. However, there has been increased criticism of these links from those concerned about alcohol abuse, and it is an issue to which sport managers have to be sensitive. The case for banning beer sponsorship is less compelling than the case against tobacco because tobacco causes diseases and illness even if it is used as intended, whereas the problem with beer is not its consumption per se, but abuse of the level at which it can be consumed safely.

It is normal practice to create different levels of benefit packages when soliciting sponsorships, so a wide range of investment opportunities can be offered. The number of levels varies but is likely to be some variation of the four categories structure of sponsorship that is commonly used: title sponsorship, presenting sponsorship, official sponsorship, and official supplier status. These packages contain different levels of benefits that are differently priced. The minimum price to be charged is the cost of providing those benefit packages. The highest price that will be accepted will be determined by the price of similar sponsorship opportunities available in the marketplace.

A short one- or two-page proposal should be sent to the targeted companies, and a follow-up call should be made a week to ten days later. There are four elements to consider in communicating a proposal. First is preparation, which involves identifying who in the targeted company should be approached with the proposal and seeking out information about him or her. This information includes determining whether the contact person is a gatekeeper, influencer, or decision maker; whether the individual is acquainted with anyone in the sport organization; and background material on the person's interests, family, and lifestyle, which will help facilitate positive personal interaction between the individual and the sport organization's representatives.

The second element is the presentation, and this should be interactive. The sport manager listens to the company's benefit needs and then explains the features, advantages, and benefits the event is able to offer to address those needs. Third, negative reactions to the proposal should be solicited, so that there is an opportunity to address and reverse them. The fourth element of the presentation is closing, which is the time when the company's representatives are asked to commit to an investment.

As recognition of the effectiveness of sponsorship has grown, companies have developed criteria and screening procedures for sifting through the multiple opportunities they are offered. They tend to focus on eight factors in their evaluation: customer audience, exposure potential, distribution channel audience, advantage over competitors, resource investment level required, sport organization's reputation, event's characteristics, and entertainment and hospitality opportunities.

When a sponsorship proposal is rejected, reasons for the negative outcome should be identified. If these can be rectified in the future, then the initial rejection may constitute the beginning of a long-term relationship. When a proposal is accepted, a written contractual document should be developed to ensure that both sides' interests are protected. To nurture a long-term relationship, the sport organization has to view the sponsor as a partner and work to help the company realize its objectives. This may be achieved by nominating a staff person to be a liaison with the company and to be its advocate within the sport organization. If multiple sponsors are involved, facilitating interaction and networking between them may be productive. Follow-up actions involve helping the key decision makers in the company evaluate the extent to which their objectives were met and initiating discussions about future investments in the event.

References

1. Kolah, A. (2001). *How to develop an effective sponsorship programme.* London: Sport Business Group.
2. Sack, A. L. & Fried, G. (2001). Pitching women's tennis to corporate sponsors: A case study of Pilot Pen Tennis. *Sport Marketing Quarterly, 10*(2), 68-76
3. Turco, D. M. (1999). The state of tobacco sponsorship in sport. *Sport Marketing Quarterly, 8*(1), 35-38.
4. Gruber, J. (2001). Tobacco at the crossroads: The past and future of smoking regulation in the United States. *Journal of Economic Perspectives, 15*(2), 193-212.
5. Koop, C. E. & Kessler, D. A. (1997). *Final report of the Advisory Committee on Tobacco Policy and Public Health.* Washington, DC: Action on Smoking and Health (ASH).
6. Siegal, M. (2001). Counteracting tobacco motor sports sponsorship as a promotional tool: Is the tobacco settlement enough? *American Journal of Public Health*, 91, 1100-1105.
7. Sparks, R. (1999). Youth awareness of tobacco sponsorship as a dimension of brand equity. *International Journal of Sports Marketing & Sponsorship,* October, 236-260.
8. Johnson, W. O. (1988). Sports and suds. *Sports Illustrated, 69*(6), August 8, 68-82.
9. Cohn, B. & Hager, M. (1993). The power of sin. *Newsweek*, October 4, 51.
10. Carmichael, M. (2003). Rx: Two Martinis a day. *Newsweek*, January 20, 48.
11. Shapiro, L. (1996). To your health? *Newsweek*, January 22, 52-54.
12. Naughton, J. (1998). Colleges eye restrictions on promotions by brewing companies. *The Chronicle of Higher Education,* January 9, A57.
13. Brooks, C. (1990). Sponsorship by design. *Athletic Business*, December, 58-62.
14. D'Alesandro, D. F. (2001). *Brand warfare.* New York: McGraw Hill.

15. IEG. (1992). Pricing: How to determine what your property is worth to sponsors. *Sponsorship Report*, September 7, 4-5.

16. IEG. (1999). Retailer takes beach event tie to "hippify" its image. *Sponsorship Report*, April 26, 1-2.

17. Aguillar-Manjarrez, R., Thwaites, D. & Maule, J. (1999). Insights into the roles adopted by the recipients of unsolicited sort sponsorship requests. *International Journal of Sports Marketing & Sponsorship, 1*(2), 185-205.

18. Weiss, K. (1999). Event horizon. *Athletic Business*, July, 50.

19. Sleight, S. (1989). *Sponsorship: What it is and how to use it*. Maidenhead, Berkshire, England: McGraw Hill.

20. D'Allesandro, D. F. (2001). Beyond the mother-in-law strategy: Avoiding consumers' indifference. *Sponsorship Report, 20*(6), 1, 4-5.

21. McCally, J. F. (1990). Corporate sponsorship and the U.S. Olympic Festival '90: A mutually beneficial marketing arrangement. Unpublished paper, Department of Marketing Mankato State University, May.

22. Poole, M. (2001). Keeping sponsors: Pitching it like you did the very first time. *Sport Business Journal*, May 28-June 3, 10.

Photo courtesy University of Oregon Athletic Department

Chapter Fifteen

Measuring the Impact
of Sponsorship

From the perspective of a sport manager, evaluation has two purposes. First, it provides a measure of a sponsorship's value. Sponsorships sometimes are dropped not because they do not have value, but because no one has actually measured the value. Evaluation answers the question: What did the sponsoring company achieve in relation to what it said it wanted to accomplish in its objectives? If the objectives were not fully met, then there needs to be a reappraisal by the sport organization of what should be done to improve the results and deliver the value a sponsor expected. The second purpose is that evaluation research provides the sport manger with information that can be used in sales presentations to potential sponsors in the future.

Despite all the lip service given to the importance of evaluation, 40% of 200 sponsoring companies reported spending nothing on research to measure the impact of their investments, while an additional 35% reported spending 1% or less of their sponsorship budget on impact evaluation. Many of these companies expressed the belief that evaluation should be the responsibility of the sport organization, and 68% of respondents reported that properties did not match their expectation in this area.[1] In contrast to the widespread lack of investment in evaluation, Coca-Cola, one of the largest and most experienced sponsors of sport, allocates between 3% and 10% of its rights fees for evaluation.[2] To remove the evaluation void, it is imperative for sport organizations to incorporate measurement audits in the proposal package that is presented to prospective sponsor companies.

Evaluations are likely to be especially credible if they are done by an external consultant, rather than in-house. The demand for impartial, third-party analyses has created a niche for companies that specialize in doing these assessments. Sometimes it may be efficient for a sport organization to coordinate a single evaluation study that services all its sponsors:

- The Toronto Raptors offered all its sponsors the opportunity to share the cost of a $50,000 survey that annually tracked consumers' recall and reaction to Raptors' sponsors. With the shared cost, it became very affordable for each company. In addition to a set of general questions, each of the participating companies added a set of their own specific questions. Annual surveys such as this enable companies to longitudinally track some dimensions of their sponsorship's impact. The survey results are reported directly to the sponsoring companies by the private company contracted to do the research. Whether the results are also shared with the team is left up to the sponsor.[3]

The usefulness of an evaluation to a company will be strongly influenced by the original specification of its sponsorship objectives. If they were SMART—specific, measurable, achievable, results-oriented, and time-bounded (Chapter 13)—then they give explicit direction as to what the evaluation must be designed to measure. Since companies seek different objectives from their sponsorships—awareness, image, demonstration platform, employee morale, product trial, product sales, etc.—different types of measures and designs will be required for each objective. However, even with good a priori specification of objectives, there are two factors that make assessing the impact of sponsorship investments challenging.

First, sponsorship is typically used as a platform for focusing the message of multiple other promotional tools. This makes it difficult to isolate the specific impact of the sponsorship. Even if other promotional tools are not being used simultaneously, there is likely to be some carry-over effect from previous marketing communications efforts that makes isolating the impact of a sponsorship difficult. These challenges can be addressed by the use of statistical models. A brand's historical sales data are likely to be available, as well as information on its historical spending on advertising, sales promotion, price discounting, and other factors. This enables statistical models that isolate the effects of each element on sales to be constructed.[4]

A second challenge in evaluation is to account for uncontrollable environmental factors. Changes in sales levels may be attributable to changes in the marketing environment (for example, an increase or reduction in the intensity of competitive effort or varying levels of discretionary income as a result of changes in economic conditions) rather than the sponsorship.[5]

The process through which companies seek to communicate a message to individuals in their target market through sponsorship is shown in Figure 15-1. The sponsor codes messages into a transmittable form (or arranges and locates those messages so that the media will transmit them). The form may include written captions, company or brand name, logo, or verbal material. The coded message is transmitted by print media, broadcast media, or personal contact. For communication to occur, individuals in the target market must absorb, receive, and interpret the message. The ultimate goal of a total communications strategy is to generate sales. A company's expectation is that its sponsorship investment ultimately will contribute to that end.

An intervening variable shown as jagged lines in Figure 15-1 is noise. Noise consists of other stimuli or communications that compete for the intended receiver's attention. A message from a sponsoring organization to its target market is subject

Linking Sponsorship to the Communications Process

Figure 15-1 Stages in the Communication Process at Which Sponsorship Effectiveness Is Measured

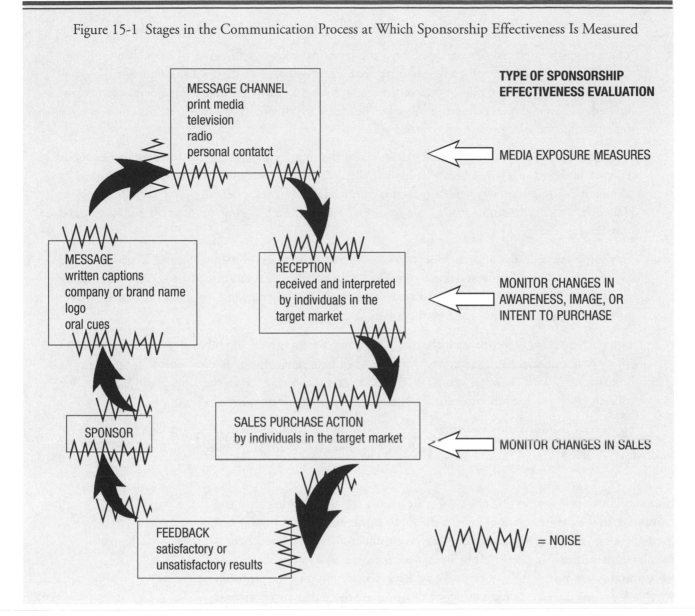

to the influence of extraneous noise and distracting stimuli that interfere with communication of the message. This noise may distort or distract attention from the transmission or reception of the message at any stage in the process. It may prevent members of the target market from receiving the message, or it may lead to them interpreting it differently from the way in which the sponsor intended. In the context of sponsorship in which the message is incidental to the main event, there may be substantial noise that causes the message to appear inconsequential and to be ignored.

Figure 15-1 shows the stages in the communication process at which the effectiveness of sponsorship can be measured. The further through the process that an evaluation takes place, the stronger the evidence of a sponsorship's contribution to increasing sales. However, emphasis on short-term sales is often not the primary goal. Rather, the general criterion may be: Does the sponsorship provide an environment in which more sales can be made and provide sales representatives for the brand with more tools in order to compete more effectively with competitor

Figure 15-2 The John Hancock Bowl: Measuring Advertising Exposure

John Hancock Financial Services sponsored the John Hancock Bowl held in El Paso, Texas on New Years Eve. One year, the company calculated that it received $5.1 million worth of advertising exposure in return for the $1.6 million it invested in sponsoring the bowl. A Hancock senior executive commented, "The bowl is an extraordinarily efficient media buy. It would cost us a great deal more money to help influence sales by normal advertising."

Hancock scoured magazines and newspapers across the country, counting the number of stories about its bowl, and measuring numbers of column inches, circulation and advertising rates. It determined its television exposure value from factors such as the precise number of times announcers mentioned John Hancock, and the amount of times the name was on screen in pre-game promotions and during the broadcast.

The company collected a seven-foot stack of newspaper clippings on the bowl game. Together with a handful of television segments, there were 7,829 stories with a total value of $1,080,995 in advertising equivalency. This refers to what Hancock would have paid to buy the same amount of commercial time on television or advertising space in the papers.

The Hancock staff reviewed each clip and placed an advertising value on it based on each publication's circulation and advertising rate. For example, a four-column, four-inch story on the John Hancock Bowl in the *Detroit News* was valued at $3,312; a two-inch item in *Time* magazine, $6,800; and a three column, seven-inch-deep article in the Laramie (Wyoming) *Boomerang*, $145.

However, the bulk of the advertising value, came from CBS's broadcast of the game. Combined with repeated references to the John Hancock Bowl, the John Hancock logo appeared at midfield, on uniforms,

brands?[6] Thus, sponsorship objectives most frequently relate to creating a climate conducive to the development of sales in the future rather than to stimulating immediate sales. For this reason, most evaluations are undertaken earlier in the communications process. If sales are not measured, then the next most convincing measures for demonstrating economic return for a sponsorship (i.e., the probability that a desired increase in level of sales will result) are those that are completed at the reception stage of the process, because this is only one step removed from the sales purchase action.

Individuals pass through a series of stages from first becoming aware of a product or company to finally making a purchase decision. These stages are generally known in the marketing field as the product adoption process. The three stages in this process that precede purchase action and that are encapsulated in the reception stage of the communication process are awareness, interest, and intent-to-purchase. These stages emphasize that a decision to participate is usually the culmination of a process that may have started long before an actual purchase takes place. Thus, sponsorship of a sport event is ultimately likely to impact sales if it succeeds in moving individuals from their present stage in the adoption process on to the next stage toward making a purchase decision.

Measuring Media Equivalencies

The most frequently used type of sponsorship effectiveness measure is taken at the message channel stage (Figure 15-1). This approach uses media equivalency val-

sidelines and scoreboards, for a total of about 60 minutes on the four-hour broadcast. The company equated this to the equivalent of $3.12 million of advertising exposure.

John Hancock Financial Services calculated the following costs and benefits of sponsoring the John Hancock Bowl:

COSTS $

Sponsorship fee $1,000,000

Television rights fee, including 10-15 minutes of
commercial time during the broadcast 500,000

Contribution to various charities, scholarships and
a game banquet in El Paso, Texas 100,000

TOTAL $1,600,000

BENEFITS: Exposure measured in advertising value, based on the amount of coverage and what Hancock would have had to pay for the same amount of advertising space in print or commercial time on television:

CBS game broadcast $3,120,000

Newspaper, television reports. 1,080,995

CBS pre-game promotions 900,000

TOTAL $5,100,995

*This case is adapted from Michael J. McCarthy. Keeping Careful Score on Sports Tie-Ins. *Wall Street Journal*, April 24, 1991, Section B, page 1, column 3.

ues to assess the value of media coverage a brand or company receives. It compares the value of sponsorship-generated media coverage to the cost of equivalent advertising space or time. It usually involves quantifying the

- duration of television coverage, including both verbal and visual mentions;

- duration of radio mentions; and

- extent of press coverage as measured in single column inches.

Typically, these media mentions are tracked, and each is assigned a dollar value based on the paid advertising rate. For example, in one year Volvo calculated that it received $7 in value for every $1 spent on its sponsorship of tennis. This resulted from 2.26 billion impressions including television, print, radio, event attendance, and promotions. These impressions were calculated to translate to $32.8 million in equivalent value, and Volvo spent less than $5 million on its sponsorship.[7] This type of analysis can provide a good longitudinal comparative measure of exposure. It enables a sponsor to conclude that the year's exposure of $32.8 million is greater/lesser than last year's exposure. It can also provide sport managers with data enabling them to compare the exposure value their property generates compared to other competing events. Figure 15-2 describes how these types of data were used by John Hancock Financial Services to evaluate effectiveness of their sponsorship of the John Hancock Bowl.

If media coverage is used as a measure of sponsorship effectiveness, the exposures should be weighted to reflect (i) the relative attractiveness of different types of media coverage; and (ii) quality of the coverage, which is likely to vary widely across companies. Because the attractiveness varies, the appropriate portion of advertising equivalency costs to use as a measure of value of media exposure will also vary. To some companies, a sponsorship mention may be worth only 10% of equivalent advertising time in a particular medium, while to others it may be worth 100%. Since tobacco companies, for example, are unable to advertise on television, sponsorship mentions in that medium are likely to be valued more highly by those companies than similar exposures achieved by a soft drink supplier. If a company or brand has very high unaided recall before a sponsorship, then the value of media exposure is likely to be relatively small. For example, Coca-Cola has an unaided recall of around 95%, so media coverage is not likely to be as important to that product as it would be to a new soft drink trying to build awareness.

Quality of media coverage is likely to vary from the highly favorable to the somewhat less favorable. Furthermore, the location and nature of coverage obtained even within a single medium will influence its impact. For example, a favorable editorial mention may be considered to be of greater value than mentions in a sports column, or a name in a headline or photograph may be given higher value than a mention of a brand in the body of a story. Some companies assign different values to different publications by using weightings. Cartier International assigned points to its print exposure by type of publication (upscale readership carried more weight than wide-circulation) and by type of mention, so the company's name in a headline or photograph rated higher than in text.[8] In summary, variables that may influence media equivalency values include quality of exposure, size of audience, audience demographics, key messages communicated, type of coverage, type of media, and prominence and position.

A final type of quality measure that is used seeks to reflect the extent of clutter encountered by a sponsorship. This measure expresses media coverage achieved by the sponsor as a percentage of total coverage of that activity and/or as a percentage of total mentions attained by all sponsors of that activity. If this percentage is reasonably high, then it is deemed more likely to emerge from the clutter of other sponsors and make an impact.

Measures of media coverage frequently inflate its real value. This inflation may occur in three ways. First, article length is measured and equated with advertising space, even though the sponsor's name may only be mentioned a couple of times in the article. Second, typically, the maximal rate card value is assumed when quantifying the cost of equivalent advertising space, and few companies actually pay these full rates.

The third and most fundamental source of inflation is the assumption that two seconds here and four seconds there of background signage or logo, when summated, are equal to a television spot that gives an advertiser 30 seconds in which to sell. Thus, a well-respective authority commenting on the use of these procedures by the John Hancock Company stated, "Ad equivalencies are bunk. If Hancock management thinks 30 seconds of ID has the same value as a 30-second ad spot, that's its problem" (p. 2).[9] Using media exposure measures and equivalences means that sponsorship is being defined in terms of traditional advertising, which is inappropriate because sponsorship and advertising are designed to achieve different outcomes. Imposing familiar advertising evaluation models onto sponsorship is of little value. Sponsorship is not merely advertising with added value, it is a qualitatively different vehicle.[10] There is a tendency to measure what is easy—visibility—rather than what is important—impact. CPM (cost per thousand people exposed to the brand name) represents only a paper justification for the investment; it does not measure its effectiveness. Experiments on the recall of visibility of signs at sports arenas compared to advertising for the same brand led to the conclusion that individuals needed ten times more exposure to signage than to a commercial advertisement to approximate a similar recall impact because of the subtle nature of the background signage exposure.[11] The issue has been expressed in the following terms:

> Measuring "visibility" leaves the real questions unanswered. Does anybody notice the logo in the background? What message about the brand is communicated by the logo on the scorer's table? The brand is paying a high price to be seen in this particular environment. Is being seen on the scorer's table at the NBA All Star game really worth any more than being seen on the side of a building somewhere? Does anyone know that the brand is a sponsor of this event? Does anyone care? These questions aren't about visibility. These questions are about impact.[12] (p. 12)

A defender of these procedures responded, "Is it better to interrupt a broadcast with your message? Is it better to upset viewers? Of course you usually won't upset them because they are probably in the kitchen or the bathroom."[13] This type of defense is not convincing. Sponsorship lacks the direct impact possibilities normally associated with direct advertising. This is widely recognized and explains why the rule-of-thumb adopted by sponsors who do use media coverage measures as their primary evaluation tool is that total exposure received should be worth at least three to six times the cost of their sponsorship.

In addition to the pragmatic limitations of the media exposure approach discussed in the previous paragraphs, there is a fundamental conceptual flaw in considering it as a proxy measure of a sponsorship's impact on awareness. Measurements of media exposure are taken at the message channel point in the communications process (Figure 15-1). That is, they purport to assess the extent of media output of the company's message that has occurred. Media output, however, does not equate to awareness in the target market, which occurs at the subsequent reception stage. It has been observed that, "While you can certainly get a guide to the visibility of your sponsorship and the potential for awareness among your target audience, you certainly cannot tell by measuring media mentions how many of your target audience saw and registered the mentions, nor how the viewers' attitude to you or your product has been influenced by the sponsorship" (p. 227).[14]

For awareness to occur, members of the target market have to interpret the message and then absorb it. There is a substantial probability that this will not occur because individuals are exposed to many more communications than they can

Figure 15-3 Using Sponsorship to Raise Awareness Levels of Cornhill Insurance Companys

Cornhill Insurance Company is located in the United Kingdom and was ranked twelfth in size among UK insurance companies. Before it committed to sponsorship, research showed that unprompted spontaneous awareness of Cornhill among UK residents was less than 2 percent. The company believed the reason for this was because insurance was sold via third-party brokers, agents or salesmen and hence the company was relatively distanced from its consumers. Most of the company's promotional activities at that time were directed at insurance brokers rather than consumers in order to influence brokers to place business with their company. Therefore, consumers lacked any direct association with the company. In addition, insurance is not a "glamor" product. It is purchased out of a reluctantly perceived necessity rather than desire.

Another influence on Cornhill's management at that time was the bad publicity generated by the collapse of a number of insurance companies. This led Cornhill to conclude that the public would be increasingly reluctant to purchase insurance from an unknown company.

At the same time as Cornhill was identifying their awareness problems, the international cricket world was being shaken by Kerry Packer and his World Series Cricket. International cricket matches for over a century had been organized by the governing bodies of cricket in each country. However, Kerry Packer, an Australian entrepreneur, announced plans to sign the best players from each country to lucrative contracts, and to promote his own series of matches independent of the governing bodies. The Test and Country Cricket Board (TCCB), which is the governing body in England, was desperate to find a sponsor who would match the salaries offered by Packer so TCCB could retain control of these players and of international games.

Cricket is a central feature of English life and this battle for the players was a major news story in all the national media. Seeing an opportunity, Cornhill made contact with the TCCB and a £1 million sponsorship fee, over the next five years, was agreed. The international matches were to be called The Cornhill Test Matches (A test match is the name given to official international cricket matches. Each match usually lasts for five days from 11 a.m. to 6:30 p.m. each day, and is televised live nationally

possibly accept or decode. Selective perception and retention means that people become aware of and retain only a small portion of the information to which they are exposed. They tend to select that which is of interest and is consistent with their existing feelings and beliefs, and ignore the rest. If a name, picture, cue, logo, banner, or other signage does not appeal, or if there seems to be no good reason why it should be noted, then an individual is unlikely to open his or her senses to it, and, therefore, it will not be received. This explains the results Coca-Cola obtained form exit interviews undertaken at a NASCAR event called the Coca-Cola 600. For seven hours, people in the stands watched cars race 600 miles around a huge Coca-Cola logo. Yet 60% of them could not name the sponsor afterwards![15] Hence, communication is not a one-way process from the sponsor organization to its target market, which use of the media exposure measure implies. Rather, it is a two-way process that depends on the intended recipients being interested sufficiently to interpret and absorb the communication.

Despite the substantial limitations associated with using media exposure and advertising equivalency visibility measures to evaluate the impact of sponsorship, these measures continue to be the most widely used evaluation tool, with 70% of

from beginning to end. There are usually five such test matches in a summer cricket season). At that time, this was one of the largest sponsorship commitments ever made to sport in the United Kingdom. Its announcement created a tremendous amount of national interest. It was made while an international match was being played, and on that day the game was stopped because of rain. This meant the media gave added attention to the sponsorship because there was no news to report from the cricket game!

Cornhill's analysis of the annual benefits from its sponsorship in a typical year showed that during 140 hours of television coverage the company received 7,459 banner ratings on screen and 234 verbal mentions. In addition, there were 1,784 references on radio, 659 in the national press and 2,448 in the provincial press. The 250 tickets that Cornhill received for each Test Match were also a valuable aid in improving relations with brokers and customers.

Cornhill launched a program to measure the effectiveness of its sponsorship that involved undertaking a research study every six months. Any increases in awareness could be attributed to the sponsorship since that, and its associated advertising, was the only promotional activity undertaken by the company. Unprompted awareness can be measured by asking respondents to mention any insurance company that comes to mind. The results of four six-monthly research studies indicated that unprompted awareness increased from 2 percent to 8 percent to 13 percent to 16 percent. Interestingly, these studies showed that level of awareness fell quite substantially in the periods between series of international matches, suggesting that awareness created by sponsorship is not long-lasting and needs constant reinforcement.

Cornhill's brokers told them that policies were much easier to sell as a result of the greater awareness of the company's name. Cornhill estimated that its investment of £2 million (£1 million in event cost and £1 million backup cost) over the five-year period, returned £10 million in increased annual premium income. Cornhill's sponsorship was especially successful because it was perceived as coming to the aid of a national institution, and was a very topical news event.

*Information for this case was obtained from material in Sleight, S. Sponsorship: What It Is and How to Use It; Meenaghan, J. A. Commercial Sponsorship, European Journal of Marketing; Hulks, B. Should the Effectiveness of Sponsorship be Assessed and How? Admap; Dinmore, F. Cricket Sponsorship The Business Graduate; and the Central Council of Physical Recreation's Committee of Enquiry into Sports Sponsorship, The Howell Report.

those companies reporting that they undertake evaluation using media equivalencies, whereas only 40% of these companies measured awareness/image, and only 7% measured changes in sales volumes.[11] There are three practical reasons for this sustained emphasis of media equivalencies. First, they are easy for management to understand. Second, these types of data are relatively easy to collect. Third, they offer quantifiable statistics that give the appearance that sponsorship decisions are being based on objective data, and thus offer peace of mind to those responsible for making those decisions. Sport managers who want to include a measure of the potential of their event in sponsorship proposal packages can also adopt this measure relatively easily. Indeed, media exposure is the only evaluative measure they can undertake without intruding into the business of the event's sponsors. Other measures requiring, for example, pre-and post-tests of awareness levels of a sponsor's product or sales performance are likely to be outside the organizers' realm of access.

The positive impact of sponsorship in creating awareness is described in the Cornhill Insurance case in Figure 15-3. Although the case illustrates an application of awareness research, it is likely to be atypical for two reasons. First, Cornhill did not engage in any form of communication except sponsorship and its associated advertising and, second, the company had a very low awareness level at the beginning of the sponsorship. These factors made it relatively easy to measure increases in awareness attributable to the sponsorship. A similar situation existed at Green Flag:

- The Green Flag company was a vehicle rescue organization that had previously been called National Breakdown. The company's goal in becoming the main sponsor of the England soccer team was to create awareness of its new name and what the company did. At the outset, national awareness of the company was 6%, and at the end of its four year sponsorship this had risen to 27%, which it considered a good return on its $1.5 million per year sponsorship fee.[16]

However, for products that do not exhibit these characteristics, the research design is likely to incorporate (i) a control group that is not exposed to the sponsorship that can be measured and used to discount the effects of other simultaneous communication efforts in which a company may be investing; and (ii) a two-part survey conducted before and after the event. NutraSweet compared results between control and treatment groups to assess the extent of linkage the company achieved between its target audience and its sponsorship of figure skating:

- NutraSweet was sole corporate sponsor of the United States Figure Skating Association, and it sponsored such events as the World Professional Figure Skating Championship, the Challenge of Champions, and national Ice Skating Month. To assess the strength of the linkage, the company commissioned a study of sales and attitudes about its association with the sport in four television markets that carried the world championships. In two of the four markets, NutraSweet commercials were deliberately blocked out, but reviewers recalled seeing NutraSweet advertisements anyway. The company considered this to be indicative of the positive image emitted from association with figure skating.[17]

This example of faulty recall exemplifies a limitation of using recall in measures of sponsorship effectiveness. Recall is notoriously faulty. People are more likely to associate a sponsor with an event based on the brand's popularity, rather than on their remembrance of seeing a company's signage on-site. For example, one study reported that only 6% of people used their actual memory of the sponsorship when asked to recall event sponsors; 42% of them recalled sponsors based on "relatedness" (that is, congruence of image, which was discussed in chapter 13) and 21% tended to assume that a market leader in a product category was the company affiliated with the event; the remaining 31% of responses were based on random guesses.[18] Another study reported that people recalled seeing the brands they used, irrespective of whether those brands were involved in sponsorship.[19]

An implication of this phenomenon is that market leaders and highly related companies are likely to receive some credit for sponsoring, whether they actually

Figure 15-4 Selected Measures of the Effectiveness of UPS's Olympic Games Sponsorship

One of United Parcel Service's (UPS) goals for its Olympic Games sponsorship was to link the Games to employee incentive programs. Winners of these programs were divided into gold, silver and bronze categories. Gold winners received tickets to the Games, including travel and accommodations. Silver winners were flown to IOC headquarters in Lausanne, Switzerland, for a special awards ceremony at the Olympic Museum, while bronze winners received a variety of Olympic memorabilia. Among the programs developed were:

Triple Jump, which was an incentive program for sales staff tied to individual goals. It resulted in 40% of UPS' sales force significantly exceeding their individual targets.

Going the Distance was a lead generation program targeted at non-sale staff designed to build business for UPS. It resulted in non-sales staff opening over 1,200 new high-volume accounts.

For drivers of delivery vans, UPS organized Gold Medal Driving, an incentive scheme to maintain a zero-avoidable accident rate. The Decathlon was a company-wide quiz designed to reinforce and extend employees' knowledge of the company, and 70% of those taking the test recorded a score of 100%.

Source: Adapted from Kolah, A. (2001). *How to develop an effective sponsorship programme.* London: Sport Business Group.

do so or not. It also suggests that any ambushing strategy these companies initiate is likely to have a high probability of success. However, another implication is that these brands will overestimate the effect of their sponsorship if they use recall as an evaluation measure. For example, if a market leader generated 60% recall from its sponsorship of an event, attributed recall might have been 20% or 30% even without the sponsorship. If recall is an important objective of the sponsorship, one of the ways to obtain a more accurate assessment is to ask respondents how confident they are in their answers. This could help determine how much of the recall is attributable to educated guessing rather than actual memory.[18] Another strategy is to use longitudinal studies, which will identify shifts over time using the first year as a baseline and measuring incremental shifts. Such studies are also used to gauge where a subsequent sponsorship is in its life cycle. They may suggest that awareness of a company through its association with the event is incrementally increasing at a satisfactory rate or that it has peaked and reached saturation level and that additional investment in it is not likely to be productive:

- Cannon made a commitment of $5 million to sponsor the major professional soccer league in England. In a three-year period, awareness of Cannon went from below 20% to more than 80%. The company decided reaching the last 15% or 20% would not be cost effective, so it withdrew from its soccer sponsorship. However, Cannon did this in a very positive way. It invited all the journalists who covered the original announcement three years earlier to a press conference and explained how successful the sponsorship had been. Coverage of its withdrawal was very upbeat, and the league was able to find a new sponsor without any problem.[20]

Awareness may also be measured by the number of visits to websites. For example, Thatlook, which is a referral service for elective cosmetic surgery, recorded more than 4 million hits in the three days following its title sponsorship of a NASCAR Winston Cup race. Normal three-day traffic averaged 260,000 hits.[21] This is a more convincing measure of awareness than recall because people have overtly demonstrated their awareness by engaging in an action. The linkage between awareness as measured by recall and subsequent purchase behavior is very tenuous. There are multiple other stages that need to be surmounted. Visits to websites places people much closer to the purchase decision (maybe only a click or two away!), making it a more desirable measure from a sponsor's perspective.

Measuring Impact on Image

Image enhancement or positive attitude change towards a product or company is a stage closer to the desired sales outcome than awareness (Figure 15-1). The distinction between these two stages is illustrated in the following example:

- A manufacturer and distributor of alcohol sponsored a horse racing classic for fifteen years in a bid to achieve a greater awareness of the company's leading brand among cognac drinkers who were followers of this sporting activity. With media coverage exposure showing an annual increase, the company assumed that the brand was achieving significant awareness amongst its target markets (a questionable assumption!). They commissioned a market research study to identify the extent of positive attitude change. The findings showed that attitudes to the brand were no more positive among those cognac drinkers who could identify the brand's association with the sponsorship than among those respondents who were unaware of the brand sponsorship. These findings suggested to the company that the sponsorship investment (which was over $500,000) had no impact on level of positive attitude to the brand, and thus the company considered withdrawing from it.[22]

Trust and credibility are components of image, so measures of these dimensions should be incorporated into evaluation of image. They are key elements in establishing relationships with consumers and the extent to which sponsorships enhance people's perception of these facets of a company should be measured.

Companies often want to know the extent to which a brand has effectively borrowed an event's image. This "strength of link" is best measured by the formula:

% of target market who recognize the link between the sponsoring brand and the event	minus	% of target market who mistakenly believe there is a link between a non-sponsoring competitor and the event

The larger the percentage who recognize that a brand is a sponsor and that its competitor is not, the stronger the link. Thus, Coca-Cola was recognized by 35% of NFL fans who were soft drink users as the official soft drink of the NFL. The company paid $250 million over five years for this right. However, 34% of the same target market mistakenly identified Pepsi as a sponsor of the NFL, which means that Coca-Cola failed to establish the link and gain value from its association.[12]

- In the context of the Olympic Games, several large companies and well-known brands that were Olympic sponsors, such as Crest, Oscar Mayer, Panasonic, Maxwell House, and Nuprin to name just a few, met a similar fate. Having paid millions for the right to say they were Olympic sponsors and to use the Olympic logo, these companies never communicated their sponsorship to the consumer.[12] (p. 14)

Another strategy for identifying how much image has been borrowed from an event is to use a longitudinal design. This was used by Visa as part of the company's evaluation of its role as an Olympic Games TOP sponsor:

- Respondents were asked which brand or company offered the best credit card service. Three months before the Games, Visa's advantage over MasterCard was about 15 percentage points. During the Games it doubled to 30 points. A month after the Games, its superiority was 20 points, still greater than the before-Games level. This suggested that Visa's sponsorship resulted in a change in its relative position in the market place, which is somewhat akin to the Intent-to-Purchase phase of the product adoption perceived stage.[12]

Measuring Impact on Intent to Purchase

The product adoption process suggests that potential purchasers move from awareness, to interest, to intent, to purchase before investing in a sales action (Figure 15-1). Hence, intent-to-purchase studies are perhaps the most useful indicators of the impact of sponsorship on future sales. Bassing America is a membership organization of 55,000 fishermen. A key to the organization's success in attracting and retaining sponsors is the research that Bassing does each year concerning its members' purchases and intentions to purchase:

- Bassing tries to find out what members own by brand, what they have purchased by brand, their intent to purchase by brand, and when they anticipate buying. The information is compared to prior years' results (looking back three or four years) to determine if sponsor's products are being supported. Findings are especially helpful when contract renewals are near. The results show sponsors how involvement with Bassing has increased their sales. For example, one annual survey showed that 15% of members owned a Ranger boat and another 21% said they intended to purchase one. Four years later, 27% owned and 43% intended to buy a Ranger boat.[23]

Measuring Impact on Sales

The most desirable measure from a sponsor's perspective is the impact that a sponsorship investment has on sales. Sales objectives may be expressed in three ways. First, they may be accomplished by boosting traffic at retail points of sale:

- Coca-Cola uses sponsorship to gain prime retail display space. The axiom in the soft drink business is that if product goes on the floor, it sells. When Coke plans an event-themed promotion, it estimates the amount of incremental cases it will sell, factors in a profit ratio per case, and evaluates its return based on actual sales and the amount it spent on rights fees. For example, through its ties with NASCAR, Coke saw incremental sales of 30 million commemorative bottles and placement of 20,000 vending machines and pop displays bearing NASCAR themes in retail outlets such as Home Depot and Wal-Mart.[24]

- DeWalt Industrial Tool co-sponsored a NASCAR Winston Cup team. They displayed the cars and drivers at major retailers such as Home Depot and Lowe's, who stocked their products. As a result of the visits, these stores featured the DeWalt products. The company's marketing manager reported this increased visibility typically led to a 30% sales increase during the promotion period. He regarded TV exposure in race broadcasts as "icing on the cake. It is new business from incremental shelf space that justifies the cost of the sponsorship" (p. 8).[25]

A less direct method of evaluating the impact of a sponsorship on retail points of sale is to compare the number of retailers or dealers participating in the sponsorship-themed promotion with the number who typically participate in a non-sponsorship promotion. This may involve tracking the number of outlets carrying their brand, or measuring incremental increase in displays at the point-of-purchase.

A second form of sales objective may be to produce targeted new leads:

- Xerox Corporation sponsored professional golf tournaments at which their managers entertained clients. Managers completed reports, three, six, and nine months after an event, estimating the impact the event had on client orders.[26]

- Ameritech Corp. received $20 million to $25 million in new business each year from its title sponsorship of a senior PGA Tour stop. The company entertained 200 CEO-types and 3,000-plus customers during event week; they alone represented about $6 billion in business. The company surveyed account executives to tally leads and new sales from the event.[24]

The third form of sales objective is an actual increase in sales associated with a sponsorship. There are two primary ways to track sales gains. The first is to tie sales directly to the sponsored event by tracking the redemption of coupons or ticket discounts given with proof of purchase:

- Burroughs Wellcome Company experimented with a women's tennis sponsorship to market a new sunscreen lotion. By distributing coupons at the venue and tracking how many were redeemed, the company found that the tennis events effectively reached the target audience of upscale women aged 30 years and over. In the following year, the company expanded its sponsorship to 12 major tournaments based on those results.[27]

- Bell Cellular Inc. co-sponsored events such as the Cadillac Golf Classic. To prompt attendees to subscribe on site, Bell Cellular offered coupons worth $110 off the first year's bill. In one year, they signed up 1,675 new subscribers, accounting for nearly $1 million.[27]

The alternative way to measure increases in sales is to compare sales for the two or three month period surrounding the sponsorship to sales during a comparable period. The comparable period may be the same months in the previous year, or a similar period at another time of the year if sales of the brand are not seasonal.

- The Guinness company's sponsorship of the Rugby World Cup was described in Figure 13-5. The company measured the impact of the sponsorship by comparing sales figures during the October/November time period when the event was held, with sales in the same time period in the previous year. The percentage increases reported included France 37%, Australia 20%, South Africa 24%, Great Britain 17%, Dubai 71%, and Malaysia 200%.[28]

- When telecom company Ameritech invests in a sponsorship, it sets a sales goal based on prior sales during the same time period. For instance, if a prior period saw 4,000 phones sold, the company may target an additional 2,000 sales from a sponsorship-related promotion.[24]

- General Nutrition Centers sponsored numerous events connected with their 2,500 stores. Typically in return for sponsorship, they offered a 20% discount on event entry fees that brought people into the stores. A computerized tracking system in the cash registers of all company-owned stores measured traffic before, during, and after an event and tracked increases over the same-period same-store levels from the previous year. For example, General Nutrition Centers provided $2,000 sponsorship to the Los Angeles Marathon Bike Tour. The discount entry opportunity brought in approximately 200 incremental customers, which, given an average purchase of $20 per visit, provided a two-to-one return on investment.[29]

Summary

Evaluation from the perspective of a sport manager has two purposes: (i) measuring the extent to which a sponsor's objectives were met and (ii) providing information that can be used in sales presentations to future potential sponsors. Because sponsorship typically is used as a platform for focusing the message of multiple other tools, it is challenging to isolate the specific impact of a sponsorship. The challenge is increased by the need to ensure valuation results are attributable to the sponsorship rather than to other uncontrollable environmental factors.

The effectiveness of sponsorship can be measured at various stages in the communication process, but the further through the process an evaluation takes place, the stronger the evidence of a sponsorship's contribution to increasing sales. The most frequently used type of sponsorship effectiveness measure is taken at the message channel stage and uses media equivalency values to assess the value of media coverage that a brand or company receives from a sponsorship. Some evaluations of this type incorporate weightings to reflect (i) the relative attractiveness of different types of media coverage, and (ii) the quality of the media coverage. There is a tendency for these equivalency measures to inflate the real value of the media coverage. In addition, this approach is conceptually flawed because it measures only the extent of media output and offers no insight as to whether or not people received, interpreted, or absorbed the message. Communication is a two-way process that is dependent upon the intended recipient absorbing the communication, and media equivalency measures fail to consider this. Despite the substantial limitations associated with using media equivalencies to evaluate the impact of sponsorship, this measure continues to be the most widely used evaluation tool because these data are easy to collect, easy for management to understand, and quantitative—giving the appearance that sponsorship decisions are being based on objective data.

Measuring changes in consumers' level of awareness attributable to sponsorship usually involves comparing responses of those exposed to the sponsorship with those of a control group whose members were not exposed to it, and undertaking a two-part survey conducted before and after the event. Most of these studies rely on people's recall of a sponsor's name being associated with the event. Recall is notoriously faulty. Responses often reflect congruence of a brand's image with an event, level of market leadership, or people's usage level, rather than their actual memory of a brand as an event sponsor. When awareness is evaluated by the number of incremental visits to a website, it is a more convincing measure.

Image enhancement or positive attitude is a stage closer to the desired sales outcome than awareness in the product adoption process. Trust and credibility are components of image, so measures of these dimensions should be incorporated into evaluation of image. Companies often want to know the extent to which a brand has effectively borrowed an event's image. This "strength-of-link" is best measured by the formula: (% of target market who recognize the link between the sponsoring brand and the event) minus (% of target market who mistakenly believe there is a link between a non-sponsoring competitor and the event).

Perhaps the most useful indication of the impact on future sales are intent-to-purchase studies since they are the stage in the process immediately preceding a purchase action. Such studies can be done by surveying a property's audience and identifying their brand and product desires and purchase habits.

The most desirable measure from a sponsor's perspective is the impact that a sponsorship investment has on sales. Sales objectives may be expressed in three ways: (i) increases in traffic at retail points of sale; (ii) number of new sales leads created; and (iii) actual increase in sales associated with a sponsorship. This latter objective can be measured either by tracking the redemption of coupons or ticket discounts given with proof of purchase, or by comparing sales during the two-to-three month period surrounding the event with sales for a comparable period.

References

1. IEG. (2002). IEG/Performance Research survey reveals what matters to sponsors. *Sponsorship Report, 21*(7), 1, 4-5.
2. IEG. (1999). Evaluation leads Coke to new sponsorship strategy. *Sponsorship Report, 18*(13), 1, 4-5.

3. Raptors arrange consumer research to show partners how their sponsorships are – or aren't – working. (1997). *Team Marketing Report 9*(9), 1, 7.

4. Horn, M. & Buken, K. (1999). Measuring the impact of sponsorship. *International Journal of Sports Marketing & Sponsorship*, September/October 1999.

5. Meenaghan, J. A. (1991). The role of sponsorship in the marketing communications mix. *International Journal of Advertising, 10*, 35-37.

6. Kolah, A. (2001). *How to develop an effective sponsorship programme.* London: Sport Business Group.

7. Schlossberg, H. (1991). Volvo proves marketing through sport pays. *Marketing News*, July 1, 19.

8. IEG. (1990). A guide to sponsorship evaluation. *Special Events Report*, September 24, 4-5.

9. Ukman, L. (1992). Assertions. *Sponsorship Report*, May 18, 2.

10. Ukman, L. (1996). Evaluating ROI of a sponsorship program. *Marketing News, 30*(18), 5, 14.

11. Poknywczynski, J. (2000). Sports sponsors know what they want. *Sports Business Journal*, June 5-11, 2.

12. Crimmins, J. & Horn, M. (1996). Sponsorship: From management ego trip to marketing success. *Journal of Advertising Research*, July/August, 11-21.

13. Urbanski, A. (1992). Fast track: Strategies for business success. What's a sponsorship worth? Supplement in *Newsweek*, November 9.

14. Sleight, S. (1989). *Sponsorship: What is it and how to use it.* McGraw Hill: Maidenhead, Berkshire, England.

15. D'Alesandro, D. F. (2001). Beyond the mother-in-law strategy: Avoiding consumers' indifference. *Sponsorship Report, 20*(6), 1, 4-5.

16. Miles, L. (2001). Successful sport sponsorship: Lessons from Association Football – the role of research. *Sports Marketing & Sponsorship*, December/January, 357-369.

17. Schlossberg, H. (1990). Sports marketing. *Marketing News*, April 2, 6.

18. Pham, M. T. & Johar, G. (2000). Research on recall rates raises flags for sponsors. *Sponsorship Report, 19*(3), 1, 3.

19. Hoek, J. & Gendall, P. (2002). When do ex-sponsors become ambush marketers? *International Journal of Sports Marketing & Sponsorship*, December/January, 383-401.

20. IEG. (1986). Evaluating sponsorships. *Special Events Report*, December 15, 5.

21. IEG. (2000). Thatlook.com sets sights on more sponsorship. *Sponsorship Report, 19*(15), 3.

22. Meenaghan, J. A. (1983). Commercial sponsorship. *European Journal of Marketing, 17*(7), 5-73.

23. IEG. (1990). Evaluation: Measuring return on investment. *Special Events Report*, September 7, 3, 6-7.

24. IEG. (1999). ROI: Sponsors share how their deals pay off. *Sponsorship Report, 18*(6), 1, 7.

25. IEG. (2002). DeWalt strategy ensures eight-figure motorsports team title pays for itself. *Sponsorship Report, 21*(20), 8.

26. McCarthy, M. J. (1991). Keeping careful score on sports tie-ins. *Wall Street Journal*, April 24, Section B, 1.

27. Lavelle, B. (1991). How Bell Cellular boosted its return from events. *Special Events Report, 19*(12), 4-5.

28. Rines, S. (2002). Guinness Rugby World Cup sponsorship: A global platform for meeting business objectives. *International Journal of Sports Marketing & Sponsorship*, December/January, 449-464.

29. IEG. (1995). General Nutrition Centers see sales increase, seek deals. *Sponsorship Report, 14*(23), 5.

Photo courtesy University of Oregon Athletic Department.

Chapter Sixteen

Fundraising

Fundraising in the context of this book is defined as the purposive process of soliciting and accepting monetary gifts, in-kind services, personnel, or materials to supplement a sport organization's existing resources.[1] Although sport organizations have had a long tradition of conducting fundraising events such as annual auctions and "Sports Days," only recently have some segments of the industry established formal, ongoing fundraising programs, often headed by professional managers. Within the last decade, collegiate athletic departments have made the most substantial commitment to fundraising among sport organizations, followed by a number of organizations from the private, nonprofit sector such as the American Amateur Union (AAU) and the Little League Foundation. Although many high school athletic programs are involved in fundraising, principally through the formation of athletic support groups (ASGs) or booster clubs, many times their efforts are more ad hoc, lacking systematic planning and structure. The intent of this chapter is to view fundraising—much the same as sponsorship—as *a purposive set of activities* for the express purpose of soliciting donations to enhance an organization's ability to sustain and/or enhance sport services.

Fundraising and sponsorship are viewed as different but related activities that are intended to acquire additional resources for the organization. Sponsorships, as discussed in chapters 12-15, focus exclusively on a two-way exchange between a sports organization and a *business* from which the company expects tangible *commercial* benefits in the form of increased visibility and sales and an enhanced image in the marketplace. In return, companies as sponsors underwrite all or a portion of the expenses associated with staging a particular special event or sports program.

Fundraising tends to focus more on obtaining donations from *individuals.* Close to 75% of the $203.45 billion in charitable giving in the United States in 2000 was made by individual donors, with corporations and foundations contributing the remaining 25%.[2] This general profile appears to apply to college athletics. For example, in 2002 the Ohio State University Athletic Department estimated that 70% of the $6.5 million received in charitable donations came from individual donors and 30% from corporations. The benefits sought by donors differ substantially from those sought by corporate sponsors. Private giving is typically characterized as a voluntary, one-way transfer of income or goods to an organization. The motives underlying donations are more altruistic than commercial. Donors are likely to contribute because of their emotional attachment to a sports organization, whereas corporations are likely to enter a sponsorship based on return on investment considerations. Although altruism plays a larger role in fundraising, self-interest still plays a role for some in motivating charitable contributions to athletic programs. As will be shown later in the chapter, the most effective fundraising programs recognize that both psychic rewards such as ego enhancement, and tangible rewards, such as preferred seating privileges, are integral components of donor solicitation.

Finally, it is important to recognize that donations potentially provide managers with much greater flexibility and independence in the way in which they can be utilized. Whereas sponsorships are sport or event-specific, charitable contributions can be unrestricted, allowing a sports organization the freedom to use the gift in any way it sees fit. Increasingly, athletic departments are providing incentives to donors to make unconditional or unrestricted donations to their programs.

This chapter initially provides a review of the nature and scope of fundraising in organized sport with a particular emphasis on its practice in intercollegiate athletics. The focus is on college sports because collegiate athletic departments have devoted the most attention and organizational resources to fundraising and, as a result, more examples are available for analysis and discussion. In almost every case, the organizational models and fundraising practices adopted by college athletic departments can be transferred to other types of amateur or nonprofit sport organizations.

The formation and operation of ASGs or booster clubs, the sport industry's most commonly utilized approach to fundraising, are discussed. Several successful models of ASGs are presented to illustrate the various ways in which sport organizations can effectively organize and conduct fundraising activities. Finally, recent and proposed changes in income tax benefits related to charitable donations and their implications for sport organizations are discussed.

The chapter concludes with a section on cause-related marketing, which describes a strategy used by corporations to tie their charitable donations directly to the sale of their products. Thus, every time somebody uses its products, the company makes a cash contribution to the sport organization. This approach first emerged in the 1980s and has become an important promotional strategy for many corporations. To date, relatively few sport organizations have developed ties of this nature, but it is an approach with considerable fundraising potential that is likely to be adopted more frequently by sports organizations in the future.

Fundraising and Intercollegiate Athletics

As hard-pressed college athletic programs have struggled to keep up with increasing costs and mandated growth in women's sports, they have become increasingly active in raising money from external support groups. One of the fastest growing areas of athletic department revenues is supporters' donations. A survey of the financial status of college athletics conducted by the NCAA reported that contributions from boosters and alumni accounted for l7% of the annual revenues of Division IA programs, an average of $3.5 million per program.[3] The importance of this source of revenue has increased appreciably over time. When the NCAA conducted its first financial assessment in l965, funds raised from alumni and boosters accounted for an average of only 5% of a Division I athletic department's budget. The growth and potential for fundraising is apparent when the most successful collegiate sport fundraising programs are considered. For example, in 2001, over $25 million in annual, capital, and endowment gifts was raised by the athletic department at Ohio State, while the Fresno State University Athletic Department received slightly over 43%, or $7 million of its annual operating revenues, from solicited monetary donations. As the importance of fundraising has become more apparent, most athletic departments have established formal fundraising programs. It is common to find, particularly within the largest athletic programs, an Associate or Assistant Athletic Director designated as the Director of Athletic Development or Fundraising. Typically, this staff member's responsibilities include developing a fundraising program, cultivating potential donors, and serving as liaison to the department's athletic support group. Most athletic departments have adopted the term *development* rather than fundraising to describe these activities to avoid the negative connotations associated with fundraising. "There is often a stigma attached to asking for money. . . (an) unwillingness to 'lower oneself' to the subordinate role of petitioner" (pp. 41-42).[4] The prominence of fundraising as an integral part of athletic department operations resulted in the National Association of College Athletic Directors (NACDA) establishing a branch affiliate organization called the National Association of Athletic Development Directors (NAADD) to support the specialized needs of athletic fundraisers.

Most athletic development officers solicit two primary types of gifts: (a) annual and (b) major. *Annual* gifts generally are solicited from a broad base of alumni and boosters. Typically, they are smaller gifts, ranging from $100 to $10,000. Annual gifts are normally used to defray current operating expenses, such as the cost of grants-in-aid, travel, and recruitment. *Major* gifts are generated from a relatively small group of donors. Generally, they are one-time donations of significant monetary value often directed at capital projects, such as a new arena. Another type of major gift that is growing in popularity is endowments (i.e., gifts that are invested to generate income, which is available for spending in perpetuity). Also included in the major gift category are *planned* or *deferred* donations. These gifts are not outright gifts, in that their benefits are deferred through legal instruments like wills and insurance policies until the death of the donor. Donors make the financial commitment during their lifetimes, but the benefits do not accrue to the athletic program until some future time, often after a donor's death. Examples of both endowments and deferred gifts are provided later in the chapter.

Annual Donor Programs

This section examines several approaches used by athletic departments to acquire both annual and major gifts. With few exceptions, the formation of ASGs is the principal mechanism through which athletic departments solicit annual contributions, but alternative models for maintaining booster support organizations are also discussed. The section concludes with the presentation of a systematic approach for acquiring major donations from individuals and corporations.

Athletic Support Groups

The centerpiece for most annual donor programs is the ASG or booster club. The fundraising capabilities of these organizations are substantial. Table 16-1 provides an indication of the size and monetary impact of selected ASGs in the United States.

Table 16-1 Examples of the Fundraising Capacity of Some of the Most Successful Athletic Support Groups

Name of Organization (Institutional Affiliate)	Number of Members	Total Donations ('02)
IPTAY (Clemson)	25,000+	$ 9.00 million
I-Club (Iowa)	10,000+	$ 15.31 million
Bulldog Foundation (Fresno State)	4,000	$ 7.00 million
Buckeye Club (Ohio State)	12,806	$6.56 million*

*Ohio State total includes only annual, unrestricted gifts to athletics. In 2002, the OSU Athletic Department received an additional $18.9 million in restricted gifts from individual and corporate donors.

A prevailing notion in the literature on ASGs is that most members are not former students of the university to which they give. One author, for example, contended that fewer than one or two percent of graduates gave to athletics. Most of those who do give direct their donations to a school's academic programs. This view asserts that athletic giving is the province of non-alumni or "boosters—rabid sports fans, who unlike alumni, never attended the institution and whose interest in it focuses almost exclusively on its college sports teams" (p. 258).[5] However, another study reported that while alumni do contribute significantly more to academics than non-alumni, graduates also donate large amounts to their alma mater's intercollegiate athletic program.[6] A study conducted at the University of Oregon tracked alumni and non-alumni giving to academics and athletics over a 10-year period. It reported that approximately 70% of alumni split their annual gift to the university, allocating portions to both academics and athletics. Further, the study found that over time, proportional giving by alumni increasingly favored athletics. From 1994 to 2003, the average size of the gift to the athletic department grew 64%, while the portion devoted to academics *declined* by a small margin. By 2003, alumni were committing 57% of their annual donation to intercollegiate athletics. Over the same time period, the average academic gift by non-alumni fell significantly. By 2003, fewer than 20% of this group allocated a portion of their annual gift to the university in support of academic programs.

The study provided evidence that a winning athletic program can have a major impact on the giving behavior of alumni. The data showed a strong association between the improved performance of the school's sports teams (particularly football and men's basketball) and increased giving on the part of alumni. As donors gave more to athletics, they tended to give less to academics. The findings reflect the giving patterns at just one institution, but the implications indicate that alumni may play a much more prominent role in athletic giving than previously considered.

However, there appears to be widespread support for the claim that a substantial number, often a majority, of those who belong to ASGs are business owners and individual fans who were never students of the university. For example, nearly 60% of the 10,000-plus members who belong to the I-Club, the primary booster club at the University of Iowa, were not graduates of the institution.[7]

Businessmen "boosting" athletic programs have long been a tradition in college athletics.[8] It was good business to promote athletics, particularly a winning athletic program. "Businessmen saw athletics as a stimulus to their profits, and because most athletic programs ran deficits, even in their early history, it was only natural that they 'boost' the activity with a financial subsidy" (p. 117).[9]

Some argue that these boosters have little concern for the educational mission of the school, often viewing their five- and sometimes six-figure donations as 'investments' in their favorite programs. In their opinion, this money not only grants them certain perks—the best seats, special parking spaces, the ear of the AD and of the coaches—but also entitles them to "a say on how the college sports franchise should be run" (p. 79).[10]

Unfortunately, history is replete with instances in which prominent boosters used ASGs to further their own interests, independent of any kind of athletic department authority or overall institutional control.

The desire of some overzealous boosters to win at any cost—even if it involves breaking NCAA regulations—has created serious problems for many universities and their athletic programs. Major institutions continue to be penalized severely for unethical practices by their boosters, typically for not controlling supporters who made illegal gifts to athletes, such as cash payments to prospective athletes and large merchandise discounts to current student-athletes. Research indicates that being placed on probation can negatively affect charitable donations directed to both athletics and academics, further raising the importance of bringing boosters under institutional control.[11]

Bringing Athletic Support Groups Under Institutional Control

In the early 1990s, increased pressure for reform led the NCAA to explicitly charge athletic directors with the responsibility for assuring that booster clubs and their members operated in compliance with NCAA rules and regulations. In a document titled *Principles of Institutional Control*, first issued in the spring of 1992, athletic programs were mandated to develop and maintain rules-education programs for all constituent groups, including boosters. To assist athletic departments with the implementation of rules orientation programs, the NCAA compliance staff established a Booster Education program. A "Resource File" containing basic information on compliance responsibilities is available on request from the NCAA.

The following steps have been suggested for ensuring greater control of ASGs at the collegiate and high school levels:

1. The first step in establishing control is for the athletic director to sit down with an ASG's board or officers to establish a written constitution or charter and by-laws for the organization. The document should explicitly define the purpose and delimit the powers of the club, including two critical provisions:

   a. a statement that stipulates the club as a subordinate group. . ."a support mechanism—nothing more" (p. 17)

   b. a requirement for "rolling board memberships" that limits board terms to no more than 3 years. "If some people are allowed to stay on the board for 10 to 15 years, they can get enough informal power so that they can run the board" (p. 17).

2. Imposition of financial control provisions that ensure that all monies raised by the ASG will be spent only with the approval of the athletic director. "Make sure all checks are processed and handled through the athletic department, not some renegade, off-campus organization" (p. 22).

3. Finally, and particularly in the case of collegiate athletic programs, it is essential that athletic directors establish a thorough rules-education program for *all* booster club members. The effort at educating boosters on their compliance responsibilities must be continuous. . ."You can't just put an article in the booster club letter once a year telling them to be good" (p. 19).[12]

The relationship between the Fresno State University Athletic Department and its primary support group, the Bulldog Foundation, provides a good example of the adoption of many of these control safeguards. The Foundation is governed by a Board of Trustees. The ASGs charter requires that four members of the university athletic department sit on the Board. Internal financial control is assured by the requirement that a senior administrator in the athletic department cosign all foundation checks, thus complying with the institutional controls mandated by the NCAA.

Gaining institutional control remains a significant challenge for all schools. In the words of former University of Michigan President James J. Duderstadt:

> . . . [I]t is clear that very few of the universities engaged in big-time sports enjoy the same degree of control over these activities as they do over the academic programs of the institution. Powerful external forces arising from fan and alumni pressure, commercial interest, the sport press, and the entertainment industry have long since eroded true institutional control. Although some University presidents have taken strong verbal positions in support of reform agendas, in reality few have chosen to ride into battle against these formidable foes. The challenge is simply too risky and intractable.[13] (p. 260)

Approaches to the Organization and Operation of ASGs

ASGs are commonly organized as either *private foundations* or *athletic department-operated clubs*. Under the first arrangement, the support group incorporates as a nonprofit, tax exempt foundation independent of the university. Private foundations have been both a blessing and a blight to athletic programs. On the positive side, some of the most successful ASGs have operated as private, nonprofit fundraising organizations. For example, in 2002, Fresno State's Bulldog Foundation and Clemson's IPTAY Foundation raised $7 million and $9 million, respectively, in support of athletic programs at their affiliate universities. Unfortunately, the independent status of these external booster groups can allow them to get out of control. Operating without any formal reporting responsibility to the university or the athletic department to which they are nominally affiliated, many "work(ed) in a clandestine manner, violating rules. . . making end runs around the Athletic Director's attempts at exercising institutional control" (p. 15).[12] However, the NCAA's efforts at demanding meaningful institutional oversight and accountability over ASG activities has substantially reduced the autonomy of private foundations, and with it their potential for committing serious rule violations.

The alternative form of booster club organization is for the athletic department to establish its own "in-house" ASG. Under this arrangement, the club "resides" within the department and is staffed by departmental personnel. This internal booster club model has worked well for many institutions, including Ohio State's Buckeye Club, Iowa's I-Club, and Oregon's Duck Athletic Fund.

Figure 16-1 Buckeye Club—Benefits by Membership Level

Benefits of Your Annual Gift	Scholar-Athlete Level $10,000+	National Champions Level $5,000–$9,999	Big Ten Champions Level $2,500–$4,999	Scarlet & Gray Level $1,000–$2,499	Horseshoe Level $100–$999
Invitation to the Scholar Athlete Banquet	YES				
Invitation to the OSU Department of Athletics Golf Outing	YES				
Opportunity to purchase a football season parking permit	YES	YES			
Two Go Bucks Cards (complimentary admission to Ohio State Olympic Sports)	YES	YES	YES		
Golf course walk-on privileges*	YES	YES	YES		
Presidents Club Recognition**	YES	YES	YES		
Ticket priority to away and post-season football games	YES	YES	YES		
Football and basketball media guides	YES	YES	YES		
Opportunity to purchase two season football tickets***	(icon)	(icon)	(icon)	(icon)	
Invitation to the annual Buckeye Club Reception	YES	YES	YES	YES	
The Buckeye Insider, the official publication of the OSU Department of Athletics	YES	YES	YES	YES	

Buckeye Club Benefits Fine Print: * Eligible to pay alumni-rate greens fees and use of the facility. Proper identification must be presented for you and your spouse. You may not sponsor a guest.
**At the $2,500 level and above, your membership includes President Club recognition, which entitles you to a courtesy campus parking permit (not valid in proximity of athletic facilities on gameday), valued at $173.
Acceptance of this benefit will further reduce the amount of your tax deduction.
*** New Season Ticket requests for football are based upon availability and level of contribution. Membership in the Buckeye Club disqualifies you from purchasing single game alumni tickets.

Regardless of organizational form, ASGs have tended to approach annual fundraising from two contrasting philosophical orientations. The first approach takes a more exclusive or narrow view towards club membership. Although any interested fan or booster may join, typically the minimum donation required for a membership starts at $1,000 a year. Membership incentives are tied to increased "perks" or benefits. As Figure 16-1 illustrates, the greater the donation, the greater the benefits. In the Buckeye Club example, individuals or corporations become "Full Members" only when they contribute at least $2,500. Not only do these members receive the full benefit package but their larger contribution substantially enhances the quality of the two season tickets they have the opportunity to purchase.

The Buckeye Club is an example of the more concentrated approach to ASG membership, which is directed at attracting boosters who have the means to make large donations. For example, in a campaign to recruit new members, athletic department staff who oversaw operation of the Buckeye Club directed a targeted mail campaign toward upper income households in central Ohio. Buckeye Club membership brochures were sent to 18,000 households in the region that had been pre-qualified as good booster club prospects on the basis of an annual household income of $60,000. In addition, the Buckeye Club placed advertisements in several "upscale" magazines throughout the state of Ohio. This resulted in over 2,800 members donating over $1,000, including 22 donors who gave over $10,000. This *concentrated* approach, in which "a relative few give a lot," has been a successful model for the Ohio State University Athletic Department. The approximately $6.6 million raised through membership contributions funded all 365 scholarships granted by the Athletic Department and helped defray team travel costs and expenses related to the maintenance of sport facilities.

The second basic approach to annual fundraising is for the ASG to take a broad view to club membership. Athletic support groups adopting this *grassroots* orientation focus on mass appeal. Rather than concentrating on a relatively small number of major donors, the emphasis is on generating broad-based involvement. Requirements for membership are modest, often in the $25-$50 minimum range. The I-Club is a good example of an ASG that has relied on this high volume-minimum contribution approach. The minimum donation required for inclusion in the University of Iowa's more than 10,000-member ASG is $40. In 2002, I-Club members donated $15.31 million to the Athletic Department. The Development Director for the University of Iowa Athletic Department recognized the trade-offs associated with maintaining a broad-based membership, "While we probably don't make much off of the minimum donor, we figure once we get them in the door, then we can work at upgrading them." A number of incentives are offered to induce larger donations. According to the Director, "While every gift entitles a seating privilege, the more you give, the higher the seating priority." [14] Preferred seating and other incentives appear to provide impetus toward upgraded or increased giving. Almost 25% of the I-Club's members made contributions of $1,000 or more in 2002.

The IPTAY Scholarship Foundation at Clemson University provides perhaps the best illustration of an ASG using the grassroots approach. IPTAY—originally I Pay Ten A Year, "inflation adjusted" to Ten Times Ten—has achieved an enviable record as the Clemson Athletic Department fundraising arm. The growth of IPTAY has been remarkable. Increases in membership, as well as contributions, have occurred in 28 of the last 29 years. The over $100 million raised by IPTAY since its inception in 1934 has furnished athletes at Clemson with a learning center, an indoor tennis center, an outdoor track, and even a 1,300-foot air strip extension. In addition to completely underwriting the $3.5 million in current annual athletic scholarship costs, Clemson's ASG assists with a number of non-athletic programs. "IPTAY has endowed a $1.6 million academic scholarship fund and hands the University President $150,000 a year in discretionary money" (p. 5C).[15] IPTAY has developed grassroots programs aimed at children, The Tiger Cub Club (ages birth to 12) and IPTAY Cats (ages 13-17), in an effort to not only broaden membership but to encourage giving from an early age.

Empirical evidence provides some insights into why the grassroots approach is effective. A number of social psychology studies have found that asking for a small donation leads to a greater likelihood of receiving a donation than initially requesting a large donation. In a series of imaginative experiments, it was found that asking for a generous contribution significantly decreased the percentage of people who donated and failed to increase the average size of a contribution by those who gave.[16] It was concluded that overall, fundraising campaigns can raise more money by asking for less. The researchers explain the results on the basis of the notion of "legitimizing small requests."[17] This notion assumes that suggesting a small amount has a legitimizing effect. "Many people who might otherwise fail to donate will contribute provided that the modest sum they are willing to give seems appropriate whereas suggesting a large donation tends to imply that modest sums are inappropriate" (p. 399).[16]

The Point System

Many athletic departments have established "point systems" as a way to more objectively assign football and basketball tickets to donors. Usually, these unpublished systems award points on the basis of the amount of annual giving, number of consecutive years of contributing, and number of consecutive years of purchasing season tickets. The more points accumulated by the donor, the better the seating location. Generally, the greatest number of points is awarded for gifts of the greatest magnitude, with each of the other categories receiving equal weight. IPTAY uses a three-step approach to calculating points based on length of membership, cumulative giving, and the amount of the current gift. Under this system, a member receives 1 point for every $250 of cumulative lifetime giving and between 1 and 50 points for the magnitude of the current gift amount. IPTAY also offers an opportunity to gain extra points through attendance at pre-selected, "Olympic sport" (baseball, women's softball, swimming, etc.) events on the Clemson campus.

The Team Concept of Fundraising

A growing number of ASGs are utilizing a "team" approach to organizing their annual fundraising campaigns. The origin of the idea has been attributed to the Louisiana State University Athletic Department. Analogous to the athletic teams they support, under the team concept, boosters are placed on teams that compete

Figure 16-2 Bulldog Foundation Annual Fund Drive

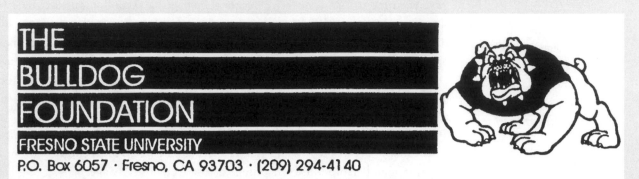

THE
BULLDOG
FOUNDATION

FRESNO STATE UNIVERSITY

P.O. Box 6057 · Fresno, CA 93703 · (209) 294-4140

FUND DRIVE

The Bulldog Foundation Fund Drive is held annually for five weeks from the middle of April to the end of May, although pledges are accepted any time during the fiscal year March 1 to February 28. During this concentrated time volunteers working under the "team concept" strive to renew the pledges of current members and solicit new pledge donors. In a spirit of competition, the players solicit funds to be used for scholarships, recruitment, and special projects by the Fresno State Athletic Department.

THE TEAM CONCEPT

Based upon the National Football League, 27 teams are established under two conferences and two commissioners. Team owners are assigned, usually from previous participation, who in turn select the volunteers who comprise their team "players." The teams are given the names of the pro football teams.

FUND DRIVE EVENTS

Events are held during the drive to further contact between teams and to promote enthusiasm toward continued success. At the end of the drive, awards are given for outstanding achievement by team and individuals. The following sections hold explanations of Fund Drive events:

- Team Owner Dinner
- Orientation Sessions
- Fund Drive Kickoff Dinner
- Report Sessions
- Awards Banquet

PREPARATION

Team Owners from the previous year are contacted and asked if they wish to again head a team for the Fund Drive. The Membership Vice President serves as the Fund Drive Chairman and selects the two Conference Commissioners with the assistance of the Executive Director. Team rosters (complete with name, address, business and home telephones) are submitted to the BDF office and players are then entered into the computer by teams. Player numbers are assigned and a master roll is prepared. Letters of welcome are sent to each Team Owner and player outlining the upcoming events.

SUMMARY OF TEAM CONCEPT OF FUND RAISING

Team Concept utilizes a Fund Drive Chairperson, two Commissioners in charge of two conferences of several teams each. The number of teams is dependent upon the number of volunteers helping in Fund Drive. There could be a Fund Drive with just two teams competing, eliminating the need for Commissioners. Each team has a Team Owner who oversees the progress of his/her team. Each Commissioner oversees the Team Owners in his/her conference. The Fund Drive Chairperson oversees the two Commissioners.

The volunteers are either drafted, assigned, or selected to teams. There are weekly Report Sessions that keep the interest piqued and the results (or lack of results) right in the face of all the volunteers showing who is doing well and embarrassing those not into some kind of action. There is a Kickoff function to start and an Awards function to end the drive. There are Incentive Awards for certain goals for reaching certain levels of pledges. There are awards for the Top Teams and Top Conference.

The Team Concept works well in athletic fund raising because most of the volunteers are competitive type folks interested in sports. However, it can be used very effectively for any cause if the volunteers have a sense of purpose and achievement.

TEAM OWNER DINNER

Fresno State coaches and Fund Drive team officials (Commissioners, Team Owners) meet for dinner to outline and kickoff the upcoming drive. Invitations and arrangements for this dinner are made by the Athletic Director's office.

ORIENTATION SESSION

One or two nights are designated for team player orientation. Orientation Sessions are mandatory for the new "rookies" to the drive and optional for "veteran" players. The first 30 minutes are devoted to new information concerning this particular year's fund drive effort. Veterans can then leave while the new players continue to be oriented in pledge levels, completing pledge cards, solicitation procedures, and donor benefits. Orientation Sessions are helpful in assuring detailed explanation of the drive and related procedures to those players who have never before participated.

KICKOFF DINNER

The Kickoff Dinner, usually held the third week of April, is for the benefit of Team Officials, Team Owners, Players, Coaches, and Administrators. Letters of invitation are mailed out well in advance with a request for R.S.V.P. in order to have an accurate count for the caterer. There is no arranged seating at this informal function, but team members usually sit together. The BDF Executive Director serves as master of ceremonies.

The evening includes a complimentary dinner, review of Fund Drive procedures, emphasis of report session dates/time/place, introduction of the head coaches, student athlete representatives, and a guest speaker if appropriate. Player information packets are distributed to Team Owners consisting of Fund Drive Team Goals; Membership Roster; Renewal Pledge Cards; New Donor Pledge Cards; Membership Brochures; Fund Drive Procedures; Map of Stadiums and Arenas.

Report Sessions are organized for the purpose of turning in pledges and monies received by the team players during the Fund Drive. A banquet room is reserved for five consecutive Thursdays beginning the last Thursday in April following the Kickoff Dinner. Individual team player printouts are grouped by teams, and used to record incoming pledges: name, amount, and money received each week. Volunteers record pledges on the tally sheets. The fifth Report Session is used as a "clean-up" session to encourage all players to submit outstanding pledges and also as a deadline for awards determination.

These weekly sessions allow the Executive Director to measure the actual incoming pledge amounts against the drive goal and that information against the same period in previous years. He prepares a weekly newsletter providing progress updates.

AWARDS BANQUET

Following the Fund Drive, a catered banquet is held to award those teams and players who assisted profitably in the drive. Those players who turned in a predetermined amount of pledges will be treated to a complimentary dinner at this banquet.

Awards are chosen according to pledge dollars raised. These awards are ordered by the players no later than the final Report Session. The BDF office staff places the orders with the specialty advertisers with an effort to have the awards available at the Awards Banquet. The awards are distributed by team.

against one another to see who can raise the most money. As the Fresno State Bulldog Foundation description (see Figure l6-2) indicates, in many cases an elaborate organizational structure is established, complete with league commissioners, team names, captains, league standings, and a sophisticated reward system.

The first year the Texas A&M-Kingsville athletic support group applied the concept, it increased its annual contribution to the athletic program tenfold, from $20,000 to $200,000. Ten, five-person teams "squared off" to compete for a number of incentive awards. According to the institution's Sport Information Director, "It gets pretty competitive. They have to switch the team members every few years to try to cool things down" (p. 21).[18]

Major Gifts Programs

No criterion exists for defining precisely what constitutes a major gift. It is generally described as a substantial, one-time contribution. For example, a capital gift campaign organized by the University of Nevada, Las Vegas Athletic Department stipulates "Major Gifts" as donations from $100,000 to $1 million. However, depending on circumstances, a major gift could be anywhere from $5,000 to $50 million or more.[19]

With major gifts, the emphasis is on targeting a limited number of prospects who have the potential to make significant contributions, rather than attracting many small gifts. Fundraisers have found that very few donors account for the largest portion of funds raised. This consistent pattern has led to the adoption of a formal principle known as the Rule of Thirds, which says you should expect one-third of your campaign goal from the top ten donors, the next third from the next l00 donors, and the remaining third from all others.[20]

The key to success in attracting major gifts is establishing a well-organized system for identifying, cultivating, and soliciting the relatively few prospects who are likely to be both capable and willing to make large contributions to the athletic department. Recently, database programs, such as BENEFACTOR, have been developed to help charitable organizations identify and cultivate donors.

Major gifts may be either outright or planned donations. In the case of outright donations, the gift is made directly to the athletic department in the form of cash or gifts-in-kind. Planned gifts, such as bequests, charitable remainder trusts, and donations of life insurance are gifts whose benefits are deferred through legal instruments (wills or insurance policies) until the death of the donor. The deferred gift is committed or established during the donor's lifetime, but the benefits from it do not accrue to the athletic department until some future time, usually after the donor's death.

Tax Considerations

Before discussing specific outright and planned major gift options available to donors, the next section of the chapter addresses the tax implications of these more substantial donations.

For some potential donors, tax considerations are the primary reason for contemplating a major donation to a sports organization or its nonprofit foundation. Even donors whose primary motives are altruistic usually will (and should) seek to derive the maximum tax benefit from their donations. Hence, taxes are a factor that sport agency managers cannot ignore responsibly. The purpose of this section is to discuss and illustrate the tax consequences inherent in various types of major donations.

It is beyond the scope of this text to discuss the tax structure in great detail because, while managers should be well informed on the issue, they do not need to be experts. Their task is to identify potential donors and then to alert them to some of the tax principles that may make it advantageous for them to donate. If interest is aroused, the donor should be counseled to retain a tax expert to recommend how the donation should be structured to the donor's best advantage. Thus, what is presented here is a simplified discussion of tax laws, which are complex and constantly changing.

From a tax perspective, it is useful to differentiate between present donations and deferred, or planned, donations. A present donation requires the donor to make an outright gift, transferring immediate possession and use of it to the agency. With a deferred donation, the donation itself is not deferred because the agency does receive an immediate gift. However, the agency's actual possession and use of the donated property is deferred to some future time. The future time may be a specified number of years of a specified future event, such as the death of the donor or someone designated by the donor. Planned gifts do not weaken the financial security of donors in their lifetime, and they tend to be relatively large. Both types of donations normally yield a current tax deduction (income or estate tax) to the donor, but the deductions from a present donation are likely to be significantly larger.

Two tax laws are particularly relevant. First, donations made by individuals to an athletic department or to a nonprofit organization are fully deductible up to 30% per year of an individual's adjusted gross income. *Adjusted gross income* is a federal income tax term that is defined as a taxpayer's annual gross income from all sources minus certain allowable deductions. One of the allowable deductions is for gifts made to government or qualified nonprofit organizations. The deduction permitted for a gift is equal to the full fair market value of the donation. If the value of the donation exceeds 30% of adjusted gross income, the excess may be carried over and deducted over the next five years until it is used up.

The value of a donation deduction to an individual will depend upon the magnitude of his or her annual adjusted gross income. The federal income tax rates and adjusted gross incomes to which they are applied that prevailed at the time this book was written are shown in Table 16-3. The gross income ranges are adjusted upwards annually, as they are indexed to inflation. By amending the adjusted gross income ranges in this way, people are not pushed into a higher tax bracket by inflation. They only move into a higher range and pay a higher level of tax when the real purchasing power of their income has increased.

Table 16-2 2003 Federal Income Tax Rates

Tax Rate	Married Filing Jointly	Single	Head of Household	Married Filing Separately
10%	$0 – 12,000	$0 – 6,000	$0 – 10,000	$0 – 6,000
15%	$12,001 – 47,450	$6,001 – 28,400	$10,001 – 38,050	$6,001 – 23,725
27%	$47,451 – 114-650	$28,401 – 68,800	$38,051 – 98,250	$23,726 – 57,325
30%	$114,651 - 174,700	$68,801 – 143,500	$98,250 – 159,100	$57,326 – 87,350
35%	$174,701 – 311,950	$143,501 – 311,950	$159,101 – 311,950	$87,351 – 155,975
38.6%	Over $311,950	Over $311,950	Over $311,950	Over $155,975

Table 16-2 indicates that a single person whose taxable income was $70,000 would be taxed at a rate of 10% on the first $6,000, 15% on the amount between $6,001 and $28,400, and 27% on the income between $28,402 and $68,800. The marginal tax rate on each dollar above $68,811 would be 30% or 30 cents on the dollar. As shown in Table 16-3, this individual would pay a total of $15,382 in Federal income taxes (an "effective" or overall tax rate of 19.6).

Table 16-3 Federal Income Tax Savings From a $20,000 Donation for a Single Individual With $70,000 in Taxable Income

Tax Rate	Tax bracket	Taxes paid	Tax bracket	Taxes paid
10%	Up to $6,000	$ 600	Up to $6,000	$ 600
15%	$6,001 – 27,950	$ 3,360	$6,001 – 27,950	$3,360
27%	$27,951 – 67,700	$10,732	$27,951 – 67,700	$5,953
30%	$67,701 – 141,250	$ 690		
Total Taxes Paid		$15,382		$ 9, 913

However, if this person were to make a donation valued at $20,000, then he or she would pay considerably less in taxes because the donation would reduce the individual's taxable income from $70,000 to $50,000. Table 16-3 illustrates the tax benefits that would result from this donation. When the $20,000 gift is deducted from the $70,000 in taxable income, the tax bill drops to $9,913. Thus, the total tax deduction of $20,000 results in a tax savings of $5,569 (from $15,382 to $9,913). The net, or real, cost of the $20,000 donation to the taxpayer, therefore, would be $14,552 ($20,000 donation less the $5,448 tax savings). The tax benefits resulting from a charitable gift increase progressively with growth in taxable income. Thus, at the highest rate (38.6%), a $20,000 donation made by a single (unmarried) individual with a taxable income in excess of $311,950 would receive a tax deduction of $7,022, so the net cost to the individual making the donation would be $12,978.

The second tax relevant to individual donors is the long-term capital-gain tax. This tax is applied to the sale of any capital asset that has been held for a period of more than 12 months. Such assets may include stocks, mutual funds, bonds, and real estate other than the primary house of residence. Long-term capital gain is defined as the difference between the cost associated with acquiring the asset and the income accruing from its sale. If an asset has been held for a period of 12 months or less (i.e., short-term) then the income is considered to be part of an individual's annual ordinary gross income and is taxed at the regular income tax rate.

The maximal rate of capital-gain tax for an individual is 20% (compared with the maximal income tax rate of 38.6% on ordinary income). Under current tax provisions, the following capital gain tax rates apply:

If you're in the 15% income tax bracket:

- Capital Gains on assets held for a year or less are taxed at your ordinary income tax rate (in this case, 15%).

- Capital Gains on assets held for more than a year, but less than five years, are taxed at a reduced rate of 10%.

- Capital Gains on assets held for more than five years are taxed at a reduced rate of 8%.

If your ordinary income tax bracket is *greater than* 15%:

- Capital Gains on assets held for a year or less are taxed at your ordinary income tax rate (anywhere from 28% to 38.6%, depending on your specific ordinary tax rate).

- Capital Gains on assets held for more than a year are taxed at a reduced tax rate of 20%.

- Capital Gains on assets held for more than five years are taxed at a reduced rate of 18%, but only if the assets were purchased on or after January 1, 2001. Assets purchased before January 1, 2001, that fall into this holding-period range are still taxed at the 20% long-term rate.

The following example demonstrates how an individual making a gift of a long-term appreciated asset can realize substantial tax advantages. Let's say the donor gave a stock purchased several years ago for $3,000 that today is worth $10,000, to an athletic department or to its affiliated ASG (e.g., the Bulldog Foundation). If the individual were to sell the stock, it would result in a capital gain of $7,000. However, by donating the stock, he or she avoids paying a federal capital gains tax of $1,400 ($7,000 x 20% = $1,400). Let's further assume, since more than 80% of the 50 states levy a tax on capital gains, that the individual will also avoid paying a 5% state capital gains tax by making the donation. This results in an additional savings of $350 ($7,000 x 5% = $350). The overall capital gains savings comes to $1,750.

Let's further assume the donor falls in the 30% federal income tax bracket. Under existing rules, the individual is eligible to take a $5,000 charitable income tax deduction that would result in an additional $1,500 ($5,000 x 30% = $1,500) savings. By combining the capital gains tax and income tax saved, the total tax savings or benefit the donor would realize in making his or her gift of appreciated stock is $3,250. By making a stock or mutual fund donation, the donor in this example is able to make a $10,000 gift that in effect costs only $6,750 ($10,000 - $3,250) after taxes.

Outright Gifts

Outright gifts include tangible assets such as cash, securities (stocks, mutual funds), and real estate. Often the aggregate benefits derived from non-monetary contributions over time also elevate them to major gift status. For example, the University of Iowa Athletic Department benefits from an extensive courtesy car program that involves more than 60 car dealers who donate more than 70 cars to coaches and administrators. In addition, Townsend Engineering Company, owned by an Iowa alumnus, has presented the I-Club with the use of its company Learjet as a gift-in-kind. Coaches have been able to use the aircraft to make quick, long-distance recruiting trips across the country.

The value of a *gift-in-kind* contribution is treated as if the athletic department had purchased the good or service itself. An example would be an individual who donates weight-training equipment that has a retail value of $1,500 as a gift-in-kind. Although the equipment may not have cost the contributor $1,500, he/she is still credited with giving a $1,500 gift. Thus, all such gifts are recorded at their relative cash value.

It is common for athletic departments to encourage booster club members and prospective donors to check if their employer offers *matching gift programs.* Many companies offer incentives for employees to make contributions to charities and nonprofit organizations by offering to "match" employee donations on a 1 to 1, 2 to 1, or even 3 to 1 basis. Marathon Oil, for example, will *double* current employees' philanthropic contributions while matching on a dollar-for-dollar basis the monetary value of its retired employees' gifts.

The University of Iowa I-Club publishes materials that encourage members "to contact their company's human resources or personnel office to find out if your employer will match your contribution to the Hawkeye Fund." However, many companies will not match employee contributions to intercollegiate athletic programs, particularly those from which employees receive direct benefits such as preferred seating privileges at football games. Many athletic departments and ASGs have attempted to overcome this objection by requesting employee-donors to stipulate to their employers that the matching gift will be used exclusively in support of scholarships.

Some donors may be persuaded to contribute *endowment gifts*. In these cases, the money is invested to generate income in perpetuity, so only the annual interest income provided by the investment is used. The principal or original amount donated is left untouched in a perpetual interest-bearing account providing an ongoing source of revenue for the athletic department. For example, the University of Southern California Athletic Department launched an endowment-by-position program campaign in 1983. By 2003, USC has endowed nearly all of the positions on its major men's and women's sports teams. The minimum requirement for endowing each position is $250,000. The interest earned from the investment of each donation funds a full athletic scholarship for each position (tuition, books, room and board), which is about $35,000 per school year. In return for the endowment gift, each donor has his or her name attached to the position. The associate athletic director who created the program attributes its success to the way it personalizes the gift, "One donor told me that if I asked him to simply donate money for a scholarship, he wouldn't have done it. But attaching his donation to a specific position made a big difference to him" (p. 5C).[21] In contrast to the USC position, Clemson University opposed the position endowment concept because of a concern that "buying" a position implied assumed ownership by the donor.

A number of athletic departments at public institutions—where the cost of a full scholarship is considerably less (from $10,000 to $12,000 for in-state and up to $25,000 for out-of-state annually) than private universities—have established full endowments at minimum levels from $100,000 to $150,000. The Ohio State University, which realized $300,000 from endowment earnings in 1993, established $100,000 as the basic requirement. Since then, through the One-on-One Athletic Scholarship Program, the endowment has grown to more than $22 million, funding 145 endowed student-athlete scholarships.

Although donors are encouraged to make the $100,000 contribution in one lump-sum payment, Ohio State, like many athletic departments, will allow contributors to fulfill their total endowment commitment over a 3- or 4-year period. Typically, the donor furnishes an initial payment of $15,000 to $25,000 and pledges to contribute the balance in equal annual installments over the next few years.

Planned Gifts

This section offers a brief review of the most common types of deferred or planned donations: gifts of life insurance, bequests, and charitable-remainder trusts.

Gifts of Life Insurance

Life Insurance is purchased by individuals to provide for the security of their families. However, if that security over time becomes adequately provided from other sources, then an individual may elect to designate a sports organization (e.g., athletic department, local Little League association) as sole beneficiary of the policy. If no premiums remain to be paid on the policy, then an individual can claim an income tax deduction equal to the replacement value of the policy for the donation. If premiums remain to be paid on the policy, then the deduction is approximately equal to the cash surrender value of the policy. If the annual premiums continue to be paid by the donor, they are tax deductible as a contribution.

Many athletic support groups and athletic departments have become very cautious in accepting insurance gifts. All too often, individuals, after stipulating an athletic program as the beneficiary so that they could receive tickets and/or preferred seating benefits, either stopped making annual premium payments or stipulated another beneficiary. As a result, athletic support groups like the I Club have now established stringent guidelines for accepting life insurance policies. The University of Iowa athletic support group stipulates, for example, a minimum cash surrender value of $15,000. In addition, to receive I Club benefits, the donor must make an annual cash contribution in addition to making annual premium payments. Further, in the event the donor should fail to pay an annual premium, the I Club reserves the right to "cash out" the current surrender value of the policy.

Bequests

With a bequest, the donor makes the sport organization, or in the case of an athletic department, its ASG, the beneficiary of his or her will. A donation can be in the form of cash assets or the transfer of real property. This type of donation may provide significant tax benefits to the donor. Under current law, the federal government (and a growing number of state governments) imposes a substantial estate or inheritance tax on the net value of an individual's assets after death. The federal government grants an exemption for inheritance taxes to each taxpayer. Since 1998, the exemption has increased steadily, growing from $600,000 in 1997 to $3.5 million by 2009. As the exclusion from estate taxes continues to increase, the top gift and estate tax rates will continue to decline over the next several years, from a high of 55% to 45% by 2007. Table 16-4 shows that current tax rates rise progressively as the value of an estate increases above the 2004 and 2005 exemption amount of $1,500,000. Currently, the inheritance of a $2.5 million estate creates federal taxes of not less than $780,800.

Table 16-4 2003 Federal Estate and Gift Taxes

Taxable gifts or taxable estate		Tentative tax is:		
Over	But not over	Tax +	%	On excess over
$1,500,000	$2,000,000	$555,800	45	$1,500,000
$2,000,000	$2,500,000	$780,800	49	$2,000,000
$2,500,000	$3,000,000	$1,025,800	53	$2,500,000
$3,000,001 and up		$1,290,800	55	$3,000,000

In addition, 17 states impose a separate inheritance tax and, in some instances (for example, New York), the tax is based on the entire amount of the property. In these 17 states, the heirs of an estate valued higher than the states' exemption amounts would owe state governments amounts ranging from $5,900 (in Nebraska) to $55,000 (in Massachusetts) in addition to their federal obligation.

Individuals who make bequests to qualified nonprofit organizations avoid paying the high federal estate taxes. The amount of the bequest is allowed as a deduction in determining the net value of an estate on which the federal estate tax is imposed. Thus, on a bequest of $100,000 from an estate on which the highest marginal tax rate of 55% is payable (estates valued at $3,000,001 and above; see Table 16-4), the tax savings would be $55,000 ($100,000 bequest x 55% tax rate = $55,000). By making the donation as part of the will to the non-profit organization, the estate avoids $55,000 in inheritance taxes.

Money in an Individual Retirement Account that is included as part of an estate is particularly prone to high taxation. Unlike other assets, if the Individual Retirement Account money is bequeathed to individuals other than a spouse, then it is subject not only to estate tax but also to income tax when it is distributed to the designee. These two taxes combined may consume more than 70% of the Individual Retirement Account assets. If the Individual Retirement Account funds are bequeathed to an athletic department or qualified nonprofit organization, then all taxes generally are avoided.

Charitable Remainder Trusts

These types of arrangements enable donors to place money, securities, or other assets into a trust account on behalf of a sports organization or its nonprofit foundation. Although the donor relinquishes control of these assets, he or she retains a life income for either him or herself or others designated as beneficiaries from the trust. Payments continue from the trust until those designated as beneficiaries are deceased. At the time of death of the last surviving beneficiary, the remainder of the trust's assets go to the designated sports organization.

Donors have considerable flexibility in designing charitable remainder trusts (CRTs) to fit their own particular needs. First, donors can decide how much they would like to put into a trust. Second, they can determine the amount of income they would like to receive from the donated assets. The income is paid annually in one of two forms. A trust that pays a fixed-annuity is called a charitable remainder annuity trust, and a fixed amount of income is received annually until the beneficiary is deceased. The annuity amount must be set at no less than 5% of the initial value of the trust's assets. If a percentage of payout is chosen, the trust is called a charitable remainder unitrust, and the annual payout to beneficiaries must not be less than 5% of the value of the trust's assets valued annually. With a unitrust, the beneficiary is paid an amount equal to a fixed percentage of the net fair market value of the trust's assets, as recalculated each year.

A donor receives considerable tax savings when he or she creates a CRT. First, when the fund is established, the donor immediately obtains the benefit of a sizable income tax charitable deduction. The amount is equal to the present value of the remainder interest ultimately payable to the athletic department or its ASG, based on Internal Revenue Service tables of life expectancy factors. In simpler terms, the older the beneficiary, the greater the charitable deduction.

The Ohio State athletic department has coupled the charitable remainder trust mechanism with its efforts to endow positions on its sports teams. Donors are encouraged to commit a minimum of $250,000 to an irrevocable unitrust, which pays them the interest earnings realized each year from the trust's assets. When the donor (or the beneficiaries) dies (die), the trust income reverts to the athletic department, specifically to endow a position in the name of the donor.

Systematic Approach to Soliciting Major Gifts

The key to successfully acquiring major gifts is establishing a well-organized program for soliciting large donations. This section describes a systematic approach to obtaining significant contributions from individuals and corporations. The approach consists of five stages that have proven effective in generating support for sport organizations. They are

(a) prospecting and targeting,
(b) preparation,
(c) presentation,
(d) closing, and
(e) follow-up.

Prospecting and Targeting

These initial stages address the first part of a well-known sales aphorism "Plan your work—and then work your plan." Often, sport organizations and athletic support groups, because of a lack of know-how or limited staff resources, tend to be reactive rather than proactive in their solicitation efforts. Some sport organizations occasionally have received unsolicited gifts from generous supporters or alumni. However, organizations that have had most success carefully target prospective donors and then design a solicitation approach specifically tailored to each prospect's needs.

Two tasks are involved in the target identification stage. The first is to compile a comprehensive list of all those individuals and businesses that appear to be potential prospects, and the second is to prioritize these prospective donors based on how likely they are to be responsive to requests for contributions.

When prospecting for major gift donors, the "Rule of Thirds" suggests the list will be short, since the most generous donors will come from a relative handful of supporters. Those inclined to give most generously are boosters who belong to the university's athletic support group. The Director of Development for The Ohio State University Athletic Department reports that "most of my major donors come directly from either the Buckeye Club (the athletic department booster club) members who have been long-time supporters of Ohio State athletics, or through referrals they make to us. Often, they'll actually have folks call us who are looking for a way to get involved." The University of Nevada, Las Vegas, Athletic department keeps an inventory of annual donors and targets them as prime prospects for major gifts. Their Director of Development noted, "Many universities have strong annual giving campaigns but never capitalize upon the success of that program by targeting top prospects for further attention, the kind that can lead to truly significant gifts."

Although existing supporters should be identified as first-line potential targets, selected alumni, such as former letter-winning athletes and those who own successful businesses, should also be given careful consideration. At this point, coordination with the institution's alumni development office is essential to avoid competition between the athletic department and the university's general fundraising department. At the University of Iowa, to ensure that the athletic department's fundraising efforts dovetail with the university's overall alumni development program, the development director for men's athletics is housed in the University of Iowa Foundation Alumni Center. Careful coordination and pre-screening can reduce the list of eligible alumni to those referred by the university development office as the very best prospects for making sizable gifts to the athletic program.

Once the prospect list has been developed, individual prospects should be assigned to one of three categories: "hot," "medium," and "cold." This rating should be based on two basic criteria: (a) their *ability* to give and (b) their *inclination* to support sport programs. The obvious intent is to identify those who are worth the most effort. An effective way to initiate a rating program of individual prospects is to seek "silent" peer-level ratings from a group of individuals who may be familiar with the prospects. This confidential process asks each individual rater to evaluate prospects as to their gift range by dollar amount and previous position to support athletics. Often, the athletic support group's Board of Directors or selected members can play a central role in this process.

Preparation

After a list of the most probable prospects has been derived, the next stage is to prepare an approach tailored to each of these prospects. The preparations commitment is time consuming but essential. Success at soliciting support is more likely to result from good presentation techniques. Three questions should be addressed in the preparation stage:

1. *What benefits does the donor hope to realize from providing the gift?* Here the intent is to try to discover donors' motivations for giving. Input from knowledgeable volunteers may prove valuable in answering this question. Individuals are not inclined to give merely because the sports program *needs* money; they contribute because they are motivated to do something special to make an impact. The opportunity to give something back to the athletic department by endowing the quarterback position in their name in perpetuity may be "that" special opportunity for certain individuals. In the case of potential business donors, the key question may be restated as, "What's in it for them?" Altruism may be replaced with a more pragmatic realization that most businesses make contributions because they believe it is in their self-interest to do so. Similar to the benefits sought by corporations entering into sponsorship agreements, businesses may seek enhanced visibility, an improved community image, hospitality, product demonstration, and/or reduced tax obligations by making a major contribution.

2. *Who should do the asking?* Research has shown that a key motivator is the person who asks. People of influence who are connected with the sports program or athletic support group are often the best people to do the asking because prospects are impressed with being asked by them. For example, the major gift campaign conducted by the University of Nevada, Las Vegas Athletic Department relied heavily on a gift committee comprised of the largest current contributors, corporate heads, wealthy people, and influentials in the community who had a genuine appreciation of the athletic department and who could articulate the department's needs to potential donors. Each of the gift committee members was matched with an identified pool of target prospects to directly solicit on behalf of the UNLV athletic department.

3. *How should they ask?* The answer to this question depends largely on the nature of the relationship between the prospective donor and the asker. Depending on how close the solicitor is to the prospect and how much is known about him, the first meeting may not be the right time to ask.[22] If the prospect does not know much about the sport organization for which the appeal is being made or appears unready to commit, the initial meeting may be best used for cultivation and fact-finding. However, by the end of the first visit, the asker should have answers to the following questions:

* How does the prospect feel about the sport organization and its needs?
* What size gift is likely?
* What giving method is most likely?
* What should happen next?

Presentation

Although the degree of formality used in the presentation at the initial meeting will depend on a number of factors, such as how well the solicitor knows the prospect and the magnitude and complexity of the type of gift being sought, best results are often achieved by a carefully organized presentation. Although there are many ways of making a presentation, one effective approach is to organize the solicitation appeal around three elements: features, advantages, and benefits (FAB). The FAB approach begins by identifying the specific *features* of the major gift program (e.g., endowment-by-position, charitable remainder trust) that are relevant to what is known about a prospect's desires for making a major gift. The *advantages* portion of the presentation addresses ways in which this unique gift opportunity is superior to other charitable investment opportunities available to the potential contributor. The *benefits* portion transforms features and advantages into benefits and directly addresses the key question, "What's in it for you. . . or your business?" (e.g., personal recognition, opportunity to give something back to your alma mater, increased visibility for the company). Guidelines for effective presentations include

* Concede points if the prospect is argumentative. Never press your views over those of the prospect.
* Be prepared to help the donor decide on the size of the gift. Do so by noting the size of gifts given by others, the average gift to date, and the period of time over which the pledge can be paid.

* Don't stress the organization's needs. Rather, seek to uncover the ways a gift could fill the prospect's personal needs. Determine which of the prospect's needs match the needs of the athletic organization.[22]

Closing

Many people find that closing is the most difficult part of the solicitation effort. They aren't sure how to ask or how much to ask for. Often, the best approach is to simply ask, "Would you consider a gift in the X dollar range?" On occasion, a prospect may not be prepared to invest in a project at the level the sport organization seeks when the question is asked at closing. However, there may be a willingness to invest either in a different project at that level, or in the same project at a lower level. Therefore, it is desirable for an organization to have more than one project and more than one investment level in mind. Then, if the main investment opportunity is rejected, the solicitor can present other options.

If the donor is willing to make a commitment, Figure 16-3 provides an example of a written pledge form that, in effect, confirms the contributor's intent to make a gift in a specific amount. Ideally, the solicitor can obtain the donor's signature on the form at the close of the meeting.

Follow-up

Regardless of the outcome of the initial meeting, the prospect should always be thanked in writing for the time he or she allowed the organization. If a commitment was made at the desired level, make sure that all appropriate parties (board chairperson, athletic director, etc.) acknowledge the contribution. And, with the donor's consent, proper recognition should be extended (news release, press conference, etc.).

If a commitment was not secured at the first meeting because the prospect either needed more information or raised certain objections, then a written response specifically tailored to the prospect's concerns should be sent. At this point, it is important to realize that early efforts may yield relatively little. A period of time may be needed for further education about the gift program and its potential benefits, and to build personal relationships before the resource support is given. The way the follow-up is handled determines the likelihood of eventually receiving some level of commitment. If the prospect needed more information, the solicitor should make sure it is sent in an appropriate format. If the prospect raised questions or concerns the solicitor could not deal with during the first meeting, then the sport organization should be sure that explanations are furnished promptly and/or by the appropriate people. A second meeting should be scheduled to discuss the proposal further.

If a negative response is received, a thank-you letter should be sent to let prospects know that the time they spent visiting with the organizational representative was appreciated. Polite persistence pays off. The organization should keep in touch with these people and proceed on the assumption that they may be prime prospects for support at a future time.

Shortly after winning the 2001 NCAA national championship, the University of Oklahoma embarked on the $100 million Great Expectations campaign with the goal of renovating or building 13 athletic facilities. The Championship Vision at Texas A&M University exceeded its original goal of $35 million in 2001 and extended the campaign goal to $50 million in support of intercollegiate athletics. While these two recent examples demonstrate the increasing popularity of athletic-specific capital campaigns, the earlier UNLV athletic department's Vision Project still serves as an exceptional model of a successful major gift campaign.

Campaign Organization

To help design the campaign, the UNLV Athletic Department retained the services of a professional fundraising consulting firm. In addition, the department secured counsel from charitable-giving specialists to clarify the tax consequences and benefits related to major gift options. A 32-member Executive Council, chaired by the CEO of a major corporation and staffed by three athletic department personnel, including the athletic director, the director of development, and the coordinator of the Vision Project, was established to oversee all matters pertaining to the planning and implementation of the Vision Project. Specific responsibilities of the Executive Council were as follows:

* Review and approve the general plan (including project elements, calendar, etc.).
* Finalize the UNLV Vision Project organizational structure and campaign goal of $25 million.
* Identify and list key leadership positions for the UNLV Vision Project Campaign (campaign chairpersons).
* Assist with the identification of top-level prospects deemed essential to the success of the campaign.
* Meet monthly during the organizational phase of the campaign.

Campaign Purpose and Appeal

The three major objectives of the campaign were to

(a) endow all of the approximately 220 athletic scholarships granted by the athletic department,

(b) build new sport facilities including a $1.5 million baseball stadium and a $2-million track complex, and

(c) secure funds to immediately enhance current sports programs.

While these concrete objectives served as the focal point for the solicitation effort, the general appeal to donors emphasized two fundamental themes:

(a) enhancing the academic reputation of the university and

(b) improving the quality of the educational experience for student athletes.

Featured in all "collateral" (e.g., brochures, videos) produced for the campaign was the theme that "intercollegiate athletics is a vital contributor to the growth and development of UNLV. . . the athletic program generates enthusiasm, pride, and support for the mission of UNLV in a manner and scope that is difficult to achieve by any other means." In addition, prospects were encouraged to give because their gifts would "create the resources that would produce exceptional achievement. It will enhance the ability of the department to attract and graduate the nation's highest caliber student-athletes, improve the quality of the educational experience afforded student-athletes, and provide the opportunity for UNLV to serve as a national leader and exemplary model for intercollegiate athletics."

Campaign Structure

Three major gift categories were established by the Executive Council: (i) Founder's Gifts—$1 million plus; (ii) Major Gifts—$100,000 to $1 million; (iii) Special Gifts—$10,000 to $100,000. Once the gift categories were determined, volunteers were recruited to serve along with selected members of the Executive Council on committees that focused on each of the specific gift categories. A *Founder's Gift Committee*, comprising 6 to 8 highly regarded members of the Executive Council, was created to seek and secure, on a face-to-face basis, commitments of $1 million or more from a highly select group of prospective donors. Members of this committee were individuals who themselves had the capacity and inclination to make their own significant contribution to UNLV athletics. A *Major Gifts Committee* composed of 15 members of the Executive Council was established to cultivate and attract gifts in the range of $100,000 to $1 million. Finally, to solicit the potentially more numerous prospects targeted for outright gifts of under $100,000, a 19-member Special Gifts Committee was organized. The targeted number of gifts in each category and their overall contribution to the Vision Project's $25 million goal are shown in Table 16-5.

Table 16-5 Targeted Gift Categories for UNLV's Vision Project				
Number of Gifts	In the Range of	Will Produce	Cumulative Production	% of Goal
2 ....@	...$2,500,000 and Above	$5,000,000	$5,000,000	.20%
6 ....@	...1,000,000 - 2,499,999	6,000,000	11,000,000	.44%
8 ....@	....500,000 - 999,999	4,000,000	15,000,000	.60%
18 ....@	....250,000 - 499,999	4,500,000	19,500,000	.78%
36 ....@	....100,000 - 249,999	3,800,000	23,300,000	.93%
100	.Under $100,000	1,700,000	25,000,000	100%

Conducting the Campaign

The identification and assignment of targeted prospects for each level of giving was coordinated by the Executive Council. Many of the prospects were initially suggested by committee members and/or identified through their history of annual giving. Once prospects were targeted for a certain gift category, cultivation activities ranged from sending birthday cards, newsletters, and invitations to arranging special events, campus/facility tours, and private dinners. Each prospect was assigned to a team of two or three committee members. Within each team, a "leader" was designated, who along with an athletic department staff member, was given primary responsibility for maintaining contact with the potential donor.

Throughout the campaign, it was imperative that staff keep committee members fully informed of the progress of the fundraising effort. Staff were directed to "pamper your committee members; allow them to enjoy the benefits of being on the 'inside' of athletic department events. Ensure that your committee members have personal contact with athletic department leaders. A very real incentive for the committee members' involvement may well be the special atmosphere of importance you create for them" (p. 15). [22]

Cause-Related Marketing

If there is such a thing as a win-win-win proposition, cause-related marketing is it. Cause-related marketing strives to achieve two objectives—to improve corporate performance and to help worthy causes—by linking donations to a cause with the purchase of the company's products or services. Discussion of it has been deferred until the end of this chapter because it's a hybrid that incorporates attributes of both charitable giving and sponsorship (which is discussed in chapters 12–15). It aligns the direct financial objective of increasing sales with corporate responsibility. Cause-related marketing qualifies as a sponsorship because it is a business relationship that is undertaken for commercial advantage. However, it meets the donation criterion of making contributions to create public benefits because corporations position their motives as being concerned with achieving socially-desirable ends (e.g., environmental protection, preservation of wildlife).

Cause-related marketing may be formally defined as the process of formulating and implementing marketing activities that are characterized by an offer from a business to donate a specified amount to a designated cause or organization when customers purchase a given product or service.[23] Most often this is done through the use of cents-off coupons: for each coupon redeemed, the business donates a fixed amount, frequently up to a pre-established ceiling, to the agency.

American Express coined and copyrighted the phrase "cause-related marketing" and has been its most visible advocate. Others have used the terms "philanthropic marketing" and "affinity-group marketing" to describe the same phenomenon. Its success is based on an appeal to the pride, attachment, and loyalty that individuals feel towards the recipient organization. In the words of the American Express CEO, "Cause-related marketing is our way of doing well by doing good." By tapping people's loyalty to their university or favorite nonprofit sports organization, corporations have an opportunity to encourage brand-switching and increase their market share. It gives people a reason to do business with one company rather than its competitors.

By offering to donate to a cause meaningful to the consumer if he or she makes a purchase, the perceived value of the product or service is increased at no additional cost to the consumer.[23]

The approach first received national prominence when American Express linked with the organization responsible for restoration of the Statue of Liberty and Ellis Island. The company's chief executive officer stated:

At first, we didn't know whether we'd found a new way to help business or just an interesting formula for giving money away. It's both. The increase in business we've seen in our cause-related markets proves the concept is as successful as any marketing program we've ever tried. We're doing good deeds, and we're also pleased with the commercial results.[24] (p. 1)

When the campaign was initially conceived, the company projected an 18% increase in credit-card transactions during that period. In fact, card use jumped 78%, and applications increased by 45%. A telephone survey of cardholders commissioned by the company revealed that those questioned had a high awareness of the widely advertised promotion. A substantial number also said that they had indeed used their card more often to help this good cause.

Each cause-related marketing program initiated by American Express begins with the announcement that the company will donate a small sum to the "cause" every time one of its clients in the area:

* uses the American Express card (typically between 1 cent and 50 cents for each purchase).
* purchases a travel package of $500 dollars or more (excluding air fare) at an American Express vacation store (typically $5 for each package).
* applies for and receives a new American Express card (typically between $1-2 for each approved application).

Thus the size of the donation to the selected cause depends on business done by the company in a specific geographic area during a set time period, usually three months.

Some advocates of cause-related marketing talk about the greater "bonding" with their brand that results when wholesalers, employees, and customers identify with the cause that is championed. Others have stated that retail chains are far more willing to adopt product promotions that are tied to a cause.

American Express was the most visible advocate of this approach. However, the principles that American Express used have been applied on a smaller scale to local businesses in all sizes of communities and can be adapted readily to meet the needs of sports organizations. The establishment of a successful cause-related marketing program between Denny's restaurants and a state high school sports organization illustrates this point.

Denny's Inc. linked with the Michigan High School Athletic Association in a cause-related marketing program. The director of marketing for the restaurant chain stated, "We're trying to dispel the impression that Denny's is just another national chain; becoming involved in the community is part of the strategy" (p. 7):

Denny's tied its athletic commitment to sales. Each time a restaurant customer presented a Training Table Membership Card, the company made a donation to MHSAA. All 49 Denny's restaurants in Michigan carried the cards and the company mailed special versions to 24,000 coaches. The program was promoted by radio and television advertisements and in-store materials. Level of involvement was tracked by card usage. High redemption from a smaller pilot program in the preceding year was the key reason for Denny's expanded state-wide program.[25] (p. 7)

The optimal length of a cause-related marketing campaign is difficult to assess. A fine line exists between maximum exposure and customer fatigue. The most common time frame is three months. That is long enough to generate sufficient publicity, establish a strong presence in the customers' minds, and give them time to buy. It is short enough that the campaign does not lose its novelty. Another strategy is for companies to link with annual events so that they reinforce previous campaigns in customers' minds. For example, Proctor and Gamble has carried out a cause-related marketing campaign with the Special Olympics annually and has raised millions of dollars for the cause. The repetition of the campaign has cemented the association between the company and the Special Olympics and has produced residual benefit to the company even at other times of the year.[26]

Cause-related marketing opens a potentially new channel for monetary support for many sports organizations. Given the emotional attachment many feel toward a community's high school athletic team, varsity team sports, and the performance of national teams at the Olympic Games, it seems likely the cause-related partnerships will be increasingly used in the future.

Summary

The intent of this chapter is to portray fundraising as a systematic, purposive set of activities for soliciting monies in support of sport organizations. Only within the last decade have a substantial number of collegiate athletic departments and selected amateur sport organizations like the Amateur Athletic Union made a significant and sustained commitment to fundraising. For a growing number of these organizations, monetary donations represent a significant portion of their annual revenues.

The first part of the chapter distinguished between two primary types of gifts: annual and major. Annual gifts are generally smaller denomination donations ($50 to $1,000) solicited on an ongoing or annual basis. Athletic support groups or booster clubs are the primary organizational mechanisms through which annual gifts are solicited. Bringing these athletic department support groups under greater institutional control is a major concern of the NCAA. The two major approaches to organizing ASGs (either "in-house" or as independent foundations) and the two contrasting philosophies (grassroots versus concentrated) for soliciting annual gifts were discussed at length.

Major gifts are substantial (depending on the circumstances, the donation could be from $5,000 to $1 million) one-time contributions. Rather than attempting to attract numerous small gifts, the emphasis is on acquiring a limited number of significant contributions. Major gifts may be either outright or planned donations. Outright gifts that are made directly to the sports organization include cash, securities, real estate, gifts-in-kind, and matching contributions. Planned gifts, such as bequests, trusts, or life insurance, are gifts whose benefits are deferred through legal instruments until the death of the donor. A systematic plan for obtaining major gifts, modeled after the University of Nevada, Las Vegas Athletic Department's Vision Program, was described in detail. The approach consists of five interrelated stages including (a) prospecting and targeting, (b) preparation, (c) presentation, (d) closing, and (e) follow-up.

The final section of the chapter described cause-related marketing, a strategy for linking a corporation's donation to a sport organization to increase sales of its product. Denny's relationship with the Michigan High School Athletic Association, in which donations to MHSAA were tied to customer purchases of the restaurant chain's membership card, is an excellent example of the concept. This form of "philanthropic marketing" has great potential for expanding the fundraising prospects for sport organizations.

References

1. Kelly, K. S. (1991). *Fund raising and public relations: A critical analysis.* Hillsdale, NJ: Lawrence Erlbaum Associates, Inc.

2. Giving USA. (2001). *Total giving reaches $203.45 billion as charitable donations increase 6.6% in 2000.* AAFRC Trust for Philanthropy.

3. Fulks, D. (2000). *Revenues and expenses of division I and II intercollegiate athletic programs: Financial trends and relationships-1999.* Indianapolis, IN: The National Collegiate Athletic Association.

4. Payton, R. L. (1987). American values and private philanthropy: Philanthropic values; A philanthropic dialogue. In K. W. Thompson (Ed.), *Philanthropy: Private means, public ends.* Lanham, MD: University Press of America.

5. Sperber, M. (2000). *Beer and circus: How big-time college sports is crippling undergraduate education.* New York: Henry Holt and Company.

6. Stinson, J. and D. R. Howard. (2003). *Scoreboards vs. mortarboards: The impact of intercollegiate athletics on donor behavior.* Paper presented at the Winter American Marketing Association, Orlando, FL, February 16, 2003.

7. *I-Club : The University of Iowa—history, structure and purpose.* (1990). Iowa City, IA: The University of Iowa Foundation.

8. Boorstin, D. (1965). *The Americans: The national experience.* New York: Random House.

9. Frey, J. (1985). Boosterism, scarce resources, and institutional control: The future of American intercollegiate athletics. In D. Chu, J. Segrave, and B. Becker (Eds.), *Sports and higher education.* Champaign, IL: Human Kinetics Publishers, Inc.

10. Sperber, M. (1990). *College sports inc.: The athletic department vs the university.* New York: Henry Holt and Company.

11. Grimes, P. W. and G. Chressanths (1994). Alumni contributions to academics: The role of intercollegiate sports and NCAA sanctions. *American Journal of Economics and Sociology, 53*(1), 27-41.

12. Bradley, M. (1993). Controlling the fanfare. *Athletic Management,* October/November, 15-21.

13. Duderstadt, J. (2000). *A university president's perspective: Intercollegiate athletics and the American university.* Ann Arbor, MI: The University of Michigan Press.

14. Telephone conversation with Mark Jennings, University of Iowa Foundation, Senior Director of Development for Intercollegiate Athletics, February 5, 2001.

15. Weiberg, S. (1991). Fund-raising arm keeps Clemson in the black. *USA Today,* October 15, 5C.

16. Weyant, J. & S. Smith (1987). Getting more by asking for less: The effects of request size on donations of charity. *Journal of Applied Social Psychology, 17*(4), 392-400.

17. Cialdini, R. B., R. Borden, A. Thirne, M. R. Walker, S. Freeman, and L. R. Sloan. (1976). Basking in reflected glory: Three (football) field studies. *Journal of Personality and Social Psychology, 34,* 336-375.

18. Bradley, M. (1993). Controlling the fanfare. *Athletic Management,* October/November, 15-21.

19. Williams, J. (1991). *Big gifts.* Rockville, MD: Fund Raising Institute.

20. Campbell, D. A. (1989, June). Second to none: If you've asked the right giver for the right amount, your lead gift will lead the way. *CASE Currents,* 22-26.

21. Davis, M. (1991). Southern California innovation: Endowments by position. *USA Today,* October 15, 5C.

22. Clontz, L. (1992). How to maximize your fund-raising campaign. *Athletic Administration,* June, 14-17.

23. Varadarajan, P. Rajan and Anil Menon (1988). Cause-related marketing: A coalignmnet of marketing strategy and corporate philanthropy. *Journal of Marketing, 52,* 58-74.

24. Higgins, K. T. (1986). Cause-related marketing: Does it pass the bottom-line test? *Marketing News*, May 9, 1,18.
25. Denny's other sponsors true to their schools. (1990). *Special Events Report*, February 12, 7.
26. Steckel, Richard and Robin Simons (1992). *Doing best by doing good.* New York: Penguin Books.

About the Authors

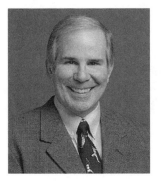

Dennis R. Howard is a professor of sports marketing in the University of Oregon's Lundquist College of Business, where he teaches sports business courses at the James H. Warsaw Sports Marketing Center. Dennis formerly served as the Director of the Graduate Program in Sport Management at The Ohio State University.

Dr. Howard is a past recipient of the Earle F. Ziegler Award, the highest honor awarded by the North American Society for Sport Management. He has authored or co-authored three books and numerous articles on sport and leisure industry topics. In 2001, Professor Howard was named a Research Fellow by the North American Society for Sport Management for his contributions to the field. He has served as a consultant to the NFL, several major league teams, and a number of intercollegiate athletic departments on a range of facility financing and development projects.

Dr. Howard is a graduate of the University of Oregon (BS), the University of Illinois (MS), and Oregon State University (PhD). He served on the faculty at Texas A&M, Pennsylvania State University, and The Ohio State University, before returning in 1997 to his alma mater in Eugene. As a member of the Lundquist College of Business faculty, Dr. Howard has received the Undergraduate Teaching Award and the Harry R. Jacobs Distinguished Teaching Award.

John L. Crompton holds the rank of Distinguished Professor of Parks, Recreation, and Tourism Sciences at Texas A&M University. He received his undergraduate degree at Loughborough College in England and completed his MS degree at the University of Illinois. He was awarded another MS from Loughborough University of Technology in business administration and later received his PhD from Texas A&M University.

Before embarking on his academic career, Dr. Crompton served as the Managing Director of Loughborough Recreation Planning Consultants, the largest consulting firm in the United Kingdom specializing in the design and operation of sport and recreation facilities.

Professor Crompton is the co-author of eleven books and a number of articles that have been published in the recreation, tourism, sport, and marketing fields. He is the past recipient of the National Park Foundation's Cornelius Amory Pugsley Award for Outstanding Contributions to Parks and Conservation, the National Recreation and Park Association's (NRPA) National Literary Award, the NRPA's Roosevelt Award for Outstanding Research, and the Travel and Tourism Research Association's Travel Research Award.

He has received the Vice-Chancellor's Award for Excellence in Graduate Teaching at Texas A&M, the Texas Agricultural Experiment Station's Faculty Fellow Award for Exceptional Research Contributions, and the Texas A&M University Distinguished Achievement Award for Research.

Index